TITANS

HOW THE NEW
CANADIAN
ESTABLISHMENT
SEIZED POWER

Peter C. Newman

VIKING

VIKING

Published by the Penguin Group

Penguin Books Canada Ltd, 10 Alcorn Avenue, Toronto, Ontario, Canada M4V 3B2

Penguin Books Ltd, 27 Wrights Lane, London W8 5TZ, England

Penguin Putnam Inc., 375 Hudson Street, New York, New York 10014, U.S.A.

Penguin Books Australia Ltd, Ringwood, Victoria, Australia

Penguin Books (NZ) Ltd, cnr Rosedale and Airborne Roads, Albany
Auckland 1310, New Zealand

Penguin Books Ltd Registered Offices: Harmondsworth, Middlesex, England

First published 1998

10 9 8 7 6 5 4 3 2 1

Copyright © Power Reporting Limited, 1998

Printed and bound in Canada on acid free paper ∞

CANADIAN CATALOGUING IN PUBLICATION DATA

Newman, Peter C. 1929–
    The Canadian establishment

Contents: v. 3. Titans: how the new Canadian establishment seized power.
ISBN 0-670-88336-0 (v.3)

1. Elite (Social sciences) – Canada. 2. Power (Social sciences). 3. Capitalists and financiers – Canada – Biography. 4. Canada – Biography. I. Title. II. Title Titans.

HN110.Z9E45 1998   305.5'2'0971   C98-931438-3

Visit Penguin Canada's website at www.penguin.ca

For my wife Alvy,
the love of my life.

Contents

"The Old Establishment was a club.
 The New Establishment is a network."

—*The Wise Men* by Walter Isaacson and Evan Thomas

Acknowledgments

IF MEN ARE FROM MARS AND WOMEN are from Venus, these Titans that I have spent most of three years trying to analyse are from Pluto. They are not just a different group of people who have seized the power that matters in Canadian society, they are a different breed.

In my attempt to describe their lives and their careers, to catch their cadence and capture their purpose, my point is to demonstrate that the Canadian Establishment—as I first described it more than a quarter century ago—is dead. Privileged birth, the best schools and membership in premier clubs don't carry much weight any more. In every branch of human endeavour except politics, Canada has become a full-blown meritocracy. And meritocracies can't be choosy: effort, luck and chutzpah determine their ranks. The men and, alas, not nearly enough women, who have grabbed power in this country, *earned* their way into exercising substantial influence, and into this book.*

Norman Mailer once pontificated that "there is no form of inquiry on earth more unwholesome than a face-to-face interview. Truth can no more emerge easily from that than any statistics on the sum of British Guyana's arable acreage might bring some cognition of life in British Guyana." That may be true, but I remain indebted to the time and energy the Titans donated to my cause. I thank them for their patience—some I interviewed through a dozen tapes or more—and I trust they will not wholly agree with my assessments. But Titans don't cry.

I have so many other debts: to my publisher, Cynthia Good at Penguin, whose patience was tried but whose friendship triumphed. She is a national treasure. That extraordinarily talented editor, Meg Taylor, gave form to this book, and I

---

* This is the only footnote in this book. Instead of the customary printing of these asides at the bottom of each page, they have been included in the text itself to save the reader unnecessary effort.

xi

bless and thank her. *Maclean's* associate editor Brian Bethune did a splendid and thoughtful job checking facts. Michael Levine, my friend and lawyer, made it happen; his chutzpah alone marks him as a Titan. That designation also applies to Julian Porter, the country's pre-eminent libel lawyer. Ray Heard, Robert Mason Lee, Jim Paupst, Fred Augerman, Vlád Plavsic, Doug Beardsley and Dan Veniez were generous with their encouragement. David Beers was an invaluable editor whose talents I admire. I am grateful, as always, to Robert Lewis, the editor of *Maclean's*, whose friendship and support have been deeply appreciated, more than I can say. To Fran McNeely, who has been my executive assistant for a dozen years and has never lost her cool, I offer my gratitude for her unfailing sense of loyalty, her kindness, patience—and blossoming computer skills.

I am determined not to taint my acknowledgements with some trivial sentiment, all too common to exhausted authors, who confess at the end of their labours that "this book could not have been completed without my wife putting up with me as I turned into a maniacal writing machine, who forgot to change his socks and never, once, took her to a Wayne Newton concert." Actually, our relationship wasn't like that—except for the socks. My lovely wife Alvy has been not only the best but the best *kind* of partner any man could have: irreverent, loving, helpful, wise, funny and patient. I thank her, profoundly, for endowing me with the rarest luxuries of life: love and laughter. This book could truly not have been done without her.

Stan Kenton's drummers, the good ones, didn't so much mark time, as mark grooves. In an art form that tends to emphasize virtuosity and showmanship, his jazz orchestras and musicians were much more concerned with depth of feeling and atmosphere than with adhering to strict musical forms.

I subscribe to a similar notion, and in writing the pages that follow, I have tried to pursue my own muse. Just as great paintings catch what the artist sees, and memorable music flows from what the composer hears, I believe that good writing depends on what the author *feels*—not only thinks. That has been my recipe for this book.

We live now at Hopkins Landing, an unincorporated village that intrudes hard into the dark cedar hills of Canada's Pacific coast. It is a good place from which to view the exotic world of the Titans who populate the pages that follow.

Love them or hate them, their future runs with us all.

P.C.N.
aboard the *Pacific Mystic*
August 13, 1998

Prologue

"Every nation needs an élite of some kind, or we are stuck with eternal mediocrity as a national fate. And every effort to construe such an Establishment is invidious, hurtful, challenging, delicious and . . . necessary."

—Novelist Scott Symons

"SORRY," SMIRKS THE HOSTESS who has just refused me a drink of water. "We never serve the stuff: fish fuck in it."

The rich and powerful really *are* different.

I'm at one of those evenings when the driveway of the Toronto megahouse I'm visiting resembles a Caddy or Rolls new-model launch. Guests stand around the patio, discussing banalities with the forehead-knotting seriousness of Euclid explaining his theorem—then leave early with their mistresses, or late with their wives. The house is decorated in Precambrian modern, combining the best of the Art Shoppe with the worst of the Group of Seven. It is filled with so many weighty objects that they seem stage props.

I am here to reconnoitre the Establishment's moods and mores. It is sixteen years since I moved from Toronto to British Columbia. My wife Alvy and I have nestled into Hopkins Landing, a quaint unincorporated oceanside village. That tiny wet dot on the Pacific coast might be a hundred leagues under the sea, so culturally distant does it seem from newly amalgamated Toronto. Yet there is a connection. In my mind's eye, I see the birds of prey that fly past my window most mornings at Hopkins—the soaring eagles that hunger through space, their talons unknotting, searching for their next victim—just like the vulpine men and women on patrol at this cocktail party. Perhaps that's why I find myself strangely comforted by the familiar chatter cascading around me.

"There's Catherine Nugent!"

"Ah yes. El Niño in heels."

Nothing has changed. Bitchiness is the order of the day. Catherine Nugent is Canada's unofficial contessa. I remember when she was between husbands—before David—and was attracting so many eligible European aristocrats, they were stacked up like 747s over Pearson airport.

Another voice: "Since we, quite properly, apologized to the Japanese for confiscating their property at the outbreak of the Second World War, why oh why don't they reciprocate and express at least passing penance for inventing karaoke?"

Most are speaking in that soft, tell tale accent peculiar to Canadians of the upper classes, best described as a mid-Atlantic twang. More accurately, it is a combination of Canadian private-school English and metaphors inherited from stints at Oxford or Harvard, or a week at *La Sorbonne* (which they pronounce "Sourbun"), where our international Brahmins rehearse for life.

The Rosedale assemblage displays the over-pampered, the siliconed, the nipped and tucked of all sexes. They are the social totems, whose bodies exude the finishing touches of yoga teachers, tennis coaches and the best-in-breed plastic surgeons.

The party is being held in honour of Maurice Strong, official troubleshooter for Kofi Annan, secretary-general of the United Nations, and World Bank president James Wolfensohn. The topic under discussion is Third World deficiencies. Strong is up to his old trick of calling world leaders by their first names, as in Saddam, Helmut, Bill, Jean, Muammar and Benjamin. Toronto entertainment lawyer Michael Levine once told me about driving with Strong to a nomination meeting in Toronto's Scarborough Centre riding. The world statesman was after the federal Liberal candidacy, so he could become prime minister of Canada. (It was one of his down times.) In the car were philosopher John Ralston Saul, renaissance person David Beatty, Levine and Strong. Being a compassionate type, Levine expressed his sorrow at the death, that morning, of Pope Paul VI, pointing out that most people would probably be mourning the institution, rather than the man, because the pontiff had been such a cold fish. "Not at all," Strong objected. "Paul was a hell of a sweet guy!"

I know that I'm at an Old Establishment event because *being there* is all that matters, not great conversation, good food or shared hospitality. Once you've arrived and been noticed by the host or hostess, the rest of the evening is superfluous. That, of course, applies equally to those who have not been invited or don't bother showing up. It's their absence that is noted and will forever define their ambivalent status in Toronto's social galaxy.

Somebody comes up and delivers a dreary *non sequitur*. Do I believe in sex before marriage? Well no, not if it delays the ceremony.

Beside me, a veteran of many a Brazilian Ball confesses that she has signed up for an extension course on spiritual awakening through organic gardening. I can see her scampering around her back garden, searching for her inner child, hoping to connect with the little bugger before he arms himself with a flame-thrower or bazooka and blasts her to eternity. But I digress.

I decide to station myself in the entrance hall. It resounds with the hollow smacks of air kisses, as guests enter and are officially greeted by the hostess (the one who displayed a propensity for quoting W.C. Fields). Air kissing is a specialty of the old Canadian Establishment. The rules are simple: man or woman, you air-kiss one cheek for casual acquaintances, two for serious prospects. But the execution can be tricky. The kiss must not really be an empty, thoughtless gesture, such as sucking in air while smacking your lips—like that loud, um-mwah sound which is a giveaway of desperate social climbers. Rather, there has to be a pretence of actually kissing, but you must avoid at all costs any area near the lips, so that you don't smudge lipstick or the powder covering the electrolysis dots. Saying "dahling" as you kiss is not recommended. Genuine Counts and European wannabes kiss women on the back of the hand while looking longingly into their eyes. Hungarians regularly empty national treasuries with this gesture. *[A rumour persists that back in the mid-1980s a visitor from Brandon, unfamiliar with the kissy-face culture, actually kissed a Rosedale hostess smack on the lips. She was never the same after that, and when last heard from was painting unicorns on a Greek island.]*

Air kisses are followed by a rapid Cold-War-in-Berlin, Checkpoint Charlie interrogation, expressing the common lust for info, passwords and countersigns that pervades Toronto social gatherings. Rumours are passed around like after-dinner mints. So and so seduces anything that isn't mineral. Will Harrison McCain marry Sis Weld? Why did Dick Thomson stick around for two lifetimes as chairman of the T-D Bank? Will Ken Thomson survive John Tory's retirement? Will Liz? Why does Izzy Asper stay in Winnipeg? Why Izzy Asper *should* stay in Winnipeg. Shouldn't I know what Murray Edwards does? How did John Cleghorn ace Matt Barrett into giving up his bank? How did Barrett meet *that woman?* *[The sequence went something like this: When Catherine Nugent attended Hilary Weston's swearing-in as Lieutenant-Governor of Ontario, she asked Matt Barrett whether he was still married, and he admitted he was available. "Well, have I got a girl for you!" she told the Bank of Montreal chairman, and phoned her friend, Ann-Marie Sten. She had meanwhile been invited quite separately by Melanie Munk to the dinner being given in honour of the Peter Munk Cardiac Centre, at the Munks' new Forest Hill house. Ann-Marie stayed with Ken and Marilyn Thomson when she first arrived from Europe, but was not particularly struck with Matt at the Munk party—though he was clearly smitten at first sight. The next day, Ann-Marie phoned Catherine, and said, "If he wants my number, he'll have to get it from you." Barrett did phone Nugent the same day. "He told me that he didn't think he'd made such a great impression," Nugent remembers, "but I said, 'Look, you're Irish. Use your charms.' And the rest is history. Eight weeks later they were married. It's so funny because they were married in the Cathedral Church of St. James, and the priest called me and said, 'Do you think it will last?' I said, 'How do I know? As much as any marriage will last, and who knows?' She had the grace to say, 'You're right!'"]* Is Charlie Baillie for real? Which CEO and his secretary went ballooning in the Loire country, and were celebrating their induction into the mile-high club when the contraption landed in an orchard, and . . .

The ever-present media consultants (gossips with connections) are casing the party, hoping to acquire enough Brownie points from clients to grab a lifestyle of their own, or at least a credit rating. The place is fuelled by mutual envy; dread of drab is what it's all about.

There is gentility here too, such as the youthful Forest Hill fiancée, her face half concealed by the Gothic arch of her falling tresses, who stands beside her man, a Wood Gundy bond specialist whose father once shot a Bengal tiger. They beam at one another, totally oblivious to their surroundings.

But mostly these are hard-core Old Establishment types. As I look into their eyes and watch their somewhat jerky limb movements, it seems to me that they are not, as they once were, relaxed in their tranquil possession of power. They are scrutinizing each other with pawnbrokers' eyes, trying to gauge whose going-rate is dropping, calculating and recalculating their net worth—and pondering even more seriously their self-worth.

This restlessness is new. They are suffering a crisis of nerve and faith, a loss of the easy self-confidence that once marked their passage. In my mind's eye I see these meticulously groomed personages sniffing the air, sitting around their campfires (those giant fireplaces in draughty old living-rooms), comparing notes, wondering where all their self-possession went. They would sooner have lunch with Mel Lastman than admit it, but they know that their world is no longer their own. And they realize, the best of them, that they ought to have perpetuated their power more purposefully, that they relied too heavily on surrogate managers, distant cousins or spoiled first sons.

They forgot the first rule of any establishment: power must be harvested as carefully as it is seeded. And then they forgot the second rule: any élite that fails to renew itself is bound for extinction.

HOURS LATER, RETURNING TO MY HOTEL in a taxi, I reflect on my own connection to Canada's establishment—keeping in mind Gore Vidal's admonition that anyone who doesn't feel paranoid about power is not in full possession of the facts. I have never considered myself the Establishment's companion-in-arms, but rather, its court jester—not in the sense of being a clown, but in the same context as Shakespeare used jesters in his plays, as bit players who deliver uncomfortable truths to the royal court, disguised as quips and fables.

The ambivalence of my relationship to the Establishment was best caught by E.P. Taylor, who was its unelected dean in the 1950s and 1960s. I had written a lengthy but not very flattering chapter on him in my first book, *Flame of Power*. When a mutual friend asked Taylor what he thought of me, Canada's most powerful businessman replied, "I've got his number—he's a goddamn Communist"—which then, at the height of the Cold War, was about as low as anybody could be ranked. But then Taylor added an unexpected codicil. "Still," he said, "I'm not taking him off my Christmas card list just yet."

My perfect epitaph.

Another apt comment was in *Time*'s review of my first Establishment book, published in 1975. After admiringly commenting on the considerable new material I had gathered, the newsmagazine concluded: "Newman's book reads as if he was invited into the Establishment's homes. Once."

Thank you very much. I stumbled into the idea of writing about the Establishment in 1969, when, after a dozen years as a political columnist, I moved to Toronto, first as editor-in-chief of *The Toronto Star* and later in the same job at *Maclean's*. Cut off from writing about federal politics, I began to meet the heads of large corporations and the chairmen of humongous banks—men who were secretive, strong-minded, puritanical, uptight, and yet, for all their arrogance, compellingly fascinating. My interest grew as I learned to discern the subtle differences between wealth and power, influence and authority, their reality and mine.

A few of the individuals I got to know were hostile, most were friendly, all were circumspect. They shared the view that if discretion was good, anonymity was best. Having confined their past dealings with journalists to muffled signals dispatched through their public relations departments, they weren't sure how to deal with me. For the most part, they treated me warily but did not exclude me entirely from their confidences.

Viewed through a working journalist's hourglass, the exercise of power is essentially a spectacle of personalities and generations in conflict, and that was what I chose to feature. The raw exercise of power fascinates because it sets in train the most compelling of human emotions: greed, the lust for power, the need for conquest.

From the beginning, I recognized the validity of the notion that power in this country resides in various élites, and have ever since concentrated on trying to define and detail the workings, origins, interconnections, rivalries and operational codes of these power cliques.

Canada's Establishment was—and is—dominated by the corporate élite, partly because its members move freely from function to function, sliding in and out of Liberal cabinets, filling seats on the boards of cultural institutions, making themselves felt within the governing bodies of universities, running most of the aggregations of power that count. "Corporate power is not tangential to Canadian society," concluded James Eayrs, the University of Toronto political scientist. "Corporate power *is* Canadian society."

This is the third of my Establishment books. The first volume in this series took six concentrated years of effort to complete and included 678 interviews, many of them with reticent individuals who had never talked to a journalist before. The critics were kind but the Establishment was highly skeptical. Some of its Toronto members, for example, put enough pressure on the bookshop at the Art Gallery of Ontario to cancel its order; others threatened lawsuits.

During the two decades between publication of my first Establishment volume and this book, I also wrote *The Bronfman Dynasty*, which first revealed how mighty whisky barons bootlegged their way to one of the world's first fortunes and became a quarrelling tribe that earned its title "the Rothschilds of the New World." *The Establishment Man* followed. It portrayed the young Conrad Black, who at that time was a real person and had just established himself in power by staging a brilliantly executed and bold grab of Argus Corp., already then one of the country's great (if leveraged) capital pools. Next on the publishing list was the second volume of the Establishment series, *The Acquisitors*, a study of the crass paladins who turned huge real-estate fortunes in the early 1980s. They tried too hard to substitute lifestyle for character, and by the end of the decade most of them—and their grubstakes—had vanished.

As I noted while attending the party that began this prologue, by the late 1990s something unexpected and exciting was happening to the Canadian Establishment. A new posse of corporate paladins rode into town—or rather, out of town. The digital revolution had made it possible for these upstarts to operate their fledgling empires on an international scale; approval of the FTA—and the North American Free Trade Agreement that followed—made it mandatory. They were swift to capitalize on new global opportunities, and absolutely mercenary in their methods, capsizing the Old Establishment with glee and not a smidgen of regret. I decided to name them Titans, referring to the mythological creatures who had created the original concept of power and staged history's first coup.

In its simplest retelling, the myth goes something like this: Uranus, the Sky God, and Gaia, the Earth Mother, gave birth to six sons and six daughters, who in Hesiod's mythology were called Titans. The entire brood revolted against their dad, because the mean old guy was locking up their brothers and sisters inside a cave. Eventually, one of the sons, Cronus, took a sickle, cut off his father's testicles, and threw them into the sea. The kids then got together and made Cronus king. This set the pattern for all future corporate takeovers. Cronus understood how power works: you retain it by eating your own. Cronus took this literally and swallowed his kids, until his wife, Rhea, tricked Cronus into swallowing a rock instead of her newborn son, Zeus. When he grew up, Zeus defeated the Titans, including Cronus, and banished them to the underworld—which only proves that no Establishment lasts forever.

This book, then, chronicles the demise of the Old Establishment and the passage from the Titans' hesitant beginnings to their current glorified status. They now run Canada's economy, and thus the country. God help us all.

Fashioning the story of how the Titans took over has occupied my literary sweat and rapt attention for the past three years. I've interviewed most members of the old crowd and the new—their critics, enemies, outriders, groupies and whisky priests. Out of those encounters, this book: the Titans' essences, methods, motives and cheatin' hearts—who they are, what they do and how they get away with it.

I | THE DEAD AND THE QUICK

1

THE NEW CANADIAN ESTABLISHMENT

"Reputation is character, minus what you can get away with."

—*Seymour Schulich, Toronto mining millionaire*

HOW FITTING TO BE THIS CLOSE to heaven, circling the globe in pursuit of Titans. I am aboard Cathay Pacific Airways, winging across the Pacific. We are still the width of Canada from Hong Kong, heading northwest towards the international dateline, an imaginary mark that slices through the narrow isthmus at the tip of the Seward Peninsula, separating Asia from North America, and one day from the next. The 747-400's four Rolls jets are bucking a headwind of 150 knots said to be blowing out of the Gobi Desert.

Across the aisle, a sleek Oriental businesswoman seems lost in reverie as she mindlessly caresses her Palm Organizer. Beside me, a Yankee trader with a cruel slash for a mouth is calling down an unnamed antagonist: "Dumb bastard couldn't count to twenty-one 'less he wuz naked," he mumbles and goes back to sleep. Midnight aboard the global express.

These sixteen hours in the sky afford me a chance to ponder the question, What is new about the Canadian Establishment that I must travel halfway around the world in my quest to pin down the source of its power? In the old days, a series of lunch dates at the Toronto Club would have told the story, so small and tight was the universe that contained much of the nation's élite.

But clubs are ponderous, heavily decorated buildings—terra firma—permanent structures with thick foundations and patrons who tend to be clay-footed (club-footed?), moving slowly along traditional paths to pre-determined goals. The networks of the Titans, who form the new-style establishment, are more like telephone exchanges that its members can plug into and out of, as required. Their users are birds on a wire, fast on both feet, corporate acrobats operating without a net. These postmodern Titans of the Info Age are joined more by their cell phones than by any sense of belonging. Their ever-shifting allegiances build empires without blueprints, as they feel their way up the corporate food chains. The Titans' motto is simplicity itself: Whatever Works.

These new "Masters of the Universe," as the American essayist Tom Wolfe named a similar group that has taken over Wall Street, know who to trust and who to betray, which deals will fly and which won't. How to get that IPO done before the CEO loses his marbles. Even at the sexual level, they operate less on their emotions than on their survival skills, quickly sizing up which partners qualify as buddies and which as potential lovers; who is symbiotic and who is toxic.

The Titans are far more worldly and sophisticated than the Old Establishment ever was. Unlike the former players, who felt secure in the backing of their peers, these new power wielders operate strictly on their own—gunslingers always heading for the OK Corral. Winning isn't important; it's everything.

Linked by the excitement of their interlocking venture of the moment, the Titans' power base is built on the shifting sands of mutual self-interest. These structures crumble the moment their usefulness is spent. Seldom is there a set game plan, let alone a book of rules; long-term planning is next Wednesday morning's power breakfast.

These sons and daughters of the new meritocracy are lethal when crossed, terminally self-absorbed and impossible to satisfy. They believe implicitly that it's never too late to have a happy childhood, and subscribe to Ashley Montagu's dictum that your goal in life should be to die young as late as possible. They live for fun as much as for money. They pursue both to the ends of the planet—with book writers trailing behind on Cathay jets.

Canada is but a dot on their virtual maps of the mind.

ONCE UPON A TIME, LONG BEFORE THE AGE of Conrad Black, Bre-X, Jimmy Pattison, Hibernia, Peter Munk and Voisey's Bay, there was a Jurassic Canadian Establishment.

The achievements of the country's earliest business pioneers were recorded with careful diligence in ledger books by clerks with fingerless gloves. Their ticks marked the acreage of fallen timber, the depth of mine shafts, the spread of harvested grain. They measured human sweat and sinew in terms of mercantile profit. The hardiest of these primitive paladins eventually formed an uneasy collective of interests, based on family rather than individual benefit, each assuming responsibility for its slice of the Canadian pie. The James Richardsons sold the grain; the H.R. MacMillans chopped down the Pacific forests; the Harry Oakeses relieved the Canadian Shield of its gold. In its frontier beginnings, this early meritocracy adopted the Darwinian edict, the survival of the fittest and the fastest. They were the swift, the strong and the brave. They became, over time, the family dynasties that made up Canada's original establishment.

That primitive establishment made up its own rules of behaviour. Its members practised insider trading with exuberance, feathered each other's nests with considerate grace, maintained their workers in patronizing insecurity and, with the instincts of an unregulated oligarchy, gleefully forced competitors out of their misery.

They thought themselves valuable and loved; in fact, they were necessary and tolerated. Someone had to organize the means of production, prime the pump of enterprise, tame the wilderness, build the factories. Someone had to buy the grain, process it, sell it back again. Someone had to keep the wheels in motion.

This early version of the Canadian Establishment represented private wealth and decision making, but it operated in what was virtually a risk-free environment. Since their Presbyterian God had lived up to his part of the bargain—placing the minerals into the rocks, spreading the rich soil across the plains and allowing the forests to sprout on the rainy coasts—members of the fledgling Establishment had few worries. They were nurtured by government subsidies, having formed a cosy marriage with the political establishment by backing those politicians pragmatic or opportunistic enough to do their bidding. They traded allegiance for handouts, while the politicians turned a blind eye to their excesses. Within this government-sponsored day-care atmosphere, Canadian enterprise grew and multiplied.

The private compacts of Canada's original commercial giants, whether of family or state, nurtured self-interested conservatism above all other personal and social values. Calmly in possession of power, the Establishment's adherents put down solid roots in their communities, regions and provinces. The arcs of their influence seemed immovable and enduring. They were the Titans of their time, supporting their crude Pantheon of commerce and industry.

The more contemporary establishment that followed became a coherent instrument of power during the 1940s. It helped deliver the country from the Great Depression—its speculative greed having helped to cause it in the first place. Its members contributed significantly to the war effort and masterminded the economic reconstruction that followed. Its influence helped Canada to become a world player in the postwar years, as a founding force in the United Nations and NATO, and eventually as a member of the Group of Seven summits.

This establishment's original members were the thousand or so business executives, nearly all of them WASPs and well educated, at a time when a university degree was still a privilege, who had been recruited to serve their country as "dollar-a-year men" after the Second World War broke out. A little older than their confrères who were rushing to enlist as officers in the navy, army and air force, these non-combatant volunteers had already found places in the country's cautious, penny-pinching business firms, many of them family enterprises. More than most men their age, they were full of ginger and ambition, set on getting ahead, not burdened with the inner conflicts and self-questioning so typical of people who grew up earlier and later. And yet, their pre-war professional lives had been muted by the pervasive Canadian colonial mentality of the period—the feeling that their country was small-time, a place where nothing important had ever happened or was ever likely to happen. They had been taught—and they had learned their lesson well—that history was made across the sea or across the border, that the best Canadians could manage was bound to be an imitation.

Their Ottawa stint turned out to be the most creative season of their professional lives, because it rid them of that deferential attitude. Their innovative talents flourished as they learned to be self-reliant and open to risk—to manage the world at large without having to copy or feel inferior to their involuntary British and American mentors.

As they began arriving in wartime Ottawa, they found themselves catapulted into a hothouse atmosphere that was confusing, frustrating, occasionally absurd, but unmistakably alive. The excitement of those times and their rapidly formed friendships would feed the participants' nostalgia for the rest of their lives. When he was into his seventies, E.P. Taylor, who spent the war in Ottawa and went on to establish Canada's most powerful beer monopoly, told me how, on the afternoon of his first day in Ottawa, he walked into the cramped office of Henry Borden, the Toronto lawyer turned dollar-a-year man. Borden was on the telephone. He gestured for Taylor to sit down and continued his conversation with the sales manager of North American Aviation Incorporated in California.

"Yes! Yes!" Borden was shouting into the mouthpiece of the old-fashioned upright instrument. "Yes, we damn well need those trainers or we can't get our air force going. We'll buy them from you. Cash on the barrel head! Of course I know about your Neutrality Act. But I've got this scheme. You deliver the planes to North Dakota, at the Saskatchewan boundary line. Have your men taxi them right up to the border. We'll have our fellows on the Canadian side throw ropes across . . . Yes, ropes. You just attach them to the undercarriages and we'll pull them into Canada. Got it? Thanks. It's a pleasure doing business with you . . ."

The man who set the style for the members of this select group, and became their deity—both as a model of efficiency and as a depository of a business ideology they could believe in—was Clarence Decatur Howe, the shrewd Yankee who became MP for Port Arthur, Ontario, later known as Thunder Bay. The single most essential lesson he taught his "boys," as he called them, was that effective networking meant power, which for its time was a remarkable breakthrough. In first reviving, then operating, a diverse economy flung across an unlikely hunk of geography, Howe's protégés identified the important decision makers across the country. They knew who counted and who didn't, who could be relied on to do a job and who was in it for the glory. They set down the rules of how to deal with one another, how to arrive at consensus views and attitudes, and how to control the country's political system without interfering too blatantly with its democratic roots.

It was this thin but essential network of connections and interconnections between businessmen from every region and each industry that evolved into the modern Canadian Establishment. It turned out to be an astonishingly resilient group.

At the close of the Second World War, the dollar-a-year men fanned out to run the nation they had helped create. Their work ethic, their mix of superior attitudes and pragmatic business methods, and the way they saw the world and one another determined the country's economic and political course for most of the next three decades. They had come to Ottawa as individuals; they left as an élite.

It was the subsequent flowering of this cadre of high achievers that altered the definition of that most elusive of commodities, the Canadian Identity. Up to then, whenever Canada was examined as a society, it was almost always in terms of its French–English problems, or its agonies as a pygmy nation in thrall to one or the other overdeveloped empires that had attended its birth. The country was rarely viewed through the prism of its true status as one of the world's most successful capitalist states. Yet that's exactly what Canada had become: a capitalist society run by clusters of interlocking élites who formed a self-perpetuating junta, in both their economic clout and their political agenda-setting aspirations.

The fiscal paladins who operate this system—then and now—are much more interested in exercising power than in analysing it. Attempts at introspection throw most of them into inarticulate confusion—with one exception. Whenever they hear the words "free enterprise," something inside them clicks to attention. Their faith is more a collection of attitudes than any carefully conceived theology, but their version of capitalism in its purest form does follow a catechism of sorts. It isn't written down, but it might read something like this:

- Good men (and presumably, good women, though power has yet to become an equal-opportunity employer) always contribute more than is demanded of them.
- Nothing improves the soul as much as a hard day's work well done.
- The marketplace rules supreme. It must govern every transaction. Everything, therefore—and everyone—has a price.
- Any incentive not based on the profit motive is hopelessly romantic.
- Since virtue can only be certified by worldly accomplishment, financial success is tangible evidence of holy favour.
- The possession of power is essential, because the exercise of authority acts instinctively to restore order, perpetuating the hierarchies inside which people know their place and keep it.
- Since economic freedom and political freedom are indivisible, democracy and capitalism necessarily reinforce one another. Private property thus becomes not only the basis for the free enterprise system, but also the source of individual freedom.
- Every piece of social legislation proposed by any government is a potential affront to future liberties and must be opposed by all available means.
- The real enemy of progress is Big Government. There ought to be a bounty on bureaucrats; they are little men and women with quartz eyes and pink hands, serving the blind dictates of the state.
- Compassion is for losers.

SUCH ARE THE GRITTY TEN COMMANDMENTS at the heart of the capitalist ethic. Out of this dog-eat-dogma emerges the business establishment's stoutest conviction: the public sector's agenda must be subordinated to the private sector's imperatives. A typical oath of allegiance to this notion was the declaration by Trevor Eyton, the sometime senator from Brascan. "A person born into this world," he told Toronto's Empire Club, "brings with him an inalienable birthright—a shadow—a simple, dark silhouette unique to him, that follows him wherever be goes. Canadians, however, have an extra shadow which follows them and walks beside them whether the sun shines or not, and unlike the first shadow, it isn't weightless, but is in fact very heavy. This second shadow can and does do incredible damage to all things Canadian—the economy, business, even our individual characters. I refer, of course, to Canada's governments . . . Dear Mr. Government, love me, but leave me alone." The sentiment was echoed by the late Roy Thomson, a Toronto barber's son who became one of the world's great press lords. "The welfare state robs people of incentive," he decreed. "If, in my early days, there had been family allowances, old age pensions and all the rest of it, I wouldn't have done what I did. They say business is the law of the jungle. I think it's the law of life. If you want to prosper, you've got to be ambitious. You've got to be ready to sacrifice leisure and pleasure, and you've got to plan ahead. I was forty years old before I had any money at all. But these things don't happen overnight. Now, how many people are there who will wait that long to be successful, and work all the time? Not very many. Maybe they're right. Maybe I'm a bloody fool. But I don't think I am."

WHAT KILLED THE OLD ESTABLISHMENT? For one thing, its members persisted in treating anyone who wasn't a member of their club with equestrian condescension—a relaxed insolence that assumed their effortless superiority. They didn't change; the country changed around them.

I well remember standing outside the House of Commons in Ottawa one sunny day 25 years ago, as Senator Norman McLeod Paterson, the Fort William grain merchant who owned 109 elevators and one of the largest merchant fleets in the Great Lakes, was having his picture taken. He had one foot on the running board of his magnificent, tug-sized Rolls-Royce. When I asked him whether he belonged to the Establishment, Paterson went berserk. All he could do was bellow a *non sequitur*—"What do you mean, we're rich old men!?"—jump into his car and roar away. He would happily have run over me, had I not jumped out of the way.

Perhaps, I speculate, even if the good Senator wasn't a great example of it, the Old Establishment believed too much in good breeding—whether it was their brood mare or Cousin Eleanor. Indeed, I sometimes nurse the vague suspicion that some misguided interbreeding might have been going on. That would account for all those gleaming, prominent overbites among Establishment brides . . .

Maybe the Old Establishment simply grew too absurd. At the height of one oil boom, I managed to chase down Bill Herron, a Calgary millionaire, to confirm that his eight-year-old poodle Peppi had a bank account, only to discover that the pooch was also the registered owner of a Cadillac with steer horns on its hood. The trail grew mercifully cold after I interviewed the daughter of mining magnate M.J. Boylen, whose whippet owned a full wardrobe, including camel-hair coat, tuxedo and yachting jacket.

No, they were not all eccentric write-offs. Too many were perfectly reasonable—but passionless. What helped defeat Canada's former élite was not that they were an establishment, but that they were the *Canadian* Establishment. Being Canadian meant that they didn't possess the passion or shrewd energy required to hold back the barbarians at the gates. They weren't élitist *enough*. More precisely, they weren't passionate enough about being élitist to maintain their supremacy. Their natural arrogance didn't carry the day. People in theatre know that it's passion that triggers the fine edge of madness which carries actors past artifice into art. That never happened. Brilliance and originality in sons and daughters were ranked well below their sense of family loyalty and occasional civilities.

THE EXISTENCE OF AN ESTABLISHMENT IS NOT SOME woolly writer's literary invention. It is real. It is the hidden hand behind the hidden hand that organizes means of production, decides who gets what and how much, when things get done and why they get vetoed. The exercise of their self-anointed authority is subtle, not always successful, but constantly aimed at fulfilling Lord Russell's definition of power: "the production of intended effects."

Establishments change. Telephones stop ringing, power shifts into different hands. Influence begins to be felt from unexpected directions. The Old Establishment's centurions die or are deposed, and their successors turn out to be not just different sets of people, but a new mutation.

There was a time when the Establishment in this country was more orderly, much easier to read. There existed an almost mystical constellation of the powerful. Everyone knew who they were: the bank chairmen, the steel company presidents, the senior partners who ran the Bay Street legal factories, the trophy accountants, the superstar stockbrokers who could move markets, and above all the founders and heirs of the Great Family Dynasties.

Every influential power holder occupied a position as specific as a piece on a chessboard. You were in or you were out. There was little truth to the notion that the Establishment was engaged in a class conspiracy to exploit the masses. Certainly, working men and women were exploited, but the old élite had little need to conspire. Its members thought the same way naturally; that's what made them an establishment. As Heward Stikeman, unofficial dean of Montreal's English-speaking élite, puts it: "The Old Establishment was a coterie of people who respected each other, worked by the same rules, followed unwritten codes and operated telepathically together."

"The men who really wield, retain and covet power in New York," Nicholas Pileggi wrote of the most power-conscious city on Earth, "are the kind of men who answer bedside telephones while making love." Pileggi ought to have included the women who have also been known to pick up receivers at crucial moments, but his statement stands as a definition of modern love and the contemporary work ethic.

Perhaps that's the real reason the new meritocracy so smoothly grabbed power from the Old Establishment: the geezers warned, "Brace yourself, old girl," and ignored the ringing phone. Well into my third shot of whatever the Cathay stewardess is listlessly handing out, the theory seems to have merit—particularly since I recall one prominent member of the new meritocracy recently telling me quite proudly, without even a wink, that he had actually placed calls during his most intimate moments.

The New Establishment is a floating crap game. Anybody can join. What counts is the margin by which your enterprise will exceed its previous quarter's earnings. In short, you are what you do—or more precisely, what you've done today, this afternoon—and achieve tomorrow.

MERITOCRACY IS A FIVE-SYLLABLE WORD with the simplest of meanings: making it on your own. Even a partial run-down of the current establishment quickly validates the concept. Craig Dobbin, the most important business presence in Newfoundland, is a lumberjack's son whose first job was as a freelance salvage diver. Harry Steele, who holds similar status in Nova Scotia, is a fisherman's son from the tiny village of Musgrave Harbour. Paul Desmarais's first venture was to take over a bankrupt, one-route bus line in Sudbury. Jimmy Pattison began by selling used cars to his college frat brothers. The late Pierre Péladeau bought his first paper with a borrowed $1,500. Jean Coutu and Murray Koffler, who have operated the largest pharmacy chains in the country, each started with one small corner drugstore. Calgary's Murray Edwards, the most interesting of the new West's money men, is the son of a Regina accountant. Peter Munk brought nothing with him when he escaped from wartime Hungary except his will to succeed.

All of these highly charged individuals and the many others who qualify as modern-day Titans have one driving force in common: they fervently believe that what can be conceived can be created.

There used to be coalitions of power brokers who ran Toronto, Manitoba, Halifax—all the parts of the economy that mattered. Their word was law. Now, there are mainly impatient individuals, negotiating. They may join together for specific projects, but their alliances seldom evolve into enduring structures. If alliances are required, they are based not on handshakes as they used to be, but on fifty-page contracts drafted by platoons of lawyers and signed with black ink in triplicate.

"If you've paid your debts in this town, you're Establishment," says Ron Coleman, the real brains behind Bobby Brown's reign at Home Oil and now a successful money man, talking to me in Calgary's Petroleum Club, where the Oil Patch Barons once ruled, and where now anybody with $65 a month in their jeans can join, the same day he—or *she*—applies.

"Reputation is character, minus what you've been caught doing," emphasizes Seymour Schulich, a Montreal investment specialist, lured to Nevada by the quality of its poker games, who struck it rich and now works in Toronto, with a six-shooter in his desk.

"The Canadian Establishment? It's an endangered species," says Matt Barrett, chairman of the Bank of Montreal, himself about to join that category.

These are a few of the voices of the new meritocracy, an awkward term that Thomas Jefferson coined eons ago. He described it as "a natural aristocracy, based on virtue and talent." Virtue? Among today's Titans? Not as Jefferson would have defined it, but the New Establishment's major players do share a loose set of character traits that help make them who they are. Their highest "virtues" are cunning, competitive fire, greased-lightning decisiveness, a passion for their quests. This, plus talent, is what separates the current power-wielders from their predecessors, who belonged to a vastly different aristocracy, one squarely based on inheritance, clubs, private schools and family connections. By definition, such an aristocracy depended for its authority on sets of assumptions;

meritocracy depends for its juice on sets of brass knuckles. It assumes nothing except that muscle and moxie are what matters.

Tracing the causes for the Old Establishment's demise, there is little doubt that it was too soft and too forgiving. For example, when Bob Rae, who is smart and charming, was a socialist premier of Ontario, the local establishment treated him as the devil incarnate, nicknaming him "the Bobarian at the Gate." As soon as he left office, however, he became the Establishment's darling, was invited to join Goodman Phillips & Vineberg, one of Canada's most prestigious law firms, and even became director of a major international bank, Crédit Lyonnais Canada, as well as Canadian Airlines and a handful of other companies.

More significant is the fact that the Old Establishment was so easy on itself. Few of its leading operatives were ever punished for being stupid, incompetent or both. When they were found out, that was usually the signal for a shift sideways, accompanied by a fat pay raise; few were booted from their positions of power. When Jean de Grandpré was ceo of Bell Canada Enterprises, he led Canada's largest firm into almost a billion dollars' worth of investments that nearly all turned sour; yet he retains an office and a secretary at BCE headquarters. (As an example of his business acumen, he purchased Montreal Trust for $875 million, invested $175 million, and sold it for $292 million.) George Petty presided over Montreal's Repap Enterprises' deep decline, yet he departed with full honours and a pay-off equal to five times his annual salary. In mid-February 1998, Ontario Hydro reported the largest write-off in Canadian history ($6 billion, plus another $3 billion pending), and not a single director, including chairman Bill Farlinger, was asked to resign or even to account for what happened. The British ideal of valuing corporate directors for their "lovable dimness" persevered even through the needless and agonizing bankruptcy of Confederation Life in mid-1994. No one, it seems, was to blame for the insurance industry's largest bankruptcy, which reduced the firm's assets from $20 billion to below zero.

The list goes on indefinitely, but my favourite example of incompetence rewarded is Hamilton's Dofasco Inc., once a model corporate citizen and employer. In the summer of 1988, Dofasco's senior vice-president, William Wallace, recommended the purchase of Algoma Steel Corp. for $713 million, cash. Only twenty-five months later, the entire investment had to be written off, and Wallace was promptly promoted to CEO and paid a $4.3 million bonus. He was succeeded by John Mayberry, who failed to meet the objectives for 1997 set by his own board, but who still took home a pay packet of $1.5 million—87 percent larger than the previous year. The list is endless.

In the end, here is what happened to reduce and finally deprive the Old Establishment's leaders of power: too many failed to take up what Henry James called "the demoralizing influence of lavish opportunity." They limited themselves to minting money instead of trying to make history. That is why, when the hungry newcomers appeared on the scene, possessing their razor-edged virtues, nothing like a war ensued. The new Canadian Establishment simply and efficiently captured most of the command posts that counted, a *coup d'état* that met little resistance. Indeed, the new meritocracy consolidated its authority without its predecessors being particularly aware of their demise. The Old Establishment wasn't murdered; it surrendered, while embalmed in a distracted stupor.

DISPLACED BY THE ARRIVAL OF THEIR POWERFUL SUCCESSORS, diminished by their shrinking fortunes and vanishing political influence, the Old Establishment continues to exist and exercise influence. There are still plenty of tough old cormorants floating about, occupying some mighty impressive roosts. Many of the vintage names still decorate the bank boards, most blue-ribbon corporations, Order of Canada nominations and the "A" lists of party invitations. But its members have increasingly become honoured bystanders.

While this ancient establishment continues to milk its sawmills and department stores, its coalmines and defence contracts, the juicy megadeals go to relative newcomers: Newcourt's Steve Hudson signs yet another lucrative deal for executive jets being leased south of the border; another British real-estate tycoon is lassoed into Peter Munk's expanding stable; one more mountain-top resort is captured by Joe Houssian. Izzy Asper is negotiating for TV rights on Mars.

The New Establishment's game? This is how some of its top players, and some of its keenest observers, define the rewritten rules:

Peter Brown, chairman, Canaccord, Vancouver. "Millionaires shop in warehouses now, and next they will do it from the television. Each technological advance creates winners and losers. If five years ago you had owned a shopping centre with two blue-chip anchor tenants, you thought, geez, that's something I'll leave to my grandchildren. Now the blue-chip tenants are bust, the shopping centres you can't give away because of technology and home shopping and the superstores. The changes in style and demographics have upset everything and everyone. There's a whole new Establishment out there."

Robert Fulford, culture critic. "Anybody today who sets out to make a deal, to sell a brewery or a piece of land or to buy a railroad, a piece of a railroad, I don't think any of them think, well, are the right people running it? They think: are they smart people, what's their experience, what's their bottom line? They never say, are they our kind of people? Because nobody knows what our kind of people are any more."

Bill Mulholland, former chairman, Bank of Montreal. "You put the country under intense economic pressure, which it is, and personal relationships become more and more expensive in terms of their performance burden. I mean, if you're screwing up, it isn't enough that you may be an old pal of mine. We don't have the margin for error and inefficiencies we once had. Recruiting and selection casts a twenty-year shadow, so you can't just look out for old friends any more. They must deserve their position."

Tom Long, chief partner, Egon Zehnder International (and senior policy advisor to Ontario Premier Mike Harris). "One of my best friends is Mike Perik, who built a little company called SoftKey into what is now quite a substantial-sized firm. He's based in Boston. He got married recently and I went to a little party that a bunch of guys threw for him down in Boston. When I looked around, I saw the wealth he had created for most of the people in that room. He's like a big speedboat pulling a lot of water skiers behind him. You can understand how someone like that could be pretty inspiring to a twenty-five-year-old MBA grad who's looking for a role model as someone who has made a difference. He's got a company that he built with his own two hands. And that's a lot of the reason why people are gravitating more and more towards commerce today, instead of politics and the public sector. They want to make it on their own."

Gordon Sharwood, financier and Bay Street guru. "I got a note from Conrad Black the other day, attached to an article from the *Daily Telegraph* written by Nicholas Harper, the editor of the *Tatler*, saying that this is the first generation of *nouveau riche* in England who were not interested in marrying their daughters off to earls' sons. 'Why go to Sunday lunch in a draughty castle,' he wrote, 'where the food comes from half a mile away and is cold and bad and you're sitting next to the earl's son who probably cheats at cards, when you can go to a renovated country inn with a Jacuzzi in your own bathroom and you know that everybody else in the dining-room is paying £250 a night and on their own merit.' That's exactly what's happening here. I mean, I've met some of these guys who are newly rich and I say, 'Why don't you come to lunch with me at the Toronto Club?' And they say, 'Where's that?' They've never been there. You see the change, when the O'Keefe Centre is named the Hummingbird Centre, owned by a guy called Fred Sorkin whom nobody had ever heard of five years ago."

French-fry king Harrison McCain. "The Establishment now is not just based on money; it's based on how well you've done in some area or another—it may be in any damn thing, even making French fries, I guess."

Paul Desmarais, chairman, Executive Committee, Power Corp. of Canada. "The old school ties are finished. It's what you do that counts. Still, if I'm friendly with somebody, well, I'll give him a break because I know him, but of course if you're friendly with a lot of people, I guess then you become a sort of Establishment on your own. But the Establishment of the old days, where I would go and sit with old Buck Crump (CPR), Earle McLaughlin (Royal Bank), Arnold Hart (Bank of Montreal) and Jean de Grandpré (Bell Telephone) and we could decide a lot of things, or you'd just sit there and say, well, we're going to do this or that, and geez, we'd do it—you can't do that today."

Hershell Ezrin, political guru and former CEO, Speedy Muffler King. "Being Establishment means that, even if we don't know each other, we share attitudes, we share friends and we share enemies. I had a dinner at my house not too long ago and a whole series of interesting and unusual people were there. There were editorial-page writers from *The Globe and Mail*, the niece of the former president of Israel—a whole series of different people. We started getting into a discussion about politics, and all of a sudden everybody was connected in one fashion or another. Now maybe it's because they're friendly with me and I'm friendly with them, we move in the same circles, but the circles are intertwined. So, even in a meritocracy we still find interconnecting relationships, though the entry-level dues are different. It's almost a bit of a Wild West for a lot of the new people."

Martin Connell, president, Calmeadow. "Being part of the Establishment these days very much depends on aggressive maintenance of your network relationships. If you're out of the loop, whether you're a cabinet minister or a captain of industry, for more than a month, you're out. Period. Your half-life is three days. You quickly dissipate your leverage. Networks are critical. To be inside the network is to be part of the New Establishment. It's very much alive. But the connecting points are different. Instead of putting your feet up in the leather chairs at the York Club, you're more likely to be found on the squash court or the golf course.

Still, it's Establishment predicated on the assumption that if you're a success, you're the tops. The nice thing is that it's now based completely on achievement."

Pierre Lassonde, president and CEO, *Franco-Nevada Mining Corp.* "Not only in Canada but throughout the world, the Establishment is being meritocratized. Even in Latin American countries, which used to be run by five families, wealth is trickling down to a whole new class."

Bill Dimma, chairman, Canadian Business Media Ltd. "The Old Establishment was on the whole more principled, more ethical, probably less dynamic and entrepreneurial than the crop moving into power. But in terms of creating wealth, a great deal more will be created in the new era."

Peter C. Godsoe, chairman, Bank of Nova Scotia. "Your Establishment keeps re-creating itself under a meritocracy. You're not born into it. I believe deeply in networks. Networks are information—people doing business with people, or working out political solutions."

Michael Cowpland, CEO, *Corel Inc.* "The Establishment has been turned into a meritocracy because it's not based on the school system or being buddy-buddy at the Rideau Club. It's based on what you can do, the functional things people do."

Bill Wilder, Bay Street financier and corporate director. "There is an Establishment, but it has been downsized like everything else and doesn't have the influence or the respect it once enjoyed. The Free Trade Agreement diminished it, because so much of business has come under foreign control. So, yes, there is one, but it's not a cohesive group that does things together very much any more. People like the Eatons have lost their stature. There are a few old trouts like me around who remember the old days, but there's no close group that's running the corporate sector now. What's taken their place are these hired guns."

Jacques Barbeau, Vancouver lawyer. "There's been a drastic change of culture, either by necessity or by desire. You can't leave the office at three o'clock in the afternoon or four, which you used to do; you can't take extended weekends. It's tough maintaining your competitive edge because it's forever changing. There's no security of tenure; if you don't perform every day, you're out."

Howard Beck, Bay Street lawyer. "How would I define the New Establishment? That you can no longer get a job in one of the chartered accountancy firms, legal firms or investment banking firms by depending on who your father was or who your uncle was. Those days have gone. A lot of people thought that Canada was controlled by a Family Compact. Well, that Family Compact has been turned upside down in the last fifteen years. But the country ends up being controlled just as tightly by different people—in fact, I would say more tightly. We now have a new Family Compact, a brand new Establishment."

John Evans, corporate director and global guru. "There is a group who perceive themselves as the Establishment in Canada and there are people who want to join that Establishment. But its shape and substance have changed. It's much more porous, it's much more all-embracing than it was before. The current transformation has changed the vertical structure of Canadian business into a very broad one, where nobody really can prevent someone from popping up almost anywhere in the scene, particularly in the industries where bright ideas, entrepreneurial zeal and just stubbornness count—that's where the new people are going to succeed."

Philippe de Gaspé Beaubien, founder, Telemedia Corp. "There will always be an establishment, there will always be people who are defined as leaders. My family has been part of that. I was the first in French Canada ever to own media in English-speaking Canada. When I lived in Toronto, it was so hard to shine, so hard to break in, because there was a cluster of a few families who were basically the same type, wore the same school ties and controlled everything. But today it has changed, not just in Toronto but all over Canada; there are so many different communities now. Things are opening up."

James Baillie, managing partner, Tory Tory Deslauriers & Binnington. "This firm is one of the two or three in Toronto that people really want to be part of, and we have a very highly organized hiring process. We have three to four hundred applications for our twenty-five articling positions every year. We then winnow those down to about a hundred twenty to a hundred thirty people, whom we interview. We then offer twenty-five positions. If I even tried, if I were to say, 'So-and-so came from Upper Canada [College] and is a friend of a friend and I think we should let that person in'—I'd have a rebellion on my hands. It's pure meritocracy."

THE CATHAY JETLINER, WITH ITS SILLY PURPLE-AND-pink fuse-lage, flying at thirty-two thousand feet above the Earth, is an aptly garish billboard for the high-riding global economy. We're over the Bering Sea now, heading towards the Sea of Okhotsk, and the cabin is dark. John Travolta is flickering on the in-flight movie screen, waving a gun at me, and I am trying to conjure up old memories of the two men who epitomized the Canadian Establishment twenty years ago, Bud McDougald and Nelson Davis. They ran the Argus Corporation before the 1978 coup that transferred ownership to Conrad Black.

I remember sitting with McDougald in the sun-room of Green Meadows, his magnificent Toronto mansion, with its Georgian stables, willow-lined drives and thirty-car garage. We were discussing his death. Since he had no children, I had asked him what provisions he was making for succession.

He began his reply with a startling proposition: "*If*, as, and when I croak . . ." he said, leaving the unfinished phrase hanging between us.

"How do you mean, '*if*'?" I asked.

He looked at me for a long, revealing moment. Then he raised his eyebrows and waved his hand in a gesture of dismissal, as if to indicate that we were both aware of the vagaries of human existence, so why discuss them.

We went on to talk of other things. But I vividly recalled that brief exchange a few weeks later, when word came that John Angus McDougald had died, and Argus went into play, eventually ending up in Conrad's eager embrace.

McDougald's death reminded me of the one major disagreement that developed when my book about that era's Establishment was done. McDougald asked to see my chapter about him. I told him that I never show anyone anything I write before publication and that he would be no exception. His eyes flashed. He rose from his desk, began shouting at me, suggesting that his purchase of my employer, Maclean-Hunter Publishing Ltd., was hardly worth the trouble to shut me up, and finally calmed down when he recognized that my position wasn't negotiable.

Bud's closest corporate buddy had been Nelson Davis, a rich and secretive Toronto conglomerateur, who was the prototype for the rich and powerful of his day. Unlike most of the Canadian Establishment, he was much more interested in spending money than in making it. "Every time I make a dollar," he explained to me, "I spend a quarter of it on myself. There's nothing wrong with that." (His personal income at the time was about $12 million a year.)

Striving for perfection in all things was an obsession with Davis: the perfect house (he had five); the perfect car (he drove six); the perfect servant (he employed eighteen); the perfect boat (he owned twenty); and the perfect golf course. A long-time member of the Rosedale Golf Club, Davis had second thoughts about the place when a duffer's ball nicked his nose. "I'll build my own," he said, and promptly bought a 350-acre tract near Markham, north of Toronto, dammed up the area's streams, moved trees, threw up hills, and created Box Grove, one of the best eighteen-hole golf courses in the country. He remained the club's only member and employed his own pro, Jimmy Johnstone. Arnold Palmer often flew up to play the course with Nelson.

If Nelson Davis had one passion besides his never-ending search for perfection, it was his yearning for anonymity. His Toronto house had five unlisted telephone numbers. His entry in the Canadian *Who's Who* was limited to name, rank and serial number. American journalists who occasionally stumbled across his name and glimpsed the extent of his fortune offered to place him on the covers of *Fortune*, *Time*, and the old *Saturday Evening Post* if he would only speak to them. But he never did. I was the only one to interview him. He was a keeper of distances and liked it that way. He died shortly after McDougald, and with the passing of these two giants the Establishment changed irreversibly.

I often find myself musing upon what that unusual pair would have thought of today's élite, whether they would have felt kinship or revulsion towards the Titans. Probably both. They would have admired the new breed's grandiose visions and appetites. Ultimately, though, McDougald and Davis were rigid men who built walls around their accumulations, around their belief systems, around their insistence that there be tradition and loyalty. They never stopped believing that they understood how the world worked and how to work the system. They would have been eaten alive in the borderless, fluid universe of the Titans.

The wheels of the Cathay Pacific jet touch Earth. Suddenly, the cabin lights are up, the movie is turned off and the heavens are aflame with a new day. We passengers grab briefcases and close power notebooks—the same dance here as on the tarmacs of Toronto, Frankfurt, Chicago, Paris, Rio.

That is the new reality the Titans know and embrace with genius. That is why they spend so much of their working lives in the heavens, alighting now and then, for profit and pleasure, in outposts most friendly to their aims. That is how the New Establishment thrives and evolves, exerting its power, still, over a very real place called Canada, half a world away.

2

EPITAPH FOR THE
FAMILY DYNASTIES

"For God's sake, let us sit upon the ground
And tell sad stories of the death of kings . . ."

—*Richard II*

IT'S LATE MORNING ON DECEMBER 20, 1996, and I am wading through downtown Toronto's Eaton Centre, swimming against the crowd, on my way to interview its namesake: Fred Eaton, titular head of the retailing empire that spawned this terrible place. The centre runs on pure energy, proof that Toronto's cutting edge is aggression. The heat and electronic impulses emanating from this crossroads of commerce could light a metropolis, and probably do.

As the crowd grows thicker and more insistent, I give in, allow myself to be carried along by the throng, and recall that I lived here once, was editor-in-chief of the GTA's house organ, *The Toronto Star*, and actually understood the dynamics of this Empire City. As I turn towards the Eatons' private offices, two young women pass by, done up in the radical chic style of a few decades back, complete with Che Guevara combat fatigues, Fry boots and expensively mussed hair. I enjoy seeing them because they represent a more familiar Toronto, a time when you might occasionally hear Gordon Lightfoot on the Eaton Centre's canned sound system, instead of the oxymoronic "rap music" that now desecrates my ears. I throw them a salute and they give me that eyeballs-rolled-to-ceiling look reserved for Hopkins Landing wharf rats loose in the big city.

When I arrive at his office to visit with Fred Eaton, unofficial dean of Canada's family dynasties, he is out. I should have known. It's five days before Christmas and he's doing his Establishment thing: cruising the stores, wishing his underpaid, non-unionized staff carefree holidays.

Once he's back, we idly discuss the retailing revolution shaking his industry, particularly the impact of Wal-Mart's arrival as an Eaton's competitor. "Our company was accused of being the Wal-Mart of its age when Timothy was running it, because it was so different from anything that had come before," he says with a shrug, walking towards the wall-mounted model of *Brave Wolf*, the pleasure yacht he enjoyed while in England as Canada's High Commissioner. "There is room for all kinds of operations—the more traditional, fashion-conscious retailers like us, and the big-box discounters like Costco and Wal-Mart."

As we stand in the back part of his office, musing admiringly over the replica of his current boat, the *Defender,* an impractical but stunningly beautiful forty-seven-foot day sailor designed for him by the naval architect Mark Ellis, I mention the rumours swirling around Bay Street. The story is that Eaton's is in big trouble, that its bankers are fed up with the store's pathetic cash flow and are planning to foreclose; that the Eaton empire is about to collapse.

"Is it true?" I ask.

"No, no," he shoots back. "Why would you think that? There are always stories about us, that we're being sold or something. Nothing to it."

I realize only later that Fred Eaton was lying, or at least, as the vernacular goes, "mis-speaking himself," which you would have thought he had learned to avoid as part of his toilet training. Fully a month before our interview, on November 21 (as revealed later in court documents), Eaton's traditional lenders, the Toronto-Dominion and Bank of Nova Scotia, had turned down the family's request for a 50 percent increase in their unsecured loan. At the beginning of the same week as I met with Fred, the family was actively discussing bankruptcy. Two months later, the once powerful clan filed a "protection from bankruptcy" document, which was accepted by the court. Its fourth page contains the phrase that shook the Canadian Establishment to its elegant roots: "The applicants are insolvent."

IF THE CANADIAN ESTABLISHMENT EVER HAD ITS OWN role models, it was these lords of the department stores, who led charmed, fairy-tale lives until they crashed to earth in the cold retail season of 1996–97. The family's pride had been rooted in the fact that, as Canada's largest private company, the details of their financial dealings were kept away from the grubby reach of everyday folk. Proprietorship guaranteed secrecy. To be an Eaton meant never having to tell your story.

A few weeks after my visit with Fred, his brother George, the only sibling by then still making a pretence of running the family shop, scrambled to recruit American vulture capitalists to lend emergency funds that would postpone the day of reckoning. With that admission, it was clear that the four brothers, in charge of the family company since the early 1970s, had achieved the impossible: run a business that had once dominated the country's retail trade, straight into the ground. The idea of being special, which was what had kept the Eaton boys' noses pointed upwards for most of their lives, was history. Now, they were just another shivering huddle of prospective bankrupts, trying to keep the sheriff at bay.

The downfall of the Eaton dynasty as a force in the Establishment was a final blow to the WASP ascendancy that had ruled the country for more than 130 years. The family's economic dominance and distinction as a Canadian role model had been the last line of defence for Canada's White Anglo Saxon Protestants who felt besieged but not yet vanquished. Now that the Eatons had "blotted their copybook," as the Establishment's severest admonition goes, it became permissible to make fun of WASPs, the only ethnic group it was politically correct to scorn.

The piteous details of the Eatons' demise are fully visited later in this chapter, because their story contains the basic plot element played out again and again across Canada in the past decade. This is an epitaph for the great family dynasties that once dominated Canadian commerce.

INDIVIDUALS DIE; FAMILIES ABIDE. Or so the theory goes. Yet what has altered the Establishment more profoundly than any other single factor has been the dramatic fall of Canada's family dynasties, which until recently were central to its power structure. The dissipation of these once closely held and carefully nurtured private fortunes has devolved power into strange new venues.

The Eatons were not alone. No longer can the patriarchs maintain the primacy of their offspring on the basis of their seeds instead of their deeds. The very idea of Canada being run by a self-perpetuating clique of family dynasties—in an age when corporate conglomerates have become as mean as they are lean—seems quaint and out of place.

Some clans, mainly in the Atlantic provinces, such as the Irvings, Grahams, Sobeys, Jodreys, Ganongs and Olands, remain in control of their business empires. But many other, once powerful dynasties, such as the Southams, Siftons, Birkses, Kofflers, Crosbies, Romans, Blackburns, Lundrigans, Reichmanns, Poslunses, Creeds, Burtons, Steinbergs,

Hermants, Gersteins, Jefferys, Iveys, McLeans, Woodwards, Crosses and Bassetts, have been deprived of their economic clout and its concomitant social stature. In some cases, they have been reduced to little more than collections of vaguely connected people with the same last names.

When they were functional, dynastic families acted as quasi-sacred institutions. They were preserved not for the filial feelings they might inspire, but as the fiscal instruments by which accumulated wealth and disposable power were transferred from one generation to the next.

The notion of business dynasties perpetuating themselves was based as much on faith as on economics. In reality, the idea that blood relatives, usually eldest sons who assumed the leadership mantle, could automatically be relied on to add value was pure bunk. It assumed that the essential life force that created a family fortune in the first place could be passed on through the genes, like blue eyes or a disposition to hay fever. It seldom happens.

The creative spark that gives birth to any great enterprise is hard to define and impossible to reproduce. Except in rare instances, succeeding generations do not spawn presiding geniuses able to expand the family enterprise. "The inheritors to large fortunes are faced with very difficult tasks," points out Sam Blyth, the Establishment's Toronto travel agent, who was married to Rosemary Bata and saw the problems firsthand. "Everybody blames them for everything that happens after they arrive, but to turn around a company which is structurally impaired is an assignment that even the most brilliant would find most difficult."

The inheritors who assume direction over "dad's estate" suffer from "affluenza," a malady that garners little sympathy in a society that treats money as the cure for all ills. Growing up in golden ghettos without walls, they don't learn to deal with real life or the give-and-jab of normal business situations. There was a time when, cradled in the endless Indian summer of their lifelong adolescence, the sons and daughters of the rich lived in taken-for-granted luxury and enjoyed every minute of it. No more. Aside from the initial rush that comes from taking over their father's or uncle's fortune, the inheritors quickly discover that merely being rich is not enough. Living on inherited money is a secondary thrill at best; it never impresses the way earned money does. While unearned fortunes don't necessarily bring uneasiness, neither do they accord their owners much distinction. *[This isn't always true. Some inheritors have an easy passage, feeling that they don't have to prove anything to anybody. Hal Jackman, who impressively expanded his father's financial empire, refused to impress his peers by spending money. "I used to have a 1971 Ford station wagon, which I stopped driving* *because it literally fell apart," he explained. "So then I bought a 1969 Lincoln for $2,000, even though it had started to rust. I hate taking cars in for repairs because the garages charge too much." Now he takes limoousines. Mostly.]*

Judging by the record, most Establishment heirs blow their financial wads with only the occasional genuflection to reality. They spend their father's and grandfather's fortunes, while exhibiting resentment that their legacy has made it so difficult to demonstrate their self-worth. They expend false energy trying to prove that they're just like anybody else—all the while enjoying the extraordinary privilege of never having to beg, steal or borrow. Their idea of going hungry is to leave uneaten a slightly disappointing *filet de sole meunière* in a declining French restaurant.

Inheritors often lose their nerve and are frightened of responsibility. They abandon their family's entrepreneurial spirit, go over the edge and eventually become paralysed in their suspicions that no one loves them, that even their friends and lovers might be there for the money. The fear of giving away the source or sum of their fortune, of committing themselves to offers of friendship, fills their minds with smoky, ill-defined resentments. They begin to feel alienated and suspicious, becoming everybody's gravy train and no one's intimate. Instead of being appreciated for the comforts it buys, money becomes despised for all the problems it didn't resolve and the magical expectations it didn't fulfil. "Having money," one inheritor sadly confesses, "is like being a beautiful woman in a romantic novel—you're always wondering whether men love you for your body or your soul. You distrust warm gestures. You search constantly for those little signals that show people's *real* intentions."

As one sage remarks: "To the founder of a family firm, the business is everything; to his children it's a challenge; to the grandchildren it's a property; and after that it's a quarrel." *[The saying goes: "Grampa starts the business, his sons make it grow, and his grandsons piss it away."]* The odds do shrink drastically. According to Gordon Sharwood, chair of the Canadian Association of Family Enterprises, only 15 percent of family companies make a successful transition to the founder's children, and fewer than 3 percent to his grandchildren. By 1925, for example, only three generations after the founding of Massey-Harris, one of this country's defining family firms, there wasn't a single Massey—or Harris—willing or able to run it. *[Third-generation heiresses tend to open florist shops or antique stores. The boys with brains become doctors; the others end up as bankers or brokers.]*

Other families have suffered from similar problems. Murray Koffler and Eddie Creed, for example, shared the experience of having their

ventures bankrupted by their children. Opened in 1988, the overly luxurious $38-million King Ranch spa, run by Adam and Tina Koffler, proved
too expensive ($2,500 per week) to sustain enough client visits, and
went bankrupt. As did Eddie Creed's magnificent Toronto fashion store,
when he turned it over to his son Tommy and his daughter-in-law Shari.
The four well-intentioned but misguided sons of Toronto optometrist
Sydney Hermant allowed the Imperial Optical chain to slide into bankruptcy. Similarly, the Billes family could not decide on succession of the
Canadian Tire empire, until Martha bought out her brothers, Alfred and
David, for $45 million. The Loebs of Ottawa, once Canada's most innov-
ative retailers, vanished as an entity, bought out by Provigo, because they
were unable to field a united front. E.P. Taylor's son, Charles, was a
gentle soul and a sensitive writer, but showed no interest in perpetuating
his father's empire. No member of Lucien Roland's family wanted to grab
hold of the family-owned Quebec paper company. The McCain feud has
still not resolved the firm's succession problem.

A model succession was being worked out at the Oshawa Group,
which runs the IGA franchise. Founder Ray Wolf's son, Jonathan, was
having to prove himself under professional management. His assignments included counting the goldfish in the sales tank at one family
store. It didn't work. Outsiders now run the firm.

Few families have quarrelled more publicly than the Krugers of Montreal, who run a $3-billion-a-year pulp and paper organization that
employs more than 9,000 workers. Founded by Joseph Kruger in 1904
and brought to greatness by his son Gene, it is now run by his grandson
Joseph II, who may well be the most nervous and most hyper CEO in the
land. *[During our interview, he kept grabbing my tape recorder and spinning it back to
hear what he had said, which was basically that he had nothing to say.]* The family was
involved in a horrendously embarrassing seven-year court case that
pitted Bernard Kruger against his late brother Gene and his son Joseph.
At one point in the court proceedings, so many documents were being
produced that fifteen large filing cabinets had to be installed in the
courtroom to store them.

One of the stranger succession stories involved Beland Honderich, the
authoritarian publisher who ruled *The Toronto Star* for most of four
decades. His son John, a capable writer but not necessarily an automatic
pick to succeed his father as publisher, had so impressed the paper's directors that he was their almost unanimous choice to succeed his father. At
the time, Beland wasn't talking to his son, wouldn't even invite him to
his house, and argued strongly against the appointment. At the same

time, John was having a major policy disagreement with his father about the sale of the *Star*'s Southam shares to Conrad Black, preferring to hold on to them as a base for the Toronto daily's future expansion. The struggle went on for three months in the fall of 1994, with neither side giving way. John Evans, the *Star*'s board chairman, finally persuaded Beland that he had been out-voted by a board he had dominated for so many years, and the father reluctantly gave way. The son has since taken the *Star* to new levels of editorial perseverance.

Marvin Gerstein, whose father, Frank, founded the Peoples Credit Jewellers chain in 1924, cast a vote against a proposed 1994 restructuring and drove the business into bankruptcy rather than have his nephew Irving continue running it. The younger Gerstein, having announced his intention of becoming the world's largest jeweller, had expanded so fast that the firm's debt ratio reached a ludicrous 72 percent of its capital structure, and the whole enterprise collapsed under its own weight.

A sad truism: each generation of the rich tends to shed its most passionate and outspoken members, too often by suicide. *[Harvey Southam, the most lively, creative and compassionate of the bunch, hanged himself from a bridge in Toronto's Rosedale Ravine. Percival Talbot Molson shot himself in his office only ten weeks after assuming the family firm's presidency.]* Families thus lose the possibility of renewal or change. The arrogance of heredity can create a sad spectacle at both ends of the generation gap. Too many rich fathers and mothers fob off the task of raising their brood onto governesses and tutors. Harvey Southam's only childhood memories of his mother were "a brush of her mink coat and a whiff of her perfume as she was going out the door." Love, unlike money, cannot be transmitted to sons and daughters through fiduciaries.

Founding fathers are hard acts to follow. "For the original entrepreneur, the business defines his position in life," concluded Harry Levinson, a New York psychiatrist who specializes in research on the corporate father–son relationship. "When a son is brought into the business, the father has all the problems of a man who introduces his rival to his mistress."

"These days," says former Ontario premier David Peterson, who has become a heavyweight Establishment adviser since being thrown out of office in 1990, "you're almost doing your kids a favour by not involving them in the family business. Let them build up their own self-esteem, doing what they want to do, instead of what their daddy did. Family companies are destructive to families. Who wants to discuss business over Christmas dinner?" Dr. Howard Book, who studies family enterprises, claims (only half in jest) that the ideal family arrangement may be the

Corleone clan, immortalized in the *Godfather* Mafia movies. "Promotions are tied to merit, not family hierarchy," he points out. "Michael Corleone, the youngest son, is chosen the new Don over his older brother because he is the most capable. The Corleone family treats all employees the same. When his older brother betrays him to a rival mob, Michael coldly kills him, just as he would a non-relative." Ted Turner, the quixotic American media mogul, followed this advice at a family dinner to celebrate his sale of CNN to Time Warner. When "Teddy" Turner IV, Ted's thirty-three-year-old son, asked his father whether his job at Turner Broadcasting was safe, the senior Turner shot back, "You're toast." And he was. *[Being part of a great dynasty starts early. When a poor Jew, walking in one of London's upper-class districts, sighted a baby Rothschild being carried into an elegant Rolls-Royce by a self-important, uniformed chauffeur, he is supposed to have exclaimed, "So young, and already a Rothschild!"]*

"These are testing times for Canada's business dynasties," recently concluded Bernard Simon, the *Economist*'s Canadian editor. "One after another the families that held sway over big chunks of the country's commerce and industry for decades—sometimes generations—are struggling to adjust to an unforgiving world in which access to capital and nimble management matter more than worship at the right church or skiing at the right private club. For many years, the odds were stacked in favour of family money. Outside shareholders, such as pension funds, were a passive bunch. Members of the Establishment (overwhelmingly white, Anglo-Saxon and Protestant) knew each other and helped each other. Much of that has now changed. Several families have tripped up trying to pass the baton from one generation to the next. Domineering old men have tried to hang on too long; youngsters have proved less talented than their sires."

In short, in the Age of Meritocracy, the family dynasty has, by definition, become a spent force.

ONE WAY FAMILY DYNASTIES ATTEMPT TO assure their survival is by going public, paying off unproductive heirs and hiring talented surrogates to exercise authority on their behalf. The Thomsons, Bronfmans, Molsons, Reitmans, Rogerses, Shaws, Moffats, Aspers, Chagnons, Westons and several others have followed that route. On the negative side, this has meant sharing secrets—having strangers inspect the family jewels. *[When they were flying high, the Reichmanns were obsessed by secrecy. So much so that when there was a minor fire at the First Canadian Place office tower in Toronto, rival real-estate executives rushed over to count the number of evacuated tenants; it was the only way they could estimate the building's occupancy rate. The found-ing brothers never did go public, but in the fall of 1997, Albert's son Michael did, and bought out the family's remaining share in the building.]*

"Those families that have gone public," points out the Bank of Mon-treal's Matt Barrett, "have had to realize that when you sell your sover-eignty, you sell the right to self-indulgence and thereby you become hostage to the interest of the people who have invested in your company. In the old days, there was sufficient capital generated within those great dynasties that they could do whatever they wanted. Today, you need access to outside capital, and the minute you go public, it's a different game."

It is easy enough to dismiss the downfall of the great business dynasties as inevitable and of little consequence. Yet this country was built on the evolution of family firms into national institutions. *[With assets divided among too many hands, family firms eventually vanish, but the families remain, even if the fortune that bonded their efforts is spent. When the Gooderhams, who dominated Canada's liquor trade before the Bronfmans and whose business was taken over by them, held a family wedding, there were so many that they had to wear name tags.]* At one point in the 1950s, nine families controlled nearly half the shares on the Toronto Stock Exchange. According to Diane Francis's *Controlling Interest*, as late as 1986, some thirty-two families, along with five con-glomerates, held sway over one-third of the country's corporate assets, and their combined income was $43 billion larger than the revenues of the federal government.

When Canada's family dynasties ran most of the economy, profit was their animating motive, but they also fostered—however patronizingly—an attitude of genuinely caring for the communities in which they lived and prospered. Established family wealth (with its palace guard of legal retainers, chartered accountants and investment counsellors) was not used only on private fripperies. At its best, the local family firm became a community trust. Because the people who lived in the surrounding region worked there, a relatively benign, neighbourly system of tolerance was in play. Family managements hesitated hard and long before laying off their neighbours, and the neighbours, in turn, hesitated hard and long before organizing themselves into unions. Whatever its faults—and the main one was the clear absence of accountability—the system worked, and it was more humane than its opposite: businesses run by multina-tional firms that switch loyalties and locales with the weather. The men and women assigned to head these transnational outposts have little interest in or knowledge of the communities to which they are temporar-ily posted. Their loyalty to Canada is at best ambivalent; their dollars seek the highest rates of return, regardless of the impact that may have on the country or the county. In Canada's case, the transnational firms are usually run by transients in any case—either bushy-tailed juniors who can't wait to move away so they can climb the head-office ladder, or passed-over managers on their pre-retirement postings.

A detailed investigation into the history of Canadian towns reveals how many local enterprises once flourished in this country, and how quickly this astonishing roster has disappeared. Ted Rushton, an impressive essayist who once lived and worked in Orillia, recalls that the little Ontario town on the shores of Lake Couchiching once boasted a prominent manufacturing base. Its factories were owned by entrepreneurs whose names have long vanished from contention, but who at the time were substantial people running substantial assets. *[They included: J.B. Tudhope, R.J. Sanderson, C.J. Miller, E. Long, W.H. Crawford, James and Sam Bailey, Alexander Ramsey, William Cars, M. Tupling, D.C. Thompson, D.H. Church, A.J. Wright, M.W. Plunkett, George Vick, J.H. Ross, C.H. Hale and T.B. Cramp.]* These families and so many others were once an important part of Canada's economic fabric; with some notable exceptions, they now count for nothing. Canada's few family dynasties that remain active and solvent are on notice. No matter how appealing the *idea* of the family dynasty might be, its reality is seldom a viable option. Too often, second- and third-generation sons and daughters simply don't possess the hunger that propelled their forefathers.

What follows are some examples of Canada's leading family dynasties and accounts of what's befallen them.

THE SIFTONS: *As If They Never Existed*

A case history of how feuds can destroy a dynasty, the Siftons, once *the* powerhouse family on the Canadian Prairies, have vanished as the influential politicians, businessmen and newspaper proprietors they so recently were. They set down the matrix for the economic evolution of the plains. Yet their only surviving monument is the skeleton of their flagship head office on Winnipeg's Carlton Street, a castle-like structure abandoned until its recent purchase for redevelopment, which once housed the mighty *Free Press*, whose editorial thunder shook the West.

Amidst stiff competition, the family's most famous character is Sir Clifford Sifton, the Edwardian statesman who, as interior minister in Sir Wilfrid Laurier's governments, opened the Prairies to rapid settlement by recruiting hundreds of thousands of European immigrants, whom he characterized as "stalwart peasants in sheepskin coats." Knighted for his civilian contributions to the First World War, he bought the *Brandon Sun*, and lived out a glorious career.

Themselves immigrants—Protestants from Ireland's County Tipperary—the Siftons arrived in Canada in the 1820s. John Wright Sifton moved from Ontario to Winnipeg in 1875 and was later named Speaker of the provincial legislature. His *Manitoba* (later *Winnipeg*) *Free Press* eventually became the most influential voice of agrarian liberalism, especially during the lengthy and inspiring stewardship of John W. Dafoe as editor, between 1901 and 1944. Dafoe attracted such stellar disciples as Bruce Hutchison and Grant Dexter. The paper transcended its provincial boundaries and became a vital national force, upholding a largely Liberal view of the world, though Dafoe also wrote good words about Clifford Sifton's favourite policies, including Sir Robert Borden's nationalism and the Progressive Party's concern with agriculture.

J.W. Sifton was succeeded by his sons. Arthur Lewis Sifton, who moved to Calgary, became chief justice of the territorial Supreme Court—a post that automatically made him the first chief justice of the newly created Alberta Supreme Court in 1905. Five years later, he quit the bench to become Liberal leader, and he served as premier of the new province from 1910 to 1917. He later moved into federal politics as a cabinet minister in the Borden government.

The two significant offspring of the next generation, Clifford and Victor, outdid their elders in many things, especially in the intensity of their rivalry. The brothers served in the First World War, both rose to the rank of major, and both were awarded the Distinguished Service Order—but Clifford won out over Victor by being wounded three times. It had been a contest, and throughout their lives they behaved as contestants. The family acquired the Saskatoon *Star Phoenix* and the Regina *Leader Post*, but the brothers' incessant quarrels made it impossible for them to work together, so Victor ran the *Free Press* while Clifford retreated to Saskatchewan. The Winnipeg side of the family lost its power base when Victor folded the paper into the newly founded F.P. chain, in return for an ownership interest that was passed on to his son John, who in turn passed it on to his son Victor. *[Perhaps the dynasty petered out because its members couldn't think up new names. Nearly all the males were named Clifford, Victor, John or Michael.]* In 1980, *The Winnipeg Free Press* was sold to Ken Thomson.

The other branch of the family prospered under Clifford's son, Michael Clifford Sifton, who moved back to Toronto, where he also ran Canada's largest privately owned airport (at Buttonville, near Toronto) and built the world's largest indoor polo field. *[When he was ill and hooked up to a kidney dialysis machine at Toronto General Hospital, Michael Sifton used to phone me to recount stories that always made out the other side of the family to be brigands. The feud never stopped.]* Michael's sons, Michael and Clifford, sold their papers to Conrad Black in 1995 for about $50 million, mainly to cover debts acquired through failed high-tech and real-estate investments. By then, the family's energy level was so low that the remaining Siftons didn't even bother trying to scare up competitive bids. It was as if the dynasty had never existed.

THE MOLSONS: *The Family That Couldn't Think Straight*

Of the surviving family dynasties, the Molsons have the deepest roots, stretching back to the eighteenth century and the earliest English settlement along the St. Lawrence. Current head of the empire—or what's left of it—is Eric Herbert Molson, an inarticulate and unimpressive character who looks as if he came from central casting in response to the call for someone who would be believable as the fumbling heir to a 212-year line of brewers. A graduate in chemistry from Princeton University, Eric, a sixth-generation Molson, fits the bill perfectly. Assessing his record makes it obvious why the Molson dynasty seems to have run its course. What he achieved was to lose control of the family brewery, so that while the dynasty still existed, it lost any reason to perpetuate itself. Then it cost him $438 million to buy it back.

The brewery was founded in 1786 by John Molson, who arrived in Montreal from England as an eighteen-year-old orphan with £250 to his name and lived to see his family take on its aura of established wealth and prestige. This first Molson not only made beer, but in 1809 built the first successful steamboat on the St. Lawrence. Its speed gave him an edge in obtaining financial news, which helped him increase his fortune during the War of 1812. In 1826, he also became president of the Bank of Montreal, following a stint in Quebec's legislative assembly. One of his sons, John, became president in 1836 of Canada's first railway, the Champlain & St. Lawrence line, while another, William, set up Molson's Bank in 1854. This significant institution, which had 125 branches when it merged with the Bank of Montreal in 1925, placed the family in the position of being able to issue its own paper money. By the end of the nineteenth century, there were so many Molsons involved in Canadian finance that few outsiders could get an accurate idea of their influence. *[The family's genealogy is difficult to trace because several Molsons married cousins. Two sisters, May-Ann and Martha, married their cousins, John and Thomas; John Molson III married the daughter of his uncle William.]*

The most conspicuous and interesting recent family member is Hartland deMontarville Molson, an uncle of Eric's who, following a distinguished military career that included flying a Hurricane during the Battle of Britain and being promoted to group-captain, became president of Molson in 1953. At ninety-one, he still goes to his Montreal office, resplendent in a three-piece, pinstriped suit and military moustache. He had nothing to do with the company's disintegration, but when asked about it, his eyes rolling heavenward say it all. The former senator sat in the upper chamber as an independent. "Because beer is sold through provincial governments of all parties, I couldn't be in Parliament and be political, so when Prime Minister Louis St. Laurent invited me to go in the Senate, I thought about it a bit, called him back and said, well, I couldn't accept to be a senator unless it were as an independent because I couldn't get mixed in the political fight and remain in our business. He very graciously said that there was no need to be a party member. And so that was what happened, I went in as an independent."

At one point in the late 1960s, the company ran out of Molsons and had to go outside for a new president. The choice was Donald Gilpin "Bud" Willmot, the capable head of Anthes Imperial, a heating and plumbing supply company operating out of St. Catharines, Ontario. He wouldn't leave, so the Molsons bought his company. They paid $74 million for Anthes, just so they could get Willmot, then gave him Molson stock worth $10 million—which yielded annual dividends of $350,000. At $84 million, it was the most expensive corporate recruitment in Canadian history. Willmot proceeded to diversify the company by acquiring a Quebec furniture manufacturing company, Aikenhead Hardware, Beaver Lumber, Willson Education Products, and Diversey Corp., a U.S. chemicals firm.

When Eric Molson became president of his family's operating company in 1980, the Montreal *Gazette* noted that "he scarcely projects the image of an imaginative, creative mover and shaker. One of his professors at Bishop's University in Lennoxville, who remembers students and their doings, says he cannot remember anything positive, negative or anecdotal about Eric Herbert Molson. His appearance is not striking. Should he ever find himself in a police line-up, witnesses would have problems remembering him."

Although he carries the nation's most historic surname and ought to have earned recognition, Eric Molson has spent the past two decades living in Toronto and Montreal and making an impression in neither. He is so far removed from the real world that in the fall of 1997 he videotaped a message to his own executives, who worked in the same building, rather than address them face to face. When Norman Seagram, the industry veteran who had spent more than twenty years in the most senior jobs at the firm and was persuaded by Eric to come out of retirement to run the company, was fired, he didn't even get a handshake. When Seagram showed up for work on May 9, 1997, only eight months after being hailed as Molson's saviour, he was handed a press release that announced his departure. Seagram was paid an astounding $2.5 million for his 160 days as the company's CEO, which at $156,000 a day was extravagant even by Molson's unrealistic reward scale. He was promptly replaced by a faceless Montreal lawyer named James Arnett.

It was no fun to work for Eric, but it certainly paid well—providing he dumped you, which wasn't much of a distinction, because everybody got dumped except him. Bruce Pope, who was let go as the brewery's president in November 1995, received $2,980,000, while Jack Edwards, a former head of the company's retailing arm, was cashiered with $6 million. Stephen Bebis, the head of another Molson subsidiary, received a cool $8 million, while Derek Cornthwaite, who ran the much troubled Diversey operation, had to make do with $3,367,550. Tough love, Molson's style.

Eric's most fateful venture was his hiring, in November 1988, of Marshall "Mickey" Cohen as Molson's president and CEO. By the time Cohen left almost eight years later, Molson had become an orphan, hobbled by a mountain of downgraded debt, owning only 40 percent of itself, its lucrative licensing agreement with Adolph Coors in jeopardy, its beer sales trailing Labatt's. Even the firm's sponsorship of the popular "Hockey Night in Canada" was aborted soon afterwards. The firm's results in Cohen's final full year—a deficit of $305,470,000—compared with a profit of $87 million the year before. That ranked Molson as the company with the third-highest loss on *The Financial Post*'s annual survey of corporate earnings; it fell sixty-seven places in the paper's overall rankings.

Cohen had sold off 40 percent of Molson's to Foster's Group of Australia and another 20 percent to Miller Brewing, a subsidiary of Philip Morris of New York. Though this all was presumably done with Eric's blessing, since Cohen's departure, the company has been desperately attempting to repurchase its birthright including a $438 million penalty. *[Announcing his departure from Molson, Mickey Cohen, who was sixty-one, cited age as the reason. "The next phase calls for a younger person," he said. He was succeeded by Norman Seagram, aged sixty-two.]* Its sales were also down from 53.5 percent of the Canadian market in 1989 to 45.3 percent by the spring of 1997. "The company has been an unmitigated disaster," concluded Jacques

Kavafian of Research Capital Corp. "There's practically nothing going in its favour. They keep losing market share and they haven't done anything to create shareholder value." Brewing expert Jamie MacKinnon echoed that sentiment in *The Globe and Mail* when he wrote: "Once a major name in Canadian business history, and so richly associated with the development of early Canadian commerce, Molson became just another rootless multinational entity."

When Molson shareholders began to object loudly and publicly that if Mickey remained in office, there would be nothing left of their company, Cohen did leave—and was rewarded for his efforts with a golden parachute worth $5.8 million. Much was made of his distaste for beer ("it makes me sleepy; it puts on weight; I prefer wine"), but that wasn't where the fault lay. Family dynasties don't bet the farm. When Cohen decided to do precisely that, by selling off control in Molson, there was no one to stop him. "The Molson family is not active in the business," Cohen told me during his stewardship. "Eric is chairman. He lives in Montreal and takes an interest in what's happening, but it's not a *participatory* interest. I talk to Eric once a week and keep him posted, but Eric is a master brewer. Molson is much more than the brewing business, but that's not his cup of tea. He's not interested in ruling the whole company. He's very hands off and the rest of the family is totally hands off. Eric behaves largely as a director, not as a proprietor. So it's a comfortable situation, but they don't act like proprietors."

It was precisely because Eric Molson stopped acting as a proprietor that he stopped being one, and had to pay the penalty.

THE BATAS: *Czech Mate*

The Batas can trace their family back an astounding eleven generations to Vaclav Batia, born in Zlin, Moravia, in 1580, who also made shoes. But the founding father of the current Bata dynasty was Tomas (1876–1932), a poor Moravian cobbler who started out with only $200—just like Frank Stronach. A dedicated proponent of efficiency, Bata copied Henry Ford's methods by applying time-and-motion studies to manufacturing, and even installed a miniature office in the elevator of his fifteen-storey factory, complete with telephone and filing system, so he wouldn't waste the moments spent travelling between floors. The firm grew so large that Zlin became a company town. Its products covered the world. "Work is a moral necessity" was the glum slogan he placed on his factory gates. "Tomas Bata felt he was sent out by God Almighty to shoe mankind," Karel Capek, the Czech philosopher, wrote of him.

The founder's son, Thomas J. Bata, was dispatched as a teenager to erect a factory in Switzerland, which would become the company's European nerve centre. *[Like every male Bata heir, Tom is endowed with a "cobbler's thumb," which can be bent backwards, almost to the wrist.]* The youngster was already well established in the business when his father was killed in a mysterious 1932 air crash, but at eighteen he wasn't ready to take over the firm, which by then was selling 36 million pairs of shoes a year. Control of the enterprise thus passed to Jan Bata, the founder's half-brother. This precipitated a family feud that ended only with Jan's death in 1957, even though effective power had devolved to Tom during the Second World War.

When the Nazis invaded Czechoslovakia in 1939, both Batas fled—Jan to the United States and Tom to Canada. Accompanied by a hundred of his most skilled workers, Tom also smuggled out plans for shoemaking machinery and much of the family's hoard of gold bullion. He used these assets to erect, equip and man a new plant at Batawa, a small Ontario town near the Bay of Quinte that duplicated the facilities at Zlin. (Batapur in India and Bataville in France would follow.) From this base, Bata eventually built up the global empire that at its height supplied one out of every three pairs of shoes sold in the world's non-Communist countries. Soon after the end of the war, the company's head office was moved to Don Mills, Ontario. Instead of following their founder's American example, the Batas opted for something closer to the Japanese model, with company songs, employees referred to as Batamen and Batawomen, and management that ran the enterprise with an unrelentingly paternalistic attitude. The Bata empire—sixty-four factories in sixty-one countries, now turning out about 270 million pairs of shoes annually—has about it a kind of divine fervour, a ritualistic devotion to the product and the family. The organization maintains its own college courses, roving inspectors, secret codes and private communications networks.

In 1946, Tom Bata married Sonja, the daughter of George Wettstein, a prominent Swiss lawyer who had set up the original family trusts. Profits of Bata Limited, the family holding company, are distributed among a private foundation in Switzerland (which acts as the banking house for the whole organization) and two Bermuda-based trusts (the repositories of the Bata family fortune). No outsider has access to their books. This tax-friendly set-up means that it is not the family but the trusts that own the business; so, legally speaking, the Batas just administer their assets without actually owning them. "We don't have a clear line of proprietorship," Sonja mysteriously confides. "I think the last thing the children expect is that they are going to be owners." An architect fascinated by design, Sonja quickly became a shrewd and knowledgeable partner in the growing business, as well as a significant patron of Canadian arts. She established a unique shoe museum in Toronto to house her historical collection of ten thousand pairs of shoes, and became an honorary captain in Canada's navy. *[In the summer of 1997, at age seventy-one, Sonja Bata, sitting in the back seat of a jet fighter, roared off the heaving deck of the USN aircraft carrier John Stennis, on patrol in the Pacific.]*

The company has declined sharply since its heyday in the 1960s, when it was making and selling a million pairs of shoes a day. That was in the days before Nike, Adidas and Reebok. *[The founder of Reebok did approach Tom Bata for a partnership, but was turned down because "he was a funny little guy and we didn't know him."]* The firm has suffered serious problems, with the bankruptcy of its French retail operation and of its eight-hundred-store Pic 'n Pay chain in the U.S. The Batas have fallen behind in their attempts to compete with other "cooler" brands that have mass appeal with the young. The Batas' insistence on vertical integration in an age of outsourcing prompted one Bata executive to explain: "We're not a true multi-national, we're a multi-domestic corporation, tied to obsolete manufacturing and trade patterns."

As the senior Batas age—Tom will celebrate his eighty-fourth birthday in 1998, Sonja will be seventy-two—their company is in a transitional mode, with no successors in sight. The couple occupy adjacent offices at the Don Mills headquarters, and they dominate the place. Others who have been brought in to run the company—their son, Tom Jr., who was CEO from 1985 to 1994, or a U.K. marketing whiz named Stanley Heath who was appointed to succeed him and lasted less than a year—are granted little opportunity to implement fundamental changes. The son's arrival and departure was particularly painful because he was born to the job, took a Harvard MBA to hone his skills, but was never given the freedom to run with his ideas, which included going partially public. *[Tom Jr. remains a director; his sister Christine chairs the Chilean company; Monica chairs the Italian branch; and Rosemarie is a successful writer-researcher in Toronto.]* "Tom," says his mother, "is a typical product of Harvard University, highly analytical and has a very quick grasp of what needs to be done, but he has difficulties implementing particularly tough programs, as we had to during his time when we had to close some companies and manufacturing plants." Rino Rizzo, an old family retainer, is currently the firm's president and CEO; chairman is Tom Symons, founding president of Trent University.

As family dynasties go, the Batas seem to have reached the end of the line. The company will in the future learn to survive outside the eleven generations that created it.

STEVE ROMAN: *Fall of the Roman Empire*

My favourite memory of Steve Roman is of being at the castle that overlooked his 1,200-acre estate just north of Toronto. He sat there, his dimpled stocky body at ease, sipping a plum brandy, complaining about why he had never made it into the Canadian Establishment. He looked like a rich peasant in one of Tolstoy's late novels, and I could visualize him in a country tavern, on the evening of market day, drinking beer out of a huge tankard and wiping chicken grease off his chin.

The house reflected the man: an in-your-face feudal castle, but not phoney, like so many of the pseudo-British country seats that decorators were then inflicting on Canada's New Rich. Like the man, the house was large (seventeen rooms), tough (wall-to-wall marble) and vulgar (plush red sofas and cathedral-size crystal chandeliers), yet functional and impressive.

Roman seemed to have it all. He was a farm-boy immigrant who had become controlling shareholder of a company worth nearly $2 billion, a fervent Catholic whose confessions were heard by a bishop in his own private chapel. But Roman was obsessed by the fact that he had not been accepted by Canada's business élite. They never granted him the right qualifying badges, never appointed him to a bank board, and rejected him for membership in the clubs that mattered. When I asked Roman which clubs he did belong to, he was reduced to mentioning Toronto's Empire Club, which is no club at all but a Royal York Hotel luncheon group that sells tickets at the door. Still, he lived as lavishly as any of the country's wealthiest citizens, flying the world in his Gulfstream jet and fervently pursuing the most élitist of hobbies, cattle breeding. (One of his three-year-old Holsteins, Romandale Reflection Cristy, had made the *Guinness Book of World Records*.)

Stephen Boleslav Roman was sixteen when he left the isolated Slovakian village of Velky Ruskov with his brother George in 1937. He worked briefly as a guard on the Welland Canal, joined the Canadian army but was invalided out, played the penny stock market, promoted a few cow pastures, and in 1953 purchased 900,000 shares (at 8.5¢ each) of a speculative mining prospect known as North Denison. It turned out to be the site of the world's largest uranium ore body. Roman's greatest achievement was to raise the $59 million required to bring the property into production without losing financial control. Initially, his mine had contracts for uranium worth $1.6 billion. "I am here to do the best thing I can and build the best company I can," was his corporate philosophy. By the 1970s he had amassed orders worth $7.3 billion from Ontario Hydro alone, and his company had quickly expanded into other ventures, such as cement manufacturing, packaging, paper-making, potash mining and, most of all, a world-spanning hunt for oil. Unlike the paper shufflers who inhabit most of the Establishment's roosts, he was a builder and a risk-taker on a grand scale. If that meant being rough along the edges—and unacceptable to the rarefied tastes of the country's Establishment—well, he wasn't going to change. "Roman is something of a left-wing paranoid's wet dream," went the perfect description by Ted Mumford in *Quill & Quire*.

Steve Roman had an evangelical faith in capitalism and no faith at all in politicians. (Except Richard Nixon, whose election campaigns he supported as the largest non-American donor.) He aligned himself consistently with Ottawa. At one point, the usually mild-mannered Lester Pearson told Roman that he was "fifty years behind the apes," and he had even rougher discussions with Pierre Trudeau, who refused to believe that anyone like Roman could be free to roam the streets. It was only with Brian Mulroney that he found peace, often entertaining the Tory PM at his palatial quarters at Lyford Cay in the Bahamas. Roman tried twice (unsuccessfully) to get himself elected as a Conservative, but his personal passions were much more closely tied to erecting his private Cathedral of the Transfiguration, near his estate. The foundations of its twenty-storey tower and dome were consecrated by the Pope during his 1984 visit. "Everybody is put on this earth to perfect a divine plan," Roman pronounced, "and mine is to save my soul."

When he died of a heart attack at sixty-six, in the spring of 1988, Denison's stock went up a full point. His body was clothed in the ornate green uniform of the Order of St. Gregory, the highest honour the Vatican can bestow on a layman. While three choirs sang and a convoy of black limousines waited outside, 1,600 mourners filed through his private cathedral as thirty priests, wearing Technicolor robes, officiated at the funeral mass.

The company was taken over by his eldest daughter, Helen Roman-Barber, but her reign was so ineffectual that by 1997, Denison's stock was worth only 30¢ a share. Donald Thain, head of the University of Western Ontario's Ivey School of Business, who served on her board, resigned in anger and frustration, calling the mess he was leaving behind "one of the worst examples of corporate governance in Canadian history." And so another potential dynasty bit the dust.

THE CROSBIES: *Down and Out on Water Street*

"To be a Newfoundland Crosbie," observed the Montreal economist Dian Cohen, "is something like being a Greek Onassis." That's only true if you place that thought in the past tense.

The dynasty's founder was Sir John Chalker Crosbie, described by his own grandson as "probably one of the biggest old pirates that ever existed on the face of the earth." When his father died, the future knight quit school to run the family hotel, Knight's Home in St. John's, and was soon involved in shipping, construction, fisheries and marine insurance, all folded into Crosbie & Co. He later went into politics, an occupational hazard for most of the Crosbies, and held several cabinet posts in the colonial government; he was Newfoundland's minister of shipping when he was knighted in 1919.

His son Ches upgraded and modernized the family's portfolio, including ownership of Eastern Provincial Airways, an Arctic shipping line, a soft drink company and even a whaling operation. His companies built the Confederation Building, which houses most of Newfoundland's government offices, and much of the Memorial University campus.

Chesley's two sons, John and Andrew, had very different lives. John, the political brother, was a highly successful—and more surprisingly, well-loved—politician, even if he kept switching parties till he found one that suited him. Voted Canada's top law student, he finished his studies at the London School of Economics and went into legal practice in St. John's before joining Joey Smallwood's Liberal cabinet as minister of municipal affairs. Six portfolios later, he quarrelled with the premier, and after sitting briefly as an independent became an ardent Tory, devoted to destroying Smallwood, his former mentor. In the 1971 election, his brother Andrew (to whom John had sold his interest in the business) managed Smallwood's campaign against him. John later went federal and became finance minister in Joe Clark's short-lived government. He ran for the Progressive Conservative leadership in 1983, but was defeated, not so much because he admitted that he couldn't speak French, but because he went on to add that he couldn't speak Chinese either, so what was the problem? Crosbie brought to Canadian politics a rare sense of humour and humanity, and managed to make very few enemies. His memoir, written with *Maclean's* managing editor Geoffrey Stevens, was 1997's top non-fiction bestseller.

Crosbie's forte was putting down his partisan attackers during the give and take of the House of Commons question period. This was a typical example: when a Liberal MP named George Baker accused Crosbie of never having got past his Dick and Jane book in kindergarten, the Newfie Tory shot back that he was sorry Baker's library had burned down. "He lost all two of his books," Crosbie explained with feigned sympathy, "one of them before he finished colouring it; the other was *Playboy*."

Brother Andrew moved the family business into flight-insurance machines and foreign exchange kiosks in airports, as well as newspapers, printing, construction equipment and the oil supply business—on top of the thriving insurance business that had created the dynasty in the first place. In his prime, Crosbie had no equal in the Newfoundland business community; his forty-nine-company conglomerate employed 2,700 and had sales of $150 million. High interest rates and the 1981 recession helped sink him, as did Richard Spellacy, the president of his offshore, oil-rig service company, who charged his Maserati, a collection of opals and many other goodies to the company. Crosbie's grand-scale mismanagement and too much time with the bottle eventually sank the mini-empire. Near the end, Crosbie owed the banks $75 million, nearly all of it borrowed at floating interest rates, so that when they zoomed into the high teens, he didn't have the necessary cash flow to cover himself. When the Bank of Montreal sent a special agent into his office to monitor his affairs, Crosbie, who had once been hailed as the youngest director ever appointed to the Montreal's board, resigned on the spot. It was his most humiliating moment. "My grandfather went bankrupt, my father went bankrupt and now—well," Crosbie mused as his office was being shuttered by the receivers' agents. "Actually, none of us went bankrupt in the true sense. We all went to the very top, and the very bottom—then we came up again." Not Andrew Crosbie. He died before he could make a comeback.

THE SOUTHAMS: *The Dynasty That Suffered Fools*

Four generations and you're out. That's the Southam story, and the blame lies in the family's sense of fairness and equality of opportunity. Instead of picking a designated hitter—like the Bronfmans, who choose one member of each generation to head the family—the Southams allowed every aunt, uncle and cousin to participate. Worse, the family Southamized in-laws instead of sticking with its own. The Southam family tree became a forest. There are so many of them—more than three hundred at last count—that each year the Southams have to circulate among themselves a privately published book so they can keep up with each other's activities and whereabouts.

Until Conrad Black took over the company in 1996, the fortunes of the family and those of its publicly traded company were inseparable. The business dated back to 1877, when William Southam and his partner, William Carey, took over the anemic *Hamilton Spectator*. Their purchase was based on the hope that Sir John A. Macdonald and his Tories would soon return to power and hand them fat advertising contracts. That was exactly what happened, and it set the pattern for the Southams' politics and their habit of buying newspapers across the country instead of starting their own.

Frederick Neal Southam, who succeeded his father, was dispatched to Montreal in 1889 to run a newly acquired printing house, and was put in charge of the *Ottawa Citizen*. The *Calgary Herald* followed in 1908, the *Edmonton Journal* four years later, the *Winnipeg Tribune* in 1920 and the *Vancouver Province* three years after that. Eight more papers, including the Montreal *Gazette* and the *Windsor Star*, were eventually acquired. The company's evolution was reflected in the changes of its corporate name: from Southam Ltd. (1904) to William Southam and Sons (1920), Southam Publishing Co. Ltd. (1927), Southam Co. Ltd. (1938), Southam Press Ltd. (1964) and Southam Inc. (1978). Headquarters moved from Hamilton to Ottawa to Montreal and, finally, to Toronto. It wasn't exactly a steadfast family enterprise.

When the founding Southam was followed as president by his son Frederick, control was consolidated within the family, but this was quickly undone when Frederick was succeeded by his son-in-law, Philip S. Fisher. The original family line took another detour when Fisher was followed as chief executive by St. Clair Balfour, related to the Southams maternally as well as by marriage. Balfour, who endowed the company with rare energy and enterprise, was succeeded by Gordon Fisher (son of Philip Fisher), whose strength of character helped buoy up the business. *[I remember congratulating Gordon Fisher when the sailboat he was skippering came in second during a particularly rough race on Lake Ontario. The weather had been so bad that most boats couldn't make it to the finish line. Instead of acknowledging my good wishes, he gave me a long, hard look and said, "Never, ever, congratulate me for coming in second," and walked away.]* But that was about it. Wilson J.H. Southam, and later, John Fisher, were the last family adherents to run the business, and their stewardships were humdrum at best. At the company's 1992 annual meeting, where William Ardell became the first total outsider named to run things, one family member, David Kerr, loudly complained:

"What William Southam had dreamed of has simply disappeared. It's not a family enterprise, it's something else."

The family had its usual quota of eccentrics, the most interesting of them being William James Southam, who characteristically wrote his bank, when he was looking for a $400,000 loan: "I have an income which is mostly outgo and then some, of $100,000 annually and I am always hard up. As to my character, I am fairly honest and an easy mark for bankers, get-rich-quick promoters and apple sellers. My habits at times are excellent. Now, do I get the $400,000?" He did.

By the time Conrad Black stepped forward to put the family out of its misery, it was falling apart. Only St. Clair Balfour, who was by then eighty-six, put up any intelligent resistance. "The spiritual force of the company," Southam director Walter Bowen told Patricia Best, the family's chronicler, "is a man in his eighties who has immense authority but no successor."

"A friend of mine who is prominent in the Southam family phoned me the other day," reported Stephen Jarislowsky during the skirmish with Black, who later named him a Southam director, "to say that they no longer care who gets the company. The idea that there exists a Southam family is a myth." And it was.

THE BASSETTS: *End of a Dynasty*

A few decades ago, when Toronto was truly bicultural—British and Irish, except for the bankers, who were Scottish—the acknowledged leader of the White Anglo-Saxon Protestant élite was an exuberant, profane, funny and charismatic animator named John White (I swear) Hughes Bassett. He died in the spring of 1998, at eighty-four, all but forgotten by the city he once dominated like a mythological Titan, running its hockey team, football team, its most exciting newspaper and most popular television station.

Toronto was a closed and provincial place in his time, and he was a fierce partisan of its absolute supremacy. When I asked him in the early 1980s what he thought about western Canada, he hesitated not a moment before booming out: "I don't care how much goddamn oil they discover in Alberta, Toronto and not Calgary is the place you do the deals. You get out to western Canada—for Christ's sake, you know, Vancouver and all those places—and you're away from the action. *This* is where it's at."

John Bassett, who cut an imposing figure (six foot four, 206 lbs.), was so interesting because he overcame his natural WASP prejudices and was, for example, an enthusiastic booster of Israeli independence. In recognition of his contributions, Toronto's exclusive Primrose Club, then just as adamantly anti-WASP as the Toronto Club was anti-semitic, made an exception and invited him to join. When his name went up on the Primrose's notice-board as a prospective member, Bassett scribbled beside his name the anonymous warning "You know what happens when you let *one* in!" and laughed uproariously as he watched members read his little message, wisely nodding to themselves as they walked away.

His family's Canadian roots extended back to 1909, when his father arrived from the north of Ireland and joined the Montreal *Gazette*, where he eventually became publisher. He served as a major during the First World War and purchased the *Sherbrooke Daily Record*, which later passed from the Bassett family to Conrad Black. In his book *Duplessis*, Black characterizes the elder Bassett as having been "political, combative, blustery, pro-French, unscrupulous, shameless"—a description that equally fit the younger Bassett.

Like his father, Bassett's time as a reporter—for *The Globe and Mail*—was interrupted by war, and he too rose to the rank of major. He purchased the Toronto *Telegram* in 1952 in a unique partnership with John David Eaton, then running the family department store. The two men signed a trust named Baton (named, according to Bassett, not after the partners' names but for the intersection of Bay and Wellington streets) leaving their corporate assets to their five children. In February 1984, the Eatons bought out the two surviving Bassetts, but in the intervening thirty-two years the families dominated Toronto's power structure.

Bassett made lightning decisions. When the CIBC was building its $100-million headquarters, Commerce Court, it needed to buy a piece of real estate he owned, but none of its executives dared approach Big John. Finally, the bank's chairman, Neil McKinnon, called him to see if a deal could be struck.

"Sure," said Bassett. "My price is $3,200,000."

"Well, my price is $2,800,000," said McKinnon.

"Let's split the difference?"

"Okay."

The transaction, a big one for its day, had taken exactly sixty seconds.

Bassett—whose second wife, the former Isobel Glenthorne Macdonald, later became an Ontario cabinet minister—was a great, if sometimes overbearing, father. Johnny F., his eldest and most accomplished son, who died of cancer in 1986, inherited his father's bluntness. "It's not a handicap being John Bassett's boy," he once declared. "I have an excellent relationship with dad. He's a hell of a sounding board and he's a bright, bright son of a bitch. I don't remember ever feeling pressure from being John Bassett's son. We're two different people. I suppose everybody in Toronto regards the Bassetts as Establishment. I don't. In 1952 my old man didn't have a pot to piss in when he bought a newspaper that, thanks to Mr. Eaton, was losing a million dollars a year." Bassett married Susan Carling of the famous brewing family, and their tennis-playing daughter Carling Bassett became the first Canadian to make it to the quarter-finals at Wimbledon.

Bassett became a partner in Maple Leaf Gardens (then known as the Carlton Street Mint) and the Argonauts football team, and was granted the city's first private TV licence, which turned into yet another mint. Bassett's *Tely* was the most exciting and eccentric newspaper Toronto ever had, reflecting its publisher's quixotic politics and *joie de vivre*. I remember being told by Beland Honderich, when I was named editor-in-chief of *The Toronto Star* in 1969, that we had one and only one editorial objective; "To beat the *Tely*." We did, and in 1971 it folded. Left without a personal platform, Big John was never the same. I recall meeting him at a party given by publisher Anna Porter. I hadn't seen him for a while, and when I asked what he was doing these days, Bassett (who had never learned to whisper) bellowed, "Oh, not much. Mostly screwing Isobel."

Bassett's son, Dougie, was equally extroverted, carrying his life in his hands like a placard, waving opinions, ambitions and shallow convictions at passers-by with infectious charm and terrier friendliness. But that wasn't enough to guarantee his future or provide a power base. Nor was he ever accused of being a great diplomat—such as the time he told Cardinal Carter, "I just can't believe that Mary was a virgin." On another occasion, asked about his cost-cutting binge at CFTO-TV, Dougie allowed that he was "chintzy, because I don't like employees at the trough, going to some goddamn film festival in Bucharest." Most of his business life, he tried to find the formula to gain control of the CTV network, but it took the Eatons' money and Ivan Fecan's negotiating skill to put that together. Having made some poor investments, he had to sell his motor boats in Muskoka and his Toronto house (to Ira Gluskin) and move into rented quarters near Ted Rogers.

The Bassetts were briefly a prominent Canadian family, representing an energetic and particularly photogenic kind of capitalism. But when their dynamic leadership passed away, so did the clan's significance. So few of our business leaders say what they really mean, preferring to defer to anyone within radar range. That's why John Bassett was a giant in a land of pygmies—and that is also why the Bassett business dynasty died with him.

THE GANONGS: *Small But Sweet*

David Ganong, who controls and runs the family's candy factory at St. Stephen, New Brunswick, is fourth generation. The company was founded by Gilbert and James Ganong in 1873, a year after the family opened a retail store and started to manufacture candy to attract customers. David's grandfather, Arthur, had in fact invented the chocolate bar—as a way of packaging candy so it wouldn't smear your pocket or handbag—and was the first to use cellophane in the packaging of candy.

"The previous generation had some terrible squabbles that just about destroyed the business," David Ganong admits. "My uncle Whidden became president, but my father Philip never felt that he should have been, and that created great animosity. Their sister Joan had inherited Arthur's shares and ended up taking the directors to court on the issue of dividend policy." David's brother Gordon worked in the firm for several years before deciding to cut his ties and move to B.C.

The company employs two hundred staunchly non-unionized workers and does not divulge its annual sales. As well as making candy, David Ganong has served on the boards of Air Canada and Mutual Life. The candy company is the smallest member of Tom d'Aquino's Business Council on National Issues (BCNI).

TED ROGERS: *The Riverboat Gambler*

In 1808, when Simon Fraser, the North West Company fur trader, was exploring the "Mysterious Great River" (later named after him) to see whether it could be used for floating merchandise to the Pacific, he had to negotiate the snarling cataracts that mark its progress. His party was forced to clamber across the precarious footholds in the rock-faces of the canyons overhanging the raging river, while portaging their canoes. "I cannot find words to describe our situation," Fraser lamented in his journal. "We had to pass where no human being should venture . . ." At one point, he confided to his journal, during the acrobatic passage of Hell's Gate Canyon, he felt as though he was hanging on by his eyebrows.

That describes Ted Rogers's situation perfectly. He is the great Riverboat Gambler of the Canadian Establishment. With his corporate debts once up to $5 billion, Rogers runs his business in a constant state of barely suppressed hysteria, while—just like Simon Fraser—hanging on by his eyebrows.

Visitors to Ted Rogers's office who are there to enquire about either his fiscal or physical health are shown a framed document, presented to

Ted in 1983 by Robin Korthals, then president of the Toronto-Dominion Bank:

"We are pleased to inform you that the TD Bank on the occasion of your fiftieth birthday is prepared to make available the following line of credit for your personal use, subject to the terms and conditions generally as outlined below:

Borrower: Ted Rogers.
Amount: $50 billion.
Lender: TD Bank.
Purpose: to help promote and prolong the state of good cheer and good health.
Availability: in amounts of $1 billion per year on demand subject to normal bank conditions, margin requirements and other security, interest rate to be negotiated in an amount commensurate with risk.
Security: one cottage, other considerations as appropriate.
Co-signers: Loretta Rogers with John Graham, repayment in full at maturity, May 27, 2033, when you reach a hundred.

We are pleased to have had this opportunity to express our appreciation and look forward to continued utilization throughout the terms of this loan. Happy Birthday."

"What prompted that offer," Rogers explains, "was a very critical loan in the company's early days. It was my wife, Loretta, who guaranteed it. But we didn't have much security, so we offered our cottage. Korthals told us to keep it, because it had such a good view."

The little joke is not typical of Canadian bankers, whose sense of humour generally ranks just behind undertakers and police sergeants. But Edward Samuel Rogers Jr. is special. Apart from his solid credentials as a patriotic Canadian, Rogers has always relied on his Establishment pedigree to get him through a wondrous life, filled with achievement and risk.

There is something of the mountaineer about Ted. It's his eyes: they have the permanent poached look of living on the abyss. He has had brushes with bankruptcy—at least three times—and has not only survived to tell the tale, but each time persuaded the same lenders to open their coffers even wider so he could spend himself dry one more time. That attitude smells of irresponsibility. But it's not. Rogers is a genuine entrepreneur, perhaps the most daring Canada has. That often means taking a corporate bungee jump, then as you float towards eternity, looking over your shoulder to see if the rope is actually attached to any-thing solid.

Rogers has a disturbing habit of being sincere against his better judg-ment. Asked about his latest electronic vision, he will go into ecstatic detail about how he intends to rewire Canada—or the universe. His bankers and shareholders read his remarks with a sinking feeling reminis-cent of the wonderful put-down that Paul Samuelson, the MIT economist, once directed at his more popular rival, Harvard's John Kenneth Galbraith. "An unguarded comment by Galbraith," cracked Samuelson, "can send the Dow off by $2; his guarded utterances send it down $5."

In permanent overdrive, Rogers's idea of reality is whatever he says it is. And he's got a point. He has been right before. In 1960, he put on the air Canada's first FM station before most of his listeners owned receivers equipped for the new radio sound, but he persisted—and even gave out free FM sets—until the operation turned a profit, and it still does. It was much the same story with cable TV in the 1970s, cellular phones in the 1980s, and fibre-optic technology in the 1990s. To be ahead of your time in Canada is a little like having leprosy: nobody wants to touch you until you're beyond help—either dead or cured.

Rogers takes a similar devil-may-care approach to his own health. He treats his frequent illnesses not as warning signs to slow down but as annoying distractions. When he underwent serious cataract surgery in the early 1980s, his pal and chief adviser, Phil Lind (who has since had a stroke) recalled seeing executives gathered around Rogers's bed, discussing a future cable project while their boss still had his eyes ban-daged. (The vision in his right eye remains at only 10 percent of nor-mal.) When Rogers suffered a coronary aneurysm several years later, he was back at work long before doctors thought it wise. His 1992 quadruple bypass surgery drove the medical staff at the Mayo Clinic in Boston to distraction; he was dictating letters before the anesthetic had worn off.

Rogers only occasionally slows down enough to be called a worka-holic. "Ted has had everything wrong with him there is, but he just keeps beating it back—he's unsinkable," says David Peterson, the former Ontario premier who sits on his board. "Everybody has been worried about his health for the last twenty years. He can never relax. He's the only guy I know who does three things at one time. He can talk to you while he's writing something, and he'll be reading something else at the same time. Honest to God, he remembers everything in all three con-texts." Tony Fell, the head of RBC Dominion Securities, who has backed

Rogers on several deals and has been out on his pleasure yacht, the *Loretta Anne*, has never seen him at rest: "Being on that boat of his is no holiday. He's got a satellite telephone and he's on it all the time." The ship is a 35-metre, $10-million floating palace with all the goodies. It could easily circle the globe, but Ted has yet to spend an uninterrupted week aboard. He even missed his own wedding anniversary after he promised to spend "a second honeymoon" with his wife, Loretta, *twice*. "My idea of slowing down," he once told me, "is to put a fax in my car."

His lifestyle matches his income. A few years ago, when Ted decided that he wanted to build a tennis court near his stone mansion in Toronto's exclusive Forest Hill district, he purchased the house next door (then belonging to Neil McKinnon, former chairman of the Canadian Imperial Bank of Commerce) and tore it down to make room for the courts. "My God," went the neighbourhood rumble, "what if Ted decides to take up golf?!" The Rogerses also own a Muskoka mega-cottage and a splendid waterfront hideout (only a three-minute golf-cart ride from the Lyford Cay Club) on the lush island of New Providence in the Bahamas, which provides safe haven for tax-weary millionaires on the wing. Rogers's travel conveyance of choice is his $40-million Canadair Challenger jet—and yes, it has a fax aboard and the best communications system money can buy.

Rogers's will to succeed against all odds is inbred. His ancestors were rebels, fighting for a place in the sun as early as 1300, when a merchant named Aaron Rogers fled religious persecution in Rome and resettled in London. He recouped his fortune, but his descendant John Rogers, a canon of Old St. Paul's, was burned at the stake in 1555, becoming England's first Protestant martyr. A half-century later, Thomas Rogers and his son Joseph, in yet another bid for religious freedom, left for the New World on board the *Mayflower*. Joseph's son, James, eventually became a prosperous merchant in Connecticut, while Robert, another family member, led the storied band of irregulars known as Rogers's Rangers during the Seven Years' War. It was only at the turn of the nineteenth century that a Rogers ventured into Canada. Timothy Rogers came to Upper Canada's York county in 1801 as the leader of forty Quaker families, settling what later became the town of Newmarket, near Toronto. During his grandchildren's generation, the family divided into two distinct branches. Elias Rogers fathered a clan that became prominent primarily through St. Mary's Cement, while Samuel Rogers's family, two generations later, produced Edward Rogers I, whose ghostly presence would dominate Ted II's life.

Born in 1900, Ted Senior was Canada's first amateur radio operator to transmit a signal across the Atlantic and the inventor of the radio tube that made it possible to build AC receiving sets, doing away with bulky, leaky and expensive batteries. The patent made him a fortune and he quickly upgraded his ham operation into a commercial radio station with the call letters CFRB (Canada's First Rogers Batteryless), which grew to command Canada's largest AM radio audience. As early as 1931, the elder Rogers was granted the first licence to broadcast experimental television, and later started to make the world's first radar set. He died in 1938 from overwork (and a bleeding ulcer) at thirty-eight, when Ted was only five. The son dedicated his life to outdoing his father, an obsession he could never satisfy. *[Ted has only three mementoes from his father: a ring bearing the call letters 3BP, which he wears daily; the first tube-operated radio; and a Valentine's card.]*

Ted subsequently attended Upper Canada College. In his final year, he was chauffeured to school each morning while his sports car was brought around during the day so he could drive himself home. *[Three years after his father died, Ted's mother, Velma, was remarried to John Graham, a clever Toronto lawyer who served in the Governor General's Horse Guards. Best man at the wedding was Donald Hunter, whose family company Rogers would purchase in 1994.]* Paradoxically, it was at UCC that Ted learned his street smarts. "I used to box at Upper Canada," he recalls, "and I got knocked out the first year. It took me five years to win my weight. I've always been a fighter."

In 1963, he married Loretta Anne Robinson, the vivacious daughter of Lord Martonmere, a former British MP who had served as governor of Bermuda. His ushers included John Craig Eaton and Hal Jackman. *[Henry Newton Rowell Jackman, better known as Hal with the sagebrush eyebrows, was once a sprightly and ambitious millionaire. In the summer of 1997, he sold his family's National Trustco to the Bank of Nova Scotia for $1.25 billion and decided to devote his life to public service. (He had been lieutenant-governor of Ontario from 1991 to 1997; later, he was made chancellor of the University of Toronto.) His greatest moment was his resignation from the board of Varity Corp. (the former Massey-Ferguson), when chairman Victor Rice decided to skip out on his Canadian government loans and move the company to Buffalo.]* Three years earlier, while still studying law at university, Rogers had bought (for $85,000) CHFI, a tiny, 940-watt station that pioneered the new frequency modulation sounds at a time when only 5 percent of Toronto homes had FM receivers. By 1967, he was in the cable television business, and he eventually put together the world's largest cable network, with 2.3 million subscribers, including systems in the U.S. and U.K. (When he sold his American systems for $1.63 billion, he convinced the buyer to base the purchase price on the number of subscribers.

He immediately sent in his crack marketers and signed up enough new connections to raise the final price by $115 million.)

Rogers kept expanding, despite the fact that his companies hadn't shown a profit since 1989. Bay Street's hopeful assessment—that cable was such a hot business, "even Ted can't lose money on this one"—didn't turn out to be true. He refused to stop growing long enough to make money. He was constantly investing, trading equity for debt, expanding assets instead of dividends. "All we have to do to make money," he would say, "is stop growing." But he never did. He moved into the Shopping Channel, bought twenty radio stations, built nearly two hundred Rogers video stores, was first into mobile phones with Cantel, got into the long-distance telephone business through Unitel Communications, and in 1994 purchased Maclean Hunter, the country's premier publishing house.

That acquisition was Rogers's largest bite, worth $3.5 billion. Maclean Hunter was vulnerable to a takeover, even though it had little debt and solid earnings, because it had no controlling shareholder. The largest block was held by Don Hunter's children, Don Jr., who had moved to the Caymans, and Margie McCallum. Rogers took Margie, who held Don's proxy, on a cruise aboard his boat and assured himself of her support before he made the offer, which was generous enough to preclude the intervention of any white knights.

Afterwards, Bill Wilder, a loyal, veteran Maclean Hunter director, spotted Margie at a party and lamented that the company's sale had been a tragedy. "It is not," said the founder's granddaughter. "I got *my* money out." Graham Savage, acting for Rogers, sold off various company subsidiaries for $2.5 billion, while retaining most of Maclean Hunter's magazine division, which publishes *Maclean's*, *Chatelaine* and *Flare*, and the company's impressive Canadian cable holdings. It was a sweet deal. At the time, Bay Street described the brief takeover battle as "the River Boat Gambler, facing off against the Village Parson." To which Rogers shot back: "I guess that's true, but I don't know why they keep referring to me as a Village Parson." The purchase drove Rogers stock into the $20 range, but characteristically, he chose not to issue any additional equity.

It also increased Rogers's cable business by nearly half a million subscribers. Although they were his cash cow, the cable networks required injections of $1 billion a year for constant upgrading. Even their generous cash flow ($2 million a day) couldn't keep pace with his ambitions. And then, in early 1995, the cable operation itself was threatened.

In the past, Rogers kept increasing the number of channels he offered, raising his monthly rates accordingly. Few objected because the only way to get a clear TV picture was to subscribe to his service, which enjoyed a monopoly everywhere he operated. But when he decided to institute a negative option—automatically billing subscribers an additional $2.65 each month for five new Canadian specialty channels, and threatening to remove some popular stations if the extra fee wasn't paid—subscribers revolted. "I was stunned," he admitted, after backing down. "From now on, customers will determine what level of service each one will get." But it was too late. The unsuccessful ploy—especially since it coincided with the financial disaster of the Unitel long-distance telephone venture, on which Rogers lost a cool $500 million—robbed Rogers of his momentum, at least temporarily. At the same time, the CRTC, having rubber-stamped his bid for Maclean Hunter by agreeing with his argument that it would allow him to compete against phone companies, offered the telephone companies entry into Rogers's turf.

By the end of 1996, his revenues were falling drastically, but worse was the loss of two of his most valuable executives: Colin Watson, who had run the cable systems, and Graham Savage, his chief financial officer. "Colin," Rogers explained, "had an opportunity to be CEO of Spar Aerospace, which is a company that has no controlling shareholder, so he'd be the boss. It was actually not bad for me. When the cable company was going through so much change, I felt its founder, the person who considers it his ultimate responsibility, should be there. We were making decisions that could wreck the company, and that's not something you can delegate."

The Savage departure, after twenty-one years of impressive service, was much more serious. It shook the banks' confidence and finally broke the shareholders' patience. Savage, who had come up through Burns Fry, had a solid investment background and was rightly regarded by Bay Street as Rogers's window to fiscal reality, holding Ted back from the most costly excesses. He was a master at conjuring up opportunities to finance the company, pulling ever larger rabbits out of ever smaller hats. At one point, Savage had to resort to dealing with junk-bond king Michael Milken, who floated $225 million of low-grade securities for the Rogers firm. On January 15, 1992, Rogers sold 2 million B-class shares in his own company because he was $75 million in debt. Typically, he had got himself into that bind by becoming overenthusiastic and buying too many of his multi-vote Class A shares. There was no more telling justification of his reputation as a control freak than the fact that he owned 91 percent of this stock and kept buying more.

Rogers's relationship with bankers has always been highly personal. "We do things on a handshake," he confides. "I've always kept my word

and I phone them first with my problems, so they don't hear about them
from others. They give me heck when I deserve heck, but they've been
unbelievably supportive. I wouldn't be here without their help. I don't
mean just normal help on loans, I mean above and beyond that." As a
director of the TD Bank, Rogers was a member of the club, even when he
was as much as $5 billion in debt and had burned out fifteen of the TD's
best credit officers who had been assigned to his account.

The day after Savage's dramatic departure—which had seriously
depressed Rogers stock prices—Dick Thomson, then the TD's chairman,
unexpectedly dropped in at Rogers's cable headquarters in suburban
Toronto. Ted was running the operation himself at the time because
he had run out of executives willing to work for him. "I was going to hold
a press conference to deal with Graham's resignation," Rogers recalls,
"and I remember being surprised when I met Dick at the elevator, and he
told me, 'You know this is the first time I've ever been in a cable
company's office.' I thought, now, isn't that something, because here's a
guy who has loaned more money to cable than any other human, ever.
[Ted Rogers should know.] And so he sits down with me and says, 'What in
the world have you got yourself into, and how can we help? You've got to
do something. We'll help you, we'll get all the people to your press conference, but you better figure out what you're going to say.' So, we laid
out a strategy. Now, wasn't that great? Thomson drove all the way out
there, didn't put on any airs, didn't act like a big shot, didn't need to
come, but he did."

The TD hung in, but gently suggested Ted might want to spread his
business around a little more. "We began to treat him as if he was Brazil,"
admitted one frustrated TD loans officer. Enter the Bank of Nova Scotia
and its chairman, Peter C. Godsoe, who had done business with Rogers
before. At the time he was buying Maclean Hunter, Rogers went to see
Godsoe on a Monday morning and by Friday, having also contacted
three other banks, he had $2 billion in his credit book. Godsoe also took
on the Cantel account. "When I was just starting out," Rogers remembers, "the Nova Scotia called a business loan, and I never complained.
They had been my personal bankers since I was five. I had an account at
their Forest Hill Village branch and never changed it. When they moved
the branch across the street, I thought, even though I'm a director of the
TD, I'd love to go to their official opening, as did Don Fullerton, then
chairman of the Commerce, who also lived in the Village. When none
of the Nova Scotia's big shots appeared, Fullerton and I stood by the
door, saying, 'Hi, I'm from the TD Bank, nice to see you,' while Don said,

'Hi, I'm from the Commerce . . .' We just had a ball. Peter Godsoe still rants about that." But not very loudly. "We're good friends," said Godsoe. "We go away every year to play tennis at Lyford Cay in the Bahamas together with our wives, and spend time with one another in Muskoka, because our kids are the same age."

In the fall of 1996, Rogers reached an agreement with Bob Allen, head of AT&T, the world's largest communications empire, for a joint marketing agreement with Cantel, and the two companies have been drifting closer together. By the spring of 1998, Rogers Communications Inc. shares were down to less than a third of their 1993 peak of $24.75. Losses were running $2 million per business day, and Ted blamed a "non-recurring charge" of $430 million for a massive write-down at his troubled Cantel division. That might have been a reasonable assumption, except that similar write-downs had been claimed during each of the past six years in various parts of the Rogers empire.

By the spring of 1998, as well as Savage and Watson, many of the other senior Rogers executives had decamped. Only the ever dependable vice-chairman, Phil Lind, and John Tory, the capable head of the company's multimedia division, remained aboard. Rogers's debt charges were increasing at $40 million per month, and shareholders were voting with their feet. The rudest prognosis came from Doug Knight, a Vancouver investment analyst, who told Douglas Goold of the *Globe Report on Business*: "If Ted Rogers died, it would be good for the stock."

That morbid opinion was not shared by its subject. "The best is yet to come," Ted Rogers kept insisting. He did reduce his debt by selling his local phone assets to the MetroNet Communications Group of Calgary for $1 billion in the spring of 1997, and pledged his company would be paying dividends on December 31, 2003. "I would then like to go into more long-term technical pursuits," he pledged, "be out of the business, move to another location, and be running some small project, just enough to keep me busy."

DAVID THOMSON: *The Reluctant Heir*

The rich don't have children; they have heirs. For the first-born male, growing up is a brief interval during which he matures into becoming his father's son, with all the baggage of continuity and the shedding of spontaneity that such a rite of passage implies. Youth involves being wafted through Father's private school and enrolled in his clubs, experiencing all the right things (doing drugs means two Aspirins at bedtime), earning a Harvard or Western MBA, and spending languid vacations at large summer homes on the manicured shores of cool green lakes. These precocious progeny learn at their daddies' knees how to exude that air of besieged innocence that marks the Canadian Establishment's young.

Unlike most of the few surviving members of this exclusive club—who are dull to the point of banality—David Kenneth Roy Thomson, the designated heir of his family empire, currently worth more than $14 billion, marches to his own drum corps. *[Since 1994, the Thomson organization has acquired information service firms worth $6 billion. According to Forbes magazine's annual surveys, that places the Thomsons seventh in their roster of the super-rich. Ken Thomson receives at least $330 million a year in dividends.]* The professional managers who run the Thomson organization regard him as "a bit of a flake," but they have no choice. Roy Thomson, his legendary grandfather who founded the family fortune, specifically anointed David, Ken's eldest son, to be the next head of the Thomson Organization. He will also assume his grandfather's title, which he will give him a seat in the British House of Lords, never claimed by his father. "David, my grandson, will have to take his part in the running of the Organization, and David's son, too," wrote the dying Lord Thomson, spelling out the rules. "For the business is now all tied up in trusts for those future Thomsons, so that death duties will not tear it apart. These Thomson boys that come after Ken are not going to be able, even if they want to, to shrug off these responsibilities. The conditions of the trust ensure that control of the business will remain in Thomson hands for eighty years." *[Ken Thomson has two other children: Lynne, eighteen months younger than David, a stunning brunette who has a drama degree from Harvard and is currently in Hollywood; and Peter, eight years David's junior, who spent most of his formative years racing in southern Ontario dirt rallies, but who is now also deputy chairman of Woodbridge.]*

David's conversation is an improbable mixture of introspective genius and postindustrial babble. Tall and wispy, with curly sandy hair and frigid blue eyes, he displays the easy grace born of his training in the martial arts. Intensity characterizes his thoughts and actions. Ask him the meaning of life or the time of day and the brows furrow into deep scars (the forehead is too youthful to show supporting wrinkles), the eyes grow reflective and the brain cells almost audibly start churning; there is never any small talk. The most private of men, David cultivates a mysterious presence. He has never given a press conference, been on TV, or said anything in public. *[His only interview to date was with me, when I was doing a history of the Hudson's Bay Company, then owned by his father. These quotes are adapted from that occasion.]*

Educated at Toronto's Upper Canada College and at Cambridge, to lighten his academic load young David played left wing on the 1976 Cambridge hockey team that beat Oxford for only the fourth time since 1930. "I like to think I was on the team because of my abilities," he laughs, "but I was the only one who owned a car—a Volvo station wagon—which afforded me a constant place."

David's most significant formative influence was the time he spent on weekends with his grandfather at Alderbourne Arches in Buckinghamshire. "He was very lonely and we conversed for hours about business and people," the young Thomson reminisces. "His curious mind was always questioning why things were done in a particular way, seeking to understand the forces that affect people's judgments. He always admired those people who could laugh at themselves amidst negative circumstances. He was an optimist with an uncanny ability to seize opportunities that others could not see. This approach was in complete parallel to my own nature."

It was at this time that David's passion for art took root. Aware that any cultural hobby pursued by a rich kid was bound to be dismissed as dilettantish, he put in a long and arduous apprenticeship under Hermann Baer, who ran a small shop on London's Davies Street that rented antique props to the film industry. The other mentor was his father, Ken, whose collection, David claims, "should be celebrated in its completeness; even the frame mouldings are harmonious. He has distilled his vision of a few artists into a handful of works by each. The result is sincere and compelling."

The relationship between the two men is close but not cloying, with the senior Thomson occasionally wondering if his son is tuned in to worldly business realities. "Our private discussions evoke mixed emotions, but once agreed, we tackle issues with a single-minded tenacity," David insists. "I love him deeply, would do anything for him, and I am not alone. Many of my cohorts would defend him to the death." Of his son, Ken Thomson says, "He's a fine young man. The same sensitivity that he relates to his paintings, he relates to people and business. It worries him if somebody isn't being treated right and all that sort of stuff."

David Thomson works in the Thomson Building across the street from Toronto City Hall, and visitors entering his private quarters are struck by the sight of three incongruous objects: a large-scale model of a 1920s U.S. Post Office monoplane, painted every colour of the rainbow, which looks as if it just landed out of a *Peanuts* cartoon; an exquisite, life-sized thirteenth-century French limestone figure that appears to be bending towards its owner in an attitude of gentle benediction; and the dark green seat from a Second World War Nazi Luftwaffe fighter.

Thomson's most valuable possession is J.M.W. Turner's magnificent *Seascape, Folkestone*, which Lord Clark, the former director of London's National Gallery, described as "the best picture in the world." David bought it for $14.6 million, outbidding the National Gallery of Scotland; it was more recently valued at more than $50 million. His real obsession is with John Constable, the miller's son who along with Turner dominated English landscape painting in the nineteenth century. He has published a lavishly printed, meticulously edited 328-page study, *Constable and His Drawings*, which has been highly praised by English art critics. "Constable's sensibility has had a strong influence on my personal philosophy, which I carry forward in all walks of life, including the business," he explains. "So few people allow themselves to openly see and question scenes and events as he did—and as I do."

The young Thomson is intensely attracted by war and danger, because those circumstances force people to harness the peak of their physical and emotional energies. "I become excited at the thought of measuring myself in varied situations, alongside Wellington in India or being in a fighter aircraft, attacking a formation of bombers and being vastly outnumbered," David confides. "It's an interesting way to test yourself."

Thomson makes little effort to separate his passion for art and his devotion to business. In his mind, the twin strands are forever intertwined. "I take art so seriously because it's one of the few pursuits in which I can totally unravel my soul," says he. "For me, the act of creation comes through in a better appreciation of business. I measure great achievements in information publishing in the same way as I view a compelling work of art." He is mesmerized by the fact that in his position he is free to make mistakes, and believes that this may be the greatest privilege bestowed on him by wealth. As part of his unusual apprenticeship, he spent ten years in the service of the Hudson's Bay Company as a full-time retailer, right down to a term selling socks at The Bay's downtown Toronto department store. "People were very careful about what they'd say to me, anticipating I would agree, that I wouldn't stay long," David recalls. "But this didn't happen because I became enthralled with many areas of the company's then-disjointed business potential." Probably his most moving experience was the time he spent at a fur-trading post in Prince Albert, Saskatchewan. "The juxtaposition was dramatic," he recalls. "On July 4, 1988, I bid successfully for a Munch woodblock in London; the following week I was in Prince Albert, and I remember being taken to the post's backyard, where ten bear claws were positioned on the cement floor, with fresh bloodstains and tissue intact. One fellow proceeded to demonstrate the various new traps and took me through the back room, where numerous shiny models were hanging. He hinged several in open positions and tossed a branch into the claw. I shall never forget the powerful crescendo of the folding pincers. For one of the first times I enjoyed a completely unfettered response to life, isolated from big cities and the diversions of money. We drove along dirt roads, watched sunsets, merchandised the store, went fishing and talked of our child-hoods. The experience was unforgettable and I developed a deep respect and empathy towards those *real* people."

Most of his co-workers grew to respect him, but he was still a Thomson. "David used to phone from Liechtenstein on a Sunday night and say, 'Hey boss, can I get Monday off?'" complained Marvin Tiller, then in charge of the HBC's Northern Stores.

David Thomson remains as unpredictable as a hailstorm. He could become the most creative representative of the failing families reviewed in this chapter, or he might seek permanent refuge in his art. He is still at the beginning of his run, with each new experience providing the bounce that will determine his ultimate direction. But his decision horizon is short: Ken Thomson is in his mid-seventies, and John Tory, the man who has so brilliantly managed the great Thomson empire, has relinquished his position.

David faces a future defined mainly by whether or not he can survive his own intensity. Perhaps he had an inkling that nothing could stop him except himself when he chose the quote to accompany his picture in the Upper Canada College 1975 graduation yearbook: "We are never so much the victims of another as we are the victims of ourselves."

Meanwhile, David Thomson is beginning to flex his expanding authority. "I wish," he says, "to prolong those inspired moments in life and see them continually manifested in all areas of endeavour. My search is always to create new wealth." Once a Thomson, always a Thomson.

THE BIRKS FAMILY: *The Little Blue Boxes*

The most famous Canadian jeweller is Birks, run by the Montreal family that for 120 years has been furnishing the wealthy with jewellery and luxury accessories. When she was given a specially made Birks diamond, emerald and platinum necklace on one of her Canadian tours, the Queen allowed that she had "never been presented with a more beautiful gift."

The Birks brand is associated with a particular shade of pale blue used on its gift boxes, a guarantee of quality and good taste. One of the few Canadian businesses passed down through five generations of the same family, its payroll has included several fifth-generation employees.

The Birkses had been in the British cutlery and jewellery trade from Elizabethan times until 1830, when John Birks emigrated to Canada. His son Henry took up the jewellery trade, at first as an apprentice and later as founder of his own firm. By 1894, three of Henry's sons had come into the business, and one of them, William Massey Birks, had two heirs, Henry and Victor, who became important in the firm. Management was taken over by George Drummond Birks after the Second World War, with the understanding that his three sons—Jonathan, Tom and Barry—would eventually inherit the growing retail empire. By the bleak winter of 1993, the family had lost that chance; their company was bankrupt.

The fate of Birks is a touching case history of how a well-meaning dynasty can lose its way and give up its mandate. Because so few members of Canada's vanquished family dynasties have talked about that awful downward spiral which choked their enterprise, here is an unedited transcript of my conversation with Jonathan Birks, the last of the once great family's inheritors, describing in intimate detail how they were brought to ground:

> We started off with one little shop on St. James Street, and then three sons joined their father in the business and wanted to see some expansion. And so we expanded by acquiring really the very finest local businesses in each city all the way across to Vancouver—which was Rosenthal in Ottawa and St. James Ryrie in Toronto and later the Ellises, and then in Winnipeg it was Dingwall, Black in Calgary and right the way out to Victoria. We kept on most of the families who owned those businesses as part of our acquisitions, and retained most of the staff because they had the loyalty of the local clientele. We had a period of consolidation from 1931 to after the Second World War, and then went into another period of expansion in 1954 with the shopping centres. It was a great move for us. By 1954, we had twenty stores, and by 1970 we had forty, with about $38 million worth of sales. The following year, by way of responding to People's, who had bought out Mappins in Montreal, we decided to go into the mid-market without knowing very much about it, and acquired O.B. Allan in Vancouver. We eventually moved it east, and then we bought out Ostrander's in Ontario and Doucet's in Quebec,

so that our mid-market operation was up very quickly to about eighty-five stores.

Until 1989, we had great growth, but the rapid expansion was a bit of a double-edged sword. We were so keen to grow the business that we had a great preoccupation about the top line and increasing market share, but we never really sat down to ask ourselves, what do we want to be? We had no game plan. About 1983, I remember a friend asking me: 'How does Birks define itself?'

'We're fine jewellers and silversmiths,' I replied.

'No, you're not. Look at the products in your shop windows; look at what you're offering in the stores. You've become purveyors of giftware. And a lot of what you're selling, you're selling at reduced prices, almost on an ongoing basis.'

He was right. And what that meant was that we had slipped into a market where we were having to compete with department stores and new kinds of operations that had come along, such as Ashley's of Toronto. This was not a market that we were prepared to compete in, because our overhead was far greater and we didn't carry the kind of inventories they could carry. Where we had always historically made good money was in quality jewellery and watches, because 85 percent of the goods we sold were set with stones that we manufactured ourselves, so we could control costs all the way through.

Our very rapid expansion was good in the sense of increasing our market share and our visibility, but was bad in the sense that we got drawn into a lot of markets where we should never have been. There was too much of a fixation on the top line and not enough on the bottom line.

Our traditional bankers were Bank of Montreal, and the Scotia came along a little bit later on. They were solid allies, but became increasingly concerned about inventory build-up and the general growth of the business. When we had our centennial celebrations in 1979, my brothers Tom and Barry and I became very keen to expand the business south of the border, because we felt that we had fairly well saturated the upper end of the fine jewellery market in Canada. We made our first U.S. acquisition in December of 1979: Shreve Crump & Low, the finest fine jewellery chain in New England, established back in 1796. The company is older than Tiffany. Then we acquired a couple of independents in Boston and northern Virginia, and in January of 1981 signed a letter of intent to purchase the Jewellery Guild division of the Dayton Hudson chain. Ken Dayton, who was chairman at that time, had a personal interest in fine jewellery stores, and much to the concern of his management team had started acquiring other firms, and built up a division of about fifty-five stores. We bought their business and that gave us seventy stores in the U.S. Then we went on to purchase J. Jessop and Son, San Diego's oldest fine jeweller; as well as Shreve & Company, which had been established back in 1857, the oldest fine jewellery in not only San Francisco but all of California. It was housed in a building that had survived the 1907 quake. After that we bought out J.B. Hudson in Minneapolis-St. Paul and C.D. Peacock, a business that was incorporated the same year as the city of Chicago. We didn't stop there. We acquired Charles W. Warren in Detroit and J. Caldwell, the oldest fine jeweller in Philadelphia. By the mid-1980s we had more than 220 stores in North America, with sales of $400 million. We had become one of the world's largest fine jewellers.

It was a huge administrative load. We had offices in Boston and Minneapolis for the American operations. Toronto was the headquarters for our mid-market operation in Canada, while Montreal remained the headquarters. And each of the offices was run on a different system.

Internally, by 1988, we had experienced twenty years of differences of opinion, to use a delicate expression, with the other side of the Birks family who were in the business. My father's uncle, Victor, had one son, Robert, who had joined the company about 1968. Things didn't work out, and after four years we asked him to leave. *[Robert Birks was dismissed from his job and the Birks board in 1976; his father was ousted two years later and asked to clean out his desk with only three days' notice.]* About the time he had come into the firm, my father and his father had hammered out a voting trust agreement, because my father felt that, if you were to continue attracting talented people into the firm, it would be very difficult to have anybody with any pride or desire show much leadership while sitting around a table with two people each having 50 percent of the common stock of the business. So my father decided that the best thing to do would be that both branches of the family place their voting stock into certificates that would mature in seventy-five years. That way, neither family would have more voting power than the other directors.

Still, with Robbie disagreeing with almost everything that was being done, board meetings were difficult and uncomfortable. We had gone through about twenty years of not being able to reconcile this situation. There weren't a lot of harsh words that were passed between the two sides, but it became increasingly difficult to continue operating on this basis. I decided, really out of frustration, that something should be done and, working with Conrad Black's support, was able to find the money to acquire Robbie's shares. *[Like most of Black's friends, Birks occasionally tries to test Conrad's legendary memory. When Jonathan finished reading a book on the Bonapartes, and with the volume's family chart in front of him, telephoned Black for a little quiz. "I figured there was no way I couldn't remember more about Napoleon than he did. So I coyly started in on the subject of Bonaparte—where his family came from, which prince had married what princess, and stuff like that. Within twenty minutes he had exhausted my chart. Obviously talking off the cuff, he went on for another half-hour, not only reciting what each man had done, but how his later absence would affect the Austro-Hungarian empire. It was a very humiliating experience."]* (It was Tom Birks who pulled the trigger. Jonathan bought out his brothers for $50 million each. At least one member of the Royal's loan committee vigorously opposed granting the loan, because he doubted Jonathan's skills as a merchandiser, but he was overruled by Royal chairman John Cleghorn, who explained, "We've been trying to get the Birks account for years. This is our chance.")

I closed the deal at Wendy's over a Styrofoam cup of coffee. So, after that, I had that 50 percent of the voting stock; plus my father, Drummond, had taken his half, retained 17 and given each of his sons 11 percent, so I ended up then with 61 percent. But in order to dissolve the trust, I needed 75 percent of the voting stock. So I went to my father shortly before Christmas 1989 to ask whether he would consider selling his shares. He wanted to know what would happen in terms of my two brothers, which was a fair question. And I said, look, I'm quite prepared to sell them on a *pro rata* basis a third of a third based on what I paid for it. He said, fine, that's all I wanted to know, here's my 17 percent. So we dissolved the voting trust and my hope was to have the three of us work for at least a year. I felt we each had the same amount to lose and the same amount to gain. The way the arrangement worked was that for the first five years of our partnership, if one of the three felt that things weren't working out, he could trigger the shotgun. I wanted 100 percent premium for my stock, because I wanted to feel some security after having gone through the exercise of settling with the Victor Birks side; I wanted to feel there was some security for me going forward. But things were triggered more rapidly than I'd expected. Within six months, both my brothers exited the business. I bought them out and reconstituted a new board, which met on the 12th of January, 1990.

The whole exercise had been a drain in terms of energy, time and money. We had to borrow substantial amounts and that added much debt to the balance sheet. By that time, we were working with the Royal Bank, which syndicated the loan. By the winter of 1990, the retail trade was taking a pretty good pounding and the banks began to suffer from overextended loan portfolios. The retail jewellery trade was one of the worst hit. Nobody needs what we sell. People require food, medicines, but not diamonds. So we were hit very severely at a time when we'd just gone through this major refinancing and when there was a fair amount of reorganizing within the business. That was from 1990 until 1992, when I was trying to consolidate the business, and I never stopped running. After thirty-five years of pretty good growth for a lot of us in many kinds of businesses, our generation could get away with Band-Aid remedies. You didn't really need to do a whole lot to make things better, because the natural process of growth worked to remedy the situation; the economy just kind of got better and better. We had been raised thinking fat. And when you think fat and all of a sudden have to start thinking lean, it's very difficult. All of a sudden, you went from Band-Aids to triple bypass surgery and a lot of the doctors were standing around saying, well, I was only trained to use Band-Aids, I don't know how to use a scalpel, don't make me open up the body, I don't know how to do that and I'll probably faint.

The analogy cuts close to home. That's what happened to Birks. Brand loyalty, loyalty to anything, had vanished. We had been used to our wives shopping in the same stores as our mothers, who shopped in the same stores as our grandmothers. There was just no question. Demographically, this country has changed radically in the last twenty-five years. When we went into Yorkdale, the Toronto shopping centre, for instance—I remember that as basically a good WASP area with a few Italo-Canadians. Look at it today, it's Asian and West Indian. You've got a real mix, and none of them were raised on our blue boxes. *[No longer can WASPS rely on their innate cultural knowledge of fellow WASPS' consumption tastes, fetishes, status markers and so on. A multicultural Canada favours global marketers.]*

By the start of 1990, I owned the entire business, which was not what I had wanted, it really wasn't, and I'm not being falsely unambitious in this. I believe myself to be a team player, beginning with my school days. But here we had this very large fine jewellery business that was doing a whole lot of different things in different offices with different systems, and what we had to do was try and consolidate. So I brought in, as my right-hand man, Bill Medes, who had been one of the top executives over at IBM. He didn't know the jewellery trade, but I thought he had a good background in areas like information technology, and ours was about fifteen years out of date. So we invested $6 million to build up our information systems. But we were trying to do too many things at the same time to do them all well. And the economy kept going south.

We had an understanding with the Royal that the American side of the business was its weak underbelly, and we almost successfully sold most of it, but the deal fell through at the last minute because of the U.S. Savings and Loans crisis. American bankers began to get very antsy and that cost us our US$50-million deal. Early in 1992, the Royal and its banking syndicate came to me and said that my business had become just too scary for them. They put on a fair amount of pressure and wanted me to do some dastardly things that I wasn't too keen to have done. I told a friend of mine in Europe that I run a business built on quality and tradition, values that I love, and so if I had to sell, I thought that Europe was probably where I should go. I thought there must be some European families that shared an understanding for our corporate philosophy. Within about a month and a half, he came back and told me about Italy's Borghesia Group, owned by the Rossi family, of Martini & Rossi fame. I'm not a martini guy, but I knew the name and felt I could become a Rossi guy, or a Martini guy if I had to.

We had promised the banking syndicates that we'd have a presentation ready for May. But concurrent with that, we were working with the Italians to try and keep their interest alive. Within a month, the banks were back at us, demanding that we provide more guarantees. I was totally naïve in this process and admitted it. I'd never had to worry about credit in the past and had no experience with managing bankers. We were not successful in controlling the bankers, even though our whole team spent all their time furnishing the members of the syndicate with information instead of running the business. That was a very critical and debilitating aspect to the entire episode. I did our presentation to the banks, and by mid-June it was evident that I had to get the Italians involved. By January 11, 1993, we had to seek protection from bankruptcy, and finalized our sales arrangements on April 17, when the business was sold to Dr. Rossi for $75 million. *[Jonathan Birks was demoted to vice-chairman, while the Rossis appointed Tom Andruskevich, a former Tiffany executive, as president. "Luckily, his first name is Tom," Drummie Birks was heard to rumble.]*

I would be less than frank if I said I didn't feel some sadness that the company hasn't remained under the family's control. But I do feel a great satisfaction and contentment that it has survived and is becoming stronger. The new shareholder has the same strong feelings for tradition and quality as the Birks family. We have two plants in France that are supplying us with exclusive products. So, yes, there is a sadness, there will always be a sadness that it was during my watch and my generation that the family lost the company. But that's nostalgia that you can't afford very much. You've got to get over it and go forward, and we are going forward.

Am I the last of the Birks? The last of the Mohicans? I am for right now, but I've got five children and one of those kids may want to come back into the business. I'd love it. We were always taught that there was no member of the family more important than the business itself. And the business has survived. That's what matters.

Like so many Canadian business dynasties, the Birks family turned out to inhabit a snow castle, which melted with the thaw.

THE DELANEYS: *The Power Couple*

They work on the top storeys of downtown Toronto buildings, each occupying most of a floor, running very different enterprises. They are joined not only by marriage, but by shared attitudes and ambitions. They are Kiki and Ian Delaney, who rank as Bay Street's favourite power couple.

"We don't think of ourselves as a power couple," says Catherine (Kiki) Delaney, who heads Delaney Capital Management, which occupies the entire fifty-first floor of the Canada Trust Tower in the BCE Centre. "We're quite normal people with our 2.1 children, though we've certainly been fortunate economically. We try very hard to make sure weekends are our own because we're very busy during the week, so we have a place in the Hockley Valley and go there virtually every weekend. There we can spend lots of time with each other and with our kids. Ian has been amazingly supportive. He is actually the person who got me to start on my own. He's the one who said, you don't have enough courage but you should have and you can do it and you've got to do it. We're fortunate because we both started out in the investment business, so we understand what the other person is saying. We don't actively seek any profile. We have normal friends, and being social is not something that we particularly want."

One thing that has brought the Delaneys even closer together is a big mother of a converted eighty-foot trawler, *Northern Song*, which they acquired in 1997. She was built as a trans-ocean fish boat, and is powered by a twelve-cylinder Caterpillar engine that drives a single screw with six-foot blades. "We have been sailing it in the Caribbean but keep her in Cuba because Ian is there every other week, so he can see it and fondle it. She reminds me of Tugboat Annie. The boat could literally go around the world—not that I particularly want to. We were aboard last Christmas time with fifteen-foot waves and that was enough for me.

There's a sense of freedom that you have on a boat that you really almost don't have anywhere else."

Delaney started her own business five and a half years ago. "I had spent at that time twenty years in the investment business. I was with Gluskin Sheff and Associates for seven years, as a partner there; and prior to that, spent fourteen years with Guardian Capital Group, and Gurston Rosenfeld, who was a real mensch and one of my great mentors. I went on my own in the summer of 1992, with the view of setting up a firm that was going to be geared to high net worth individuals; and my view was that, while there were people in the business serving that market, there were not a lot of firms serving it the way I thought it should be, which was to give not only returns but excellent service, and to be there at all times for your client. What happened after that was sort of a fairy tale, because I got a call before I'd actually set up the office from a mutual fund company that had lost their two managers to Mackenzie, and they asked if I would manage their funds on a contract basis. And so before I actually opened up Delaney Capital, we had $200 million under management. We now run around $4 billion, which is staggering and a testament to what's gone on in the mutual fund business."

Confident and self-assured, Delaney claims she operates at only two speeds: all-out or asleep. And it's the latter state that she believes describes most Canadian bankers. "They have allowed the likes of Steve Hudson to become huge. They're struggling to get into the twentieth century before we move into the twenty-first. My take on the banks today is, they're no longer in the lending business; they're not interested in lending you or me any money. They would like to sell you mutual funds, they'd like to sell you high net worth services, because they want the fees, and they're starting to do a good job at it."

She believes the Establishment changes every ten years. "If you look at who's powerful today, had anybody heard of Steve Hudson ten years ago? A meritocracy eventually becomes an establishment, but the door isn't locked and nobody has thrown away the key—so that's the main thing. You can tell your children that you can become part of all this with determination and hard work."

Her husband Ian works out of a round room on the top floor of a security-conscious building that his company bought in a distress sale for $3.5 million (it cost $17 million to put up). He appears to be seven feet tall, has arms like windmills and penetrating blue eyes. The walls of his office are resplendent with pictures of Fidel Castro posing with various members of the Delaney household.

Ian earned his title "The Smiling Barracuda of Bay Street" when he was president of Merrill Lynch, just before joining Peter Munk's empire. In 1990, he launched a proxy fight to take over the Canadian operations of Sherritt Gordon, a nickel refinery that for forty years had been a partially owned subsidiary of Newmont Mining in New York, and which suffered from underperforming management. He took the company over on September 19, 1990, when it had a capitalized value of $230 million—compared with close to $4 billion now. Sherritt had a serious problem finding ore to refine. That was solved by getting into business in Cuba, which led to other things. Delaney has since acquired an oil and gas company there, and is into the cellular telephone market, hotels, market gardening and power generation.

From the start, Delaney dealt directly with Fidel Castro. "He is an affable guy, but he doesn't really run the country," he says. "Cuba is run by people in their forties and fifties who cut the deals with foreign companies. Fidel's method of administration is to pick out and follow consensus pools. He holds himself above the fray. I've never negotiated with him, but we get along and I find him enormously engaging and amusing. He gave up smoking his long cigars long ago, but when he sees one sticking out of my top pocket, he taps it and says: 'We only sell those to our enemies now.'"

The American political opposition to doing business with Castro has resulted in the Delaneys being barred from the Unites States. "Washington is a pretty formidable adversary," he says. "But I can never walk away from a fight, and I have the high moral ground here. History is on my side. I don't like what's happening, but buggered if I'm going to get off the case. It's not going to happen.

"I am vastly amused that I'm being interviewed for a book on the Establishment," he interrupts himself. "That gives me all sorts of amusement, because I don't consider myself that way. Classical economists always talk about the enormous concentration in the Canadian economy, but that's been true for more than a hundred years. The neat thing is that every twenty-five years we change the guys who own the concentration. It's amazingly fluid at the top. And that creates an openness and an opportunity that doesn't exist in any other country in the world.

"Kiki works a lot harder than I do," he admits. "She's just a demon for work, and she not only does her business but is the centre of our household, around which we all revolve. She also carries an enormous load outside her office, such as being chairman of the National Ballet School. We do enjoy the new boat, and took her from Vancouver to Cuba through the Panama.

"Our future," says Delaney, "is only limited by our imagination. We're financially extremely strong."

For a minute you're not sure whether he's talking about Sherritt or the Delaneys. Doesn't matter; both versions are true.

THE WESTONS: *A Royal Family*

The Westons are proprietors of one of the world's largest family-controlled businesses, George Weston Ltd., a multinational food processing and food retailing company with 1997 sales of $14 billion.

The family's course was set in 1868 when George Weston arrived in Toronto from Oswego, New York, with his English-born parents. Young Weston apprenticed to Toronto bakers and at age eighteen became an independent businessman by purchasing from his employer one of the bread delivery routes he had been servicing. He quickly added more routes and later entire bakeries, including the so-called Model Bakery, an innovation at the time in hygiene and efficiency, which opened in 1897.

Weston was an active player in the game of shake-out and rationalization that affected industries such as baking around the turn of the century. When he started out, neighbourhood bakeries were common, but by 1900 a few large firms, his own included, dominated the scene. In 1903, he sold his bread business to a group that formed Canada Bread. Part of the deal was that Weston had to refrain from selling bread for ten years, so for the next decade he concentrated on biscuits and confections. By 1913, when he could begin making bread again, he had been a Toronto alderman, and was a Methodist church leader and businessman whose name was synonymous with baked goods. Weston died in 1924, of pneumonia he caught while walking miles through a blizzard rather than spend money for cab fare or overnight accommodation. By that time, effective control of the company had already passed to his son, W. Garfield Weston, who had been born in 1898 in the family apartment above the Model Bakery. It was he who put the family and the company into the running, nationally and internationally.

Weston served with the Canadian Engineers during the First World War, mainly in Britain, where he became enamoured of both British baking methods and British society. Much of the mammoth empire he built would eventually be centred there, run from an office on the top floor of Fortnum & Mason, which he owned. His company went global in 1928. Most of Weston's international ventures were takeovers rather than startups. During his fifty years at the helm of George Weston, Garfield purchased control of more than two thousand businesses, an average of one acquisition every ten days. Most of the acquired companies were in Commonwealth nations, and they operated everything from fishing fleets to traplines. The Depression brought him temporary setbacks, but also quickened his pace because so many bargains were available. It was in the 1930s that he moved boldly into the British market, taking over major bakeries and quickly becoming a public figure. In 1940, he was elected as a Tory MP and throughout the Second World War was involved in wartime assignments on both sides of the Atlantic.

After his Canadian bakery began to flourish, he bought out the well-known Scottish biscuit-making firm Mitchell and Muil, and Chibnall's of London. He moved to England in 1934 and started on a rampage of food firm acquisitions. When Matthew Halton, the Canadian journalist, toured one of his plants, Weston pointed out a small air jet he had installed at the end of the production line. "I see, that's blowing the extra chocolate off," Halton observed. "Oh, no," Weston replied. "It's blowing the profit on!"

Until 1943, Weston had acquired only bakeries and other food-related businesses. That year, he persuaded R.B. Bennett, the former Canadian prime minister, to sell his majority interest in the E.B. Eddy paper company. This was the only major departure in the long-standing pattern that brought him control of, for example, the Loblaws supermarket chain (1947), the William Neilson candy company (1948) and the National Tea Supermarkets in the United States (1956). *[Garfield Weston once bought an Irish castle after he saw two donkeys at the gate. When he enquired about their names, he was told that they were called Fortnum and Mason, his London store.]* Although a genius at acquisition, Weston was less gifted at management. There was little visible orchestration of the empire from above, and Weston's companies became notorious for competing against one another and getting in each other's way. His annual reports read like telephone directories.

Their father's legacy of disorganization was felt by Garry Weston in Britain and W. Galen Weston in North America following his death in 1978. While still in his twenties, Galen Weston, using his own funds, built up a chain of supermarkets in Ireland, and after Garfield's death, Galen and his team resurrected the Loblaws chain and returned it to prosperity. They pruned the company of superfluous branches, sold such businesses as the Tamblyn drugstore chain, and turned the food company into a bonanza. Under the inspired management of Richard Currie (who earned $6.8 million in 1997, plus stock options worth more than $100 million) and Serge Darkazanli, the Loblaws chain now commands fully one-third of the nation's retail shelf space.

Galen Weston—whose homes include an Irish manor house and an English castle—has played polo in the same league as Charles, the Prince of Wales. *[Fort Belvedere, the castle in which Edward VIII abdicated for the love of Wallis Simpson, sits on fifty-nine acres of parkland at Windsor, near the Queen's residence.]* He remains as elusive and mysterious as ever. When architects were completing the blueprints for his company's new head office on St. Clair Avenue in Toronto, about a mile to the north of his apartment, he had them install a private elevator strictly for his own use, so that he could come and go without being seen. He drives a different route to work daily in case he might be followed. He walks like a wolf, with darting, glancing eyes, and always has his guard up, sitting only at corner tables in restaurants and trying hard not to be recognized—which has become more difficult since his wife, the former Irish model Hilary Mary Frayne, became lieutenant-governor of Ontario.

THE EATONS: *The Big Ones Go Down*

There are family dynasties. Then there are the Eatons. Their fall from grace was even more momentous than it appeared. True, even though they lost control of the family asset, so carefully tended by four preceding generations of less careless forebears, there still is an Eaton's—at least until the next cash crunch. But if the stores haven't disappeared, the family dynasty as a meaningful economic unit has.

Canadians always felt a special relationship with the Eatons. As late as the mid-1970s, the family's department stores dominated Canadian retailing. Eaton's set the national style, while the family lived like merchant princes, occupying private castles and even erecting their own church and hospital. In its heyday, Eaton's was the country's fourth-largest private-sector employer, ranking just behind the two national railways and Bell Telephone. The company's sixty-three stores moved goods worth $25 million a week—half the merchandise sold across the country—while its catalogues enjoyed annual distribution of more than 18 million copies. No rural outhouse was complete without an Eaton's catalogue. *[Inevitably, Eaton's archives contain letters from farm bachelors who, having leafed through that season's catalogue offerings in the women's underwear section, sent in orders such as: "send the second lady from the right, on page 261."]* The family's well-earned reputation for honest dealings had turned its sales pitch— "Goods Satisfactory or Money Refunded"—into a phrase as familiar as the first line of the national anthem. Four busy generations of Eatons had extended their department stores across the country, and through mail order offices they had reached even the tiniest hamlets.

The store was founded in Toronto in 1869 by a pious, teetotalling Methodist named Timothy Eaton, who had immigrated to Canada following the potato famine in his native Ireland. The retail operation, the first in Canada to offer fixed prices and guaranteed returns, was brought to its full flowering by his son, Sir John Craig Eaton, then extended across the country by a nephew, Robert Young Eaton, and modernized by John David, leader of the third generation. In 1909, the family decided to build its own church, Timothy Eaton Memorial, in midtown Toronto, and it quickly became the Establishment's place of worship.

Probably the best-known Eaton of them all was Florence McCrea, youngest daughter of a carpenter from Omemee, Ontario, who married Sir John in 1901. Lady Eaton always retained the fifty-cent cheque issued to her when she served an hour behind the ribbon counter during the opening ceremonies of the family's Winnipeg store—her only work experience. She built a Norman castle with seventy rooms at King, just north of Toronto, travelled about the country in her private railway car, and during the Great Depression of the 1930s leased a summer villa in Florence (originally built for Queen Elizabeth of Romania). Interviewed by the *Toronto Daily Star* after her return from Italy, she praised dictator Benito Mussolini's reforms, smugly reporting: "No more do the beggars around the cathedrals annoy anyone."

Flora's eldest son, Timothy, became Master of the Hounds at the British school he attended, but never did much after that except stay home and operate his one-eighth-scale toy trains. His house in King was filled with miniature tracks for his tiny steam engine, fuelled by special coal imported from Nova Scotia. He searched five years for an appropriate ship's bell, finally found one in Moncton, and installed it on the back of his Cadillac with a rope running to the driver's seat. That way, whenever a streetcar pulled up behind him and went, *clang! clang!*, he could *clang* back. At sixty-eight, he bought his first motorcycle, took it out and broke both his legs.

Timothy's father (Sir John Craig Eaton was knighted in 1915 for his civilian contributions to the war effort) wrote a will stipulating that the family's stock in the company be kept intact until one of his four sons was chosen as his successor by his executors. The mantle fell on John David Eaton, who had been raised at Ardwold, a Toronto mansion with fifty rooms, fourteen bathrooms and its own hospital. In 1933, John David Eaton married Signy Hildur Stephenson, a Winnipeg beauty he courted while he ran the family's downtown store.

John David also kept a mistress in Montreal, whose special allures were practised in the mink-lined bedroom of her Côte-des-Neiges apartment.

He gave her an Eaton's credit card, grandly instructing her to order any-thing she wanted. The practical lady promptly phoned Eaton's, request-ing "one of everything in the store," but decided to have the deliveries stopped when she was nearly crowded out of her apartment by a load of bicycle tires.

Though he suffered from an increasingly serious drinking problem, John David remained in charge until 1969. He lived like an Eaton, maintaining a large house in Toronto's Forest Hill Village, a country seat in the Caledon Hills, a villa in Antigua and an island in Georgian Bay, com-muting between his various pads in a Hughes helicopter he'd learned to fly. The *Hildur*, a diesel yacht with accommodation for half a dozen pas-sengers and six crew, was his prize possession.

The faith that Canadians placed in the Eatons is hard to exaggerate. Although they lived in private enclaves, out of reach and sight of more ordinary mortals, whenever they appeared, they were treated as aristo-crats worthy of absolute trust. Everything they did seemed magical. Like nearly every other department store, they hired a Santa Claus at Christ-mas. "We always knew that Eaton's Santa was the real one," Rick Rabin recalled of his Toronto youth. "You can't fool kids about anything as important as that." *[Fred Eaton remembers how impressed he was as a child when he found out that Santa worked for his father.]*

The family seemed invincible. "Nobody will ever beat them," pre-dicted Steve Juba, a Winnipeg retailer who later became one of the city's best mayors. He told Ted Byfield, founder of *Alberta Report*: "Here's what they do. They'll buy a bunch of, say, dresses from a manufacturer after squeezing the price down so low the guy can barely make a nickel on them. Say they buy sixty at $8 each. They put them up on their prime fashion floor for $49.50, and in the next two months sell maybe twenty of them. Then they have the Trans-Canada Sale and they offer them at $24.95 and unload twenty more, announcing—accurately—that the price has been reduced by 50 percent. Finally, they clear them off in the basement at $9.95, broadcasting this price through a flyer in type six inches high. Meanwhile, the little retailer down the street goes wild. He bought the same dresses at $12. Here's Eaton's selling them at $2 below his cost. That's how they do it, and they can never be stopped."

When it came time for John David and his advisers to choose a successor, none of his sons—John Craig, Fred, George or Thor—were ready, so the store was turned over to professional managers. "They are rich men's sons of the most attractive sort," wrote the late Alexander Ross of the privileged quartet. "Handsome, soft-spoken, unobtrusively well-mannered, utterly assured and quietly confident of the fact that being born an Eaton is nothing to be ashamed of. They would not be out of place as constitutional monarchs of some clean little country like Denmark or Holland."

The boys' education was not promising. George Galt, a master who taught John Craig Eaton at Upper Canada College, remembered years later how much trouble the youngster had differentiating between "there" and "their," finally deciding to spell both "thair." John Craig later failed at Harvard. Young Thor, who was sent to Forest Hill Collegiate, complained that he alone of all the kids in his class didn't have a bar mitzvah. Fred was the only brother who managed a degree—at the University of New Brunswick, after getting special dispensation for not having passed Ontario's Grade 13 exams.

The most interesting of the Eaton boys—who are still called "boys" though all but one are just over or just under sixty—Fred was anointed the company's CEO in 1977. At first he did well, turning a profit of $60 million in 1979, opening Toronto's Eaton Centre and expanding the chain into new sales territories, with an eventual total of 108 stores and warehouses.

As Fred quickly discovered, to be an Eaton meant garnering unwanted attention. The mansion he occupied in the heart of Forest Hill Village was burgled so often that at one point he went to consult his neighbour, George Cohon the hamburger king, and asked him what he did about thieves. Cohon, whose love of practical jokes comes close to his worship of Big Macs, allowed that he really did nothing.

"You mean that you don't have any alarms, no guard dog, no protection of any kind?" Eaton demanded.

"That's right, Fred. All I do is, before I go to bed at night, I hang this little sign on my front door."

"What's it say?"

"Fred Eaton lives one door south of here."

Despite his good start, by the mid-1980s, Fred seemed to lose interest in the stores, spending increasing time sailing and hunting. As well as shooting ducks at the Long Point Company at Point Pelee in southern Ontario and gunning down hand-raised pheasant and tame deer on Griffith Island in Georgian Bay, he went on regular elephant-shooting safaris to Botswana with the King of Sweden. He quit the firm in 1991 to take up Brian Mulroney's patronage appointment as Canadian High Commissioner to the United Kingdom. When he returned three years later, he rejoined the Eaton's board, but took only a token interest in its affairs. By then, his main preoccupation was to move the family fortune out of department stores into Baton Broadcasting, the television arm of the Eaton empire that he and his brothers had founded in partnership with the Bassett family in 1960.

During Fred's absence in England, George Eaton, whose only previous claim to fame was as an unsuccessful Formula One racing driver, took over store duties. Thor, the youngest brother, built himself a French chateau in the Caledon Hills north of Toronto that actually has a moat. He devoted most of his time and all of his energy to raising thorough-bred horses.

The disintegration of Eaton's had many fathers. The once immensely profitable catalogue division was closed in 1976, although catalogue selling across North America has since grown impressively in revenues. The Santa Claus parades were phased out in 1982 after seventy-seven years, though they regularly drew crowds of more than a million.

The primary problem was the absence of strong leadership at the top. The enduring impression was that the boys drew straws and the loser got to run the stores. "George Eaton," wrote Andrew Vajda, Eaton's former national purchasing manager for supply services, "had no merchandising experience and limited education. He surrounded himself with managers who would not threaten his every move, while selling him on the concept of 'everyday low pricing.' That's when the fortunes of the company really started to diminish." There was no end of silly decisions. Grunge fiddler Ashley MacIsaac, who had publicly confessed that he favoured being peed on during sex, was hired to star in TV commercials designed to bring in family shoppers. Montreal's Eaton Centre was seized by creditors in 1992, while the Montreal store confused shoppers by moving on-sale merchandise out of the bargain basement and up to the eighth floor, calling it The Basement on 8th. "At the same time," reported Lysiane Gagnon of *La Presse*, "the ladies' lingerie department was moved to the main floor, next to one of the main entrances, so that passers-by could watch women choosing their panties and bras."

Everybody had their favourite Eaton's story. The fatal flaw was the absence of shareholders who might have forced the board of directors to be accountable for their actions, or lack of them. Between 1991 and 1996 (the year the company suffered a pre-tax loss of $128 million), Eaton's sales dropped by nearly 50 percent. As late as 1996, *The Financial Post* listed the family as Canada's fourth wealthiest, with assets of $1.7 billion. In fact, the stores were scrambling to stay open, and the brothers had to fire-sell $100 million worth of real estate. Market share had shrunk to 11 percent of national department store sales, one-third of the total reported by Wal-Mart's three-year-old Canadian operation. After an aborted attempt to merge with Sears Canada in the fall of 1997, even the Eaton boys realized their jig was up. "At times," concluded *The Globe and Mail's* investigative team, assigned to report on the state of Eaton's empire, "the four Eaton brothers have seemed to consider retailing a chore that took time away from broadcasting, thoroughbreds, politics, patronage appointments, and charity gold tournaments. They have been as warm and communicative as the government of Albania."

Until the final crisis, Eaton's had never gone to market for investment capital; and being a provincially chartered corporation, it was not required to make public disclosures of its operations or board membership. One of the great mysteries about the Eaton empire was how the family managed to pass it on intact from generation to generation without paying the succession duties that cripple enterprises many times ~~smaller. The secret was a process called "income freezing," which involved~~ hiving off assets to a holding company (Eaton's of Canada). The holding company controlled the common stock, which was placed in the hands of each succeeding generation after payment of a modest gift tax.

Despite their critical situation by the early winter of 1996–97, the Eaton name still counted for something. The Toronto-Dominion and Scotia banks had extended the boys a revolving credit line of $168 million, unencumbered by any pledge of store assets. But the bank float proved insufficient, and by Christmas the banks reluctantly ballooned their loan to $250 million, later increasing the amount to $360 million. It still wasn't enough: another $100 million had to be found—fast—to keep the stores afloat.

That was when the fateful phone call was made that signalled the death of Canada's WASP establishment. On February 5, 1997, George Eaton telephoned Stuart Armstrong, vice-president of commercial finance of GE Capital, begging for cash to tide the company over long enough to seek bankruptcy protection from the courts. Three weeks later, the other brothers resigned as Eaton's directors, leaving their patrimony adrift. Once the rulers of the country's most profitable enterprise, the current generation of Eatons had been so reckless that by the time Brother George had to make that fateful phone call, they owed their creditors a cool $480 million.

At a crucial moment in the proceedings, the Eatons' clout was tested one last time. On February 26, 1997, Justice Lloyd Houlden of the Ontario Court's General Division was asked to adjudicate when the

Bank of Nova Scotia, one of the Eatons' banks, threatened to send back an $8-million payroll cheque that exceeded the store's exhausted credit line. Unchallenged, that event would have been enough to sink Eaton's permanently. "I was almost on my knees, asking the bank not to do that," the usually impartial judge recalled. It had been a close call. Later, the judge explained that he and his wife had bought their first kitchen set from Eaton's, and when one chair didn't match, the store had replaced it, no questions asked. You never know what will turn history's crank.

Bankruptcy protection was granted under a statute that allowed the company to postpone the due date of creditors' accounts for six months. But as journalists, particularly the *Globe* investigative team (John Heinzl, Carolyn Leitch, John Saunders, Marina Strauss and Paul Waldie), began to look into the events surrounding the Eaton's rescue, they discovered that the company had approved an astonishing $50-million charge to cover George Eaton's liabilities as CEO. Worse, a secret $10-million dividend had been transferred from the troubled firm into the family's private holding company—to be split four ways—just before Christmas. Faced by this damning disclosure, George Eaton could only stutter, "We have a history of moving funds . . ." At the same time, the Eatons wanted to distribute $9 million to the firm's former non-Eaton directors.

Most disturbing of all was the fact that, only sixteen months before reaching insolvency, the Eaton family had enough cash on hand to pay $106 million (through Baton) for the television arm of Electrohome Ltd., thus helping to consolidate their hold on the CTV network. Two months later, they offered $166 million to buy out Baton's minority shareholders, and on February 26, the day before the Eaton insolvency became public, Baton won control of CTV. Within a year, the Eatons sold the television network for $339 million, thus successfully transferring most of their funds out of the family's foundering department stores. Ironically, that amount, added to the available bank loans, would have been more than enough to prevent the bankruptcy procedures, and would have saved the family's heritage. But that would have required a dollop of creative energy, and that the Eaton boys no longer possessed.

The suicide of Eaton's as a family enterprise was not marked by any sense of mourning; the brothers had been much too arrogant for that. Their final group photograph shows John Craig, Fred, George and Thor standing in front of the bronze statue of their great-grandfather, Timothy, that greets shoppers at their main Toronto store. They look embarrassed and confused in the founder's presence. They know that soon they'll have regained their privacy, but be invincible no more. Not sure what to do, they stand there as one and stick out their chests, waiting for the ordeal to end. "The boys look like ballet dancers with falsies," dismissively decrees one Establishment wife. "Stuffed shirts," says another.

And that's how Establishments die.

3

BOARDING UP THE
PRIVATE CLUBS

"Personally, Your Admirable, I light up one big motherfucker at 7:30 in the morning, and that keeps me in orbit all day."

—*Marvin Schanken, publisher of* Cigar Aficionado, *addressing Canada's governor general at a Cigar Dinner in Montreal's venerable Mount Royal Club, after being asked which cigars to smoke at various times of the day.*

IT IS HIGH NOON IN OTTAWA. "Real time," as the local power brokers like to remind visitors.

I am patrolling the Rideau Club, trying to discover why people pay $2,140 to belong to this historic dining establishment. It's beautiful. The view is the best, a full-Monty of Parliament Hill. The design—by Giovanni Mowinckel, who later became Mila Mulroney's personal decorator—is perfect. The stately panelling and antique fireplaces are set off by slightly threadbare carpets and fading prints. I keep glancing from one to the other, and it strikes me that they're interchangeable: that you could cover the floor with some of the prints, frame and hang squares of some of the carpets, and no one would notice the difference.

What makes the Rideau Club different from, say, an amateur theatre set for an Hercule Poirot mystery or one of those Hy's Steak Houses with the *Titanic*-before-she-sank décor, is the stillness that pervades the place. This is what once passed for the holy hush of power and privilege, the feeling that great events were unfolding here, that affairs of state were being negotiated among the *cognoscenti*.

Now that pregnant hush is just silence, the absence of sound. It's almost as if puffs of nerve gas were wafting through the halls, reducing the speed of members' limb movements. Two exceptions prevail: the bar, where real people are sipping real single-malt Scotch and smoking real cigars, and the club library, where real people have basically passed out. Most of the club's *habitués* move as if they were preserved in aspic. There is not much visible energy here; few are talking as if they mean it or gesturing or doing very much except whispering and raising eyebrows. The pale sunlight filters through the club windows, dyeing the gloom under the oxblood leather chairs, glancing off the overly waxed furniture. The club-men claim their reserved tables, order a T-bone medium-rare, and wash it down with an amusing little St. Emillon, wishing it was a pre-Mussolini Brunello, while puffing their Monte Cristos.

It is very much yesterday's power arena. The issues being negotiated in the main dining-room may or may not be affairs of the flesh, but they're almost certainly not affairs of state. *[The favoured hangout among Chrétien cabinet ministers is Mamma Teresa Ristorante on Somerset Street.]*

I know because I was a member of the *real* Rideau Club, when it was Ottawa's cockpit of power back in the 1950s, 1960s and 1970s. That was a time when Rob Bryce, the Robertsons Gordon and Norman Ed Ritchie, John Deutsch, Bud Drury, A.D.P. Heeney, Ross Tolmie and all the other great mandarins of the postwar generation regularly lunched at the "Cabinet" table in the left-hand corner of the ornate dining-room. There was a kind of inner glow that illuminated the faces of members then, especially when they were exchanging cabinet secrets, real or imagined. The place was alive with rumours of war and pestilence, of Quebec lieutenants who would be cashiered at dawn and of some clown of a British Columbia premier who claimed to have confounded fiscal gravity. Again.

The club was then strategically situated across Wellington Street from the Parliament Buildings, where it belonged. "The South Block" it was called, and it was a hive of considerable influence. *[The Rideau Club was founded by Sir John A. Macdonald in 1865, two years before he started the country. Obviously, a club-man who had his priorities straight.]* With its processional staircase, Corinthian pillars and ruby-red carpet sweeping upwards to its drawing-rooms and dining lounges, the Rideau Club was the ideal setting for exchanging confidences. Those with access to power—who weren't sure how much their listeners knew—circled one another like forest animals that smell a hunter: nose down, tail up to catch the scent. A German ambassador to Canada at the time briefed his successor: "Whenever you want to report on the reactions to any important policy, wander into the Rideau Club, take a seat at one of the large tables for members without guests, and chat with the senior civil servant inevitably eating next to you. This is the only capital in the world where you can gauge the government's attitude over one lunch." Regular members greeted each other with hearty voices and that possessive pat on the shoulder, followed by a tight grip of a hairy forearm that constitutes the club-men's gesture of belonging. *[Canada's quintessential club servant was Joseph Arthur "Archie" Lacelle, who served as the Rideau Club's hall porter for fifty-seven years. His only recorded mistake was in 1908. He put the home address on a letter that had arrived for a member, letting the wife in on her husband's secret love affair. Rebuked by the club executive, he never again admitted to a female enquirer that a member was in the club until he had checked and found out the desired reply.]*

The club may have been powerful, but like most of its sister institutions at the time, it was anti-semitic. The understandable fear of being blackballed kept so many distinguished Jews from applying that in 1964 a rump of enlightened club regulars did away with the rule of having memberships approved by secret ballot among the entire membership, and allowed the less Precambrian directors to approve applicants instead. The Rideau was not unique. Montreal's Mount Royal Club didn't admit its first Jewish member, super-lawyer and future senator Lazarus Phillips, until 1966, when he couldn't be denied because he had been nominated by the Montreal Establishment's two most powerful figures, Senator Hartland Molson and Earle McLaughlin, then chairman of the Royal Bank. Montreal's most important businessman, Sam Bronfman, the founding father of the Seagram empire, never did get in; his son Charles made it in 1970.

Among the worst offenders was the Vancouver Club, and I well remember having lunch with Walter Koerner at the Shaughnessy Golf Club, listening to his elaborate and studied explanation why it was a more convenient spot to meet than the Vancouver Club, where in his final years he wouldn't even go as a guest. The West Coast's most generous philanthropists, the Koerners, were never allowed to join the Vancouver Club, even though they tried to get around its prejudices by pretending to be Anglicans. *[The first Jew to join the Vancouver Club was Nathan Nemetz, who was difficult to ignore since he was B.C.'s chief justice, chancellor of the University of British Columbia, and a great charmer.]* Ironically, the Vancouver Club now exhibits nil prejudice, but as recently as 1990, the Shaughnessy Golf Club blackballed Caleb Chan, one of the Vancouver Chinese community's most significant businessmen and most generous philanthropists, having, among many other gifts and achievements, sponsored the University of British Columbia's $10-million Chan Centre. *[The Shaughnessy charges $48,000 for a membership, compared to the Capilano Golf Club's $50,000 and the Point Grey Country Club's $35,000.]* After being denied use of the Shaughnessy, Chan promptly built his own golf course, Nicholas North, at Whistler. Chan may not have been good enough for the nabobs at the Shaughnessy Golf Club, but when Jean Chrétien came to Vancouver for the first time as PM, he picked Caleb as his golf partner—and beat him 90 strokes to 92, winning $5.00 (no GST). *[The Rosedale Golf Club recently was the last to stop discrimination against Jews. As other clubs have allowed Jews to join, the community's own clubs, such as Toronto's Primrose Club, have had to close.]*

An equally serious problem was the discrimination against women as club members. Until recently, most clubs treated women with as much grace as your average Islamic state. They were barred from entry, except at Saturday-afternoon weddings of members' sons and daughters, when nobody else was using the facilities, or they were admitted for dinner, through side doors, with their husbands before horse shows or art auctions. Even when allowed inside to use their cordoned-off facilities, they were treated as backstairs creatures, permitted to appear only under cover of darkness, entering through separate doors into segregated quarters, their washrooms done up with marble sinks, tortoiseshell combs, silver powder boxes, flecked wallpaper and Pears soap. For a time, the only exception was the Ranchmen's Club of Calgary, which actually allowed women to hang around most of New Year's Day. It took the Rideau Club exactly fifty-eight years to act on a 1921 resolution calling for full female membership. At a 1964 reception tendered by the Department of External Affairs for U Thant, then secretary-general of the United Nations, two women MPs, Pauline Jewett and Margaret Konantz, were prohibited from entering the club's main premises. As soon as they had been sighted, club stewards hustled them out of sight into a pantry. They coolly declined the offer of a sandwich to go, as they were ushered through the kitchen and out the back door. Finally, on March 28, 1979, a reluctant club admitted women—and the sun came up next morning, right on schedule!

First to apply was Jean Pigott, a feisty member of one of Ottawa's most distinguished families, then a senior adviser to the prime minister of Canada, and later chair of the Ottawa Congress Centre. There had been a warning of sorts issued to her by a retired Supreme Court justice. She was walking up the club staircase, just a day or so after having been admitted, when the jurist stopped her. "I voted against you joining the club," he said, not sounding the least embarrassed. "I play high-stakes poker on Monday nights, and I'm a very nervous player. When they announced that women would be taking over the second-floor washroom, I cast my ballot against you because that washroom's very important to me and my poker game."

A few months after being anointed, Jean Pigott was relaxing in the club with political activist and feminist Laura Sabia. They were having a good laugh about the absurdity of their situation. "I wonder what the ghosts of all those old gentlemen are thinking?" Pigott recalls saying, as they bade one another good night. The next day—October 23, 1979—the Rideau Club went up in flames. Its hallowed premises were totally destroyed. "When the fire marshal reported the blaze had been caused by spontaneous combustion," Jean Pigott remembers, eyes a-twinkle, "I immediately felt a great surge of guilt." Some of the more fusty club members actually claimed the fire had been "started by Mrs. Pigott burning her bra."

Such silliness aside, the fire destroyed not only the club's premises, but its glory. It moved into much less prepossessing quarters on top of a downtown office high-rise and began to reflect a very different Ottawa.

Political Ottawa has no memory and no retroactive loyalty. When anyone of importance leaves, they are promptly forgotten; and if they return, they must start their climb all over again. The Rideau Club's membership still includes some of the city's powerful decision makers—Tom d'Aquino, Rod Bryden and a few others—but mostly, its membership roster represents local instead of national influence: lobbyists, real-estate operators, lawyers, accountants and political groupies of all stripes and persuasions. *[In a December 9, 1997, recruiting appeal, W.H. Stevens, Jr., chair of the membership committee of the Rideau Club, listed "the club's roster of leading Canadians" as the nineteenth reason for joining, after mentioning such higher-priority lures as free evening parking and discount access to health facilities. Corel CEO Michael Cowpland admits he joined mainly because the club has "three great snooker tables."]*

There, too, dine Ottawa's former political and public-service stars who have remained in the capital city beyond their allotted time in power. These once-dominant mandarins have retained their dignity and reek of wisdom. Unlike their successors, they hold in their minds specific notions of what Canada could be and should be—might have been, had their advice been followed. Still, they miss the game. Once they had a devil-may-care approach to politics, convinced that it was a sport, not a religion. But now that they're out of it and are feeling excommunicated—that is, their phones have stopped ringing—they're not so sure.

It's mainly inside the Rideau Club that they maintain their due. Every Wednesday at noon, they gather in the Sir Wilfrid Laurier Room and for two hours hash out the nation's problems. *[Around the table sit, among others, Mitchell Sharp, who first came to Ottawa in 1942 and is still senior spiritual and ethical adviser to the reigning prime minister; Robert Stanfield, the best prime minister Canada never had; Simon Reisman, the angry godfather of the Auto Pact and the Free Trade Agreement; Brian Dixon, the former, wise-as-an-owl chief justice; Louis Rasminsky and Gerald Bouey, much missed former governors of the Bank of Canada; Gordon Robertson, former Clerk of the Privy Council and CEO of Canada's constitutional industry; Max Yalden, former chief of the Human Rights Commission; Arthur Kroeger, former deputy minister of Employment and Immigration; David Golden, former head of Telesat Canada and once a military prisoner after the fall of Hong Kong; Beryl Plumptre, former chair of the Food Prices Review Board; Monique Bégin, the gutsy former minister of national Health and Welfare; Jake Warren, former deputy minister of Trade and Commerce; Basil Robinson, former under-secretary of External Affairs and the man who made John Diefenbaker almost understandable; Marshall Crowe, former chairman of the National Energy Board and cattle farmer extraordinaire; Roger Tassé, former deputy minister of Justice and a great Mulroney champion; Russell Mills, publisher of* The Ottawa Citizen; *Bertha Wilson, Supreme Court judge and former member of the Royal Commission on Aboriginal Peoples; and Gordon Ritchie, author and former trade negotiator and deckhand on a Hudson's Bay Company freighter.]* The current chairman of the group is Tom d'Aquino, the peripatetic CEO of the Business Council on National Issues. *[d'Aquino's favourite hide-out is the Sand Hill Fishing Club on the east coast of Labrador.]* Jack Pickersgill, the patron saint of the governing party, who was a member of this round table until a few weeks before he died, referred to his luncheon companions as "extinct volcanoes." But that wasn't quite fair. When Pierre Trudeau was searching for a sounding board to try out his contrarian position on the Meech Lake Accord, he chose to audition before this group. And they shot him down.

My walkabout of the Rideau Club is just about over and it has revealed few surprises. Until I decide to have lunch.

My memories of the club are coloured by its goofy struggles to keep out Jews and women, since I am one of the former and sympathize with all of the latter. Every time I revisit the place, I find it hard to get my mind off the prejudiced ways of the old Rideau Club.

Then, I enter the dining-room, and am welcomed by the club's *maître d'*. Instead of the superannuated army majors who had once, stiffly, performed that function, a young woman leads me to my Rideau Club table. Black and gorgeous: Álmaz Belay, a Whitney Houston look-alike from Eritrea, deep in the heart of Africa. At that moment I realize how profoundly Canada's private-club scene has changed.

CLUBS SUCH AS THE RIDEAU, AND IT WAS among the best, were the flagships of the Old Establishment. Apart from their status functions, they often served as sanctuaries for members who felt under siege. Most of the clubs had upstairs rooms reserved for members who required temporary escape hatches. More often than not, these lodgers were fleeing angry wives, demanding mistresses or both. Such comforting grumbles as "Never mind, old boy, Matessa is bound to come to her senses," were offered by fellow old boys, as the exiled member sheepishly moved into one of those Spartan, attic cabins. If the wife or mistress didn't manage to "come to her senses," the lawyers at Blake's or Gowling's sorted out the damage.

The clubs were significant instruments of acceptance and exclusion, providing the social measure of a man, granting an imprimatur to those who belonged. Being a member meant you were recognized for *who* you were, not merely for what you did—which, of course, is precisely the opposite qualification of today's meritocracy.

It is difficult now to comprehend the significance of the clubs at the height of their influence. I remember being in the office of Bob MacIntosh, a relatively enlightened Toronto money man who later became head of the Canadian Bankers Association and was then the Bank of Nova Scotia's deputy chief general manager. He had been trying for years to get into the National Club, a second-tier institution on Bay Street, whose façade faced his window. He stopped our conversation as he spotted the hall porter climbing onto the club's roof and lowering the flag to half-mast. "I'm moving up the list!" he gleefully exclaimed. *[The witty essayist Kildare Dobbs once described the chief requirements for club membership as "Dress British, think Yiddish, but keep quiet about the second part. Voice boring opinions as though they were novelties. Marry the chairman's daughter."]* In those days, the *maître d'* of the nearby Albany Club complained that the King Street streetcars were jostling his cellar stocks of port and demanded they reduce speed as they rattle by the club's premises. City hall agreed.

Toronto's most beautiful club is the York, a stone mansion in the university district that was once the home of the Gooderhams, Ontario's premier distilling family. Sir Albert Gooderham, worried about his wife's aversion to the chilly morning walk to her morning bath, evolved an elaborate plan to ease her discomfort. Each morning, a manservant would fill the tub with steaming water and discreetly withdraw. With a flourish, the husband would then push a bedside button, and the tub, mounted on narrow-gauge rails, would pull itself up to the bedside, so that his wife could descend directly into its comforting warmth. The house-proud host was once taking a group of friends on a pre-dinner tour of his mansion. To show off the "world's smallest railway," he pushed the button, and out of the bathroom rumbled the tub, filled with steaming water and a screaming Lady Gooderham.

When the clubs really counted, applicants denied membership suffered genuine anguish and occasionally exacted elaborate revenge. When William Myron Keck, the wildcatter who struck it rich in the offshore rigs he floated on the Gulf of Mexico in the 1950s and later on Lake Maracaibo in Venezuela, was refused entry to the California Club in downtown Los Angeles, he bought the club's air rights through an intermediary and built his Superior Oil headquarters on top of its premises. "That way," he explained, "I can piss on it."

The devotion of club members is hard to exaggerate. On May 3, 1997 when Ray McQuade knew he was dying of cancer, he drove himself to the Manitoba Club on Broadway Street in Winnipeg. He spent most of the day there, making preparations for his final journey. First, he played a farewell round of billiards, then he spent an hour with *maître d'* Gerry, making the arrangements for his own memorial service and for the reception to follow. Three days later he was dead, and ten days later his friends gathered at the club to celebrate their friend's life and to mourn his passing in what, they all agreed, had been his second home. That sense of belonging was surpassed only by Alan Kelly, another Manitoba member who lived in the club for thirty-nine years.

The Old Establishment's emphasis on private clubs as the symbol of its authority turned out to be a serious miscalculation. The *nouveaux riches* of the 1970s and early 1980s, who had their noses pressed against club windows, were easily co-opted. The Establishment took most of them in, only to discover that its real antagonists were not these turbo-driven but harmless acquisitors. Its serious rivals, who have now replaced them, are the Titans who have moved into the top roosts of corporate power, simply because they're damn good at what they do.

If members of that rampaging new meritocracy—the Titans—give any thought to the clubs that had so enchanted their fathers and uncles, it is to dismiss them as quaint watering holes with middling dining-rooms. Some have joined, but mostly they have chosen to bypass the experience as being irrelevant and boring.

The worst fear of the original club *habitués* was that "hooligans" (anybody not wearing a tie) would one day burst through the doors and grab all those little silver cups that marked club occasions with the names of past recipients engraved into them. They imagined these intruders would then throw these trophies into rivers or melt them down for coin, like the statues and angels stolen from cathedrals during the French Revolution. It never happened. The little silver cups are still there. But as club membership has declined, no one bothers to dust, polish or covet them.

And that, of course, turned out to be the club-men's ultimate nightmare.

Writing in *Country Estate* magazine, Jane Litchfield hit on the perfect description of how the members of Canada's clubs falsely view progress: "It's like they're sitting in a train, looking out the window at another moving train, thinking that they're moving, when they're not."

Apart from such sociological and anthropological reasons, these once-great lunching clubs are fading away because most of the people who count don't take time out for elaborate lunches. Those who do, prefer eating in the smart places with menus dedicated to their waistlines. In restaurants such as Canoe, Jump or Prego in Toronto, Chartwell's in Vancouver, the Palliser in Calgary and Rae & Jerry's or Dubrovnik in Winnipeg, they can sniff out the fast money and look past their luncheon companions' shoulders to see who's breaking bread with their competitors. In the club culture, the elaborate meal was a sign of power. *[There was a certain comfort in chomping salmon flown in from the Dee that morning, Bay of Fundy lobster so fresh it still had seaweed on it and Alberta prime filet dripping with hot blood—and washing it down with a Bâtard Montrachet 1973 (with the fish), a Château Beychevelles 1966 (with the beef) and Dom Pérignon 1971 (with Marnie, later).]* Now, the more you eat, the less powerful you are. The Establishment drink used to be Cutty Sark or Chablis; now it's Evian or Perrier with rocks and a twist of lemon. "No longer," says Red Wilson, chairman of BCE Inc., Canada's largest corporation, and a recent head of Montreal's Mount Royal Club, "no longer are there a lot of guys up for extended lunches. We're eating sandwiches in our offices and meeting for specific purposes, not simply to eat. The clubs are now mostly used for taking out-of-town guests to lunch or as elegant places to host private dinners or receptions. There aren't too many members who use clubs just to munch food together."

In 1993, before he became chairman of the Mount Royal, Wilson sponsored a black-tie Cigar Dinner with Marvin Schanken, the editor and publisher of *Cigar Aficionado*, as speaker. The guest of honour was Ray Hnatyshyn, then governor general, an office that the Brooklyn-based magazine editor had never imagined existed and didn't know how to address. For reasons known only to himself, Schanken kept addressing the G-G as "Your Admirable," instead of "Your Excellency," but things ran pretty smoothly until the question period. The room was filled with the aroma of forty-five cigar smokers exhaling the luxurious fumes of their smelly habit, when one member harrumphed and asked which cigar to smoke at various times of the day. Marvin stood up and went through the liturgy on how people are usually advised to have a small cigar in the morning and work themselves up to a fat, full-flavoured cigar after dinner. But looking straight at the governor general of Canada, Marvin said he didn't believe in any of that. "Personally, Your Admirable," he said, "I light up one big motherfucker at 7:30 in the morning, and that keeps me in orbit all day."

To replace their vanishing constituencies, clubs are trying to attract members with every activity short of sponsoring striptease performances—unless, of course, they happen accidentally, such as the time a dishwasher in the Manitoba Club got himself tiddly by swallowing the remnants in members' wine glasses and streaked the main dining-room, on the evening the club was holding its annual Ladies' Night. Meanwhile, the Rideau Club has opened a Friday-night piano bar, with Jim Brough tickling the ivories; the Saskatoon Club sponsors monthly lawyers' nights, with the lawyers providing their own entertainment; Montreal's St. James's Club has wired itself into a fibre-optic network so it can offer its members thrills in cyberspace; the Halifax Club has conscripted its chef to hold cooking classes. The Manitoba Club is the most successful in these diversifications, with events planned for nearly every evening, ranging from readings by Carol Shields to pre-game Blue Bomber dinners.

Gordon Sharwood, a former banker with one of the sharpest minds on Bay Street, who devotes most of his time to raising funds to maintain mid-size businesses in family hands and keeps up with the habits of the new players, reports that none of them show the slightest interest in any of the private luncheon clubs. "The only place they ever meet Establishment types is at the Jockey Club, because they like horse races," he says. "They're very reluctant to mix. They'll have a boat up in Georgian Bay, at Ontario Place or down in Florida. And that's where they really want to be. It's happening all over." All of the private dining clubs except the Toronto and the Manitoba are in financial crisis. Even at the Toronto Club, the limit of two members per bank or accounting firm has had to be eliminated. The highest fees charged by any of these institutions is at Toronto's Rosedale Golf Club, which has an entry fee of $40,000; 1,300 members have paid that levy and there remains a ten-year waiting list. Strictly women's clubs have fared very badly. Toronto's McGill Club has been bankrupt three times and has been torn by dissention since it was started. The Georgia Club in Vancouver was recently absorbed by the Vancouver Club.

"I'm old enough that I belong to some of these clubs," says James Baillie, the head of Tory, Tory, DesLauriers & Binnington, one of Bay Street's Establishment legal factories, "but my partners who are in their thirties just don't care. It's not a matter of their thinking, Oh, I'd never get into the Toronto Club, so I won't apply. They just couldn't be less interested. 'What would I want to have lunch with those old stodgies for?' they ask me."

ONLY ONE OF THESE INSTITUTIONS STILL harbours significant disposable clout: the Toronto Club, established in 1853 by members of Upper Canada's Family Compact. A Victorian pile at the corner of York and Wellington streets, it has 450 members. There's still a waiting list of a year or so, unless you're Steve Hudson, the genius who put together Newcourt Credit (Group)—then they want you aboard fast. "I'm on the executive, and when we see somebody we feel should be a member, we'll go and get him," says Fred Eaton, who serves as honorary secretary.

Eaton's own membership dates back to the time Bud McDougald, who preceded Conrad Black as head of Argus and Hollinger, was the chief animator of the Toronto Club. A member since 1933, McDougald had been asked to head a committee charged with reorganizing the club. He agreed. But it never met. "The only kind of committee I join," he once confided to me, "is a committee of one." And that was how he ran the club. To become a member required his blessing. Fred Eaton recalls being called by his mother one evening in 1966. "Your father and I had dinner with Mr. McDougald last night, and he thinks you should be a member of the Toronto Club, and he's going to call you this morning," she reported with scarcely hidden delight.

"So I waited," Fred remembers. "Bud wasn't a friend of ours, but he knew us. And sure enough, he called on schedule and invited me to join, suggesting that Allan Lambert, then our family banker, would nominate me. And that was that."

Ted Rogers was similarly blessed, but it took a little longer. The father-in-law of his friend Jim Wood had put him up, but nothing happened for six years. Rogers had a meeting with McDougald at about that time— because Bud had bought his father's radio station, CFRB—and ventured a question: "Sir," he hesitatingly demanded, "I was put up for the club six years ago, and I'm not asking a favour to be in, but if I'm not going to be able to join, I want to know so that I can go somewhere else."

"You mean that you'd rather get a no, than a continued delay?" McDougald barked back.

"That's exactly right, sir," Rogers replied, certain he had blown his chances. "When I walked out, I thought, Jeez, what an idiot. I'm out now. But three weeks later, I was in."

Contrary to prevalent rumours, Conrad Black was not born in the Toronto Club. His father, George Black, then a senior associate of the Argus Corporation, was involved in a spat, and McDougald, to help get him onside, sent Conrad a plain white envelope on his twenty-first birthday; it contained a membership card to the Toronto Club. There never was a nominating process or nonsense like that. Conrad took part of the Toronto Club to London with him by hiring Ingo Schreiber, its former secretary-manager, to be in charge of his domestic catering. *[Conrad has nominated many new Toronto Club members. His most questionable project was helping the late Nelson Davis get his son Glen admitted. The younger Davis, who is a former history professor and not very interested in business, didn't really want to belong and was sure he'd be rejected because he sports the last brush cut in captivity and dresses like a long-distance canoe racer who's been on the river for six months. But since it was Conrad who put him up, no one dared object.]*

In his declining years, McDougald spent nearly every lunch hour at his beloved Toronto Club, but it just wasn't the same any more. I remember lunching with him just a few months before he died. "My God, it looks like a convention of plumbers in here," he complained. "People are actually coming into the Toronto Club wearing wooden shoes!" That lament reminded me of another criterion McDougald had used in determining the club's membership. He would never allow anyone to join who wore white or diamond-patterned socks. His wife Maude, known to everyone as Jim, had told me of an occasion when a man's socks had ruined his career: "They were looking for quite a top executive for one of the Argus companies, and they had tried everybody," she recalled. "Finally, this chap seemed as if he were going to be simply perfect. Some of the other executives had met and interviewed him and the poor fellow came into our living-room, hitched up his trouser legs and sat down, showing his white socks. My husband turned to the others and just said, 'Out. . . . Useless.'" *[A quarter century after McDougald's death, veteran Toronto Club members still pay homage to his memory. They nod as they pass his special table, the only one with armchairs.]*

The big hitters still lunch at the Toronto Club. Peter Munk is on the management committee, the first Jew ever to be so honoured. The club's roster carries a dozen Jews and a half-dozen women; discrimination is no longer an issue. *[More of an issue is the $20,000, non-deductible entrance fee. This compares with only $3,000 for the Metropolitan, New York's best club. North America's most expensive club is the Sherwood Country Club, outside Los Angeles, at $150,000—U.S.—membership.]* There is a comforting sense of continuity about the place. Rod McQueen of *The Financial Post* recalls seeing three successive chairmen of the Toronto-Dominion Bank—Allan Lambert, Dick Thomson and Charlie Baillie—lunching in various corners of the dining-room. "The Toronto Club," says Tony Fell, the head of RBC Dominion Securities and its current president, "is in outstanding shape. The physical quarters are superb, we have money in the bank, and we still have a good waiting list, even if it's not as long as it was five or ten years ago." One problem is that the club strictly enforces a rule that no member can discuss business at lunch, which means not being able to take a scrap of paper out of your pocket or daring to touch a pen, even to jot down a phone number. "I'm surprised you're not frisked at the door," complains Ed King, a former head of Wood Gundy, who has been a member since 1989. The Toronto Club also has nearly 200 out-of-town members, including Harrison McCain, the French-fry king, whose most valuable other club affiliation is Annabel's, one of London's grooviest hangouts, favoured by young royals.

Montreal's icon club is the Mount Royal, which once managed to combine virulent anti-semitism with the exclusion of French-Canadians. As late as 1975, there were only nine Québécois members. Now three-quarters of the new recruits are French speaking: Jean de Grandpré (BCE), Paul Paré (Imasco), Roger Beaulieu (lawyer), Jacques Courtois (lawyer), André Bisson (corporate director), Pierre Des Marais II (corporate director), Jacques Menard (investments, Hydro-Québec) and Guy Saint-Pierre have served as chairmen. Lodged in a vintage building designed by the American architect Stanford White, who also did the Metropolitan Club in New York, the Mount Royal is the most elegant of Canada's clubs, but its fortunes run with the dubious future of the city itself.

Montreal's St. James's Club, started in 1857 by local businessmen fed up with eavesdropping waiters at commercial restaurants, has found new life catering to a lower rank of entrepreneurs. It's still true that its members break down into two groups—those who wish they belonged to the Mount Royal and those who are glad they don't belong to the Mount Stephen Club—but less true than it used to be. *[The St. James's Club recently borrowed $700,000 to renew itself. The unexpected source was the solidarity fund of the Quebec Federation of Labour, from which the club will elect no members.]* The Mount Stephen is housed in the magnificent mansion that was the original residence of CPR godfather George Stephen, who headed the Bank of Montreal as well as the railway. It features a five-inch-thick front door with a knob and hinges plated in 22-carat gold and a magnificent staircase hand-crafted out of Cuban mahogany, but not much else. It is rented out for the shooting of films that feature old mansions and is used for wedding receptions (including Brian Mulroney's), but by 1994, membership was down to forty-four and there wasn't even enough money to preserve its wooden panelling. The Montreal club with the best kitchen is the University, though there was an uproar when the new francophone chef admitted that he not only didn't know how to make steak-and-kidney pie, but was blissfully unaware such a dreadful concoction existed. The most popular club with francophones is the St. Denis, which not only has a noble kitchen but a bowling alley. The Montreal Hunt Club is virtually comatose, though there still are Hunter Trials and a Hunt Club Ball.

Most Montrealers reserve their club activities for the country. Still solidly enjoyed are the Hermitage Club at Lake Memphremagog, which has a couple of dozen cottages on its site, but also plays host to many Establishment types who summer nearby. Yves Fortier and his wife Carol are the dominant presence—there is even a tennis trophy named after him. Other Montrealers who belong include: David Angus, Claude Castonguay, seven members of the Coutu family, Paul Desmarais, Jr., who is building a palace nearby, Guy Forget, Pierre Michaud, Beatrice Molson, Jean Monty, Pierre Nadeau, Alex Paterson, Boris Reford, Ron Riley (two of them), Guy Saint-Pierre, Guthrie Stewart and Michel Vennat.

The Mount Bruno Country Club at Hudson, which is at the opposite end of Montreal, has the best view of any Canadian green—all the way to the mauve hills of Vermont and New Hampshire. It's mainly a golf club, which also has a couple of Rileys. It's expensive (the entrance fee is $18,000, plus $4,000 annually), and although there are no stated restrictions, perusal of a recent membership list reveals few Québécois. Some of the Establishment's favoured holiday spots are Matisse Beach (Con Harrington, the surviving Refords and a sprinkle of Birkses), Ste-Agathe (David Culver), Murray Bay (Paul Desmarais, Sr.), Magog (David Angus), North Hatley (Norman Webster), Sutton (John Cleghorn), Drummond Point (Guy Saint-Pierre), Stowe (Arnold Steinberg) and Montgomery, Vermont (Gord Sinclair), where Pierre Trudeau once skied.

Of the several East Coast clubs, only the Halifax remains in serious contention. Dating back to 1862, when the city had already passed its centenary, the Halifax preserves the best of what remains of club life. Its past minutes of annual meetings are highlighted by an exchange in the early 1950s, when a new member dared suggest that the menu was too fattening and should include some light soufflés on the dessert tray. For some reason, Bob Nelson, then president, took this as a personal affront and cut off the discussion with the comment, "Soufflés? A soufflé, my friend, is nothing but a baked fart." When another member had the poor sense of timing to expire in the arms of Halifax's most popular prostitute, she notified the club, and a posse of well-fortified confrères ambled over to her familiar address. They collected his remains, which they parked on the club steps. The following day, local papers touchingly reported how fitting it was that the poor man had met his maker at the portals of the club he held so dear.

The Halifax Club commemorates the great family dynasties that once ran Nova Scotia. The Morrows, Camerons, Connors, Olands, Robertsons, Smiths, Jodreys, Frasers, Browns, Gordon Archibald and the grand R.B. Cameron are on its lists, even though their time of influence is over. The member who has had more to do with reviving the club than any other is Stewart McInnes, a lawyer and former minister of Public Works in the Mulroney government, who reduced its stuffiness by adding jazz nights, dancing lessons, bachelor dinners and visiting lecturers.

At mid-country the Manitoba Club, established in 1874, is one hangout that has maintained not only its reputation but its membership, due mainly to the inspired managership of Michael Cox, a British chef who trained in Switzerland, learned his management skills in Sweden and spent considerable time in Africa as a purchasing agent for a mining company. Out of that varied experience emerged a talented diplomat whose high sense of decorum is tempered by a touch of mischief. A typical example from one of his internal bulletins dealt with the club's soap situation: "Members will be happy to note that we have secured another source for the supply of Pears soap and that they will no longer have to suffer using environmentally friendly Ivory soap. Our thanks for bringing this unbearable situation to our attention are extended to Judge Philip Ashdown."

Calgary's Petroleum Club has probably made the best adjustment to the 1990s. Since it hasn't had a waiting list for nine years now, it has, in effect, ceased being a club (its entry fee is down to $2,000, with special discounts for quantity purchases, plus $65 per month) and has become a pleasant place to eat. Not that you have to: so many people were staying in their offices for lunch that in 1997 manager Rod Thomas started a popular takeout service, dispatching sandwich lunches all over downtown. Women have been admitted since 1989, though the place retains its decidedly masculine icons such as bronze cowboy sculptures, acres of brass and marble, heavy furniture and drive-in fireplaces. The club's significance as a roost for Calgary's power brokers is derived from its mornings. "The Pete Club became an epicentre for breakfast," says John Brussa, one of the city's Titans, "with a lot of networking going on, especially by the First Energy guys."

Very different is the Ranchmen's Club, founded in 1891, which is on the edge of town and not on everybody's flight path. Recently reactivated as a status-enhancing dinner venue, it bears a heavy burden of history. Its archives still contain the boiled tuxedo shirt autographed by the future King Edward VIII and the names of club members who attended a wild party to mark his visit as Prince of Wales. To the Ranchmen's also belongs the distinction of having had the member who remained longer in residence than any other member of an Alberta club. Dudley Ward, whose wife took up with the Prince of Wales, left England in order not to embarrass the royal family and spent much of the last twenty-five years of his life living on the club premises.

One *habitué* most succinctly expressed the Ranchmen's Club ethic: "By belonging, you take the guesswork out of friendships." Less pleasant is the club's anti-semitic history. "When I came to town in 1962, I passed an interview with one of the largest firms in the province and when they invited me to the Ranchmen's Club, my brother-in-law said, 'They must not realize you're Jewish or you wouldn't be there,'" recalls Bruce Green, an establishment lawyer. "I asked J.J. Saucier of Bennett Jones if he realized that I was Jewish, and he said, 'Oh, that doesn't matter.' But it did; they had no Jewish members at the Ranchmen's Club in those days. But there's none of that now." *[Jack Pierce of Ranger Oil was the first Jew to join the Ranchmen's; Harold Milavsky of Trizec was second.]* Still, it's significant that Brett Wilson, one of Calgary's most powerful Titans, hasn't been at the Ranchmen's for the past four years. Ken King of the *Calgary Herald*, who comes as close to being a Titan as any publisher in the country, generally avoids clubs, but has his own table in the kitchen of La Chaumière, the best restaurant in town—though many Calgarians swear it was better before it changed locations. Earl's at Banker's Hall, the Rimrock and the Palliser are also popular.

The Vancouver Club is a good example of how these once-sacrosanct institutions have faded into insignificance. It was once a luxurious and much sought-after hide-out. What characterizes the West Coast is activity. Everybody feels obliged to be doing something every waking minute. Other clubs cater to such habits: the Royal Vancouver Yacht Club sponsors the best races and runs the most romantic outstations in the universe; the University Club (amalgamated with the Vancouver Club in 1987) concentrated on good conversation; the Terminal City Club (currently being reincarnated) had a pool and gymnasium; and the Lawn Tennis & Badminton Club gives its members hefty workouts. *[Its original lawn-bowling turf came from the gardens of Colonel Victor Spencer, who with his brother*

Chris sold the family department store to Eaton's in 1948.] The Vancouver Club was useful as a good place for wastin' time—just a-sittin' and a-rockin', watchin' the ships go by. Members felt protected there, away from the rush of business, out of the reach of marital wars.

To keep up with the times, the Vancouver Club, which enjoys the most beautiful vista in the country, not only let in women and Jews, but the Chinese. The sanctuary has been breached. "It isn't the power centre it was," says Ron Cliff, the chairman of BC Gas. "Even if the most powerful people in town all belong there, they don't meet there and do things there any more; it just doesn't happen. I'd rather go to maybe a nice restaurant, a different one every day of the week, than go to the same place and talk to the same people." Peter Brown, chairman of Canaccord, agrees: "That business about allowing women into the Vancouver Club as a seat of power—what a joke that was. The profile of the average new member of the Vancouver Club is assistant manager in British Columbia for Manufacturers Life."

As in most cities, Vancouver's Titans lunch in the fun places: the *nouvelle cuisine* Diva's on Howe Street, Gianni's on upper Granville, Il Giardino's where Umberto rules (when he's not in Tuscany), the Cannery, Elaine Skalbania's elegant Wedgewood, the much under-rated Ivy on Fourth and most frequently at Chartwell's. Capably hosted by Susan Minchin, who knows nearly every important player in town, this Four Seasons outlet has become the new Vancouver Club. "Many customers have their usual tables, and it seems as if there are very few big deals made in Vancouver that don't start here," she says. "It's very much like a club; we see the same faces three and four times a week."

Beyond the downtown lunching clubs, there is a covey of sportsmen's hideaways, such as the Restigouche Salmon Club in northern New Brunswick, located at the aptly named Million Dollar Pool, and the Long Point Company on the north shore of Lake Erie, where an English member, J.T. Lord, once shot 3,300 ducks in one season.

In the age of networking, it's the golf clubs that are the most popular. The longest waiting list—five years—is at the Calgary Golf and Country Club. Halifax's original Ashburne Golf Club ranks with the best, as do the Laval-sur-le-lac and the Mount Bruno near Montreal, the Rosedale in Toronto, the St. Charles in Winnipeg and the Capilano in Vancouver. "There are more business deals done on golf courses than in boardrooms," says David Ho, who heads a Vancouver conglomerate that includes ownership of a luxury golf course. "You have a relaxed atmosphere, and when you're walking all those miles from hole to hole, all you can do is talk." In the Chinese glossary of gaining face, golf is also important because it shows that you must be very successful if you can afford to take so much time to play a game instead of working.

The country's most powerful club has nothing to do with dining, buildings or the fine points of exclusion. It is the Trilateral Commission which sits annually in secret in secured quarters on three continents, discussing trade patterns, fiscal dues and political endgames. The group has no fixed agenda, but wields heavy influence, especially with the G-7 prime ministers. The Trilateralists' self-imposed mandate is nothing less than to restructure the global economy and redirect the policies of member states—including Canada—to implement their recommendations. Established in 1973 by David Rockefeller, then chairman of the Chase Manhattan Bank, the Trilateral Commission is dedicated to free markets, which means opening up new territories for its member corporations, with little regard to national interests. The commission's corporate members are the new proletarians of the global economy.

The chair of the Trilateral's Canadian section is Allan Gotlieb, the driven ex-diplomat who never strays far from the centre of action, especially if he's creating it. Canadian members, past and present, include Conrad Black, Paul Desmarais, Harrison McCain, Jimmy Pattison, Yves Fortier, Michael Phelps, Ron Southern, Red Wilson and Alcan's Jacques Bougie. *[Their titles, as well as a list of the Trilateral Commission's membership, is published in Appendix 1.]*

Canada's most exclusive club, the Forum Group, which is affiliated with the Young Presidents Organization, has only six members. They meet once a month at one of the exclusive Toronto lunching clubs or in each other's homes. They are the very best of Canada's young entrepreneurial crop and include Steve Hudson, the most successful of the new money men; Michael McCain, now CEO of Maple Leaf Foods Inc.; Larry Stevenson, the presiding genius of the Chapters book chain; Tony Graham, who is running his family's impressive investments, including parts of the Holiday Inn chain and the Scott Hospitality operation (Colonel Sanders' chicken); Greg Wilkins, who is spearheading the expansion of Peter Munk's Trizec-Hahn into the world's largest real-estate company; Neil Shaw, who handles an international portfolio for British investors; and Sam Blyth, the establishment travel agent. "We act as a sort of personal board of directors for each other's companies, and hopefully we'll spend the next ten years together," says Blyth.

Many other such groups are being formed out of the ceaseless networking that has become the New Establishment's lifeblood. But the classic men's dining clubs have become relics of another age. Like the Old Establishment's adherents whom they fed, housed and cosseted, these institutions depended on exclusivity for their justification. Now that the Establishment is open to anybody, regardless of their pedigree or school tie, the clubs that perpetuated those notions have lost their reason for existence. To be clubbable means precisely nothing.

Good breeding is for horses.

4

RIDING THE
MONEY CULTURE

"My God, man, have you lost all sense of the value of money? Why, I know people who haven't paid that much for a house!"

—*Comment by a fellow tax exile at a Canadian cocktail party in Bermuda, after a fellow guest revealed he had just paid $11 million for an antique armoire.*

HIS EYES ARE LIKE BOUNCING LOTTERY BALLS.

Anything might come up. A mixture of vanity and fun, Peter Nygard is showing me his new home. House? Villa? Mansion? Palace? Coliseum?

What do you call a structure that spreads over four acres, its habitable area covering 100,000 square feet? *[The only house that compares to Nygard's Bahamas abode is the luxurious compound built near Seattle by Bill Gates. It is less than half as large, but it cost three times as much because of higher real-estate values.]* How do you describe a residence that requires guests to drive electric cars to their bedrooms, located somewhere in its suburban extremities?

In Nygard's case, what you call this architectural monstrosity is a temple. It's a place to worship his outsize personality; a shrine to his remarkable success as one of Canada's largest manufacturers of ladies' quality garments; a cathedral for a man whose appetite for women and in-your-face architecture knows no bounds.

Nygard takes me on tour. His athletic six-foot, three-inch body is crammed into a pink silk shirt, a pair of fashionable short pants and label running shoes. He watches for my reaction as I stumble around his acreage, at first trying hard not to laugh, but gradually realizing that while a place this size is strictly looney tunes, it is bold in concept and stunning in its execution. Located on the western tip of New Providence Island in the Bahamas, on a cay that Nygard has named after himself, the

building is a lavish labour of love that has taken him a decade of planning and work, plus an estimated $12 million to put together.

"Is this," I ask, exhausted from hiking across the living-room, "is this
the world's largest house?"

"No," he acknowledges. "Buckingham Palace will always be bigger."
Right.

"Actually," Nygard goes on, "it's sort of wrong to call my place a
house. It's more like a resort."

Actually, the place sort of gallops to infinity; it's a series of intercon-
nected pods that house his entourage and fourteen guests, plus profes-
sional-size tennis, volleyball and basketball courts that can be
transformed into covered runways for fashion shows. The dominant
motif is sensual curves and secret places from which to watch a sunset,
hear the ocean, make love. There are bending roadways everywhere to
carry the narrow-gauge electric cars that interconnect the sprawling
structure's outlying regions. (I can visualize some exhausted guest, roused
from deep slumber by a call of nature, complaining, "Damn it, now I
gotta drive to the bathroom.")

"I'm trying to go back to nature," Nygard insists. "It's as if Robinson
Crusoe had found a huge shipwreck and built himself a home."

Well, not exactly. As far as I remember, Robinson Crusoe's wilderness
bedroom didn't have a mirrored ceiling. I also doubt whether that primitive castaway could relax, as Nygard does, in an exquisitely carved stone
sauna built for twenty-five of his best naked friends. Chances are that
Crusoe couldn't avail himself of a double-storey, treehouse office, accessible only by cable car, furnished like a Fifth Avenue penthouse.

But I quibble.

Much like Crusoe's island, Nygard Cay is self-sufficient, producing its
own electricity, fresh water and soil. (The soil is refined from palm
leaves, which when mixed with water, become a fertilizing agent, so that
the once-arid cay has grown green and lush.) Nygard loves rock gardens,
but nature's available boulders are the wrong shape and size. That's why
he has a "rock factory," which uses intense heat to mix real stones with
fibreglass and iron-reinforcement rods to create rocks of specific bulk
and contours. Nygard has thrown up massive cliffs with overhangs made
out of this remoulded substance and claims it has the strength to hold
up eighty-storey skyscrapers. The miniature, 50-foot-high Matterhorn
he built has special significance. "I had a girlfriend once who liked
mountain climbing," he confides, "and so I said, 'I'll build you a mountain.' She left me, but I thought the mountain was a good idea anyway.

It will have a huge 35-foot-deep lagoon underneath it, so you can dive into a cave where there'll be a little discotheque and a wet bar that you can sit in."

The entire peninsula will eventually be turned into a bird sanctuary, with free-flying peacocks, parrots, flamingos and other photogenic species. "I'll have a skywalk above their nesting space," Nygard rhapsodizes, "so that at sunset we can play classical music and watch the birds preening underneath." He also promises to turn part of his property into a retirement home for ageing circus animals and already has his eyes on a couple of white Bengal tigers.

When I ask him who built his tropical dream, he becomes surprisingly defensive. "I'm the best bloody crane operator on site, lifting those 7,000-pound palm trees," he boasts. "I run the biggest crane here."

Then, he grows very quiet. "When we first came over from Finland in 1952, I was ten," he recalls, "and our family lived in a converted coal bin ௵௵ ௵ ௵௵௵௵, ௵ ௵௵௵௵ ௵௵௵௵ ௵௵ ௵௵௵ ௵௵௵௵௵௵ ௵ ௵௵௵௵ ௵ ௵௵௵௵௵௵௵."

Nygard pauses, and for a moment the mask slips. "I didn't have a crane when I was a little boy," he confesses, sounding very much like a little boy. "I didn't have a choo-choo train or a treehouse either. But I've got a *big* crane now."

An official resident of the Bahamas since 1975, Nygard divides his time among luxury pads in Winnipeg and Toronto, his Caribbean extravaganza and another gigantic tranquility base he has built out of two seaside condos at Marina Del Rey, near Los Angeles.

A curious mixture of macho posturing and artistic posturing, Nygard is built as solidly as a wrestler, with wavy blond, Samson-like hair. His creations—whether they're $799 cocktail dresses or $12-million houses—are endowed by his superb Finnish sense of colour and design. Inordinately vain about his appearance, he panics when I want to take his snapshot. "I don't look good in pink," he shouts over his shoulder as he rushes away to change. He reappears in a blue tunic that makes him look like a Scandinavian sea dog, straight out of *Gentleman's Quarterly*. *[At his annual reception for fashion buyers, Nygard usually rents an elephant or camel, and paints it white.]* Scattered among his various *pieds-à-terre* are five Excaliburs. The $70,000 automobiles (fibreglass reproductions of Adolf Hitler's 1920s Mercedes SSK roadster) are carefully colour-coordinated with Nygard's wardrobe and the dominant colour of his various domiciles. "The cars have to suit the clothes I wear," he patiently explains, "because I'm in the fashion business." *[The hues of his current Excalibur fleet include fawn brown, silver, burgundy, white and beige.]*

He can afford to finance these and other luxuries out of the double-digit millions he nets as majority owner of a $350-million-plus international empire that employs 2,500 people and ranks in the top ten among North America's most profitable fashion houses.

He sold his Morgan-51 sloop that he used to moor in the Bahamas, but maintains his status as an Olympic-class sailor by keeping a sailboat at each of his locations. Starting out in twenty-two-foot Tempests on the Lake of the Woods, he won the Manitoba championship, eventually became a North American gold medalist and was ranked as the world's fifth-best Tempest racer.

While growing up in Winnipeg, he married his friend Helena Jaworski and later Carol Knight, one of his in-house models. He purchased the former Gilbert Eaton mansion on the city's Wellington Crescent as his matrimonial home with Carol, but never moved in. "All of a sudden," he says, "it became a struggle as to which society I would belong to. I've never subscribed to the Establishment's rules and regulations. I don't really know what they are and haven't bothered to learn. I find them kind of boring." At the time, Carol complained to a friend that before he proposed, Peter wanted it clearly understood she would get only 6 percent of his time. There were no children from that misalliance, but Nygard has had at least two daughters and two sons by other women. He claims that another marriage is not part of his life plan. "Fortunately," he confesses, "at a very young age, I got totally in tune with myself. My mind and my body are very much in harmony. I've got complete freedom. I don't want to be married and be running around with other women. My whole attitude is that I really can't tell a person that I'll live with her happily ever after. But I really go out and spoil my women. I create an environment where they prefer my company. I say, 'I'm going to make it difficult for the next guy to top this.' I hardly ever break up with them any more. I just have more of them. I'm not jealous. And that's because of my sense of security. There's a certain air of excitement I create because I'm always on the move."

He has squired glamorous women such as Elke Sommer, Jaclyn Smith, Jane Kennedy, Joan Collins, supermodel Iman, Cybill Shepherd, Maude Adams and Ann-Marie Pohtamo and a Miss Universe or three; squads of blonde knockouts seem always to be in reserve. To an outsider, they appear to be more of a menagerie than love objects, props for his extravagances. "Some are better friends than others," he acknowledges with one of those looks that implies everything or nothing. One of Nygard's Winnipeg acquaintances who made a casual study of his female companions was lost in admiration for the functional criteria he applied to his choices: "For example, when Peter was training for the sailing Olympics in boats that required frequent hiking—which means hanging far out over the edge of the gunwale, squirming around with all the weight you can muster—he was always taking out girls with legs six feet long and big bottoms. I don't know how he does it." *[Alan Sweatman recalls, "I remember Peter racing his catamaran. He always had a lot of women and picked them for whatever the other activity was, but he had a girl on this thing with legs right up to her ears and a round hard bottom. The idea was, he'd put her out in a trapeze, and Christ, there was all that weight out there. I don't think he ever saw her face! He had a luxury boat that followed him, so that at night he'd have caviar and . . . . He is quite a guy."]*

Peter's family emigrated from Finland before he was a teenager and started a bakery at Deloraine, eventually moving to Winnipeg. Young Peter was on the go almost as soon as he got into long pants. At twelve he was already subcontracting four newspaper-delivery routes, selling them to immigrants who wanted their sons in business but didn't know how to go about it. He would lend money to his sister Liisa, then charge her interest in the form of claiming half the candy she bought with it. Summers he worked as a carnival age-and-weight guesser, lifeguard and supermarket stock boy. He studied business administration at the University of North Dakota, became a management trainee at Eaton's and listed his name with a firm of corporate headhunters. He happened to be in bed with the then-Miss Sweden when the telephone call came notifying him that Nathan Jacob, a local clothing manufacturer, was looking for a sales manager. Over the next seven years he bought out the firm, altered its merchandising patterns and expanded east and south. "Luck," he philosophizes, "is the crossroads of opportunity and preparation." He changed the company's name from Jacob Fashions to Tan Jay and completely reoriented its product line. "Everybody was telling me that half the market was under twenty-five and that to survive you had to sell to that sector. I cleverly figured out that if half the population was under twenty-five, the other half must be over twenty-five, and that they probably weren't being properly catered to. I jumped into an industry that was ripe for change."

Peter Nygard is a movable zoo. He has achieved spectacular success in the most competitive of industries, and he did it his way. A hedonistic workaholic, he gives free rein to all his senses while minting millions in the process. If the compulsion to flaunt his wealth annoys his peers, that's just too bad. "And anyway," he sensibly concludes, "I have no peers."

IF HE IS NOT A CHARACTER OUT OF F. SCOTT Fitzgerald, Peter Nygard certainly is a lively affirmation of the author's best known aphorism: "Let me tell you about the very rich. They are different from you and me." That oft-repeated snippet from a short story titled *The Rich Boy*, published in 1926, leaves out the most astute part of Fitzgerald's rumination about the mentality of the very rich, which still rings true today. "They possess and enjoy early, and it does something to them, makes them soft where we are hard, and cynical where we are trustful, in a way that, unless you were born rich, it is difficult to understand," runs the rest of the quotation. "They think, deep in their hearts, that they are better than we are because we had to discover the compensations and refuges of life for ourselves. Even when they enter deep into our world or sink below us, they still think that they are better than we are. They are different."

Fitzgerald's literary canvas—the America of the 1920s—was a giddy time. Youthful inheritors staked their lives and careers on the kind of epic emotional gestures that moved Fitzgerald's people to their final-chapter denouements. They were mostly playboys and playgirls, but they injected new energy and new dances (the charleston instead of the waltz) into the old milieu, re-energizing fortunes and loosening social taboos.

Now, seven decades later, the 1990s are proving to be an equally giddy time, with another ageing establishment being arm-wrestled into submission and a new generation of self-made up-and-comers taking over. A striking similarity between the 1920s and 1990s is that business in both ages became a spectator sport, with its dominant players—heroes and villains alike—gaining superstar status. Canada has no money kings, like the Rothschilds or Rockefellers, but we have princes: the Bronfmans, the Westons, the Desmaraises, the Thomsons, Peter Munk, Issy Sharp, Gerry Schwartz, Izzy Asper and Conrad Black. There are even unexpected touches of glamour, such as when Bank of Montreal chairman Matt Barrett, who was raised in an Irish monastery, overnight married a rural Ontario lass-turned-international-playgirl—whose last publicized affair was with an Arab arms dealer—then, mysteriously gave up leadership of the bank he had helped build by submerging it into the Royal.

There has been no shortage of dastardly villains to give capitalism a bad name. Among them the crew of slovenly attired guys from Calgary whose Bre-X shenanigans triggered a $6-billion fraud; Robert Campeau, the unstable egomaniac who spent $11 billion he didn't have to buy department stores he couldn't run.

There was Don Cormie, whose Edmonton-based investment empire—
The Principal Group—cost 67,000 pensioners most of their life savings,
while he retained his extravagant lifestyle (six houses, a yacht, etc.) and
Christine, his ("we are just good friends") companion, a Scandinavian
woman he referred to as "Cupcakes." *[The very same week that Cormie was
charged with seven criminal offences, he was restoring his hideaway at Cameron Lake,
northwest of Edmonton. After the collapse of his Principal Group empire, he was left with
houses worth at least $6 million and had $5 million stashed away in U.S. and Swiss bank
accounts.]*

Bay Street stockbrokers and lawyers keep being fined or carted off to
jail at irregular but frequent intervals for cheating their clients. In one
ruling about the questionable activities of Toronto lawyer Glen Erikson,
the Ontario Securities Commission dented his defence by coming down
with a judgment that stated, "We have trouble with Mr. Erikson's asser-
tion that this disclosure was made to shareholders at the meeting, when
he, in fact, was the only person at that meeting."

More than a hundred CN workers were laid off on Christmas Eve 1997
with no explanation for the cruel timing. When the real-estate giant
Bramalea Ltd. went bust in December 1992, president Marvin Marshall
couldn't even be bothered to interrupt his Colorado ski holiday, and
addressed a Toronto news conference on his company's downfall by
speaker phone from his luxury hideaway. (It was the largest bankruptcy
court filing until Eaton's came along five years later.) British teenager
Cathy Shephard was fired by McDonald's for eating two extra chicken
McNuggets (eight instead of six) on her lunch break. The beat goes on.

Private-sector heroes and anti-heroes may have dominated the news,
but the public felt more revulsion than admiration for the miniature
Citizen Kanes who dominated the economy. There were some notable
exceptions, but most of the corporate paladins stopped polluting and
obeyed rudimentary safety codes, mainly because government regulations
demanded it. They were society's icons in the sense that sports figures
become metaphors: winners are glorified; losers, denigrated. It all comes
down to the growing disparity between rich and poor. John Kenneth
Galbraith, the expatriate Canadian who became one of the masters of
twentieth-century economic thought, expressed it best when he told his
audience at the 1997 Keith Davey Memorial Lecture, "We won the war
on poverty. We beat the poor." During a decade of mostly rapid economic growth, the gap between rich and poor has become a chasm. As
Mel Hurtig and others have pointed out, the rate of unemployment in
the age group between fifteen and twenty-four has been running at 28.5

percent. Having been promised that their lives would be better and richer than those of their elders, many young Canadians gave up the struggle. "Party hearty and die young," became their motto.

The Establishment's new meritocracy follows its own agenda, and compassion is seldom on the menu. "The new managers of information and money—unlike the old élites of bloodline and land—feel no sense of attachment to community or devotion to such traditional virtues as prudence, obligation, charity, or loyalty," wrote University of Toronto philosophy professor Mark Kingwell. "We cannot imagine them caring for indentured servants, taking part in village fetes, or collecting for rummage sales. Worse, their vaunted meritocracy is 'a parody of democracy,' in which the privileged take refuge in abstract equality of opportunity when confronted with the less well-off."

Becoming adult exempted no one from such disparities of concern and opportunity. Following the 1990–92 recession, corporate profits enjoyed an unprecedented updraft, but that didn't disrupt the ceaseless round of downsizing; professional economists, always ready with an appropriate oxymoron, labelled it a "jobless recovery." That's the equivalent of "sanitary landfill" or "British engineering."

Idols or bandits alike, we follow the Titans' deeds and misdeeds and are swept up, however reluctantly, in the notion that money has become the cutting edge of Canadian society. Careers and cash are worshipped as things in themselves, rather than as means to a better life. We pretend it isn't so, because it sounds so American, but it is an irrefutable fact that many, if not most, Canadians live in a money culture.

The money culture took hold of this country at some point in the spring of 1997. That was the moment when, for the first time, Canadians as a people received more income from dividends, commissions, capital gains, rents, interest and so on, than they earned through wages and salaries.

Cash is king. The only club worth joining is Money. Self-worth equals net worth.

That deadly equation implies that self-enrichment can replace emotion, faith, thought—and the other denominations of human experience. While money is no surrogate for humanity, kindness, love or ecstasy, the Titans who dominate the current business scene carry a deadly virus: the monetarization of feelings—the notion that only those sentiments fuelled by money are worth following. They seem genuinely to believe that if they had twice their money, they would be twice as happy, no matter how much they already have. There is never enough of anything:

success, love, Jaguars, fame, golfing trophies, Dom Pérignon. Money is being poured into $2- to $3-million condos with such tight security that no guest cars are allowed into their underground garages; the bill for a gourmet dinner for three couples at Montreal's Les Chenets recently came to $5,500, plus tip; the waiting list for Porsche Boxsters ($62,000) at Vancouver's MCL Motors was so long that an underground ($18,000) bonus was established to buy out the person at the head of the line.

That gluttonous attitude is reflected in the ease with which most Titans make more money—they shuffle more paper. *[Canadian essayist John Ralston Saul goes one step further: "Money plus power equals more money."]* Whatever their occupation or expertise happens to be, they are not basically in the oil, real-estate, fast-food or film industries; they're in the money business. Theirs is the currency of the fast deal; their instinct is to hype underutilized pools of corporate funds and spin them out to exponentially multiply their original investments. "In the last decade," complains ⟨illegible⟩, "great financial reward has not accrued to those who manufactured things and sold them. Rather, the best profits have gone to those involved in financial engineering, such as leveraged buyouts paid for with junk bonds, and they are often only successful at the expense of thousands of workers."

Most of the Titans described in this book create personal fortunes instead of jobs. While Issy Sharp builds new hotels, Peter Munk has exploited mines, Laurent Beaudoin turns out commuter jets, and Conrad Black's writers and editors publish worthy newspapers, most of the other entrepreneurs who people this book are involved in financial manipulation, in buying and selling companies and each other for maximum profit and minimum tax.

Their mentality is plugged directly into the same circuit that powered Lee Iacocca, the former Chrysler chairman and free-enterpriser, who said, after being questioned about his $20.4-million salary, "That's the American way. If little kids don't aspire to make money like I did, what the hell good is this country?" As the money culture takes over, there has been an accompanying quantum leap in the calculus of wealth. Millionaires are no longer defined as Canadians fortunate enough to have assets of $1 million; now, they must earn that much or more annually. In this fiscal stratosphere, annual incomes become irrelevant, indicating only how much money they've taken out of trust accounts, tucked away in income-deferment plans or which stock options have been cashed.

The money culture is everywhere. Lawyers, consultants, literary agents, accountants, speech writers, itinerant preachers, call-girls, lobbyists, swamis, tennis pros, dieticians, futurists, freelance metaphysicians and all those who work for fees and retainers have quickly realized how the new system works. They know that in a money culture their income is set, not by the value of what they do, but by their clients' perception of what that service is worth. In other words, the legal adviser who charges $500 an hour is half as valuable as the lawyer who costs $1,000, regardless of the quality of their counsel. The call-girl who doubles her fee, even if she reduces her feigned ardour by half, is twice as desirable. This weird upside-down logic is the money culture's prevalent ethic. Money is invested with magical qualities, and as such it begins to own the people who hoard it. The Indian sage Rabindranath Tagore touched on this impor-tant notion when he mused, "I thought that my invincible power would hold the world captive, leaving me in a freedom undisturbed. Thus night and day I worked at the chain with huge fires and cruel hard strokes. When at last the work was done, I found that it held me in its grip."

Belonging to the money culture also means speaking its language, based essentially on using words to hide real meanings. It's a form of expression reminiscent of the U.S. Central Intelligence Agency's comi-cally skewed death warrants. Whenever American spooks were ordered to murder perceived enemies during the hot or cold wars, the assassina-tion was described as "termination with extreme prejudice." That double-speak has been adopted by modern companies desperate to hide their true intent. Bankrupt businesses are described as having "non-per-forming assets," when they, in fact, have nothing but debts. The phrase "going back to basics" means cutting the losses on a previously announced "synergistic move into high-tech"; when a company admits it is experiencing "a period of accelerated negative growth," sell the damn stock. Quick.

It's a way of life that taints the soul. "The secularization that has come over practically the whole world has had a bad effect," maintains G. Emmett Carter, a prince of the Catholic church. "The only thing that seems desirable is to make money. The bottom line is the only one that matters, and that's why you have such a serious breakdown in morality."

The fast, young and brittle new knights of the meritocracy know that nothing is inherited any more and that only their abilities will make the difference. Because time is so much more precious and so very much more exhaustible than money, they place great emphasis on its expendi-ture. They worship efficiency in all things, whether it's a turbo laptop computer that takes only ten milliseconds to boot up, or the gadget that allows them to turn on their bathtubs at a pre-set temperature from their cars when they're still ten blocks from home. *[Probably the silliest time-saving invention is the automated, odour-free, scoop-free cat-litter box, which uses sensors and computers to run an automatic sifting comb through the sand at crucial moments, or more precisely, just after crucial moments. It is guaranteed not to stink.]* They think nothing of hiring stretch limos to bring over the latest issue of *Barron's*, return a T. Boone Pickens video, fetch little Amanda's babysitter or deliver cartons of chocolate-chip Häagen-Dazs. But they won't sit still for being overcharged by a tradesman, barber, hairdresser or banker. Once they've reached a certain plateau, luxury is their addiction of choice, and it's harder to shed than heroin.

The St. Vitus dance of materialism never stops. At some point, money ceases to have much meaning. When Calgarian John Hagg (the founding chair of North Star Energy) and his beautiful Swedish wife Kristin were visiting Bermuda in the winter of 1997, they found themselves at a lavish party in the home of expat Canadians. John Scrymgeour and his *[entire wife were introduced. Scrymgeour, international chairman of Teredo International, an oil/gas exploration and service firm, as well as the world's largest plumbing supply company, left Calgary for the Bermuda tax haven in the early 1970s. He commuted in style aboard his private, luxuriously appointed Boeing 727, referred to as* Air Force One, *a $20-million jet that would ordinarily accommodate 146 passengers.]* But what struck the Haggs was the guest who was boasting that he had just purchased an antique armoire for $11 million. Someone exploded, "My God, man, have you lost all sense of the value of money? Why, I know people who haven't paid that much for a house!" That was tough to take, even for the Alberta big-money crowd.

WHAT SEPARATES NEW MONEY FROM OLD IS mainly the time frame in which they operate. The Old rich seldom need to defer desires. Their wealth gives them authority to purchase the time and services of others—at the office, around the house, in bed, at the golf course. In contrast, New Money is always scrambling to keep up, to make that extra deal that will provide enough disposable income and reaffirm its self-worth. There are many other differences that count. Adherents of both groups give themselves away in all sorts of subtle ways: where they summer or winter, how they decorate their houses and offices, what they wear, drive and eat, whom they marry and sleep with.

An inevitable if subtle partnership exists between the two groups. Old Money needs New Money for validation, and vice versa. It's the upstarts' envy of the Old Establishment's social legitimacy that maintains the geezers' sense of self-importance. Even if it means extending their sense of condescension to its limit, they enjoy reminding members of the new meritocracy that they may be rich, but that's all they are. The point is badly taken but well understood. At the same time, no meritocracy can exist unless some outside agency endows it with merit. To grant the new arrivals acceptance once they've earned it is the only remaining power of the Old Establishment. But it's a blessing seldom refused even by the proudest of Titans.

The Old and New Establishments spend their money differently—the former much less conspicuously, the latter much more intensely. What New Money can never grasp is that the surest way of losing respect is to compare possessions. By specifying the exact square footage of a new house or by boasting about the horsepower of their latest car, the cruising speed of their yacht, a girlfriend's measurements, or the cost of a French Impressionist canvas, they betray a gauche insecurity the Old Establishment never feels. This is not to equate the Titans in any way with the vulgar *nouveaux riches*, which one of their number once told me was not very comforting, but better than no *riche* at all.

It all depends on what makes the blood pump. When it comes to automobiles, New Money prefers Range Rovers, Lexuses, Porsches, Beamers, Jags, Mercedes (particularly the new SUV model), and the Infiniti Q-45, with its steering wheel covered in leather that, promises Nissan, "comes from the same animal, thus not upsetting the driver's tactile balance." *[Pity the drivers of luxury vehicles not thus equipped. You can imagine them complaining, "Damn it, Maggie, I feel every which way but loose. I bet more than one antelope hide is on this dang steering wheel." Infinitis are mostly bought by drivers with money who like quality but don't believe in cars as status symbols.]* Lincolns and Cadillacs with elk-grained cabriolet tops and regency custom grilles still occupy Old Money garages, plus the odd Rolls-Royce, though Turbo Bentley Azures (at $467,000 a shot) are more in demand. *[It's fast (0 to 60 kilometres per hour in 6.3 seconds) but wildly inefficient (13 miles to the gallon), has plug-ins for fax machines, VCRs and laptops. If you're not great at backing up, a rear-fender mounted video camera—with a monitor in the foot well—will show you what you're about to hit.]*

Canadian sales of Porsches, especially the Turbo model at $172,000, zoomed 87 percent in 1997, but the vehicle that some Titans aspire to most is the Hummer. The 3.5-ton, rugged, over-sized 4-by-4 can climb 60-percent grades and costs $93,400 for a hardtop. One Bay Street bond dealer executed a much-admired triple play, when he traded his Jag for a dark green Hummer, then switched to a black turbo Hummer, as well as grabbing a Harley. *[There is very little correlation between cars and wealth. Barry Sherman, who graduated in rocket science from MIT and now runs Apotex Inc., one of*

Canada's leading generic drug houses, last year made an after-tax profit estimated at $60 million. Yet he drives a 1997 Oldsmobile that keeps stalling on him.]

Sailing yachts are out of favour with the new crowd. They're too slow and inefficient. Something is always going wrong. They require too much fussy tending. The old saying that owning a sailboat is like standing in a shower tearing up hundred-dollar bills is *passé*. Now it's thousand-dollar bills. But help is at hand. Corporations with sleepy shareholders can be used to finance private yachts. For example, Raymond Loewen, the Burnaby, B.C.-based CEO of Loewen Group Inc., a publicly listed company that buries people, sold his 110-foot yacht, *Alula Spirit*, for $7.2 million to his company, after buying it for $5 million. The boat, the crassest luxury yacht ever built in Canada, has seven staterooms, ten bathrooms and a helicopter-landing pad. It's about as cosy as an aircraft carrier.

Private jets are a high priority item with both Old and New Money. The rationalization is that they're an essential time saver for busy executives. Canada is the third-largest user of business aircraft in the world. Bombardier's Global Express is the favourite choice ($37.5 million plus GST). It can fly from Toronto to Tokyo non-stop. Vancouver's premier entrepreneur Jimmy Pattison owns a Bombardier Challenger and has crossed the Atlantic twice in one day. Increasingly popular with the New Money crowd are helicopters, those improbable, whirling machines that shout clout. You can feel their horsepower in the small of your back as the rotors rev up and lift you into space—in contrast to those jet engines on fixed-wing aircraft, which just sit there and buzz. Canada's most distinguished helicopter pilot is Michael Davies, the former publisher of the Kingston *Whig-Standard*, who used to own *Archangel*, the most beautiful sailboat ever built in Canada, and who now swoops across the country in his 206B-3 Bell Jet Ranger—also and more appropriately named *Archangel*.

The differences between New and Old Money abound. Old Money drinks Glenfiddich, vacations in Palm Beach, wears three-piece suits with Oxfords and believes in Tom d'Aquino; New Money wears fancy belt buckles, cowboy boots or iguana sandals, drinks Evian (or if pressed, Perrier) and believes in Charles Darwin. Old Money has hairy ears, wants to do its duty and plays polo. New Money has pierced ears (is on the waiting list for a cell-phone implant), snowboards, bungee jumps and couldn't care less about duty. Old Money follows the supermarket ads and knows when 170-gram cans of Clover Leaf flaked white tuna are on special. New Money tips lavishly and regards waiters as buddies. Old Money tips with a dismissive wave of the hand and treats waiters as self-propelled furniture. Old Money prefers subdued shades of pastel;

New Money loves electric colours and comprehends that polyester can be the stuff of *haute couture*. New Money women dress for themselves; they feel liberated from fashion. They know it's impossible to look dowdy if you don't feel it. Old Money prefers dry goods made out of anything that once lived: wool, leather, silk and fur. Old Money affects deliberate shabbiness, such as wearing swamp-cured duck-hunting hats and Windsor-knotted regimental ties while carrying Grandfather's walking stick. Howard Webster, one of the country's richest and most secretive tycoons during the 1970s, used to travel on business wearing tennis shoes and carrying his files in a Loblaws Supermarket shopping bag.

New Money savours the pleasures of ordering only the top vintage trophy wines, because it's a handy way of instantly demonstrating you have both money and good taste. ("Excess cash flow seeking social vali-dation," is how Vancouver food-and-wine critic Jamie Maw, one of the best in the country, describes the process.) If it's really well informed, New Money will order Cheval Blanc 1947 or a 1978 Chassagne-Montrachet; in the reds, Château Margaux 1953 or La Mission-Haut-Brion 1961. The trick is to ask for the brand, then gracefully—and knowledgeably—bargain about the actual vintages. Bay Street traders go mainly for Dom Pérignon 1976 or 1982. This is very different from Old Money which placed lubrication ahead of sophistication, indulging in such pedestrian Scotches as Dewars or the Famous Grouse as starters, and no-name claret with dinner, concentrating on the after-dinner ports (Newman's—no relation) and various liqueurs, preferably made by monks under vows of silence living on top of mountains.

Both New and Old Money prefer puffing Cohiba Robusto cigars. They were Castro's favourites before he gave up smoking in 1985. But there's a difference. New Money half believes the legend that these stogies are made by beautiful young Cuban women, who roll the raw tobacco leaves against their bare thighs. Old Money just wants a great smoke. New Money loves great sound systems; one Toronto broker had the floor of his pad mounted on springs so it wouldn't distort the music. Old Money is just getting into CDs.

Old and New Money use Sam Blyth to plan their holidays. He is one of the Canadian Establishment's genuine totems. An army brat who attended Cambridge and the Sorbonne before starting a modest travel agency with a difference, he sells "experiences" instead of journeys. *[He has had a few of his own as Margaret Trudeau's sometime escort, the man Barbara Amiel left husband poet George Jonas for after one date and as the husband (now ex-husband) of Rosemarie Bata.]* He runs a shipping line that organizes round-the-world voyages and owns most of another company that has the world's largest ice-breaker fleet under charter (six former Russian Arctic exploration vessels), which he uses to take passengers through the North West Passage and into Antarctica. *[His fleet includes a flotilla that will take Young Presidents Organization members from 82 countries to Antarctica, the only piece of non-sovereign real estate on Earth, to celebrate the Millennium, on December 31, 1999.]* Although he dominates the Canadian exploration and adventure-travel business, only 15 percent of his sales are domestic. He plays a lot of tennis, caters successfully to the carriage trade and has three adopted Bhutanese children. *[Bhutan (pronounced like the stuff you pump into portable hair dryers) is a tiny republic in the Himalayas which is probably the world's most primitive country.]*

New and Old Money share the excitement of flying to and from Europe aboard the supersonic Concorde, which wings across the Atlantic in three hours and twenty-five minutes ($12,539 per round trip). *[New Money inevitably liberates one of the Concorde's tulip-shaped champagne glasses as a souvenir.]* New Money knows the guy who can get a discount on Giorgio Armani's special Black Label line of suits. Old Money knows the curator of teapots at London's Claridge's Hotel by his first name. When New Money moves into a new dwelling, it calls in a professional decorator, orders her to "do it up right," talks about drapes, chesterfields and homes. Old Money employs decorators as consultants to find specific pieces and talks about curtains, sofas and houses.

Old Money knows not to wear diamonds before dinner, not to carry unfinished cocktails to the dinner table and that Thursday is the maid's night out. Its chauffeurs never slam doors or walk around the front of the family car when opening doors. New Money collects watches and covets a Blancpain, the last of Switzerland's handmade models, which take four months to produce. Old Money plays tennis; New Money hires an exercise trainer to make house calls. New Money gets the best tickets to the Super Bowl.

Old Money rents boxes at the Kentucky Derby and arranges foursomes at Burning Tree. New Money uses caterers and invites a few business associates so that it can write off its cocktail parties. Old Money engages a middle-of-the-road combo and refers to them as "the music"; New Money boasts, "We've got the Barenaked Ladies!" Serious New Money buys good art; serious Old Money buys great artists. Old Money turns to public service if it gets really exercised or really bored. New Money believes the public sector is for losers.

Both New and Old Money play competitive croquet; New Money always wins. The Great Gatsby-style game has been turned into a macho event, even though it's played while sipping champagne and munching caviar. "It's just like warfare on the corporate battlefield," says Jack Osborne, one of the founders of the U.S. Croquet Association, which has 350 clubs in North America. "In golf, you play against the course; in croquet, you play against your opponent. You can really screw somebody over if you want to. The game mimics office politics."

In the bedroom, Old Money urgently whispers: "Brace yourself, old girl." New Money lovers compare daytimers, diarize mutually convenient times to rendezvous and go for it.

THE RICH HAVE A DIFFICULT TIME SEPARATING THEIR money from their manliness. In the proving ground of their souls the two are indivisible. If the man makes the money, he is in charge. There's almost always trouble if the wife earns more than the husband or if their wealth comes by inheritance from the woman's side of the family.

With some exceptions, Old Money treats its wives as baubles, as if they were flesh without magic, fulfilling a purely decorative function. The wispy women who married into the Old Canadian Establishment have triple-A-width feet, straight hair and lanky tennis-honed bodies that never sweat. *["Horses sweat," goes the saying, "men perspire, women glow."]* Their walk is a kind of golf lope. They betray moments of deep thought by idly fingering opera-length strands of freshwater pearls and spend hours perfecting their natural look—applying seasonal shades of lipstick and thin bands of pale eye-shadow with fingers as steady as those of elephant hunters. *[Michael Thomas, the best of the Wall Street novelists, once described a merchant-banker's wife as having "come out of the womb in a twin set and pearls."]*

By the 1990s the style in wives had shifted. The Titans' women of the New Establishment still show the time-honoured effects of good nutrition, good posture and good genes, but in few other ways are they similar to their predecessors. No longer preoccupied with either museum-quality or trendy collectibles, they live interesting, crowded lives and collect memories instead. Gone are the neurotic Lhasa apsos as pets and all those airy trimmings that made up empty lives. Instead of shying away from work, they are energetic, gregarious, ambitious and tough. If they don't "go to business," they are equally active as volunteers, social animators and fund-raisers.

They tend to be suavely international, belonging not so much to any international jet set as to a coterie of mobile Canadians who can afford to expand their perceptions via quick trips to Gstaad, golf rounds at Hilton Head or four days floating down the Irrawaddy River and its tributaries from Mandalay to Rangoon tacked onto their or their husbands' business week in Hong Kong or Singapore. These women know a great deal about how power works in this country, including the nuances of convertible debentures and federal-provincial cost sharing. Instead of the cultivated helplessness of their patrician mothers and grandmothers, they know precisely what they want from life and how to get it. What they want is balance, the specifics of which they insist on defining for themselves. They are proud, creatively protective of the insecurities of their men, determined to fulfill their individual destinies and are never, ever afraid to go their own way and speak their own minds. They dress for themselves instead of their mates; menopause is a starting gun instead of a last-post salute.

The wives of the new power holders are defining themselves not through their husbands, but with a well-honed sense of their own worth. Their newfound self-esteem has altered the calculus of family harmony; coming to terms with marriage as a true partnership is a prerequisite of altered lives. Monogrammed his 'n' her towels no longer do the trick.

Constantly weighing the costs/benefits of the dilemma of time versus money, Establishment couples thrive for—but seldom achieve—that desirable but elusive objective of relaxed achievement. It's an oxymoron. *[The author cannot allow this opportunity to pass without recording the best of the best oxymorons: Microsoft Works.]* The idea is for ambitions not to diminish but to grow more focused. Vitality is a must. Couples of the 1990s follow vitamin regimes and jogging paths. They know it's essential to sidestep burnout by pacing, but they don't always manage it.

The Establishment has finally begun, hesitantly, to cross gender lines. Women are gaining power and wealth, as is their just reward in any society that operates on merit. But even if the source of the most creative energy lighting up the business scene is female, vestiges of male monopoly of authority remain in place. Much is made of the promotion of women to essential Canadian economic command posts, such as those occupied by Maureen Kemptson Darkes, president of General Motors of Canada; Diane McGarry, CEO of Xerox of Canada; Sheelagh Whittaker, head of Electronic Data Systems Canada; Annette Verschuren, president of Home Depot Canada; Bobbie Gaunt, CEO of Ford Canada; and others. But what these executives have in common, apart from their obvious ability and drive, is that they head the Canadian subsidiaries of American multinationals, and thus do not exercise ultimate authority. Whittaker, the most articulate of these great dames, once aptly summed up the state of play: "We'll have true equality," she declared, "when we have as many incompetent women in positions of power as we have incompetent men." That won't be easy. Peggy Wente, managing editor of *The Globe and Mail*, got it right when she described how a former boss tried to instill in her a sense of urgency during a corporate crisis. "He pounded his fist on my desk," she recalled, "and declared, 'Our balls are on the line here!' That was when I knew I just didn't have the equipment for the job."

THE LARGELY MALE RANKS OF THE TITANS have assumed the power of the Church in the Middle Ages. "CEOs have become our contemporary priests," notes Richard Gwyn, *The Toronto Star*'s wise columnist. The high priest of how to succeed in twenty-first century business without really trying is American management consultant Tom Peters, who has redefined power inside the restructured corporate world. "It's not ladder power, as in who's climbing over adjacent bods, that counts," he maintains. "It's not who's got the biggest office by six square inches or who's got the fanciest title. It's power that matters. It's influence power—being known for making the most significant contributions in your particular area—or reputational power that count. You're measured by the number of CEOs who have your card in their Rolodexes or, better still, the number who know your beeper or cell number off by heart."

Peters points out that while there may not be many jobs available, there is lots of work: "It's a project world out there, and that means most corporate tasks are subdivided into individual tasks, which provide a rapid method of recording measurable and braggable successes. That's what makes the best power résumés."

Corporate loyalty, according to Peters, amounts to indentured servitude. "Loyalty today," he insists, "isn't blind obedience to the company. It's loyalty to your colleagues, to your team, to your project, to your customers—and loyalty to yourself. I see that as much deeper than mindless loyalty to the company logo."

The evidence suggests that he is right. There was a time when corporations—especially those listed in *The Financial Post* Five Hundred—were like mighty ocean liners. You secured a berth straight out of university or high school, put in your forty years and disembarked wearing a gold watch. Now, with great good fortune, you get to change ships two or four times; if you're unlucky or back the wrong side in an office feud, they heave you overboard. Or if everybody guesses wrong, the ship sinks right under you. Agile corporate survivors know when to grab a life jacket and leap onto the next vessel.

The scenario Peters paints is of a work world manned by free agents, men and women who believe in themselves, are proudly independent, but whose services are always for sale to the highest bidders. Careers are daisy chains, forged by networking. "Linearity is out," Peters concludes. "Careers are now checkerboards, full of moves that go sideways, diagonally, even backwards when that makes sense. A career is a portfolio of projects that teach new skills or sharpen old ones, that reinvent the individual involved. There is no single path to success. Except this: start today. Or else."

The New and Old Establishments clash on many issues, but on none more fiercely than the concept of loyalty, so airily dismissed by Tom Peters and his disciples. To the Old Guard, being loyal meant everything. Wealth and power were regarded as forms of stored possibilities, not meant to be spent but to be savoured and treated as patrimonies held in trust by each generation for the next. That loyalty to family, company, community and country was what held the old élite together, and it was not negotiable. In its heyday, the Old Establishment held common assumptions so profoundly that its members could communicate handily through raised eyebrows and shared silences. Its members looked out for each other and deals really were done on a handshake—over J & B with rocks.

Education counted high among perceived priorities; work experience did not. The rich and powerful kept out of sight and sound, lived in country houses at the far end of curving driveways and practiced a self-effacing, who-me? approach designed to keep the *parvenus* at bay.

Most of their decisions evolved from the style in which they allowed things to happen. Pleasures and splendours were made to seem effortless rather than planned, ordinary instead of ostentatious. They took everything for granted. They would talk right through ringing telephones and doorbells, because they were so used to having them answered by assistants or servants. They believed that doors would always be opened for them, and would drop their winter coats without a backward glance, sure there would be someone there to catch them. They enjoyed a surprisingly stylized, if highly sybaritic, existence that touched only tangentially the mainstream of everyday Canadian life.

Connections were used but never paraded. Everybody was somebody's cousin; kinship reigned supreme. They treated each other as extended family and thus extended their loyalties. Marriages often meant corporate mergers and vice versa.

What they suffered from most was the fear of intimacy. They only hesitantly committed themselves to offers of friendship, never certain whether it was they or their money that was the source of affable overtures. Such smoky, ill-defined resentments made them feel so alienated and suspicious that they withdrew into themselves. They often kept their distance, even in family situations, displaying little talent for tenderness. Nobody ever genuinely hugged anybody. Even in their most intimate moments they seemed to regard love—as well as birth and death—as quaint accidents.

TO THOSE OF US TOILET-TRAINED IN THE PURITAN ethic of English Canada, the Titans' materialism seems crude, even offensive. They despise boundaries. They made it their way, and if their passionate grab at life builds strange monuments, like the monstrosity constructed by Peter Nygard on his Bahamian atoll, so be it.

Another bizarre personification of same phenomenon is Frank Stronach, the perambulating ego who runs Magna Inc. That neither Stronach nor Nygard have been accepted by the Canadian Establishment—Old or New—makes them valuable witnesses. They represent legitimacy's outer limits. The tales of the two eccentric but gifted tax exiles perfectly bracket this chapter on the wilder shores of Canadian capitalism.

Somebody once quipped that as he ages, Stronach looks more and more like Little Orphan Annie, what with the curls, the pouts and the childish behaviour. That's hardly a fair description of the founding genius of Magna International and one of this generation's most successful entrepreneurs. But the man is his own worst enemy. He creates hostility effortlessly in his quest for establishment recognition. His demands that Fair Enterprise—his business philosophy that can best be described as Ayn Rand with balls—become the dominant creed of the Canadian economy dominates his personal and public agendas. The born-again capitalism that Stronach preaches, not just for Magna but for all Western democracies, has been dubbed by just about every business writer in the universe as his Magna Carta. It consists of nine edicts that he modestly describes as "the most important chapter in Western industrial society." He spends inordinate time and trouble drumming up support for his scheme, and even made a move to try to become Canada's prime minister. That would have given him a great platform to spread his gospel, despite the drastic pay cut involved. He did run unsuccessfully for the Liberals, but his politics are flexible. Just after Pierre Trudeau left office, Stronach was accorded the honour of being placed at the head table of his official farewell dinner; only a month later he appeared as one of thirteen members of a blue-ribbon committee to advise Brian Mulroney how to push his Conservative Party into power.

The explanation for his obsession with spreading the word about Fair Enterprise is vintage Stronach. "If I didn't," he confides, "I would look at myself in the mirror and say, 'You son of a bitch. Life's been great to you. You're copping out.'" The creed, published in ten languages, is a simplistic profit-sharing formula that presupposes every Magna employee will devote similar energy to his job as Stronach. That would translate into at least seventy hours a week of eating, drinking, dreaming and talking Magna—with a thick Austrian accent.

Within the confines of Magna's corporate culture, the scheme works, mainly one assumes because those who refuse to subscribe to its dictates don't last long on the payroll and seek alternate salvation by joining unions, which is strictly *verboten* in the gospel according to Frank.

I remember asking Stronach, with feigned innocence, whether or not the racehorses he breeds are on a similar incentive program as his workers. He gave me his hardest stare, flashed his profile as if he were posing for a Roman coin, then sourly replied, "I hope so. I try to instill it."

Stronach's achievements at Magna are impressive, particularly since he arrived in Canada from Austria in 1954 (as Franz Strobsack) with only his machinist's papers and $200. The automotive-parts company that evolved from that humble start now has annual revenues of $8 billion and employs 32,000 people in 118 factories. This represents no mean turnaround, because in 1990, Stronach's extravagances and misconceived diversification strategies plunged Magna into near bankruptcy. Losses totalled $190 million for the last quarter of 1989, and accumulated debts of more than $1 billion were on the books. At one point things became so precarious that the Bank of Nova Scotia wanted to install Earl Joudrie, Calgary's yet-to-be-shot turnaround artist, as the company's CEO. Ed Lumley, then vice-chairman of Nesbitt Burns, recalls going to see Ced Ritchie, the head of Scotiabank, on Stronach's behalf: "I asked Ced, 'Is Magna's problem Frank Stronach?' And Ritchie said yes. So, I said, 'Is Magna's solution Frank Stronach?' He said yes and granted the credit."

Stronach slashed costs, made some profitable deals (such as buying the Michigan seat-maker Douglas and Lomason), appointed his then son-in-law Don Walker to the presidency and turned the company around. Magna shareholders have since enjoyed annual returns of about 30 percent. No one has benefitted more than Stronach, who in 1996 paid himself a record-breaking $47.2 million. That didn't even include the huge dividends Stronach collects from his 64-percent hammerlock on the company's stock. (Each of his class-B shares carries 500 votes.)

Sometime in the mid-1990s, Stronach became a tax exile and moved into a magnificent castle with two-foot-thick walls in suburban Vienna.

("I needed a large piece of land—it just happened that there was a castle on it," he lamely explained.) One recent Christmas, he ran out of the 181 days Immigration allows tax exiles for Canadian visits and had to celebrate the holidays with his family via video clips. As well as the Austrian castle and his mega-mansion north of Toronto where he stays during his increasingly rare Canadian sojourns, he has stables in Kentucky and Florida where he breeds some 500 thoroughbreds, 120 of them for racing. Stronach runs the world's most profitable horse business (he earned $4 million in the 1997 racing season), having won the Belmont Stakes, the Kentucky Derby and two Queen's Plates. But it took a full twenty years of lobbying before he was invited to become one of the trustees of the Ontario Jockey Club.

More recently, with $1 billion in cash and no debt, he has been expanding in Europe, buying parts manufacturers such as Austria's Steyr works (which assembles 500,000 vehicles a year for Mercedes-Benz and Jeep Cherokees for Chrysler, as well as rifles, tractors and armoured vehicles) and Marley PLC in the United Kingdom; as well, he has the body contract for the European Smart Car. He has also been awarded the contract to manage and design a new interior for all Ford sports utility vehicles.

His most controversial purchase is a 270-hectare plot at Ebreichsdorf, 30 kilometres south of Vienna, where he intends to build a $787-million theme park, which will feature a 140-metre-high globe that will depict the history of mankind. He was also planning a luxury airline with private cabins (Magna Air), a five-star resort in southern Austria, the $1.3-billion renovation of Vienna's historic Prater amusement park, plus a first-class executive retreat at Lake Rosseau, north of Toronto. All this was planned to be purchased through Magna. "I don't see why we should pay for this man's late-life crisis," Montreal money manager Roch Bedard told *The Financial Post*'s David Olive. "If he wants to go ahead with these crazy stunts of flying bedrooms and resort hideaways, let him do it with his own money." That, in fact, was what happened. Under pressure from shareholders, Stronach backed off and spun his fantasies into personal holding companies. "Frank Stronach," concluded David Berman in *Canadian Business* magazine, "is the kind of entrepreneur who leaves observers wondering whether he is as canny as his track record suggests or as crazy as some of his public pronouncements would indicate. Ask the 64-year-old about his retirement plans and he looks at you as though you are stuck in another era. Not only is he in terrific shape, he says, but he intends to remain that way for the next hundred years."

Jawohl!

5

FUCK-YOU MONEY WITH
A SOCIAL CONSCIENCE

"This goes back to the Medicis—buying your way into heaven."

—*Gordon Floyd, Canadian Centre for Philanthropy*

BACK WHEN TELEVISION EVANGELISTS had private sex lives and Billy Graham was still a prime newsmaker, he decided to launch one of his revival crusades in Canada. *Time* magazine asked me to cover his Toronto visit for its American edition. My evangelism has its limits, but I had always thought of Graham as being superior to the righteous opportunists who pollute the Sunday-morning airwaves.

It isn't hard to tell the good Bible-thumpers from the bad. The voices of those who are in it strictly for the money seldom come from deep inside them. Theirs is the nasal twang of insincerity as they singsong their way through sermons, bellowing *Jaysus!* Or *Ahmen!* whenever they lose their place. Their body language screams for attention (remember the Jimmy Swaggart crouch?) as they prowl the stage—hollerin', stompin', prayin'.

Not Graham. When I interviewed him, the man's deep voice and subdued grace were impressive. I figured that his burning eyes reflected either deep religious conviction or not enough sleep. Being the representative, however temporary, of a major U.S. magazine, allowed me access to his entourage. When I visited them backstage at the close of the first night's activities, the Graham people were a gloomy lot.

The Canadian National Exhibition Coliseum, which they had turned into a makeshift place of worship for the occasion, was still reverberating with the echoes of Graham's sermon. More converts for Christ had come forward than at any other first night of the Graham crusade. I had watched in awe as ordinarily reticent Canadians ambled toward the dais, displaying the appropriate symptoms of loose-limbed ecstasy. But when it came around to collection time, the crowd responded with nickels and dimes, instead of the more substantial contributions Graham was accustomed to Stateside. Since I happened to be the only Canadian behind the curtains, Graham came over and asked me what the trouble was.

"Billy," I said, "this is Canada. Before you ask for money, make it clear you'll issue tax receipts. Even when they're saving their souls, Canadians want to be damn sure it's deductible."

"Bless you brother," a couple of Graham operatives mumbled, and the next evening, after the appropriate announcement . . . Oh Lord, how the money rolled in.

Hallelujah!

That inbred Canadian attitude of being generous only with Revenue Canada's blessing hasn't changed. But giving money away—why it's done and who gets it—goes to the heart of how Canada's establishment has reinvented itself.

Money and class are not interchangeable. Most Canadians, regardless of their birthright or financial standing, modestly claim membership in what George Orwell, greatest of the British essayists, called "the lower, upper, middle class." That's the class that helps give its offspring a higher education, but not the head start of inherited wealth. Making money is seldom useful in upgrading one's social class, but *giving* it away earns the Establishment's blessing. *[There may not be a recognized Canadian class system, but sometimes it seems that the country has split into two classes: the overworked and the underemployed.]* The Old Establishment may not have much residual day-to-day clout, but it retains the power to confer membership on its successors. That's not an inconsiderable gift; certainly no one refuses it. And it is philanthropy that legitimizes the new contenders.

In an age when governments must ration their generosity, the unexpected rush of gifts from the newly wealthy is significant. The freshly minted Titans quickly realize that earning sizeable fortunes is not enough. They learn to appreciate that there is nearly as much satisfaction and a great deal more acceptance in giving money away—with the appropriate write-offs, of course—as there is in making it.

They insist that their motives are pure: that they want to "give something back," and it's true. Whether it's to ease their conscience or because they genuinely want to make a difference, there is little doubt that Canada's newly wealthy support worthy events and institutions because they know it is expected of them. They don't need to be told that their ascent into Establishment ranks has little to do with the size of their Swiss bank accounts, and everything to do with donating serious money to high-profile causes. They are well aware of this trade-off, and they act accordingly.

The actual organization of the Titans' donations and the fund-raising they are called to do is taking up an increasing amount of their time and energy. It is more than *noblesse oblige*. It has become an essential source of their self-respect. "What matters these days is the ability and willingness to write a cheque for the right causes," says Ira Gluskin, an irreverent Toronto investment adviser reaching for Establishment status. "If you can't produce a generous gift, you get banished. Power is related to how much business you hand out and how much money you donate." Gluskin took his own advice when he and his partner Gerry Sheff spent $1.5 million to sponsor the opening-night gala for the showing of the Barnes Collection of French Impressionists at the Art Gallery of Ontario on September 12, 1994. The partners, who had earned more than $15 million each that year, were celebrating their firm's tenth anniversary and wanted to imprint the firm's name, Gluskin Sheff, on Bay Street's consciousness. *[Gluskin Sheff & Associates manages the private funds of some of Canada's richest individuals, including Galen Weston, Richard Ivey and themselves.]* Prompted by another of their partners, Alan Schwartz, who is an ardent collector and on the board of the AGO, they shelled out $1 million to help pay for the exhibit itself. Then they stood proudly in the receiving line in the 14,000-square-foot tent they had rented for the occasion, welcoming Conrad and Barbara Black, Ted and Loretta Rogers, Ken and Marilyn Thomson, Edward Bronfman, Sylvia and Bernard Ostry, Irving and Rosie Abella, Murray and Nancy Frum, Galen and Hilary Weston and 3,000 other establishment guests. *[The complete menu is reproduced in Appendix 2.]* The invitations, engraved in gold on luxurious paper and accompanied by a handmade wooden box that contained a stunning coffee table book on the exhibition, cost $200 each. The dinner featured racks of New Zealand lamb, accompanied by South African gooseberries, strawberries handdipped in Belgian chocolate and dozens of other culinary delights, all washed down with magnums of Pol Roger. According to *Toronto Life* magazine, it was the most lavish black-tie party in Toronto history. "The symbolic end to the recession," the magazine called it, "a milestone in Toronto society, a coming out for the new power élite. The old WASPs were there, but it wasn't their night." As Robert Fulford, the literary critic and chronicler of Toronto's contemporary scene, wisely noted: "That was a euphemistic way of saying that the evening illustrated one of the most significant changes in the history of the city, the absorption of a remarkable number of Jews by the late twentieth-century equivalent of the Family Compact." *[Joe Rotman, the Toronto financier who was then president of the Art Gallery of Ontario, was also in the receiving line, but the previous evening he had held a dinner-party of his own in the garden of his Forest Hill home. His guests included Hal Jackman, then lieutenant-governor of Ontario; Bob Rae, then premier of Ontario, and his wife Arlene; Peter Munk, the mining and real-estate magnate, and his wife Melanie; J. Carter Brown, director emeritus of Washington's National Gallery of Art; Frank Cahouet, chairman of Pittsburgh's Mellon Bank; Richard Glanton, president of the Barnes Foundation; Third World philanthropists Martin Connell and Linda Haynes; impresarios Garth and Pearl Drabinsky and David and Audrey Mirvish; Toronto developer Morton Rapp and his feisty wife Carol; plus those ubiquitous* boulevardiers *Allan and Sondra Gotlieb.]* The gesture was typical of Titan-style philanthropy: thoughtful, elegant, expensive, yet "putting-the-firm-on-the-map" useful. The trick is not merely to shovel cash into a preordained list of humdrum write-offs. To these new givers the call to alms has become a field of dreams that allows them to use generous impulses and imagination in fascinating new ways. For example, Scott Paterson, the thirty-four-year-old chairman and CEO of Yorkton Securities, has found a highly rewarding charitable niche for himself. He has created the Merry Go Round Children's Foundation to distribute free computers to promising, yet disadvantaged, students in Toronto's impoverished Regent Park area for use in their homes. Paterson's Foundation is partnered with the 51 Division of the Metropolitan Toronto Police, whose officers are online Big Brothers to recipient children. "We're levelling the playing field for a few financially disadvantaged children, hopefully changing their lives," he says.

ANY SOCIAL OR ECONOMIC SYSTEM REQUIRES sustaining myths to give it life and legitimacy. With all of its excesses, tax shelters and on-the-edge ethics, the Canadian Establishment in the late 1990s has chosen philanthropy as the rationale for its exercise of power. "This isn't exactly a new practice," points out Gordon Floyd of the Canadian Centre for Philanthropy. "This goes back to the Medicis—buying your way into heaven."

And heaven can't wait.

As they turn into givers as well as takers, these Titans do not for a minute abandon their basic philosophy: that you can't do good unless you first do well. But they're also convinced that buying status through giving away money is a good investment.

"It's really fuck-you money with a social conscience," a Bay Street Titan explains, requesting anonymity in return for his frankness. "Besides, it's a hedge against mortality." More serious-minded peers realize that their wealth carries civic obligation. The gap left by a largely bankrupt public sector must be filled by private donations if the system is to survive. Across the country, the rich are donating millions of dollars to shore up universities, hospitals, opera companies, ballet troupes, little theatres, children's charities and other cultural and scientific institutions worn thin by the retreat of financial support from public treasuries. The process has established a new pecking order, with certain money-raising functions recognized as more desirable than others. Culture outranks diseases. Sponsoring a Writers' Development Trust dinner is worth two fund-raisers for diabetes or multiple sclerosis, though AIDS benefits remain popular. Large cheques are also written to support political parties, which hardly rank as charitable institutions, but they still earn write-offs. *[Political contributions were most adroitly handled by Ian Sinclair when he was chairman of the CPR. He didn't fool around with ideological subtleties. When Liberal fund-raisers came to see him at a time when a new air-route agreement was being considered in Ottawa, Sinclair made it easy for them by suggesting he would give the party either $5,000 or $50,000, depending on how many new airports CP Air could add to its schedule. He was later rewarded with a Senate seat. In 1996, when the Conservative party reached its lowest ebb, its leader Jean Charest contributed $960 to its survival, Brian Mulroney $2,500, Conrad Black $3,875 and former leader Kim Campbell, "nada."]* The most popular venue for new, big-money donations is higher education. Those Titans with either "fuck-you money," or a conscience— or both—are racing to name university buildings and academic chairs after themselves.

"We've never used the words," admits Jon S. Dellandrea, the country's most successful fund-raiser, in charge of the University of Toronto's epic $575-million-plus 1997–98 campaign. *[See Appendix 3 for a list of Titans who served on the campaign's executive team.]* "But certainly by inference you are saying to potential donors that by joining a group of leading Canadians who support a great institution such as ours, they will become part of that magic circle and be recognized as being in the ranks of Canada's establishment."

Those who can't perpetuate themselves through blood-lines do it through monuments, mainly at Canada's ninety-one universities. The process is complicated, but the price is always right. Having a whole faculty named after you runs from $10 to $16 million; academic departments cost $5 million; lecture rooms, $500,000; science labs, $250,000; administrative areas, $100,000; offices, $10,000; student carrels, $5,000. *[Vancouver's Simon Fraser University is even selling the space above the urinals in its men's washrooms to local advertisers. Presumably these messages are read in short, concentrated spurts.]*

One good reason New Money has jumped into the financing gap is that Old Money donations have been drying up. Kathleen and Muriel Richardson in Winnipeg; David and Maggie Fountain in Halifax; Joan Chalmers, Hal Jackman and Bluma Appel (who gives her soul as well as her money) in Toronto; Charles Bronfman, Phyllis Lambert and Paul Desmarais in Montreal; Don Harvie, Martha Cohen and the late Francis Winspeare in Calgary; and Charles Mitchell in Saskatoon are perpetuating their forebears' generosity. But they are the exceptions. Most family dynasties are either dispersed or no longer viable, and of those that remain, several have gone underground or offshore. Much of Canada's dynastic wealth is either tucked away in tax-friendly foundations or safely lodged in anonymous trusts in the Caymans, Bermuda, the Bahamas, the Channel Islands and in other tax havens. Neither the Irving family, Galen Weston nor Conrad Black are known for their philanthropy.

The most frustrating target of Canadian fund-raisers is the man who controls the country's largest fortune, Kenneth Roy Thomson, second Lord Thomson of Fleet, or "Young Ken" as he is still called, though he has already celebrated his seventy-fifth birthday. By the best estimate of *Forbes* magazine, which keeps track of such things, Thomson is sitting on about $12 billion, a sum that's multiplying by about $350 million a year from dividends alone. He gives nothing away. His tight-wad habits are legendary, but some figures high in the Establishment have occasionally taken up the challenge of trying to hit him up for a donation.

Back in 1990, Dick Thomson (no relation), then chairman of the Toronto-Dominion Bank, and Fred Eaton, who still had a considerable power base, called on Thomson to solicit funds for the Toronto General Hospital, a favourite Establishment charity. They had been warned by mutual friends that they would only get money out of the pet-loving Thomson if they promised to add a veterinary wing to treat Ken's dog Gonzo. They thought it was a joke, but came back empty-handed. Thomson's only major excursion into philanthropy was his 1982 effort to have Toronto's most prestigious concert hall named after his father Roy. "Young Ken" shelled out $4.5 million for the project, the largest donation ever granted to the performing arts up to that time. But the naming of Roy Thomson Hall caused a furore, because the Thomson family got all the glory, while paying only a minor part of the bill. Of the $40 million required to finance the building's construction, $26.5 million had already been allocated by federal, provincial and municipal governments. Another $12.5 million had been raised from corporate donors and individuals, not including Thomson. Ken's contribution was a welcome, but hardly essential, windfall, and it was budgeted mainly for future improvements. *[Thomson's $4.5-million donation was divided into five annual instalments of $900,000, so that, as well as saving him $450,000 a year in deductible taxes, the delayed instalments earned annual interest of more than $500,000, leaving the estimated size of his gift at a relatively modest $2 million.]* Tony Fell, the presiding genius at RBC Dominion Securities, the country's premier stock-brokerage firm, augmented his reputation considerably in 1994, when he pried $50,000 out of Thomson for Toronto's Princess Margaret Hospital. "It was incredibly unique," he admits.

Fell's philanthropic activities date back to his support of the Arthritis Society in the 1970s. He was the chairman of Toronto's United Way Campaign in 1989 and for five years after that headed the Princess Margaret campaign, which is still the talk of the town. Funds were slow rolling in, so Tony took a day off and phoned thirty of his best customers, harvesting donations of $50,000 to $100,000. He didn't get a single turndown, and that put the campaign over the top. To Bay Street's inner circles who know the story, that *force majeure* exhibition of fund-raising was a raw and rare display of Fell's power. They were mighty impressed. "He didn't lose any business doing it," notes Stanley Hartt, one of Bay Street's few intellectual resources. "He was still Tony Fell when he finished, owing nothing to anybody. Tony's a great example of meritocracy in action. He's not just lucky; he has earned his reputation." RBC Dominion Securities puts aside 1 percent of pre-tax profits ($497 million in 1997) annually for its own foundation, which distributes grants mostly to universities and the United Way. "Fund-raising is a game for the rich," says Fell. "It's reciprocal. We support what our best customers are doing, and they support our causes. Certainly, you're expected to participate. If you want to be accepted, if you want to get inside the circle, you must become a generous giver. There's no question about that."

Collectively, Canadian corporations endow universities, preserve landmarks, donate artworks and raise money for appropriate charities, but their impulse towards creative generosity is hardly overwhelming; corporate charitable donations account for barely 1 percent of profits.

Canada's top corporate contributors are the large banks, with the Royal leading the way ($17 million) and the Commerce close behind ($16 million). *[Other leading corporate donors include Bell Canada ($13 million), Imasco ($10 million), Imperial Oil ($6 million), the Bank of Nova Scotia ($6 million), Noranda ($4.5 million), Nova ($4 million), Merck Frosst ($4 million), Power Corp. ($4 million), Shell Canada ($3.5 million), T-D Bank ($3.5 million), Canadian Pacific ($3 million) and Bombardier ($3 million). The leading foundation donors are the Vancouver Foundation ($2.7 million), the J.W. McConnell Foundation ($1.5 million) and the Jackman, Beaverbrook, Edmonton, Calgary, Eaton, Laidlaw, De Seve and Samuel and Saidye Bronfman foundations, which hand out $5 million amongst them.]* "More and more corporations are tying their giving to their marketing strategies, seeking ways to align their self-interest with the public good," admits Matt Barrett, chairman of the Bank of Montreal, which gives away $10 million annually.

One of the largest and most imaginative recent donations was the $8 million Nortel gave the University of Toronto to establish a communications institute. Largely because of the inspired lobbying efforts of Don Johnson, vice-chairman of Nesbitt Burns, Finance Minister Paul Martin used his 1997 budget to increase charitable tax write-offs. He allowed donors of publicly traded securities a 64 percent tax credit, instead of the usual capital-gains penalty, and raised the ceiling for charitable credits from 20 percent to 75 percent of taxpayers' individual incomes. Winnipeg's Izzy Asper immediately took advantage of the loophole by donating CanWest Global shares worth $665,000 to the University of Manitoba. Harry Hole, head of an Edmonton mechanical contracting firm, similarly gave away most of his family's founding shares in Neutrino Resources Inc., a gift worth $5 million. Bill Wilder, a former head of Wood Gundy and one of Bay Street's most enlightened financiers, donated a building to the Harvard Business School, his alma mater, but had less luck trying to collect $1 million from Bay Streeters to keep Canada's dormant two-party system alive. "It was Fraser Elliott's idea," he recalls, "to get ten people to donate $100,000 each to help out the Conservatives, because it's the only viable national alternative to the Liberals. Well, I didn't get a million; I got $850,000, and it was a really tough sell."

The scale of the new givers is breathtaking. Peter Munk, who has donated $6 million to the Cardiac Centre at the Toronto Hospital and nearly $10 million to the University of Toronto's new Centre for International Studies, also runs a private foundation that makes many imaginative gifts. Jim Gray, a leading Alberta oil man, devotes almost as much energy raising much-needed money for the Calgary Academy, a school for children with learning disabilities, and the Calgary Women's Emergency

Centre for battered women as he does to his job as chairman of Canadian Hunter. "There is no question," he says, "that if I had nothing to talk about but the oil and gas game, it would have been a pretty damn boring life. Besides, being engaged in your community is a business advantage—and not in any indirect way, either."

True enough. Giving money away not only opens the door to Establishment membership, it impressively extends the donors' networks, which are the lifeline of business success. "No question about it," says Martin Connell, a former mining company CEO who has turned a strong personal commitment to philanthropy into something close to a full-time occupation. "It's a fast track into the new networks," he says. "The people who are aggressively involved in their communities become part of the networks that count. You can see it happening all the time. People who are extremely wealthy, extremely successful, but known only to a handful of insiders, suddenly get discovered by being brought into some major charitable activity. The next thing you know, they're named to more significant directorships, become board chairmen and skyrocket into prominence."

Connell himself is a good example. He has become the most creative philanthropist in the land, while at the same time expanding his reputation and influence. One of Canada's more fortunate inheritors, Connell succeeded his grandfather, who founded Conwest Exploration (assets $130 million), which brought several Timmins and Cobalt, Ontario, mines into production. After graduating from McGill, Connell became an integral part of the Toronto bar scene. With two partners, he introduced pizzazz and high-tech décor to such popular hangouts as the Boiler Room, the Coal Bin, the Jarvis House, Ports of Call, Bemelmans (Garth Drabinsky's favourite bar), the Bellair Café and Toby's Good Eats. His day job was selling bonds at McLeod Young Weir, but he also invested in Twenty-One McGill, the club whose members sought to establish an "old-girls network," but got caught up in internal cat fights instead. *[He guaranteed a bank loan for the club's operating head Isabel Beveridge, his live-in companion at the time.]* Connell eventually joined the family firm and by 1974 had been named president. Five years later, fed up with the piranha-like ethics of the mining game, he was in the process of reassessing his life when he met Linda Haynes, who would become his second wife. Connell was flying home from Palm Beach, where he had been visiting his grandfather, when he spotted her. "I couldn't believe such an attractive woman would be going to Toronto," he recalls. "I sent her a note and asked if she wanted to come back and join me for a drink. I'd never done anything like that in my life, but she came by, checked me out and our courtship began." They were married six months later. Linda Haynes had just returned from El Salvador, where her father Cedric Haynes (former president of Orange Crush) was serving as a volunteer. She was full of stories about the orphanages she had visited and the poverty she had witnessed, and vowed to dedicate her energies to helping the underprivileged.

"I had reached a stage in my life, in my early forties, where I was ready to recognize that I wasn't going to be satisfied being in business for the rest of my life and knew I needed a radical change," Connell recalls, "so I kicked myself upstairs as chairman of Conwest and began to travel. Linda had awakened my fairly deep-down abiding interest in the plight of man. We went to Calcutta and walked along the Hugli River, where refugees from the 1971 Pakistani civil war lived in huts, and all you could see were little pots of fire with families huddled around them. It was an epiphany. It gave me insights into the human condition I had never even dreamed of. Once you've done that, there is no going back."

Connell disentangled himself from the corporate world (Conwest was sold to Alberta Energy), and with his wife and $1.3 million of his own money, he established Calmeadow, a private non-profit organization that provides "micro credit" to self-employed entrepreneurs. Based on the old Jesuit principle, "Give a man a fish and you feed him for a day; teach him to fish, and you feed him forever," Calmeadow deals with people in Canada, as well as in Third World countries, who have no collateral or credit histories and are outside the fiscal range of regular banks. Loans average $500, and so far nearly a million customers have been helped. "We have $70 million worth of loans out on the street and a 98 percent pay-back rate," he reports. "Three-quarters of our clients are low-income, self-employed women. It's a model we're pushing hard to replicate in other places. I'm a sustainability hawk." Branches are growing in Bolivia and South Africa.

With his Armani suits, patrician manner and Cartier watch, Connell is an unlikely do-gooder, and he makes little fuss about his charitable works, becoming much more agitated when describing his bakery. For a long time Connell's hobby had been baking bread, and he built a wood-burning stone hearth at his country place in Caledon, north of Toronto. For his fiftieth birthday, Linda took him to New York, where two of Gotham's best bakers became his mentors. When they returned, Martin and Linda opened a small Toronto bakery, which has since become a large business, catering to 120 restaurants.

In all he does, Martin Connell is driven by memories of his 1980 visit to a small village in Bangladesh. Inside a thatched hut he watched a man standing over an open brick furnace blowing glass globes for lanterns.

Behind him, women scrambled through piles of garbage searching for shards of glass that could be recycled for the venture. Nearby, another man was folding cardboard into boxes for packing the lanterns. That primitive example of entrepreneurship became Connell's guiding light. "Talk about grass-roots entrepreneurs," he says. "You can't get more bootstraps than that."

THE HUSH WAS PALPABLE ON MARCH 5, 1996 at the reunion of business school alumni at York University. These were the best and brightest of Dean Dezso Horvath's shock troops. Never put a Hungarian in charge of a business school if you don't want to graduate warriors. Hungarians really aren't Europeans at all, but descendants of the wild Asiatic tribes that invaded the Danube River basin in the ninth century. They thrive on violence and are as tough and resourceful as any race on Earth. For instance, after Hungarian landlords caught Gyorgy Dozsa, who had led an unsuccessful peasant revolt in 1514, they chained him to a red-hot iron throne, then made his followers eat his fried remains. Hungarian history books bulge with scenes of flesh-eating vultures hopping around the country's many battlefields, too bloated to fly. That bird isn't the mascot of the York Business School, but it could be. Students and professors here compete with a Hungarian *esprit de corps*, which means, "watch out!" An electrical engineer from Sopron, with two PhDs, Dean Horvath is a fairly typical Hungarian, one of those aggressive egomaniacs who gets into a revolving door behind you, and emerges ahead of you. At York, a campus built entirely out of cement that straddles the exact border between Greater Toronto's 416 and 905 telephone exchanges— and reflects the cultures of both—Horvath has moulded Canada's most enterprising business school.

Now Seymour Schulich is getting ready to speak to York's business school alumni. It's the first chance the graduates will have to meet their benefactor, the Canadian who struck it rich in Nevada and was persuaded by Horvath to give the business school a cool $15 million.

And there he is, the great benefactor in the flesh, boogieing towards the dais. The music he has chosen for this occasion is a track from the Beach Boys, "True to Your School." He goes on a bit about what the song means, then explains that he has spent "much down time in rural Nevada, a land rife with sin, where I am known as a Texan hold 'em poker player of some renown."

"This news of my endowment," he admits, "did not bring unlimited ecstasy to the academic folk at York's senate."

"What to do?" he asks rhetorically, pretending to be one of the grey savants who run York, smell of water biscuits and now find themselves embarrassed by his lively presence. "How to turn this sow's ear into a silk purse?" he says, mimicking their concern. "The solution is to enrol him—that's me—in media training. Now, media training is the art of transforming honest, candid, God-fearing people into politicians. Rule number one is no matter what the media ask you, give them the message *you* want. And so they dragged me out of the closet of peace and anonymity and thrust me into a world of chaos. Ever since I've been busier than the proverbial one-legged paper-hanger in an ass-kicking contest."

It's vintage Schulich, and the alumni eat it up. Seymour is an original, a Jewish kid from the streets of Montreal—Richler country—who got into mining, never discovered an ounce of anything, but cut himself in on the action through royalty arrangements so that he became Peter Munk's senior partner in the fabulous Goldstrike property, and now he's worth at least $500 million. Stock in one of his companies, Franco-Nevada Mining, has been the biggest price gainer on the Toronto Stock Exchange in the past fourteen years. Except that he keeps a six-shooter in his Toronto office desk, he lives a very ordinary life, having occupied the same Willowdale bungalow for the past two decades and having been married to the same woman, the former Tanna Goldberg, for twenty-eight years. He is unpretentious even in the choice of his toys. Three years ago, he traded the Cadillac Seville he had driven for ten years for a Ford Lincoln, but it still only has 16,000 kilometres on it. "They say that people who know how to make money sometimes don't know how to spend it," he says. "I've never learned how to spend. I'm not particularly comfortable with money."

After graduating in science and taking an MBA at McGill, Schulich joined Ned Goodman and Austin Beutel in a money-management firm, in which he still retains an interest, and then moved to Nevada. "I like tournament poker, and I like to ski; Nevada is one of the few places where you can do both," he explains. "I used to go to Reno a lot, and I kept thinking, my God, this is terrific. If only I could find a way to write these chips off. There were so many old shafts there, I figured there must be something left in one of them." With his partner Pierre Lassonde, he started buying up royalties in mine prospects and in 1983 went public. *[Lassonde gave $5 million to the Mining and Geology Department at the University of Toronto, on behalf of himself and his wife Claudette McKay-Lassonde.]* The original market capitalization of his two companies—the other is Euro-Nevada Mining—was $2 million. By the spring of 1997, their worth had reached $4.2 billion.

Schulich is a cowboy capitalist with no hidden agenda. What you see is what you get—and what you've got is a compassionate, interesting guy who has been lucky beyond his wildest dreams, and who now wants to grab himself a bit of *civitas*. His two-year odyssey into the minefield of university philanthropy—how he tried vainly three times to give his money away—is not a subject he will willingly discuss. The fact is that he involuntarily sprung loose millions in university donations, before settling his own $15 million on York. The story is fuzzy on detail, but accurate in substance. Because he had originally gone to McGill, Schulich had planned to donate the funds to the university's mining school, with the understanding that the faculty would be named after him. That wasn't possible, he was told, even though the university's school of commerce had been named after the late Samuel Bronfman. *[Later, McGill phoned Schulich and said they'd name the mining department after him if he gave $25 million. He declined, but gave $1 million to the McGill Library. Meanwhile, McGill's mining building was named after Man Hung "Jimmy" Wong, a former engineering student who left the funds in his will.]* So Schulich took his offer to Rob Prichard, president of the University of Toronto, who said, well, no, he was hoping to get $18 million from Joe Rotman, the Toronto merchant banker. Having been made aware of the competition, Rotman promptly wrote his cheque, and the Joseph L. Rotman Faculty of Management was born. *[Schulich maintains his counsel, but every once in a while the bitterness comes out, such as when he refers to the University of Toronto as "Prichard's Palace."]* Undaunted, Schulich drove to London, Ontario, and tried to get the business school at the University of Western Ontario to accept his $15 mill. No dice. The possibility of his alma mater accepting the Schulich option triggered Richard Ivey, current heir of the family that originally founded Empire Brass, to donate $11 million to UWO's newly renamed Richard Ivey School of Business. Increasingly exasperated, Schulich met Horvath, York's Hungarian business dean, and the deal was quickly done. "They suit my temperament and my background," he says of the York warriors. "Their president came to see me, as did the chairman of the board of governors and their vice-president of donations. They're hungry. They're my kind of people."

A very different style of benefactor is Joe Rotman, who silently runs Toronto's Clairwest Group, a merchant bank used by its main shareholders to reinvest their fortunes. They include classy multi-millionaires such as Issy Sharp of the Four Seasons, Michael Bregman of Second Cup, Tom Beck of Noma Industries, Lionel Shipper, a founder of the Sun newspapers and such private investors of note as the Heffernan brothers, Eph

Diamond and Syd Cooper. Rotman owns 38 percent of the $200-million pot. One of the firm's most successful startups was Barrick, the gold-mining giant, which Peter Munk, the controlling shareholder, freely admits would never have been possible without Rotman's then-risky backing. *[With Schulich sponsoring York's facilities and Rotman financing the U of T's, the funds for both of Toronto's great business schools have been provided by Nevada gold.]* Rotman has been inordinately swayed by his father's obsession with higher education. After working his way up from pushing a coal cart, the senior Rotman saved enough money to enrol in university at the age of 66, and he graduated four years later with a BA. "He left in all his children a tradition, a culture, a belief that we live in a great country and that we have an obligation to maintain its quality and make it better," says his son proudly.

Another philanthropist carrying on his father's tradition is Joey Tanenbaum, who has done more to support Canadian art and artists than any other private donor. His father Max, who also gave considerable money away, arrived in Toronto from Poland in 1913 and went to work at the family junk yard at age fifteen. A stooped man with the powerful hands of a stonemason, Max slowly built up a personal empire worth $400 million, which included huge slabs of undeveloped Toronto real estate, a stock-market portfolio run by his friend, the late Bay Street guru Andy Sarlos, and York Steel. He operated out of a messy back office in his steel yard, spending most of the day on the telephone making deals. "One thing I've never needed was window dressing," he once told me, sitting there in his fedora and spring-clear-out Tip Top Tailor suit, sipping Scotch and munching on one of the chicken legs he brought to work in a brown paper bag. Despite his wealth, Max took the bag home every night for a refill. He drove a ten-year-old Cadillac, but rather than pay for a parking meter, he left it across an abandoned railway track near his office—until a runaway freight car hit it. "Max is not exactly the 'champeen' of finesse," observed one of his friends, commenting on Tanenbaum's habit of wiping the chicken grease off his chin with the sleeve of his jacket. Endearing he may have been, but his competitors claimed Tanenbaum would chop you up for liverwurst if it served his purposes.

Max Tanenbaum's nineteen descendants fought bitterly over his estate, but they've since settled down and have themselves become philanthropists, led by the eldest son Joey and his wife Toby. "Money," says Joey Tanenbaum, "is like dung. If you keep it in a pile, it only smells. If you spread it around, it fertilizes the soil and beautiful things come from it, magnificent things—paintings, opera, ballet—all the great arts." He started to collect, not the popular French Impressionists, but their teachers, who were selling for one-thousandth the price of their pupils' canvases. His first major purchase was a Jacques Joseph Tissot that he bought for $1,750 in 1968 and sold to Freddie Koch, the New York collector, for $1,050,000 in 1983. Three other Tissots followed, purchased for $175,000 and sold at auction for $4,800,000. He has since donated paintings and sculptures to the Art Gallery of Ontario and to the National Gallery, which are worth at least $80 million, including the only major Bernini in private hands, a bust of Pope Gregory XV, carved in 1623. "I say, 'Court me!'" Tanenbaum exclaims. "Why not? What the hell! It's incumbent upon the wealthy to give major works of art to public institutions, but each institution has to create compelling circumstances in order to convince donors that *it* should be the one to receive them."

AT THE OTHER END OF THE COUNTRY, David William Strangway, who retired in the summer of 1997 after a dozen years as president of the University of British Columbia, has been fielding his own brand of miracles.

Strangway transformed a ponderous and inefficient regional institution into a national university that regularly ranks near the top of *Maclean's* annual surveys. His greatest success was raising close to $500 million for new buildings, academic chairs, professorships and endowments. At the same time, Strangway forged partnerships with private enterprise to explore nearly 200 technologies developed on campus. More than seventy spin-off, high-tech companies were established, ranking UBC third in North America (after MIT and Stanford) in terms of technology transfers to business. These were impressive achievements, since Vancouver has few head offices, and its paltry Establishment platoon boasts little spare change.

There was little tradition of philanthropy on Canada's West Coast before the Koerner brothers—Walter, Leon, Otto and Theodore—arrived from Czechoslovakia in 1938 and began marketing the lowly western hemlock as "Alaska pine." A new fortune earned, the Koerners spent most of three decades making imaginative donations to the University of British Columbia, culminating in the gifts that formed the heart of the Museum of Anthropology collection and the new humanities and social science sections of the UBC Library. One of the Koerners—Leon—actually moved on campus, to live on the top floor of the Graduate Student Centre.

One of the more unusual UBC donors is Jack Bell, who made a fortune selling peat moss, then switched to cranberries with the same result.

Strangway had been pressuring the retired entrepreneur to make a gift, but all he could confirm was lunch at the English Bay Café in Vancouver's West End. At the end of the meal, Bell leaned over and said, "David, if you pay the bill, I'll hand you this envelope." Strangway did, and the envelope contained a handwritten cheque for $1 million, destined to finance a First Nations longhouse for the UBC campus. "It was typical of the man," Strangway recalls. "He did it with no fanfare, fuss or bother, but rather because he wanted to help perpetuate the heritage of our First Nations students."

The UBC president's success with Asian donors quickly became legendary, as he persuaded many a Hong Kong family dynasty that they had been allowed to prosper strictly so they could make sizeable donations to his campus. Early on, Strangway realized that the peer pressure that was so effective in North American fund-raising cut no ice in Asia. Instead, careful building of relationships was the key, and that approach worked because Strangway is one of those rare academic executives who can draw out people's psyches, take their dollars—and make them feel good about it. In everything he did, Strangway was backed by his vice-president of external affairs Peter Ufford, a professional fund-raiser with a highly evolved sense of integrity in an industry known for fast talking and cutting corners. All in all, Strangway moved his institution from fifteenth to the top, in terms of the endowment funds collected during his stewardship. He now plans to do it all over again as head of the private university he is planning to build at Whistler.

Joe Cohen, the jovial head of the Vancouver branch of the Cohens' Winnipeg-based empire, recently spotted Strangway casually walking along a downtown street, hands in pockets, deep in thought, with a beatific smile on his face. "How ya doin', David?" Cohen said, as the two men passed one another. Then speaking for many of his Establishment colleagues, he added, "Great to see you with your hands in your *own* pockets for a change!" But Cohen didn't really mean it. Joe Cohen, like most of his peers who give their time and money to the new philanthropy, know that the Canadian social critic Margaret Visser got it right when she wrote in *Saturday Night* magazine, "It isn't enough to own a fortune; you must also be persuaded that you deserve it."

6

THE ESTABLISHMENT
GOES GLOBAL

"What is a borderless world? It is a world emptied of every value and principle except one—accumulation."

—*Eric Kierans, one-man think-tank, Halifax*

PHOENIX. EARLY MORNING. Don Hannah, CEO of U.S. Properties Inc., and the actress Daryl's father, has invited me to a nondenominational service on his impressive spread. We are here to toast the dawn on Easter Sunday. It's all very spiritual. A turbo-charged Bible-thumper keeps yelling, "He is risen! He is risen! He is risen *indeed!*" My host reminds me that we live for love, and I keep trying to forget that these guys are all developers. They greet the sun by holding their arms out to the cloudless sky, while attending gurus and gurettes chant that getting in touch with your "spatial boundaries" will expand your "emotional pastures." Or perhaps it was the other way round, but an urban cowboy standing beside me, Stetson pushed back on his head, fails to clue in to the message. "Hell," he says, raising his glass to the sky in a perfect *non sequitur*, "life is too short to drink bad wine."

Deserts are ugly, and this one is no exception, but during the long, languid evenings when the scent of jasmine, orange blossoms and jojoba bushes flavours the night air, Phoenix seems like a splendid place. Locals drive their air-conditioned El Dorados and Jags across the iridescent desert with Episcopalian grace, while on the far horizon, like giant fire flies, executive jets take off and land at Phoenix's Sky Harbor International, the country's busiest private airport. The moonlight glints off the jets' wings and the sky is alive with their roaring. Two million passengers move in and out of Phoenix every month. Six flights daily unload incoming Canadians.

By the time you get to Phoenix you realize why this desert city of nearly three million is the most popular American haven for Canadian entrepreneurs on the lam. What they're running away from, they insist, is not only high taxes but "the Canadian attitude."

"A lot of it," says Peter Thomas, the Vancouver entrepreneur who moved his $100-million Samoth Capital Corporation from Vancouver to Phoenix in 1994, "is the perception that has been created by Canadian governments that you can't win. Nobody I know in Phoenix has left Canada because they think it's no good, but you can't make any sizeable money there." If Ottawa's anti-business attitude bothers the snowbirds, the Phoenix ethic is more to their liking. "When a developer puts a plan to the council here, and he hasn't heard back in two days, he's all over them, insisting, 'Where's my answer? What's going on here?'" says Thomas. "In Canada, you just stay quiet and wait forever, because you don't want to get the guy with the authority mad at you."

The Arizona imperative is to create your own future instead of waiting to have it shaped by circumstance. As in any meritocracy, what matters is now. "You're only as good as your last song," says Thomas. "You have to earn your right to be here and stay here. Nobody gives a damn about family trees or historical niceties." Because the migrating Canadians are, like almost all Phoenicians, recent arrivals, they face few hierarchical barriers and establish themselves quickly. Certainly the Canadian presence is felt heavily in every branch of local business, especially real estate.

Life is not free but it's easy. There is little time or chance for pretence in these dry, stony canyons. Wealth means status. You're either up or out. The Arizona state motto says it all: *Ditat Deus* (God enriches).

Like most of the American Sun Belt, Phoenix is filling up. Every night the fourteen-wheelers push south along Interstate 10, and the following day race back north, high and empty, to load up again with one more migrant's belongings. Apart from its obvious growth potential, what attracts Canadians to Phoenix is the weather: 315 sunny days a year— with summer heat occasionally at a broiling 122 degrees Fahrenheit, the sun is an ever-present fireball in the sky. Rainfall averages only seven inches a year, less than the Sahara. *[When the locals talk about a three-inch rain, what they mean is that there are three inches between raindrops.]*

Life in Phoenix combines the self-determination of America's hard-rock conservative spirit with the gotcha opportunism of the frontier. Feeling secure in their big-buck ostentation, these gunslingers are hard right politically. A radical is anyone who frequents bookstores. Their cropped hair leaves their ears exposed and that lends them a deceptive air of friendly candour, but inside they're crude and unforgiving. Conversation is as strong as horseradish and gets straight to the point. ("Burglar alarm? You betcha. Keeps the house shut tighter than a bull's ass in fly time.")

From the air, Phoenix is one giant golf course with live-in privileges. Greater Phoenix has 245 links utilized to capacity from sunrise to sunset. The best way to tell when newcomers have become real Phoenicians is when they start squinting at night. Indoors. With shades on.

MOVING TO THIS VERY UN-CANADIAN PLACE is for exiled Titans like Peter Thomas a very Canadian solution. You gain entry into the international marketplace and leave behind the burdens of heavy taxes, overregulation and winter snows—all without a significant switch in language or culture.

Until recently, there was something vaguely un-Canadian about going global. If we display excess energy and imagination abroad, went the subliminal argument, we might be expected to do so at home. We would thus quickly lose our inferiority complex, which apart from Medicare is the only national identity we've got. Besides, the idea of doing business in far-away places with strange-sounding names sounded risky and pretentious.

One of the defining differences between the Old and the New Establishments is the extent of their global thrust. Without exception, the Titans profiled in this book have climbed aboard the global express train. That, more than any other criterion, is what qualifies them as Titans. They know that globalization will be the life force of the twenty-first century—and so they work with it and harness it. Conrad Black cuts a more imposing presence in London and New York than in Toronto; he has become a world player of singular significance. All of Peter Munk's most valuable gold mines are outside Canada, while his real-estate empire straddles the world. His home and his office are in Toronto, but the prodigiously successful Gerry Schwartz runs only one major asset in Canada. Issy Sharp's invaluable Four Seasons franchise has a larger presence in every other industrial country than it does in Canada, where only two hotels—in Toronto and Vancouver—sport his logo. Frank Stronach is a tax exile living in Austria and Switzerland. Jimmy Pattison has moved most of his remarkable conglomerate south of the forty-ninth parallel. The largest and fastest-growing sector of Paul Desmarais's impressive corporate empire is in Europe. The Irving money is in Bermuda. Harrison McCain spends most of his time aboard his $30-million jet, inspecting his empire of food operations in ninety countries. Robert Friedland has gone native in Burma. Until recently, Izzy Asper expanded his television empire everywhere but Canada. Between 85 and 95 percent of Canada's high-tech production is sold abroad, and that's where the industry has developed its most strategic networks. Terry Matthews, commander-in-chief of the besieged Newbridge Networks Corp., once confided to me that his main local activity in Kanata, Ontario, where he lives and works, is getting his hair cut.

At some point in the mid-1990s, Canada's Titans decided to take on the world. Now, they are in flight mode, living aboard their trans-ocean private jets or in the first-class cabins of 747s, chalking up so many airline points that giving them away has become a major philanthropic undertaking. They are investing more of their capital funds abroad than in Canada; their mind-set is focused on Berlin, Buenos Aires, Bombay or Boston, as they exploit the one-world marketplace. In the process, they are becoming impressive international traders. A recent survey by the World Economic Forum ranks Canada third (just behind Singapore and Hong Kong) in overall quality of corporate management. The Swiss-based International Institute for Management Development, which measures world competitiveness, ranks this country tenth, up from twelfth in 1996. A Deloitte & Touche Consulting Group survey of 12,000 publicly traded corporations doing business in fifty-six countries places twenty-three Canadian firms near the top of the globe's 200 fastest-growing companies. "It's only Canadians who consistently put down Canadians," points out Jeffrey Gandz, associate dean of business at the University of Western Ontario. "Our business sector is extraordinarily well recognized outside our country."

The new power-wielders know they have no choice. Export or die is the governing mantra of the twenty-first century. Limiting themselves to the Canadian market is like refusing to use computers. It can be done, but economically it's suicide.

And yet, even for the most adventurous of the Titans, going international is daunting. That's not because of language problems—English is the universal business language in every corner of the world except Quebec. And it's not because bribing government officials is occasionally part of a foreign business deal. *[Most bribes are tax deductible.]* The problem is psychological. The global players must steel themselves against the very different rules by which international business is played:

- It means having to compete, *really* compete, down and dirty, with rivals ten times your size, whose ethics hark back to the pirates who once swept the Caribbean, brooms tied to their masts and mayhem in their hearts.
- It means coming to terms with the notion that the world is run not by the United Nations, not by the presidents, dictators, prime ministers or parliaments of member countries, but by corporations. They call themselves multi- or transnational, but they mostly roost where taxes are the lowest and worker protection laws the meanest. According to the United Nations, fully one-third of the world's private-sector productive assets are already owned by these new-breed mega-companies. They practise "free production," which means that they have removed the notion of borders in their strategic considerations. All that counts is where something can be made most cheaply and most efficiently. They are held together by fibre-optic circuits and private computer networks. Encryption reigns.
- It means realizing that those corporate playing fields that may not have seemed quite level in Canada are really pretty good. Once abroad, the playing fields are so tilted towards the big guys that you feel lucky if you can get into the stadium. The giant transnationals are subject to virtually no accountability, except to their owners, which are ultimately numbered companies. Eric Kierans, Halifax's one-man think-tank who has studied their behaviour, concluded: "What is a borderless world? It is a world emptied of every value and principle except one—accumulation."
- It means that you're not only competing with other companies in your industry, or even with other industries, but against entire ecosystems—those new organizational life-forms that extend across many markets and are based more on waves of innovation than on product lines. (Bill Gates's Microsoft Inc., for example, is not a corporation but an ecosystem on the march.)
- It means joining what Nobel laureate economist Paul Samuelson describes as "the ruthless economy," which views employees as expendable factors of production. People are retained on payrolls only until they can be replaced by cheaper alternatives, including child labour in some far-off sweatshop.
- It means the end of civic responsibility, even among enlightened managers. Brownie points for good corporate citizenship mean nothing when the score is kept in a numbered bank account in the Seychelles Islands, a Liechtenstein trust, or the office of some lawyer

in a Panama hat in Labuan. Frank Stronach, who knows these things, said it best when he told one of his shareholders, who had been enquiring about why he was investing outside Canada: "Money has no heart, no soul, no conscience, no homeland."

• It means understanding that the lifeblood of the global market is mobility. Successful international entrepreneurs must be as free to resettle as migratory birds with constantly changing nesting grounds. In other words, forget your personal life, or grab a new one.

Despite these and other hurdles, the Titans are going global. "Canada is becoming the first truly post-modern society," claims Michael Adams, the national pollster. We have mastered the modern world's common currency: we speak English, express the right kind of knowledge at the right moment, and are able to apply and market it.

The Canadian companies that have caught the global bug measure their effectiveness by international, not Canadian standards. "Within our group of companies the rule is that if we are not within the top 25 percent in the industry on a world basis, measured in world currencies, then we shouldn't be in the business, and we get out of it," says Trevor Eyton, who along with Jack Cockwell runs the $36-billion Edper empire, formerly headed by Peter Bronfman.

As well as moving their business talents abroad, the Titans are taking a dramatic new approach to trade. Anything goes. When Victor Young of Newfoundland's Fishery Products International was faced with vanishing fish stocks, he negotiated deals to buy frozen-at-sea stock off Alaska, shipped it for processing to China, and still managed to sell fillets at a profit in the North American market. Art DeFehr, CEO of Palliser Furniture in Winnipeg, completely retooled his product line after the Free Trade Agreement, limiting his run to oak and cheap particle board, quadrupling his U.S. sales. The railways may be a sunset industry in Canada—unable to run a decent train across their own country—but as continental carriers, they're booming. The CNR has changed its name to CN North America and is busy buying up American railway lines, as is CP Rail System, which collects 40 percent of its revenues from American traffic. Under Derek Burney, the former diplomat, now CEO of Bell Canada International, the once-staid telephone company is expanding to other continents, building cellular networks in Brazil, India, Colombia, Chile and China that don't require the complex infrastructure of standard telephone exchanges; they operate on BCE nets. Philip Orsino, CEO of Premdor Inc., with executive offices in Mississauga, Ontario, turned the mom-and-pop door-making business into a giant niche-manufacturing operation, and is now the world's largest door supplier with forty international manufacturing facilities. Vancouver lawyer R. Stuart "Tookie" Angus's business card lists a dozen business addresses on three continents.

Another subtler effect of globalization is that many of Canada's most important corporate decisions are being made by foreign surrogates. Two-thirds of Canada's largest corporations are owned outside the country. Even if local managers exercise apparent autonomy, their authority is not final; they answer to foreign proprietors. The CEOs who run these companies act as colonial administrators. The Americanization of this country under the Mulroney and Chrétien regimes has been profound and disturbing. Many of Canada's defining companies are now run by Americans. *[They include Tom Stephens at MacMillan Bloedel, Lamar Durrett (and Hollis Harris before that) at Air Canada, Roger Parkinson at* The Globe and Mail, *Stephen Bachand at Canadian Tire, Bill Fields at Hudson's Bay Company, Frank Hennessey at Coca Ltd., John Boland III at Dominion Textile, George Petty at Telus Corp, and many others.]*

Domestic unemployment remains an unresolved issue, but healthy exports have given Canada the best job-creation record among the G-7 countries. According to the International Monetary Fund, Canada's economy was the fastest growing in the world during 1998. The number of new jobs in Canada from 1970 to 1995 increased by 65 percent, compared to 59 percent in the U.S. and only 6 percent each in Britain, Italy and France. Few Canadians, obsessed with domestic political problems, are aware that their country is the most trade-intensive industrialized nation on Earth. Only ten years ago, exports accounted for 25 percent of this country's gross domestic product; by century's end, that ratio will be close to 50 percent.

In the process, Canada is becoming part of the borderless world described by Japanese management consultant Kenichi Ohmae. He maintains that in a global economy nation states have been rendered obsolete and national economies nonexistent, since both have been eclipsed by transnational corporations.

"I'm a passionate believer that you can't be any nationality any more," says Victor Rice, the CEO of Varity Corp., whose chilling employment history—he has laid off a conservatively estimated 60,000 workers—amply documents his claim. Rice heads what's left of Massey-Harris, once Canada's premier farm implement manufacturer, and gives evidence of being a haunted man, on the run from himself and the misery he has inflicted on so many of his one-time employees. He abandoned Massey's pensioners to their own meagre devices, accepted $200 million in tax breaks and loan guarantees for his company from Canadian governments, then skipped the country by moving the firm to Buffalo. More recently, he captured control of Lucas Industries PLC in Britain, and now lives the existence of a typical global entrepreneur—as ruthless with himself as he is with his people. He allows himself precisely four hours and twenty-three minutes sleep a night, is permanently on the road, and has time for his hobby—tending his perennial garden at Niagara-on-the-Lake, Ontario—only late at night, under special floodlights. Those courageous few who continue to work for him compare Rice to the anti-hero in Joseph Heller's novel *Something Happened*. In it, the fictional boss tells one of his underlings: "Goddamn it, I want to see you right on the verge. I want to be able to hear it in your stuttering, flustered, tongue-tied voice. I don't trust flattery, loyalty, sociability. I don't trust deference, respect or cooperation. I trust fear."

The twenty-four-hour work alert is common among the global players. Tom Long, a senior head hunter with Egon Zchnder, a Swiss-owned, Toronto-based personnel consulting firm, begins working the phones to Europe at dawn and finishes late in the day, on the line to Australia. "I work sort of constantly," he says. "I'm always on call. That's the exciting part of belonging to a global organization."

The scope and size of these global elephants is difficult to grasp and even more difficult to credit. Of the world's hundred largest economies, fifty-one are corporations. Wal-Mart, for example, is larger than 161 countries, including Poland; General Motors is larger than Denmark; Toyota dwarfs Norway. Philip Morris is richer than New Zealand. *[Three Canadian corporations rank among the world's top fifteen: Thomson Corp., Seagram Inc. and Nortel.]* As the world's seventh-largest industrialized country, Canada is a member of the club, but with a limited bar bill.

Gerry McGoey, a corporate gunslinger with many notches in his belt, got a taste of this country's insignificance while he was raising money for BCE in California, late in 1996. "We saw a number of the important pension funds and weren't getting too far when I remembered there was a small fireman's fund running about $150 billion in a San Francisco suburb, on the second floor of a strip mall," he recalls. "We introduced ourselves and they said, 'Well, we don't know why you're down here.' And I told them that I wanted to talk about raising some money. So they summoned a fellow from the far corner of the office, a young kid in his thirties who had his tie undone, and they said, 'Well, this is Bill. He's in charge of Canada. How much money do you run overall, Bill, including

Canada?' 'About $6 billion,' he said. They apologetically explained that Bill was just learning. Then they asked Bill what he knew about our company. 'Bell is the biggest business in Canada,' he replied. 'Well,' they said, 'we wouldn't invest in you fellows up there anyway because, first of all, we'd have to make the decision, do we want to be in Canada? and secondly, do we want to be in a regulated industry? and thirdly, we'd have to know about the government's position on monopolies. There are too many decisions involved, so we don't bother with Canada. We don't really care what's going on up there.' They asked Bill how much he had invested in this Bell thing, and he said, 'Nothing.' 'Well, that's all we'll probably do,' they said, ending the conversation. My fellows just sat there with their eyes bulging out."

Currencies, commodities, derivatives, stocks and bonds worth $1.5 trillion are traded daily, the buy and sell bids orbiting the Earth via satellites, as the major markets move in their never-ending twenty-four-hour cycle from North America (New York), to Asia (Singapore), to Europe (London). The amounts are dazzling. I was on the Toronto trading floor of Nesbitt Burns one summer day in 1997, not a particularly busy time, yet $35 billion flowed through the room that day. And this was only one of Bay Street's four major trading floors. It dealt only in currencies, bonds and derivatives; the equity books were being traded elsewhere. *[It's the value of currencies that more and more determines the economic destiny of a country, but it's difficult to divine what each currency is actually worth. A surprisingly accurate indication that shows just how much a currency's daily quotes deviate from its real value is the "Big Mac Index," developed by* The Economist *in Britain. Calculating that the average price of a Big Mac in the United States was $2.42, that compares to $4.02 in Switzerland and only $1.16 in China. The index assumes that if a Big Mac costs less than $2.42 under current exchange rates in another country, the local currency is undervalued. In 1995, the Index indicated the Japanese yen was being valued at almost twice its real worth, which turned out to be fairly accurate.* The Economist *proudly pointed out that when eight major currencies rose or fell by at least 10 percent in value, the Big Mac index got the direction right for seven of them. That record, it boasted, "is better than most highly paid currency forecasters."]*

The best-known Canadian in the highly volatile occupation of trying to gauge international business trends is Ken Courtis, who was educated at Laval University and has links into every level of the Canadian Establishment. When *Asiaweek* was hunting for the most authoritative economist in the region to comment on market trends just ahead of the 1997 currency crisis, the newsmagazine chose to interview Courtis, whose full-time job is as the Tokyo-based strategist and chief economist for

Deutsche Bank, Group Asia. He predicted that stocks and currencies would perform "like Chinese firecrackers" and warned the magazine's readers to "get out before everyone decides the party's over." Within a week of the article's publication, stock markets began their massive correction, and currencies plunged to unprecedented lows. Courtis spends at least 250 days a year on the road, searching for signs and portents that will confirm his suspicions.

His work has become his life. "Deutsche Bank only has me from 7 a.m. to midnight," he quips. "The rest of the time is my own." He may well be the world's best-connected economist. The reason that just about everybody in top political and economic posts will talk to him is that he hands out useful fiscal advice gratis while gathering his data. (A typical Courtis prescription: "Short the Japanese yen against the Italian lira—that will make you a possible 15 percent.") A leading mover inside the Trilateral Commission, he is listened to carefully because he has become one of the few economists whose views can move markets, a phenomenon business papers have labelled the "Courtis effect." The forty-eight-year-old economist may well be the prototype twenty-first-century man. Born in England, raised in Canada, educated in Paris, he speaks five languages. (His Japanese is so fluent that he teaches at Keio and Tokyo universities.) "Ken thinks in three dimensions—historical, current and future," notes Jeffrey Carten, a former U.S. undersecretary of commerce. "He has the keenest sense of the interconnection between political and economic forces of anyone I know."

Those vital links are intimately explored and exploited at the most important of the international conferences: the World Economic Forum held annually at Davos, a quaint village in the Swiss Alps. Highlighted by the elegant dinner Peter Munk hosts for Canadian delegates in his winter home at nearby Klosters, the conference is nothing less than a yearly convention of the industrialized world's Titans.

"Davos people control virtually all international institutions, many of the world's governments and the bulk of its economic and military capabilities," rightly claims Samuel Huntingdon, author of *The Clash of Civilizations*, who has written extensively on the "Davos culture." Roughly a thousand executives, at least four dozen heads of government (plus a scattering of robed bishops and dictators wearing generals' uniforms) and any number of panting power groupies gather to trade gossip, lies and videotapes. The really significant networking is transacted in the village cafés, away from prying competitors. "When Jimmy Goldsmith bought Lord White's interest in Newmont Mining," recalls Bill Turner, the

Montreal corporate director, "he and the chairman of Newmont were at Davos and we had a board meeting on the spur of the moment. We just went to various rooms and called out our South African director, the English board member, me from Canada and so on. Once we were together, we talked to Jimmy so we could find out what he intended to do. There aren't many place in the world where you could have done that." Davos is unique. It's the place Canada's Titans increasingly treat as their home base away from home. *[Canada's 1997 Davos business delegation had twenty-six members: Conrad Black (Hollinger), Jacques Bougie (Alcan), Michael and Marlen Cowpland (Corel), Tom d'Aquino (BCNI), Nan and Philippe de Gaspé Beaubien (Telemedia), Jacques Lamare (SNS Lamare), Brandt Louie (London Drugs), John McNeil (Sun Life), Ron Mannix (Loram Inc.), Jacques Menard (Hydro-Québec), Jan Peeters (Fonorola Inc.), Don Reimer (Express World Corp), Jean-Claude Scraire (Caisse de dépôt et placement), Jim Sheppard (Finning Tractor), Charles Sirois (Teleglobe), Don Sobey (Empire Co.), Brian Steck (Nesbitt Burns), David Strangway (University of British Colum-bia), Maurice Strong (CEO of the World), Don Tapscott (Alliance for Converging Technolo-gies), Paul Tellier (CNR), André Tremblay (Microcell Telecom Inc.), Bill Turner (Exsultate Inc.), and Don Walker (Magna Inc.).]*

Canada's growing cadre of international traders live and deal in a world where nothing is as it seems. It is an arena of big wealth and bigger deals. The seriously rich who inhabit these rarefied latitudes are highly allergic to taxation. *[Being a tax collector these days is not a healthy occupation. In Russia during 1997, some twenty-six tax collectors were killed, seventy-four injured and six kidnapped. "The art of taxation," advised Jean-Baptiste Colbert, Louis XIV's legendary treasurer, "consists in so plucking the goose to obtain the largest amount of feathers with the least possible amount of hissing."]* Owners of the transnational corporations, including a growing number of Canadians, tend to live in one country, manufacture in a second, sell their products in a third, invest the proceeds in a fourth, and collect the profits in a fifth, which usually is a lush island haven, where wealth never emerges to be counted, taxed or recorded. Income is assigned to any of these five domiciles, and profit centres are moved to escape the cash flow. The popularity of tax havens depends on whispers. In this underground world, it's the rumours that count: Who is investigating what? Is the IRS really closing down the Seychelles? How safe is safe? How much do the local lawyers charge? Can the trust's shares be held in bearer securities? The black islands of the Caribbean are considered safer than Bermuda and the Bahamas. Many of these tax havens have passed laws not merely protecting the identity of tax exiles but coming down hard—such as life sentences in local jail—for any lawyers or bankers who might be tempted to reveal anything (including rank, name and serial number) about the names on the trust accounts in their tender care. Among the most welcoming jurisdictions are the British Virgins, Gibraltar, the Isle of Man, Jersey, the Turks and Caicos, and of course the Pacific's beautiful and mysterious Cook Islands. *[The Royal Bank of Scotland's offshore branch at Jersey, in the English Channel, is never closed. Its phone number, 724365, stands for seven days a week, twenty-four hours a day and 365 days a year. In the Cook Islands, fifteen tiny dots in the South Pacific, somewhere between Hawaii, Polynesia and New Zealand, the local tax laws are so lax that not only are there no taxes of any kind, but the international trusts lodged there require no local directors and no annual statements. There are no minimum capital requirements and annual meetings can be held by an exchange of faxes.]* The least regulated tax haven on earth is the Seychelles, a cluster of 115 tiny islands north of Madagascar in the Indian Ocean. The minuscule republic sanctions and even welcomes not merely tax avoiders, but self-confessed money launderers. Another increasingly popular spot is Labuan, a former steamship-coaling station off the coat of Sabah, in East Malaysia. The largest offshore banking centre in Southeast Asia, it houses the offices of fifty international banks and has a five-star hotel to accommodate their clients. Local menus feature such delicacies as fish 'n' blue chips, trading burgers, Chase Manhattan pizza, and a noodle dish dubbed "*mee* make more money."

Of all the world's tax havens, none is more glamorous or more closely connected to Canada than the Bahamas. In 1954, E.P. Taylor, whose Canadian Breweries group was then selling suds worth $1 million a day, formed the Lyford Cay Development Company to start converting 2,800 previously uninhabitable acres into one of the world's most luxurious communities. He eventually sank $35 million into the project and earned a generous return. Originally, Taylor invited George Black (Conrad's father), Bud McDougald, W. Eric Phillips, and M. Wallace McCutcheon (his Argus partners) to put $1 million each into the Lyford project, but they turned him down. Phillips told Taylor at the time: "Eddie, I'll give those islands twenty years. After that, the cruise ships will come and the natives will get hostile, and they won't be worth a damn." When Taylor began to discuss the notion of transferring his citizenship, Black exploded: "You're out of your skull, Eddie. For God's sake, your people have lived here for a long time. Why are you so bloody jumpy about taxes? Don't you think that the country where you made your money is where you should keep it?" To which, Black remembered Taylor replying with a sigh, "I can't afford to die in Canada."

Tired of paying high taxes and flying restlessly between board meetings aboard his Hawk-Saddle jet, Taylor sold Canadian Breweries for a

$118-million profit in 1969 and moved permanently to the Bahamas. Lyford Cay on New Providence Island was established as a private preserve where millionaires could sun themselves in an atmosphere made almost piously tranquil by the absence of refinements of civilization such as income tax and death duties. Taylor became a Bahamian citizen in 1977 and gradually phased himself out of any Canadian involvement. He enjoyed a happy exile and died at eighty-eight, in 1989.

Apart from its obvious fiscal benefits, Lyford Cay has several distinct advantages over other tax havens. It's close to those Canadians who live east of Winnipeg (three hours' flight from Toronto; thirty minutes from Miami); it has a modern communications network (its telephones are tied into the North American system as area code 809); and it's in the same time zone as New York and Toronto.

The Bahamas depends for much of its thriving economy on tax exiles. Nassau, the islands' bustling capital city, is home to more than four hundred chartered banks, a hundred trust companies and fifty insurance firms. New offshore trusts can be incorporated within twenty-four hours of obtaining proper documentation—or twenty minutes if you're really in a rush. The system is so efficient that investors fly into Nassau for morning meetings with their portfolio managers and return to Florida in time for lunch, or Toronto in time for dinner.

As tax exiles have built their dream houses in every imaginable architectural form except thatched huts, Lyford Cay has become a picture-book island resort of 250 mansions, set on manicured lawns, with ruby bougainvillea hanging off every balcony. The community's centrepiece is the confectionery-pink clubhouse and its nearby pool complex, where languid bodies stretch out on green-towelled chaises. The Planter's Punch and conch salad are the best there is. The club's three dining-rooms offer dancing under open skylights, and the nearby Yacht Club boasts a view of fantasy yachts at sunset while you enjoy roast Eleuthera chicken and sumptuous strawberry shortcake. "It's the only really private place left in the world today," Baroness Meriel de Posson, a long-time Lyford member who returns year after year from London, told *Town & Country* magazine. Among the many Canadians who call Lyford Cay home is Arthur Hailey, the best-selling novelist who moved there with his wife Sheila in 1969. Unlike most tax exiles, Hailey talks unabashedly about his decision to leave Canada:

"In 1969, after many years of writing with only moderate returns, two of my novels—*Hotel* and *Airport*—hit multi-million circulation numbers around the world. There was a Niagara of earnings expected to come in over the following two years. At a consultation with my lawyer and accountant in Montreal, I was warned that on those earnings I could expect to pay 70 to 77 percent in income taxes over the next two years— that tax total being a larger sum than I had ever dreamed of earning. Something else: when you create a successful book, it is not like building a widget factory that continues making widgets, producing profits in the future. For an author, when fortune smiles broadly, you never know if it will happen again. Very often it does not. So the advice from my lawyer was specific: 'If you want any of those earnings left for your family and your old age, get out of North America fast, and move to a tax haven.'"

Which was exactly what the Haileys did, and lived happily ever after.

Another fascinating Lyford resident is Charles "Chuck" Rathgeb, who lives in the magnificent villa once occupied by Sean Connery when he was shooting the James Bond film *Thunderball*. Rathgeb's half-dozen bracelets of gold and leather jangle like a belly-dancer's charms when he moves his left arm. *[It's the Big Six. Each bangle, awarded by the Explorers' Club in London, denotes that Rathgeb has shot, single-handedly, one of the world's great animals: a lion, a leopard, an elephant, a buffalo, a tiger and a rhino. He bagged the tiger in the Himalayan Hills, the others in either Kenya or Tanzania, and has since given up hunting.]* One of the business community's most influential members in the 1970s and 1980s, Rathgeb was the Establishment's resident jock. His Toronto office featured floor-to-ceiling blow-ups of him hunting, parachuting, tuna fishing, bobsledding, car rallying, ballooning, mountain climbing and racing motorboats, airplanes, horses and several other speedy conveyances. He won the London-to-Monte Carlo power-boat race, was a member of Canada's 1964 Olympic bobsled team and in 1967, became the first Canadian to fly over the Alps by balloon, from Zurich to Milan. An experienced climber, he abandoned his 1975 assault on Mount Everest only because Ottawa wouldn't lend him the appropriate re-supply aircraft. In 1973, at the age of fifty-two, he became the first Canadian to drive in the Targa Florio road race in Sicily; his car finished tenth out of eighty entries. A year later, he took part in the arduous Trans-Sahara World Cup Rally. He has flown jets solo across the Atlantic, operates racing stables and captained the first Canadian entry in the International Tuna Championships. President and sole shareholder of Canada's largest contracting company, Canadian Comstock, he sold out to Newfoundland's Lundrigham family in 1979 for more than $140 million, and eventually retired to Lyford Cay. Recently, at age seventy-five, he took part in the gruelling 19,000-kilometre London-to-Beijing auto race. "That was a rough go," he sums up. "I'm not doing that again."

More recent tax exiles have included Michael deGroote and New Brunswick billionaire K.C. Irving, who both chose Bermuda. DeGroote, the former controlling shareholder of the Ontario-based waste management firm Laidlaw Inc., never denied the Ontario Securities Commission's allegations that he had made a $17-million profit short-selling Laidlaw stock after learning internally that some of its dump sites were about to be declared toxic. He proved his innocence, if that's what it was, in a strange way. DeGroote paid a $23-million fine for contravening the OSC provisions against insider trading, but his lawyer insisted that the transaction had been an "honest mistake"—whatever that is.

When he died in 1992, Irving willed the bulk of his wealth, estimated at $7 billion, to a Bermuda-based trust he had set up twenty years earlier. He left precise instructions that it be jointly administered by his three sons but there was a catch: they could only claim the fortune if they became non-residents of Canada, to ensure that Ottawa never received a penny of his holdings.

The most visible tax exile of the 1990s is, of course, John Felderhof, who made a pure profit of at least $42 million selling his stock in Bre-X where he was chief geologist before the scam became public. The owner of three luxurious properties worth $5 million inside the gated communities of George Town in the Cayman Islands, Felderhof escaped before any of the $270-million class action suits against him could be heard. Although he went on record to claim that the Bre-X deposit contained 200 million ounces of gold, he later denied knowing anything at all. About anything.

Settled by pirates, deserters and other undesirables during the eighteenth century, the Caymans haven't changed much. This tiny pup of a country has no economy (except making the odd pot of turtle soup), yet an incredible 550 banks have offices there, including forty-five of the world's top fifty banks, Canada's Big Five and the Bank of China. In terms of the value of monetary transactions, nearly all done through heavily secured modems, the Caymans rank as the world's fifth-largest financial centre, just after New York, London, Tokyo and Hong Kong.

Grand Cayman Island itself is only 32 kilometres long and from six to 11 kilometres wide. It has a population of 25,000—that's less than half the number of football fans who attend the average Grey Cup game. What holds the local community together is the island's only daily newspaper, *The Cayman Compass*, which runs a regular column on teaching your parrot how to talk better.

Its owner?

You guessed it, Conrad Black.

Now, *that's* globalization.

7

TAKING OVER
THE NATIONAL AGENDA

"If you ask yourself, in which period since 1900 has Canada's business community had the most influence on public policy, I would say it was in the last twenty years. Look at what we stand for and look at what all the governments, all the major parties . . . have done, and what they want to do. They have adopted the agendas we've been fighting for in the past two decades."

Tom d'Aquino, CEO, Business Council on National Issues

I HAVE A FRIEND who finally figured out a practical approach to the eternal dilemma of how the private and public sectors ought to deal with one another. "Whenever I go to the dentist," he explains, "just as he is bending down to put that nasty drill in my mouth, I grab him by the balls, and I say, 'Now, we're not going to hurt each other, are we?'"

"Works every time," boasts my friend. "That's how business and government should treat each other. Carefully."

Maybe. But the relationship is a little more complicated than that. Certainly it has been complicated in Canada, where governments have alternated from being regarded by business as essential partners in laying down the vast land's initial infrastructure—roads, canals, railways and so on—to devilish nuisances by taxing away incentives and over-regulating industries.

During the Second World War, government and business behaved as one, equally dedicated to beating the Nazis. But after that, a decidedly chilly polarity set in. At first the rift was gradual, because C.D. Howe, the "Minister of Everything" who was an intimate of the business community and looked after its Ottawa interests, retained most of his power right up to the Liberal defeat of 1957, which sent him back into the private sector. There followed the election of John Diefenbaker, who ranked "the Bay Street Boys" just behind the Liberals on his list of favourite villains. That was followed during the Pearson years by the brief nationalistic flowering of Walter Gordon, a man of conscience and mission who tried to keep alive the flickering flame of Canadian owner-ship and domestic control. Next was the confrontational style of Pierre Elliott Trudeau, who mistrusted businessmen and found being in their company offensive—a sentiment that was enthusiastically reciprocated.

The alliance between the public and private sectors was shattered. Big business dug in, dismissing Trudeau as "a Communist," and mounted campaigns to cut his government "down to size." That was a code phrase for removing Ottawa from any meaningful economic involvement, leaving the public sector with little to do, except for such mundane func-tions as deciding which side of the highway Canadians ought to drive on. *[Except in rural Alberta, where even this edict was regarded as interfering with an individ-ual's freedom of choice.]*

Then, with the unexpected 1984 electoral sweep of Brian Mulroney and the Tories, the private sector switched tactics. Mulroney had a pecu-liar connection with the country's business establishment. He was in it but not of it, having grown up in Baie Comeau, a hinterland company town on Quebec's North Shore, and having had to claw his way to the top of Montreal's legal fraternity. When his *habitant* face first hove into view, he could do no wrong. The Establishment's initial mood of eupho-ria was best caught by Mulroney's friend Ross Johnson, the anti-hero of *Barbarians at the Gate*, who introduced him to the Economics Club of New York as "the former head of the Iron Ore Company of Canada" and got appreciative chuckles from his tuxedoed audience when he cooed, "Having another CEO of a multinational become the head of a govern-ment gives us all an unexplainable tingling feeling." Next morning, Johnson purchased a full-page ad in *The New York Times*, proclaiming Mulroney to be "the right man in the right place at the right time."

As far as the business community was concerned, he was precisely that. Once in power, Mulroney did everything the Establishment wanted—he negotiated and signed a free trade deal with the Americans, castrated the Foreign Investment Review Agency, killed the National Energy Program, de-regulated Canada's financial sector, and cut corpo-rate taxes from 15 to 7.5 percent. His official quarters at 24 Sussex Drive became an Establishment hangout.

He was, in fact, not so much a convinced philosophical conservative as a politician without ideology, as his often repeated statement, "I am not ideologically opposed to anything, unless it doesn't work," made clear. The definitive statement about his thought process was the verdict of Charles McMillan, his chief policy adviser, who told me in the fall of 1984, "Brian? He's about as ideological as that coffee pot."

Most Canadians assumed that Mulroney had come to political leadership from his Montreal law practice. That was not the case; he had given up practising law seven years before he became Tory leader. In the interval, he had been running the Iron Ore Company of Canada, a subsidiary of Hanna Mining of Cleveland, Ohio—and had been very good at it. When he took over, the company had debts of $400 million and a dismal labour relations record; by the time he left, the debts had been paid off and the iron mines were spinning off dividends of $300 million a year, more than ever before. Only a year before his switch to politics, Mulroney was a director of ten major companies, including Conrad Black's Standard Broadcasting; the giant supermarket chain, Provigo Inc.; United Provinces Insurance; the Canadian Imperial Bank of Commerce; and, predictably, the Ritz-Carlton Hotel Company of Montreal. These were useful instruments to broaden his contacts but none more so than the Commerce, which allowed him a seat at the very marrow of the Establishment's decision-making process. Equally important were the contacts he made in the U.S., sitting in at the board meetings of his parent company in Cleveland. Meeting with Hanna's partners and directors brought Mulroney in direct touch with the paladins of American business. As well as the crop of Hannas and Humphreys, who then held control of the company, there was Peter Grace of the New York mercantile family; Stephen Bechtel, Jr., head of the San Francisco-based master builders with annual revenues of $12 billion; Nathan Williams Pearson, who ran the Mellon fortune out of Pittsburgh; Charles Ames, head of the Acme-Cleveland Corporation; and William Boeschenstein, chairman of Owens Corning Fiberglas. They took to the charming young Canadian Irishman as if he were the son they never had (an impression Mulroney did nothing to dispel), leaving him in the enviable position of having one of the highest-quality business networks on the continent. He was a Canadian business Titan before the category existed, and he went into politics very much as their ambassador—and in fact, was suitably rewarded for his dedication to the cause of big business by being showered with directorships, stock options and plum legal and speaking assignments once he had left office.

WHEN THE ESTABLISHMENT RECOGNIZED Mulroney for what he was, big business in Canada decided it had at long last found its Margaret Thatcher or Ronald Reagan. Since they had one of their own in charge,

went the establishment mantra, why not impose on governments legislation favourable to business, just as had so successfully been done in Great
Britain and the United States.

Without anyone outside the magic circle being conscious of the consequences, Canada's business establishment deliberately began setting
Ottawa's political agenda, in effect taking over the country's economic
governance. It was the mildest *coup d'état* in history, dealing as it did
with a compliant political authority and a prime minister who was its
unindicted co-conspirator.

The animating agent of that silent but highly significant upheaval was
Tom d'Aquino, the messianic president and chief executive officer of the
Business Council on National Issues (BCNI), whose 150 members control
$1.7 trillion in assets, earn annual revenues of $500 billion and have 1.5
million employees. Never elected to public office, he exerts an influence
over Canadian public policy that C.D. Howe, even at the height of his
wartime powers, would have envied. Much reviled by his enemies,
d'Aquino is very good at what he does. He is not your average lobbyist.
In the fall of 1997, when he was preaching a reduction in Canada's environmental goals at the Kyoto Conference on global warming, no fewer
than seventeen Ottawa deputy ministers gathered to watch his slide show,
a record seldom surpassed. A tall, humourless gent who treats his briefs
like papal bulls, he outsmarts the few bureaucrats who dare take him on
by the simple gambit of being smarter—and faster—than they are. Raised
in Nelson, B.C., he attended the London School of Economics and
later worked for three years in Pierre Trudeau's Privy Council Office. *[Tom
d'Aquino's wife, Susan, is also highly influential as an assistant deputy minister of finance
responsible for federal-provincial relations and social policy.]* "I took one of the very
first courses that was offered on the law of European institutions, which
really focused on European union," he recalls. "That got me very interested in the role of transnationals operating within the European Union
and then when I went on to do management consulting in Paris, I worked
only for transnational companies, primarily in Europe. That and my studies
at LSE hooked me into this idea that the winds of change were already
sweeping over Europe and ultimately would sweep over North America."

The BCNI had been established three years before d'Aquino was
recruited as its CEO in 1981 by such Establishment pillars as Earle
McLaughlin of the Royal Bank, Ian Sinclair of Canadian Pacific, Bill
McLean of Canada Packers, Paul Desmarais of Power Corporation, Roy
Bennett of Ford, Tom Bell of Abitibi Paper, Peter Gordon of the Steel
Company of Canada, Alf Powis of Noranda, and Bill Twaits of Imperial

Oil. d'Aquino set out to create a parallel government that would be more than just another lobby group—though he once explained that he didn't really mind being called a lobbyist, since "the Pope is a lobbyist too." It's a valid comparison: both men treat their positions not as a job, but as a mission, and it's a toss-up which of the two is the most dedicated and the most effective.

The BCNI's operational code is not so much to impose the government's agenda as to provide pro-business policy options, making them available at crucial moments in the Ottawa timetable. The BCNI's researchers are always ahead of the game, providing useful detail and handy rationales that outline—and suggest—the bureaucrats' and politicians' choices.

The dedication of BCNI's members to their cause is hard to exaggerate. When Arthur Child, the CEO of Calgary's Burns Foods Ltd., died in the spring of 1996, he bypassed some family obligations to leave a cool $1 million of his personal wealth to propel d'Aquino's efforts. *[To qualify as BCNI members, CEOs must preside over double or at least $100 million and be judged acceptable by their peers. So far, only two applicants have been turned down. Annual fees are $50,000. The BCNI's current membership is listed in Appendix 4.]*

The BCNI's initial involvement with federal policy in a proactive way was in persuading the Trudeau government to maintain its Six-and-Five wage-restraint policy as a voluntary instead of a mandatory program during the great battle against inflation in the early 1980s. Not only was the idea of a voluntary business-supported initiative to reduce inflation hatched at the BCNI, the first person asked to chair the program was Gordon Fisher, the Southam CEO, who turned the offer down in favour of fellow BCNI member and blitzkrieg specialist Ian Sinclair. The battle was fought and won; the BCNI took and deserved much of the credit.

The Business Council's next intervention was to help negotiate the end of the National Energy Program that Brian Mulroney had promised the BCNI he would eviscerate. D'Aquino then turned his attention to revising Ottawa's competition bill, the federal legislation that is supposed to keep the business establishment's piratical instincts in check. "We had previously decided that Canada needed a new competition law," he recalls. "Attempts to bring the business community to heel on the issue had all failed. When André Ouellette was named minister of consumer and corporate affairs in 1981, we had lunch in his Centre Block office and he said, 'Look, one minister of consumer affairs after another has tried to bring amendments to the competition law, and they've all failed. What are we doing wrong here?'

"'André,' I said, 'the time has come for Canada to have a new act that is not antiquated, but I can tell you something right now: if you pursue what has been the historical approach—that business is bad, and we've got to bring in a law to tame them—it will never work. If you bring in a different approach, I'll turn the business community around and we'll work with you.'

"The new approach I had in mind was that instead of having a director of Combines who treated us as if we were gangsters, Ottawa should look at the positive side and, if necessary, get rid of the Combines branch and put somebody in there who'd be more constructive."

The minister, according to d'Aquino, replied, "That's fine. You've got a deal." Incredibly, they did.

During the next three years, the BCNI spent $1 million on the project, hired its own team of twenty-five lawyers headed by Toronto's Bill Rowley and by 1985 had produced a 236-page master plan, which became Canada's new competition law. There were no provisions for class-action suits; conspiracies remained just about impossible to prove; and prosecutions were moved from criminal to civil courts. It was the only time in the history of capitalism that any country allowed its anti-monopoly legislation to be written by the very people it was meant to police.

These and other successful lobbying efforts had been private and highly confidential. d'Aquino went public on the issue of who ought to govern the country in a little-noted 1985 speech to Toronto's Board of Trade Club. "We are 2 million strong," he warned, presumably including the employees of his member companies, "and we are bound together by certain shared values . . . Let's be more wary of public-sector imperialism. Let's defeat those with statist ambitions, whatever they may be!"

What happened next proved his point. In the Great Free Trade Debate of 1985–88, the BCNI became the pivotal advocate, spending $20 million in the largest and most powerful lobby effort in Canadian history. d'Aquino was everywhere, taking on all comers with his continentalist patter.

He had quietly launched the idea as early as 1981, when both the Liberals and the Conservatives were against even exploring the prospect. At that point the BCNI itself was split on the issue. Only a handful of members—Rowlie Frazee of the Royal Bank, Alf Powis of Noranda, David Culver of Alcan and a few others—supported the idea. Most important, Brian Mulroney, the incoming prime minister at the time, was dead set against free trade. That is, until his street-corner conversion by d'Aquino.

"After he was elected but just before Brian moved into 24 Sussex, and while he was still living in the Opposition leader's house at Stornoway," the BCNI CEO recalls, "I was walking along Acacia Avenue and ran into him."

"'Lookit,' he said, at one point in our conversation, 'I know you people have been promoting this idea of free trade now for a couple of years and I've read your most recent paper. It's got a lot of appeal and I'm really looking at it with great interest.'

"That," d'Aquino exulted, "was within ten days after the election and it was the first favourable sign that I had seen from any of the Conservative leadership. Brian had sufficiently high regard for the BCNI that if we thought it was a really important issue, he felt he should at least take a good hard look at it. And he did. By the end of that autumn, he had bought the argument. The Shamrock summit followed in April, and the rest is history. The free trade idea didn't start among the senior civil servants at External Affairs, as they contend. It was ours." *[According to the Canadian Centre for Policy Alternatives, the U.S. Free Trade Agreement prompted thirty-three BCNI members to slash their workforce by 216,004 jobs, while eleven members upped their payrolls by 28,073.]*

BIG BUSINESS EVENTUALLY ABANDONED Mulroney because he didn't prove to be a long-distance winner. But it didn't matter, because Jean Chrétien was standing in the wings. This was the Jean Chrétien who masqueraded as a rube from Shawinigan, fresh off the turnip truck. Yet he had big-business credentials at least as valid as those of his predecessor. Having been beaten by John Turner for the leadership, Chrétien retreated to Bay Street, where he became a senior adviser to its premier stock-trader, Gordon Capital; he joined the board of the Toronto-Dominion Bank and was a director of other corporations with assets of $60 billion. *[Including Viceroy Resources, run by his friend Ross Fitzpatrick, whom he later named to the Senate, and Stone Consolidated of Chicago, the company that sold its 18-hole golf course at Grand-Mère to him and some friends for $1.25 million.]* Chrétien's daughter had married the son and *dauphin* of Paul Desmarais, one of his most enthusiastic and most generous backers. As minister of finance during the late 1970s, Chrétien had publicly confessed, "I don't do my budgets without consulting with de Business Council on National Issues."

That was not his mood when he was back in Ottawa as Opposition leader on a memorable winter evening in 1992. At one of the European ambassador's residences that dot Rockcliffe, there was a shouting match between d'Aquino and Chrétien that shook those who witnessed it. "There were four tables set out for dinner," d'Aquino recalls. "Jean and I were at the same one, but he was at one end and I at the other, talking with the ambassador. I could overhear him saying, 'You know de business community of Canada, it's done me in. I been trying to raise money for de party and I can't get no pennies out of dose guys, after all I did for dem. Dey're against me on free trade, dey're against me on inflation, dey're against me on the deficit, dey're against me on the constitution, where dey got no business sticking their nose. See dat big shot d'Aquino over dere? He's my problem cause he's leading dose big business guys!'

"It was becoming somewhat embarrassing," d'Aquino recalls, "so I said, 'You know, Jean, I really don't know why you're so up in arms. You've accused us of being great supporters of Brian Mulroney. Let me remind you that corporate Canada was largely supportive of John Turner, not Brian Mulroney. But that situation turned around very quickly because the party of Mitchell Sharp, the party of Bob Winters, the party of Paul Hellyer, the party of C.D. Howe, the party that had worked in a symbiotic relationship with big business in Canada to make this one of the wealthiest countries in the world, totally went off the deep end and started acting in a highly aberrant way. You want to fire John Crow, and we believe his policy on inflation is right. You want to rip up the Free Trade Agreement, and we are dead opposed to that. You said the deficit wasn't a problem, and you're dead wrong on that too. Instead of saying that you're glad to see that businessmen care about trying to keep this country together, you condemn us for sticking our nose in the constitutional debate.'

"The discussion got so heated that at one point I said, 'You know, Jean, the party you lead bears no resemblance to the party I once served, none whatsoever. In fact, you people are not qualified to run Tanzania!'"

The feud didn't last very long. One summer day after the Liberals had been elected, Chrétien called d'Aquino and asked if he and Aline could come over and see his house. *[The d'Aquinos live in a house designed by Hart Massey, cantilevered over McKay Lake, in the heart of Rockcliffe. When not occupying an official residence, the Chrétiens also own an Ottawa home built by Massey, purchased from Barney Danson, a former Liberal defence minister.]* The two couples spent three hours in pleasant chit-chat. After that, the Prime Minister had little problem implementing the BCNI's agenda. The circle had closed. *[John Crow was fired, but he was replaced by his deputy and think-alike clone, Gordon Thiessen.]*

The top BCNI priority at the time was to popularize the fight against the deficit. "We started right after the MacEachen budget in 1981," d'Aquino remembers. "At the time, we were constantly being dismissed by both the Liberals and the Conservatives, not to speak of the NDP. They said that we owe the money to ourselves, and that it was no big deal. I ran into Bob Rae within days of his election as premier of Ontario, and he pointedly told me, 'I guess you must have had night-mares about my being elected.'

"'On the contrary,' I replied, 'social democratic leaders all over the world today are fighting deficits. If that's the kind of social democracy you're bringing to Ontario, you're going to have my support.' He just walked away, but shortly after that, a small group of us went in to see him to make a strong argument that Ontario was heading for a very, very bad situation deficit-wise and he should do something about it. 'Tom,' he said, 'you've failed to make the intellectual case that there's any linkage between high interest rates and high deficits.'

"Now, Bob Rae doesn't believe that today," d'Aquino insists. "He and I were at the World Economic Forum together in Davos for several years running, where he saw the world was going in a different direction. By the time Rae left office, he had changed his mind.

"The Mulroneyites, for all their rhetoric that they were incredible slashers and burners, missed their deficit-cutting targets every single budget," d'Aquino complains. "People used to say that the business community and the Conservatives worked hand in glove. But some of the toughest letters I've written in my career were to Brian Mulroney, warning him again and again and again to cut the deficit. The long and the short of it was that after Chrétien was elected, we took that campaign in hand, and we scared the hell out of people. We said it over and over and over again for so long that people began to believe the deficit really was wicked. And so I look with great satisfaction on the fact that we are going to reach zero financial requirements federally by 1999, and that we have seven out of ten provinces at a fiscal balance. In very large measure that has been the BCNI's accomplishment. If you ask yourself, in which period since 1900 has Canada's business community had the most influence on public policy, I would say it was in the last twenty years. Look at what we stand for and look at what all the governments, all the major parties including Reform have done and what they want to do. They have adopted the agendas we've been fighting for in the past two decades.

"And we haven't finished. There's one last battle we have to win, and that's national unity. We've devoted an enormous amount of time to quiet diplomacy. People like Ted Newall in Calgary, Peter Bentley in Vancouver, Jean Monty and Guy Saint-Pierre in Montreal, Al Flood in Toronto and many others have led the way. No business community in the world at the CEO level has taken such an active interest in politics. We were very heavily involved promoting the Meech Lake and Charlottetown accords, and now we will be there for the last round-up.

"After the defeat of the Yes forces, on the night of the 1995 referendum, the entire BCNI membership was meeting in Toronto, at the Four Seasons Hotel," d'Aquino continues. "Mike Harris was with us, and it was an evening of great emotion. The next morning, Mike went off to Queen's Park to handle the media and we said to ourselves, this must never happen again—that this country would be caught as unprepared as we were this morning. We commissioned a major task force to study the rebalancing of the federation, including a devolution of powers that would strengthen the federation in three or four areas. We also talked about some very significant initiatives that would deal with the recognition of Quebec. Senior BCNI members in each province then met with all the premiers except Lucien Bouchard to push the idea—and that became the Calgary Accord of 1997.

At the end of June of that fateful summer, d'Aquino sent a seven-page letter to the prime minister. What it said in effect was, "Get out of the way." The Business Council on National Issues, speaking through its chief executive officer, made it crystal clear that the country's top 150 chief executive officers doubted the PM was up to the job. "The efforts made by your government to date are insufficient," d'Aquino admonished the prime minister, going on to request he bug out so that the provincial premiers could get on with the real nation-saving exercise. "The needs of Canadians must come before either partisan or jurisdictional interests," d'Aquino emphasized, urging the PM to "give heartfelt support to any worthwhile initiatives that may emerge from other levels of government."

WHOEVER HAS THE MONEY HAS THE power. With governments at all three levels deep in debt, the private sector had moved in to grab control. By the late 1990s, the conflict between the public sector and big business had largely evaporated. The same establishment that had reacted to the initiatives of the Trudeau Liberals with self-righteous rage was happy with the budget-slashing extravagances of Paul Martin. *[A former member of the BCNI, incidentally, during his time as CEO of Canada Steamship Lines.]* When the finance minister produced his deficit-slashing 1995 budget, d'Aquino awarded him the BCNI's ultimate imprimatur. "The Liberals," he decreed, "are now in the camp of correct economic thinking." Under Chrétien's sponsorship, the Liberal party had returned to its favourite pre-Trudeau political position of striking the most marketable balance between élitism and egalitarianism. That meant moving to the right of the political centre, but not far enough to allow a popular swing to develop behind the NDP. That formula made Tom d'Aquino's heart sing. His long day's journey into might had produced dramatic consequences.

The most far reaching of these was the Multilateral Agreement on Investment (MAI), which, until public protests started and eventually forced a postponement, the Chrétien government was prepared to sign.

A secret PMO (Prime Minister's Office) memo, leaked in *Maclean's* when the Canada–U.S. Free Trade Agreement was being negotiated in 1988, advised Brian Mulroney, then prime minister: "It is likely that the higher the profile the issue attains, the lower the degree of public support will be. Benign neglect from a majority of Canadians may be the realistic outcome of a well-executed communications program." That was certainly the approach adopted by Liberal trade minister Sergio Marchi, and it worked up to a point. Considering that twenty-nine countries, including Canada, had been negotiating the trade accord since May 1995, the proceedings were kept so secret that there wasn't a parliamentary debate on the issue, even though MAI represented the greatest threat to Canadian sovereignty since Canadians traded Pamela Anderson for Howard Stern.

It was as if the direction of Canada's future had surreptitiously been relegated to the BCNI—with a mandate to sign the country away. While nobody wholly understood the likely impact of the MAI, it amounted to Tom d'Aquino's dreams come true. He kept insisting that it simply formalized previous trade treaties, and that only through this kind of economic emancipation did Canada have a chance of protecting its independence. But in fact, no self-respecting country could sign such an agreement because its provisions robbed national government of the ability to impose even the most basic elements of sovereignty. The heart of the MAI was the edict that there ought to be no difference between domestic and foreign investors in any of the twenty-nine countries that make up the Organization for Economic Co-operation and Development. That would mean an end to protection of the economy, including the cultural industries, covered by domestic ownership rules. Everything would be wide open, up for grabs to the highest bidder, which in all likelihood would be some U.S. trans-national. Carla Hills, the U.S. trade representative, gave cause for concern when she summed up American trade intentions. "We want our corporations," she declared, "to be able to make investments overseas without being required to take local partners, to export a given percentage of their output, to use local parts or to meet a dozen other domestic restrictions."

The MAI went even further than that by endowing privately owned corporations with the power—but not the accountability—of nation-states. *[It was no coincidence that 488 of Fortune's 500 leading global corporations are domiciled in OECD countries and have been pushing for the MAI's ratification. Only five Canadian companies—BCE Inc., CIBC, George Weston Ltd., Royal Bank of Canada and Seagram Ltd.—make the list.]* The MAI would remove any remaining barriers and compromise the ability of governments to impose environmental standards, labour laws and patent exclusions that adversely affect foreign investors. The MAI battle has yet to be waged, but its objectives have not been abandoned.

Meanwhile, under Tom d'Aquino's leadership, the members of Canada's business establishment have good reason to believe they are running the country's economy. They formulated a solid agenda, put their muscle, their brains and their dollars behind it. Then they declared war on governments and battled out each outstanding public policy issue. Without ordinary citizens becoming aware of it, Ottawa capitulated. The regimes of Brian Mulroney and Jean Chrétien came to agree that what was good for the BCNI was good for Canada.

Tom d'Aquino had proven himself to be not only a brilliant political strategist on behalf of big business, but he emerged as the most powerful influence on public policy formation in Canadian history.

The Canadian Establishment is thus no longer merely a social group or a high-octane debating society. Operating through Tom d'Aquino and the Business Council on National Issues, its members have become a coherent instrument of unprecedented political power. A silent, seemingly bloodless war has delivered Canada's government into the hands of its former enemies—the market-worshipping Titans of the new economy.

2 THE TITANS

Introduction

THE HALF-DOZEN TITANS WHO ARE PROFILED here represent the most successful and fascinating of the new breed taking over Canada's Establishment. Each is a strong individual who has bullied his way into contention and lives by no rules except his own. Each has succeeded to the point where money is nothing except a way of keeping score. Each finds it difficult to feign humbleness and tends, like most self-made men, to worship his creator. Each operates outside Canada—some, like Issy Sharp and Gerry Schwartz, almost entirely outside the land of their origin. Nearly all run conglomerates, which are out of fashion because their earnings stream is too unfocused; yet there are few more successful Canadian-owned operations than Paul Desmarais's Power Corp., Gerry Schwartz's Onex or Peter Munk's ventures into gold and real estate.

My decision to select these particular Titans for closer attention is based on twin criteria. First, even though they run public companies, they act as proprietors, not only because they hold majority stock positions, but because they feel secure, if not always tranquil, in their possession of power. The second reason is that I have followed each of their careers from conception, and want to take a shot at adding to a fuller understanding of their lives, companies and operational codes. They are no angels, but as the Orwellian expression goes, I would happily go tiger hunting with any of them, if ever I went tiger hunting, which I won't.

8

KING PAUL

"My enemy now is time."

—*Paul Desmarais*

THE OLD TITAN REMINISCES AS WE SIT on his front porch. "I had the great advantage of being born in Sudbury," he says, "which is a truly bilingual community. So I could speak English and understand the English mentality. I grew up hanging around garages, drugstores and pool halls, fighting to speak French, yet going to school and playing hockey with mostly English-speaking kids." Few Canadians are more smoothly bilingual and bicultural than Paul Desmarais. But he is French. His ancestors came to Canada from Paris in 1657 and settled in Verchères, on the south shore, close to Ville-Marie at the foot of Mount Royal. In 1905, his grandfathers moved from Gatineau to northern Ontario as foremen for the CPR, supervising cuts of timber for railroad ties, and later owned a general store and a sawmill in the village of Noelville.

The assets he controls add up to $100 billion; his annual income is more than $33 million. *[For an outline of Desmarais's empire, see Appendix 5.]* The boy from Sudbury is now very rich and very powerful—and something more: he is a key political player in the matter of Canada's survival as a nation. Paul Desmarais grew up to be not only the dean of Canada's establishment, but a bold advocate for federalism. Canada as Sudbury. One nation, in which Quebec fought to speak French, surely, but not to secede.

His political convictions have long driven the radical nationalists wild. During the FLQ crisis, Paul Desmarais was regularly burned in effigy;

165

he was threatened with assassination so often that the Quebec police bluntly informed him they could not guarantee his safety. None of it cowed Desmarais, who made it his business to know and gauge the characters of Pierre Trudeau, Daniel Johnson (Sr.), Robert Bourassa and René Lévesque, and who chose to register his vote on separatism by all but ceasing to invest in Quebec, routing billions into new enterprises outside Canada for much of the past two decades.

Given that history, the "porch" on which Paul Desmarais and I speak is aptly located. This is actually the marble terrace of a 12,000-square-foot neoclassic manor house designed by the kid from Sudbury himself, and modelled on Thomas Jefferson's magnificent Monticello. Desmarais built it nowhere near Sudbury, but in Palm Beach, Florida, where the climate, political and otherwise, is nothing like home. *[Several Canadians regularly winter in this self-indulgent paradise, among them: from Montreal—Charles Bronfman, Marjorie Bronfman (Gerald's widow), Jonathan Deitcher, the RBC Dominion Securities investment dealer to the Canadian rich, Senator Normand Grimard, some Reitmans and Cummings; and from Toronto—George Mann, Steve Stavro and Conrad Black.]* Desmarais went to extremes to control every detail, even throwing up an artificial hill precisely high enough to cut off views of the road, so that from the house you may see, without distraction, straight out to the Atlantic.

All the better to contemplate Europe's gain and Canada's loss, for during those long years in which Paul Desmarais largely opted out of his native land's economy, he built instead a new business empire across the Atlantic. All the better to wonder, with Lucien Bouchard the latest prophet of Quebec separation, why the boy from Sudbury, now in his seventies, has lately been bringing his money back home again, to Canada.

AMONG TITANS, DESMARAIS IS IN A CLASS OF his own. He is the only major establishment figure whose hold on power has bridged all of my books, having been featured in my first volume, published nearly a quarter of a century ago, just as prominently as he is in this one.

Over the years, I have enjoyed a stormy relationship with the man whose aptly named Power Corporation ranks as the most remarkable example of how business power has been wielded and expanded in twentieth-century Canada. He seldom speaks to journalists, but Desmarais did open up to me when I was researching my original book. After he heard that it was locked up, but before he had seen its contents, he scribbled me a note: "If it's good, I'll buy five hundred copies. If it's no good, I'll buy all the copies."

He never made good on his promise, which was too bad because we were ready to keep the presses rolling. Instead, he decided to sue me. At issue was my description of one of his more intricate financial manoeuvres. He instructed his Toronto legal adviser, the formidable J.J. Robinette, to demand an injunction that would have prevented the book's publication.

Since the volume was already printed and awaiting distribution, the only way to deal with Desmarais's threat was to alter the text. To await litigation would have killed the entire project. So on a rainy October weekend in 1975, a dedicated group of McClelland & Stewart employees hand-pasted 75,000 paper patches of ten lines of reset type, one by one, over the offending paragraph. Desmarais later accused me of using bad glue. When I objected that we had tested it to make sure the sticker couldn't be ripped off, he exultantly exclaimed: "A friend of mine put your goddamn book in the freezer for two weeks, and the damn sticker just peeled off!"

Twenty years later, his dominant features seem ageless: the lively brown eyes disengaged from whatever may be occupying his mind; his almost successfully disguised stutter when he is emphasizing a point; the long, sensitive fingers and the thumb that curves outward, signalling a hot temper.

As we begin to talk, Desmarais's infectious enthusiasm takes over. When I tell him some high-level gossip about Conrad Black, his eyes widen, his eyebrows shoot straight up, his mouth opens in astonishment and he exclaims: "Well, what do you think of that!" He is not the richest Canadian—that honour goes to Ken Thomson—nor is he the most powerful, a distinction that can be claimed by Conrad, because he can make his influence and ideas felt through his newspapers. Yet Desmarais is the dominant role model for today's Titans. He elicits the same respect from them that climbers feel when they face a challenging mountain.

He has suffered several serious heart attacks and survived two major bypass operations. But Desmarais's sense of fun has hardly diminished. About halfway through our sessions, he launched into the previously untold story of how he saved Power Corp. from being taken over by the CPR—and just how close he came to losing his company.

This happened in the late 1970s when Ian Sinclair was the CPR's president and CEO. "Big Julie," as Sinclair was known, was a primitive corporate marauder, his ruthlessness softened by a sense of humour and a grudging respect for his tough opponents. Those whose businesses he coveted lived to regret any hopes of trying to best him. During one negotiation to buy the 25 percent of Algoma Steel held by Germany's

Mannesmann for $60 million, Big Julie came face to face with Egon Overbeck, then considered Germany's toughest industrialist. Overbeck had served as a member of the German general staff during the Second World War and had been wounded in action seven times. After four hours of having his arm twisted by Big Julie, the German caved in, confessing he had met his match. *[My own experience with Sinclair was typical. He at first adamantly refused to be part of the CBC's "Canadian Establishment" television series based on my first volume. Once he'd agreed to participate, he threw himself so enthusiastically into the project that he virtually took over its production. He invited the CBC unit into so many actual CP Ltd. board meetings that he had to swear in the camera crew as "insiders" to meet securites regulations.]*

At the time, Peter Thompson, one of the earliest Power partners, had a bar in his office at Power Corp., and Montreal Establishment types would gather there on Friday afternoons at five o'clock to talk about what had happened during the week. Desmarais went to one of these informal gabfests and found that Ian Sinclair was there, asking heavy questions about Power. As direct as always, Desmarais demanded, "Ian, are you trying to buy my goddamn company?"

"You either sell me Northern & Central Gas or I will bloody well buy your goddamn company," Sinclair replied.

Desmarais knew that he couldn't defend himself against any onslaught by the mighty CPR, but he shot back, "It's not for sale."

And so the two men decided to spend the evening talking about it, and started to drink. They went to the Château Champlain, which was the CPR hotel in Montreal at that time, and drank their way through a meal, then they went up to the hotel's roof, where there was a private club that Sinclair belonged to, and drank there. Afterwards, the CPR CEO ordered a suite in the hotel and they drank some more. It was three o'clock by the time they finished, and both men were very drunk. They went to Desmarais's house, but he couldn't find his key—or even his pocket—and when he finally did, he couldn't find the keyhole, so the staggering pair of corporate heavies used their shoulders to break down the front door. A startled Jacqueline Desmarais threw Sinclair out on the street.

The next morning, Desmarais, feeling very hung over, reserved a room at the Queen Elizabeth Hotel, and told his secretary that he was going to be at an important business conference all day. He slept for most of eight hours, but not before phoning his secretary and asking her to call Sinclair to tell him that he was at a conference all day, that Power Corp. was definitely not for sale, and that he'd get back to him later in the afternoon. Finally, at five o'clock, Desmarais went over to Windsor Station to see

Sinclair, who was sitting behind his desk, looking green and almost comatose, the sweat pouring off him. He had worked all day, and was so upset when his eyes focused on the smiling and vibrant-looking Desmarais that he gave up the whole scheme and Power Corp. was saved.

The anecdote tells a lot about Desmarais, but to conclude that he built his empire by bluff and the quick strike would be wrong. Desmarais is extraordinarily well focused and seldom rushes decisions. When he has a significant choice to make, he'll pick up the relevant file, examine the issue from every angle, put it aside until the patience of those around him has been tested beyond endurance, then postpone the decision one more time. Desmarais allows schemes to marinate, like pickled herring. *[Another mark of the Desmarais technique is the intricate and horrendously complicated corporate structure he employs to maintain control (see Appendix 5). For example, Power Corp. owns 67.7 percent of Power Financial, which owns 50 percent of Parjoint, which owns 55 percent of Pargesa Holding, which controls Desmarais's rapidly expanding companies in Europe.]* "I'm basically very conservative," he admits, "People say I'm a big risk-taker, but I'm not and never have been. I was very impatient when I was young and rushed the fences a lot. You think that if you push hard you can get things done efficiently. Taking your time is not always very efficient, but sometimes it's absolutely the necessary and best course." His deliberations are greatly enhanced by the think-tank that makes up Power's tiny head-office staff, currently including Jim Burns, Robert Gratton, Michael Pitfield, John Rae, Peter Kruyt, Michel Plessis-Bélair, Paul Morimanno and Denis Le Vasseur. One of the most valuable players, until he died in the spring of 1998, was Frank Knowles, a rare creature in that he was an enlightened and thoroughly human accountant.

Desmarais is always being accused of having cashed in on his good fortune, but luck had nothing to do with it. "It's the kind of luck," explains Jim Burns, Power's deputy chairman, "that strikes only when the co-ordinated planning, arithmetic, preparation and patience of the dozen minds that constitute Power Corporation are transformed into action by opportunity."

The best examples of Desmarais's superb timing were his sales of Montreal Trust and Consolidated-Bathurst in 1989. The paper and packaging company, one of Power's core holdings at the time, suddenly went into play early that year and was peddled sight unseen to Roger Stone, a Chicago entrepreneur. The price: $2.6 billion—50 percent over market value. Stone paid Desmarais a 50-percent premium over market value for his Connie-B shares and pledged to spend an extra $1 billion on modernizing the company's infrastructure—plus his $2.6-billion purchase price—without ever doing any due diligence or visiting any of its facilities. Stone paid out that much cash simply on Desmarais's word that the assets were as he described them. At about the same time, Desmarais sold Montreal Trust (at 23 percent over market value) to BCE for $547 million. These transactions left Power Corp. armed with a war chest of $1.5 billion in cash, and immeasurably enhanced Desmarais's reputation as a financial wizard—especially since pulp and paper prices dropped soon after the deals were closed, and a severe recession followed that seriously drove down the price of both companies.

With $1.5 billion in his jeans during an economic downturn, Desmarais appeared to be either a genius or inordinately far-sighted. "I was neither," he says. "I did my homework. I studied in detail Connie-Bathurst's goddamn cycles. Looking back, I found that every time I got my cash flow and profits up, the engineers at Connie-Bathurst would take over and say, this damn mill needs this and we've got to expand here and if we're going to be a global player we've got to do this or that. Jeez, we'd spend the money before I could lay my mitts on it. So I thought, to hell with it, if I get an offer I can't refuse, I'll take it."

That formula of homework plus timing has allowed Desmarais to negotiate some of history's most astonishing and complicated business deals. For the most part, he has expanded his company—and captured its original assets—through reverse takeovers. This is twentieth-century capitalism's favourite parlour trick: the target company pays for its own demise. "What you do," Desmarais explains, "is sell your assets to a company and with the proceeds buy the shares of the company that just acquired you." Simple. It's the minnow swallowing the whale, with the whale's consent. In other words, it's a leveraged buy-out under a less notorious label.

"Paul has the knack of making people believe in his vision, even when it's against their self-interest," I was told by one observer of his methods. "He is probably the only businessman in Canada who can make a pitch to a board of directors for the takeover of their own company and leave them in heat." Not coincidentally, he is the Titan with the longest pedigree, having been Power's chief shareholder and animating force for twenty-eight years. He built his once-modest company into Canada's premier financial conglomerate. (In the interval, he increased Power's market capitalization from $61 million to $2.6 billion, thus blessing shareholders with compounded annual returns of 16.4 percent.)

On May 10, 1996, the old Titan officially resigned his management positions at Power Corp. But this is no lion in winter, licking his paws, reflecting on past glories. Without a doubt, when Desmarais turned over the offices of chairman and CEO of Power Corporation to his sons, Paul Jr. and André, it was a genuine transfer of power. The two younger Desmarais are now running the company. But they don't own it. Their father walked out of that emotional 1996 annual meeting the same way he walked into it: with his controlling 64.7 percent of votes and 30 percent of equity shares of the company (that give him solid control) firmly tucked into his trouser pocket. Power Corp. of Canada has 12,213,693 participating preferred shares issued, with 10 to 1 voting rights. Paul Desmarais holds all of these. Another 98,538,201 subordinated voting shares (one vote per share) have been issued, with the senior Desmarais owning 21,343,925 of these, for a grand total of 33,494,773 shares in his account. This gives him 64.7 percent voting control, and the largest block (30 percent) of equity holdings. Since all shares pay a 90-percent dividend, his annual income from that source alone totals $31,145,285. His sons, both in their forties, are in charge, but it's Paul Senior's phone calls that cast deciding votes. He is chairman of the board's executive committee and holds the proxies. He plays at being retired, or as he says with an appropriate smirk, "semi-retired." But the eight bulging briefcases in his living-room say otherwise.

Paul Desmarais is still *Le Patron*.

IS IT SOMETHING SHREWD OR NEEDY IN THE man that makes him prefer the company of politicians? He collects them like rare butterflies. Most Desmarais receptions and boards of directors resemble parliamentary reunions. At one of his New Year's Eve parties at Palm Beach, his guests included Brian Mulroney, Pierre Trudeau and former Ontario premier Bill Davis, not to mention Dinah Shore, Estée Lauder, Douglas Fairbanks, Jr. and former Trudeau counsellor Jim Coutts.

"To hell with people who say I do it for political favours," says Desmarais. This, obviously, is a strong incentive, but it's not the whole story. He enjoys being part of history as it is being made, especially when heads of government consult him on various policy options. He loves being in the know. Since he regards himself as a platinum patriot, he sees nothing wrong with trying to influence national policies his way. While Desmarais treats political leaders with deference, it is the kind of deference due sleepwalkers—sleeping giants who must be led, ever so gently, lest they wake up to the fact.

Conrad Black explains Desmarais's affinity for politicians differently. "I suppose we're all unlicensed psychiatrists," he once told me. "Paul has a liking and envy for the positive way politicians can get up and easily present themselves to an electorate and stand there commending themselves to the voters' good consideration. He feels much more self-conscious than he should be about his slight speech impediment. It's like when you were a teenager and you have a blemish or something and worried about it, thought that it was much bigger than it was. But the reticences of other people rarely are logical. Paul really, in an odd way, is intrigued by politicians and always has been."

Whatever the reason, Desmarais has known every PM since Mackenzie King, and despite his later Liberal connections was particularly fond of John Diefenbaker. When he was a student at the University of Ottawa, his father would come from Sudbury once or twice a year to the nation's capital on business. Young Paul had recently written to Diefenbaker, asking to see him, and had received an invitation to lunch. "I was talking to my father, boasting how well I knew Diefenbaker, while we were at the Château Laurier hotel, when the elevator door opened and there was Diefenbaker. My father said, 'Would you present me?' So I said, 'Sure. Mr. Diefenbaker, I'm Paul Desmarais, I'm from Sudbury, and I would like you to meet my father, Jean Desmarais, who is a lawyer in Sudbury.' Dief, using his usual mangled French, said, 'John Des Mair, you've got a fine son here. I'm having lunch with him next week.' After that, I thought Diefenbaker really put the water in the ocean!"

One of Desmarais's favourite collectibles is Pierre Trudeau, who remains on Power Corp.'s international advisory board. They became close only after he reached power, but plans for Trudeau's candidacy had first been hatched in early 1968 at the offices of Power Corporation, at Friday-night meetings presided over by then-Power vice-president Claude Frenette. In August of that year, two months after Trudeau swept the country, the new PM flew to visit Desmarais at Murray Bay, where he has a summer home. When Desmarais picked up the PM at the airport in one of his two Rolls-Royces, Trudeau casually enquired what it was like to drive a Rolls. Desmarais promptly stopped the car, got into the back seat and, as Trudeau took the wheel, exclaimed, "This is the first time I've ever been driven by a prime minister!" Who says he's not a power groupie?

Only three years before, Desmarais had gone to Hawaii at a crucial moment in Quebec history. A semi-official Union Nationale document had come to light outlining the provincial government's confidential five-year plan for Quebec independence. After refusing to disown the scheme, premier Daniel Johnson had flown to Hawaii for a rest. Desmarais promptly joined him there, taking along a reporter from *La Presse* (which

Desmarais owns) and Marcel Faribault, the Montreal constitutional expert. The three men walked along the beach and debated the issue. Later Johnson told the journalist he would support a federalist constitution and that his administration had been given no mandate "to build a Great Wall of China around Quebec." It was easier back then to be a one-man rescue squad for Confederation.

The first time Desmarais met René Lévesque, who later became the province's first separatist premier, was comically strange. "I wanted to talk to him when he was a minister in the Lesage government, because we were thinking of buying the Dosco steel mill in Cape Breton. He was trying to build a steel mill when he was taking over Shawinigan Water & Power, because in those days every state wanted to have their own steel mill as a symbol of nationhood. So I thought the best way for him to do that was not to build anything new, but to buy Dosco, which was really defunct. My idea was to bring steel billets from Nova Scotia and turn them into usable steel in Quebec, where they already had a laminating plant. I knew that if we could put such a deal together, it would be a great thing. The federal government could come into it: we'd need lots of subsidies of course, and so on. And it was not too large an investment from our point of view. But René didn't understand financing very well. So I called him and said, 'I'd like to come and see you.'

"He said, 'No, I can't meet you.'

"And I said, 'Why?'

"And he said, 'It's none of your goddamn business.'

"'I have to see you.'

"'Well,' he said, 'I can't, my evening is taken.'

"I said, 'I'll go wherever you are.'

"So finally he said, 'I'm babysitting at my house in Outremont.'

"So I said, 'Well, I'll come and babysit with you.'

"He said, 'No, no.' And I didn't even know if he had any babies or what, but he was sitting. Anyway, finally he said, 'Okay, come over and see me, I'll give you half an hour.'

"So I went over. It was a very modest home, and we're sitting in this living-room and he said, 'Would you like a cup of coffee?' I said, 'Yes, thank you.' So he got up and he made the coffee. We kept on talking, and it finally got to be seven o'clock and he said, 'Would you like a little bit of cheese?' I said, 'Yes.' 'Would you like a beer with that?' I said, 'Sure.' So we had beer and cheese and crackers. And we kept on talking, had more cheese, more beer, more crackers, and we talked about all kinds of things. I stayed there till around midnight.

"And by that time, I said to myself: 'My God, this guy is a real social-ist! If he ever gets control, there will be nothing left in this place. I've got to get the hell out of this province.' I went home and called my partner, Jean Parisien, and I said, 'Jeez I've just finished talking to René Lévesque. Boy, is that guy a goddamn socialist!'

"As soon as he was elected premier, I saw René at the goddamn Mount Royal Club. The goddamn Montreal WASP establishment rushed to give him a reception, and I was kind of annoyed that they did that the day after his election as a separatist premier, and I didn't want to go. But I went over anyway, and I remember walking into the red salon. They had removed all the furniture and people were kind of circling him. As I walked into the room, he was standing alone right in the middle of the room, so I walked up to him and said, as loudly as I could, 'Bonjour, René.' He burst out laughing, but the English guys were all bothered about it . . ." True to his thoughts after his initial meeting with Lévesque, Desmarais stopped making major new investments in Quebec and Canada once the separatist politician was elected as premier, and in fact did not make a major domestic investment until the spring of 1997, when he bought control of London Life.

AFTER THE FIRST REFERENDUM ON QUEBEC SOVEREIGNTY, in 1980, Power's Canadian activities were put on hold. Without much fanfare, Paul Desmarais transferred his activities to Europe. There, he owns assets ranging from that continent's largest TV network (Compagnie Luxembourgeoise de Télédiffusion SA) to a Swiss salami maker (Rapelli). He has parlayed a $20-million transatlantic investment into yet another empire, duplicating his achievements in North America.

The turning away from his Canadian base really began, ironically, years before with a visit to Napoleon's old haunts. "Jackie and I went for a trip to Europe in 1959," he recalls. "In Paris, I visited the Paribas bank because I wanted to see the room where Napoleon had married Josephine, which is now the bank chairman's office. When I went there, they said I couldn't see the room unless I had an appointment with the chairman. So that was arranged, and when I went in I was told the room hadn't been changed since Napoleon was married in it. When I left, the chairman said, 'If you're ever in Paris again, come and see me.' So then I got to know those guys, and finally they invited me for lunch to tell them what I was doing in Canada, and of course I was progressing, and we started to talk business. That's when I began building my web of European connections and knowledge.

"I originally bought 5 percent of Paribas for $20 million in 1981 and was named a director. But we were turfed out, because France nationalized the banks. The opportunities came through the nationalization, because we were all turned out, we were all friends, we all had money, and the government paid us back the money we had invested."

When it came to getting his money back, it paid to know a few world leaders. "There was a meeting of the Group of Seven in Montebello in Quebec," Desmarais recounts. "We had been nationalized in France for about a year and hadn't been paid. I wanted my money, so I told Trudeau about it and he invited me, with about 150 people, to come to the Governor General's for a garden party held for the G-7 heads of government. Jean Chrétien had been assigned to take [then French president] François Mitterrand around the party. We were having drinks when there comes Jean with Mitterrand—so I told Mitterrand how we had been unjustly expropriated. But Mitterrand wasn't flustered at all. He was such a cool cat, he just looked at me and said, 'Pardon, monsieur.' And his security guys were getting very excited, but we had a good talk. Two days after, I got a phone call. The French ambassador came to see me, and within two weeks I was paid—all cash, in U.S. dollars!

"That was why we all found ourselves together, because of the nationalization. My friend Albert Frère had also been a director of Paribas. We ended up controlling Paribas's Swiss subsidiary bank, Pargessa. Then we formed the Groupe Bruxelles Lambert, which is kind of the Power Corp. of Belgium, of which we own 57 percent. Then there's Parfinance, our holding company in France, which controls Imetal, the old Rothschild group of companies. We also ended up controlling PetroFina, the world's eighth-largest oil company, with major holdings in the U.S. [It had sales of $28 billion in 1997.] We're partners in the largest European broadcasting network, with twenty-two TV and twenty-two radio stations in a dozen European countries. We also have 12 percent of the company that owns the Suez Canal. We now have $3 billion in cash in our European companies. And no debt."

ONE WAY TO MEASURE THE WILY TITAN'S LONGEVITY is by the missed opportunities and near disasters he has survived financially. The first was his attempt in the early 1980s to grab control of CPR.

To allay the boredom he felt at university, young Desmarais had worked out a complicated but feasible scheme by which an outsider might be able to capture stock control of CPR, and in August 1981 he decided to put it into effect. He bought, for $174 million, a 4.4-percent interest in the railway, and with his allies (mainly the Caisse de dépôt) eventually controlled more than 8 million shares, or 11.73 percent.

"They wanted to keep me the hell out," he recalls, "but they'd always say it in a very friendly, diplomatic way. They never said you can't have this goddamn company, or you can't do this or you can't do that. And I just pursued it. I'd go and see Ian and I'd say, hey, I'm going to buy some shares and he'd say, well I don't know if you should do that, what's it going to give you, what are you going to be able to do? Of course, after I bought them, he'd tell me, well then you might as well be on the board and then we'll see. Since I was an important shareholder, they sat me down next to Ian. To his right was Earle McLaughlin, then chairman of the Royal, as the senior director, and myself on the left.

"I probably could have done it, could have taken them over, but one day I decided I'd been at it a long time and I was either going to really participate in it or quit. I told Ian I wanted to be chairman of the executive committee, and they hesitated a great deal and asked me if I was going to buy more shares. I didn't think that was their prerogative, so I said no, I'm not going to buy any more shares. I went to see them a couple of weeks after and told them, I have to be chairman of the executive committee or I'm going to leave. When they said, we don't think we'll do that, I said, well that's fine, I'm gone. I had arranged to sell my shares that day, through Gordon Capital. I got $195 million and the stock went down after that quite a lot. But anyway, that was the end of that episode." . . . *[Not quite. In 1983, when Pierre Trudeau was spending Christmas with Paul Desmarais in Palm Beach, he decided to name Sinclair, who had just retired as CEO of CPR, to the Senate, and it was his task as prime minister to inform the lucky Ian. But Desmarais persuaded his friend Pierre that he should make the call, so that it looked as if he were making the appointment, and Sinclair had to thank him. That Christmas, Desmarais also called another Montreal pal, Leo Kolber, to announce the same honour, on behalf of an amused PM. Desmarais himself has been offered a Senate seat several times, but has always turned down the opportunity.]*

IN THE EARLY 1990S, DESMARAIS WENT INTO two highly risky ventures with equally dismal results. The first was a 1992 investment in three million shares (worth $1 billion) of Time Warner Inc., which if successful would have given him and his partner, Belgium's Albert Frère, control over the world's largest multimedia operation.

"Steve Ross, the chairman of Time Warner Inc., came to see me in Canada and we hit it off," Desmarais recalls. *[As part of the price for its merger with Warner Communications, Time Inc. agreed to pay Ross, then the Warner chairman,* *annual compensation that eventually reached $180 million.]* "I really liked him, and he appreciated what we were doing. We had long discussions. They were too long as a matter of fact. We were offered a very good first position in Time Warner, and I wanted to bring some of my friends in. We needed to make quite a substantial investment, which we could afford to do, and it would have given us effective control of the company. By putting in US$1 billion, we were offered twenty-year rights to buy shares at a fixed price. Steve Ross wanted to have me follow in his footsteps. Then he became ill. He had cancer of the prostate, and he still desperately wanted me to do it, but the idea died with him. I should have made that investment, but it took too long to do."

The other adventure was potentially much more lethal, because it involved the explosively controversial Drexel Burnham Lambert Inc., home office of convicted swindler Michael Milken, and a brokerage that ended up triggering the biggest Wall Street scandal of the 1980s. It never made the news, but it was a fact that through his European companies Desmarais was the firm's largest shareholder, with nearly 40 percent of the equity at one point. He very nearly became its majority owner, which would have placed him in serious legal jeopardy.

"Groupe Bruxelles Lambert, one of our European partners, had a merchant bank in New York which merged with Drexel, and that was how we initially became 20-percent shareholders in Drexel," Desmarais explains. "When they were making billions of dollars, we were making good money. When they made $2 billion, we made $400 million. But the people running it were taking out such large bonuses—they paid $1 billion to Mike Milken, for example—so that by the time they were finished, there was very little profit left. They were in control of the company and we couldn't do anything about it. They were financing the takeover of America with these junk bonds they had originated. I even had dreams that maybe I should get on that bandwagon and take over General Motors, but I never did do anything with junk bonds; I was too afraid of the high interest rates they charged. I'd met Milken and found him a brilliant man. He'd do three things at the same time. You'd be talking to him and he'd have at least two other guys there and be talking to all of us. I had trouble concentrating, but he didn't. *[Actually, he did. During his subsequent trial, Milken testified that he could not recall many details of his trading activities because when he was talking to someone, he would usually be carrying on several conversations, either in his office or on his bank of telephones. Testified Milken: "I would say that I listened to no more than 25 percent of the conversation I had during my trading days. I would tune in and out, buy and sell securities during any conversation." That may even have been true. During one interview with* The San Francisco Chronicle, *Milken couldn't recall the name of the best man at his wedding or his wife's middle name.]*

"Anyway," Desmarais recalls, "I invited the guy who was running Drexel, Fred Joseph, to Murray Bay. He was a very nice man, a charming young fellow and very straightforward. But when Ivan Boesky testified that he had been involved with Drexel Burnham, the American Securities Commissions and everybody else got into it. I was horrified to discover that we owned 39 percent of Drexel, because its partners had been cashing in their shares.

"One day, I was in New York and had lunch with that nice young man Fred Joseph. As a joke I said, 'Fred, I think this month you're going to lose $100 million, next month you'll lose $200 million and the month after that you'll lose $300 million.' It had been said in jest, but all he answered was, 'Yeah, maybe so.' I didn't say anything but just continued eating, then quickly got a room at the Waldorf Towers and called my Paris office and told them, 'You guys are crazy! I'm telling you, Drexel's going broke, sure as hell.' And they said, 'Well we're thinking of contributing to their request for increased capital.'" As late as January 9, 1989, Gerard Eskenazy, the head of Power Corp.'s Swiss holding company, told Mathew Horsman of *The Financial Post*, "We have a great deal of confidence in Drexel's future and in their ability to overcome their present problems."

"How much?" Desmarais yelled into the phone. The answer was $150 million, "just a drop in the bucket," by Desmarais's figuring, compared to what Drexel was about to hemorrhage.

His response: "'You're goddamn *not* going to put in $150 million, and you're going to tell them that we're not going to participate in any damn increased capital!'

"The whole Drexel thing was shut down the next day. That was the end of Drexel Burnham. It could have lasted maybe three more days if we had put the money in, and we'd have been in for over 50 per. Jeez, it was close."

By the end of 1989, Drexel Burnham Lambert had pleaded guilty to six felony counts, five of them involving fraudulent transactions with the notorious Boesky. The charges outlined a pervasive pattern of illicit practices by the junk bond dealer, including elaborate schemes to gouge Drexel's own customers. Massachusetts congressman Edward Markey, who headed a congressional subcommittee on finance, charged that the single most successful firm on Wall Street during the 1980s had "built its fortune largely on a foundation of criminality." Connie Bruck, the lawyer-author who wrote a book on the subject, described the firm as "the brass knuckles, threatening, market-manipulating Cosa Nostra of the securities world"—and went on extensively to document her thesis.

Drexel's punishment for its thuggery was a fine of $780 million, the largest ever levied in any stock fraud case, but small change for that "nice young man" Fred Joseph, who had already created a reserve within company accounts for the fines he expected to pay. It was one time that Desmarais had badly misjudged his partners, and it was only because Drexel was run not as a Power subsidiary but as a free-standing company that none of the mud stuck to him.

IT WAS ANOTHER UNHAPPY EXPERIENCE THAT CEMENTED Desmarais's sometimes strained bond with fellow Titan Conrad Black. The entwinement began when Desmarais attempted to grab Bud McDougald's Argus Corporation in 1975. *[The full story is told in the first volume of my Canadian Establishment series.]* He purchased 51 percent of the holding company's equity, but gained only 26 percent of the votes. That obvious bias against Desmarais prompted an Argus board member to ask chairman Bud McDougald why Fred Eaton, who had just been named to the Argus board, had become a director when he didn't own any shares, while Desmarais, who had a lot more than the chairman, was being kept out. To which McDougald's entire reply was, "Some are asked and some are not." Later, when Conrad Black took over Argus, he repurchased Desmarais's shares, and the two men grew closer together.

Desmarais's most vivid memory of Conrad Black is of the time he tried to console him—and how it backfired. "I was in Paris and Conrad was really in the dumps. He was trying to buy this goddamn newspaper in the United Kingdom and everything was not going right. So I called him in Toronto from Paris.

"'Well,' he said, 'I'm trying to do this and do that and the banks won't lend me the money.' 'Look,' I said, 'I'm going back to Montreal next week, I'll come and see you and we'll get more details about what the hell you're doing.' I saw all this mess and I figured Jesus Christ I'd better talk to him and see what I could do.

"Anyway, I went to see him. Flew into Toronto when it was snowing. I can't remember the date. I get to the airport, couldn't get a goddamn car, had a hell of a time. Finally, I got a taxi and arrived at his place. It was seven or eight o'clock. His gate is half open, so I had to get out of the car—I'm in my shoes in the snow—and push open the gate. We get to his house and there's snow against the front door. I bang on the door;

no answer. Goddamn, was I mad. And all of a sudden, the door opens and it's his kid, Jonathan, saying, 'How do you do, sir, come in, Mr. Desmarais. My father is waiting for you in the library.'

"Conrad is sitting there like the bloody King of England behind his desk in his pope's chair and all the flags behind him. So I said, 'Conrad, what the hell are you doing? Why are you goddamn depressed?' 'Ah,' he said, 'I'm having problems . . .' So anyway, he needed money from the bank and nobody would give him any. I said, 'Jesus Christ, things have a way of working out, and you'll be okay.' It was just a friendly visit. We had a couple of Scotches, I left there about 11:30, went back to the airport in the snow, got home.

"The next day, I talked to the prime minister and I said, 'Brian, jeez, Conrad's having a tough time, why don't you call him?' And that was the end of it.

"But when I read his damn book, Conrad says that Mr. Desmarais came to visit me and it was quite nice of him to do that, but I resent his indiscretion in having spoken to the prime minister of Canada to tell him I was in trouble! So I called Conrad and I said, 'Are you crazy? I'm a friend of yours, you're making other people believe that I'm a shit that I would go and find out that you're not doing well. Don't you realize everybody in Canada was saying that you're going broke, for Christ's sake, and that if I talked to the prime minister of Canada, don't you think that he already knew, and did he not call you?'

"'Yes,' he says, 'the prime minister is the one who told me that you said I was having problems.'

"I said, 'You see, you're such a negative son of a bitch, such a schemer, that you always think people are after you. Goddamn it, why can't you believe that somebody is nice and wonderful and a great friend? One of these days, something is going to go wrong and there will be nobody there to do a damn thing for you.'

"When we bought our shares in Southam, Conrad and I became partners," Desmarais goes on. "But our methods of operating were different. He wanted us to cut more costs in a more brutal way than we were thinking of doing. So at one point I said, 'Look, you're going to run it or I'm going to run it, but we both can't do it. So why don't we split it, and I'll take the larger newspapers and you take all the smaller ones. He said, 'Well okay.' But the Southam board of directors was against it. So I called him and I said, 'Conrad do you want to buy goddamn Southam today?' And he said, 'Yes, I do.' I said, 'Okay, the company is yours.' And when we decided to get out, it was done efficiently, effectively and quickly.

"I enjoy Conrad. I like his turns of phrase. He has the most convoluted vocabulary in the world, and he loves it. I'm like an uncle to him now and we laugh a lot, though he occasionally says some nasty things. When Conrad decides that he's going to do something, he surrounds himself with tough cookies and lets them take the rap. But he's very tough himself, of course he is."

WITH A SURROGATE NEPHEW LIKE CONRAD BLACK, YOU LEARN TO appreciate a mate like Jacqueline Desmarais. She is a talented singer, plays championship bridge, has a 12 handicap in golf and is the vibrant centre of Paul's life. *[She has cut half a dozen privately distributed albums, including* Back to Dry Martinis *and* Songs I Love to Sing, *backed by a twelve-piece band. Her voice is a rhythmic mix of Ella Fitzgerald and Edith Piaf. She frequently sings live duets with Robert Charlebois.]* "If I was to say, look Jackie, I'm going to start a passenger service to the moon tomorrow, she'd say, that's a great idea, babe, why don't you do that," proudly boasts her husband of forty-five years. "She seems to think that I can do anything." (So does he.)

When Paul wants to surprise Jacqueline, as he did on one of her decade-marking birthdays, in 1988, it's not a let's-order-pizza-in affair. On that occasion, he took over Montreal's Windsor Hotel. Guests gathered along its long marble promenade, among its ornate mirrors and columns, with specially mounted gold trellises spilling freshly opened roses, and fancily clad hussars opening the doors to a ballroom where a symphony orchestra played Viennese waltzes. Later in the evening, Ella Fitzgerald and Robert Charlebois sang for the crowd, which included the governor general, the prime minister and Quebec's premier, plus their spouses.

They're a closely knit family. Daughters Louise and Sophie lead private lives. The boys have been groomed for their ascent to the Power throne for the past fifteen years. "When I was growing up," Desmarais recalls, "I was the fourth of eight children, right in the middle, so I was the one who was ignored all the time. The younger ones didn't want to play with me and the older ones always told me to buzz off. So my father took me with him wherever he'd go, to the courthouse and even fishing. I was with older people most of the time and learned a lot. I've done that with my sons, taking them everywhere. I enjoy it, but a lot of people were kind of annoyed that they'd invite me and I'd say, is it all right if I bring the boys? They'd say, oh shit, not those two little kids again." It seems to have been worth it. The Desmarais boys today are both intelligent, lightning fast with figures and capable of negotiating with anybody; they seem born to rule.

When not in Palm Beach, the Desmarais family is to be found at one of three Canadian dwellings or, if in Europe, at Claridge's Hotel in London or the Ritz in Paris. The Montreal house on Westmount's Ramezay Road was originally decorated by Lou Edwards, E.P. Taylor's daughter. The large living-room, done in lemon and pale aqua, has a stunning Diego Rivera canvas as its centrepiece.

Desmarais's favourite *pied-à-terre* is La Malbaie (Murray Bay), near the mouth of the Saguenay River. It was once a prestigious resort, the home of the Cabots of Boston, the Tafts of Ohio and the Hamilton Fishes of New York. Desmarais bought the house for $60,000 from Leo Timmins, of Hollinger Mines fame. It's on the Boulevard des Falaises, on a bluff overlooking the St. Lawrence. He has added a swimming pool, sauna and tennis court. The garage holds his 1906 Cadillac, a motorcycle and two Rolls-Royces, one of which is fitted with a horn that sounds like a steam locomotive. "This is the place we're happiest in," he says. Inland from La Malbaie is his château, a country estate with a hunting lodge that can accommodate forty guests, built on a wild stretch of land—a 10,000-acre property with fifty lakes on it—that once belonged to Canada Steamship Lines.

Moving from place to place, especially when he's doing business in Europe, Desmarais climbs aboard his Challenger jet, which he is upgrading to a Canadair Global Express in 1999.

The Desmarais offices in Montreal are like nothing else in Canada (except perhaps Peter Munk's private study in his new Forest Hill mansion). On first impression, Power Corp.'s building resembles one of the minor, outlying pavilions at Versailles; on closer inspection, it resembles Versailles itself—but with the patina of good taste. Done in a classic Louis XIV style, its creamy pillars and long marble corridors with arching, ten-metre ceilings, the richness of its plush velvet drapes, scattered sculptures and weathered woods lend the place a solemn, almost churchly resonance. The walls are crowded with the most valuable corporate collection of Canadian art in the country—dozens of canvases by A.Y. Jackson, Clarence Gagnon, Maurice Cullen, Goodridge Roberts, Frederick Varley, James Wilson Morrice (a whole wall of them), David Milne, Tom Thomson, Homer Watson, Jean-Paul Lemieux, Franz Johnston, Arthur Lismer and Jean-Paul Riopelle. The boardroom has forty-five exquisitely mounted Cornelius Krieghoffs.

ALL OF THIS IS A LIFETIME AND A WORLD away from the pool halls of Sudbury, certainly, but the popular myth that Desmarais's success was totally self-made is nevertheless a stretch. He did grow up with certain privileges. The Desmarais family was well respected and relatively well heeled. Paul's grandfather had helped found the local Sacred Heart College, formed the first local Caisse DesJardins co-op and helped finance the St. Joseph Oratory in Montreal. He became a quite prosperous lumberman through his wooden-tie contracts for building of the CP and CN from North Bay to Winnipeg. His uncle was mayor of Sudbury in 1939—the only year it mattered, because that was when the King and Queen came to town, so the family had their pictures taken with the royal pair. Paul's father was a successful Sudbury lawyer who helped found Laurentian University. Out of that background plus his own success came the self-confidence that allowed Desmarais to grow personally and professionally without having to overcome the deference that marked his generation.

"I had no trouble going and sitting at the goddamn Mount Royal Club and telling the chairman of the Royal Bank or anybody else, what the hell is wrong with you that you keep complaining about 'those damn French Canadians'." Diehard members of English Canada's Establishment regard him as a welcome ambassador from Quebec, a part of the country most of them view with only slightly less comprehension than some distant Transylvania.

While Quebec does loom large in the accent of Paul Desmarais's speech, he is more properly reckoned with as one of the planet's best-connected inhabitants. Among a circle of prominent advisers nurtured by Desmarais are the following, formally gathered in his Power advisory committees: Pierre Elliott Trudeau; Helmut Schmidt, who was federal chancellor of Germany from 1974 to 1982; Gustavo Cisneros, the head of a huge industrial complex in Venezuela; Wei Ming Yi, Chairman of the China International Trust & Investment Corporation in Beijing; Junichi Amano, president, Nihon Unisys Ltd.; Ross Johnson, formerly with RJR Nabisco; Charles Bronfman, co-chair, Seagram's; André Levy-Lang, chairman of Compagnie Financière de Paribas; Sylvia Ostry of the University of Toronto's Centre for International Studies; Sheikh Ahmed Zaki Yamani, chairman of the Centre for Global Energy Studies, Saudi Arabia; Paul Volker, former Federal Reserve Board chairman; Lord Armstrong of Ilminster, Rothschild & Sons, London; Viscount Rothermere, chairman, *Daily Mail*, London; and Baron Frère, chairman of PetroFina, Belgium.

With the current Liberal administration in Ottawa, Desmarais enjoys his usual gold-plated access. Apart from the fact that Jean Chrétien's daughter France is married to Desmarais's son André, the old Titan is extremely close to Finance Minister Paul Martin, who spent most of his working life at Power Corp., running Canada Steamship Lines. (In a classic reverse takeover, Desmarais allowed Martin to buy CSL from him, and even signed a bank note on his behalf to help cover the $195-million purchase price.) One of Power Corp.'s senior vice-presidents is John Rae, who served as executive assistant to Jean Chrétien in Indian Affairs and managed his triumphant 1993 and 1997 election campaigns. The bright and affable older son of former ambassador Saul Rae, and brother of the former Ontario premier, he provides the intense and high-brow headquarters gang with a human face. Other political operatives who have worked or are working for Desmarais include former Ontario premiers Bill Davis and John Robarts, former Quebec premiers Daniel (Jr.) and Pierre-Marc Johnson, former Trudeau aides Ted Johnson and Joel Bell, former Liberal cabinet ministers Maurice Sauvé, Jean-Luc Pépin and Bryce Mackasey, and all-round Liberal party guru Claude Frenette. Most recently, Don Mazankowski, deputy prime minister in the Mulroney government, joined the Power board.

"Paul is a master manager of the political process," says Michael Pit-field, Clerk of the Privy Council during the Trudeau years, whom Des-marais tagged to be deputy chairman of Power Corp. in 1984. The scion of a wealthy and influential Montreal family, Pitfield was a public servant most of his life, but once freed of his responsibilities (and wafted off to the Senate) he began to appreciate the private sector's role. "It never ceases to amaze me that so few people recognize that businessmen are responsible for shaping the whole country's infrastructure."

Exhibit A is his own boss. "The easy thing to think about Paul is that he has the politicians in his pocket," continues Pitfield, "that he's a sort of master of marionettes. But he's not. He's a player. He never disengages; he never withdraws from the arena. He made an enormous fortune by age thirty-five and has ever since been engaged in the active governance of this country. Most people automatically assume that Paul's policy involvements are designed to make him richer, that he tries to control people and events to get some desired, selfish result. In fact, he's an active participant, using his power base to press for what he thinks are desirable policies. It's very important to understand that distinction."

When Pitfield was hired, he was handed two assignments: to be an in-house guru for Power's operational activities, and to mastermind the transition from Desmarais to his two sons. As a private tutor for the boys, he has massaged their views on economics and political science as well as instilling in them a feeling for Canada that they might otherwise have lacked. Of Pitfield, the elder Desmarais says: "He's a very intelligent, a far-seeing fellow. He's very tedious in the sense that, if you ask him a question, he's got three answers or four possibilities, maybe ten, and if you listen to them all you have to be patient. But it's wise to listen to him because sometimes he brings up things that you'd never think of. It's good to have somebody to talk to in great confidence about what you're planning to do or what you're thinking about doing, and he'll shoot you down very fast or he'll show you how to do it in a more practical way. That's why I wanted him—plus he has a profound knowledge of how Canadian government functions."

Desmarais's most profoundly personal friendship with any politician is with Brian Mulroney, who, after he left office, was appointed to several important European boards within the Power Corp. empire and resumed his function as one of its chief legal advisers. "He may turn out to have been a great prime minister. We need more time to assess his record," says Desmarais. "If you look at the big things—Meech, free trade, our relationship with the U.S. all that was much improved by him. The trouble is that he was too loyal to his friends, and some of his friends people he shouldn't have been too loyal to—took advantage of him. He should have told them, look, this is where you get off, I'm prime minister of Canada, I have a job to do and you have your own goddamn interests, so look after your interests but don't come to me.

"I always thought," continues Desmarais, "that I couldn't impose on political figures and ask them to do something for me and still be a friend of theirs. If I was going to render any service to the country, I could do it by giving these guys my policy positions. Now, if there was really a socialist elected, I mean, it would be no compromise. I wouldn't believe in it and I wouldn't have anything to do with him. I'm not going to participate in policies that I think are going to destroy the country. With others, I try to help."

Not surprisingly, the advice Desmarais renders inquiring prime ministers is that business in Canada must be allowed to grow bigger and bigger and bigger. While he has no problem with policies that guarantee every Canadian an equal start in terms of education, health care and job opportunities, he draws the line at equal outcomes. "Canadians," he asserts, "not only want everybody to start together, they want everybody to finish at the same time in the same place. And if somebody wins, then they take it away from them, so there's no incentive to do anything. Canadians always think that if something is accomplished, it's because you've got an in with somebody, with a boss or a politician. Hell, it's hard work, it's persistence, it's patience, it's vision."

The funny thing about Paul Desmarais is that, while he is adroit at amassing political capital, he has often failed to convert it into outright capital. In fact, a case could be made that he has had very little luck getting politicians to support his schemes. Robert Bourassa, for example, proved almost perverse in his non-cooperation. It began back in 1973, when Desmarais had made a bid for the UniMédia chain of newspapers, then owned by Jacques Francoeur, which included *Le Soleil* and *Le Droit*, in Quebec City and Ottawa. Conrad Black was bidding for the property at the same time and Bourassa backed his position, telephoning him after every private visit from Desmarais, urging him to keep up the pressure.

"Bourassa really didn't want me to have *Le Soleil* and played his cards in such a way that anybody but me would get it. 'You shouldn't have all the newspapers in the province,' he kept telling me, and I said, 'Look, it doesn't make a damn bit of difference whether I have all the newspapers in the province. Jeez, there are so many other papers and so many other ways of getting news, for God's sake.' But he had that fixation. And when Conrad bought it, I said to Bourassa, 'Well, Jesus Christ, are you happy now—you have an English instead of a French Canadian in charge!'"

Not only did Robert Bourassa stop Desmarais from acquiring Uni-Média, but along with Ottawa he also vetoed Desmarais's intended purchase of Montreal's powerful Télé-Metropole and seven TV outlets. The feds ignored his application to buy Teleglobe, and though he was granted a licence for direct-to-home satellite television, the CRTC's stringent conditions made the venture unworkable. "Maybe I went a little too fast," Desmarais admits in a Titan's rare concession to critics of mega-capitalism. "After I bought the newspaper in Sherbrooke, I decided to buy every damn newspaper in the province because it was such a good business. When I got going, I had them all on option and the government moved in and stopped me. Maybe," he muses, "there *was* a little too much concentration of power."

In the end, he concludes, it all comes down to who you know and how you play it. "A lot of politicians think you're a pain in the ass if you're trying to give them too much advice, so I try to avoid that. I've never held it against them when they did unkind things to me, and they've done plenty. Bourassa did and so did Brian Mulroney. We got some real good kicks in the ass.

"Still," Paul Desmarais admits, bringing his theories of politicking back to certain facts of life that are indisputable and eternally motivating, "it's been a great advantage to be able to say, 'Well I know the prime minister of Canada, and I know what he's thinking.'"

WHAT, THEN, WAS PAUL DESMARAIS THINKING in the autumn of 1997, when his Power Corp. suddenly lunged to life after a long sleep in the land of his birth? Power made a pre-emptive $3-billion bid for London Insurance Group Inc., after the Royal Bank had already claimed its possession through an earlier offer. When the smoke cleared, London was merged with Great-West Life, another Power holding.

The contest between Desmarais and the Royal Bank was particularly fascinating because that was the bank that gave him the credit to start Power Corporation. At the time, Earle McLaughlin (who was the Royal's chairman) and Desmarais were good friends, but joshingly kept threatening to fire each other. "Earle," Desmarais recalled, "who was a Power director, told me that if I didn't have those ten-for-one votes to maintain control, he would have voted me out long ago, and I told him that if banks didn't have that goddamn 10 percent rule, I would have fired him. And then we both laughed." This time, nobody was laughing. "I should have bought the Royal a long time ago," says Desmarais.

The Desmarais move on London Life was exquisitely timed, jibing with the public sentiment against the idea of the big chartered banks taking over all of the country's financial services. The insurance firms were the last holdouts. Great-West and London Life also enjoyed great synergy in their corporate cultures, since their areas of specialization— London is largest in individual life, while Great-West leads in group policies—melded beautifully. The merger, the biggest commercial transaction of the year, formed the country's largest insurance company. It was Power's first major Canadian expansion in more than two decades.

Couple with that Desmarais's successful initiative to form business connections between his homeland and China. He was one of the first Canadian businessmen officially to visit that country, setting up the China Canada Business Council, ably run by Jack Austin. Desmarais is in partnership with Peter Munk to develop China's gold mines and with Laurent Beaudoin to sell railway cars to the Chinese. First among Canadian businessmen, he has managed to attract major Chinese capital into Canada: $50 million to build a pulp mill in Castlegar, B.C., in partnership with one of his companies.

Since Desmarais stopped investing in Quebec in the early 1980s (his only significant holdings there are a dozen small radio stations and the newspaper *La Presse*), his Canadian base of operations has shifted to Winnipeg. He controls the Manitoba capital's Investors Syndicate, the country's largest and most successful mutual fund operation (assets of $34 billion), run by Sandy Riley, which will be a major investor in London

Life. Winnipeg is also the home of Great-West Life, which has assets of more than $53 billion after its London acquisition. A tip-off to Great-West's significance within the Power group is that Desmarais usually assigns two or three of the holding company's directors to serve on the board of each subsidiary; but the Great-West board includes nearly the whole Power house—not only Desmarais and his two sons, but Power CEO Robert Gratton, vice- and deputy chairmen Michael Pitfield and Jim Burns, chief financial officer Michel Plessis-Bélair, as well as Power director Don Mazankowski.

So how to read this great homecoming of Paul Desmarais's investment and attention? Does it portend more than profitable opportunities seized? Might the old Titan find in today's Canada, run by his favoured Liberals, with Lucien Bouchard's separatists on the defensive, a shining example of his Sudbury dream renewed?

Desmarais is not willing to make such sweeping pronouncements—yet. Within Quebec, he still is considered something of an outsider—a man who was born and raised in Ontario, who established and enlarged his impressive credit sources entirely through sympathetic support from the major WASP financial institutions. To those Quebeckers who believe in both federalism and capitalism, he provides a useful symbol of what can be achieved within the system, though Laurent Beaudoin of Bombardier and several other, younger entrepreneurs are now competing for that crown.

"Of course, in rural Quebec there is still the power of the nationalists, which is the old power of the Catholic Church that keeps French Canadians in the background. To them, it's the Jacques Parizeaus of this world that say: 'This is my parish, the province of Quebec. Stay out of there and I'll negotiate because I'm the big shot.'"

The conversation turns, again, to his old antagonist, a dead politician who left Paul Desmarais some surprising words at the end, even if he never did much to help while in office. "Robert Bourassa," says Desmarais, "really was a balancing act. He had his heart split in two. First he was a Canadian and then he was a Quebecker, and he kept puzzling if he was a Canadian first or a Quebecker first. He never resolved that. When I spoke to Bourassa, only three days before he died, he said to me, 'You know, the province of Quebec has all the powers it needs to accomplish what it wants to do, all the powers it needs to protect its language and its culture—if we would only get on with it.' If you say that in your book, people won't believe it—but that's what he told me.

"I would like to see the separatist issue resolved sooner rather than later so that we're not left behind the eight-ball and are treated like a bunch of hicks by a group of nationalist dictators in a separate Quebec," declares Paul Desmarais, warily staring out at the Atlantic from his Monticello terrace in Palm Beach, USA. "I'm still not sure about Lucien Bouchard, whether he's a real separatist or not."

WE HAVE BEEN TALKING FOR MOST OF TWO DAYS. The Desmarais household is reclaiming the living-room, which was our debriefing chamber. Desmarais is in his summing-up mood.

"I've been like a fisherman who goes out and puts out a net, and if he's lucky, he gets a good catch. But sometimes, even if he's a good fisherman, he gets nothing. Well, I spent a lot of time putting out nets and finally, over a long period of time, I've been lucky. But it's not just luck; it's hard work. You've got to expose yourself to the fish precisely when circumstances are favourable . . . We have a lot of capital now, much more than I ever dreamed possible, really. There are a lot of things I'd like to accomplish still. I sometimes ask myself, why don't you stop? With everything you have, there is a corresponding responsibility—and after a while it becomes a heavy burden. But the fascination to go on never stops . . ."

He trails off and I notice that night has come. There is no wedge of light remaining between the ocean and the horizon. "My enemy now is time," he says as we part.

There will never be another Titan quite like this one. He was the forerunner. Long before the Titans came along, he showed them the way. He demonstrated that you could outwit and outcharm and, if necessary, outbully your competitors, annihilate them, have fun doing it, and never feel a moment's guilt. The other Titans watch him, study him, try to copy him—like apprentice Sioux learning to shadow a great buffalo—but his essence remains elusive and inviolate. In a world filled with corporate honchos who act like constipated eagles, Paul Desmarais is a refreshing exception.

I climb into my rented car and drive back to my hotel, past the darkened Palm Beach mansions. It was an interview to remember. Now, I just hope the mighty Paul doesn't put this damn book in his goddamn freezer.

9

MUNKY-SEE,
MUNKY-DO

"The goddamn real-estate business. It's the graveyard of the human ego."

—*Peter Munk, chairman of TrizecHahn.*

IAN DELANEY, FIDEL CASTRO'S FAVOURITE CAPITALIST, won his corporate spurs working for Peter Munk. He was for a time second in command of Munk's formidable empire as president and chief executive officer of Horsham Corp., its central holding and management arm.

He got to know his boss well. "There aren't too many people I've worked for," he says, "who I am prepared to admit have altered my view of business, but Peter Munk is certainly one of them. His style, his energy, his inability to ever stay down when he's been knocked over, the brilliant way he articulates objectives—both internally and externally—and changes them if necessary. He is absolutely undaunted by the size and scope of any project. He thinks on a scale that would stagger most people. His forbearance and his generosity, his judgment, his . . ."

Delaney goes on citing Munk's stellar qualities as if he were reciting some sort of pagan catechism about a long-departed hero or martyr.

"But," I say.

"Oh yeah, well, of course, he fired me," admits Delaney. "He was the controlling shareholder, and I was the chief executive officer, and I wanted to have things my way. Obviously incompatible. So he fired me."

Why hasn't that made Delaney bitter?

"Frankly," he says, "I would have fired me a year and a half before he did."

A small taste of the Munk magic.

SIMONE SIGNORET, THE FRENCH FILM STAR, ONCE observed that trying to explain the secrets of acting was impossible. "You shouldn't try to explain the mystery inside you," she said. "You either have it, or you haven't."

Peter Munk has it. It's the perfect analogy. Munk is an actor. He has a dozen faces. His expression seldom changes, but his appearance shifts with his moods. One moment he looks as confused as an usher at a shotgun wedding, so uncertain of his cause that he stutters and stumbles. Ten seconds later, he has the magisterial bearing of a pope presuming worship. Same guy, different mood. Those who know him most intimately—all three of them—swear that he is a false extrovert, aggressive and demonstrative when the occasion requires visible strength. But more often, he is remote and private, a man whose countenance betrays the fact that he has travelled some lonely terrain in his time. He has been at the top, and he has been at the bottom, and has successfully confronted and absorbed both experiences.

Out of that catharsis has emerged the hard core of the man's character. It took most of three decades for Munk to acquire the self-esteem that now fuels his final venture: to own more of the world's urban real estate than anybody before him, and if possible, after him. His motives aren't as innocent or uncomplicated as making money. It's restitution, redemption, revenge—the three great *R*s in Peter Munk's life. It's about giving the finger to all those snotty guys who never waved goodbye as he snuck away for his twelve-year exile in the South Pacific after the Clairtone fiasco back in 1967. That's the essence of the Peter Munk story. All else is detail.

"IF PERSONALITY IS A SERIES OF UNBROKEN, successful gestures, then there was something gorgeous about him," F. Scott Fitzgerald wrote about Jay Gatsby, "some heightened sensitivity to the promise of life, as if he were related to one of those intricate machines that register earthquakes ten miles away." Peter Munk can claim kinship with Gatsby. He, too, is possessed by a heightened sensitivity that endows him with the power of second sight so he can see through things and people to unexpected meanings.

Munk is not physically beautiful, but he is daring—and that makes him beautiful. When he gets excited he becomes an emotional hangglider, talking so fast that you can hardly follow him. Yet when he's sharing hopes or secrets, he dramatically lowers his voice, as if he were a Cold War spy confiding the address of his East Berlin safe house.

Spending time with him is exhilarating but exhausting, because Munk doesn't treat visitors as merely listeners. They must become co-conspirators in whatever crusade is occupying his attention at the time, or their stay is abruptly brief. Those callers who come bearing new deals or supportive messages are rewarded with rapt attention. He welcomes old friends with a smile you could auction at Sotheby's.

The once widely circulated comic strip *Li'l Abner* featured a sad character named Joe Bfstplk. Whenever Joe appeared, trouble was sure to follow. His gloomy approach to life poisoned the mood of anyone unfortunate enough to meet him. To signify that misanthropic outlook, Al Capp, the strip's creator, always painted Joe with a black rain-cloud hovering over his head. If there were a comic-strip creation with the opposite characteristics, its inspiration could have been Peter Munk. He creates an intense, yet festive, atmosphere wherever he goes. The ingredients that allow Munk to light up a room with the grace of his presence are not easy to isolate; maybe it's his air of ingenuousness, those beseeching eyes and mock sighs, the way he rolls words and favourite phrases around his tongue as if they were chocolate-dipped maraschinos.

Munk's Messianic side is seldom on public display. But at least twice a year at the annual meetings of his two companies, when he rises to address his shareholders, he lets go. His appearance is preceded by servitors from Barrick (his gold-mining company), who flood the room with so many upbeat statistics that by the time Munk stands up to speak, the shareholders seem to be holding themselves back from shouting, amen! or hallelujah! It was at the 1996 Barrick annual meeting that Munk made news by unreservedly praising the record of Chilean general Augusto Pinochet for his economic reforms, glossing over his bloody record on human rights. I once asked Munk why he had appointed former prime minister Brian Mulroney to his board. "He has great contacts," was the reply. "He knows every dictator in the world on a first-name basis." After not very convincingly explaining to the crowd how truly humble all this success has made him feel, Munk confesses, as he did at the 1992 annual meeting, "Barrick is my life. It's something I created, I conceived, I conceptualized, I lived. It's a miracle not to be repeated. It will go down in the annals of business history."

Within twenty months of that oration, Munk had switched his attention from gold (and Barrick) to real estate (and TrizecHahn), by acquiring the near-bankrupt real-estate empire of Peter Bronfman's Trizec Corp. and turning it into a bonanza.

"The goddamn real-estate business," he complains in pretend anger. "It's the graveyard of the human ego."

Why then is he devoting the rest of his life to it, while taking a $600-million hit by shutting down half of his gold mines? "Why did I switch? Because I'm not going to go bust. With Trizec, we're building the first global real-estate operation. Just give us two or three more years, and you won't believe what we can do. We're already second in North America in terms of our market capitalization, and we haven't really begun."

Since Munk bought Trizec and two years later changed its name to TrizecHahn to accommodate the name of its American partner, he has expanded its downtown holdings in Canada and the U.S., acquiring US$3 billion worth of properties while selling US$2.6 billion. TrizecHahn now owns 50 million square feet of real estate. The company has bought such high-profile structures as Toronto's CN Tower, which is being renovated as a retail-entertainment destination; Mann's Chinese Theatre in Hollywood (which will be turned into a $200-million entertainment centre, including a new auditorium for future Oscar ceremonies); Desert Passage on the Las Vegas strip, which is being redeveloped as a retail-entertainment complex; the West End City Center in Hungary, next to Budapest's main train station, which is being turned into a typical American mega-mall; and Chicago's mighty Sears Tower, the world's second-tallest office building.

"Euphoria is so common in real estate, because the more you win, the bigger bets you place," explains Munk, sounding appropriately euphoric. "But I don't see this as a gamble. Gambling is when you roll the dice and double your assets if you win; and if you don't win, the banks and shareholders lose. But I don't confuse gambling with doing business. Gambling is when you roll the dice; business is when you control the dice. When I decided to buy Trizec, there wasn't a Canadian real-estate company that could raise a buck. Half my board, led by Jim Tory, threatened to walk out on me when I suggested doing it, because they thought real estate was dead forever after the Campeau and Reichmann disasters. We injected some serious money and now have almost unlimited access to capital in this low-interest-rate environment.

"Why am I not staying only in gold?" he demands. "We're still the world's most profitable gold company, but gold by definition is a limited commodity. We've built up a $14-billion mining company in a business that has total market capitalization of $110 billion—that's less than Microsoft. In real estate, at $10 billion, we haven't scratched the surface. It's the world's biggest business. It's been around since the days of

Cleopatra. At $100 billion, you're a factor. We want to become the General Motors of real estate, the fastest-growing and most international leader in three categories: entertainment destinations (like Toronto's CN Tower and our Hollywood project); a mix of office and shopping spaces (like Calgary's new Bankers' Hall or Montreal's Place Ville-Marie); and we want to push the envelope to see where else we can combine entertainment, shopping and other functions such as airports perhaps. Real estate is not a defined entity any more."

Whatever he does, Munk will move TrizecHahn's emphasis outside his home continent: "Why would I fight for the North American market, which is overbuilt and over-malled, with nearly zero growth of people's disposable incomes, especially at a time of rapidly rising Internet and catalogue sales? I'm going to concentrate on Prague, Budapest, London and other great European cities where the populations—and car ownership—are doubling every four years and the kids have spent their lives sucking on a giant hind tit, not able to buy what they see on TV. That's changing. Now, they want to visit Planet Hollywood, buy Nikes and Big Macs, shop at the Gap and Ralph Lauren. Where are they going to go? Those old dusty streets where you can't even park a car? Most of these historic cities are ossified, remaining just like they were fifty years ago. Four of the world's largest mall-construction companies are as American as apple pie and too far removed from people outside North America to know what they want. We're the only ones who can put it all together, turn shopping into an entertainment and vice versa. I come from an international background, speak other languages, and thank God, haven't been spoiled yet . . . Anyway, don't let me get carried away." (We won't.)

Since he can spout with equal, volcanic enthusiasm on gold and real estate, is he in the gold business or the real-estate business? Neither. Peter Munk's business is business. His personality is the opposite of Donald Trump's—he is introspective, moody, intellectual, something of a dreamer in the land of hard sell. Yet they have one thing in common: both are obsessed by the art of the deal.

Munk has been deeply involved in at least four unrelated lines of work: consumer electronics, hotel ownership, gold mining and real estate. While the detailed technical knowledge required in each industry only bored him, he has, with one or two exceptions, negotiated deals that have taken his competitors' breath away. He operates at the very top levels of the international business world with the skill of a champion swordsman, a Zorro who knows precisely when to feint and when to thrust.

He has a deserved reputation for lightning mega-deals that turn industries on their heads, but he is really surprisingly conservative, only appearing to be bold. Every step of his corporate forays is planned to the last detail. And if he does make a mistake, as he did with Clairtone by allowing others to control his destiny, he never makes it again. "I look at every business like skiing a very steep new hill," he says. "The key is to look down, laugh and tell yourself it's just like any other hill. You use the same techniques. The moment you panic—the moment you think, Oh God, this is broken powder, there are rocks—you aren't going to make it. I don't make a deal a minute; I have long-term objectives. I do *business* deals, not deals *per se*. Some people are deal junkies—they carry fifteen pieces of paper around, each with a different proposition. I never do that. I know where I want to go, because I'm convinced that I'm right."

Such confidence is based, not on any feeling that he possesses ultimate wisdom, but on his record of buying in when an industry, such as gold mining or commercial real estate, is bottoming out, then surfing the crest of its comeback. "I'm not one of these guys with a super IQ," he says. "I don't sit around working out mathematical formulas. I'm not a workaholic. I never miss four weeks skiing in the winter or going to my island on Georgian Bay in the summer. I love women. I love good food. I love great wine. I love good friends. I am so focused, so consumed, so excited about what I do. I love my family. I love my wife." (Don't you hate these simple men of God who've gone uptown?)

Peter met his wife, the former Melanie Bosanquet, while skiing in Gstaad, where she operated a boutique in the Palace Hotel. He had gone in to buy something for his then-wife Linda and took Melanie out for a drink. They lived together for a few years and got married in 1973. It's a happy partnership. "Melanie," he exalts, "is a super girl. Great wife. Fun. Good partner. Likeable. Worldly. Not pretentious. Warm. Thoughtful. She is very important to me." They have two daughters, Cheyne and Natalie; Peter also had two children—Anthony and Nina—with his former wife Linda. *[What few people know is that Linda remarried and had another son, Marc-David, by her second husband, who died. So the boy doesn't feel left out, Munk invites him to every family function and treats him in every way as his son. He even carries the Munk name.]*

MUNK LIVES WELL BUT NOT EXACTLY EXTRAVAGANTLY. *[Sir James Goldsmith, one of Munk's peers in the gold-mining business, who died in the summer of 1997, owned six houses, including an estate called Cuixmala on the west coast of Mexico, 16 kilometres north of Carreas. It consisted of 18,000 acres of jungle and wetlands—*

filled with wild zebras, monkeys, and big cats, as well as 400 crocodiles—and 2,000 acres, enclosed with barbed wire, where the main house was situated. He employed a hundred servants and at least the same number of gardeners. One visitor described it as having all the splendours of the Taj Mahal. It had a golden dome and enough rooms to comfortably accommodate fifty guests, or a hundred in a pinch. That's the kind of luxury Munk could afford, if he wanted to.] Munk's attitude to money is as non-chalant as that of most inordinately wealthy individuals. "I'm worth more than $100 million but that doesn't particularly turn me on," he says. *[He is actually worth well over $400 million.]* "To me, money is like the points you win in tennis. If I hadn't earned that first $5 million long ago, I probably wouldn't feel that way, but I did that when my Southern Pacific Hotel chain went public thirty years ago, and I haven't changed my lifestyle habits since."

The year he received $32 million in compensation from Barrick (because he cashed in some of his stock options), Munk was attacked by an angry shareholder at the company's annual meeting, who thought it was "wicked and wrong." Munk paused for thirty seconds before he responded. "Well, I'll tell you what I think," he shot back. "I did make $32 million, and I deserved it, and here's the reason why: I've created $12-billion worth of value, and so from that I took a small piece." Then he had an afterthought. "You know," he said, "as I think about it, what this country needs is more Peter Munks, not less." The objecting share-holder sat down, and the room burst into prolonged applause.

Munk maintains a house (with tennis court and pool) in Toronto's Forest Hill Village, a farm in the Caledon Hills, an apartment in Paris, a chalet at Klosters, Switzerland, as well as the island on Georgian Bay. *[This is his favourite sanctuary. It's an old, many-times-expanded cottage (originally built for $9,000) that now covers most of his private island, bought for $1,200 in 1958. "That's been my real link to Canada," he says.]* But it's at Klosters that he comes into his own. One of the world's premier ski resorts, which draws both social and mountain climbers, Klosters' nearby Parsenn region has the world's wildest Alpine ski runs. One of the Parsenn runs is in the *Guinness Book of World Records* as the world's longest (at 14 km) and toughest ski slopes. It is his daredevil approach to the most hazardous of these suicide trails that prompts some of his friends to enquire, after a few drinks, why he is trying so hard to kill himself. "I do take risks," he admits. "It's one way of fooling myself that I possess eternal youth. We all like to believe that we're forever in our thirties, whether we chase girls—which I don't do any more because I am happily married—or chase mountains. Skiing is the only thing in life I do well, apart from business.

I can still power ski with any twenty-five-year-old. I can get through any trees, can handle anything, so can Melanie. I know I could have a major accident, but life is full of risks. That's the exciting part. After a day on the slopes, I feel elevated, youthful, sexually invigorated, physically rejuvenated, intellectually ready to tackle anything."

Klosters is the winter residence of the kings of Sweden and Norway, as well as Prince Charles, who has become a Munk intimate. Munk subsidized a hard-cover publication of Charles's collection of his own watercolours and offered to hire David Wynne-Morgan of Hill and Knowlton, one of England's most astute public-relations experts, to help the disgraced Prince regain public confidence, but the Prince chose to flounder on his own.

In 1993, after the episode in which Charles was overheard in a tapped telephone conversation telling his beloved Camilla that he wanted to be reincarnated as her Tampax, Munk spent four days with the depressed heir to the throne. "I was very sad," he recalls. "The man was being hounded. If my cleaning lady had her phoned tapped, had her conversation recorded and given to the newspapers, the whole world would back her up in claiming that she had a right to privacy and no one, but no one, can invade her fundamental rights. Prince Charles wasn't even given the chance to defend himself, because he's unable to sue. He tried six different ways, but wasn't allowed by Buckingham Palace. I know the conversation was quite shocking. Okay, but I asked this of a hundred friends of mine and people in Klosters: you name me a normal man who, at one time or another when he is totally assured of the privacy of a single one-on-one affair, in a moment of passion, did not say things which taken out of context and put into a newspaper would not be highly embarrassing. Why, then, are we so hypocritical in the late twentieth century, when we're protecting every goddamn minority group, imagined or otherwise, but Prince Charles, we don't give him the same kind of courtesy? I did everything to try and build up his ego, and I kept on telling him that he represents an institution in whose name people died or sacrificed their lives and ultimately, because of those sacrifices, defeated Hitler. I mean you've got to stand back and think of those concepts. I tried really hard. He became so emotional, smashed the table with his fists, spilled our wine. Then I couriered him a long letter, and he sent me back a handwritten note six pages long. But nothing worked. He can't recapture people's confidence until he regains his self-confidence."

One of Munk's favourite visitors to his place at Klosters is Conrad Black, who drops by annually while attending the Davos conference nearby. "I adore him," Munk exclaims. "He should be our prime minister.

I know he's pompous. When he was thirty he behaved as if he was sixty-five. He is outrageous in every respect, a snob, rightwing, aggressive—all the wonderful things that we Canadians have given up being. And yet he's as Canadian as maple syrup. He could rejuvenate this nation if he was prime minister. Every time he makes a speech, I send out a thousand copies. I love the guy." Munk was a guest at Black's wedding to Barbara Amiel in London and decided to give them a grand present: their honeymoon. He knew they were flying to Australia anyway, where Conrad then owned newspapers, and Munk's original partner, the elegant David Gilmour, runs a luxury private resort, called Wakaya, on one of the Fiji islands. *[Gilmour lost his young daughter Erin, who spent her last Christmas with him at Wakaya, and it was in her memory that he built the club. There are eight exquisitely designed and luxuriously appointed bureys (huts), one per couple, on the island's beaches. Wakaya features four chefs to cater to the guests, fourteen sporting activities and every other imaginable luxury.]* Munk gave the newlyweds a week's holiday there, but they almost didn't make it.

When the blissful couple got to the Fiji airport, after a gruelling twenty-hour flight, Conrad headed for the local VIP lounge, which didn't exist, Fiji's airport being furnished mainly with a few plastic chairs and many buzzing flies. "Conrad was angry," Munk recalls, "because he had never not been treated as a VIP. The Fiji airport is no Heathrow. It's a big room with natives trying to hustle you to buy candies. It was over a hundred degrees, and there was no air-conditioning." Finally, Gilmour's plane arrived to take them to the resort, but it was a bumpy ride, and all that anyone remembers is Black muttering, "I'll kill Munk." But then the plane landed, the newlyweds got out, and Conrad, though absolutely frazzled, spotted a familiar-looking figure leaning against a nearby palm tree. "That," he said to Barbara, "looks like a better-looking Tarzan version of Michael Heseltine!" *[Heseltine is a leading British Conservative, then trade minister and rival for the succession of Margaret Thatcher.]*

"Well, it is," Barbara replied, and Conrad felt that at last he was back in civilized company.

"Conrad was a sight," Gilmour recalls. "I couldn't imagine him in short pants, but by the fourth day he looked like he totally belonged. Actually, he looked like he owned the island. He went from totally cynical to totally happy, and though he and Barbara came for a week, they stayed twenty-two days."

ONE ATTRIBUTE MUNK SHARES WITH BLACK IS THE ability to formulate long-term strategies and then stick to them. "Peter can pick up on his mental radar screen the essential priority, then identify and analyze it as the tip of the iceberg—or once, of the pyramid," says his partner Gilmour. "His ability to think originally stems from the composition of the business experiences of his life."

Munk's Hungarian background as the son of wealthy and divorced Jewish parents, and the story of how he escaped the Nazi invasion when his grandfather bought a place on the last train out of Budapest bound for Switzerland, have become familiar territory. "I don't really consider myself Hungarian; I feel much closer to being Swiss," he says. After the end of the Second World War, he followed two of his relatives to Toronto and studied electrical engineering at the University of Toronto's postwar Ajax campus. The details of how he and his friend David Gilmour launched Clairtone, with $3,000 of borrowed money as North America's first manufacturer of top-quality, solid-state radio/record player consoles, has been told many times. Less familiar is the profound psychological impact that venture had on his future. "It was my first love, my first infatuation with the romance of business," he recalls. "It was unrequited, it was immensely uncompleted, and maybe that's why it made such a major impression on me. But it was an experience that formed the foundation for everything that I have accomplished in my life."

Clairtone went from making four sets in 1958 to selling a hundred thousand units a decade later, winning worldwide recognition along the way. Frank Sinatra ordered a Clairtone, as did Hugh Hefner, Sean Connery and Dizzy Gillespie. "Listen to Sinatra the way Sinatra does— on a Clairtone!" went the ads. The most fashionable New York department stores sold the units, while sound-conscious Japanese and German consumers recognized the sets as the world's best. Clairtone was hailed by the Canadian government as the leading example of what imaginative industrialists could accomplish in a country then better known for its fur, lumber and iron-ore exports.

As their company grew, the partners were so determined to keep expanding ahead of the market that they decided to establish a new, modern factory to manufacture all of the components of their sets under one roof. They were too severely undercapitalized to finance a plant on their own, so they applied for a grant from the government of the job-hungry province of Nova Scotia to subsidize its construction. The inexperience of the local labour force resulted in heavy cost overruns, but worst of all, the government insisted that the firm move quickly into the colour-television market, which was then supposed to be opening up. The expected boom didn't materialize; most consumers held off buying

their sets until prices dropped, while the Clairtone units suffered crip-
pling technical and marketing problems. When losses mounted to unac-
ceptable levels, the Nova Scotian politicians fired Munk and Gilmour.
The government took over the operation, and in two short years, ran it
into the ground. Meanwhile, the two young entrepreneurs had lost their
money and their reputations. They settled an insider-trading charge out
of court and felt they had to leave the country.

"It was the classic impossible dream," Munk later recalled. "Everything
I've done afterward has been child's play compared with Clairtone. My
ego was destroyed. What I learned was never to give away your destiny.
Don't put control into the hands of a body that doesn't have interests
aligned with your own."

That searing experience is still never far from Munk's thoughts. In
1996, for example, when both Barrick and Horsham, the holding
company that had recently bought Trizec, were resounding successes, the
Wall Street Journal decided to publish a Munk profile.

"Hello, Mr. Munk. Some analysts say that they don't fully trust
Horsham," the *Journal* reporter started off her interview.

"What would you like me to say, madam?"

"Well, what is your comment?"

"I have no comment. If they don't trust it, they must not buy it. Only
those who trust it should buy it."

"Well, some people talk about your record in Clairtone."

"Madam, you know I was fired from Clairtone in 1967. That is a generation ago. In the meantime, I started Barrick, which has been the best-
performing stock on the New York Stock Exchange for two of the past
five years."

"But how do you feel about Clairtone?"

"I'm exceptionally proud of it. For nine years, Clairtone represented a
unique Canadian achievement. Both in design and in technology, we
won the highest accolades. Never have Canadians produced a product
with such sophistication as this. It failed, and to the extent that I was the
founder and CEO, I accept all the responsibility, but you know, I hope I
have learned from my mistakes. That's all I have to say to you."

Following the Clairtone disaster, Munk and Gilmour went into exile
halfway around the Earth in Fiji, and in the next decade, they built up
Southern Pacific Hotel Corporation, a remarkable chain of fifty-four
resorts that fetched an impressive $128 million when they sold it in
1981. Along the way, Munk had picked up another partner, the Arab
arms dealer Adnan Khashoggi. At first he was a welcome source of

investment funds, but his personal habits soon got on Munk's nerves. There were reports of his cavorting with ten prostitutes at the same time and of his regularly ferrying Playboy centrefolds to his Spanish villa aboard one of his four private jets. He had just taken delivery of the largest and most luxurious private yacht ever built, when Munk visited him in Monaco. The ship had every imaginable luxury, including a computerized deep-freeze with frozen animal carcasses hanging from hooks. Depending on the number of guests Khashoggi was bringing home, the chef could punch, say, A-32 into his computer, which would produce an eighty-pound lamb, or B-41, which would provide half a side of beef. "I sat with Adnan and Melanie at the ship's launching party, and as he took us into his bedroom which was four times bigger than my living-room at home, I noticed on his coffee-table a glass box and inside was a model of a huge yacht.

"'Is this a model of the *Nabila*?'—which is the boat we were on, I asked him.

"'No,' he said, 'it's my new one!' [*This yacht turned out to be half the length of the* QE2.]

'But you've just finished paying $35 million for this one. Adnan, why do you need a new boat? Is there something wrong with this one?'

'No, but you know I like growing.'

'Adnan, you've got the world's biggest yacht. You just took possession, you just paid for it. Why on earth would you spend your time on designing a bigger boat?'

"When his helicopter took us away, I said to Melanie, 'There's going to be big trouble,' because this was sheer insanity." [*Khashoggi later ended up in a Swiss jail, and Munk paid his bail.*]

But Khashoggi remained a partner for one more venture. In 1974, Munk and Gilmour decided to erect the ultimate luxury resort. With a projected final price of US$400 million, it was to stretch over 10,000 acres and be built on the banks of the Nile in the shadow of the great pyramids. These elaborate plans were enthusiastically approved by Egypt's then-president Anwar Sadat, who later backed away from his commitment. It took nearly twenty years before the courts vindicated Munk and Gilmour with appropriate damages.

When Munk and Melanie arrived back in Canada in the fall of 1979, they were not exactly welcomed. He went, brown fedora in hand, calling on the Canadian Establishment, but they turned up their noses. "Most of Bay Street," he recalls, "treated me like a fugitive and a loser. Not a word of my achievements, which had been forgotten by all except the very few who had been a part of them. I had made it big in the South Pacific, but back home I was still a pariah. I remember being invited to have lunch in the boardroom of McLeod Young Weir, and on the appointed morning they phoned and said the directors were all busy and couldn't do it. Despite my requests, Wood Gundy never did talk to me. I knew that if I wanted to be at peace with myself and build an international business presence, my home port must be Toronto. That was where I had to clear my name."

After a false start in the oil business, he decided to go into gold mining and established Barrick. His first major purchase was the Camflo gold mine, which had a tiny producing shaft 13 kilometres west of Val d'Or in northern Quebec. The cost of the acquisition was to pay off the $100-million loan Camflo's former proprietors owed the Royal Bank. The Royal, then headquartered in Montreal, wouldn't even talk to Munk about it, after letting him wait for an hour past his appointment time. He had to get his friend Joe Rotman to fly to Montreal to vouch for him before they agreed and gave him only a year to repay what then seemed like an enormous amount. *[In 1989, after Munk agreed to include the Royal Bank in the largest single gold loan ever—US$420 million—senior vice-president Brian Gregson gave a lunch for Munk at the bank's headquarters. The visitor took all of twenty seconds to remind the Royal executive of the Camflo incident, an admonition to which Gregson replied, "We know what you're talking about, but I just want to tell you that we would love to do this business with you; we would like to be amongst your lead bankers. We checked on the behaviour of the bank and you in connection with the Camflo deal and would like to say that, despite the fact that we work here for the Royal Bank, between the two of us, you were much more of a gentleman."]*

How Munk raised these funds from a standing start—allowing him to move into the big time—may well have been his greatest achievement. Camflo was insolvent at the time, though its stock was still listed on the TSE at $1.75. By persuading fifty investors to pay $2.10 each for Camflo treasury shares, which they could have bought for 35¢ less on the open market, he closed the deal and bought the company. Even in retrospect, that seems the most questionable of bargains, but those investors—and the lucky few who bought Barrick shares from its modest beginnings—exhibited blind faith in Munk, which was well repaid.

Along with Camflo's modest cash flow, Munk obtained the services of its three most important executives, mine manager Bob Smith and geologists Brian Meikle and Alan Hill. They became his key executives in the drive for gold. Smith, a compact, muscular hard-rock miner (who insisted that his favourite girlfriends were Lady Luck and Mother Nature) became president of Barrick in 1985 and was the mining brains of the outfit. The industry was then in deep trouble, but Munk was convinced that European pension-fund managers, who always maintained some gold shares in their portfolios, would have to switch to North America because of mounting political unrest in their previous favourite investment region, South Africa.

One of the benefits of buying Camflo was its 26-percent interest in the Pinson mine, just east of Reno, which led the Barrick team to Nevada. The saga of the Goldstrike deposit, which was the lucky break that transformed Munk into a financial powerhouse, had none of the romance usually associated with mining. There was no grizzled prospector, fluent in authentic Western gibberish, who struck it rich, no platoon of hardy miners drilling some dimly lit mine slope who found the motherlode. The discovery of Goldstrike took place not in a blinding flash of recognition but in a slow, thirty-year process of advance and retreat, faith and doubt, opportunities seized and missed, careful diamond drilling and meticulous assaying. Barrick—the ultimate winner—had nothing to do with discovering the property, but everything to do with making it economically feasible and fully exploiting its potential. Located on 6,870 acres at the north end of the Tuscarora Spur in Nevada's Eureka County, an hour's drive from Elko, Goldstrike turned out to be North America's richest gold deposit.

Although the first serious exploration of the site dated back to 1962— it had been staked by several companies, and there was a small producing mine on the site—it wasn't until Smith and his Barrick crew arrived in 1987 that the full dimensions of its deposit became clear. Barrick had purchased the mine for US$62 million, mainly on the hunch of the Camflo trio. The great strike occurred on March 24, 1987. Smith was in Florida on holiday when Meikle telephoned with some unbelievable news. "Bob," he said, "we've pulled a hell of a hole. It's 600 feet, averaging 0.36 ounces of gold per ton!"

"Brian, that's bullshit," Smith replied. "Some son of a bitch salted the core. We better go back, resample the whole damn thing and drill another hole." Smith didn't dare tell Munk, because the news seemed too good to be true. The second hole showed even better results. Eventually, eleven diamond drills were honeycombing Goldstrike's bottom layers, and one 450-foot length of core averaged 1.089 ounces of gold per ton. For an amazing fifteen months, the drill crews were confirming a million ounces of new gold every thirty days. Even now, after more than a decade of mining, the property (with 10 million ounces already sold) still contains gold reserves of 29.3 million ounces, the largest gold cache in North America.

The Barrick miracle won the acceptance on Bay Street that had eluded Munk for such a torturously long time. "For years," wrote Ira Gluskin in *The Financial Times*, "I used to hear that there was a Peter Munk discount. It was only four years ago that Barrick was at a discount to its peers because of the alleged moral deficiencies of Mr. Munk, incurred in the year 8 BC. Today, Barrick sells at a premium, and the very same Peter Munk is a national hero and credit to his race, creed and lineage."

Munk's other great contribution to the industry was hedging. Because he had put all his own money into Barrick and couldn't afford to lose it, he devised a scheme that made gold mining independent of gold prices. It involved selling the shiny stuff three years forward to banks willing to be locked into their loan positions. In the summer of 1998, when gold was selling under US$300 an ounce, Munk was getting more than $400 and had reduced costs to below $150, except at his Pierina mine in Peru, which was getting ready to pour gold at an unbelievable $50 an ounce. That prospect, originally owned by Arequipa Resources, was purchased in 1996 for $1.1 billion from Catherine McLeod, a young Vancouver mine finder, who personally made $9 million on the deal. Two years earlier, Munk paid $2.1 billion for Lac Minerals, which included some underdeveloped mines in Chile. And he bought the sad remnants of Calgary's Trizec Corp., once Canada's prime commercial real-estate company.

THE FORMER PRIDE OF THE PETER BRONFMAN empire was now run by Jack Cockwell and Trevor Eyton and was actually bankrupt, kept alive by the Royal Bank to protect its loans. Cockwell had been pumping so much money out of Trizec to save another of his failing properties, Bramalea, that the company lost its cash flow and its credit rating. But it still owned a portfolio of good properties, and that was what attracted Munk. It was Tony Fell of RBC Dominion who brought the Trizec opportunity to Munk's attention at a specially arranged Horsham board meeting on February 7, 1994. Eventually Munk made an offer of $661 million for a controlling position, with Jeremiah O'Conner of New York as a partner. Two years later, Munk merged Trizec with Horsham—which cashed in its ownership of Clark, its Midwest American refinery, and its 15 percent holding in Barrick—and created the cash-rich real estate company known as TrizecHahn.

Greg Wilkins, a former racing-car driver who was named company president, insists that he's not trying to collect marquee properties for publicity or ego reasons. "A marquee property," he says, "is generally sought after because it is a great physical specimen in a great location, which attracts tenants and gets higher rents. The difference is that we are not going to pay an ego premium for them just because we want to have ownership of the greatest tower in the city. Our strategy is that we want one of those marquee properties only if we get them at the same financial returns that we get on lesser properties."

No question, the Munk company's marquee building in Canada is Place Ville-Marie, architect I.M. Pei's famous crucifix-shaped skyscraper in downtown Montreal. Built in 1962 on a vacant lot owned by the CNR, the forty-three-storey building, which comprises 3 million square feet of prime office space, remains the head office of the Royal Bank, among many other firms. Built on top of the city's main commuter railways, it pioneered the construction of the underground shopping malls that now spread below most of the downtowns of North America.

Unlike every other Canadian real estate firm, including those based in Quebec's largest city, Trizec has expanded in Montreal. "Prices are so far down, the only way they can move is up," says Munk. "Besides, Montreal has a terrific location, a good airport, and the advantage of the French presence. For conventions, hotel rooms are half the price of New York, and it's fifty minutes away. Houses are cheap, the schools are fabulous, there's great skiing, the girls are better looking, and there are great restaurants—all at a third of the cost of New York and half as expensive as Toronto. Why wouldn't you go to Montreal? You'd have to be a nut case."

That geography lesson ignores the threat of separatism, which Munk dismisses as a non-starter. Trizec floated a $250-million debenture to refinance the debt of Place Ville-Marie and is upgrading the building itself, including construction of Pei's original lobby ceiling, which was specified but never completed. Munk is proud to be finally acknowledged as the building's owner. It wasn't always the case.

In 1994, when Munk had just closed his bid for Trizec, he flew into Montreal with some of his senior executives to do a presentation on behalf of Barrick for his intended takeover of Lac Minerals, then in play. The group was driven from the airport to the Ritz-Carlton Hotel in an airport limousine, Munk riding shotgun in the front seat.

"Hey, how is Montreal doing?" he asked the driver.

"Nothing's doing," was the glum reply.

"Any exceptions?"

"Yeah, Place Ville-Marie. It's rented."

At that point, Munk wasn't quite sure what he owned in Montreal as part of his new Trizec acquisition, but he knew that Place Ville-Marie was top prize of his local portfolio, so he asked the driver why it was the exception. Why was it rented when every other building was in trouble?

"Look," the driver pointed, "it's right there. You can see it sticking up. It's the biggest building in Montreal."

"But why is it full?" Munk repeated.

"Well," the driver confided, "it's the ownership. You see Place Ville-Marie is owned half by the Pope and half by Paul Desmarais. So what would you expect?" Montreal's two popes. You can't do much better than that.

I was *Maclean's* business editor when Place Ville-Marie was first proposed, and I interviewed Bill Zeckendorf, the legendary New York developer who won the building contract. Zeckendorf worked in a huge round office on the top of one of his downtown skyscrapers, and while we were talking, he was carrying on two telephone conversations simultaneously and giving his secretary instructions about a future lunch date. At the end of my visit, I couldn't resist asking the harried tycoon if he got ulcers working at such a frantic pace.

"No," Zeckendorf replied. "No, I don't get ulcers. I *give* them." But the New York developer met his match in James Muir, the no-nonsense Scotsman, then chairman of the Royal Bank, which was financing the project. "Jim keeps things simple," Zeckendorf told me. "If you're his friend, you can do no wrong; if you're his enemy, you can do no right. And if you're worth considering at all, you're in one category or the other."

The many differences between the two Titans were resolved only when Muir agreed to become Place Ville-Marie's lead tenant for a then-unheard-of annual rental of $2.6 million. The bank chairman was partly persuaded to move in because Zeckendorf assured him that by using a telescope from his top-floor office, he would be able to see down in the financial district and into the private dining-room of the rival Bank of Montreal headquarters, so he could identify the clients its chairman Arnold Hart was entertaining for lunch. And that's how Place Ville-Marie was born. *[It was Zeckendorf who formed Trizec Corp. in 1960, when he joined with Second Covent Garden and Eagle Star Insurance, both of London, to provide the final financing for Place Ville-Marie.]*

IN 1996, BEFORE BRE-X WAS DISCOVERED to be a fraud, Munk felt that Barrick was the obvious company to go after the so-called world's greatest gold mine and did his best to negotiate a deal.

Bob Lee: hip leader of Vancouver's Chinese Establishment

Stuart Davis/Vancouver Province

Charles Bronfman: the son also rises

Bill Becker/Canapress

John Cleghorn: first bank chairman to carry his own luggage

David Lam: the conscience of Vancouver's Chinese community

Malcolm Pe[...]-Vancouver Sun

Erica & Caleb
Chan: *refused by
one golf club, they
built another*

Canapress

Galen & Hilary
Weston: *the cowboy
and his lady get
hitched*

*George Eaton: he
and his brothers
wasted their legacy*

Frank Gunn/Canapress

*Fred & Nicky
Eaton: golden
no more*

Trisha Hickey/Toronto Sun

Shaun Be— T ronto Star

*Izzy Asper: battling
the status quo from
Winnipeg*

Chris Beeger

*Jim Gray &
Wayne Perkins:
Calgary's early
morning networkers
in full regalia*

Jimmy Pattison:
doing it his way
and buying
Frank Sinatra's
home to boot

Brian Kent/Vancouver Sun

Lyall Knott:
Vancouver's Ace
networker making
another connection

Courtesy of Langara Fishing Lodge

*Murray Edwards:
Calgary's chief
money mover
never stops*

*Paul Desmarais
and sons: a dynasty
with assets worth
$100 billion*

Peter Eng: proving that even developers can be intellectuals

Courtesy of Peter Eng

Peter Godsoe of Scotiabank: no mergers for him

Tom Hanson/Canapress

"I had a handshake with David Walsh and J.P. Morgan [the Bre-X advisers], who recommended our deal," Munk says. "All the controversy would not have happened because their [Bre-X's] investment bankers gave them the full go-ahead, and this would have been a beautifully done, smooth deal. But those guys who knew it was a fraud hadn't sold enough of their shares—and I am referring to that crowd on the property in Indonesia—and they needed more time. They knew that if they signed up with us, the first act after the signing was due diligence. Felderhof and de Guzman could not afford due diligence.

"I wasted months and months of time, and I was very disappointed, heartbroken, because it just didn't make sense that we couldn't make a deal. We had all of our field engineers, our drilling rigs were on the ground in December, because J.P. Morgan and the government and us had agreed. But Felderhof shut the door on us, sent our people back and abused Bob Smith, our president.

"It wasn't until that morning when it was announced on BBC radio that it was a fraud that I jumped for joy. Everything I had done for a year—I couldn't understand why it wouldn't succeed. Suddenly, the whole thing became crystal clear.

"When they were forced at the end, because they were threatened with a withdrawal of their licence—when they were forced by Bob Hasan to sign with Freeport—that was when the suicides and the escapes to tax havens began. They knew that Freeport would go out and drill . . .

"They were absolutely paranoid, and that was why they kept on saying that there was more and more gold and got their shareholders to say, 'don't force us into this deal.' I had been in bed with depression when I lost the deal in February. I had never tried so hard, and I just couldn't understand it . . . Nothing worked, and suddenly, the moment it was announced as a fraud, I went from a deep depression and a psychosomatically induced flu to health in fifteen minutes. It was like someone opening up a window on a totally dark tunnel. Everything—all the meetings, all the delays, all the incompatible little details—everything totally made sense."

That was the sad ending of the Bre-X saga.

MUNK IS SEVENTY, BUT HE IS NOT IN A retirement mode. "I feel more energized," he says, "more enthusiastic. This is not a time to worry about biological age, about chronological age. It's a time to enjoy life and do things better than you have before. I've got the experience and the ability—the best of both worlds." In the fall of 1998 he was planning to establish a base in London, so that he could personally direct TrizecHahn's assault on Europe.

Except for his son Anthony, who has been a director of Horsham, none of his children are involved in his business, and they will not inherit his companies. His fortune will be left mostly to the foundation he has set up to encourage the spread of "liberty, freedom and free enterpise."

Munk won the acceptance he so treasured long ago, but somehow it's never enough. In the spring of 1993, he was appointed an officer of the Order of Canada and cried through most of the ceremony. "Peter Munk is well respected because of the super jobs he did with Barrick and Trizec, and nobody can take that away from him," says Bill Wilder, the former head of Wood Gundy and one of Bay Street's High Establishment figures. "But he's never going to be one of the boys playing poker at the Toronto Club. He's a cold-blooded, tough Hungarian who is going to paddle his own canoe." Munk has since not only joined the Toronto Club, but is the first Jew to be a member of its executive. He does not stay after lunch to play poker.

What separates Peter Munk from the usual run of successful tycoons is his hard-won self-knowledge. "Whenever we complete a large deal," he once told me, "I always tell my people not to get too euphoric and remind them not to get caught up in the deadly sin of hubris. I keep drumming into them—and make them repeat it back to me, so I'm sure they've got it—that we're still the same human beings we were fifteen years ago when we were struggling. Balance sheets may change, but people don't. We'll never get too big for our britches."

10

THE MINNEDOSA KID

"We've never been able to say exactly where we think CanWest will wind up, because people would put us in a straitjacket."

—*Izzy Asper, founder of CanWest Global*

SOMEBODY IS ALWAYS LECTURING Israel "Izzy" Harold Asper, founder and chief animator of CanWest Global, patiently trying to explain why he can't do something he has just finished doing. He sits there, in good humour, pretending to be going along with the gag, never bothering to remind his well-meaning intervener that you've either got chutzpah or you haven't, and that if you've got it like he's got it, the ordinary rules of doing business don't apply. "We've never been able to say exactly where we think CanWest will wind up," he confesses, "because people would put us in a straitjacket."

To define a corporate culture suitable to the late 1990s, that iconoclast philosophy is about as good as it gets. For Izzy, it's been gospel. His personal fortune, approaching $1 billion, proves it. For the shareholders of CanWest, the $5-billion Winnipeg-based television broadcaster, it has meant a bonanza.

Asper is one of a kind. Mini-titans by the dozen enjoy the good life where the Assiniboine River meets the Red, but only one Titan bestrides Winnipeg: Izzy Asper, who controls and runs the country's most profitable and most international television network. A Titan of his own making, he is solidly in the New Canadian Establishment, but not of it. A graduate of his unique school of meritocracy, he tries hard to ignore most establishment rites, and whatever establishment still exists in Manitoba returns the favour, by trying to ignore him.

Since he started CanWest twenty years ago, he has written his own operational code and marched to his own groove. From the very first, he was never interested in running merely a successful company; he was always intent on creating a world-class media empire. And he has.

"Izzy is brilliant, mercurial and inspired," says Ray Heard, a former head of Global News, who remains one of his policy advisers. "He could shave a beaver off a nickel. He's good to his friends and brutal to his enemies—and he has plenty of both."

Modesty is not one of Asper's dominant traits, but he is not wrong to credit Lady Luck for a goodly slice of his success. "I regard myself as the luckiest human who's ever lived," he says. "Every adversity has turned out to have not only a silver, but a golden lining."

From a modest beginning—running a tiny independent TV station out of a converted Winnipeg supermarket back in 1975—he has created four international TV networks that reach 42 million viewers in markets that generate $5 billion annually in advertising revenues. Bay Street's assessment of his company's worth has grown exponentially. Investors fortunate enough to have invested $1,000 in CanWest's initial 1991 public offering have seen an amazing increase in the value of their shares to $15,309 by May 1997. The firm's market capitalization totals well over $3 billion; its stations rank among the industry's most valuable franchises. His networks in New Zealand, Australia and Ireland contribute well over half of CanWest's profits.

As Canada's most lucrative private-sector broadcaster, CanWest Global is, outside of the United States, the single largest buyer of American-network series television programming in the world. During a fairly typical week (October 20, 1996), Asper's mini-network was carrying nearly all of North America's fifteen top-rated shows, among them "Seinfeld," "NYPD Blue," "The X-Files" and "Beverly Hills 90210." Global also won awards for its excellent series "Traders," but Canadian production has not been a major element of his success. Asper turned many of the country's cultural mavens against him when he boldly asserted that "television is not a complicated business. TV stations are gigantic advertising machines there to be filled with product."

In assessing Asper's life and career—and it's difficult to separate the two—his achievements must be set against his modest background and formative circumstances. He was born in Minnedosa, Manitoba, a peppy frontier settlement on the Little Saskatchewan River that was once a setting-off point for the great buffalo hunts. It was a good place for him to simmer up, because the town instilled ambition in its young to leave, at any cost. His father, a Russian-born classical musician, was the proud proprietor of the only movie house in town, where Izzy's first job was scraping the chewing gum off the bottoms of the theatre seats. ("I was too dumb to realize you weren't supposed to chew it.") Eventually he was promoted to usher and doorman, but never cashier, because his approach to mathematics was—then and now—deliberately vague.

Unlike most of the upwardly mobile tycoons who populate Canada's corporate landscape, Izzy has never forgotten his roots. Minnedosa and then Winnipeg, where he moved when he was still in his teens, are his touchstones. This is true even though the young Asper experienced many instances of anti-semitism. Winnipeggers knew only too well how to apply cold showers to douse the ambitions of upstart Jew boys. "It was just a given that Eaton's didn't hire Jews for summer jobs, and neither did the banks or insurance companies," he bitterly remembers. "Local universities at the time had strict quotas, and there were no Jews allowed into the Manitoba Club."

Remaining in Winnipeg removed from the geographical mainstream has been an essential yet paradoxical element of Asper's success. If Izzy had become an average Bay Street trader, doing the deals that define life in the fast lane, he would not have accomplished nearly as much. It is precisely because he never stopped thinking of himself as the Minnedosa Kid—too much of a hick to realize what logically can't be done, yet willing to bet on himself at every turn as the one to do it—that he made so many of his impossible dreams come true.

Like most successful Winnipeggers, Asper has been plagued all of his professional life by the eternal cry of Canada's Empire City: "If you're any good, why aren't you in Toronto?" He has consistently refused any position that would mean leaving Winnipeg, although he has been offered prestigious slots as chairman of major Canadian companies, ambassadorships and even the federal ministry of finance, if he had been willing to run for the Liberals.

Instead, he stayed home and made the world come to him. For Asper, remaining in Winnipeg is gospel. "And I'm stubborn about it," he declares, as if that were a surprise. "I remember one night, about two in the morning, I called up Sam Walton in Bentonville, Arkansas. He was sick with the cancer that eventually killed him, but he took my call. And I asked him why he ran what was then the most profitable U.S. company out of a place that was away from everywhere and not even big enough to have its own Wal-Mart store. We talked for quite a while. He was very forthcoming, telling me, for example, that rent at his rural head office building was $3.17 per square foot, compared to $55 in New York. Talking to him, I realized how important decentralization in a country can be. Sure, we could all pack up and move to Toronto, which would become as big as New York. But what would that do for nation building? If the objective is to have a country, why isn't the Bank of Nova Scotia's head office in Halifax? The Bank of Montreal's in Montreal? And the Royal Bank's in Winnipeg? We've got to keep the country together the hard way, because it's no fun doing it the easy way."

Asper's patriotism hits close to home. When, in October 1983, he had a serious heart attack at age fifty, he rejected the easy alternative of immediate attention at the well-known, relatively close and, to him, affordable Mayo Clinic and insisted on being treated in Winnipeg, even though that meant waiting in line. "I wasn't going to the United States. I'm a Canadian, damn it," he insists. "I trust the system, so I had my surgery in Winnipeg, even though I had to wait around for six weeks, doing nothing."

Despite his heart trouble, he never slows down. He's more of a blur. "I have an overwhelming failing that has been the bane of my life," he confesses. "Whatever I'm doing so preoccupies me that I drown in it. I just get immersed to the exclusion of everything else, whether I'm playing jazz or doing business. I've never had much sense of balance."

That may be why the CanWest chairman tackles most business problems with the grace of a tank. He is virtually immune to criticism or even physical pain. When he had his heart troubles, Asper recalls seeing a letter in his medical file from a specialist to his own doctor that reported, "This is the most stoic patient I've ever met. Nothing bothers him. Nothing fazes him. He accepts with equanimity everything I tell him. There are no recriminations." His friends worry that he won't quit chain smoking, but have given up trying to persuade him to stop. When one of his kids talked him into visiting a hypnotist, the experiment backfired. "I hypnotized the hypnotizer and got him to start smoking," boasts Izzy.

"I'm relentless," he admits. "I get so focused in corporate situations when I don't get the answers I want, and I keep going at it until I do. While I expect full commitment from everyone who works for me, I'm harder on myself than everybody else. When I do something wrong, you don't have to give me hell, because I've already given myself greater hell than anyone else could possibly give me. But I make no bones about being tough on management and tough on my kids. Life is tough. It's tough on me, too.

"I absorb blows well and roll with the punches," Asper continues. "But at times I do need emotional support. I've had some very lonely, isolating periods. I need a sanity check every so often to answer the question, 'Is there something wrong with me?' People like Don Gordon, my dear friend who was my partner in the Minnedosa distillery; Stephen Gross, who was such a loyal executive; and Yale Lerner, our lawyer—those were some of the people who saw me through. At the end of the day, I usually get things back in balance, and I realize how funny everything is. When somebody threatens your corporate life, you certainly focus on that. But then you stand back and realize that even if you get slaughtered, nothing is that serious. I can always go out and do it all over again."

Asper makes the most of his world, not so much by challenging the status quo as by ignoring it. Instead of trying to alter existing realities, he prefers to create his own. And he never gives up. If acquiring CKVU from its former owners took nine years of legal mayhem that cost nearly as much as the Vancouver television station was then worth, so be it. If taking over ultimate control of Global TV took fourteen years of brain-numbing, soul-testing manoeuvres and the payment of enough lawyers' fees to finance their kids and grandchildren through university in perpetuity, well, that was the going price, and Izzy paid it. In that case, he paid in full measure, not only in dollars but with the psychic agony involved in suing former friends and colleagues. But he knew it would eventually be worth the money and the trouble. And it was.

Although Asper spent most of a decade studying at the University of Manitoba to be a lawyer—and in the process became campus and Western Canadian debating champion—the most significant aspect of his education was to nurture his affinity for jazz. Writing the column "Words on Music" for the student newspaper gave Asper an entrée to New York nightspots, where he interviewed the likes of Duke Ellington, Dave Brubeck and George Shearing. As he immersed himself in the music, he began to feel its cadence and became inordinately influenced by the meaning and nature of the music he loved.

A quarter-century later, after he became an overnight success, whenever writers tried to divine Asper's complex motivations and unique business methods, they usually speculated that he doesn't do it just for the money, but for the fame or "love of the game." They ignored the fact that, while chutzpah may define the style, his inner voice swings. "My greatest love in life is music," says Asper, "and that means jazz." He is an accomplished lounge-style pianist, and at least once, at the Starlight bar in Minneapolis, he actually played for a paying audience. (It was the house pianist's night off, so he just sat down, began improvising and was invited to stay.) "The thrill of a lifetime," he recalls, "and best of all, I got asked back."

But the impact of jazz on the man has only partly to do with playing or listening to it. The essence of jazz is improvisation. Musicians call it jammin'. It happens when they gather in late-night sessions to express their feelings. It's the only time they play for themselves, which is why these are toe-tapping, finger-snapping odes to joy. "We play life," Louis Armstrong replied when asked to define jazz, and no one has coined a better explanation since. While jammin', musicians remain true to a tune's rhythmic impulses, but dismember its tonal core, pass it around, turn it over, play it forwards, backwards and sideways, blow it out of sight, then, finally, home in on it and transform a standard melody into new and exciting sets of sounds. That's what makes jazz an art form and allows it to regenerate itself.

Asper appreciates all that, as does anyone who understands jazz, but he is almost alone in applying the notion of jazz improvisation to business. To put the most creative spin on business strategy in the late 1990s requires the same style of loosey-goosey discipline as jazz music. Everything must be negotiable, the elements of any deal need to be shaken up and put together again in totally unexpected but creative ways. Jazz, like business, involves inspired improvisation, plus a series of trade-offs. The music may be spontaneous, but it has limits: the originating melody, its harmonics and time signatures. The size and temper of the audience determine a concert's reception, as does the talent and mood of the musicians.

CanWest's growth and profit potential has similarly been limited by the disposable energy of its chairman, the daring of its bankers, the faith of its directors and the patience of its shareholders. The point is that to be successful, neither business nor jazz can rely on established formulas or conventional wisdom. Reading sheet music gets you nowhere. When Asper is off on one of his existential rants and no one can follow his thought process—which is most of the time—he's jammin'. That's how his most daring corporate strategies are born. "Jazz," he says, "allows you to approach any issue on the basis that nothing is too outrageous to consider, or too ridiculous to try. You begin with a coherent proposition, but admit you have no idea where it's leading. In the process, you may go down blind alleys. Jazz musicians do that all the time: take off on a lick and push it to the absolute limit."

That's a tough formula on which to build a corporate strategy, particularly when you're asking for big money from a bunch of sober bankers who think that jammin' means spreading something sweet on your toast for breakfast. Asper couldn't care less. He resolves the inevitable tension between cold-blooded analysis and hot-blooded passion by granting each emotion equal time, often with impressive results. And that's jammin'.

ASPER APPLIES THIS UNIQUE APPROACH TO BUSINESS in his various incarnations, and there have been many. "If *Trivial Pursuit* had been invented in Winnipeg," wrote Michael Hanlon in a *Toronto Star* profile, "the name of Israel Harold Asper—lawyer, newspaper columnist, author, politician, international tycoon—would be found among the answers in just about every category. There might even be a special Izzy edition, and one of its questions could be, 'Who stayed up all night memorizing the answers so he could beat his buddies at *Trivial Pursuit* the next day?'"

After graduating as class valedictorian from the University of Manitoba, Asper rapidly built up a successful corporate practice in Winnipeg, while also writing a nationally syndicated legal and tax column. Even though he was netting $200,000, he decided to leave the law to try his hand at business. Canada's most successful company at the time was Seagram, so naturally Izzy decided to challenge the Bronfmans by building a distillery—where else but in Minnedosa. "The town fathers came to me and said that Minnedosa was dying, needed new industry and that they had this fab-quality water that could be turned into great booze," he recalls. "Don Gordon and I got a bunch of guys together, and we spent a summer reading up on how to make liquor. This was not going to be just another whisky plant; this was planned as a world-class operation—another Seagram, but bigger. We drew up a thirty-three-year business plan, so elaborate that its outline, written on large sheets of paper, covered every inch of the walls of my recreation room."

It was vintage Asper, and surprisingly, the scheme worked. The little company, known as Canada's Manitoba Distillery, produced liquor entirely for export, which meant that it didn't have to carry inventory. The operation was profitable in its first month. "What a schmuck I was," Asper laments. "At the start, my partners told me, 'Yeah, yeah, this is great. Let's go, let's go.' But nobody really believed me that it could actually be done. When it began to happen, they weren't willing to stay the course."

The distillery is still there, but his partners insisted on selling out when Melchers of Montreal made an attractive offer only eight months after it went on tap. "I learned a sobering lesson," Izzy grieves. "No matter what your partners agree to do when they go into a transaction, ultimately they forget what they had for breakfast when it comes time for lunch. I learned the hard way that amnesia is the curse of the business world."

Since he couldn't save his company, Asper decided to save Canada instead. That was just as prime minister Pierre Trudeau, one of Izzy's favourite sparring partners, was beginning to tinker with the constitution in a way that the Winnipegger found distasteful. Asper believed that he could influence national affairs in an enlightened direction only by becoming Manitoba's premier, and very quickly found himself leader of the province's all-but-defunct Liberal Party. (The contest amounted to the possible candidates throwing dice, and the loser taking the job.) The Manitoba New Democratic Pary, led by Ed Schreyer, was firmly ensconced in power, while the Liberals had only three seats in the legislature. Asper got into the act by winning a by-election and fully expected to be swept into office in the next provincial campaign.

When he did run for office, Asper promised Manitobans such grandiose schemes as the abolition of capital-gains taxes and Senate reform (neither exclusively within provincial powers); he pledged that people would work for welfare and that he would triple the province's population through massive industrial-expansion programs. When the votes were counted, Liberal support had indeed multiplied, just as he had promised. The party's representation in the legislature grew by 25 percent—from four to five seats. While Izzy won his own riding, it was only by four votes, eternally earning him the nickname "Landslide Asper."

"Everybody else wanted to talk about paving Main Street, while I wanted to discuss climbing great political mountains," he explains. Realizing that politics was not his destiny, Asper shortly afterwards went back into business by establishing the company that eventually became CanWest Global Communications Corp.

Asper's determination to overturn the established disorder of the Canadian TV industry is legendary. In order to prosper in Canada's communications industry, which is uncomfortably lodged between a rock (its powerful American competition) and a hard place (the CRTC, which regulates the possible and vetoes the desirable), Asper has often had to draw on his overdeveloped sense of the absurd.

It comes out at unexpected occasions. To fill the spare time he didn't have, Asper agreed, in the late 1980s, to serve as an honorary lieutenant-colonel in the Canadian militia. On October 20, 1987, the day of the steepest market crash since the Great Depression, Asper found himself participating in NATO war-games in Europe, as part of a Canadian infantry regiment operating out of Lahr, West Germany. "It's five in the morning and we get our Canadian Army breakfast," he recalls. "It's gruel straight out of *Oliver Twist*. Then the Americans arrive for our final planning rendezvous, accompanied by McDonald's and Wendy's concessions mounted in armoured trucks, serving delicious-looking cheeseburgers. It was brutal. Anyway, our troops have these other guys surrounded and are going to fry them, because the pretend war has to be over that evening.

"Our general is junior to the American general, but he's all spiffed up, ready for the big battle. So we walk over to the U.S. command tent, and our general clicks his heels, comes to attention and reports that he's ready for war. The American commander, who hasn't shaved and is pacing his tent with his jacket and tie off, snaps back, 'What the hell are you talking about? This is finished. I've packed in the war-games. We're going back to the main base right now. Haven't you heard the news? The Dow has dropped 508 points!'

"The Canadian general, looking dumbfounded, manages a mild, 'Sir?'

"'Don't you know, man? The Dow is crashing!'

"'What's the Dow, sir?'"

It was not Canada's finest moment.

Meanwhile, Asper is trying to find a phone so he can postpone two CanWest stock issues due to hit the market that day, but has trouble because just about every American soldier is phoning his broker. After a while, the U.S. general decides that the market has stabilized enough for the battle to begin. "Let's go get the buggers!" he yells out, and the war-games resume. Asper treasures the memory: "You've got to appreciate the absurdities of life, otherwise things become too painful."

ASPER'S CAREER IS HECTIC BEYOND THE point of common sense, but he does find solace at home with Babs, the former Ruth Miriam Bernstein, his wife of forty-one years. "I wouldn't have any quality of life if it wasn't for Babs," he confesses. "She runs the home part of my life. If it wasn't for her making the arrangements, I'd probably never see my mother or my kids—and never take a holiday."

This latter claim is a bit of a stretch, since the idea of taking holidays ranks on Asper's personal agenda somewhere below being locked in a room with the heavy-metal rockers of Metallica. He not only doesn't indulge in spare-time activities, he doesn't indulge in spare time. The exceptions are the odd game of tennis and his annual summer sojourns at Falcon Lake, on the edge of the Canadian Shield, just northeast of Winnipeg. Asper Park Lodge, as he calls it, is his haven there, even if he does arrive most weekends hefting two full briefcases.

Trying to build Canada's third television network often threatened to drive him certifiable, but if that was the price, Izzy seemed willing to pay it. He finds it hard to comprehend why it took him only a year to establish a private TV network across New Zealand, yet it has taken him twenty years to pull it off in his own Canadian backyard. Until recently, because federal regulators had refused to grant him the Alberta licences he needed for national coverage, he had been forced to cover off the province by signing a much less lucrative program distribution deal instead. Still, he had hammered together a remarkable and unique Canadian television operation, and called it a network, even if the CRTC wouldn't officially recognize it as such.

That achievement was and is a commercial proposition of astounding potential, but Asper believes that he is doing it for his country as well. He is a fervent nationalist and recognizes the correlation between Canada's future and the need for more electronic highways from east to west and back again. "Countries are united by national bonds," he maintains. "Sometimes those bonds are made of steel, like railways or pipelines; sometimes they consist of common affection to a person or symbol, like the Queen, or whoever. But in Canada, a new coast-to-coast broadcasting system is the most significant device for achieving a greater sense of citizenship. We badly need a new national window. And that window should be Global, Canada's third network. We've been in training for this moment for twenty years."

That's true enough. But so is the fact that in the late 1990s Canada is on the verge of gaining access to a 500-channel TV universe, bound to compete fiercely with existing TV stations and their networks. Not to worry. Asper is ready for that eventuality, and plans to devote the rest of his professional life to the making of programs on which future competition will turn.

The Minnedosa Kid is going Hollywood. "One of my great failures," he confirms, "is that I didn't do what I personally set out to achieve, which is to create great television programming. My last hurrah will be in the creative field. I've told everybody that we must reinvent ourselves as a network, and that decision is sacred. How we actually do it remains negotiable. We're now, finally, in the business of finishing the great Canadian dream. I want to go out as a champ."

11

THE ONEX
JUGGERNAUT

"I am so anti-establishment at heart that I find it hard to believe I
would have been tricked by life into being part of it."

—*Gerry Schwartz*, CEO *of Onex Corp.*

WHEN THE LIST OF CANADA'S HIGHEST-PAID EXECUTIVES for 1997
was published, I noticed Gerry Schwartz's name, and felt momentary
sympathy for the man. True, his compensation of $18,775,640 was up
124 percent from the year before. Yes, he did manage to pay himself
three times as much as, say, Conrad Black, even though the Hollinger
chief had more than doubled his own pay. True, Schwartz was well ahead
of Jean Monty, who runs Canada's largest corporation, BCE Inc., and
Laurent Beaudoin, who masterminds the world-class aircraft and every-
thing-else-that-moves company, Bombardier Inc.

Still, no matter how impressive, the size of Gerry's pay-packet placed
him behind Robert Gratton, CEO of Montreal's Power Financial Corp.,
who won the year's crown with a tidy $27,395,123 stuffed into his piggy
bank. There was no way to disguise it: Gerry Schwartz had come in
second. I could visualize the poor guy trying to explain to his father what
had gone wrong. Hence my sympathy.

The previous year, when Onex Corp., Schwartz's conglomerate, made
it to number fourteen in *The Financial Post* list of Canada's top 500 companies, the CEO allowed himself to feel happy—excited even. After all, in
the *FP*'s listings, Onex had come in just behind Imperial Oil, the biggest
of the energy majors, and just ahead of Canadian Pacific, the country's
defining corporation.

Now, no one has ever mistaken Gerry Schwartz for a soul without ambition, but he does not show his feelings easily. At moments of stress, joy, sorrow or excitement, he can appear stiff, holding himself with what a friend describes as "the impeccable posture of a hand puppet." Not that morning. If he hadn't been in his Bay Street office forty-nine floors above ground, he might have done a little cake-walkin' in the spring sunshine, so exhilarated did he feel. He couldn't resist calling his father in Winnipeg to share the thrill.

When Andy Schwartz came on the line and Gerry announced the great news, the phone went silent for a split second or three. Then his father issued rather subdued congratulations, and they talked of family things. The younger Schwartz knew only too well what that hesitation meant. He had come in fourteenth, and fourteenth wasn't first, which is what every Jewish father expects of his son.

Now, to make things worse, he had come in second in his pay-packet, stuck at a lousy $18 mil. "There's an apocryphal story of the kid who comes home after he gets 98 in his exams," Gerry Schwartz says. "Of course his Jewish father says, 'Why didn't you bother to think about the area where you lost those two marks? Why didn't you study that? At least for the next exam, prepare yourself.' The kid goes back, studies like crazy, comes home after the next exam and says, 'Pop, I got 100.' 'So,' the father replies, 'don't rest on your laurels.'

"The morning that *FP* list came out was a very defining moment for me," Schwartz vividly recalls. His father's "sort-of lukewarm" voice on the phone caused all the other sort-of lukewarm moments to well up in his memory, like the time "when I was going to law school in Manitoba. I stood first for a while, and then in the final year, I was fifth or something because I was engrossed in a couple of business deals.

"My father didn't come to my graduation or talk to me for a couple of months. He kept saying, 'You could have been first. All you had to do was work hard enough. You knew how to do it—you already proved you were smarter than the others.'"

No wonder Gerry Schwartz is so mysterious a package to contemplate from without. He's a man who honed his skills in the nastiest of shark pools, the junk-bond frenzy of the 1980s, the leveraged-buyout game that *Harper's* editor Lewis Lapham called "the capitalist system at its worst." He's a man who has been accused of outlandish greed at the expense of his own shareholders, a charge easy to level at any CEO who pays himself $75,000 every working day. He's a man ardently loved by his formidable wife, Heather Reisman, and revered for his Zen calm by his business partners. He's a man who has pulled off some of Canada's most lucrative mega-deals. He's the same man who hesitated and let slip away what might have been the best deal of all.

"There is a buffed Schwartzian veneer that envelops the small tight figure within it," wrote Jennifer Wells in *The Globe and Mail's Report on Business*. "It must be kept intact, and so an orchestration of the corporate and personal tableaux must be conducted." He is, in short, a Jew burdened with a Presbyterian conscience, which is a tough burden to carry for any man.

STARTING OUT IN WINNIPEG AFTER GRADUATING in law, Schwartz found himself articling with one firm while being attracted to the style and expertise of Izzy Asper, already a well-known tax lawyer and destined to become a broadcasting Titan.

"One day Gerry just showed up on my doorstep, introduced himself, told me he was going to article with me, learn everything I know, practice law with me, and we would do beautiful things together," Asper recalls. "A bit pushy, I thought, but his determination intrigued me. I didn't have any openings, so I sent him on his way. He kept coming back until I finally caved in, and he did article and graduate with me. Then, in 1968, he decided to leave for Harvard Business School."

While studying at Harvard, Schwartz operated a chain of small carpet stores in Winnipeg, Calgary and Edmonton and used to fly up on weekends to take care of business. Peter Herrndorf, the television guru who was at Harvard at the same time, remembers bumping into Gerry at the business school library. While everyone else was studying case histories, he was working over his companies' real cash-flow statements.

One of the advantages Schwartz enjoyed at Harvard was running the business school's Speakers Club. That gave him the chance to have a private dinner with each guest. One of those speakers was Bernie Cornfeld, the former New York social worker who had become the high-flying head of Investors Overseas Services, which, before its spectacular collapse, was the world's largest group of mutual funds with 85,000 salespeople in a hundred countries on its payroll. The youthful Gerry made such a good impression that Cornfeld offered him a summer job in Geneva.

"Cornfeld looked like a little rabbi from Philadelphia," Schwartz recalls. "He knew nothing about business, knew nothing about finance, but he knew everything about what motivates individuals and what they most fear. He was Rasputin-like and could transfix you with his eyes, like he was looking into you. One day he was having a fit because one of his underlings wasn't following his marching orders. He was screaming at this guy, and the guy wasn't paying much attention, until Cornfeld said, 'I'll send you back where you came from. You'll be in Kansas City the rest of your life!' The guy wilted because it was the one thing he really feared. One lesson it taught me: nobody is better than anybody else. There are no geniuses out there. It was an eye-opener to see a lot of these big shots humble themselves to Cornfeld.

"I shared his office, and every trip he took, every place he went, he took me with him. It was fun, and the people I spent time with were unbelievable." Like the time Schwartz was sent to Rome aboard the Investors Overseas Services jet so he could meet with a cardinal in one of the hallowed rooms at the Vatican to dispense financial advice to the Holy See. Or another time, when the most coveted of smuggled goods appeared in Geneva. "I remember going out to the airport to meet Charles Bluhdorn, chairman of Gulf & Western. When we arrived back at the IOS mansion, Bluhdorn put his briefcase out on his knees, and Cornfeld said, 'Well, Charlie, did you bring it?' Bluhdorn grinned and brought out not one but two giant salamis from a New York deli for Cornfeld, who hugged him and danced a little jig of joy."

Schwartz was grateful to his mentor, but not to the point of emulation, for Bernie Cornfeld was, in the words of his protégé, "a Lothario" who "could be something of a pig." Schwartz remembers the two of them leafing through a copy of *Life* magazine one evening, finding special interest in an article on bathing-suits in far-away Fort Lauderdale. "There was a picture of one gorgeous, absolutely gorgeous woman that Cornfeld kept coming back to and looking at. Three days later, she was living with us in the Geneva house. Victoria Principal, the actress who later appeared in 'Dallas,' spent the summer there, and in fact, there was a picture in *Newsweek* of the three of us—Bernie, Victoria and me—sitting at the end of a long table.

"I was the young *dauphin*," Schwartz recalls. "I had the run of the place." What became increasingly clear, however, was that Bernie Cornfeld took the same blithely reckless approach to mutual funds as he did to mutual fun. "IOS actually wasn't a scam; it was unbelievably badly managed. There were no budgets, no controls, no anything, because so much money was coming in that they were always ahead of the game. We used to have dinner at his beautiful villa that Napoleon had originally built for Josephine on Lake Geneva, and Cornfeld always had four or five girls living in the house who were available to everybody. There were usually three or four businesspeople in town who we entertained in a constant round of big dinners, a party every night. The scene could get sickening. One night, I was sitting there and had my feet up, just watching the goings-on, and I thought to myself, This is really stupid. I just stood up and walked out the back door and headed to the office, because I had left my car there. A light misty rain was falling, and I'm walking on the gravel at the side of the road when I hear this crunch-crunch behind me. I turn around and there's Cornfeld. He puts his arm on my shoulder, walks me back to the office and says, 'I know you hate this.'"

At the end of the summer, Schwartz headed back to Harvard, got his MBA and hit Wall Street. At Bear Stearns, he was assigned a desk next to Henry Kravis, then in training to become the leading leveraged-buyout specialist in the country. Schwartz learned his lessons well and was involved in some of the first LBO takeovers. He was a good friend of the not-yet-imprisoned Mike Milken and later did three or four new junk-bond issues with the rogue trader.

Schwartz was searching for something permanently entrepreneurial to engage his talents when Izzy Asper was visiting New York. While dragging Gerry to yet another jazz joint, Asper hit upon the idea of starting a Western-based merchant bank. On January 17, 1977, they received a federal charter to set up CanWest Capital Corporation. Its structures reflected an intriguing marriage between institutional financiers and entrepreneurs, with the former putting in most of the money but the latter making most of the decisions. Investors were pledged to stay in for ten years without taking out dividends, though results were monitored annually. By the summer of 1981, the young firm's assets had exceeded $2 billion, with revenues of $700 million. Izzy teed up the purchase of Monarch Life, through Brigadier Dick Malone, then publisher of the Winnipeg *Free Press*. But it was Schwartz who engineered the financing through the sale of preferred shares guaranteed by the Toronto-Dominion Bank.

Schwartz and Asper formed a nearly perfect working team, though their ebullience made it difficult to tell which one of them was holding the other back. When they moved in to jointly occupy the chairman's office of Crown Trust, which they bought from stuffy predecessors, they had a large Mickey Mouse telephone installed. A visitor asked Schwartz, "Why the Mickey Mouse telephone?" Schwartz replied, "Because I do Mickey Mouse deals." The partnership broke up over the sale of one of their best holdings, Monarch Life. Asper, ever the Winnipeg patriot, wanted to keep the company in their portfolio because it was, outside the

Richardson empire, the last major Winnipeg-owned financial institution and because he saw it as a future Great-West or Manulife. But when North American Life bid for Monarch at a price that gave the partnership a cash gain of $36 million on a $6-million investment four years earlier, Izzy was voted down by his own board, nine to one.

"I've never been so wounded, despondent, almost suicidal in my life," Asper recalls nearly twenty years later. "That was my big break with Gerry. I couldn't believe it. When he threw his vote in to sell, that was the rupture of our relationship, because to me it was a violation of what we had agreed to do. The only thing that makes me mad at anybody is when he or she wastes my time, because it's all I've got. And here I'd spent seven years building this thing, only to see it unravel."

Schwartz tells it differently. "The sale of Monarch wasn't just a loose event," he claims. "The TD Bank was pushing us very hard to repay the loans in the holding company from a U.S. investment we had made in the pay-television business—it was disastrous, way ahead of its time. TD was pressuring us to pay as a way of settling that loan. It's true that Izzy and I didn't agree, but I think it was more a matter of what we each wanted to do with our own lives than how we wanted to run the business. The board had kind of lost faith in management's ability to run the company because these losses were just mounting every week. Once we made the decision to sell Monarch, which Izzy opposed and I supported, that was the end. But the actual sale of Monarch was simply a result of all those other things; it wasn't the triggering event."

THAT SAME UNNERVING DISPASSION IS THERE when he is presented with the outrage of others. It's in Schwartz's voice when he tells critics how he built his current empire, Onex. The attacks have centred on the pay he has drawn out of his firm, especially during its first lean years when there was a general feeling that Onex was good for Schwartz but not so good for its shareholders. "That just burns me," he says, "because it was good for the shareholders who have gotten between 30 and 60 percent compounded returns. We took Automotive Industries public at $11, we did a secondary at $24, and we sold the company at $33. Johnstown America we took public at $9; we got out of it at $28. We took Dura Automotive public at $13, and the stock today is around $28, something like that. We took Tower Automotive public at $11, and the stock went up to $41. People have done fantastically well by investing alongside me. Secondly, we've got scads of guys who have made a lot of money either running our businesses or being in Onex itself. And in every case, they are guys who had previous careers with other people and might have accumulated a $1.5-million net worth elsewhere; with us, they've accumulated a $10- or $15-million net worth. Tony Johnson, our partner in the automotive business, for example, has probably made $50 million in the eight years that we've been together. Before that, he ran Cummings Engine for North America and probably had a net worth of $1 million. So the people that I've worked with have done well. The people who have invested with me have done well. And I've done enormously well, too."

Gerry's annual income from Onex includes not only his salary, bonuses and expenses, but the dividends he receives on the 10 million subordinated voting shares he owns, plus all those multiple voting shares, which also allow him to unilaterally name two-thirds of the directors. That amounts to an additional $4.5 million or so; his annual take now seldom dips below $20 million. Up until 1994, Onex had a unique compensation package. At year end, auditors would value the portfolio asset growth, with management receiving 20 percent of the increase and Schwartz getting the lion's share of that payout.

If certain critics choose to find fault with such an enormous income, Schwartz is content to chalk it up to "Canadians' desire to bring successful people down. If I earn a $4-million bonus, that's a lifetime's income for most people, and they like to read that I'm a jerk for having done that. It makes them feel better."

As for those who would cast aspersions on his leveraged-buyout pedigree, Schwartz is equally sanguine. "There were some LBO excesses that were enormously negative," Schwartz agrees, "but the technique also had huge positives which helped reshape American business."

Leveraged buy-outs have been characterized as trading the short-term expectations of your stockholders for the short-term expectations of your bankers. Technically, they involve the purchase of an undervalued company by a small group of investors, financed largely by debt, the cost of which is borne by the acquired company, either from its treasury or by selling off its assets. (The LBO experts who do the deal usually charge a 20-percent premium or fee.) Properly done, it's as close to an infinite money machine as you can legally get, because you grow by using somebody else's money. In other words, LBOs are the corporate equivalent of that country-and-western ditty about becoming your own grandpaw.

Schwartz had a tough launching period with Onex in 1984 because it started as an acknowledged LBO play, making him the Canadian wizard of leveraged buy-outs. This, right at the time of the aborted *Barbarians at the*

Gate RJR Nabisco deal, and a whole series of Boone Pickens–Carl Icahn–Henry Kravis LBOs that left even the most adventurous investors with a bad taste. To quote more fully the view of Lewis Lapham, LBOs are like "cutting up the carcass of a sperm whale, and selling off the parts. These predators repay the debts they accumulate through flash asset dispositions, sweetening the process by providing golden parachutes for displaced executives worth many millions—written off as tax-deductible opportunity costs, of course. It's neat and tidy and the capitalist system at its worst, because it destroys companies instead of creating value."

Because the LBO business in the U.S. was ultra-competitive yet superlucrative, it attracted some questionable operators willing to accept its high risks and higher rewards. *Fortune* magazine compared running an LBO to "crossing the Atlantic on a high-speed catamaran. You're screaming along at twenty-five knots with the windward pontoon flying above the wave and the leeward hull underwater. It is the ultimate test of seamanship, recommended only for expert helmsmen."

Which some might agree describes Gerry Schwartz in action during the building of Onex. He makes no apologies. "What characterizes an LBO is two things: using the assets and cash flow of the acquired company to support a substantial portion of the purchase price in the form of debt; secondly, the original LBO firms invested other people's money and earned a fee for doing so. LBO firms were driven to sell the companies they acquired to realize a profit from their participation in the sale. At Onex, we were never really in the LBO business because we didn't fit the second characteristic, though in the early days we bought and sold many companies to increase our capital base." Another essential difference is that Onex raises permanent capital instead of depending on temporary investment partnerships, affording it the luxury of taking a longer point of view.

Today, Onex is worth $11 billion. Gerry Schwartz makes no apologies for that whatsoever. Except maybe to his father.

SCHWARTZ AND HIS MULTITALENTED wife Heather have scythed their way into Toronto society, pleased to do whatever was required to be accepted. They lead charmed lives, indulging their private and commercial fantasies, with Heather running Indigo, an exquisite book and music mini-chain, while Gerr, as she endearingly calls him, is making Hollywood movies with artistic bounce. Once a month or so, they co-host Toronto's most prestigious literary salon in their Rosedale mansion. Its walls are crammed with medieval paintings and ancient Oriental *objets d'art*. There's a Gulfstream II jet to carry them between their Nantucket and Bel Air houses. They know how to live. For Heather's fortieth birth-day, he flew in the Kingston Trio to serenade her. They were her favourite group when she was growing up. That year for his birthday, she gave him a red Porsche 911 Targa.

The initial meeting of Gerry Schwartz and Heather Reisman, niece of free-trade negotiator Simon, is a matter of some dispute.

His version: "I was in Montreal seeing my friend Claude Frenette [the financier and Global director], when he said, 'Let's go out tonight. We'll go out with two beautiful women, and we'll have a wonderful time.' I thought that was a great idea, but I didn't know any women in Montreal. Claude said, 'Oh look, I have two fabulous women who work for me, and I'll call them both into my office so you can choose.' So he calls the first one in on some trumped-up excuse, and in my opinion, she's absolutely gorgeous. *[She was Marie-Josée Drouin, later Canadian director of the Hudson Institute, a leading American think tank, and even later — after having married and divorced Mon-treal Symphony Orchestra conductor Charles Dutoit—the wife of Henry Kravis, the great American king of the LBOS, who had two wives to go before he would meet Marie-Josée, but was at the time working with Schwartz on leveraged buy-outs.]* As she leaves, I say to Claude, 'Skip the second one!' He said, 'No, no, you must meet the second one.' Heather was the second woman, and that's the end of the story. I took Heather out that night, and that was it." A hundred days after they met, they knew they would be married, and a thousand days later, they were.

Her version: "Claude Frenette did introduce us at the Inter-Group office where I worked. But he introduced Gerry to me first. And Gerry said, 'That's okay, I don't have to meet the next one.' The first real date we had, he invited me to meet him in New York for the weekend. We went to see *Annie*, which had just opened on Broadway. And we weren't into the play fifteen seconds when he started crying, because it's such a poignant opening, and I remember thinking to myself, Well, any guy who would cry within fifteen seconds is definitely worth getting to know better.

"There's no question that Gerry has a very, very soft centre, wrapped in lots of layers of insulation that create a legitimate interface between the essence of his emotions and what he's experiencing—the barrier between feelings and knowing. It is a really effective interface. From a business point of view, its value is that while he's always processing at an intellectual level, he never seems bogged down by an emotional reaction to something that could in any way deter his intelligent judgment in a strategic situation. His outward lack of emotion prevents outsiders from sharing his vulnerabilities, so that he comes off as much more cerebral than he really is."

If that seems an oddly analytical way for one soul mate to describe another, consider the source. At first glance, Heather Reisman seems soft and shy. She is not. She is whip smart, fiercely ambitious and constantly testing herself. She profoundly loves her "Gerr," but is very much her own woman. She is an optimistic feminist who believes in the inevitable empowerment of technology, and thinks that the resulting meritocracy cannot and will not be based on gender. *[That's one area of conflict with Gerry, who is unable to comprehend the notion that not everyone can become empowered at the present time.]* Because of her brains, energy and forest fires of ambition, Heather will never achieve the empty glories of Jewish princesshood. Though she now enjoys a life of wealth and privilege, she knows about struggles and down times, about being a single mom without a car to take the kids to school. She dresses modestly, with as much taste as insight, knowing that comfort is more important than fashion. The effect is understated elegance, throw-away cool.

The daughter of a small-time Montreal developer, she graduated in social work from McGill and worked with foster kids, helping them to cope with life and to find jobs. She married a fellow student; they had two kids, then divorced. She later dated Sonny Gordon. *[Dating Harold P. Gordon, an attractive lawyer who spent twenty years as a partner at Stikeman Elliott, was a rite of passage in Montreal during the 1970s and 1980s. He now lives in New York and is a certified mogul of the U.S. toy industry.]* Heather subsequently trained in computers and polling and eventually co-founded Paradigm, a successful consulting company with a $10-million annual turnover.

"She is really a stupendous woman," Schwartz confirms. "She is all she seems to be, but she's a huge amount more. She appears to be smart, vivacious, interested, but she's also cheerful, a great support system, a great partner, a great leader. Most people say she's the best thing that ever happened to me, and she really is. She and I are alike in so many things; our values are the same. I may not know what she's going to do, but I always know where she's coming from, and I think she always knows where I'm coming from.

"There's also a whole side to Heather that's very soft and gentle. She says I cry in movies, and I do, but try going to a movie with her. She's impossible. She talks out loud, and you really can't go to a movie with her unless there's nobody within twenty seats of you. I mean we always have somebody turning around and saying, 'Sshh!,' because Heather's commenting on the film, like when somebody's about to get hurt, she's yelling, 'Don't do that! Don't hit him!'"

All tears and inner goo aside, these are the two that *Toronto Life* magazine has named the city's number-one establishment power couple.

"THE WEIRDEST THING ABOUT GERRY," SAYS his regular tennis partner, Ray Heard, "is that in the middle of winter, when it's minus thirty degrees on a Sunday morning, and I'm picking him up in my Acura, he'll be waiting on his front steps, wearing shorts and a T-shirt, raring to go."

At fifty-six, Gerry, who carries his 160 pounds on an athletic frame, plays tennis earnestly, skis recklessly and sails experimentally. His game of choice is tennis, and his partners swear that he plays exactly as he does business. "Schwartz is the most unpredictable tennis player I have ever played against. He never gives up," claims Heard, a former media executive, now senior adviser to the chairman of the Royal Bank. "He's terminally tenacious; sometimes I have him, five to three, and he'll come back from nowhere. He will return anything. I don't particularly mind if I don't win, but Gerry likes to win, I tell you."

In tennis as in business, Schwartz is a paradoxical combination of ruthless energy and inner calm. Probably his favourite literary quotation is from Pascal: "It has struck me that all men's misfortunes spring from the single cause that they're unable to stay quietly in one room." He uses that quote with the guys around the Onex offices when advising them not to jump at companies, lecturing them against the mad notion that "just because we've got money to spend, we've got to find something to buy." The maxim he coolly preaches is: You're usually sorrier for the mistakes you make than you are happy for the great deals you conclude.

His most significant recent purchase was Celestica Inc., the manufacturing and service arm of IBM Canada, which Schwartz acquired for $750 million on October 6, 1996. Of that amount, $150 million came from Onex and the balance from the Bank of Nova Scotia and the Hospitals of Ontario Pension Plan. Through multiple voting shares, Onex retains control in the company, which has revenues of more than $2 billion and unlimited prospects. "There were a dozen bidders, but we got it," says Schwartz, "because we probably have the best reputation in North America for buying divisions of large companies that are required to go on supplying their former parent company—Sky Chefs continues to supply American Airlines, ProSource continues to supply Burger King, and now Celestica continues to supply IBM. In each case, we've done well for ourselves and have very happy customers." Celestica has since expanded into Europe, and Schwartz's goal is to at least double Celestica's revenues by century's end. In the spring of 1998, he successfully sold a Celestica IPO worth $570 million, the biggest high-tech initial public offering in Canadian history.

The Celestica deal transformed Onex from being regarded as merely a fascinating conglomerate with growth potential into a certified winner that will grow exponentially from now on, with its stock soaring 62 percent in the hundred days after the Celestica purchase.

Gerry's sweetest deal was his original purchase of Sky Chefs Inc., the company that dominates the oxymoronic airline food business. It is now the world's largest in-flight caterer, serving 600,000 passengers on 250 different airlines daily—from 139 kitchens in twenty-eight countries. Onex bought the company from American Airlines for only $19 million and seven months later sold off its airport concession division for $175 million, repaying its purchase price as well as eliminating its entire debt load.

Other Onex holdings include ProSource, which distributes food to such chains as Wendy's, Burger King and Red Lobster and turns out revenues of $5 billion; Hidden Creek, which runs half a dozen auto-parts factories; Vencap Equities Alberta Ltd., a venture capital fund; and Scotsman Industries, which makes ice machines.

All of its activities are carried out at the operating level so that Onex itself employs only a dozen executives and their secretaries. *[Besides Schwartz, they are Ewout Heersink (the CFO), Mark Hilson, Anthony Melman, Seth Mersky, Anthony Munk, Donald Lewtas, Tom Dea, Andrew Sheiner, Nigel Wright, John Elder, Eric Rosen and John Troiano.]* All staff members share in Onex's generous profit-sharing expressed through stock distribution. "As a result," says Anthony Munk, one of the senior vice-presidents, "there's more pressure on people to perform. They have their own money at work, and now they're virtually running their own show. It's amazing the impact that has on a management team. I mean, suddenly you have guys working at night, suddenly you have guys cancelling their holidays, suddenly you have guys turning the office lights off at night, suddenly you have guys driving home from work thinking about ways they can make more money for the company."

"A lot of what I do," adds Gerry, "is shape the edges of the playing field to allow the team to keep playing on it, and if the ball gets snapped to me, my job is to hand it off and put it in the hands of whoever can best run with it. The world is a very tough place; you really need to trust people."

His staff respects Schwartz, though he can be a demanding boss. What they admire—and copy—most of all is that he does what he damn well pleases. "If you're so hung up on what people think, you end up chasing your own tail," says Munk. "The way Gerry lives exemplifies that he's different. He chooses his own time and place for vacations, his own friends. From a business perspective, he is not afraid to challenge the status quo, and in that way, there's a degree of contrariness to him.

"You can see that in some of the deals we've done. In 1990, we formed a partnership with Tony Johnson to do acquisitions in the automotive industry, though people at the time thought we were crazy because GM, Ford and Chrysler were supposed to be going bankrupt. Yet on that deal, we probably generated the greatest return we've ever made.

"There's a degree of rebelliousness to Gerry," Munk continues. "He takes pride in doing things differently from the Establishment. And I don't know whether it's from his background or because he loves the success he's attained without having to have gone through all that stuff. He's not necessarily thumbing his nose, because we need the Establishment at Onex. It's more him saying, 'I'm going to do it my way, and I want to maintain a strong relationship with all of you, but you have to accept me as I am, because I'm not going to conform to your ways.'"

Schwartz himself sums it up in a kind of Zen koan for the global Titans: "I suppose there is an establishment, but I am so anti-establishment at heart that I find it hard to believe I would have been tricked by life into being part of it."

"I remember him as quiet, disciplined and very focused when he was in partnership with Izzy Asper back in Winnipeg," says Bill Mingo, dean of the Halifax legal corps, whose mutton-chop whiskers may be the last one in captivity, outside remakes of *Mutiny on the Bounty*. Mingo knows Schwartz very well, having served on various boards with him for the past two decades. "He appeared largely uninterested in creating a business presence or empire for himself. He wanted simply to be a merchant banker who created value. I remember him mainly as possessing one of the clearest minds I've ever encountered, encompassing complex transactions effortlessly, the flow of his articulation balancing easily the nuances of his thoughts."

"His main attribute is discipline," adds Brian King, an Onex director. "If prices climb too high, deals aren't done; the adrenaline of the chase is never allowed to dominate."

Schwartz has done many deals with adrenaline-pumping speed. In October 1994, Robert Lantos, the Toronto entertainment czar, called

Michael Levine, the country's busiest entertainment lawyer, and asked him to arrange a meeting with Schwartz because he was intrigued by the Onex operation. "I called Gerry," Levine recalls, "and he invited us to his home for breakfast. In the middle of the meal, after Robert described his company—where he was going and what he wanted to do—quite unexpectedly, Gerry said, 'I would be pleased to advance $16.5 million for a convertible debenture. According to my calculations, that will buy me about 8 percent of your company.' Lantos said yes. And I said, 'What's for lunch?'" The stock has since sky-rocketed.

SWEET DEAL. YET SCHWARTZ IS THE FIRST to admit there have also been several inexplicable fumbles—and one outright choke that tears at him to this day.

Among the fumbles, count his unwillingness to bid for Budget Rent-a-Car, which was dangled before him many years ago. The rental firm was then owned by Transamerica, whose president Art Van Leuven entered negotiations with Schwartz. He grew fond of the Winnipeg entrepreneur and mentored him through the process. Schwartz offered $100 million cash, plus a $25-million note. "I remember," Schwartz recalls with horror in his voice, "Van Leuven telling me in exasperation, 'Gerry, this is yours on a platter and I promise you it's a wonderful company, but the price is $150 million cash. You can't keep on trying to buy it for less. Make up your mind, and if you don't pay that, we'll hire an investment banker to do the selling.' I finally got up to $125 million cash. They opened it up and had all kinds of bidders. We revised our bid to $185 million, and the company sold for $225 million. The guys who bought it resold it for $400 million."

The big one that got away was Schwartz's failure, in the spring of 1995, to buy Labatt Breweries and its ancillary operations—including the Blue Jays baseball team, which Gerry badly wanted. It was a complex and puzzling heartbreaker.

"The night before we made our offer, I called and asked to see [Labatt CEO] George Taylor that evening. Taylor said no, that he and Sam Pollock [chairman of Labatt] were going to the hockey game, and he couldn't see me.

"'George,' I pleaded with him, 'I have to see you tonight. It can't be tomorrow morning. It's got to be tonight!'

"'Ah, Christ, can't it wait? I'll see you in the morning . . .'

"'I've got to see you tonight.'

"'Oh, okay, come up to the hockey game.'

The two men arranged to meet in a suite at the Four Seasons. But by now they were both in a foul mood. It was then that Schwartz told Taylor that Onex would be making a takeover bid the next morning.

The offer amounted to $940 million, of which Onex was putting in only $106 million cash, with the balance being contributed by strategic partners, including Gordon Capital, TD Securities, the Ontario Teachers Pension Plan and Quilmes Industrial S.A., an Argentinian brewery. Schwartz intended to sell off most of the brewery's non-beer assets, then privatize it and move it inside the Onex stable. His bid amounted to $24.00 per share, while Taylor insisted that the business was worth a bid of $28 to $32 per share and accused the Onex crowd of trying to steal the company.

During the next few weeks, while Taylor and Labatt management were searching for a better offer, Schwartz found himself operating in a vacuum. Nobody would speak to him.

"It was largely a personality thing," Schwartz maintains. "I tried to get three or four people on the Labatt's board to get me together with George Taylor to say, 'Let's work together.' And I couldn't get them to do it, because George had taken the view that anybody who talked to us was a traitor, that his board should stay intact and keep up a façade of not wanting to deal with us. So the people I knew pretty well who were on the board actually wouldn't help me.

"The same thing with Peter Bronfman. I called and spoke to Peter, but George had just shut everybody down. Peter wouldn't go to bat for me. The interesting thing was that after the Labatt sale, Peter called me two or three times and asked me for favours to do with the prime minister. But he wasn't there when I needed him."

On June 6, 1995, Taylor triumphantly announced the sale of Labatt to Interbrew S.A. of Belgium, which bid $28.50 per share, though Holland's Heineken NV was also in the race. Schwartz was devastated.

"It took me a long time to get over it," he admits. "In Los Angeles, Rolling Rock, the local Labatt brand, is fairly popular, and whenever I'm in a bar or a restaurant and it's on the menu or I see someone at the next table having it, it's like a little knife in my heart. I'm not kidding; it feels like that. It's the one thing I really wish I'd done. I'd love to have spent the next ten years building a beer company—building that particular one—because everything about it was right."

The smallest of consolations came during Christmas week in 1995 at a Florida dinner party at Lost Tree, hosted by Jack Lawrence, the former chairman of Nesbitt Burns, held in honour of golf pro Mike Harris, who happens also to be Premier of Ontario. Schwartz found himself there with Trevor Eyton, who as the head of Labatt's former parent company, retained considerable clout on its board. Gerry had always considered him a friend, but during the takeover battle, Eyton had refused to take his calls.

Just before dessert, Eyton came up to Schwartz and asked to have a word with him. "I know that you called during the Labatt takeover and wanted me to intercede with George," Eyton told him, "and I didn't do that because Taylor was so adamant we mustn't talk to you. Andy Sarlos called as well, asking me to help get the two of you together. I just want you to know that I consider it to be one of the great mistakes of my business career. Everybody would have been better off if you'd bought Labatt. It was the right thing to do. It was a mistake on my part, and I've regretted it ever since."

Schwartz remains haunted by the possibilities. Could he have had Labatt if he'd started out with a bid of $26 or $26.50? "I don't think that was the issue," he argues, although the battle was decided by price. "We made a terrible mistake. About six or eight weeks before we made the bid, George Taylor called me and said, 'I hear all over the place you're going to make an offer for the company. That would be terrific. Let's get together; I'd like to talk to you about it.'

"Our two leading professionals, a world-renowned investment banker and our head lawyer, both said, 'Absolutely don't do it. You cannot go and talk to him. He'll take whatever you say, twist it into what he wants and you'll read about it in the newspaper the next day. You cannot go and see him until we are ready to launch the bid.' So against all my instincts, I listened to that advice. And I was stupid. Had I sat down with George when he wanted to . . . he would have wanted to be part of what we were doing. He knew his company was going to be in play. George wanted to be an ally, but the way it happened, in typical deal style, I saw him the night before the offer to notify him that we would be making a bid the next day. Of course he was infuriated. And he then worked tirelessly, ceaselessly, to find an alternative. And I don't think it was just price. The tragedy of it is that we would have been by far a better home for Labatt than where it went. It would have remained Canadian, and the senior management team would have been owners in the company instead of continuing to be employees."

Why did the famously independent Schwartz suppress his instincts? Why did he step so far out of character by letting an emotion very much like fear paralyse his decision making? Here's an intuitive guess: what so intimidated him was the silken hand of the Canadian Establishment.

Gerry Schwartz wasn't dealing with a sheik in a far-off land or some first-generation cowboy capitalist from Dallas who wore sunglasses with the mirrors on the inside. He was dealing with the Establishment in his own country, and even though he knew it was largely a paper tiger, these were the guys who had kept him out of the Manitoba Club. These were the self-possessed WASPs who hung out at the Royal Lake of the Woods Yacht Club and thought LBO stood for Liquor Board of Ontario.

"Nobody is better than anybody else. There are no geniuses out there." Gerry Schwartz briefly forgot that lesson, learned so long ago in the Rasputin-like presence of Bernie Cornfeld. The price paid: he lost faith in his own judgment and allowed the Labatt guys to intimidate him, not realizing that the only thing they had over him was that they wore red blazers to the annual ball at the London Hunt Club, where most of them belong, while he didn't have a red blazer or go to hunt clubs.

If that speculative scenario is true, how ironic a series of events for an operator many see as the walking embodiment of the muscular Canadian Establishment, 1990s version. Schwartz himself disparages the fading old-boys' network. All that Bud McDougald shit is gone," he says. "It used to be that you couldn't get a great job in a big company unless Bud said you were okay. That doesn't exist any more. I can phone anybody in this country and get my call returned quickly. It's not that old nonsense that you have to be introduced to somebody in order to get him or her to return your phone call. I don't believe there is much disposable power floating around any more. I can get people to call me back, but I sure as hell can't get them to do anything that's against their better interests.

"Whatever influence I have is not based on power," he insists, "it's based more on notoriety. It's not because we've got 42,000 employees and run a $12-billion portfolio that I get a serious hearing. It's all those newspaper articles, bad as they've been sometimes. It's the notoriety that makes people take you seriously."

Right, Gerr. Of course, it can't hurt that Gerry Schwartz happened to be Canada's chief Liberal bagman for most of a decade, taking over that function during John Turner's time as leader. Prime Minister Jean Chrétien asked him to stay on, but he demurred. Heather was co-chair of Paul Martin's first leadership bid, and both Schwartzes remain close to him. Heather almost ran for the leadership of the Ontario Liberals and remains one of the party's wisest policy resources. Whenever Chrétien hits town, the Schwartz parlour is a compulsory stop. The Schwartzes are also close to Liberal strategist Keith Davey, who even in retirement remains the political conscience of his party.

And power networking surely has nothing to do with the fact that Schwartz has earned a reputation as a take-no-prisoners fund-raiser for this or that cause. "He phones me up and says, 'You bank with the Nova Scotia, don't you? Good, you've just committed to being on the tribute committee for Peter Godsoe, because I'm running this thing,' recalls Hershell Ezrin, a friend who shares synagogues as well as banks with Schwartz. "And I said, 'Well, what am I expected to do?' He said, 'We want you to buy five tables.' When I started to object, he said, 'We've got to get more than that, so I don't want to hear any of your stories.' That's Gerry."

"Schwartz is very smart," says Ira Gluskin, the investment guru, getting right down to the nub of how Titans tend to keep and wield power. "He is probably smarter than anybody on Bay Street. He's got a real sense of who's important. And he knows them all."

ONE OF THE PEOPLE GERRY AND HEATHER knew all too well was Gerald Pencer. Probably the least ethical of the contemporary business executives never actually jailed, Pencer is responsible for the most traumatic event in the Schwartz's professional lives, namely Heather's agonizing term as president of Cott Inc., the private-label bottlers.

A former associate of William Obront, the Montreal butcher with proven underground connections, Pencer moved through many financial incarnations, leaving a trail of broken promises and bankrupt investors. He was bad medicine, and if anyone should have known it, it was the Schwartzes. Heather had been a director of Pencer's Financial Trusco Capital; Gerry had introduced Pencer to the fast and loose Milken crowd at Drexel Burnham. Heather never felt comfortable with Pencer, whose idea of fun was to tell dirty jokes, but he had been a satisfied client of her consulting firm, and when he asked her to become president of Cott, she accepted.

Pencer proceeded to behave in character as CEO of Cott, milking the company's treasury by creating for himself stock options worth an incredible $106 million. "I never felt comfortable in my skin as president of Cott," Heather recalls. "There wasn't a day go by that somebody wouldn't say to me, 'Heather, what are you doing working with Pencer?' At one point, Tom Kierans asked me to go on the board of Manulife and a few days later called me back to explain apologetically that, even though he was head of the nominating committee, the Manulife board refused to appoint anyone who was associated with Pencer."

For the same reason, when the Royal Bank was on the verge of making her a director, the formal offer evaporated. Six other boards passed her by. "Heather was incredibly hurt by the whole Cott episode," Gerry sympathizes, "and I know better than anybody else what the truth was. She came to me in April or May and said that she was really unhappy working at Cott. She didn't like the environment; she wasn't happy working with Gerry. She was forty-five and wanted to get on with something else. We talked about it, and I said, 'Look, quit. Just quit. You don't have to do it.' So she spoke to Pencer, and he said, 'Ah, no, you can't leave right now; we're just about to do this and that.' Pencer made one excuse after another, begging her not to leave. Finally during the summer, they picked a date: the end of August, about a month away.

"She and Gerry agreed on the wording of a press release, which announced that Pencer would assume the president's title himself. When she came in on the agreed-to Monday morning, Pencer handed her a new press release announcing that Dave Nichol, formerly of Loblaws, would be appointed president to replace her. There was no discussion with either of us about Nichol joining the company or becoming president. That suddenly placed a totally different meaning on Heather's departure, and Pencer knew exactly what he was doing. The impression was that she had been fired. Everybody called to sympathize. She was devastated; she was beside herself.

"Worse yet, the Friday before, the *Globe's ROB* magazine came out with her on the cover and a big story about how she was rebuilding Cott. And it looked as if she was fired the next day. It just couldn't have been worse; her psyche was really hit. She didn't recover for probably a year."

Some time later, Pencer added a coda to the ugly tale. Stricken with a brain tumour, Pencer was interviewed by *The Financial Post*, and he took the occasion to double-cross Heather once again. "He said how touched he was that Heather had been the first person to call him, and what a true friend she was," Schwartz recalls. "He then went on about her departure from Cott, explaining with a shrug that there just wasn't room at the company for three entrepreneurs. Heather went wild all over again. He had a chance to correct what had happened and came out with the same bullshit."

Shortly afterwards, Nichol was fired as president of Cott, and Pencer was dead of a brain tumour.

"DID YOU EVER SEE A WOMAN WHO'S QUITE beautiful, but she's wearing a funny beehive bouffant hairdo?" Gerry Schwartz ruminates, trying to explain something about himself. "And you realize that in the 1960s when that hairdo was stylish, she saw herself as the most beautiful she would ever be, so she maintained that style, never changing. And of course, she's quite unbeautiful now with that stupid-looking hairdo in the 1990s. People like that don't get it; they don't keep growing. You have to get a haircut at some point. You've got to put yourself into a position where you're back in kindergarten, learning."

Instead of a haircut, Gerry has gone into the movie business, which amounts to the same thing. "For me, part of it is the absolute joy of being back in kindergarten," he confesses. "Here's a trade where they talk a different language, where the whole business rests on relationships, where the values are different than anything I've seen before, where it's largely a creative adventure rather than a numbers-driven process. So, I knowingly put myself into kindergarten and have been trying to work my way out of it ever since. It has made me grow enormously as a person. Having to deal with creative people, creative issues, people who don't understand or care about the things that I have traditionally cared about, who don't measure success at all by the same standards that I do—that's growth.

"We made *The People Versus Larry Flint* and lost money on it. The film had a very narrow audience, but Milos Foreman, the director, and the actors who were in it and my partner Mike Medavoy—they're all thrilled that they made it. They don't care if it lost money; they made a wonderful movie. And actually, it was a wonderful film."

Schwartz put $20 million into Phoenix Pictures, a partnership with Medavoy, formerly one of the extravagant honchos who ran Sony's ill-fated Tri-Star Pictures Inc. into the ground. The new movie company, Phoenix, is due to make $60 million worth of pictures, which already includes Barbra Streisand's *The Mirror Has Two Faces*, which grossed about $45 million. "Barbra," he says as diplomatically as possible, "being the commanding force she is, many people want to accede to not only her every wish but to what they might perceive as her every wish. Because of this, the studio out-spent what it should have on promotion and our costs were enormously high, so the film didn't do well financially." That was also true for *U-turn*, the Oliver Stone movie Schwartz did, as well as several smaller films.

In his Hollywood incarnation, Schwartz has become friends with Robert Redford and bought 15 percent of his Sundance Resort in Utah. So are we witnessing Gerry's "soft, soft centre" finally oozing out, the guy who cries at movies, letting dread emotion mess up his business instincts? Not really.

"What I want to do here with Mike is build a sausage factory that makes sausages called movies," Schwartz told Jennifer Wells. "The value isn't going to be in the given movie. The value is going to be in the factory. If we can create a factory that has the infrastructure, the capability to keep on making four or five movies a year, there's a huge capitalizable value. Some other entity is gonna want to own all or part of our business. There are so many people who are desperate for the output, we'll sell 30 percent of this company for half a billion dollars."

The Schwartzes recently purchased a house in California to be closer to the movie industry. They are building a replica of a 1940s California clapboard home, with a low shingled roof and a couple of dormers across the top, which will appear conspicuously incongruous among Bel Air's pseudo French châteaux and Spanish castles-to-go, designed to show off their occupants' importance. "It was the first property we were shown, but we couldn't get into the house to view it. From the moment I saw it to the day I put up the money was about six days. I don't care about the original house; I didn't even go inside. I'm going to tear it down, but the land is magnificent; it's four-and-a-half acres right in Bel Air, and the lot is flat as opposed to those huge hillsides that you can't touch."

Apart from his Hollywood ventures, Schwartz also runs Waterloo Capital with Steve Gross, a lawyer friend from his Winnipeg days who now does real-estate equity lending, largely in Toronto. Schwartz also controls Vincor International Inc., Canada's largest winery, which he acquired by coming to the aid of Leland Verner's T.G. Bright & Co. and combining it with Cartier Wines, which Don Triggs had spun out of Labatt. Combining these wineries, plus the prestigious Inniskillin, Dumont and La Salle labels, has been the industry's greatest success story.

A lot of the best vintages get poured whenever Heather and Gerry alight at home in the Rosedale mega-house they have turned into a weekly salon for the hip and lit. The place is a showpiece, far removed from its days as a run-down rooming-house. Gerry and Heather gutted the old pile, bought the large house next door, tore that down and extended the dream house into a tasteful chateau. The Schwartzes now buy mainly British sculptures and sixteenth-century Chinese pottery. Beautifully decorated, the mansion is large enough to comfortably entertain 200 guests. (The 200, for example, who paid $1,000 each to be there one evening in 1995 for a Liberal fund-raiser featuring Chrétien and most of his Ontario ministers. "God, it was boring," remembers Schwartz. "It was in June, and the rain just kept coming down in torrents, buckets; everybody was soaked.") As well as his Porsche, Gerry has a Ferrari, a 1957 Thunderbird and a 1967 Austin-Healey that he restored himself. He has his certified auto mechanic's papers and is definitely eyeing a Rolls-Royce. Heather doesn't own a car; she borrows one of his.

The couple's attention to esthetics extends to the Onex offices. For years Schwartz admired Toronto's Carswell House on the corner of Richmond and University, a Georgian building across from the law courts. He wanted to locate his offices there. Instead, he rented quarters on the forty-ninth floor of BCE's Canada Trust tower and built a Georgian office suite inside it. Nothing has been forgotten. The floor is fashioned out of rough-hewn planks of old chestnut scavenged from a 150-year-old Alabama farmhouse. Ancient shutters surround double-hung windows, which give the appearance of being open, but aren't, because there's a plate-glass window behind each one.

"We're in the business of giving people confidence," Schwartz explains. "When a guy comes up to your office who wants to sell you his company for $600 million, it helps to be in surroundings where he can implicitly assume that we can pay for it—and he kind of understands we don't need to buy his business. So we built what is basically a theatrical set to support that thesis."

Standing in that world of Georgian fakery encased by a smooth skyscraper, listening to Gerry Schwartz theorize about the usefulness of façades, the mysteries of the man tantalize all the more. How soft, really, is the centre of any guy who's been an LBO SOB? I muse about that for a while. And then I ask him when was the last time he cried.

"I was up at IBM headquarters recently," he replies, matter-of-factly, "which is near West Point. So I drove over. It's up on a very high bluff overlooking the Hudson River and out to Tarrytown, and it's gorgeous, really magnificent. I kind of wandered around, saw the parade grounds, the superintendent's home and the barracks. Then I went up on this lookout point, and there were these brass plaques put in at the top of the stone wall. I stood there crying as I read the dedications."

For more evidence of softness, there is, as well, Heather's assurance that Gerry Schwartz really is "empathetic and sensitive to what other people go through. For example, we had a young woman who worked in our garden—I'm a very committed garden person —and one day I was talking to her, and she told me that she was so excited because she had been accepted into graduate art school in New York. I was saying how fantastic it was, when she said, 'Of course, I can't go, because I don't have any money. But I just wanted to see whether I could get in.'" Heather mentioned it to Gerry at dinner that night. "Without telling me first, he called her up, and said he would send her to school for two years, all expenses paid. "No one," says Heather, "knows that he does such things." Another kind gesture that received no publicity was the time he gave a free office to Bob Donaldson, a leading Bay Street lawyer who got caught cheating on his expenses and was prevented from practising for two years. When Donaldson's former associates would rather cross the street than say hello to him, Schwartz helped to get him back on his feet.

And then there is that other mystery, the question of what professional reward will prove enough to satisfy not just Gerry Schwartz, but his father.

"I haven't actually celebrated any victories, such as selling a company for a tremendous profit," Gerry confides in a quiet moment. "One of the things that people do in this business is have these closing parties. They're unbelievably boring. It's a bunch of people who happened to work together on a single transaction and have nothing in common with each other except that they did a particular deal. So they get together, make silly toasts, drink and then go away never to see each other again. Actually, I even avoid going to our own closing parties."

One gets the impression that all the slaps on the back from colleagues will never compensate for that brief parental hesitation on the phone, that "sort of luke warm" tone in his old man's voice.

When good things happen, that's when Gerry's Presbyterianism kicks in. Those born into that barren faith know only too well that you must never appear happy or relaxed, because that's the moment the bearded deity chooses to pounce. So if you don't celebrate too much, there's not too far to fall, should things go the other way. If you don't say you want something very much, you don't feel you've failed if you don't get it. That fear is buried deep in Schwartz's psyche. And he has no intention of tempting the fates.

"It's lousy in a way," he admits, "because you never feel the exuberant joy of revelling in your success. Like when I'm buying some company, people call and congratulate me: 'Hey, you've bought BC Sugar—isn't that great!' And I'm thinking these people don't get it. Anybody can buy a company; all you do is pay for it. What determines the success of the deal is what we do with it. We've got to fix it, make it run better, get the costs down, straighten out its market position; there's real work to do. So I never feel good when I've bought something.

"And I never feel good when we sell something, even if we make a big profit, because I don't feel that legitimate about it. Often the payoff is much bigger than I expected it would be, but I realize that I wasn't as smart as people say I was, because I didn't know I was going to make that big a profit. I didn't buy it knowing I'd make ten times the money. I wasn't a genius."

Maybe not. But take heart, Gerr. Nobody's a genius, remember?

12

A MAN FOR
FOUR SEASONS

"Power is that which you never use. If you use it, you lose it."

—*Issy Sharp*, CEO, *Four Seasons*

"WHETHER MR. SHARP IS JEWISH OR NOT JEWISH, that's the least of my concerns . . ." The voice on the phone, speaking from a desert encampment east of Riyadh, arrives in Hopkins Landing, B.C., startlingly clear. But then, why wouldn't it? That voice on the phone has his own area code, and spends $120,000 a month on calls. When you are His Royal Highness Al-Waleed Bin Talal Bin Abdulaziz al-Saud, son of Prince Talall bin Abdulaziz, brother to the King of Saudi Arabia and grandson of King Abdulaziz, the kingdom's founder, the connections (telephonic or otherwise) are always superb.

The day I make my connection, the Prince is having dinner with the *khawian*, his rowdy retinue of Bedouin outriders, some wearing silver-handled Colt .38s, who regularly join him for evening meals served on exquisite hand-woven silk rugs.

This, he tells me, is the time he has set aside for *majlis*, which is his way of interacting with his people. "It's part of the duty of a member of the royal family," he explains, "to see what their needs are, and to fulfil them." They line up, a hundred at a time, chanting and bowing, trying to enlist his mercy and his cash. He gives away about $260 million a year, receiving the petitioners with dignity but hard questions in his white caftan and bright red-checked Lawrence of Arabia head-dress. Like everything else about the Prince, his philanthropy is a mixture of the modern and the ancient. To avoid repeat donations, he keeps track of his recipients' social security numbers by computer.

After these preliminaries, I ask the Prince why, as a fundamentalist Muslim, he saved the ownership position in the Four Seasons chain on behalf of Isadore Sharp, an orthodox Jew.

"For me," the answer comes back, "there is nothing unusual about a Jewish businessman dealing with an Arab prince. I am dealing with a human being; religion is not on the table. But since you ask, I must say that I really admire Isadore. The most important thing is, I'm a businessman and he's a businessman; he's a gentleman and I'm a gentleman too."

The two men first met aboard the Prince's pleasure yacht, *Kingdom*, off Cannes, in southern France, in the spring of 1994. A floating pleasure palace originally built for Arab arms dealer Adnan Khashoggi and later owned by Donald Trump, the 282-foot yacht is only one of the Prince's indulgences. He also owns three hundred cars and a fleet of jets, including a forty-three-seat Boeing 767, a Boeing 727 and a Challenger 601. He is about to move into a 317-room palace that features 1,500 tons of Italian marble, specially woven silk carpets, golden faucets and 250 television sets.

The Prince ranks among the world's richest individuals; only Bill Gates has more camels.

His assets are estimated at $13 billion, and the Prince keeps $3 billion in cash lying around, so that he can move in and out of stock markets at a moment's notice. His single most profitable deal was buying US$590 million worth of convertible preferred shares in New York's Citicorp, one of the world's largest banks, which was close to bankruptcy because of Third World loans that had turned sour. Six years later, that stake is worth US$6 billion. On October 20, 1987, when the New York Stock Exchange suffered one of its worst declines, the Prince placed a buy order for $1.2 billion—the largest transaction ever by a private investor.

The Canadian hotel-chain owner had requested the shipboard meeting off Cannes with the Prince. Four Seasons was in a financial bind because the recent recession had cut cash flows. In addition, Sharp felt compelled to do some planning of his estate, which would require him to sell off his control position in Four Seasons unless he could find an investor willing to buy 25 percent of his stock. That meant investing US$250 million without diluting Issy's control position. To accomplish this, a new class of shares would be created that would keep Issy in control at his then two-thirds percentage, regardless of future financings. It was a mighty tall order. Still, it was true that Sharp could have made a lot more money had he sold control of the chain outright. "Everybody thought I was just manoeuvring to get a higher per-share price to sell out," Issy recalls. "Even the Prince's advisers believed that."

This was the tricky proposal the two men discussed that day aboard *Kingdom*. Ownership of Sharp's empire was at stake. No other investor would touch the deal. But the Prince could afford to take a longer-term view. He realized that Four Seasons with Sharp was worth a lot more than Four Seasons without him. So he took Issy at his word. "We hit it off right away," he recalls of their meeting. "Actually, the money I put in [$334 million] didn't go to the company but to its shareholders. From day one, I understood Issy's objective. He wanted a strong shareholder who would not only help with his estate problem, but also assist him in expanding the chain in the Middle East, Europe, Africa and the Far East. We're doing just that. For example, I recently purchased the George V in Paris, the world's leading hotel, and it will eventually be transferred under Four Seasons management. I wanted to have an investment in the real-estate side of a luxury hotel chain that's as solid and well known as Four Seasons. I did a lot of homework on the company. It's the best." As well as 26 percent of Four Seasons, the Prince also owns the Plaza Hotel in New York, the Copley Plaza in Boston, San Francisco's Fairmont Hotel, half of London's Inn on the Park, one-third of Switzerland's Mövenpick hotel chain and half of the Fairmont hotel chain, as well as large investments in Donna Karan, Saks Fifth Avenue, Norwegian Cruise Lines and Apple Computers. Along with Michael Jackson, he is building a $500-million theme park in Vancouver. This is only a partial list; the Prince seems to have invested in everything except Bre-X.

The Prince's high opinion is shared by most Four Seasons guests (who pay an average of US$680 per night) and investors, who have seen the stock more than double in the past year. *[Top price in the chain is for a suite the size of a three-bedroom house at the Pierre in New York, which rents for $1,980 a night, and is seldom empty.]* The five-star hotel chain that Issy Sharp has put together, since he built his first motel on Toronto's prostitute runway in 1961, now totals sixty hotels in twenty-six countries. It is a crown jewel of hospitality. Four Seasons units were included in the 1997 Condé Nast list of the ten best North American hotels; fifteen of the chain's hotels made it into Institutional Investor's "World's Best Hotels" survey; the Vancouver Four Seasons, run for a dozen years by Ruy Paes-Braga, has been voted Canada's best hotel.

The deal between Sharp and the Prince was signed a week after their shipboard meeting. It allowed Issy to convert his multiple (twelve-for-one) voting shares into a new and highly unusual class of variable voting shares. They're equal to common shares in value, don't trade, but increase in number to retain his—and his heirs'—two-thirds control position in perpetuity. He thus sold a quarter of his holdings yet retained undiluted control of his company, without investing any new money. It was the deal of the century. The Prince did okay too: the shares he bought in 1994 for us$14.50—a 50-percent premium over market value—had jumped to us$35 by the spring of 1998, a 140-percent increase.

Partly due to the Prince's efforts—he has two representatives on the Four Seasons board, Chuck Henry and Simon Turner—the chain is in an unprecedented growth mode. He is personally investing in seven of the new units and helping to facilitate several more, although he has taken a complete hands-off attitude in terms of management, and has visited the Four Seasons head office in Toronto only once. His target for the chain is eighty luxury hotels by 2005. As well as five new units under way in India, others are being opened in Damascus, Riyadh, Dubai, Amman and Sharm el Sheikh (Egypt), and at least two in Cairo; others are being readied in Caracas, Prague, Las Vegas (an extension of Circus), San Francisco, Aviara (California), Scottsdale, Punta Mita, Mexico and Lisbon. A few of the hotels are conversions, not new construction. The Milan Four Seasons was a fifteenth-century monastery; the Istanbul hotel was, until 1970, Sultanahmet Prison, a notorious Turkish jail. Sharp also runs a joint venture franchising five-star Regent hotels with the giant Carlson Hospitality Worldwide marketing organization, which already owns 427 hotels in thirty-nine countries and handles such mega-events as the Super Bowl in return for 35 percent of profits.

Typically in this age of globalization, Sharp's operations are growing apace almost everywhere except in Canada. The chain has only two Canadian hotels—in Toronto and Vancouver—and Sharp has no intention of building any more. And true to this age of specialization as well, Sharp actually owns only three of his five dozen hotels: Vancouver's Four Seasons, the Pierre in New York and the Four Seasons in Berlin. It's the contracts to manage the other fifty-seven that produce the generous profit flows. The hotels are in fact owned by international investors, who rake in a minimum 20-percent return on their outlay. The hotels belong to anonymous-sounding groups, such as HPL Ltd. of Singapore, the Blackstone Group of Atlanta and JMP Inc. of Chicago. Toronto's Four Seasons is owned by Lew Wolff, whose firm Maritz Wolff & Co. also has the Four Seasons units in Nevis, Santa Barbara and Austin. When he was visiting his Toronto property in the fall of 1997, Wolff cut himself while shaving and phoned down for a fresh shirt, without revealing that he owned the place. It arrived within the hour. "If I were back home at a hotel in California," he remarked, "I'd probably get my shirt back a month later with a note pinned to it, saying they couldn't get the stains out."

"Selling off the real estate has nothing to do with management contracts," explains Sharp. "We control the brand name and every aspect of how our guests are treated. At the core of our corporate culture is the golden rule: do unto others as you would have them do unto you. I know that sounds simplistic, but we employ so many people representing such diverse cultures and religions, that we can only unite them behind a universal value system."

Issy has no trouble being an apostle of the obvious. He is true to the Titans' animating philosophy: anything that works. Asked about the vision that drives his corporate world, he shrugs: "There is no vision. It's just an idea that grew."

And part of what works is choosing the right employees. No astronaut has ever had to endure a more rigorous selection process. Take the new Four Seasons flag-carrier in New York, which opened last year. "Because nearly every New Yorker has a chip on their shoulder, we actually interviewed 17,000 people," he explains. "The 400 we finally hired were each interviewed at least five times, the last time by the hotel's general manager. One result of all that trouble is that we generally get the best people. The great fringe benefit is that, once they've been named one of the chosen, they feel highly motivated from their first day on the job."

When Sharp was recently planning a resort hotel on Hawaii's Big Island, he wasn't too happy with the local labour pool; most hotel employees had two jobs and weren't performing particularly well in either. So he bypassed the industry and sent recruiters into the sugar fields to sign up harvesters who wanted to improve their status, taught them the required skills, outfitted them in fancy uniforms and spectacularly improved his hotel's service potential. "We don't motivate people," he says. "We hire and train motivated people."

The trick is whether he can maintain that pace in sixty hotels—or nearly twice that number if long-term projections are realized. "I remember people asking me when we had five or six hotels," Sharp recalls, "'How much bigger can you get and still retain quality control?' But it's not just me. We have thousands of people [the chain employs 22,000] who have been brought up in this culture; some have been with us a couple of decades or more. In a sense, they're my children: all equal and all different. Years ago, when I started talking about how we're going to make service our competitive edge, it was a soft option. Today, as competition grows in our sector of the business, it is no longer something we have to be convinced about. Now, it's our people who are carrying the message." No detail is too small to be fixed. When he was visiting the Four Seasons in Boston, a housekeeper drew his attention to what she thought was a misprint in the guest bibles. He had it fixed. The formula seems to be working: the Four Seasons occupancy rate in 1997 was 75 percent, the highest of any luxury chain. Four Seasons guests are loyal to a fault. Some find the experience so enchanting, they ask for "take-out" service: most hotels sell at least eight beds a month, complete with Frette linens, duvets and down pillows, at US$3,725 a shot.

Regular guests make strange demands. Rod Stewart once wanted a bagpiper to visit his room at midnight; Elizabeth Taylor needed a new cage for her pet parrot, Alvin; Mick Jagger must have his room darkened through the daylight hours. When the chain still had a hotel in Montreal, its deliciously named guest relations manager, Brigit Nubile, received a telephoned request from an incoming Calgary guest at 10 p.m., to arrange a lobster dinner for forty of his pals at midnight. As he spoke, the would-be host was coming in for a landing aboard his executive jet at Dorval Airport, half an hour away. The hotel had only a few of the crustaceans left in its fish tank, so the upwardly Nubile Brigit dispatched a fleet of taxis to collect the lobsters from Montreal's late-night restaurants. That image of lobsters gasping for water as they're ferried by taxi from all corners of Montreal to meet their midnight date with destiny defines what Four Seasons is about.

ISSY HAS BEEN MARRIED TO THE FORMER Rosalie Wise, a successful Toronto interior decorator, for forty-three years, and his idea of a really wild time is to play bridge with her as his bidding partner. "You get caught up in the game," he declares with what one must assume is a quickening pulse. "It cleans your head."

There is something very special about the Sharps' marriage; at sixty-seven, he's demonstrably in love with Rosalie, and Rosalie thinks he's one cool dude. "The most important lesson I've learned from him is, be cool," she says. "During one negotiation for some new hotels, one of his competitor's board members turned red with rage and exploded at Issy, who replied with calm logic. He got the deal because the other side's chairman decided Issy was the kind of self-possessed guy to be partners with.

"What I really love about Issy," she confides," is his grace on the ballroom floor. When we waltz, I'm transported and need to keep my eyes on a fixed point, as they say in ballet—in this case, his nose. And you should see him on the tennis court, when he arches to deliver a powerful service, and his opponents have to scramble to receive it . . ." Lucky man.

"Whenever I reflect on Issy's open-ended capacity for love and his gentle but sometimes arbitrary leadership, I am reminded of his Yiddisher mother from Ostrowitz, Lil, the consummate mom," Rosalie goes on. "A lady with no doubts, like a great big mama bear, she would swat her cubs or defend them to the death. The first time I met her—she was wearing her usual tent-size housedress—she lifted me off the floor as she clasped me to her bosom, and exclaimed, 'Welcome to the family!' Lil's four children don't drink, smoke, see shrinks or leave their spouses. They *do* call their mother every day."

Born in 1931, the son of a Polish plasterer, young Isadore did not attend university, but got an architectural diploma from a local vocational college, where he was known as "Razzle-Dazzle-Issy" and made his mark in hockey and football. He went to work in his father Max's small construction firm, which built upscale houses, one by one. Max built new houses around his family; during the first sixteen years of his life, Issy lived in fifteen places. After a decade of valuable apprenticeship, Issy built his first hotel, right on Toronto's Jarvis Street, then the sweaty HQ of the city's hooker row. Issy's least favourite memory of the place was the time the night security manager informed him that so many couples were in the habit of making out under the grand piano in one of the reception rooms, he was missing out on room revenues, $9 a night. Called the Four Seasons Hotel (after the famous *Vier Jahreszeiten* in Hamburg), the hotel had an inner courtyard and a high-voltage ambience.

His next project, the suburban Inn on the Park, moved his business up several notches. From the beginning, Sharp's partners included Eddie Creed, who owned the city's most fashionable clothing store, and Murray Koffler, the founding genius behind Shoppers Drug Mart. Nearly four decades later, they're still board members.

Sharp's great breakthrough occurred at the climax of the six years it took him to open the Inn on the Park in London, his first international venture. It was his defining moment, because it was the hardest thing he ever did, and it proved to him that nothing was impossible. Every knowledgeable expert, including his own consultants, had advised him to throw up a Holiday Inn on the Hyde Park space he was lucky enough to option, because no upscale hotel could compete with such nearby classics as the Savoy, Connaught, Dorchester and Grosvenor House. Instead of the 320-room building allowed by local zoning, Issy went against all the rules and applied to put up a luxury structure with only 225 suites—a decision that earned him the nickname "that crazy Canadian." It was a close call. The fortune already spent on the hotel meant that, to stay afloat, it had to operate at full occupancy rates from the day it opened— which was exactly what happened.

In the next twenty years, Issy took advantage of the wave of conspicuous consumption sweeping the continent to establish Four Seasons outlets in a dozen American cities, and an equal number of overseas outposts. But the deep recession of the early 1990s drove down occupancy rates, almost bankrupting the chain. Four Seasons went into a serious loss position in the third quarter of 1992. That was when Sharp realized he would be far better off running the chain for management fees instead of building and owning all that risky real estate.

During its evolution, Four Seasons has pioneered many innovations that have since become commonplace, such as free newspapers, European-style concierge service, alternative cuisine, phones in bathrooms, computer programs that keep track of customers' preferences in whichever Four Seasons they patronize around the globe—and overnight golf-shoe repairs.

The Four Seasons hospitality compulsion grows absurd when it comes to dogs. While their owners are registering at the Four Seasons, Washington, for example, pets are presented with a silver tray with rawhide chew sticks, Milk Bones, toys and bottled water. *[For dogs' birthdays, their owners can arrange a special feast that includes a beef patty birthday cake complete with candles and an "Every Dog Has Its Day" card.]* At the Pierre in New York, the welcome amenity is a dog biscuit shaped like a bone, with the canine's name spelled out in edible letters. At night, the pampered pets "sleep in comfortable wicker bed-baskets, with Italian linen mattress covers, and pass the time playing with toys provided by the hotel." Room service will even create a "doggie bag" for the furry guests' excursions away from the hotel. Diet-conscious pooches will prefer to stay at the Four Seasons in Boston, which offers weight-watchers' choices: Barnyard Chase (grilled chicken with fresh corn) or German Shepherd's Pie (ground beefsteak with potatoes). Rough.

ISSY SHARP LEADS A CHARMED LIFE. But not everything has come up roses. The family was devastated when their seventeen-year-old son Christopher died in 1978 of melanoma. Partly in response to that ordeal, Sharp was the corporate sponsor of Terry Fox's original 1981 odyssey, and later founded the annual Terry Fox runs that have become the world's largest fund-raising event, so far having raised $190 million in sixty countries. Only Anthony, among his three surviving sons, has joined the company. His eldest son, Jordy, is a bluegrass banjo picker; the middle son, Gregg, is into computers in Minneapolis.

As CEO and majority owner of the world's most successful quality hotel chain, Isadore Sharp could be a big player in Canada's Establishment, a Titan of the first rank. He certainly qualifies as one. Apart from his personal clout, he retains 4 million shares in his company and is easily worth $250 million. He lives extremely well, but with little ostentation. Issy knows the essential difference between excellence and extravagance—in both his hotels and his personal life.

He is not modest about his accomplishments, but Sharp deliberately avoids trying to spread his influence or visibly exercise his authority. "Power is that which you never use," says he. "If you use it, you lose it."

Socially, he is all but invisible. Even the one club he reluctantly joined, Toronto's unpretentious Oakdale Golf and Country Club, rarely sees him. He has, in fact, only been there once, to celebrate his father Max's ninety-sixth birthday. Issy did make a surprise appearance at Malcolm Forbes's legendary seventieth birthday bash in Morocco, but that was it.

Issy Sharp is an elusive character. Nan Wilkins, his British-born executive assistant since 1980, caught him best when she said, "Issy is a man who has control of his spirit."

The Four Seasons empire, designed specifically to pamper the Titans and their wannabes, is all but off limits to us more ordinary mortals. Behind the warm graciousness of Issy Sharp and the phenomenal success of his hotels lies a hard-edged truth: the customer is always right—as long as he or she is rich enough. Issy's world is full of princes, ego-driven enough to believe they need and deserve all that regal attention.

13

THE AGONY AND THE
ECSTASY OF BEING BLACK

"I went down to the Southam office to welcome him, and the first
thing I noticed was what a charming gentleman he was. But he had
the coldest eyes I've ever met."

—Ron Cliff, fired Southam board chairman

IF THE CANADIAN ESTABLISHMENT HAS A ROYAL PRESENCE, it is provided by Conrad Black and Barbara Amiel. Regal fodder for the gossip
mills, their every twitch makes news. Black once told me that whenever
somebody asks him if he is *the* Conrad Black, he smiles politely and
replies, "No, I am *a* Conrad Black." But he couldn't get away with that
now. He has become a metaphor. Being Conrad Black is no longer a
name, but an occupation.

The truly powerful—and Black wields more disposable clout than most
heads of state—are always more interesting than the merely rich. No businessman in Canadian memory has attracted, and deserved, so much attention. In the fall of 1997, when the Reverend William Phipps, Moderator
of the United Church, speculated publicly about Jesus Christ's divinity,
hinting that he may not have been God, CTV's "Double Exposure"
comedy team of Linda Cullen and Bob Robertson immediately picked up
the cue. "Great news," they chuckled. "Conrad's back in the running."

Unlike most of Canada's celebrity business personalities, Black fits the
stereotype only partially. He looks and walks and puffs himself up like a
mogul, but he doesn't think or talk like one. Most Titans are ambulatory
money machines, about as introspective as heavyweight boxers or lion
tamers. Not only is Black a certified intellectual with a master's degree
and a scholarly book to prove it, but he conducts an active inner life that

he shares with the world—through his own books and those of others, *[Including my book,* The Establishment Man, *published when he was thirty-five and had just taken over Argus Corporation.]* through speeches, sermons, articles, rants, letters, libel suits and admonitions of various kinds. Just by being there. Or not being there.

He intimidates just about everybody, even when he's not present. I vividly recall a Canadian Imperial Bank of Commerce director complaining to me that during an executive committee meeting of the board, which Black did not attend because it dealt with a sizeable loan to Argus (his holding company), "the room reverberated with Conrad's absence." The loan, of course, was hastily approved.

He seems unable to take a single step that isn't aimed at his personal or corporate aggrandizement. A mixture of calculation and boldness, he is not particularly attracted by modesty and feels little ambivalence about being rich. Beyond money and even beyond power lies his obsession with deal making, the thrill of living on the edge by negotiating against seemingly impossible odds, as a city or industry—and sometimes a country or continent—waits to see what he'll do next. Since 1985, he has bought over 300 newspapers around the world.

As far back as his student days at Carleton University in Ottawa, young Conrad was determined to turn himself into a Canadian version of William Randolph Hearst, Col. Robert McCormick or Henry Luce, the American media moguls who lived on a grand scale and used their publications to propagate their personal agendas. Black looks and acts the part of Press Lord, with his majestic bearing and hypnotic eyes. Predictably, arguments rage about the colour of his eyes. "I think they're hazel," he himself says. "I'm not sure. Even Sir Neville Henderson in his memoirs refers to Adolf Hitler's eyes as being surprisingly blue, so blue one could become quite lyrical about them if one were a woman. Hitler, of course, had brown eyes. And Henderson's embassy wasn't very successful, in any case." When Black gets bored or angry, his eyes become as blank as the gaze of a Las Vegas croupier. In fact, his eyes are the hue of grey found inside gun barrels. Six feet tall and appearing pudgier than he really is, he has the body language of a puma in heat. His face is a mask.

Among the tiny echelon of genuinely creative and articulate Canadian business leaders (you can count them on one hand and one toe), Black stands out as a supremely self-assured operator. In public, he is always on stage. Joanna (née Shirley), his first wife, maintains that Conrad acts out his own script of how a great man ought to live and talk. "Everything he spoke about was quotable," she says. "Not to me—he'd say, 'Let's get a pizza'—but if he was being interviewed by somebody or if he was at a dinner party with people there of interest or influence, he would get very quotable."

The first Mrs. Black, snazzy lady though she is, hardly fit the role of model wife Rosedale's mavens had preordained for the youthful Black. The grand-niece of Robert Stanley Weir, the Montreal judge who wrote the original words to "O Canada," she moved to England with Conrad at a time when they were both preparing themselves to receive a British title. Feeling that Lady Shirley just didn't have a regal ring to it, she changed her name to Joanna, but the marriage ended when she decided to leave Conrad for a Catholic priest she had been seeing for spiritual advice. At about this time, Dan Colson, CEO of Black's *Telegraph*, went for a holiday in southern France. When Conrad asked him how he enjoyed it, he quipped that it was great, especially a concert by the singer Joanna Bassey. Black admitted he had never heard of her, and Colson smilingly shot back, "She used to be called Shirley Bassey!" Conrad gives off an aura similar to that which encircles Hollywood stars, Himalayan prophets and Mafia bosses, having mastered the theatrical trick of creating space around himself. I've interviewed him many times and even when there were only the two of us in his home or office, he would act out his answers to my questions, rising in his seat to imitate Charles de Gaulle or Napoleon Bonaparte, two of his favourite role models.

His presence is charged with an expectant air that invites confidence. Because he withholds so much of his real self, his interviewers, dinner guests, stock analysts, diplomats—everyone—rush in to fill the void. Visitors confide in him, hoping he will reciprocate. He seldom does, releasing instead clouds of marginally meaningful verbiage. During business deals, he is decisive and tough, using short, hard words, like a Hemingway hero caught in a defining moment. His verbal gymnastics can also be lyrical. Anna Porter, who has served on his boards and is a writer, publisher and editor, admires his "astonishing command of the language. He is not at all like any other businessman I've ever known. His use of the language is really beyond delightful. I mean, it is also delightful, but it's enjoyable and it's interesting and challenging in the sense that everybody is challenged to be as witty and respond in kind."

On most occasions, however, Black rolls out phrases that submerge their meaning in many levels of obscurity. He once called Australian prime minister Paul Keating the "king of all larrikins, a coarse autodidact with a wicked wit and a tongue that could clip a hedge." Then he added, as if to explain all of that gobbledegook, "I find it hard not to like him."

When he wants to hurl insults, he tends to become more direct, as in this put-down aimed at Tony O'Reilly of Heinz, who was bidding against him for an Australian newspaper property: "Our principal rival, the florid and talented Irish chairman of the H.J. Heinz Company, had appeared to exercise the saturnine influence of a Mephistophelean leprechaun on prime minister Bob Hawke. He had convinced many Australians, prior to my arrival, that he was at least partially Australian, a substantial newspaper owner and a serious academic doctor. It gave me the most exquisite pleasure to puncture those impostures, and in the ensuing five years he has given new and comical meaning to the concept of the poor loser." The Australian venture was abandoned because Black was not allowed to acquire majority ownership of the Fairfax papers. But Hollinger made a profit of more than $300 million on its investment.

In Canada, he regularly attacked Ontario's NDP premier Bob Rae for "sodomizing" the province's economy, and when his pal Hal Jackman agreed to serve as lieutenant-governor during the Rae regime, Black wisecracked: "Hal takes care of himself. If he signs decrees that do savage violence to the financial interests of his friends, at least he'll give us a viceregal wave from the back of his limousine." He once described former Quebec premier Robert Bourassa as "a poltroon masquerading as a chief."

In his memoirs, Black describes wife Barbara as being "preternaturally" sexy, which according to the dictionary means "something above and beyond nature." He once chided former Ontario premier Bill Davis for his "psephological" objections, which means "having to do with elections."

IN THE LATE 1990S, NO OTHER TITAN HAS nearly the impact of Conrad Black. He is everywhere. Others have more material possessions and command greater corporate clout; but no one comes even close to Conrad in terms of encapsulating the public's best and worst perceptions of the rich and powerful. There is about him a certain *droit de seigneur*— the man who has so much that he believes he deserves it all.

Choosing a musical metaphor, Black's operational code is reminiscent of a comment made by the jazz singer Cassandra Wilson, who was interviewed by *The New York Times* in the fall of 1997. Asked about sexism in jazz, she wisely replied that her gender actually gives her a decided advantage. "Jazz is like a good-old-boys club," she said. "It's very difficult to get into and it has its own secret language. But once you're inside of it, you gain a certain freedom. You can hang out with the guys. And you can be one of the guys. But they can never be one of you. Being a woman and a singer, I'm kind of an outsider. So I've never felt I had to abide by any rules." That's Black. He can behave like his fellow Titans; but they can never be like him. Gene pools spit out a Conrad Black every hundred years or so, as a reminder that anything is possible. But mostly, he remains the figment of his own imagination, and is thus an original.

He makes up his own rules and creates his own challenges. One reason he decided to launch a new national newspaper in the fall of 1998 was that he felt he must prove himself to the one audience whose applause has so far eluded him: the folk of his own country. This, even though the Black empire, which sounds like something out of *Star Wars*, now controls some of the world's great newspapers, with Darth, er, Conrad private-jetting from one home to another in Toronto, London, New York and Palm Beach. The mansion Black owns in Palm Beach was purchased from John R. Drexel III, a descendant of the Philadelphia banking family. The New York apartment now occupied by Conrad and Barbara is one of the largest and most luxurious in the city. Peter Munk had originally suggested they buy the condo owned by his partner David Gilmour (and previously by David Niven), which combined three full-floor layouts with internal staircases and huge French windows overlooking Central Park. But the Blacks said it wasn't big enough.

Conrad Black's publishing empire currently ranks as the world's third largest, right after Rupert Murdoch's and the Gannett chain in the U.S., which owns *USA Today*. During 1997, it ground out revenues of more than $3 billion, nearly twice as much as the year before, producing a net profit of about $1 million every two days. His corporate structure is a tall ladder, with Hollinger Inc., Hollinger International Inc. and Hollinger International Publishing Inc. at its top rungs. All tightly controlled by Black and his partners, David Radler and Peter White, through their ownership of Ravelston Corp., their private holding company. Black personally owns 62.6 percent of the shares of Hollinger Inc., which in turn controls 83.6 percent of the voting rights of Hollinger International. These holding companies in turn control subsidiaries and associated companies that publish 350 newspapers in six countries with a combined circulation of more than six million. That roster includes London's daily and weekly *Telegraph*, the largest-circulation broadsheet in the United Kingdom; the *Chicago Sun-Times*, the Windy City's most popular newspaper; the *Jerusalem Post*, Israel's highest-circulation English-language daily; the Sterling Group, which publishes four dozen papers in western Canada; UniMédia Inc., a Quebec-based publishing outfit that includes a religious book operation; and a myriad smaller dailies and weeklies, such as the *Stillwater* (Minnesota) *Gazette*, Pennsylvania's *Sykesville Post*

Dispatch (circulation 712) and *República*, in San Jose, Costa Rica; plus various literary public-affairs magazines, like *Saturday Night* and the *Spectator*; and, of course, Southam Inc., Canada's largest newspaper chain. In Saskatchewan, Black enjoys something of a print monopoly, since he owns the dailies in Regina, Saskatoon, Moose Jaw and Prince Albert, plus the weekly in Swift Current. Bill Peterson, one of his former publishers, is challenging the status quo with lively independent weeklies in Regina and Saskatoon.

None of it is enough for this particular Son of Canada, and so Black, via Southam, set about launching a new national newspaper for the fall of 1998, thus extending nationally the boast of one of his smaller papers, Prince Edward Island's Summerside *Journal-Pioneer*, which promotes itself as covering "the Island like the dew." His sixty dailies reach 2.4 million Canadians, nearly half of the country's newspaper readers.

"The subliminal plot, as Dr. Freud could tell us—and all of us who know and secretly love Conrad know—is that he has an ego larger than the *Titanic*," explained Allan Fotheringham in *Maclean's*. "When on his visits to lunch at the Toronto Club from across the waters, it matters little that he owns *The Ottawa Citizen* or *The Edmonton Journal* that all the tycoons in their six-piece pinstripe suits have never read. He has to have a Toronto rag for bragging rights." ("I've had several set-to's with Fotheringham," says Black. "And I suppose I'm glad that Allan doesn't think I'm a bore. I wish I could say the reverse were true.")

THE BLACK FORMULA FOR THE NEWSPAPERS HE acquires is steely and razor-edged: assign budgets to each department and audit their results; shift administrative functions to a central accounting office; replace obsolete presses and upgrade the layouts; strike a deal with unions to cut staff positions; freeze salaries; eliminate most expense accounts; force the paper to buy editorial copy from the Southam and *Daily Telegraph* syndicates; centralize purchasing; give the former owner/publisher a fancy title with no executive power—and that's it. New paper; new owner; double the profit.

The directors and members of the advisory boards that supervise Black's various companies number some of the business and political world's most celebrated totems. They constitute Conrad's court, and it is only fitting that he is listed among their number as "the Honourable Conrad Moffat Black," a distinction he owes to Brian Mulroney who appointed him a member of the Queen's Privy Council for Canada in 1992, an honour usually reserved for cabinet ministers and governors general. *[Mulroney also conferred the same distinction on Power Corp. chairman Paul Desmarais and the international real-estate tycoon George Vari.]* The blue-ribbon members of Conrad's court have included: the Rt. Hon. the Baroness Thatcher, who served as prime minister of Great Britain from 1979 to 1990 and is Black's intellectual godfather; the Rt. Hon. the Lord Carrington, former secretary-general of NATO; Henry Kissinger, the gutturalvoiced former American secretary of state, and last of the Vietnam hawks still flapping his wings; Giovanni Agnelli, the worldly chairman of Fiat, from Turin, Italy; Chaim Herzog, former president of Israel; David Brinkley, the ABC news commentator; Zbigniew Brzezinski, former U.S. national security adviser; William Buckley, the David Frum of American journalism and founding editor of the *National Review*; half a dozen British gentry, such as the Lords Hanson, Weidenfeld of Chelsea, Swaythling, Rawlison of Ewell, Tebbit, and King of Wartnaby, who heads British Airways; Bob Strauss, former head of the U.S. Atomic Energy Commission; Richard Burt, former chief negotiator for strategic arms reduction with the body; Sir Evelyn de Rothschild, chairman of London's House of Rothschild; Paul Volker, former head of the U.S. Federal Reserve Board; Major-General Shlomo Gazit, former chief of Israeli military intelligence; columnist George Will; Leslie Wexner, who heads something mysteriously called The Limited Inc., which retails "apparel and personal care items," and who is a director of the intimately branded Intimate Brands Inc.; and, of course, Allan Gotlieb, the former Canadian ambassador to Washington, whose approbation at such gatherings ranks second only to that of His Eminence G. Emmett Cardinal Carter, whose name has also decorated one of the Hollinger boards. They're an awesome crew all right, but their average age leaves the impression they would feel winded playing chess.

This group, together with the editors, columnists, commentators, hangers-on and assorted groupies who work for him, makes up Conrad's retinue. It obeys its own political imperatives, not dissimilar to those of the Vatican, whose power struggles have always intrigued Black. *[According to an apocryphal tale, during one of the papal elections, when cardinals are locked into a chamber until they pick a new pope and release a puff of white smoke, one of their members has a heart attack and dies. As his body is being carried out, a cardinal turns to his seatmate and whispers, "I wonder what his motive was?" That air of intrigue is how one former member describes the Byzantine atmosphere of Black's retinue.]* As well as conducting his internal court, Black plays a leading part in the Western world's two most influential secret societies: the Trilateral Commission and the Bilderberg Conference. *[The Trilateral Commission is described in Chapter*

3; its membership is listed in Appendix 1. As well as Black, who heads the local chapter, Canadian membership of the Bilderberg Conference, named after the Bilderberg Hotel in Oosterbeek, Holland, where it first met in 1954, includes: Fred Eaton, formerly dean of a well-known Canadian department store; Al Flood, CEO of the Commerce; Tony Griffin of the Guardian Group; Red Wilson of BCE; Ted Rogers; Sylvia Ostry of the University of Toronto Centre for International Studies; and, of course, Allan Gotlieb.] Consisting of 120 of the industrialized world's most profound doers and thinkers, the Conference meets annually under tight security, to discuss current issues. There is no formal agenda or tabled set of recommendations.

Achieving fame in Conrad's view is about lounging in the back of his Phantom VI Rolls-Royce with the built-in telephone and hooded reading light, and being chauffeured through the narrow streets of the City, London's financial district. In few former seats of empire is there so much to occupy the eye, the imagination and the memory. The men who built London's magnificent office structures, and whose descendants still occupy them, brought a touch of civility to the rough-and-tumble world of commerce. Former U.S. secretary of state Dean Acheson, who knew his history, once remarked that he could think of no more delightful period or place in which to have lived than mid-nineteenth-century England, when the country was run by a small group of highly intelligent and largely disinterested individuals. That notion appeals to Conrad, even if he is anything but disinterested. He fits perfectly into the British milieu, having already been the confidant of two former prime ministers, a friend to some members of the royal family, and welcomed everywhere he appears. People on both sides of the Atlantic observe his every move and follow his gaze, hoping to be noticed.

In the past half-decade, Black has grown up, become more interesting, less self-obsessed. His imperious bearing remains intact, but he no longer seems so mesmerized by his own rhetoric. He can laugh—well, at least chuckle—at himself, and occasionally manages to sound downright human. "I feel myself very fortunate," he admits. "I have a position perfectly suited for me that I've worked rather hard for a number of years to design. I do pretty much what I like and don't do very much that I don't like. I don't mean that in a social, hoity-toity way, but I'm personally happy with my lot." *[He should be. Apart from his more than $3 million a year in compensation, he benefited in the spring of 1997 from special Hollinger dividends worth $70 million.]* His juices have cooled. The rigid guardsman's posture has softened, and he allows himself the traces of a slouch, the way old ball players do, once their mug goes up in the Hall of Fame. He is no longer as obsessed with his image in the media as he once was, except when

Linda McQuaig writes one of her broadsides. He has become convinced that most journalists suffer from incurable dementia, and pretends to ignore their achy-breaky ravings about him.

That has been especially true since he married Barbara Amiel, then the lead political columnist for *The Sunday Times* and one of the most sought-after and talked-about charmers in London, as well as Toronto—and St. Catharines, Ontario, where she simmered up. There is no doubt that she has added joy to Conrad's life. They have become an almost required presence at the very top levels of London society. ("As soon as you see the names Conrad and Barbara on the guest list, you know you're at the right place at the right time," says one dowager.) They fit right in. Ideologically, she is far to the right of Conrad, being a libertarian instead of merely a conservative.

Amiel is a classic example of a woman whose goods looks have made her vulnerable to false accusations. One example was the time she was named editor of the tabloid *Toronto Sun*, taking over from founding editor Peter Worthington.

"On her first day as editor of the *Sun*, I took Barbara for lunch at Winston's," recalls Doug Creighton, who was then the tabloid's publisher. "I was toasting her, telling her to be her own person, that there was nothing really scary about us, that we weren't going to go left wing or anything like that, and if there was something that she was trying to change which potentially was an embarrassment to me or the paper, she just had to give me a call. I kept saying, just be yourself.

"When Barbara talks to you, it's right up close and you can hardly hear her.

"'Why do you keep mentioning Peter Worthington?' she asked me at one point.

"'Well, he was your predecessor, he hired you, and he's trained you as editor. I'm just trying to say he's gone, that's done.'

"So she leaned back in the booth and said—just at the precise moment when everybody in the restaurant had stopped talking for a split second—'You think I'm fucking him, don't you?'

"'Jesus Christ, that isn't what I was saying, but I suppose your question demands an answer, and I would say yes,' I remember saying.

"'Well,' she said, 'I'm not.'

"'That's a great waste of journalistic effort,' was my reply, and I remember that the lawyer Fraser Elliott was sitting at the next table. He heard the question, but he didn't hear her answer, and his eyes were just bugging out."

That seems long ago. The Blacks now live in a four-storey mansion purchased from the renegade Australian financier Alan Bond for $7 million, with as much again spent on massive renovations. It is divided into eleven bedrooms, eight bathrooms and an indoor pool and has two elevators plus every luxury known to man. Wherever the Blacks travel, a cook and a butler precede them to assure their every comfort. When Barbara and Conrad visited Peter and Melanie Munk's hideaway island in Georgian Bay, they were astounded that the Munks didn't have a staff and everybody had to do their own dishes.

For Conrad, his social and business success in Britain has been the ultimate triumph. His purchase in 1986 of one of the world's greatest newspapers, the *Telegraph*, gave him an unparalleled international power base, a private intelligence network and an impressive cash flow that needs investing. The late Robert Maxwell, who was no slouch at buying newspapers at discount prices, described Black's purchase of the *Telegraph* in 1986 as "history's biggest fish, caught with history's smallest hook." The paper cost Black $67 million; its franchise is now estimated to be worth close to $2 billion. To be the proprietor/publisher of the *Telegraph* is to be perceived as powerful—not in the way politicians enjoy their often brief fling with fame, but in the more permanent manner of being, *and being recognized as being*, the "power behind the throne." That is sweet indeed. And for Conrad to have earned that enviable insider status in the Mother Country of the land of his birth—the one place left on Earth where behaving like an aristocrat is still permissible—is as good as it gets.

IT HAS TAKEN BLACK MOST OF THREE DECADES to finally pacify the feeling of revenge for the slights inflicted on his father. A Winnipeg-born accountant, George Montegu Black had been fired as head of Canadian Breweries by E.P. Taylor at age forty-seven, after a dispute over his reorganization of the company, though he had turned it into Canada's most profitable brewery. During the next eighteen years, until his death in 1976, George Black seldom strayed from the living-room of his Toronto house, except for the odd round of croquet in his garden. He spent his days smoking (sometimes puffing two cigarettes at the same time) and ringing for Fernando Aranda, his Spanish butler, to refill his martini jugs. He had a ticker-tape installed at home and turned a fortune by buying undervalued stocks and bonds. He used the money he made from the turnaround on Alberta bonds and Abitibi Power & Paper second-preferreds to amass shares in Argus Corp., the company that Conrad would capture in 1978. The senior Black became an Argus director in 1951 and eventually some of its board meetings were held in his living-room.

Many writers have speculated on the major influences on Conrad's tangled thought process, citing almost everybody from Charles de Gaulle and Sigmund Freud to Napoleon Bonaparte and Donald Duck. The answer is simple and irrefutable: his humbled father was the youngster's chief mentor and soul mate. The father lived through the son. It was during their many evenings together that the elder Black spun the tales of corporate derring-do that ignited the youngster's imagination and would eventually dominate his life. Unlike most Establishment patriarchs, who rush to endow their favourite offspring with the material rewards of their own hard-won success, George Black gave Conrad something much more valuable. He taught him the fundamentals of the market economy, steeped him in the lore of Argus, and explained to him how stock-value fluctuations can be forecast and exploited. He instilled in the boy an appreciation for the relevance of historical perspective and, most important of all, trained him in the art of seeing through human deception. Father and son relaxed by playing chess. They pitted their talents against history's great masters, replaying gambits devised by José Raúl Capablanca, the Cuban child prodigy who started playing the game at the age of four and became world champion in 1921.

Conrad learned his priorities early. By his own admission, he first became determined to be chairman of Argus Corp. (the predecessor company of the current Hollinger) when he was only seven years old. Laurier LaPierre, the historian–TV commentator who taught Black at Upper Canada College, remembers him well. "Even then," LaPierre recalls, "Conrad was like a champion runner. I sometimes watch those contestants at the Olympics and find myself fascinated by the tension as they wait to spring into the pool or onto the running tracks. Conrad was like that, except that he seemed to know precisely when the starting gun would go off. His entire sense of life revolved around the idea that through a combination of circumstance, accidents and evolution, God had granted him this extraordinary power that he must guard well and pass on. He always felt himself to be a genuine instrument of history, with the capacity to create events."

Conrad was only eight when, of his own accord, he saved $59 in pocket money and bought a share in General Motors. "When I purchased that share," he would later recall, "it was for motives that were then widely held by my elders. The Korean War was on at the time; Stalin was still in power; it was the height of the Cold War. To buy stock in General Motors was a wise means of participating in the growth of capitalism, supporting a great institution and casting one's vote with the side of justice and freedom in the worldwide struggle with the Red menace which was then generally assumed to be lurking behind every bush and under every bed. Notwithstanding my extreme zeal as a stockholder and as a Cold Warrior, I was appalled when the president of General Motors, Frederic Donner, announced that the U.S. automobile industry's policy was one of planned obsolescence. He claimed that because of the beneficial effect of this policy on the American economy, it should be described not as planned obsolescence but as dynamic obsolescence. I was young and reasonably credulous, but I instinctively knew that this was nonsense. Still, I always felt I was better off investing in General Motors, despite my reservations about management, than in record albums and the like."

Conrad emerged from his father's intense tutorials too undisciplined and mentally overheated to handle more conventional schools. He managed to get himself expelled from two private schools (Upper Canada College and Trinity College School in Port Hope), failed his law courses and endured rather than absorbed his formal education. Part of the problem was that Upper Canada at the time was designed to appeal to the Toronto élite, who wanted their sons to learn how to be unobtrusively rich. The school taught them about authority and money and how to cope with having it, instilling in graduates the need for perpetuating establishment values. This was not a skill or an attitude that Conrad required any lessons to master.

John Fraser, the journalist, essayist and Master of Toronto's Massey College, was one of the few good friends Conrad made at UCC's prep school. "My earliest memory of him would be in about grade six and how terribly, terribly conscious he was of wealth and power," Fraser recalls. "We were walking around the school grounds one day and Conrad was raving on about the stupid masters. At one point, he swept his hand to indicate the whole of the college and said, 'E.P. Taylor could buy this silly place fifty times over. He'd subdivide and make some money off it.' He was constantly sketching scenarios for taking over the college. Childhood was a prison for him. I remember Conrad as someone whose head was practically splitting because he was so impatient to get out into the real world and away from this nonsense of a boys' school." The climax of Conrad's dubious career at Upper Canada College occurred in the spring of 1959, when he broke into the principal's office, discovered some exam forms, had them copied and sold them to fellow students on a variable price system, charging less to kids who couldn't afford to pay and more to students he felt were certain to fail. It was his first business venture and resulted in his expulsion.

After barely graduating from Ottawa's Carleton University, Conrad left Ontario for Quebec, where he spent eight years learning French, getting two degrees (in law from Laval and history from McGill), discovering the world of women, and becoming a newspaper publisher.

On his twenty-first birthday (as described in Chapter 4), Conrad received a plain white envelope from Bud McDougald, the Argus executive then trying to undermine the authority of the founding chairman, E.P. Taylor. Inside was a membership card for the Toronto Club. Conrad thus slipped past the club's cumbersome admissions procedure and became its youngest-ever member. When the story was told by a mutual friend to Paul Desmarais, who would later have run-ins with both McDougald and Black, the Power Corporation chairman quipped, "Hell, Bud probably signed up Conrad the day he was born!"

It was his sojourn in Quebec that ignited Black's intellectual affinity for Charles de Gaulle, the charismatic French general who ranked along with his father as one of his idols. De Gaulle had initially fascinated Conrad because of his unusual career as army strategist, exile, recluse, saviour, savant and saint. Although he never reached the stage of sharing the general's ecstatic vision of France as "the Madonna in the frescoes," he was immensely attracted by the idea that the esthetic of French civilization is based on the creative faculty of choice. According to this notion, options are exercised not in response to an individual's tastes and preferences, but on the basis of what the French call *mesure*, the proper proportion of things. As part of that view of life, Conrad subscribed to the comment by the seventeenth-century French satirist Jean de La Bruyère, who wrote that "life is a tragedy for those who feel, and a comedy for those who think." He believes that and acts accordingly.

Intellectuals are confused by Black because he is so far to the political right that he ought to be dragging his knuckles, yet he is more cultivated in the arena of ideas than most of them can ever hope to be. "Still," as Murray Kempton, the American essayist, wrote about de Gaulle, "one senses that he is most approving when he watches intellectuals marching in formation." That's a thought that Conrad would certainly support.

Though de Gaulle insisted to the end that he was France's "only true revolutionary," once in power he entrusted management of France's economy to a vice-president of the Rothschild Bank. Conrad would have approved of that too. (Yet unlike his French role model, who was much more interested in what could be preserved than in what could be created, Black does not fear the future. He is willing to create, providing it is for his own account.)

De Gaulle's claim to *be* France struck Black as not in the least pretentious. That illusion dates back to a cool morning in June of 1940, when *Le Grand Charles*, alone in London but assuming charge of France's government in exile after the fall of his country to the Nazis, set aside his own lack of electoral legitimacy and decided that "it was up to me to assume I was France." There is some disagreement among Black-watchers about whether Conrad sees himself as Canada personified. I have never subscribed to that silly notion for the simple reason that if Black were to personify any country, he would pick a grander, better-managed and less untidy nation than ours. Still, he appreciates the concept, and may one day choose to exercise it.

DURING HIS TIME IN MONTREAL, BLACK was attracted to the city's French-speaking business élite because they were nearly all self-made and had worked their way up against tough odds. He constantly stressed his identification with these *arrivistes* rather than align himself with the WASPish Westmount establishment. He insisted on explaining to anyone who would listen that he had made it on his own, and that, while he might have been born to privilege, he had started his own business and its success had been based on his own merit, his own brain, his own ability to function. This interpretation of Black's founding of the Sterling newspaper chain, which was the object of his boasting, magnified somewhat the series of events involved. Moreover, as his friend, the late *boulevardier* Nick Auf der Maur, loved to point out, "Conrad had a slightly better line of credit than most of us."

It was mainly in Auf der Maur's company that Black found the courage of his condescensions—such as the time they met on Sherbrooke Street and decided to have a drink. "As a lark, I took Conrad to the Truxx Cruising Bar on Stanley Street, then Montreal's most notorious homosexual hangout," Auf der Maur recalled. "It was three flights up, an awful place, raided by the morality squad a couple of weeks later. I knocked on the door, but they wouldn't let us in; with his three-piece suit, Conrad looked much too straight. He went through this hilarious transformation. For the first thirty seconds, he was totally indignant because we were standing at what he later called 'the portals of depravity.' He then turned just as indignant because as a free citizen he was being refused entry. He got quite confused because he couldn't quite decide which to be more indignant about. We never did go in, but I remember that wonderful moment of consternation."

Peter White, Black's friend from their days at Carleton, had purchased for one dollar a tiny, decrepit Quebec weekly, the Knowlton *Advertiser*, which claimed a summer circulation of three hundred. He persuaded the youthful Conrad to run it. Black changed the paper's name to the *Eastern Townships Advertiser*, decided to publish year round, bought a companion French-language weekly in nearby Cowansville, and within six months was turning a monthly profit of $350. Black moved into a boathouse belonging to Peter White's mother on the shores of nearby Brome Lake. What had started as a lark gradually turned into a business. With a staff of only two, Conrad wrote most of the copy, sold much of the advertising and looked after subscriptions, which climbed to 2,100. Through the brooding solitude of a Quebec winter, Black lived in cramped quarters, spending the long nights by himself. A snifter of Napoleon brandy at hand, he would muse about his future, gazing across the frozen lake towards Tyrone, the baronial summer house of the late John Bassett, a real publisher, who had commanded the Montreal *Gazette* and owned the Sherbrooke *Record*. "I may have been tempted to shake my fist at it many nights," he later recalled, "but I don't think I ever actually did."

DURING HIS EIGHT YEARS IN QUEBEC, BLACK also came in close touch with the Catholic Church, mainly as the self-appointed campaign manager for the Nobel Peace Prize on behalf of Paul-Émile Cardinal Léger, then in charge of the Quebec diocese. He began by all but worshipping the cardinal, and learned much about Catholic politics and religion, but became nonplussed when the churchman decided to abandon his powerful post to care for lepers in Africa. "I always felt that Conrad intended to be Léger's campaign manager for the papacy," commented Nick Auf der Maur. "He would have liked nothing better than to have access to the Pope. He was endlessly fascinated by how a guy such as Léger could reach the bearing and natural grace of aristocracy without having been born to it. But when the cardinal gave up his post to become an ordinary parish priest and went to look after lepers in Africa, Conrad felt he'd blown his chance for the Holy See and got quite exasperated. He saw his whole entrée to the Vatican going down the drain. He kept complaining that Léger wasn't being consistent, that nobody was going to take him seriously any more. As the whole thing disintegrated, Conrad got increasingly short-tempered, and whereas he'd once spoken in total awe of Léger, he would mutter about the cardinal having become a bit eccentric and how he'd better clean up his act."

In an age when the meltdown of moral absolutes is a common occurrence, Black has maintained a private spiritual dimension, which has led him to ditch his Anglican upbringing and join the Roman Catholic Church. After he returned to Toronto, G. Emmett Cardinal Carter, the Archbishop of Toronto, became his spiritual adviser and confidant. The two men spent many a long evening debating the finer points of Vatican intrigue, Quebec history and the theological verities. "It was a highly intellectual conversion," Carter recalls. "Conrad never expected anything in return; he really is a spiritual man. I believe he converted from the Anglican Church because he found there was more historical background when it came to Catholicism. I think he found that very strong.

"Conrad could easily have been a Jew, because the Jewish religion has a background that goes way back to the prophets and the Psalms, all the way back to Abraham and so forth. Conrad used to come to see me, before his conversion, almost every week, and we didn't always talk theology, but we did do a lot of deep probing of theology, and he was very good. He has a very wise grasp of the teachings of the Church; he has studied it deeply. And I gave him some books to read which he faithfully read, and then we discussed this point and that point. There were some things he didn't agree with, but they weren't matters of doctrine, and of course he knew a lot about ecclesiastical history and the errors that the Church made over the years, which are multiple. But that didn't throw him off to the point where he was discouraged with the Church. He had really no problem with its basic teachings, though he disagreed with some of the Vatican's politics—some of which I disagree with myself. After they made me a cardinal, I couldn't talk very much about it. Somebody said to me once, 'Rome must have had a hard time with you.' I said, 'Well, they shut me up by making me a cardinal.'

"Conrad really is extraordinary," recalls Carter, warming to his subject. "But he puzzles me. I don't know how he does it. I can hardly bring up a subject he's not up on. I lived much of my life in Quebec, and he knows more about French Canada than I do. One day he recited the popes for me from the beginning, from Peter all the way down to the present pope, just like that. He is very history-conscious, in some ways more of a traditionalist than I am. He loves to talk about what goes on among the cardinals, and is always fleshing out some historical church figure I didn't remember anything about or had only heard as a name. He certainly knows more about how the Vatican worked in the eighteenth century than I do. He is quite incredible. In business he's tough, no question about that. But I think he's fair too. I told him, when he was younger, 'Conrad, you've committed a very serious sin.' He said, 'What do you mean?' I said, 'You're too successful too young, and they're not going to like it. But that will go, don't worry, it will disappear after you get a little older. They'll get used to you and forgive you.' That's what happened. There was a lot of jealousy the first years, but not now."

At one of his Hollinger Dinners at the Toronto Club, which are the equivalent of annual coming-out parties for the Canadian Establishment, Black described Cardinal Carter as "being dressed tonight in his raiment as the ecumenical chaplain of 10 Toronto Street [Hollinger's headquarters] as well as the ecclesiastical Toronto stringer for the *Jerusalem Post.*"

The cardinal has also been a friend and adviser to Barbara Amiel, long before she met Conrad. "She was marrying a Catholic at that point," he recalls, "and she came to me to ask me how it would work, because she's Jewish and she wanted to know what the difficulties would be. I explained the whole thing and I found her very affable, charming, bright. She's good for Conrad. She's an intellectual equal, and he needs that. I like to hear them argue together; she never backs down. She's never taking her hat off or curtseying to everything he wants to say or do."

APART FROM THE CHURCH, THE most profound influence on Conrad Black has been his partnership with Franklin David Radler, a street fighter with fastidiously tuned intuitions, who is his *alter ego*. Radler's father owned a Montreal restaurant called *Au Lutin Qui Bouffe* (The Elf Who Eats Too Much), which attracted customers by allowing them to play and pose with piglets that wandered among the tables. After graduating in arts from McGill, Radler took an MBA degree at Queen's, and while still at university was asked to create a handicrafts marketing program for the Curve Lake Indian Reserve north of Peterborough, Ontario; he later developed similar schemes for thirty Native communities.

The ambitious trio (Black, Radler and Peter White) bought the Sherbrooke *Record* in 1969 for $20,000, cut the payroll in half (from forty-eight to twenty-four), found a cheap press to print the paper in Vermont, and reduced costs by rationing the pencils and rolls of toilet paper used by reporters. Black has a difficult time dealing with the concept that newspapers need to employ reporters and editors. "It is one of the great myths that you need journalists to produce a paper," he blandly declared when one of his papers, the strikebound *Le Soleil* in Quebec City, kept on publishing with a tiny skeleton staff. On other occasions, he has merely condemned the profession for being "heavily cluttered with youngsters who substitute 'commitment' for insight and with aged hacks toiling through a miasma of mounting decrepitude. Alcoholism is endemic in both groups." At one point, when an employee came into Radler's office with a petition of grievances, he was fined 2¢ for wasting a sheet of paper. Within a year, the paper had turned the corner. "After we saw the profits coming in, we said to ourselves, God, where has this business been all our lives?" Black remembers asking himself — and that was the beginning of the Sterling newspaper chain, which grew into today's giant Hollinger holdings.

In the subsequent quarter-century, Black was the front man, doing most of the large deals, while Peter White tended to busy himself on public affairs issues. It was the third partner who did most of the tough hiring, firing and operating. Radler laid off 300 of the *Jerusalem Post's* 480 employees, and in Saskatchewan, 183 staff members of the dailies bought by Hollinger were herded into a hotel room and fired without appeal or warning. The writer Jennifer Wells has described Radler and his crew as "corporate Reservoir Dogs," while Adam Zimmerman, the Southam director who was fired by Black, accused him of "showing no class" and described Hollinger's executive as "some very tough guys. They're not people. They're torpedoes."

Radler sums up his theory of newspapers and democratic ideals thus: "The buck stops with the ownership. I am responsible for meeting the payroll; therefore I will ultimately determine what the newspapers say and how they're going to be run. If editors disagree with us, they should disagree with us when they're no longer in our employ."

Certainly the newspapers in the Southam chain have felt the Black/Radler regime's presence since the purchase was completed in the summer of 1996. While they have installed new editors closer to their ideology, they have also purchased new presses and spruced up the layouts. Some of the papers, especially *The Vancouver Sun* (under the inspired editorship of John Cruikshank) and *The Ottawa Citizen* (guided by Neil Reynolds), now qualify as serious reading. But is it all at the expense—as some critics charge—of political independence at those same papers?

Radler disputes that notion. "Too much is made out of that," he says. "Ask the guys in Vancouver if I've asked for a change in ideology. It may be that some of these editors see us and suddenly see the light; there might be some of that. But no one has been ordered to change ideologically. When we brought Reynolds into the *Citizen*, that wasn't primarily an ideological change. I was actually shocked when I found out that he was a libertarian." Ken King, publisher of the *Calgary Herald*, supports that point of view. "Black's interference consists of expecting you to deliver a high-quality product," he says. "On a day-to-day level, he interferes not at all."

The Southam takeover had all the elements of a classic Black manoeuvre. The pattern had been seen so often before: with the Smith sisters during the original Argus takeover; the Humphreys and the Hannas during the Hanna Mining grab in Cleveland; with the comically inept Berry family at the *Telegraph*; the pitiful remnant of the Fairfax family in Australia; and the Fields of Illinois, who had allowed the *Sun-Times* to slip badly. Each of these once glorious enterprises was held in the feeble grip of a fading family or dynasty. They were ripe for the picking. Like these clans, the Southams had fathered too many heirs, diluting their genes and equity positions. Only a decade earlier, the Southams still owned 44.9 percent of the company's shares, their loyalties reinforced by a privately published guide, issued once a year, that gave news of what every family member was doing. By the time Conrad arrived on the scene, their holdings were down to 17 percent, and nearly every shareholder wanted to sell. In fact, two Southams—Christopher and his sister Ann—sued National Trust for $7 million for holding too much Southam stock in their trust accounts instead of making more profitable investments. The family's inability to speak with one voice or to field strong management had left their chief assets bereft of adequate profits or sustaining energy. The fight was led by eighty-two-year-old St. Clair Balfour (related to the Southams maternally as well as by marriage), who had been the company's president and chairman between 1961 and 1985. "You can't have family members selling down their shares and claiming the firm is still ours," he conceded. "The first job of any company is to operate at a profit, which Southam has not done for the last two years."

Back in 1991, the board was dissatisfied with the company's performance (John Fisher was president and Hugh Hallward was chairman). Nothing was going right, so directors formed an ad hoc corporate governance committee, which recommended that Southam hire a new president and appoint a new chairman. These two positions came to be occupied by Bill Ardell, from the company's Cole's division, and Ron Cliff, a professional Vancouver director.

A partnership formed with Torstar in 1985 hadn't worked. The idea had been that the companies would at some point get together so that Southam would gain a Toronto outlet or the *Star* could head a national chain, but nobody made the first move. In November 1993, Torstar sold their 20-percent holding to Conrad Black.

"I went down to the Southam office to welcome him, and the first thing I noticed was what a charming gentleman he was. But he had the coldest eyes I've ever met," Cliff recalls. "At any rate, he started musing a bit. He likes to use the word 'muse' and 16 million other words. And as he was musing about what he saw at Southam, he was sort of hinting that he would like to take some of his papers and roll them in for Southam shares and that way get control of Southam. So we set up a committee of one—me—to strike the Southam–Hollinger agreement. He and I, with the help of his lawyers and Gar Emerson on our side, worked to get this agreement, and I can remember the closing moment. I was down in Barbados and I got a call at a cocktail party at the hotel, and I went into a luggage room, where there was a telephone. So Conrad and I agreed to call it the Luggage Room Agreement.

"We settled all the final outstanding things as to board representation, and it was very clear that he could not take control of the company, even if he owned 40 percent of the shares. Neither could he take control of the board. What he got out of that was the fact that we weren't going to fight him, that we'd put him on the board, work with him, welcome him and one thing and another."

By 1993, Cliff had invited Paul Desmarais's Power Corp. into the company by selling them a 20-percent share, partly as a cash infusion and partly to keep Black at bay. Paul and Conrad had agreed that Cliff should continue as chairman and that any English-language print media in Canada would be offered to Southam before either Power or Hollinger could buy them. But Black bought several Thomson papers without formally offering them to Southam, though Roy Megarry, who was handling the sale for Thomson, claimed that Southam could have made a bid but didn't.

"Time went along," Cliff recalls, "and Desmarais, who has never sold anything for a loss, I suspect, in his life except maybe a school bus, gave us ample warning that he didn't want to be in business with Conrad. And he gave us ample time to try and figure out how the company could buy him out. Really, there was no way in which we could figure out how to buy his shares, worth two hundred and some-odd million, so he sold to Conrad and made about $60 million. Meanwhile, Conrad bought the *StarPhoenix* and *Leader-Post* without consulting anyone. So Desmarais sold out and made his money, and that voided the Southam–Hollinger agreement. But who cared at that point?

"The four or five directors Conrad wanted to fire chose not to step down, except for David Johnson, who resigned. The rest of us said, 'Well, we just got re-elected and you only own 40 percent of the company.' It was Adam Zimmerman who led the charge, but they threw us out and fired Bill Ardell. All very unpleasant. Conrad is a very brilliant guy," says Ron Cliff, "but he's as ruthless as they come, and doesn't believe in corporate governance."

Radler has a bitingly fast reply. "Ron Cliff," he says, "goes down in our corporate history as one of the builders of the empire. We wouldn't own Southam if he hadn't been there, if Ardell or Zimmerman hadn't been there. We could never have been able to afford the shares if Southam had been well run."

Conrad Black's seizure of the Southam publishing chain was typical of the man and his methods. He scooped up control of Canada's largest newspaper chain after a behind-closed-doors stock deal with Paul Desmarais, pledged that he would preserve Southam's integrity, then promptly fired its independent directors, replacing them with his own choices. As such, it was a fairly routine corporate takeover, but because Conrad Black was involved, it quickly became headline news, prompting calls for stern investigations into his motives and methods. Dark accusations were voiced that he might use his clout as owner to dictate what his newspapers would print.

THERE WAS NEVER, OF COURSE, THE SLIGHTEST DOUBT that Black intended to use his newspapers to influence public opinion towards his conservative view of life. A clue to his publishing philosophy is contained in a private letter he once wrote to William F. Buckley, Jr., of the *National Review*, house organ of that sector of the American right whose adherents are moderate enough not to require distemper shots. Black was preparing to purchase *Saturday Night* magazine and wanted advice. "I take the liberty of writing to you on behalf of many members of the journalistic, academic and business community who wish to convert an existing magazine into a conveyance for views at some variance with the tired porridge of ideological normalcy in vogue here, as in the U.S.," he wrote Buckley. "We are people of some means and convictions and intend to persevere with our plans. It is in that context that we would like some advice from you, as we will at least partially emulate your example at the *National Review*."

Black did buy the magazine, then edited with grace and verve by Robert Fulford, who was not precisely asked to leave but found it philosophically uncomfortable to work under its new owner. It wasn't until Black appointed the capable Ken Whyte, a graduate of the Ted Byfield School of Alberta-centred Journalism and later appointed editor of Black's new national daily, that *Saturday Night* reflected more closely its owner's approach. Between Fulford and Whyte, *Saturday Night* was edited by John Fraser, Black's Upper Canada College school chum who was the exception that proved the rule, and who ran the magazine with cheek and verve but no particular ideology.

That is the extent to which Black interferes with editorial departments: he appoints editors whose ideology he trusts, then allows them their freedom. That may not be desirable, but neither is it unique. Most of Canada's great publishers—Joe Atkinson, J.W. McConnell, Jacob Nicol, Pamphile DuTremblay, Max Bell, Victor Sifton, John Bassett and R.S. Malone—regarded their newspapers as extensions of themselves. Questioned about using his paper to attack his foes and praise his friends, John Bassett asked with genuine astonishment, "Why else would I own one?" *[I know how the process works. In 1969, before I was offered the job of editor-in-chief of* The Toronto Star, *Beland Honderich, then its publisher, quizzed me in great detail about my attitudes on his paper's prevailing ideology, which was highly nationalistic and slightly to the left of centre on social issues. Nobody pretended we were neutral. In 1970, when, along with the late Walter Gordon and Professor Abe Rotstein, I founded the Committee for an Independent Canada, which became the chief lobby group for government action on increased domestic ownership of our media and resources, I wrote the CIC's manifesto at my editor's desk, and shamelessly used the paper to promote our cause.]*

Even though he runs so many papers that he has become more of a corporate being than a publisher, Black is perpetuating, or at least trying to keep alive, the old-fashioned notion of proprietorship. "I don't intend to be some swashbuckling, absolute proprietor," says he. "But I do believe that proprietorships are better run because the motivation is greater. Every cent wasted comes eventually from your pocket." That penny-saving syndrome allows Black and his cohorts to control the contents of their papers in another essential way: reducing budgets means they can't afford too many investigative initiatives. When a PWA jet crashed near Cranbrook, B.C., back in 1978, the Black-owned *Daily Townsman* had been trimmed down to four editorial employees, so that the paper had to cover the tragedy mostly through dispatches from the Toronto-based Canadian Press news agency. That too is the proprietor's prerogative.

IF CONRAD BLACK DIDN'T EXIST, HE WOULD invent himself—and he has. His career has progressed through a series of carefully planned and meticulously executed moves. He has done it all—and it's not enough. Never enough. And yet he's well aware, as he once told me, that it was "the compulsive element in Napoleon that drew him into greater and greater undertakings, until he was bound to fail." Black likes to describe his career as having been conducted according to "the expanding-funnel offence" conceived by the British military strategist B.H. Liddell Hart: "I keep advancing like a platoon of men through a forest, parallel lines moving in various directions—and wherever there is a breakthrough, I try to exploit it."

That says nothing about his intentions or the boundaries—if any—to his goals and ambitions. Meanwhile, he goes on, decanting himself out of the leather seats of private jets, the teak bunks of luxury yachts, the back benches of Rolls-Royces, the sofas in the office or the eighteenth-century cardinal's chair he keeps under the rotunda in the library of his house in Toronto. He is in some ways Canada's only true Titan, because unlike Paul Desmarais or Peter Munk, who rival him most closely for that honour, he deliberately behaves like one. Conrad has attained that rare state of grace that finally allows him to capitalize on his aura. He is what he has always wanted to be.

The definitive description of Conrad Black remains a 1979 Montreal *Gazette* cartoon by Aislin, showing him in a pinstripe suit, pondering his future. "So, at a very early age, I had to make the decision," he is saying to himself in the cartoon's caption. "Did I really want to be Prime Minister? Shit no, I thought. I'd much rather be powerful."

3 GUNSLINGERS IN RED SUSPENDERS

14

THE ANATOMY
OF BAY STREET

"Most of us enter the investment business for the same sanity-destroy-
ing reason women become prostitutes. It avoids the menace of hard
work, is a group activity that requires little in the way of intellect, and
is a practical means of making money for those with no talent for anything else."

—*Richard Ney*, The Wall Street Jungle

THEY SAY TORONTO IS CANADA's eleventh province, so powerful is
its sway over the rest of the country. "How many Torontonians does it
take to change a bulb?" goes the hinterland joke. "One—to hold the bulb
still, while the world turns around him."

But looked at more dispassionately, it's not Toronto that decides who
wins and who loses in the country at large; it's Bay Street. Those twenty
downtown blocks inside the rectangle formed by University Avenue and
Queen, Front and Victoria streets—where $100 billion (including cur-
rency and derivative trades) changes hands most working days—is home
base for the majority of Canada's most active Titans.

It's inside those golden acres that many of the men and women who
make things happen in this country finance, exploit, sustain, chisel and ride
close herd over Canada's economy. This is where the price of money is
set. Jean Giraudoux, the French savant, once described Paris as "the twenty
square miles of the world where the most thinking and the most talking is
going on." That's how Bay Street's twenty-block abattoir views itself.

Bay Street, of course, is less a place than a state of mind. It is where
you can become a millionaire in one lucky stab at the stock charts, or be
reduced to a bum—just as quickly. Young stockbrokers, often inexperi-
enced, unseasoned and not possessing much of an IQ, can make $250,000
a year within twenty-four months or so of being hired. In a way, it is
Canada's version of Hollywood, a mythical domain where dreams may be

dashed, but still a place where dreamers test themselves against their destinies. They come every day aboard the more than 500 jets that land at Pearson Airport, disgorging new Bay Street hopefuls, ready to do a little strip mining in the big city.

Once settled into their slots, the 52,000 or so inhabitants of this crammed financial district seldom give much thought to the country beyond their immediate horizons, except to acknowledge at every month's end the profit centres quietly bubbling out there among the provinces. When they do take a nanosecond to consider the Canadian reality, their image of that large and splendid patrimony encompasses what they can see from the fifty-fourth floor of the TD Centre, at a window table of Canoe restaurant.

Bay Streeters' motivations are easy to understand. The place is populated by impatient men and women with six-figure salaries who would kill for seven-figure incomes. Their religion is money, and their patron saint is Mike Milken—not the one who went to jail for twenty-two months after being convicted of securities fraud, but the inventor of junk bonds, a financing craze that in one year alone earned him an income of $660 million, which was $2 million more than McDonald's made that year. Milken is also the patron saint of workaholics, having figured out during his early years how to work while riding on an early-morning bus from his home in Cherry Hill, New Jersey, to Wall Street. To enable him to study the financial data he always carried with him in a mailbag, he strapped a miner's lamp on his forehead and read by its beam without disturbing the other passengers. Virtually bald, Milken was so vain that he owned thirty toupees, of slightly varying lengths to that he could simulate monthly hair growth. Bay Street's operators are so deep into money that it sometimes seems as if they inhale the stuff. It's not that they're dedicated to their work; it's that their souls would wither without it. Most have no institutional memory, little sense of loyalty or duty that transcends their quest for material well-being. They exhibit scant pride about their places of work (most Bay Street firms are revolving doors), but boast shamelessly about the deals they've done. *[Milken also set the standard for celebrating successful deals, with his anything-goes Predator's Balls, held annually in Los Angeles. The entertainment provided for jubilant clients celebrating major transactions included prepaid "starlets and fashion models" hired as available sex partners. Just goes to prove that gentlemen don't always prefer bonds.]* In 1996, Midland Walwyn traders were hired from Lévesque Beaubien on the basis of generous guarantees, and soon afterwards moved over to First Boston for newer and richer guarantees. "All you need to become a world-class financier," Michael Thomas, the best of the Wall Street novelists, once prescribed, "is the chutzpah of a car salesman, the moral sensitivity of a stone crab and a line of credit." Bay Street's most successful habitués qualify on all three counts.

The Bay Street operatives who live the culture can rationalize themselves into almost anything. Keeping a mistress as a hedge against inflation can be made to appear only mildly absurd, should they take the time to think about it—which they don't. They're deep into fitness, mostly by flexing their muscles at the Cambridge Club (or the Fitness Club on top of the IBM Tower). The Cambridge, run by Clive Caldwell, claims more young Titans than any other organization in the country—mainly because it has barbells instead of bar bills. Its diehard adherents claim that they enjoy a certain comfort zone because membership is limited to men. *[At one point, Cambridge Club membership included three Eatons, two Bronfmans, two bank presidents (Robert Korthals of the TD and Bill Barford of the Montreal), one bank chairman (the TD's Dick Thomson), a former finance minister (Donald Macdonald), as well as Pierre Berton and Gordon Lightfoot.]* Dr. Jim Paupst, one of Cambridge's founding partners and until recently its medical director, found the reaction of its members to pain singular and alarming. "Pain is not recognized as a messenger but as an ominous threat to their finely balanced daily ritual," he reported. "They become extremely uncomfortable when the concept of rest is presented as part of the therapeutic solution."

These Bay Streeters are strangely interchangeable agents of opportunity, set loose in the money fields. Being cool is the order of the day, and being cool means being true to yourself—and only to yourself. Power on the Street works strictly on a barter system. Whenever deals are transacted, both sides keep scrupulous accounts of the debits and credits accumulated in the process. Favours granted and indulgences withheld are reserved for future redemption. Having power on Bay Street means getting through on the telephone to anyone at any command level, including Tony Fell, who heads RBC Dominion Securities, and John Cleghorn, chairman of the Royal Bank. These two are the acknowledged power twins, who are constantly in motion and whose every move makes waves. That kind of clout must constantly be used or it atrophies, which is why power on Bay Street flows like mercury, seldom standing still, continuously shifting to where it can be applied for maximum gain. It is not a way of life for the weak or the sensitive. There is a profound chill of the soul that surrounds this endless money making. In private moments, even the crudest of the Bay Street players feels flashes from the primeval past, when men and women treated one another as prey instead of as fellow humans, and wonder how far beyond that primitive station they have evolved.

The animators who make the stock markets churn are the head traders at each brokerage—the Big Swinging Dicks who set the Street's frantic pace. Their field of dreams includes not only stocks and bonds and fiscal instruments denominated in recognizable values, but also swaps in that slightly elevated form of Monopoly known as derivatives. Their role model is Marty Stephens (played by Patrick McKenna), the charming rat-fink who propels the action and draws out the killer instincts of the characters on "Traders." This successful Global series may be the only TV drama that has ever understated the feeding frenzy it is pretending to portray. "Traders" and traders proudly share a distinctive symbol of their authority: suspenders, usually red or black, and customarily worn over white shirts. "Wearing suspenders is a statement," admits Scott Paterson, the chairman and CEO of Yorkton Securities, who owns fifty pairs. "There is a high degree of self-confidence or power associated with them. If you wear suspenders on Bay Street and you're not a hitter, you look like a joke. People quickly assess you and think, yes, he can wear suspenders, or no, he can't. Having plaid or multicoloured suspenders takes away from the power message. I can't remember a day when I've worn a suit without suspenders in thirteen years; I'd feel naked without them." When Prime Minister Jean Chrétien was speaking to the Economics Club of New York in the spring of 1998 and attacked "the guys in red suspenders" for driving down the value of the Canadian dollar, he was aiming at the right targets, even if he couldn't deflect their currency-destroying actions.

While there is little hierarchy on Bay Street itself (as contrasted with the fairly strict patriarchal structures within each firm), the financial district is tied together by a network of directorships. The process of choosing new directors, which perpetuates the power of this essential daisy-chain, is best described by Stanley Hartt, a former federal deputy minister of finance, who now chairs Salomon Brothers Canada Inc. and is a director of half a dozen firms, including Sun Life, Gulf Canada and Montreal's Ultramar Inc. "What do you do when somebody says, could you give me ten names to consider for my board?" he asks, rhetorically. "People like me don't think, wouldn't it be nice if you had a woman of colour who'd only arrived here two years ago, who is under thirty and who didn't have a job that sort of associated her with the powers that be—wouldn't it be nice to have a director like that? Nobody thinks that way. You go to the bible, *The Financial Post Directory of Directors*, and you

leaf through it and you reject some names as inappropriate for the circumstances and you make your list. So the Establishment still feeds on
itself. In the eyes of the public, this is treated as the old boys' network,
but it isn't intended that way, it's not done to exclude young women or
people who aren't in the network; it is intended to assure *reliability*. If I
tell my friend that the following ten people would be good candidates for
his or her board, I don't want one of them to be an unknown quantity. I
don't want one of them to be someone who basically doesn't deliver. I
know what the expectations are, because my friend has told me. He's
kind enough to seek my advice. I don't want to let him down, so I'll give
him known quantities. This is not good, because it's self-perpetuating;
but it happens all the time. Once I got my first two boards, I got my next
three and then I got my next two—and they keep coming. The offers
now come faster. Two begets five, five begets nine, nine begets twelve,
and so on." Former Ontario premiers Bill Davis and David Peterson are
in heavy demand as directors, but Trevor Eyton, the chairman of
Brascan, who sits on twenty major boards, probably holds the record.

What drives responsible Canadian directors to distraction are the
unrealistic expectations of investors. "There is lots of room for well-
managed companies to grow," points out David O'Brien, CEO of Canadian Pacific Limited, "but not at 40 percent a quarter in an economy
expanding by 4 percent or so a year, which some investors seem to
expect. Canadian Pacific has been growing at a compound rate of 8
percent in the last few years, and that's been wonderful. But we're nearly
half American-owned and under huge pressure from U.S. institutions,
which are much more demanding than our own. A few years ago, there
was no pressure, and not much performance either. It was a nice, clubby
atmosphere. Well, it's not clubby any more."

THE STOCK MARKET IS A GAMBLING CASINO. That used to be the
claim, but it no longer applies. Casinos have rules; stock markets don't.
The irregular but inevitable roller-coaster rides in share values ought to
have imprinted that essential fact into every investor's brain cells, but it's
news every time share values take a dive. Andrew Willis, *The Globe and
Mail's* Streetwise columnist, keeps warning his readers not to mistake bull
markets for brains, but few pay heed to his sensible warnings.

For reasons that remain obscure, investors like to pretend that there
exists some connection between share prices and the state of the Canadian or world economies. There was a time when this was true, when
people bought common shares in blue-chip companies as a hedge against

inflation. In those days, a sharp shift in market indices was a fairly safe predictor of an economic upturn or downturn six months later. Nothing that sensible applies in the 1990s. What runs the market now is mostly emotion, a deadly mixture of greed and fear that guarantees overreaction at both ends of a narrow spectrum. Stock prices have become disconnected not only from economic realities, but from corporate earnings. The most astonishing aspect of the Bre-X story was that investors drove the stock up to a peak of $288 a share before the company had any earnings, or had even begun to dig into the mountain of gold that turned out to be pure mud.

A few diehards who exist outside the blinkered orbits of Bay Street, spending their days drilling for oil in Alberta, mining coal in British Columbia, harvesting wheat in Saskatchewan or cutting trees in New Brunswick, may find it hard to believe that Canada has moved beyond the stage of being a provider of raw materials to world markets. Long may their labours continue, but inside Bay Street there has been a seismic shift: it's the knowledge and information technologies that count now, and none is more in fashion than entertainment—television and films, the glamour industries of the twenty-first century. *[Unlike most fields, where legal work is spread amongst many lawyers, Canada's entertainment industry is dominated by Michael Levine, who represents most of the writers (including this one), actors, studios and financing angels. His life and career define the word ubiquitous.]*

Bay Street's excitement about the entertainment industry, is inspired not by its cultural dimension, but by the fact that its Canadian companies raised close to $1 billion in the past four years and expect to finance themselves at an ever accelerating rate in the future. That means new business, and a fresh and unexpected source for fat commissions. Frank Giustra's fledgling Lions Gate Entertainment, for example, got off to a running start with financings of $130 million. *[No conflict of interest exists, but the author is a director of Lions Gate.]* Some other players—Michael MacMillan of Atlantis ("Traders") Communications Inc., who spun his company through a reverse takeover into control of Alliance; Michael Hirsh of Nelvana Ltd., an animation house; Michael and Paul Donovan of Salter Street Films ("This Hour Has 22 Minutes"), who work their magic in Halifax; Baton Broadcasting, run by that mighty negotiator, Ivan Fecan; Jay Firestone's Fireworks (bought by Izzy Asper's CanWest); Coscient Group Inc. (acquired by Charles Sirois); and a few others—have gone public in their search for funds, but the industry is overshadowed by Alliance Communications Corp., built up by Robert Lantos into the only Canadian company that sustains a major film portfolio, with such hits as *The English Patient* and *The Sweet Hereafter*.

The late Andy Sarlos was always being asked how he made so much money on the stock market, mainly by people who didn't know or remember that he had made three large fortunes on Bay Street and lost two and a half. "Asking me how and where to invest," he would tell his inquisitors, "is like asking an opera singer or a parachutist how they practise their trade. The former needs a lifetime of study and devotion to practice; the latter requires nerves of steel and the willingness to take risks. For the stock market, you need both. It's as much an art as a science. John Maynard Keynes, the British economist who was also a highly successful investor, once defined the process as 'anticipating the anticipation of others,' and that's a pretty good rule of thumb to follow. In the end, putting your hard-earned money into the cold, cruel marketplace comes down to a choice of wanting to eat well or sleep well. I've been lucky enough to do both, probably because I'm not really an investor, but a speculator, and I know the odds. The ordinary investor's chances of winning are no better than those of a casino customer betting against the house—and as any seasoned gambler knows, over the long term, the house always wins." Gambling is a zero-sum game and the stock market is not. Quite.

THE MOULD USED TO BE SET IN ASPIC. Up to the early 1960s, Bay Street operated like a well-ordered club, with Wood Gundy, Dominion Securities and A.E. Ames (the only underwriter in Bay Street history that had carpeted washrooms) forming the holy trinity of desirable brokerages. Their clans perpetuated themselves by pedigree, instinct and fellowship. Having been a boarder in the same house at Upper Canada, Ridley College, Trinity or some of the other nearby private schools, and being able to qualify for Toronto Club membership—that was enough to guarantee a rewarding pew at one of these vintage firms. The members of this protected enclave flourished without straining their brains or muscles, except during bouts of bridge at the Toronto Club or tennis at the Lawn and Tennis. They felt like, and behaved as, members of a privileged community and competed in the usual Canadian way: mildly.

That all changed in 1961 when Bill Wilder, a Harvard MBA with brains and guts to burn took over Wood Gundy and introduced Harvard Business School management techniques to the Street. His decade-long tenure ignited the first sparks of genuine competition along Bay Street. His firm was finally overshadowed in 1981 by a merger between Ames and Dominion Securities and he departed to build an ill-fated pipeline in the North. Other houses that grew significantly included Midland

Doherty (not very spectacularly revived by David Weldon and Phil Holtby), Burns Fry, an outgrowth of Burns Brothers (founded by the innovative Charlie Burns in 1932), and Fry, Mills, Spence, which opened for business on January 3, 1925 and was rejuvenated under the leadership of Latham Burns (Charlie's nephew), Peter Eby and Jack Lawrence. McLeod Young Weir struggled under the stormy stewardship of Austin "Firp" Taylor, the heavyweight from Vancouver who attended UBC and Princeton, but didn't graduate from either, and always felt more comfortable on the back of hunting horses than behind his desk, particularly after it was owned by a bank.

The next big shake-up came with the ascent of Jimmy Connacher's Gordon Capital, which broke the syndicates in 1983 when he introduced block trades and bought deals (the notion that new issues required no fixed commissions to brokers and could be guaranteed by the issuing house with its own funds). That permanently reduced the size of dealers' commissions. Connacher, who is a first cousin of ex-prime minister John Turner's wife, Geills, always had a brooding anti-establishment cast to him. He spent weekends at his farm in Vermont and lived in a house in Toronto's Moore Park that looked like a hyped-up space station. He could be spotted most trading days hunkered down behind red-and-white venetian blinds, seated beside an ornate naval chest, under a blue-wash Tanabe painting, watching the world go by.

Except for Midland (which was taken over by Merrill Lynch in the summer of 1998 for at least three times its book value), the once feisty independent brokerage houses were quickly submerged in the banks that absorbed them and diluted their cultures. Competition became even less gentlemanly. The effects were most easily observable in the tombstone ads that appeared in newspapers' business pages to announce new corporate issues, spelling out the leaders of each underwriting. Instead of passively falling into line, investment houses began jockeying for position, like Hollywood stars vying for billing on movie marquees. Brokers started to hang Lucite cubes containing miniature versions of these ads in their offices to trumpet their triumphs. At one time, it had been a more or less friendly round of musical chairs, but with deregulation and the bank acquisitions, it became war.

To be lead underwriter and have your firm's name on the top left-hand column in the tombstone ad recording the major financing of a *Financial Post* 500 company is a trophy whose value only diehard Bay Streeters can comprehend. But it defines their lives. "The lead underwriter has the greatest liability, so it makes the most commission," explains Scott Paterson, the chairman and CEO of Yorkton, who owns many a Lucite cube. "People want to do business with the brokerage leading the transactions because they drive the whole process: the marketing, the timing, the accounts and pricing. The rest of the syndicate usually just respond to what the leader advises them to do. But the main reason you want to lead is that you're in the allocation position, so that if you have a hot deal, the lead determines which institutional accounts get the stock— and how much. That's the power that counts."

THERE IS SO MUCH TALK, BUT THE ACTION on Bay Street is real. The Toronto Stock Exchange alone moves as many as 180 million shares worth $3 billion per day. The sell-side traders try to endear themselves to the buy-side traders and portfolio managers. "The world of the traders is pure meritocracy," wrote Gregory J. Millman, in his authoritative *Around the World on a Trillion Dollars a Day*. "Here the race is to the swift, rather than to the well born, properly schooled or decently acquainted."

Millman is dead on. Like a band of latter-day knights entering the lists, Bay Street's warriors ride into battle each morning aboard their Beemers, Mercs and Porsches; by the time the markets open, the underground parking lots of the bank towers look like luxury car dealers' lots. All the traders have going for them in the deadly equation between greed and fear is that these emotions inevitably intersect at a point that will yield one of the parties in any transaction more profits than losses. And then there's "liability trading," which has exploded in recent years. Liability trading is an almost instant execution of transactions using the brokerage's own capital, often undertaken (even when losing money) to maintain market share rather than make a profit. It's also a sign of how deadly competition has become on the Street.

The men—and it is still mostly men—who dominate this commerce are caught up in a macho view of existence, convinced that masculinity is not something they're born with, but a badge of honour they must earn. Keeping your nerve means everything; most deals involve split-second decisions that would put high-wire trapeze artists to shame. The available response time to offers and counter-offers is usually something like ninety seconds; "the long run" means the next ten minutes.

The metaphors most commonly used to describe these shirtsleeved Cossacks are derived from war. "Today's businessman," says Dr. Paupst, the athletic physician with the Bay Street practice, "is often an exemplar of the warrior system: the high-rise office buildings are the ramparts of his business; his company logo, a personal emblem; more often than not, the boardroom is a war-council chamber. His plan of action, even though it involves corporate ritual, is still one of combat and winning against his adversaries. Because his daily conduct is characterized by aggression and in many instances retreat, his body continues to react in a primitive way."

BATTLE LINGO PERVADES BAY STREET TO AN astonishing degree. Bank chairmen used to be as discreet and soft-spoken as delegates to Presbyterian synod meetings. Now, when first discussing their proposed merger, for example, John Cleghorn and Matt Barrett of the Royal and Montreal sounded like spaced-out acid-heads, accusing their critics of "dicking around on the beach" and promising "to kick ass" in the global marketplace. The late Yves Landry, chairman of Chrysler, declared "the mother of all wars" against Japanese car makers. Canon (a military-sounding brand to begin with) advertises its new line of printers with the slogan, "Choose your weapon!" Head-hunting Caldwell Partners runs ads for new vice-presidents of corporate affairs, headlined "High Noon."

These muscular slogans are reinforced by such outfits as Performex Management Services Inc., which runs military manoeuvres for Bay Street warriors. Charging up to $3,000 per participant, the personnel-training firm supplies khaki uniforms, military equipment and facilities, hiring off-duty Canadian army personnel to conduct such realistic exercises in and around Camp Borden, Ontario, as cleaning up simulated toxic spills, rescuing downed pilots in situations that require the building of rafts from local materials, crossing deep ravines on single rope bridges and waking up at 4 a.m. in a forest, in the rain, lost and hungry. "Something like Desert Storm," claims Chuck Reynolds, a McGill engineer who runs Performex. "It's outside everybody's comfort zone."

At Niagara-on-the-Lake airport, another outfit, calling itself Air Combat Canada, straps the Bay Street warriors into aerobatic fighter planes (accompanied by real pilots) so they can replicate dogfights at 12,000 feet. They simulate missile weaponry by shooting laser beams at one another while pretending to be Top Guns at 400 kilometres an hour, and chalk up the number of downed opponents. (When a target aircraft is hit, smoke spews from its tail.)

That's one approach. But having interviewed dozens of Bay Street's regulars, both field marshals and spear carriers, it doesn't ring true—not for the serious hitters who make the markets. Warriors they may be, but the senior movers on Bay Street would feel silly in any organization as disciplined as an army or air force that pays heed to Geneva Conventions and takes prisoners.

The Street's true paladins can more aptly be compared to the gun-slingers who flourished briefly across the American West in the postbellum period between 1868 and 1885. "The gunslingers weren't in fact very good shots. They were fast on the draw, but their duels were fought at such close range, they could hardly miss. Movie audiences think they were daring; in fact, they were a pretty desperate crowd, not romantic but often cow-ardly, dirty and usually, very drunk." So claimed Jimmy Stewart, who played many a gunslinger in his time. And yet, the legend lives on. Their exploits have since been kept alive in countless horse operas, such as *Shane, Gunfight at the OK Corral* and *3:10 to Yuma*. The gunslingers prob-ably never actually said, "Reach for the sky," or boasted that Luke was "dayed 'fore he hit the ground," but they did exist and the code they lived by finds resonance on Bay Street in 1998. *[No one will admit to having been the first Bay Street trader to carry his cell phone in a leather holster, slung from his belt, but it's not uncommon. There is a special Toronto gesture, which takes years to perfect, that involves rolling out of a limousine while talking on a cell phone, without breaking stride.* The gunslinger metaphor applies because there is a restless and unruly frontier approach in play on global markets these days. It doesn't involve Colt 45s, but the sudden-death ethic on which it's based is not that differ-ent from shootouts in *The Cisco Kid, The Magnificent Seven* or *High Noon*. The mark of the gunslingers was their courage in the early morning. They were loners who risked life for pride, facing deadly challengers while hung over and dog-tired of it all. Instead of being scraped off barroom floors, modern gunslingers die with their computers disconnected. In the fall of 1997, when Gordon Capital was undergoing its rapid deterioration from power player to bit player, seventeen of its top executives were called to a meeting away from their offices, where they were unceremoniously fired by CEO Brad Cameron. Twenty minutes later, when they returned to their desks, their computer access codes had been changed. Most Bay Streeters enjoy brief careers, their *High Noon* ethic a subconscious part of nearly every initial public offering floated on Bay Street. As the self-appointed vigilantes in charge of preserving Canada's capitalist system, Bay Street's gunslingers enforce the rough economic justice of the marketplace. Money, not purpose, measures the metabolism of the stock market.

The gunslingers are Titans by another, perhaps more appropriate name. Their corporate loyalties fade as fast as Zellers aprons. What drives their ambitions is the same force that controls their emotions—and the life they miss enjoying is often their own. Many regard conscience, but not honesty, as a floppy disk that can be inserted into commercial transactions at will. They take good care to obey Ontario Securities Commission regulations, but wouldn't necessarily disagree with former Gulf Canada chairman J.P. Bryan, who told a 1996 Senate committee in Ottawa that corporate governance was "just a load of guacamole."

Because there are relatively few top professionals in the game, Bay Street's four dozen most powerful shakers follow each other's every move. The place is a huge whispering gallery where gossip—wafting from building to building like summer butterflies—can jump-start reputations or ruin careers. Sometimes it seems as if all of Bay Street is connected to one mammoth conference call, buzzing with inside information and rumours. Nobody's secret is safe. *["A secret," John le Carré once explained, "is something revealed to one person at a time."]*

Despite their warlike poses and noises, most Bay Streeters dress conservatively, even on so-called casual Fridays. "The well-tailored approach to dressing could not be stronger than it is on Bay Street," says Harry Rosen, whose shops outfit most successful investment bankers. "A variety of dark blues and greys, single and double breasted, remain the most popular. Changes are generally in the preference to finer fabrics, which look richer in superfine wools. The senior people on Bay Street will be buying more of the same and add vests to their single-breasted suits. Along with this tailored clothing, most men will wear suspenders to support their trousers, which is most appropriate. The suspenders should complement the shirt and tie."

THE TORONTO THAT ALLOWS BAY STREET to flourish consists of a quarter Canadian WASPs, a quarter Third World arrivals, a quarter Italians and a quarter Space Invaders who have yet to be identified. By the year 2000, visible minorities will make up 54 percent of the population of the Greater Toronto Area, up from 30 percent as recently as 1991. Immigrants come from 169 countries and speak 100 languages, with 42 percent understanding neither French nor English. Toronto has a higher proportion of foreign-born citizens than any other city, including that giant melting-pot, New York, where only 28 percent are foreign born. "Toronto is a city in the process of becoming," wrote Morley Callaghan, the novelist who best captured its essence. "But I don't know what it's becoming, other than rich and opulent. Watching Toronto grow and change is like watching a cake in the oven, wondering when it will be done. I don't know if it will ever be ready, if it will ever be cooked, or what kind of cake it will turn out to be."

Toronto is a board game. Everyone is constantly reaching for more money, more fame, more power, more glamour, more parking, more health,

more orgasms, just *more*—all the while demanding a recount, because more
is never enough. Toronto's unfashionable suburbs and the bungaloids who
occupy them aren't even on the radar screen. Scarborough is as far from
the Eaton Centre as Hopkins Landing, B.C., where I now live. Further.

Bay Street is the city's epicentre, and the earthquake that has shaken
it to its once tender roots has been globalization. Toronto's status as the
world's seventh-largest financial capital is secure, and that's not good
news. It now has access to every economic zone on every continent, but
it's not first in line anywhere. Still, Toronto remains Canada's Empire
City, the nation's commercial hub and cultural headquarters. More than
half the country's one hundred leading financial institutions live here, as
do 40 percent of the five hundred top industrial companies, two-thirds of
the accounting firms, all of the top advertising agencies and three-quarters of the major law firms. Toronto architects know how to cater to the
whims of the powerful. The Scotia Plaza, for example, the last of the
great bank headquarters buildings, was designed with sawtooth walls so
that there would be twenty-two corner offices on each floor.

In the rest of the country, Toronto was once envied, then hated, later
pitied, and now it is reluctantly tolerated, even occasionally admired.
Whatever the depth of its arrogance—and no one has yet plumbed its
limits—Toronto alone maintains the twenty-first-century infrastructure
that other Canadian cities can only reproduce in miniature.

Within sight and sound of Bay Street are the posses of "hired guns"
who make it tick. Here are the fountainheads of Canada's surviving chartered banks, the great brokerages, the money managers, the legal factories and the accounting wizards who, in one shirtsleeved weekend can
throw up a high-tech plant in Kanata, open a tax-haven trust account in
Belize or finance a Benny's Bagels outlet in Outer Mongolia. There isn't
much that the Toronto money movers can't do or arrange to have done.
The Bay Street lawyers understand their fundamental assignments very
well: to preserve the value of Old Money and to keep New Money from
being indicted.

THE REST OF THE COUNTRY MAY NOT know or care who Bay
Street's new Titans are. But Toronto does. The pages that follow describe
a representative selection of these individuals and their power sources.
Unlike the Old Establishment, whose members were socially prominent
in their communities without necessarily possessing much economic
clout, there is now only one list and if you lack the necessary economic
muscle, you're not on it. "There's so much New Establishment money in

Toronto," says Catherine Nugent, the Toronto establishment's unofficial gatekeeper. "Be it from Canada or anywhere else, it's intermarried, intermingled and a whole new story. The young people don't want to buy into its rules any more. They have different agendas and are much more interested in what you do and where you're going, not where you've been or all that Old Family stuff." *[The most sought-after invitations are to parties thrown by the Nugents (which can take place at a moment's notice on any of the explored continents); the expanding receptions thrown by Conrad and Barbara Black; and for the vintage establishment, Nancy Phillips's garden galas, which include rides on her wonderful merry-go-round.]* Catherine Nugent's husband, David, who was once an officer in a crack regiment of British commandos, still finds it strange that, unlike in Europe, the first question a stranger asks in Canada is "What do you do?" He has some fun with that. "I always say I run a small chain of brothels in the south of France—that they're very clean and very profitable," he quips. "Usually I get back a sickening smile, but others say, 'Really?' and want to know their exact locations." *[Until recently, Nugent ran Riviera Concepts, a highly successful perfume company, with sales of $100 million in sixty-eight countries.]*

The following are some of the essential Bay Street players and institutions (see also Appendix 7):

JOHN CLEGHORN

John Edward Cleghorn, who presided over his first annual meeting of the Royal Bank of Canada in Montreal on March 6, 1996, is very different from the proud roosters who customarily occupy the gilded cages of Canada's most influential corporate chairmanships. He takes nothing for granted. Unlike most bank chairmen, who believe that it takes only one person, themselves, to change the nation's light-bulbs, Cleghorn rejects any image of being an imperial, all-knowing presence. While he is obsessively interested in the private truths that underlie the social and economic pressures that bedevil his job, he is basically an ordinary guy who has been picked for an extraordinary assignment. As CEO of the merged Royal and Montreal banks, he would represent the greatest source of non-governmental power in this country. He would automatically become the Titan of Titans, with the clout to decide which companies and individuals are granted the credit necessary to multiply their assets, and whose expansion plans would be postponed or vetoed.

A McGill commerce grad who started out in banking with Citibank in New York and joined the Royal only in 1974, Cleghorn is an extraordinarily capable banker, but not very good at hiding his occasional bouts of boredom. At one 1997 meeting to discuss how to improve the Royal's image, he quickly decided that the room's potential for producing exciting new ideas was dangerously close to zero. To keep himself awake and alive, he broke into a lengthy soliloquy about the Fuggers. "The Fuggers," he kept saying. "Love those Fuggers. They began in 1367 to dominate most of Germany's commerce, expanded into trade, even leased the Roman mint, influenced the election of the Holy Roman emperor. Then they had the sense to get out of banking and move into real estate." The assembled bankers harrumphed at appropriate moments, but had no idea their boss was talking about the legendary Fugger family, history's first merchant bankers, who were central to European commerce between the fourteenth and sixteenth centuries.

For students of history like Cleghorn, the merger with the Montreal is the culmination of a dream. The Royal was founded by the upstart Merchants Bank in 1869, when the Bank of Montreal was so dominant that the new bank's first branches bypassed Montreal and Toronto, to open in Bermuda and Vancouver. Some 129 years later, the Royal seems finally to have triumphed. "People ask me, why now?" he says. "Look, we've been sitting on our hands since 1925, and we didn't know what the value of acquiring another bank was going to be, except that it would probably be too expensive. So, the only hope we had of building a serious global presence was this merger. Also, the Montreal and ourselves have a similar view of the future as corporate investment bankers. It's a natural fit." That may be, but as Deirdre McMurdy of *Maclean's* has pointed out, "corporate loans are typically syndicated by one lead bank, which then spreads the risk among others. But with fewer players, there are fewer opportunities to spread the risk—and financial institutions are likely to become much more stringent about lending and underwriting."

His blushing cheeks and granny glasses make the Royal Bank chairman appear deceptively accommodating, and up to a point he is. John Cleghorn has the knack of being who you want him to be—but only up to a point. He is not a man to fool with. As the lightning rod for the bank mergers, he is charged with nothing less than persuading ordinary Canadians to love their banks enough to allow them to become at least twice as large and many times more powerful.

His dilemma brings to mind the story of the Canadian soldier on peacekeeping duty in the Middle East who stumbles onto a genie in the desert. "I'm not like most genies," warns the little magician. "I only grant one wish, not three. What's yours?" The soldier pulls a map of the region out of his back trouser pocket and says, "Look, genie, here's Iraq, Jordan,

Syria, Israel and the Palestinian territories. Everybody's fighting all the time. My wish is very simple: bring peace to the Middle East." The genie is flabbergasted. Most of its supplicants request sexual fantasies or obscenely large material possessions, and here is this Canadian private asking for peace in the Middle East. "Look," replies the genie, "I really admire your unselfishness, but it's very difficult, even for us genies, to bring peace to a whole region." The soldier is visibly disappointed. He refolds his map, puts it back in his pocket and starts walking away. "Come back," says the genie. "Since you seem so enlightened, I'll grant you a different wish!" The soldier is delighted. "Look," he says, "I come from Toronto, and I want the Maple Leafs to win the Stanley Cup!" Oh, all right," says the exasperated genie, "let me see that damn map again."

That's a fairly accurate assessment of Cleghorn's dilemma. He knows that the public perception of Canadian banks is set in concrete: they are too big and much too powerful; they make huge profits and pay minimum taxes; they short-change small business, charge their customers extravagant service fees, and would gladly tax sex if that would expand their already bloated bottom lines. He also knows that such perceptions are as difficult to change as the blood feuds that keep Arabs and Jews apart. And yet that's what he must accomplish. Is he the genie who can pull it off? Don't bet against him. Mergers are in the air, and if he can make a credible case by going over the politicians' heads it might work.

Journalists, desperate to endow the Royal Bank chairman with a colourful personality, are reduced to reaching back thirty-eight years, when the young Cleghorn was playing centre on the offensive line of the McGill Redmen. He was the guy who hunched over the ball, snapped it to his quarterback, then hurled himself against the opposing team's front line like a human missile. History records no miracles (or touchdowns) scored by Cleghorn. Yet a thousand metaphors were born on the turf of Molson Stadium that sunny afternoon to explain his later success and tough-minded ways.

To sum up: Cleghorn's football career was short and uninteresting—as opposed to his banking career, which has been long and has now turned out to be fascinating.

THE PROCESS OF HISTORY IS DETERMINED by how individuals react to the unusual circumstances in which they find themselves. That's why Cleghorn's determination to turn the Royal, Canada's largest financial institution, into one of the world's truly humongous banks adds considerable interest to his fate and Canadian banking's destiny.

Paradoxically, his partner in the project, the Bank of Montreal's chairman, Matt Barrett, might have been a persuasive force in such a crushingly difficult crusade. Unlike Cleghorn, who measures the effectivenes of his speeeches by how many statistics he can cram into each paragraph, Barrett has the Irish trick of being able to appropriate his surroundings. His gusts of blarney puff up his arguments with built-in levitation. He is cool and has a sly moustache, which makes him ideal for TV. But it was not to be: Barrett unexpectedly became a bit player in the game, preoccupied with a personal merger of his own. Cleghorn became the point man. As the debate developed, it became clear that he is a man with remarkable heft *[A definition of "heft" is "what Joe Clark doesn't have."]*—an inner strength that will not let go of him. Shy and introverted he may be, but like most WASPs, Cleghorn's root belief system is not negotiable. Somewhere in his past, he became convinced that big was beautiful.

Cleghorn's urgency is based on his understanding that banks have lost their unique ability to create money, credit or anything else. Their rivals are no longer other banks, but firms like Steve Hudson's Newcourt, which replicates most banking functions with minimum overhead, or Microsoft, which, if it had been allowed to acquire Intuit, would have become a virtual consumer bank. This informal "debanking" of the financial system has prompted futurists such as Britain's Hazel Henderson to question how long conventional banks anywhere can retain their fiscal supremacy, however impregnable they may appear. Asked by the magazine *Wired* what was the biggest economic shift she could see coming, Henderson flatly predicted: "The demise of banking. If money isn't democratized, we'll go around them by using high-tech bartering. We couldn't go around the money system until people had computers and the Internet, because bartering is clunky. But now you can do four- or six-way trades. We may want bananas, these people have tin, and those people have copper to sell—computers keep track. We really need three currencies. A global reserve currency for trade transactions. We need national currencies, in which I include food stamps, student loans, vouchers for this and that. And then there are locally based systems— computer barter and local currencies. This would allow a huge paradigm shift, because money wouldn't be scarce. The old giants can't turn their ships around fast enough. Their business is the business of scarcity. What we're talking about is the abundance of business, where anyone can make a market in *anything*. Companies are terrified of this. They're offering cash accounts and smartcards, but this is simply recycling. They can't get the idea that we don't need the money loop any more."

Cleghorn understands all that, and knows how to deal with it. He was a key negotiator in the $1.6-billion acquisition of Royal Trust in 1993, but it was also Cleghorn who lost the $2.5-billion offer for London Life to Paul Desmarais. Now, he wants to consummate the proposed merger with the Bank of Montreal, so that his Royal (in terms of market capitalization) would become the tenth largest in North America and twenty-second in the world.

There was a time when banks got bigger by being better; now, it seems, they need to be bigger to get better. It's a tough sell. As it is, the Royal isn't exactly a mom-and-pop operation. The Bank has 10 million Canadians as customers and total assets of well over a quarter of a trillion dollars. In 1997, it recorded a net profit of $1.679 billion, the largest by any Canadian enterpise ever, ranking first for the second year running. Canada's banking system is already the world's most concentrated. In 1995, the pre-merger Big Six (including the National Bank) controlled $739.7 billion of Canada's total $740.4 billion in banking assets. Canadian banks among the largest providers of bank services in the world. Despite the growth of electronic banking, the country still has more bank branches than pubs and taverns.

THERE ARE ONLY TWO BANKS that are certain never to merge: the food banks and the sperm banks; it would simply be too messy. With the proposed marriage of the country's four largest banks creating two elephants with assets of $500 billion each, the amalgamated institutions would have assets of nearly a trillion dollars. But what is it, specifically, that they would then be able to accomplish that they can't accomplish now—except, of course, bring peace to the Middle East?

Despite his grand intentions, Paul Martin's windy pronouncements on the issue remind me of the British policeman in a skit by Robin Williams. The cop is chasing a thief. Since the bobbies in England are unarmed, all he can do is keep yelling, "Stop!" The thief keeps running. The exasperated bobby finally yells out: "If you don't stop, I'll yell 'Stop' again!" Martin is determined to emerge as Jean Chrétien's natural successor as prime minister. That's why he can't allow the banks to ride roughshod over him. The finance minister and Cleghorn often play together at the Knowlton Golf Club near their summer homes; but this is no game. Martin will no doubt demand strict limits on the newly merged banks' abilities to lay off redundant employees, and will probably permit more foreign banks into the country; but whether he dares rend asunder the love match already joined by Bay Street remains an open question.

MONEY IS NO JOKE IN THIS COUNTRY, and banking is very much more than just a business: it is a calling. Senior bankers regard themselves as chief custodians of the free enterprise system and take inordinate pride in operating the levers of the machinery that keeps business expanding, consumers spending and the economy functioning. They discharge their powers with the self-conscious virtue of Jesuits serene in the security of their faith. Never for a moment would they concede that they exercise power, even as they're vetoing some poor dreamer's plan to build a summer resort on Baffin Island. Exercising *responsibility*, the supreme middle-class virtue—that's what makes their blood pump. No matter how high they rise, Canada's bankers retain a kind of green-eyeshade, good-boy-who-got-terrific-marks aspect about them. They are dutiful soldiers, dutiful sons, dutiful husbands—steadfast ecclesiastics in a heretical world. Just like John Cleghorn.

He has sold off or done away with nearly all of the perks that Royal Bank chairmen so recently enjoyed. No more private barber, no more limousine (he drives his own Chrysler), no more Challenger jet, no more free chairman's mansion in Toronto's plush Rosedale, and no more tennis-court-sized office with chintz drapes and a desk mounted on a platform so he could look down on his visitors. *[I have had some personal problems with the Royal's overdecorated executive floor at its gold-towered Toronto head office. When it first opened, then chairman Earle McLaughlin had me over for lunch, and I later wrote in* Maclean's *that it reminded me of a Turkish whorehouse. For some reason, Earle took great exception to this, and phoned me. "Newman," he bellowed, "when were you last in a Turkish whorehouse?" He hung up before I could answer.]*

THE MAN WHO HAS THE BEST CLUES TO WHAT MAKES John Cleghorn tick is Don Wells, who until recently occupied a key post as the Royal's executive vice president of strategic planning. The two men go back thirty years together, when Cleghorn was a sugar trader with Ridpath and later a young executive with the American-owned Mercantile Bank of Canada. Back in 1974, the two friends had a long, liquid evening at the Hilton Hotel bar in Quebec City, and by about 5 a.m. Cleghorn admitted he'd like to join the Royal. Wells immediately recommended him to Deputy Chairman Doug Gardiner, who hired him shortly thereafter. (Wells was so hung over the next day that he had a minor car accident that cost him a $150 fender-repair job.)

"One of John's key attributes," says Wells, "is the balance he maintains between his job, his family, his friends and his community. He takes every single day of every vacation he's entitled to. He's very tidy, very organized, can synthesize both hard and soft information very quickly—but above all, he's genuine." Wells experienced a good example of that when he was invited to the 1996 wedding of Cleghorn's daughter Andrea. What struck him was that he was the only Royal Bank guest there, that John didn't try to use a social occasion to impress his peers, but instead saluted his friends.

Cleghorn has always felt that he owes much to his friend for helping him into his present position. On the day Cleghorn became CEO, Wells received a hand-delivered envelope: it contained a cheque for the eight-year-old $150 fender-bender and a note thanking him for his help. Later, he sent him the interest as well. Wells, who is not sentimental, cried a little and wished his friend Godspeed. He'll need it.

ANTHONY SMITHSON FELL

If Bay Street has an acknowledged leader—the head of a brokerage house who sets the pace and is the competitor to beat in almost any deal that's in play—it's Tony Fell, who runs RBC Dominion Securities (DS). Producing total revenues (in 1997) of $1.9 billion and a 32-percent return on equity, the firm is almost obscenely profitable, virtually doubling its returns after taxes for each of the past three years, and paying out distributions since 1992 of $678 million to its shareholders, a roster that includes 148 happy, if constantly rotating, vice-presidents.

The company is also more profitable than any U.S. brokerage firm by a considerable margin. Typically, DS led the field by raising $12.6 billion of the total $47 billion in financings floated in 1997. Its branch system of two hundred offices takes in just about every Canadian burg between Port Alberni on an inlet of British Columbia's outer coast to Rothesay in Newfoundland, as well as two dozen foreign posts, including Grand Cayman, the Bahamas and the Turks and Caicos.

At first meeting, the secretive yet purposeful field marshal of all this activity appears to be a self-deprecating and not very impressive fellow. Fell tends to answer questions in the third person, as if he were dictating a memo about himself to a secretary, and outlines his remarkable career with all the flourish of a maiden aunt describing her gout or arthritic knee. He will list, for example, the nine firms that DS has absorbed over the years, and make each merger sound offhand and inevitable, instead of the gut-wrenching decision it must have been for the proprietors and partners in each deal. Between 1973 and 1996, DS absorbed Harris & Partners, Draper Dobie, A.E. Ames, Pitfield Mackay Ross, Molson Rousseau, Pemberton Houston Willoughby, Marcil Inc., McNeil Mantha and Richardson Greenshields. DS was itself acquired in 1988 by the Royal Bank which paid $390 million for a 75-percent stake. At the time, Fell said rather incautiously, "The real reason we did the deal was to get a firsthand look at how to nickel and dime our customers." The absence of visible ripples as these investment houses became submerged in DS is deceptive. Fell seized on every merger as an opportunity to upgrade his staff, so that the best performers in each acquired firm gained favourable slots at DS, while veterans of the firm with middling sales records were dropped off the end of the wagon. Within nine months of Ames's takeover, for example, all the executives who had joined DS as part of the deal were gone, yet DS had kept virtually every one of the defunct firm's accounts. Half the senior Richardson Greenshields staff were let go twenty weeks into its "merger" with DS. "There's a distillation after every one of our mergers," Fell admits. "That's what has enabled us to build up a reservoir of talent."

Fell is underwhelmed by the forecasting abilities of his analysts and other support staff. "The more researchers and economists you have," he decrees with a wit drier than any martini ever shaken, "the better are your chances of one being right." The late Sandy Ross, as usual, touched the heart of the matter when he wrote about DS in his seminal book *Traders*. "No other investment firm so perfectly embodies the verities of the Canadian financial establishment: its integrity, its good manners, its damnable caution, its occasional ruthlessness and above all, its ability to survive." One of the black marks of Fell's stewardship was the $250,000 fine levied by the Investment Dealers' Association for DS's part in allowing Christopher Horne, later convicted on charges of embezzlement, to defraud clients of at least $5 million during his employ.

Fell's salary, which first topped $5 million in 1996—a 140-percent raise from the previous year—hardly reflects the worth of his contribution. He is not above having fun at his own expense. At one of the annual DS dinners celebrating annual bonuses, he deadpanned: "If we ever have a record year return on equity, which means over 40 percent, I will retire immediately. Which is good news for you and gives everyone lots of incentive to work like hell. The bad news is, with my salary and bonus, you'll never make it." At the same dinner, after the rough-house activities got out of hand, he wryly commented, "I've always said a well-run investment firm is like a zoo without cages, and this dinner proves it." "Tony has earned his way to the pinnacle of influence, having built DS from basically nothing," says Stanley Hartt, the Canadian chairman of Salomon Brothers and himself one of Bay Street's most sought-after advisers. "He is a superb manager, and rigidly controls costs in an industry highly suscepti-ble to excesses. His reputation is that he never goes into a corporate boardroom for a business meeting and comes out empty-handed. That's true, but his real strengths are as a manager and cost controller."

The economies certainly show. DS may have the newest-generation computers and mach-speed modems, but most of its office furniture looks like a collection of rejects from an office-wrecker's auction sale. The carpet in Fell's private office may not have holes, but it is so faded that its original colour, if it had one, is impossible to guess. His chair needs mending too; but what counts is its location. Fell works in a tree-house office overlooking his trading floors. "You're right on top of things," says he. "Right there, look, we have 340 trading positions, and they handle $75 to $80 billion-plus a day. Over there are the bond and money market traders, and at the side are the risk management systems and technology people. This place closes around 5:30 p.m. and all our trading inventories then go to Singapore, and when night-time comes to Singapore, the trading book goes to London. They book it during their day, and then when we come here in the morning, around seven o'clock or shortly thereafter, the trading book comes from London to here. So it's a twenty-four-hour trading operation.

"I like this office because I've got an escalator right out here. I can be on that floor in about a minute flat, and I make a tour at least three times a day. Every time I walk through that room, I'll talk to about four of my people, just at random. I find out fast what's happening or what's wrong or what's going right or what the current deals are and which way they're heading.

"These trading rooms are an example of our partner, the Royal Bank, coming together with DS. In the future, there's going to be more and more of a merging of the two and eventually we'll all be one. There's not enough spread to make profit in lending money any more; it's too com-petitive. So you either have to become a trading business with your cus-tomers or an investment banking business like new issues, bond issues, or mergers and acquisitions.

"We're entering the age of investment banking, not a commercial banking culture. When you sweep away the politics, Canadian banks will have to be allowed into the insurance business and car leasing. We will have a universal banking system very similar to what they now have in Germany and Switzerland."

Fell predicts equally sweeping changes for his own industry. "The price of technology is coming down. We can process business now for almost nothing and the only thing we're going to be paid for in the future is giving advice to clients. We'll be paid as long as we can make money for our clients and when we can't do that, we'll be out of business. It's a narrowing field. The biggest challenge we have is keeping up with changing technology, because it's a tidal wave. Our average customer in this firm is about sixty and not computer literate. As they pass on money to people in their thirties, who are totally receptive to new ways of doing things, there will be a sea change in this industry. The TD has been brilliant in developing its discount brokerage business, because it provides them access electronically to customers without branches. Now they've got a network they can build on."

It had been a long lecture, but no one else I met on Bay Street seemed to have as clear a view of the future. Perhaps one reason Fell can look forward with some wisdom is that he is one of the few current Bay Streeters with a past.

His father, Charles Percival Fell, was with Dominion Securities from 1917 to 1929, opened its New York offices, then moved over to Empire Life Insurance, which he sold to Harry Jackman in 1959. Tony has one son, Geoffrey, formerly of Wood Gundy and another, Graham, with Lehman Brothers Canada. His brother Fraser recently retired as chairman of Gentra, the residue of Royal Trust's real-estate portfolio, and his other brother, Albert, headed the philosophy department at Queen's University.

The Fells have a cottage on Georgian Bay where they go most summer weekends, but he plays neither golf nor tennis and, except for the past two years, has spent his Christmases at Mauna Kea on Hawaii's Big Island.

"Yes," he says of his business, "I suppose it's a game, but it sometimes seems more like a war. Perhaps quite often, now that I think of it. You get a shot of adrenaline almost every day: something new is going on, there's a new deal, there's a new competitive bid for a major piece of business from Scotia McLeod, or somebody is trying to take one of your accounts away, and so you marshal your resources and go to war."

Ira Gluskin, the Toronto financier who understands how power works on the Street, pins Fell's strengths to two main sources. "Tony can go to any one of these big-time charity events filled with Establishment types, and he alone will know them all by their first names—and will probably have done business with them. Secondly, *he* is the one everybody phones for advice. You can just see a Lord Thomson Junior or Galen Weston thinking, I wonder if I should put in a bid for General Motors ... why not call Tony, see what he thinks. Fell will give them good advice, then subtly hand them over to one of his senior people. If anybody on the Street has respect and pedigree, it's Tony Fell."

STEVE HUDSON

One of the still-relevant differences between New and Old Money is the meaning ascribed to office furniture. New Money tends to treat offices as personal statements. They're places to show off that great panoramic shot of their maxi-boat, riding the Bermuda surf under full spinnaker; or a canvas by the inevitable Riopelle; lots of low-slung leather desks, chrome and glass, including those fancy clocks with no numbers on them that make it impossible to tell the damn time; or just a table with a portable Eurocan computer to demonstrate that they're international players and the office is only another pit stop on their global rounds.

In contrast, the offices that either house or hope to attract Old Money carry the burden of pretending to be British turn-of-the-century merchant banks. They project a mood of heavy oak venerability, like drawing-rooms borrowed from road companies doing George Bernard Shaw plays, complete with Adam sideboards, doilied Sheraton tables, paintings of anemic hounds chasing exhausted foxes, and the warming lustre of burnished bronze.

The notion that any mega-account customer would entrust his or her funds to Bay Street's money manipulators because they're greeted in an office made up to look like a BBC stage set is, of course, absurd. But it works. There's a flourishing cottage industry of decorators with three names who profitably cater to this nonsense. They have convinced most CEOs of financial services firms that such artificial baronial surroundings close sales. The tradition continues unabated. There is hardly a boardroom on Bay Street that doesn't attempt to instil an old-fashioned hush that allows deals to be transacted away from the vulgarity of modern commerce. Discreet lunches are served on silver platters and escutcheoned china to heighten the effect. If anyone had the nerve, office sound systems would probably be tuned to martial versions of "Rule, Britannia!"

The main entrance to the offices of Newcourt, Bay Street's most phenomenally successful new financial group of the 1990s, is no exception. To gain access to the firm's receptionist, visitors must pass through a kind of tunnel made up of showcases housing swords that speak of brave deeds by great admirals of the fleet, beating off armadas of howling infidels who would never be admitted to hallowed quarters like these. Tastefully displayed under glass is a sword supposed to have been worn by Sir William Hall Gage, Admiral of the Blue, 1846. Other weapons are ascribed to totally obscure British swashbucklers of the eighteenth and nineteenth centuries. The hallway leads into half a dozen richly panelled board-rooms—the Nelson Room, the Albany Room, the Churchill Room and so on—of various sizes and pretensions, generously endowed with elegantly subdued paintings ensconced in glorious frames.

It's only after walking about a bit and looking closely at Newcourt's ambience that you realize that's all it is—ambience. The canvases are bought from young Canadian painters, with the understanding that if they become famous they can repurchase their art from Newcourt at the original purchase price. Nobody works here—except the receptionist. (The real work goes on in mundane parts of the floor, away from all this pretence.) Unlike most of these artificial set-ups, Newcourt's front office is not a stage set pretending to be an office; it *is* a stage set, pure and simple. Well, not really pure, because this is Newcourt's way of giving Bay Street's old-fashioned financial institutions the finger. And not that simple either, because the irreverent approach epitomized by this bit of trickery is the secret of Newcourt's astounding success.

THE ACCUMULATION OF SERIOUS WEALTH in this country used to be a gradual process of unfolding possibilities, like climbing a mountain or reading a book by John Ralston Saul. But fortunes these days are made by entrepreneurs whose ideas and energies are revolutionizing their industries by dumping traditional methods and discarding conventional wisdom. The most impressive of these new-style financial warriors is Steve Hudson, founder and resident warlord of the Newcourt Credit Group, which in the fall of 1997 acquired an American company nearly twice its size, through the largest bought deal in Canadian history. The $2.2-billion transaction that saw Newcourt take over AT&T Capital moved Hudson, an impish and amusing forty-year-old workaholic, into the major leagues. With a combined market capitalization of $7 billion, the takeover created the world's largest publicly traded commercial finance company.

Without so much as a "by your leave," Hudson has successfully invaded the traditional territory of the chartered banks, competing toe-to-toe with most of the services they offer, yet unhampered by the expensive bricks and mortar of the branch system they require to support their efforts. Hudson has placed Newcourt in the fortunate position of being able to do just about everything the banks can accomplish, while they are not allowed into most of the leasing areas where he turns some of his biggest profits. More important, the banks have yet to grab hold of, or even fathom, his methods and efficiencies. "In contrast to a traditional bank," he says, "where a customer walks in and gets a loan to purchase a car or whatever, in Newcourt's case, our loans officers are out in the field, so that when a Western Star truck is being sold in Kelowna, for example, we're right there at the dealership; or when a Herc aircraft is being marketed in Atlanta, Georgia, our loans officers make the sales calls along with the local agents. It's point-of-sale financing done entirely outside the branch system employed by the banks. We don't have the overhead, and with the AT&T deal we have become something like Ford Motor Credit; we are now the captive financing arm to more than 320 of the world's most significant companies." One example is Dell, which is the fastest growing of the computer hardware companies. Each mail-order unit sold is financed by Newcourt.

Hudson's success depends on the health of the partners he picks, but his choice of secured, amortizing loans is the safest category of loans, because they avoid revolving lines of credit, which often cause problems. Newcourt's progress has been not so much rapid as instant. The company was founded in 1990, went public four years later, and that same year completed its first major deal, becoming the preferred financing source of John Deere industrial and farm equipment, an arrangement worth an initial $400 million. Business has expanded so fast that by May 1996, Hudson was able to negotiate a $1-billion credit facility with twenty-three of the world's leading banks. Earnings for the second quarter of 1998 were up by a whopping 71 percent and the merger arrangements with AT&T Capital, occupying a team of 150 specialists, were ahead of schedule.

Hudson first got into the field as a financial analyst at Toronto Hospital, which was acquiring an MRI imaging machine. The banks wouldn't finance its purchase, so Hudson persuaded the hospital's doctors to get together and finance it, which they did. Hudson was started in the non-bank credit business. He launched Newcourt as a way of providing health-care credit, thus creating his own market niche. Later, while he was working for Clarkson Gordon (now Ernst & Young), Hudson performed audits for life insurance companies, and realized that they would be the perfect source for the funds he needed to expand his rapidly growing agency. "They had been mostly invested in mortgages and we provided an alternate form of secured investments," he recalls. "On a risk-adjusted basis, it's about equal to mortgages, but more importantly, it provides them with diversification."

Not being able to beat him, at least two banks—the Montreal and Commerce—have joined Hudson, becoming partners by joining the Newcourt capital pool or taking up equity positions. (The Royal had a separate deal with AT&T Capital, which was folded into Newcourt.)

While Newcourt now ranks second in global vendor financing, with owned and managed assets of $34 billion, it's far behind the industry's leader, GE Capital, which enjoys an asset base worth more than twice as much. "Size is not our absolute driver; focus is," Hudson insists. "We have no ambition to close that gap, but we do want to be Number One in our chosen markets. As consolidation in the industry continues, I expect people to merge with us."

The combined Newcourt and AT&T Capital operations employ five thousand, with only 27 percent of business in 1997 originating in Canada. Ownership is split between Nomura Securities (12 percent), Newcourt employees (10 percent), CIBC (9.5 percent), Janus Capital (5.8 percent) and Mutual Life (1.6 percent). Hudson himself owns 2.3 percent of the issued shares, worth $236 million.

Hudson takes little time out from work. "Newcourt is my hobby and passion," he admits. "Its progress has been much like rearing a child. Seeing it through its babyhood and teenage years took seventy to eighty hours a week. I'm a lousy golfer, like to ski, enjoy French wines, but try to spend prime time with my new wife and our two children. I can't deny that Newcourt's success has come at a high personal cost." Those who know Steve Hudson well are not overly awed by his astonishing success. They know he is just beginning his run.

MOSES ZNAIMER

The Wesley Building in downtown Toronto was erected in 1913 for the Methodist Book Publishing House, named for John Wesley, founder of the Methodist Church, which spawned a type of revolution in its own time. Now, it's the docking station for a spaceship that goes by the call letters Citytv, the world's first television facility without formal studios or formalized programming. It airs a movable feast of actual events and live spectacles over a dozen channels that are revolutionizing not just TV but the media world in a way that hasn't been achieved since Marshall McLuhan was at the height of his prophetic powers.

Moses Znaimer, the reigning monarch and resident guru of this electronic empire, is the contemporary inheritor of McLuhan's mantle. A Zen-like figure in a black suit, he has managed to marry culture and technology into a seamless continuum—and made it pay. His version of McLuhan's "The medium is the message" is "The process is the product." That's an important qualification, because that's what makes him a Titan in the context of this book: he is as interested in being a prophet as in making a profit. "He doesn't just treat culture as an artifact to be anesthetized," points out Grant McCracken, director of Toronto's Institute for Contemporary Culture. "He lets it take place on the screen and flow through the viewer."

"I like to be in the grip of historical forces," Znaimer admits. "I love the gadgetry of the future, and we've carved quite a position as being the expression for the new media. The primary use of real-time interactivity has to do with being able to step into the flow of a program—let's say it's a concert—and give an opinion, ask a question, in full video with a form of eye contact with the person who's watching. We just finished a Madonna special in that form. And yet we're moving away from the idea of the one big machine that does everything—some kind of tele-puter omni-single machine on the desk—to a lot of distributed intelligence, where all kinds of objects will have some kind of memory, some kind of function buried in it and it will be very good at doing that one thing."

"We didn't get Vancouver," he says of the historic 1996 refusal by the CRTC to approve his application for a new TV outlet on the West Coast, "but we're about to do something big in Brazil. São Paulo is the third-largest city in the world, 17.7 million people, and about thirty-odd clicks down the road is another million and a half in a place called Santos, so the better part of 20 million people, that's just about the population of English-speaking Canada—and we already have the licence."

Znaimer is constantly seeking the innovative, treating Citytv not as a station but as a laboratory. "My personal taste," he says, "has always been to seek out the different. That's not perversity, it's just that if lots of people are doing something already, nobody needs me to do more of it." Apart from such pioneering projects as the country's first watchable cultural channel (Bravo!), simulated trips to Jupiter, interactive theatre and a Space Channel, plus a twenty-four-hour news station that actually works, Znaimer is the perfect role model for the twenty-first-century Titan. "The new meritocracy is not only internationally minded but, if you take me as an example, we commute internationally. It's a normal way to live; you move between the big cities of the world," he says. "It has always been my view that the political formations that matter at this point in history are either larger or smaller than countries—that the hegemony of the nation-state is over—and personally I'm not that nostalgic about it, even though I'm happy to say that Canada is perhaps the most benign of countries. Culture is created in cities, the modern world is created in cities. The G7 has already been replaced by the C-24—a couple of dozen of the world's largest and most functional cities."

He recognizes the inevitable evolution of today's meritocracy into a future establishment, but points out that it's not so entrenched and isn't passed on in the same unearned way that, say, land titles can be conferred. "Generally speaking," he contends, "merit has to be won and re-won, and therefore it shifts much more often. You've got to be fluid; you have to enjoy a certain ambiguity. It's the modern idiom, and that's why rootless cosmopolitans such as myself feel very comfortable with it. In fact, all the things for which cosmopolitan people, notably Jews, have been blamed are actually a particular kind of agility, which is a great advantage in this more fluid society. And if you're busy, having a good debate with somebody, and you're getting laid every day, you're just not going to pick up an axe and do somebody in."

Right. And that's why everything's coming up Moses.

PETER C. GODSOE

When Peter C. Godsoe (who recognizes a winning middle initial when he sees one) opened his Bank of Nova Scotia annual meeting in the spring of 1998, he had a welcome message: "I'm not here to announce the merger of Scotiabank with the rest of the world. We're big enough now." The chairman of Canada's fourth-largest bank went on to argue that the Scotia was happy with its asset base ($195 billion) and welcomed the prospect of competing with global giants. Shareholders gave Godsoe a round of applause, approved a two-for-one stock split and awarded the bank's directors a healthy pay increase.

Godsoe was actually second choice on the Royal's dance card, had Matt Barrett of the Montreal not chosen to waltz with John Cleghorn. Strengthened by its $1.2-billion 1997 acquisition of Henry Jackman's National Trust, the Scotia had been flexing its overseas muscles, particularly in Latin America. "Roughly half of our assets and revenues are international now," says Godsoe, "and I fully expect that sometime soon in the next century, we'll end up with more people working for us in South America than in Canada. We have joint ventures or own quite large banks in Argentina, Mexico, Peru, Venezuela and El Salvador. We joint venture—anywhere from 30 to 70 percent of the equity—for cultural reasons and to add leverage to our capital. Everybody focused on our purchase of National Trust, but we've been doing much more growing internally.

"Are we big enough to compete globally?" he asks rhetorically. "Sure, we're certainly big enough to compete in our own country, and there is no question that we can compete with some of the global giants. We've tripled our market capitalization in the last four years. Do we need to merge? I suppose that if you were a dictator for a day and you looked at this game of creating headquarters for Canadian multinationals, you would encourage mergers, which is what the Dutch, the Belgians and the Swiss have done. On the other hand, if we opened everything up totally, we'd probably lose two of our banks to big foreigners, one of which would be the Hongkong Bank, now the world's biggest. They would buy a Canadian bank without a blink."

Unlike most Canadian chairmen, Godsoe got his banking start outside the country. He grew up three blocks from Toronto's Upper Canada College, tried it for one week, then switched to the less prestigious but academically superior University of Toronto Schools, going on to study math and physics at the University of Toronto, and later taking an MBA at Harvard. *[Toronto-Dominion Bank chairman Charlie Baillie was at UTS, the University of Toronto and Harvard at the same time as Godsoe, and they were both members of the Delta Epsilon fraternity. Yes, Virginia, there is a Canadian Establishment.]* After taking an accounting degree, Godsoe's first major job at the bank was at its New York office, where he was up against the big-time money men at Citibank, Bank of America and Chase Manhattan. "I came out of the U.S., knowing we could compete with the Americans," he insists. "I also learned what competing internationally really meant and that if we couldn't, we'd lose our bank."

Godsoe is the most international of Canada's bank chairmen. In the past decade, he has averaged 270 days a year on the road, doing deals for the Scotia's global treasury department, which he ran, and later for the Far East, Middle East and Latin American sections, which he also ran. His clients include Hallmark Cards in Kansas City (for global banking) and Quk Leng Chan, one of Malaysia's great tycoons, who owns, among many other assets, air-conditioning factories in Dallas. Regional lending limits have been increased to $10 million; a risk control committee in the Toronto head office only vets the bigger loans. "We're on the defensive the way we never used to be," Godsoe admits. "The popularity of the big banks is unbelievably low. If Canada doesn't come up with an industrial strategy that takes account of its financial services sector, it will keep receding in importance and ultimately will be taken over by foreigners. God help us if everything is owned by Americans. We don't have very much that's big and you can't build a whole country on small; it just doesn't work."

Godsoe is Canada's Establishment banker. He still hasn't got over the Eaton boys abandoning his bank when they were in trouble and opting for American vulture funds instead. "We got hurt on Eaton's," he says, *sounding* hurt. "Why, my mother and Signy were like sisters, and I grew up with the Eaton boys . . ."

Godsoe is a middle-of-the-road banker who doesn't believe in confronting governments or issuing ultimatums. But he also realizes the importance of Canadian banks becoming much more international, and if his plans for expansion south of the Rio Grande come true, his successor will have to be truly bilingual: English and Spanish.

FRANK MERSCH: *The Man Who Fell to Earth*
Bay Street's big shooters like to say they're in it for the game as much as for the gain. But they're not. Their greed is endlessly creative and their motto, if they have one, is Victor Hugo's sexist dictum, "Imagination is intelligence with an erection." Even that scrambled bit of logic seemed to fail Altamira's Frank Mersch, the most charismatic and successful Bay Street superstar of the mutual fund decade, who once recorded gains for his clients of 40 percent-plus annually. Despite his successes, he ended up as the industry's most spectacularly disgraced victim.

In the early 1990s, thousands of investors had flocked to his seminars, throwing money at him, virtually begging to join his funds. "He was like a rock star," recalls Stephen Kangas, vice-president of external funds at Canada Trust, who also points out that near the end of his run, the same funds were earning only 17 percent annually, compared to the 28-percent return on as mundane an index as the TSE 300.

Certainly, a good part of Altamira's problems were self-inflicted in the sense that the company was constantly on the block, with the TD Bank and Manulife among its most active suitors. At the same time, the firm's partners spent most of their energies attacking each other in public, so that the last thing on their minds seemed to be gaining greater returns for their clients. At issue was the fact that the flagship Altamira funds managed by Mersch had seriously underperformed, and that in 1996 the total invested in his funds increased by only 17 percent, compared to the industry's growth rate of 45 percent. Mersch didn't help his cause by blaming his bad performance, while talking privately group of Edmonton lawyers, on the fact that he was spending too much time with lawyers. That may have been true, but most of the issues being discussed were his own tangled legal problems.

Even taking for granted that money is Bay Street's driving force, it was difficult to comprehend why Mersch, an intelligent and personable money manager, behaved as he did. When Altamira Management was sold to TA Associates of Boston, Mersch, as the Canadian firm's largest shareholder, realized a profit of about $45 million. Yet he gambled his career and reputation on a $3,375 stock purchase in a penny-stock transaction. The Ontario Securities Commission later proved that he had quite simply lied about the transaction, claiming it had been made by a grade-school friend of his named Peter Cunti, though Mersch had paid for the purchase with a cheque on one of his own numbered companies. The osc promptly barred him from trading for 182 days, one of the harshest punishments imposed on any major Bay Street figure.

Perhaps there was a clue to his fall from grace in Mersch's confession to *Maclean's* in the winter of 1997. "We're not God; we make mistakes," he said, employing the royal "we." Since no one on Bay Street had been aware of Frank Mersch's holy or regal pedigrees, his reluctant admission that he might, after all, be prepared to consider himself a vulnerable mortal struck a bizarre note.

Ensconced in the catseat of his seventy-line private switchboard, Frank Mersch had become a ball himself. Hubris had struck again. His rise and fall bracketed a crazy time on Bay Street, when even greed got out of hand. Frank Mersh thought he had touched the hand of God; instead, he committed a stupidity that was less a crime than a natural outcome of the value system in play on Bay Street in the wild 1990s.

MERITOCRACY'S FATHER

If there is one person who changed Canada's corporate culture overnight, it's Ed Waitzer, one of the few highly intellectual Canadian lawyers, who ran Stikeman Elliott's New York office before becoming chair of the Ontario Securities Commission. On October 31, 1993, just as he was taking over as head of the osc, a new rule was put in force: henceforth, all publicly listed Canadian companies would have to publish the total salaries, bonuses and stock options awarded annually to their top five executives. Thus was born a revolution. For the first time, not just directors or shareholders but everybody could see the outrageous rewards paid to some owners and executives. More important, Canadians would discover something that insiders have known all along: executive remunerations bore almost no correlation to how well or badly they had done their jobs.

Out of that perception grew the notion of Canadian business as a meritocracy. Pressure grew to marry performance with reward, so that some common sense would return to Canadian capitalism and there wouldn't be such absurd compensation packages as that of Robert Gratton, CEO of Montreal's Power Financial, who led the payroll stakes in 1997 with

$23.5 million—plus $94.8 million in unexercised stock options. That was the equivalent of being paid more than $2 million per week. Jim Buckee, the head of Calgary's Talisman Energy, saw his company's earnings drop by 19 percent in 1997, while his pay package shot up by 155 percent, not including options worth $4.4 million.

"We knew of course that the Securities Exchange Commission in Washington had required disclosure of salaries for a long time, and as more and more Canadian companies listed in the U.S., many of our senior issuers were obliged to make that disclosure under the U.S. requirements, so the question started arising, why don't we have those requirements in Canada?" Waitzer recalls. "When I was asked to become chair—this would have been, say, August of 1993—one of the discussions I had with the Bob Rae government was to ask what they were planning to do with this executive compensation thing, because the word was out on the Street that the government was going to disregard the previous OSC's advice to issue only collective compensation, and go ahead with U.S.-style disclosure."

The abuse of the system has been startling, even for capitalism's critics who expect its practitioners to be greedy and selfish. Peter Allen awarded himself a 1,567-percent raise while he was head of the floundering Lac Minerals, while Mike Sopko, INCO's CEO, saw his profit drop by 58 percent while his pay went up 14 percent. Some executives, like Paul Tellier (who turned around Canadian National), deserved their raises; most did not. When Ted Sherman left as chairman of Revenue Properties, a Toronto developer, in November of 1996, his bonus of $1.4 million pushed the company from a profit into a loss position. In 1996, Laurent Beaudoin, the head of Bombardier, rewarded himself with a 1,335-percent raise to $19 million, plus his $33 million in unexercised options—which for that year happened to be (like Frank Stronach's earnings) more than the combined salaries of the American executives in charge of the parent companies of General Motors, Ford and Chrysler.

The examples are endless. At least four hundred Bay Street stockbrokers were paid more than $1 million in 1997, led by John Hunkin, head of the CIBC's investment and corporate banking arm, who got $10.5 million—three times as much as the salary paid Al Flood, the chairman of CIBC. "Excessive pay for CEOs has become the mad cow disease of North American business," decreed Richard Finlay, head of Toronto's Centre for Public and Corporate Governance. "It moves from boardroom to boardroom, infecting directors whose actions defy any notion of good judgment or common sense."

"There are signs this gravy train is nearing the end of its line," wrote David Olive in *The Financial Post*. "Stock market analysts are raising concerns and institutional investors are agitating for reforms. Ordinary shareholders are glaring up at embarrassed CEOs at annual meetings, and shouting—or at least, being good Canadians, thinking—'Earn it, baby! Our company lost money, so how dare you grab a bonus? You better tell us what you did to deserve that fat pay-packet!'"

And that's how meritocracies are born.

THE $60-BILLION MAN

His office is where the Toronto subway line ends and the driver walks back through the length of his train to steer it back to where things are happening. This is the outer fringe of North York. On the fifth floor of a nondescript building, working in a nondescript office that has a nondescript carpet and a nondescript desk, sits a nondescript gentleman named Claude Lamoureux, who controls investments worth $60 billion. That makes him the most influential and least-known investor in Canada. He is also the only power player in the country whose daily trades average 4 percent of the TSE's quoted market value yet who takes the subway to work and buys most of his lunches in his building's basement food court.

As CEO of the Ontario Teachers Pension Plan Board, Lamoureux runs Canada's largest portfolio next to Montreal's Caisse de dépôt et placement du Québec, which has a different mandate since it looks after the revenue stream from Quebec's entire provincial pension plan. This is a new and impressive source of institutional power in the country. OMERS (the Ontario Municipal Employees Retirement Board), with nearly $30 billion in assets, is another contender, as are several other large pension plans, which together with mutual fund managers control well over half the equity values of Canada's publicly traded companies. "The real power base in Canada today," says Gerry McGoey, a corporate director and former chief financial officer of BCE Inc., Canada's largest company, "are the pension funds and the professional managers who run them. They have far more clout than the Old Establishment ever did at the height of its power, because they're not really accountable since they have no shareholders. Even in the glory days of Bud McDougald and Argus, he may have had a lot of friends on his boards who were large shareholders, but he still had to hold public annual meetings. The pension funds are faceless and don't have the same discipline that publicly held companies do. They're already flexing their muscles and will be expressing more of their discontent with the way some companies they invest in are run."

"We try to use corporate governance to affect turnarounds in troubled corporations," is the polite way Lamoureux puts it. But it's much more brass knuckle than that. The Teachers have made a pact with the Bass Brothers of Texas jointly to buy large minority positions in Canadian companies not meeting their potential. "We'll still continue to do it with the Bass Brothers, but some on our own too," says Lamoureux. "We've tended to be fairly quiet about it, but if we think that a company is not running the way it could be, we'll talk to the management or to the board quietly, not with guns blazing, but to see if these boards would implement some of our ideas."

Lamoureux, who is paid $780,000 a year, is not a power groupie. He doesn't have to be; the powerful come to him. Red Wilson drops in to report on what's new at BCE. Wallace McCain arrives to brief him on the latest at Maple Leaf Foods. Ted Newall wants him to know how Nova will fare in the impending split. Paul Reichmann arrives (one assumes by subway) to explain how he intends to re-establish himself. One time, Isiah Thomas sauntered through his door to explain the future of the Raptors. ("He's 6 feet 2 inches, but his lawyer is 6 feet 10 inches, so they were hard to miss.") In recent times, Lamoureux has gone into town only once: to spend an hour with Charles Sirois, who plans to wire the Earth with his long-distance webs but couldn't make it out to North York.

Lamoureux is charming and he's having fun, even if he has trained himself well not to display any apparent pleasure in the extraordinary power he wields. During my visit only one statement took my breath away. In his 1997 annual report, Claude Lamoureux states: "We use derivatives to reduce risk." Wow.

THE PENSION FUNDS ARE ALSO beginning to do their share of original financing. Among the most successful was the $43-million initial public offering put together by Phil Doherty of Canadian General Capital (owned by the Ontario Hydro and Hospitals of Ontario pension funds) for Larry Stevenson, the founding chairman of Chapters Inc. Another $140 million was raised over the next four years to buy out Coles and Smiths and build the initial fleet of superstores. Doherty remains deputy chairman of Chapters. "Had there not been pension fund money available, Chapters wouldn't exist," Stevenson states flatly.

The son of a northern Quebec bush pilot and former Hudson's Bay Company post manager, Stevenson attended Royal Military College, went into the Canadian military, where he rose to be a captain in the controversial Canadian Airborne Regiment and served two tours of duty as a peacekeeper in Cyprus, then switched to Harvard, where he got an MBA. He joined Bain & Co., a U.S. strategic consulting company, first in Europe, where he ended up being in charge of the firm's merger and acquisition activity, and later in Canada. With his partner, the capable Harry Yanowitz, who became the number two in Chapters, he won ownership of the two existing independent chains, Smiths and Coles. "I based my idea of bookselling," says Stevenson, "on Foyle's, the great London bookshop. You can wander in Foyle's forever. It has almost random access and seems to have every book there is. I wondered why there wasn't a Canadian equivalent. It came down to the fact that there were two major players, both owned by conglomerates that had no intention of investing further in books. So that's how I ended up in the book business.

"I'm an entrepreneur, I didn't have access to the sort of money that would be required, so it was a legitimate partnership with Phil Doherty's pension fund. It was like going into a game and needing a partner without knowing exactly how the game would unfold. For us, it turned out great. Phil has been there at every turn, including some pretty risky ones. I remember we had to sign the deal for our Toronto store at 110 Bloor West, which was probably the biggest single investment made in the history of the book industry. We were signing a lease for about $20 million, which at that point was effectively more than the net worth of the company, and we hadn't yet built our first suburban superstore to test the idea." The fees and cost of the money came out in the form of common stock for Doherty's capital fund, which now owns a majority of the bookstore chain, leaving Stevenson with about 9 percent.

He has revolutionized the book-buying experience in Canada by fielding stores with alluring selections and well-informed staff. People often ask him about their aunt or father who has written a book, and why doesn't he just buy some copies and put them in his 350 stores, which would make it a best-seller. "Actually, no," he replies, "you have an amazingly light view of how important the Canadian consumer is. They read the books *they* want to read. Sure, they must have access to them, but the access is a small piece of the puzzle. Me buying a thousand copies and putting them in 350 stores doesn't guarantee anything at this stage of the game."

Stevenson is no intellectual, but he does love to read, especially Canadian fiction, which is the seldom-seen romantic side of him. Actually, it's on display most clear mornings when he jumps on the ferry to Toronto's Island airport and takes up a rented Cessna 172. Up in the clouds by himself, he feels contact with his mentor and hero, his late father who used to be such an avid reader that when he went flying with young

Larry, he would let him take the controls, even when the kid was too small to see over the plane's coaming, and sit there reading while Larry flew the plane. The father rationed himself, tearing out fifty pages of a book at a time, so that he didn't have to tuck too bulky a volume into his flying suit. "I love the solitude," Stevenson says. "When I'm having a horrible day, if I just go up and fly around for an hour and a half or something, it clears everything for me. I often do it early in the morning; it's just a great way to start the day. But my most fun since being in the book business is that at two in the morning, when I'm reading, I can tell my wife I'm working."

EDDIE COGAN

Eric Ambler, the novelist, once wrote that "a man's features, the bone structure and the tissue which covers it, are the products of a biological process; but his face, he creates for himself. He wears it like a devil mask; a device to evoke in others the emotions complementary to his own. If he is afraid, then he must be feared; if he desires, then he must be desired. It is a screen to hide his mind's nakedness. Only painters have been able to see the mind through the face."

Ambler would have appreciated Eddie Cogan's face, a mask of his own making, with the contours of a backwoods map where roads follow topography instead of planners' patterns. His skin is as hard as flesh scourged by the Spanish Inquisition. The face is the ultimate testimony to the proposition that form follows function.

Cogan is not muscular, but his poise and elegance suggest an athlete or dancer. He has occasionally allowed himself to be used by lesser men, but he is honest and has done much for his home turf, the Bay Street area of Toronto where he grew up and which he helped shape as its most imaginative and successful real-estate animator. Most of downtown Toronto's best features owe much to Cogan, though he will probably never receive the acknowledgement he deserves.

Cogan is in pretty good shape for the shape he's in. His body is still drum-tight (he takes an off-the-rack 34), his blow-dried hair almost covers his bald spot, his eyes are as clear as telescope lenses. He subscribes to the Humphrey Bogart dictum that what's wrong with the world is that it's always one drink behind. There is a jungle essence about him that intrigues and makes him seem bigger than life—which of course he is, providing he has an audience to hear his stories, which include hilarious encounters with Margaret Thatcher, Frank Sinatra and Brian Mulroney, among a thousand others. Cogan is one of those rare people whose coffee-break chatter can be converted into seed money for new enterprises—or visions for a new city.

Cogan's ego dilates and contracts like a Portuguese man-of-war; he feels that he is either the king of the castle or finished, never to be heard from again. Most of his days fit both categories. Cogan's manner has a subtle yet discernible intensity, a suggestion of pent-up heat. He is kind to his friends and charming to his enemies. He has many more of the former than of the latter, but he has a phantom quality, so that he always seems on the verge of disappearing—until he emerges in some new, unexpected incarnation.

Cogan's best friend and associate was the late Edward DeBartolo, the largest shopping-mall developer in the U.S., with fifty-one regional malls and fourteen strip plazas under his umbrella. He also personally owned the Pittsburgh Penguins hockey team and the San Francisco 49ers football club. He put in a $20-million offer for the Chicago White Sox, but was voted down by eleven of the fourteen club owners in the American League. The two DeBartolos did much business together, and DeBartolo, who knew about these things, thought Cogan was the best deal-maker he'd ever met.

Cogan is constantly patrolling himself, having at least twice been hours away from bankruptcy. He now has enough money that he can spend himself dry one more time. But he's not. He's doing deals again: rebuilding Niagara Falls, New York; handling the Canadian franchise for the House of Blues; expanding a chain of turkey restaurants; and always planning the bigger, better city of his dreams. In permanent overdrive, he seldom relaxes except when he is squiring one of his ladies to the Founder's Club at the Dome or some similar venue.

Cogan's love life is not simple. At one point he had ten "wives" and several children, and supported these extracurricular families faithfully— well, at least constantly. He maintains all these relationships including that with his original wife, the only one he legally married, who remains a good friend. "If I were a homosexual," he laments, "I would be a billionaire." Cogan sends out a thousand roses every Valentine's Day.

Cogan feels most alive when he is testing his nerves, waiting out offers, juggling at least three balls in the air. His thrill is in losing as much as in winning, because he is a professional deal-maker, addicted to trading real estate as the best game in town. He always comes back, and that's where the excitement comes in. He lives by his ticker file, spending most of each day on the phone, his second most legendary appendage. His telephone voice is a cigar-cured purr, conspiratorial yet demanding. He is in the business of selling himself. He never stops and seldom fails.

To hear Eddie tell it, things just happen to him. The Feds buggered up the Pearson Airport modernization; who but Cogan could manipulate a deal to rescue the situation? The promoter of the Donovan Bailey sprint runs out of money and energy; why not get Eddie? You want to put up a $300-million casino in Niagara Falls? Get Cogan to buy up the town. He is always on the go, and no one, including himself, knows how many of his deals have actually happened—because it's the next deal that grabs most of his energy and interest.

When he's negotiating, Eddie's body language becomes deafening. As he listens to a proposal, his hands lock in pretend prayer, his shoulders contort, his torso writhes, his eyes beseech. He abruptly changes the subject, tells a tale about the time he was helping to open a Penthouse Club in London and created his very private United Nations. At the end of that long and lascivious recitation, you know that anybody who tells a story like that about himself wouldn't lie to you. He has confided in you; you must be his friend.

He has seen it all, but not quite done it all. Not yet. A sweet man, at once good and terminally mischievous, Eddie Cogan is an original. Only those who really know what makes Toronto tick, like Diane Francis, know much about Cogan, and yet, during the past four decades of Toronto's downtown history, he has been everywhere. He reminds me of Duke Ellington, who cast himself as "the cool one" in a play he wrote, *The Man With Four Sides*, which was never produced. In it, a character, obviously modelled on himself, describes his approach to life. "I don't need a watch," he says. "I'm so hip that I know what time it is, all the time, everywhere. I know what's happening every place. I got a million fingers, dipping into everything. Just call me ubiquitous." That's Eddie.

CHARLIE BAILLIE
The April 10, 1998, issue of *Canadian Business* magazine carried an interesting profile of Charlie Baillie, chairman of the Toronto-Dominion Bank, in which he was asked by author Jonathan Harris whether he believed in bank mergers. "We like being independent," Baillie insisted. "If this Royal–Montreal merger thing goes through, they will have tremendous market dominance. But we've always thought that by being nimbler, we could outperform the others." Author Harris rightly concluded that "Baillie is not interested in looking for a merger partner." In a separate interview at an even later date, Baillie said, "Our plan is to

become so profitable that our stock makes us too expensive for anyone to buy. That's our best, maybe our only, hope of not losing our independence."

The magazine was barely off the newsstands when Baillie not only changed his position 180 degrees, by agreeing to a merger between the TD and the Canadian Imperial Bank of Commerce, but emerged as the architect and future Chairman and CEO of the new union. It took the Toronto-Dominion Bank board of directors just half an hour to approve the proposal.

Baillie's turnabout may be the most mysterious aspect of the strange Canadian bank merger saga. Baillie, who took over the TD from Dick Thomson in 1997, doesn't fit the traditional mould of Canadian bank heads, even if he does work in a Toronto high-rise office the size of a tennis court. With fourteen windows, it tops the count for any banker's office in the country. "It's not my fault," he explains. "This office is really a museum, because Mies van de Rohe, the great American architect who designed the TD's head office building thirty years ago, insisted this space be kept intact, exactly as he planned it. Even the flowers have to be placed in a certain way." You sense that Baillie is uncomfortable here because of the extravagant space he has to occupy. It's only a slight exaggeration to report that, when he got up from the conference table where we were talking and went back to his desk to fetch a piece of paper, Baillie moved so far away that he seemed to disappear behind the earth's curvature.

As CEO of the smallest of the Big Five banks (the TD has assets of $151 billion), Baillie used to insist that he couldn't afford to be obsessed with size for its own sake. In fact, he had a nicely honed sense of the absurd regarding size. On the morning I dropped in to visit, he took great delight in telling me about a consultant who was making the rounds of Canadian bankers. Spotting a canvas by the Quebec artist Riopelle outside Baillie's office, the consultant exclaimed, "So that's the one! When I was at the Commerce just now, they were boasting that their Riopelle was bigger than yours!"

In keeping with his then-modest priorities, Baillie sold TD's corporate jet and continues to occupy the family home he has lived in for the past twelve years. "My wife owns our house," he says.

What makes Baillie so different and so interesting is the depth of curiosity revealed by his highly unbankerish hobbies. He has acquired a copy of every issue of *Punch*, the British humour magazine, dating back to its origins in 1841. He loves reading modern accounts of history and then comparing them with reports from contemporary magazines. "I'll be reading about, say, the great mutiny in India, and I can look up the stories and cartoons in *Punch* for 1857 at the same time," he says with obvious excitement.

The kind of holidays Baillie takes also reveal an unbankerish turn of mind. Together with his wife and four grown children, he enjoys bird-watching expeditions. These aren't leisurely country walks: they have trekked through the jungles of Botswana and Zimbabwe. "I saw 192 varieties of birds in two weeks!" boasts Baillie. The family has also walked through Kenya and Papua New Guinea, and when the TD opened its office in Chile, Baillie snuck in an extra few days to go bird snooping in the Andes. Who knows where Charlie will turn up next?

TOM LONG

Bay Street's grey eminence behind Mike Harris, and in some ways the resident philosopher of the country-wide neo-con movement, is Tom Long, the new boy wonder of Canadian politics. (He is forty but looks thirty and has been immersed in Tory Party matters since he was fourteen.) A lawyer who came to Ottawa on the Mulroney wave in 1984, he worked for the next two years in the Prime Minister's Office with Peter White, who was in charge of running the government's patronage shop. On his return to Toronto, he rose to become managing partner of Egon Zehnder International, the world's third-largest firm of executive talent hunters, with forty international offices. A former president of the Ontario Progressive Conservative Party, Long became Harris's campaign chairman and heavily influenced the drafting of his platform. His greatest joy was winning a Tory election in Ontario without once calling for help from the Big Blue Machine that had dominated the party back rooms since the Ice Age. "It's the nearest to a religious experience as I've ever had," Long confessed right after the cabinet swearing in ceremony.

It was the last epiphany he had for a while, as the Harris agenda unrolled and managed to alienate nearly everybody without really trying. That wasn't too surprising, since he was pledged to balance the budget and reduce taxes by a third, while cutting already trimmed provincial expenditures by $6 billion over three years.

"It just isn't true that Ontarians are social democrats at heart," Long insists. "What you saw in the election was the silent majority backing not just Harris, but his ideas. What Mike has done is establish a new coalition of people who aren't the stereotypical conservatives. He challenged almost every aspect of Ontario's conventional political wisdom, and got 45 percent of the vote, more than any Tory since Leslie Frost in 1955."

Long predicts that unlike most politicians who slip unexpectedly into office and promptly disappear into cabinet echo chambers from which they seldom emerge, Harris will continue campaigning, trying to expand his coalition. "Mike doesn't just want to change policy; he wants to change the political goalposts," he explains.

What Long had in mind when he was first drafting Harris's strategy papers was something he called realignment politics. "I've never understood why working people didn't see themselves as Conservatives, and Mike Harris is just the brand of populist who can make it happen. One of his overriding objectives is to prove to people that how you vote actually makes a difference."

Although he seldom appears in public with the Ontario premier, Long has remained one of Harris's most trusted advisers, and thus has moved up within the Establishment. It was Long who organized Bay Street behind Harris in the first place, by putting on pre-election fund-raising dinners, fronted by the Eaton boys, especially George. (Harris's mentor was actually Bill Farlinger — later appointed Hydro chairman — who is an uncle of Harris's longest-serving staff member, Bill King.)

"The Establishment has now embraced Harris," Long insists, "because they see him as a winner, but at the start of his leadership that certainly didn't include everybody. There are at least two dozen very prominent business people who now keep saying they knew Mike was going to make it all along. But when I asked them to help during the campaign, they turned me down flat, because they didn't think he was up to the job. The late Sean O'Sullivan had a great phrase: forgive your enemies—but remember their names. So I kind of time-stamp his supporters, because I remember when they came into the thing. But that's the nature of the Establishment in this country. They're camp followers."

UPPER CANADA COLLEGE

A lifetime ago, when I arrived in Canada during the Second World War, not speaking a word of English or knowing a soul, my parents wisely sent me to boarding school at Upper Canada College. They realized that, if I stayed home and spoke Czech and German, I would never get rid of my accent or find a girlfriend. In 1945, Upper Canada had an informal wartime scholarship program, so I only had to pay half the fees.

It was the kids, not the teachers, who made me feel like an outcast by teasing me about my accent. They were all rich and WASP and I was Jewish and poor. But for me, the biggest drawback of UCC was that it wasn't coeducational. To come out of that all-male environment into university, where suddenly there was no structure and women were all over the place, made me feel like an alien from another planet. I was terribly shy, and it took me years to come to terms with the startling fact that under their clothes, women were naked. In the summers, during my last two years at UCC, I worked in a gold mine in northern Quebec and made enough money to pay the rest of my tuition, so that I am one of the few boys who actually worked his way through UCC.

I remember writing in the old boys' directory, "Like war, I'm proud of having been at UCC—and prouder still of having survived it." I got beaten up two or three times, and the overall experience wasn't that happy; but the other side of the quote is relevant too. I'm glad that I went to UCC because I learned how to survive in Canadian society and lost any awe I might have had of the Canadian Establishment. When I came to write about its members, I could be very objective, because I'd seen them in showers, I'd seen them cry when their football or hockey team lost, I'd watched their growing pains. There was nothing extraordinary about them—then or now.

Returning to the school to research this book, I found many changes, the most surprising being that it was at last trying to live up to its motto: *Palmam qui meruit ferat* ("May he who has deserved it, win the prize"). Under its current principal, Douglas Blakey, the emphasis is on academic achievement. "There's quite a bit of concern among some of our old boys that they are losing Upper Canada as their kind of establishment school," I was told by Blakey. "And to some extent that's true. The emphasis is on academic achievement. We're raising the merit hurdle. You have to have a certain level of ability and talent to get in here. So just because you're an old boy or just because you can afford to pay doesn't mean you're going to get in. Our last entry point is really Grade 9, and every boy has to go through an entrance examination and a series of interviews and references and all that sort of thing. So it's a fairly detailed screening process."

But the approach hasn't changed entirely. "Pedigree of family backgrounds still has a significant influence through contacts and financial resources that can open up doors and provide opportunities," says Blakey. "At UCC we have worked pretty hard to build up our endowment so that we can provide financial aid and keep the doors open to some families of boys who might not have the wherewithal to afford this kind of education. We believe that it will be important to provide opportunities to get to know some of the other people who aren't the more traditional, establishment kind of families."

UCC is more popular than ever. With an enrolment of 1,065, it receives hundreds of applications each year for its one hundred openings. (It costs as much as $15,690 for day boys and $27,120 for boarders.) "We do give benefit to old boys, sons of old boys, or relatives that are connected to the school in some way," explains Blakey, "particularly for those families that have been consistently supportive of the school, who have taken an interest and so forth. But everybody has to get by those academic hurdles."

One thing hasn't changed: there are still no girls. "Ridley has gone coed, Trinity is coed, Lakefield is coed and so is Appleby, but my concern is that they've done it primarily for economic reasons, in order to double their applicant pool and be able to keep the calibre of student fairly high," says Blakey. "We're not in that situation." The big change is colour. Instead of the pale sea of white-bread WASPs I remember, there are students from twenty different countries in the student population now, mostly from Korea, Hong Kong, Taiwan, places like that. Also—hallelujah! the morning meetings are now called assemblies instead of prayers. At least four students have been caught using drugs and one was expelled. The staff nurse now distributes condoms.

In a way, it's an amazing school, because any list of business leaders on Bay Street or in the rest of the country inevitably contains an inordinate number of UCC grads, including twenty-two Rhodes Scholars and thirty-eight recipients of the Order of Canada. Now that's clout.

CREAM OF THE MBAS

They turn them out like sausages, but at least they know something about the real world of business. When I got my MBA at the University of Toronto (an MBA then going under the slightly more dignified title of Master of Commerce), I knew next to nothing about becoming a businessman except that I didn't want to be one. Now, it's a goddamn religion.

On nearly every list, national or international, that surveys Canada's graduate business faculties, the Richard Ivey School of Business (at the University of Western Ontario in London) is first or near the top. One in six of the school's twelve thousand graduates carries the title of CEO, COO, president or managing director (see Appendix 6 for a partial list of distinguished grads). It's the Harvard of Canada (the average Ivey MBA's first-year salary is $76,000, compared with US$88,000 for Harvard), producing the second-largest number of case-method studies anywhere. *Business Week* has ranked the school with the three best outside the U.S., while *U.S. News & World Report* numbered Ivy fifteenth in executive education among thirty-three U.S. and international schools, the only Canadian institution to be included.

Headed by Lawrence Tapp, whose cv mentions no degrees but points out that he led an aggressive $552-million leveraged buyout of the Lawson Mardo Group and transformed it into a successful international packaging company with sales of $1.5 billion, the School features an Institute for Entrepreneurship, Innovation and Growth. "For many years," says Tapp, "we were a big fish in a little pond. All we had to do was to keep on doing what we had done so well for decades. But when we did an environmental scan several years ago, we found that our pond had turned into an ocean. We saw increased competition for students and faculty and growing pressures on Canadian business from globalization. We decided that the only way to survive was to become a bigger fish, and prepare to compete with the top business schools in the world."

"My first class," recalls Michael Clements, an Olympic sailor from Vancouver who took an Ivey MBA, "was with Roger Moore, the call-it-as-he-sees-it, take-no-prisoners marketing professor, whose sole focus in life was Total Margin Dollars. There we were, all seventy of us, petrified to the core and mute. In later sessions it became clear that the classroom was an artificial place, which caused strange behavioural changes in some people, especially the introverts in real life, who in class became tigers, always fighting for air time. I viewed myself as going to war each day, armed to the teeth with all of the weapons I had at my disposal: my Hewlett-Packard calculator, my textbook on methodologies and my brain. The classroom was the battle zone, my classmates were the competition, and the professor was God, arbitrating the battle. Victory was one or two minutes of uninterrupted air time. Those moments were rare, and treasured accordingly. Anyone who could perform in such an atmosphere would be totally at home sitting in a boardroom of a large corporation. When I finally graduated and found that I had made the dean's honour list, it was the proudest moment of my life."

Another MBA grad sums up his experience more succinctly: "What you learn is that it's not how you play, it's whether you win the goddamn game."

SAM SLUTSKY: *The Interlocutor*
If the Old Establishment was a club and the New Establishment is a network, the personification of the latter is a jovial lawyer from Winnipeg named Sam Slutsky who has become Bay Street's ultimate networker. That's what he does, seven days a week, round the clock:

network. He doesn't tell anyone—including authors of books on the Establishment—who his contacts are, but he knows nearly everything that's happening on Bay Street's and Canada's corporate command posts, and he lets slip just enough tidbits that you know he knows. He is a member of four bars—Ontario, Manitoba, Alberta and Prego—and his official title is managing director of Equimar Capital Inc., which he loosely describes as being in "investment and merchant banking." His partners include former deputy prime minister Don Mazankowski, chairman of the firm; Michael Mackenzie, the former superintendent of financial institutions; and Brent Hollis, a corporate finance lawyer who is also an accountant.

"I come from a culture where we're interested in people and interested in life," he explains. "We like to get involved, we like to find out what's going on, to focus on relating to others. I believe that you must set yourself up in life so that you do business with people you like, because you can develop trust and figure out how to advance ideas. You can have a good mix of professional and personal lives and enjoy going up to people and saying, 'Hey Red, how you doin', what's going on?' *[Lynton Ronald Wilson, chairman of BCE Inc., who is one of Slutsky's main contacts.]*

"I'm genuinely interested and curious about what people are doing," Slutsky emphasizes. "Why be in business if you're not there to make friends? I'm viewed as a bit of an oddity that way because there is hardly anybody I don't have some link to and there isn't anybody I won't seek out, from CEOs to line people. I've been doing this now for twenty years, and one step at a time I've built up this huge network of people who are interrelated, so that there is hardly a front-page event that goes on that doesn't involve somebody I know and have a relationship with. The matchmaking I'm doing now is quite interesting. I'm putting together people who have not yet realized the opportunity to take the initiative themselves, but who jump at the chance once the logic of a linkage is suggested. Networking is what it's about, and in a true network people enjoy the company of its other members, and that's been the success of my business. More and more business, particularly the largest deals, are based on relationships and trust, and that's the basis on which we get involved in them.

"One of the strengths of this approach is to be able to talk to people in organizations about what is really going on and avoid being obsequious. Business people, particularly CEOs, need to be alerted to sensitive matters that are part of the flow of the street. We are confidants to about a dozen CEOs across the country and help them explore different initiatives before they broach them internally or take them to the board. Sometimes there's a transaction in it for us, sometimes there isn't, but we manage to be involved at the CEO level with some of the most significant players in this country."

Slutsky's skill at networking—which amounts to making sure the recipient of the advice he proffers gets the credit for any favourable consequences, while paying Slutsky a consulting fee—flows out of his experience in politics. As a lawyer who specializes in taxation, he was probably the author of as many significant changes in Canada's tax system as most ministers of finance and revenue. He did it by being their personal adviser, being at their side during the interface with their departments, explaining the political effects of policies, saying, "Look, here's what this really means, guys. Here are the benefits. This is how it's going to help you politically, and this is how it's going to make the system better—or worse." He acted as tax counsel for the federal government in the Hibernia negotiations, and was the first to suggest the transformation of the National Revenue Department into a non-political government agency.

"The more powerful a CEO, politician or public servant becomes, the more isolated they are, surrounded by people who will not risk their jobs to tell the truth and be straight with them," he contends. "Even in my own organization, when I suggest to my partners that I'm going out to talk to some CEO and I'm going to discuss his company's troubles or his personal problems, they say, How can you do that? You're talking about some of the most sensitive stuff there is about him. My answer is that if you really want to help somebody, you address the bad as well as the good. It doesn't make sense to sit around when someone is heading for trouble without trying to be of help. In Europe, this approach is part of the fabric of life. They take it for granted, everybody does it. In New York, it's the same thing at the highest levels: you do business by relating to people. In Toronto, less so. People are more inclined to stay in their own sandboxes.

"I have a great competitive advantage: I work on a model that makes sense for living. In Canada, the norm is not to be curious, and to be uncomfortable with people who are. I don't get along with everybody. There are a lot of people who don't like my forthrightness or my aggressiveness, and I accept that. Success in life depends on how well you can deal with rejection.

"The joke goes like this: people say, what do you do? I say, well, I'm a merchant banker. They say, oh, so what do you do? Basically, I go to work every day and I get on the phone; I laugh, I joke, I try to figure out new initiatives. We are also involved in a fair bit of international corporate finance on the frontier. While most people are flying at 33,000 feet, many of the people we're dealing with are in the Concorde at 50,000 feet. We do some very eclectic and interesting financing. We restrict our business to relatively large transactions where we have the experience and expertise, and our activities often involve some of the most sophisticated players in the world—smart money. For example, we're working with partners to set up a new insurance company offshore to provide residual value insurance for equipment finance transactions. It involves the largest insurance companies in the world, but our main partner is a Finnish fellow who is one of the leading international tax structure engineers. His relationships in that world are remarkable.

"Going to work every day is fun," he concludes, mysterious as ever. "I spend probably 60 percent of my time networking and 40 percent actually getting involved in the mechanics of deals. But it's the greatest of lives for me. I talk to all sorts of people around the country and the world, get involved in exciting and cutting-edge initiatives at top management levels. I have a damn good time—and I get paid for it."

TOM KIERANS

If the Canadian business community has an operational guru, he is Tom Kierans, president of the Toronto-based C.D. Howe Institute, a think-tank with balls, which during his decade-long stewardship has become the country's most consistent, if largely academic, policy-research source.

Like his role model—his father, Eric, the one-time Trudeau cabinet minister who had too many fresh ideas to feel comfortable within any political context—the younger Kierans has drifted between the private and public sectors, leaving a considerable mark on both. An MBA who became an important activator in Nesbitt Thomson and Pitfield MacKay Ross before joining McLeod Young Weir as president and organizing its sale to the Bank of Nova Scotia, Kierans was one of the first to predict the anatomy of Toronto as a deregulated financial centre. "These are the last days of Bay Street as a club," he declared in 1987. "Who cares whether you lunch at the Toronto Club with some likely client? His treasurer will call for tenders anyway."

During his corporate career, Kierans has headed half a dozen public policy committees, contributed thoughtful articles to academic journals, and served as chairman of Petro-Canada, First Marathon Securities, Ipsco Inc. and Moore Corp.

It was his reputation for knowing exactly what's what and who's who on the Canadian business scene that led him to be chosen as the primary contact for the entry to this country of the Bass brothers, those legendary Texas billionaires busy shaking Canada's corporate family tree, in the company of Claude Lamoureux. "Back in 1990, when Ced Ritchie was still head of the Scotiabank, he suggested I brief Tom Taylor, the Bass brothers' investment point man," Kierans recalls, "because he was thinking of taking the Bass operation into Canada. Taylor is wealthy himself— and I don't mean just rich—and invests along with the Basses. They identify companies where they see stock-market values being depressed by poor corporate governance and buy a 5- or 6-percent holding. They then tie themselves in with one of the big pension funds, which buys an equal amount of stock. Together, but led by Taylor, they then attempt to convince incumbent management to see things their way. If that fails, they meet with directors, and Taylor is granted a seat on the board to help implement his strategy. Taylor is not a hostile-takeover artist but management's departure usually follows."

That tactic has allowed the Bass organization to turn the profit picture around at such basket cases as MacMillan Bloedel, the giant West Coast forest company; Trimac, the Calgary-based transportation firm; Encal Energy, an Alberta oil producer; United Dominion; and Agrium, as well as Moore Corp. The Bass family fortune, estimated at more than $6 billion, was inherited from their great-uncle, Sid Richardson, the legendary Texas oilman, who died in 1951. His estate is now spread between father Perry Bass and his four reclusive sons, Robert, Lee, Sid and Edward, who live in Fort Worth, where they build humongous residential communities and casino resorts, as well as redeveloping forty-one downtown blocks. The original family fortune has grown exponentially, their $400-million investment in Walt Disney Co. now being worth at least $3.5 billion. Sid's wife, Anne, received 1.38 million Disney shares as a divorce settlement, worth $525 million. The Bass family still owns 5 percent of Disney, worth $2.5 billion, the La Quinta Inns chain and Bell Atlantic. The brothers also built the $150-million Biosphere-2, a flawed but imaginative self-contained ecosystem in Arizona. Their Canadian investments included the 1995 purchase for $1.6 billion of North America Trust's Canadian real-estate portfolio and the sale of Stella Foods, a large U.S. cheese producer, to Montreal's Saputo Group Inc. for $563 million.

One reason Kierans has been able to place himself in the epicentre of Canadian business is that his opinions, on whatever subject, are usually worth hearing. "Everybody in Montreal understands the extent to which power has shifted to Toronto, because that's a straight number," he says. "Even Ottawa understands that. But neither Ottawa nor Montreal understands the extent to which power has shifted from Toronto to the West. The federalists are supposed to be flexible, yet we've got this old Montreal–Ottawa–Toronto axis still controlling the country. Whether it's Liberal or Conservative doesn't matter, and it's quite right for people to become alienated from that axis when so much reality has changed."

Despite his disillusionment with active politicians of all parties, he defends the system. "I give lots of speeches to lots of kids, and I tell them, if you opt out of politics, the grey hairs are going to run everything and you're going to get screwed, so make sure you grab a stake in the system while you can." He unexpectedly jumped into the dispute about RCMP headgear, siding with Alberta's rednecks. "The mythology of any system is crucially important. The people who objected to the RCMP wearing turbans instead of the hats they've worn since 1910 were called racist. They're not. Those Mountie hats are an inherent part of the Canadian mythology, which knits the nation together."

Tom Kierans is an ardent Canadian, but occasionally questions the depth of national commitment. "We're the only people in the world," he complains, "who feel compelled every six months to dig up our roots and look at them, just to make sure we're still here."

ABUSING THE SYSTEM

I have a friend in Calgary named Ralph Hedlin who has had great success playing the stock market. His winnings are based on never buying into a company until he does his own due diligence. He was having lunch at a downtown bar a couple of years ago when in staggered a paunchy and dishevelled gent who spent the next hour or so perched on a bar stool, knocking back drinks until he keeled over and passed out. When Ralph enquired about the drunk's identity, he turned out to be a bar regular, David Walsh, the head of Bre-X, then starting its climb to infamy.

"Well," Hedlin said to his companion, "that's all the due diligence I need," and he never bought a single share of the Indonesian swamp that turned out to be the greatest mining swindle of all time.

Walsh died in the spring of 1998, but his legacy survives. Whether he was involved in salting the core samples that convinced investors there was real gold at Busang will never be known, but he certainly took advantage of his insider knowledge concerning other matters that share-holders should have known about to mint a personal fortune. During 1996 alone, Walsh and his wife, Jeannette, cashed in Bre-X options worth $34.9 million—many originally purchased for one cent each as options from treasury stock controlled by Walsh. In December 1995, while the stock was still flying high, Walsh purchased his luxurious seaside villa near Nassau, in the Bahamas.

Only forty-one days before its crash, Walsh allowed his chief geologist, John Felderhof, to issue wild estimates claiming that Bre-X's Borneo discovery contained 200 million ounces of gold. That meant its open-pit mine would have been history's richest find, containing gold worth $100 billion. To put this figure in perspective: the world's largest existing open-pit gold ore body, being mined in Irian Jaya, Indonesia, by Freeport-McMoRan of New Orleans, has reserves of 55.3 million ounces of gold. Bre-X, as invented by its founders, would have been nearly four times as rich.

Until Walsh looked up Indonesia in his home atlas, Bre-X was a worthless Alberta Stock Exchange shell, selling for two cents a share—which is a couple of pennies more than it's worth now. Yet at its height, Bre-X had a stock capitalization that exceeded that of Molson, Chrysler Canada and Coca-Cola Beverages combined.

There have been other recent scams, such as the First Marathon involvement with Cartaway Resources, a company that originally rented out garbage containers in Kamloops, and whose share values went from $26 to $2, and Yorkton's Timbuktu Gold, which turned out to be another salting operation. But Bre-X was in a class by itself.

If there was anything admirable about the Bre-X débâcle, it was the way it demonstrated how easy it is to fool the experts. John Doody, editor of Wall Street's monthly *Gold Stock Analyst*, who did a detailed study of how the swindle worked, estimates that it took only $40,000 worth of real gold to salt all 268 drill holes. What was most disturbing about the Bre-X fraud was how gullible—or stupid—the Bay Street gurus were in backing a company run by Walsh, who, only weeks before he discovered what he modestly called "the largest gold deposit in history," was driving around Calgary in an ancient Buick Regal held together by duct tape, and a year earlier was so maxed out on his fourteen credit cards that he had to declare personal bankruptcy.

The analysts managed to achieve an unblemished record for being wrong about Bre-X. Egizio Bianchini at Nesbitt Burns, touted as Bay Street's top gold-mining analyst, declared after a visit to Borneo: "I know for a fact there's gold. I've seen it." Only days before the stock went into the dumpster, he was still calling for the shares to double to $29. Even after chief geologist Michael de Guzman jumped to his death, Bianchini further strained his credibility by telling his clients that the idea of samples having been salted was "so preposterous, I am not even going to address the possibility."

How can anyone believe what Bay Street analysts say and write ever again? The best advice was published in *Barron's*, the authoritative New York City investment weekly: "When the lead geologist of a speculative gold-mining company falls out of a helicopter—sell the stock." A variation on this useful counsel came from Vancouver's "Tookie" Angus, one of Canada's most knowledgeable mining lawyers. "I have a cardinal rule," he once told me. "I never buy gold-fields from guys in Calgary, and I never buy oil wells from guys in Vancouver."

Everybody was fooled, but no one more so than Paul Kavanagh, who hung in as an independent Bre-X director until the bitter end, fully supporting the firm's initiatives, introducing and hyping the stock to Bay Street's trend-setters. Kavanagh had been senior vice-president of exploration at Barrick for six years and held top management positions at leading mining companies like Kerr Addison, Newmont (where he was president for two years) and Rio Algom before his stint at Bre-X. How he could have gone along with Bre-X's 200-million-ounce reserve estimate—which made no sense at any level comprehensible to a professional mining man—remains a mystery.

Equally incomprehensible was the decision by the Toronto Stock Exchange to include Bre-X in its prestigious 300 Index, where it joined such venerable institutions as the Royal Bank, even though it was at best still an unproven gold prospect.

The Bre-X tragedy was best summed up by Dr. Eugene Newry, the Bahamian physician who attended David Walsh during his fatal illness. "Aside from the aneurysm," the good doctor concluded, "Walsh was in excellent health." Exactly. But then, aside from the fact that it was a flat-out fraud, Bre-X was an excellent gold mine.

THE BRE-X AFFAIR WAS THE DARKEST side of Canadian capitalism, but the wrong people garnered most of the blame. The renegade geologists may have thought up the swindle, but they didn't drive Bre-X's market value to $6 billion; that was Bay Street's accomplishment. Such leading houses as Nesbitt Burns, First Marathon, Midland Walwyn and Lévesque Beaubien were still recommending Bre-X only hours before its dramatic tumble.

A strange aspect was the defence entered by Nesbitt Burns to the $3-billion class action suit it was facing. Because it is the clients and not the marketers of shares who have the final say about purchasing, claimed the Nesbitt defence, its own salesmen (like Egizio Bianchini, who pushed Bre-X the hardest of any dealer) had no fiduciary responsibility to investors.

THE SCARLET PIMPERNEL

Of all the cheeky new recruits who have arm-wrestled the Old Canadian Establishment to the ground, it's Robert Friedland who provides the most persuasive argument that a new meritocracy is taking over. He is extravagant proof that to make it big in the 1990s requires neither class credentials nor private-school education, neither mentors with patrician pedigrees nor memberships in exclusive private clubs.

Friedland's idea of a great hangout is to slip on his sandals and roam the fields of abandoned eleventh-century Buddhist temples at Pagan in northern Burma. He belongs to no clubs, owns only two suits, and grew up in Chicago as a hippie amongst the free love, loose batik blouses and fluffy philosophy of the turned-on, lava-lamp 1960s drug culture. He was a master of ceremonies at the legendary 1969 Woodstock music festival, was later arrested for dealing in LSD and served time at a Virginia youth corrections facility, but later had his conviction legally expunged. He was educated not at Harvard, though he earned the marks to get into its medical school, but in the Himalayan foothills, by Neem Karoli and other remarkable gurus of the 1970s. His soul mate and travelling companion at the time was Steve Jobs, the godfather of Apple computers.

Friedland drifted into mining promotion on the Vancouver Stock Exchange and for the next two decades roamed the Earth's crust, ballyhooing and occasionally finding minerals: the hint of diamonds in the sandy sea bottom off Namibia, and serious gold deposits in Alaska and showings along Latin America's Guyana Shield. Then he suffered his great flameout at Galactic, which sounds like an incident out of *Star Wars*, but was the tragic story of the gold-mining company at Summitville, Colorado, which he headed, allegedly not cleaning up a spill of cyanide. That much-misunderstood and misinterpreted event was a defining moment in his business career. He was never guilty as charged, but he was charged. The Galactic episode turned his name into a curse: Robert Friedland, Enemy of the Earth. His mine tailings were said to have devastated Colorado's calendar-art hinterland. It was never true, but the accusation stuck. Only in the summer of 1998 did he get court permission to sue the U.S. Environmental Protection Agency for defamation.

Shortly after that came the dramatic Labrador base-metal strike, and that meant redemption on a grand scale. No one, ever, has enriched more members of Canada's Establishment than Friedland and the elephant-sized ore body his prospectors discovered in north-central Labrador—the $30-billion-plus base metal deposit near Voisey's Bay. Shares in his company, Diamond Fields, zoomed from $3.00 to $176.50. He was the guy who realized everybody's wet dream.

Since finding the mineral strike of the century during the autumn of 1994 and selling his stake for $600 million, Friedland has become the elusive Scarlet Pimpernel of Canadian business. A seldom-seen or -heard presence, he has virtually ceased to exist in the Canadian consciousness, except as a distant and receding legend. He is so afraid of being misunderstood that he shuns the media—and then, of course, is even more misunderstood. But to his coterie of Bay Street friends, clients and partners, Friedland remains a voice in the dead of night, whispering advice, Buddhist incantations and other instant sermons into his Ericsson cell phone from the distant hills of Kazakhstan, the outbacks of Tasmania or the trading floor of Singapore's financial district, where a billion dollars' worth of securities changes hands every twelve minutes, even during the height of Asia's recent flu.

Mystery has its own currency, and Friedland makes the most of it. He nurtures the existential aura of a man who shares urgent secrets with the universe, and in a way he does. Since Voisey's Bay, he has ventured into some highly speculative but potentially exciting chunks of geological *terra incognita*. Working out of his Singapore headquarters or one of his five houses on four continents, he quietly goes about his big-game mine hunting. He spends most of his time in the air, aboard his luxuriously appointed $30-million Falcon 2000 jet, on the lookout for new mineral plays that, if successful, will extend his reach to the wildest shores of capitalism.

Friedland has a strange effect on people: they don't believe he's real. He comes across as a philosopher with a whoopee cushion. They want to preserve him as evidence of a lusty, roguish past, when tycoons really were pirates, and easily visualize him with a patch over one eye and a squawking parrot on his shoulder. The only aspect of that fantasy that touches reality is the parrot. He does keep parrots and spends hours grooming them and teaching them to expand their vocabulary. His favourite is Ozzie, a Canadian-born Hyacinth Macaw, who says things like, "I can talk—can you fly?" The most articulate bird is Romeo Friedland, who can give stock advice—"Listen, buy low—sell high"—or even help out his owner—"Help, let me out! I've been framed! Call my lawyer. Get Huberman!" *[David Huberman, one of Vancouver's best, was Friedland's lawyer for most of twenty years.]*

Is he a billionaire? "All depends which day you ask him," says his personal financial adviser and senior vice-president A.P. Singh, a Sikh from the Punjab, the son of an Indian army general, who after he immigrated to Canada rose to be in charge of Bank of Montreal's private banking operation in Vancouver, and now spends his entire time and energy with Friedland. He has known him for seventeen years, worked for him full-time for three, and has a private bedroom in each of Friedland's houses. "Robert's secret," he says, "is that he's incredibly focused on everything he does, whether it's a multimillion business deal, or teaching his parrots new tricks, or feeding their recently hatched chicks with an eye-dropper." *[When I tried to interview Friedland's parrots about their keeper, they were resolutely close-beaked, not even bothering to throw a "No comment" my way, though I tried bribing Romeo with two big walnuts.]*

Singh is an exception. Accompanying most of the people who work for Friedland is the buzz of drones tending a queen bee. He doesn't demand it, but there's a kind of group drool that goes on whenever he arrives at one of his many offices. His exacting schedule reflects his impatient appetite for life, and he's impossible to keep up with; even he can't manage it most of the time. Friedland is handsome and lithe, has deep, sunken eyes and speaks in a lilting monotone that can become mesmerizing.

Dr. Roger Morton, the former dean of the economic geology department at the University of Alberta, who has worked with Robert in Latin America, concluded, "He is a person endowed with infinite energy. He runs on his own kind of metabolism, which is about five times the speed of everybody else's. Why is he unpopular in the industry? Because success is something that society despises through envy in most cases." Trevor Wilson, who did business with Friedland when he was deputy chairman at Yorkton, puts it this way: "I have a high regard for Robert, but he is one of the most difficult men I've ever dealt with. Somebody asked me once about his personality, and I said, he has sixteen, and two are great." Another mining man has a simpler explanation: "Robert is perfectly balanced: he has a chip on each shoulder."

To burden Friedland with titular membership in the Canadian Establishment may shock what remains of its self-selecting clique of family dynasties. And yet there is a certain rationale in claiming that, if he isn't another Conrad Black, Paul Desmarais or Galen Weston, his financial score and his twenty-first-century lifestyle—running a risky, global business that recognizes few geographical or fiscal limits—is where the future points. If success among the new Titans is measured in the number of dollars minted, as it assuredly is, Robert Friedland has to be the pick of the litter.

I spent several days with Robert Friedland in Singapore, preparing this book, and found him to be as compelling as anyone I've run across during four decades of practising the black arts of investigative journalism. Rich and powerful enough to shape his own destiny, Robert Friedland knows exactly what he wants to be when he grows up: Robert Friedland, playing the odds. And yet there is something indefinably poignant about this forty-eight-year-old fortune-hunter, with his achy breaky heart, trying to connect with the universe, never giving up his quest for love and dollars.

THE BAY STREET CROWD

Appendix 7 lists some of Bay Street's essential players, as do the preceding pages of this chapter. *[Another guide to the Bay Street establishment is Appendix 3, which lists the Dream Team that Jon Dellandrea, the University of Toronto's chief development officer, gathered for the 1997–98 fund-raising campaign that collected an unprecedented $400 million.]* But there are a few others desribed below:

IT'S THE AGE OF THE BANK-OWNED BROKERAGES, and no one can top such mega-deals as Wood Gundy's $2.2-billion Newcourt Credit financing, but it is at the boutiques that most of the exciting new ideas are being spawned. For example, Newcrest's Bob Dorrance (formerly of Nesbitt Burns) was chosen to do a $176-million bought deal for Gerry Schwartz's Onex Corp. Formed in 1995 by nine refugees from the large houses, Newcrest's seventy employees prosper purely on the basis of imaginative suggestions to their clients. Elsewhere in town, the combination of Brad Griffiths and Gene McBurney—and their thirty-eight partners—has been potent and obtrusive. The firm's reputation as "the bad boys of Bay Street" hasn't prevented them from consistently being among the top ten houses based on their share of equity trades. The $50,000 invested by each of the two founders in 1995 was worth $10 million by the spring of 1998. First Marathon, headed by Lawrence Bloomberg (who owns 27 percent), was Bay Street's first discount brokerage and remains innovative, but it has been hurt by the shenanigans in its Vancouver office and the emphasis on its trading of shares in Bre-X. Some impressive intuitive leaps have been taking place at Yorkton Securities, under its chairman and CEO—and largest shareholder—Scott Paterson, who is the subject of Chapter 15. Among the buyers of securities,

Ira Gluskin occupies a special pew because he is not only successful but generates so many great stories about himself. (Sample: Chuck Winograd, deputy chairman of RBC Dominion, swears that Ira once phoned him to say, "I'm just calling to let you know I've got Peter Bronfman on hold.")

Amongst the enlarged presence of American merchant banks, the most impressive is that of Salomon Brothers, headed by Stanley Hartt, whose background in law (Stikeman Elliott), Ottawa (deputy minister of finance), politics (chief of staff to the prime minister) and salvage (Robert Campeau's Camdev Corp.) has equipped him to be one of the few philosophers on Bay Street. His accounts include CN, the telephone companies and Ontario Hydro. Peter Dey, Canadian head of Morgan Stanley (who went to kindergarten with Gar Emerson) ably represents the Wall Street merchant bank on Bay Street. His clients include Four Seasons, Ballard Batteries and Clearnet Communications. Barbara McDougall has, along with Michael Wilson and Don Mazankowski, been among the few cabinet ministers from the Mulroney administration to make a successful switch to civvy street. Chair of AT&T in Canada, she holds half a dozen other blue-ribbon directorships—as does Anna Porter who is emerging as a real force, not only because of her prize-winning publishing house, but her top-line directorships (Argus, Alliance and *The Financial Post*).

Allan Gotlieb is in a class by himself. He appears in so many guises that it is almost easier to list those few companies or committees that have *not* felt the weight of his influence. He is a parody of the man of affairs, who has to be involved in everything that moves or feel left out. "He has become a one-man industry, creating more employment than the entire island of Newfoundland," noted Allan Fotheringham. "My favourite Gotlieb story is the description of him, deep in thought, standing on an Ottawa curb through three green lights and then stepping out—on the red." He is very much the intellectual. A fussy man with fusty tastes—in other places and times, he would have been a Talmudic scholar—he seems constantly apprehensive; he is not a man you warm to easily.

When the Europe's Rothschild Group (the family's financial arm in the United Kingdom, France and Switzerland) decided to set up a Canadian "advisory firm" in 1990, they wisely chose H. Garfield Emerson to be their Canadian representative. The chair of Rogers Communications and a distinguished corporation lawyer, he has been chief adviser on such deals as the partial privatization of Petro-Canada, the debt restructuring of Magna, the takeover of Maclean Hunter by Ted Rogers and the acquisition of Royal Trust by the Royal Bank. Dominic D'Alessandro, who was passed over by the Royal Bank in favour of John Cleghorn, is making his own yards as CEO of Manufacturers Life, the first Canadian life insurance company due to be de-mutualized. Miles Spencer Nadal, whose MDC Communications occupies the most beautiful head office in Toronto (at 45 Hazelton Avenue), reports that the 1997 sales of his security and marketing operation were up 77 percent. His subsidiaries employ three thousand people in sixty-five countries. A university drop-out, he donated $1 million to York University's business school, with the proviso that its downtown campus be known as the Nadal Management Centre.

Dale Lastman, who at thirty-six was named CEO of the Goodman Phillips Vineberg firm and negotiated the sale of *The Financial Post*, is emerging as the best of the new generation of Bay Street's securities lawyers. Like his father, the mayor of Toronto, he has a sense of humour. During a retreat at Deerhurst Lodge for the firm's lawyers, he was asked to host the Goodman Awards, which were supposed to be mock prizes to lighten serious study sessions. "I decided we would have this award called the Lawyer of the Year," he recalls. "So we wrote a separate letter to each of the lawyers in the firm saying, 'As you know, this weekend at Deerhurst we will be announcing our annual awards which are of a humorous nature, but there is one serious award, Lawyer of the Year, which pays tribute to that person's dedication to the practice of law, and stands them apart from all others. After serious consideration we've recommended that you be the first winner of the annual Lawyer of the Year award.' And I added, 'We ask you to keep this in confidence because we want to enjoy the moment, but we're telling you in advance so that you can prepare a short response.' And we had the then managing partner, Herb Solway, write on the bottom of each letter, 'Not my choice, but congratulations.'

"In any event, we then took these letters with us and, about four-thirty on the afternoon of the award ceremony, dropped them under each lawyer's door at Deerhurst. That evening at the mock awards ceremony, I stood up and said, 'We're now at the point in the program where we have one serious event, recognition of the Lawyer of the Year, the person whose dedication to the practice of law stands them apart from all others. The person who won this award has been notified in advance. Will he please step forward.' Much to my shock and horror, about twenty-five lawyers started walking toward the head table with speeches in hand, and there was a dead silence in the room. I realized I had made a serious mistake; nobody was laughing. I mumbled something about there appearing to be co-winners and sat down at my own table, where my wife looked at me and said, 'You're in deep trouble.' *[Lastman knows about such*

*things. He had to survive his parents' arrangements for his bar mitzvah, when father Mel
and mother Marilyn insisted on redecorating the whole second floor of the Royal York
Hotel as Camelot, with young Dale sitting atop a golden throne, wearing a crown, while
seven hundred guests gawked.]* Later, some partners actually wrote Herb
demanding his resignation for being a part of the send-up. One lawyer
had phoned his kids that afternoon and said, 'Your daddy has just won
Lawyer of the Year.' At any rate, it was a lot of fun. Now it's folklore."

Others making yards: Hymie Belzberg's son Brent; Sun Media's Paul
Godfrey, who has become recognized on the Street as a major facilitator
and, with his newspaper domination of central Ontario, rivals the power
of *The Toronto Star*; Michael Bregman of Second Cup; Ron Joyce, the
former policeman and donut king who sold Tim Horton's for a world-
class fortune, after collecting $30 million a year in dividends; Don Green
and Michael Budman of the Roots organization; John Tory, steadily
reviving the fortunes of Rogers-owned Maclean Hunter; and Larry Tan-
nenbaum, the civilized half of the Stavros partnership that controls
Toronto's sports future, who owns two American basketball magazines
and a paving company. Jim Baillie, chairman of the executive committee
at Tory, Tory, Deslauriers & Binnington and former head of the Ontario
Securities Commission, continues to exert his moral suasion, as do Sheila
Block, Lorne Morphy and Bob Armstrong in his firm. Alan Lenczner,
Edgar Sexton, Jake Howard, David Drinkwater, Peter Beattie and Ted
Donegan lead Bay Street's legal battalions.

Former premier David Peterson occupies a unique slot as a corporate
catalyst and someone in whom everyone confides. He has collected
sixteen top boards and likes to compare his current incarnation with his
political career. "You don't have the scrutiny, so that's a very nice part
about it," he says. "But you don't have the real power that you do as first
minister either. The similarity is that you have to read the road map on
extraordinarily complex situations with an awful lot of people, so that in
the end, politics amounts to institutionalized human behaviour—just like
business. In retrospect, I got thrown out at a very good time." Fellow
Liberal Ed Lumley, the former owner of a small wood-finishing plant in
Cornwallis, Ontario, who became Pierre Trudeau's trade minister, became
Nesbitt Thomson's deputy chairman and one of its most aggressive producers. He sits on the boards of Magna, Trilon, CN and BCE Mobility.

Another very special presence is John Evans, a Rhodes Scholar,
former president of the University of Toronto, chairman of New York's
Rockefeller Foundation (giving away $120 million a year), and chair of
Torstar, Alcan and Allelix Biopharmaceuticals. "A lot of people who are

successful don't listen because they feel that *they* have a lot to tell the world. I don't think I have a lot to tell the world, but I'm really interested in many areas and love to listen." There's much more to it than that: Evans has become a touchstone for his generation.

On the multicultural front, among many others, Vic De Zen, CEO of Royal Plastics Group, threatens to become the richest of all, sprinkling the Third World with his inexpensive but functional plastic houses. He owns 20 percent of his $1-billion company and controls 80 percent of the votes. Fred Sorkin is the CEO of Hummingbird Communications, which makes network connectivity software; his purchase of the right to rename the O'Keefe Centre after his company was a perfect symbol of the times. Prem Watsa, the head of the quixotic but phenomenally successful Fairfax Financial Holdings, has no problem settling his executive salary: he simply informs his dummy board what he plans to pay himself. Suresh Bhalla, who has three sons at Upper Canada College, has been the Royal Bank's most successful trader, minting millions, mostly on real-estate play. (The father, as it turns out, was the only pilot to fight in the Battle of Britain, and eventually headed the Indian air force.)

Among the interesting comebacks is that of the new generation of Reichmanns. Albert's son Philip, for example, had been working for his father for fifteen years when the empire collapsed in 1992 under its $18-billion debt load. The following year, Philip and his partner Frank Hauer (Paul's son-in-law) bought O&Y Properties Inc. from its creditors for $18 million, and were managing 9 million square feet of office space. That was eventually doubled, and with Sam Slutsky acting as go-between, they purchased Camdev, the remains of the Campeau empire, for $76 million. They also bought Paul Reichmann's remaining 28-percent interest in Toronto's First Canadian Place. "What Frank and I have accomplished wouldn't have been possible without the 1992 meltdown," says Reichmann. "And we can't be accused of being secretive any more, because we run a public company now." His nephew, Abraham, is building a huge indoor recreation park, complete with ski hills and hang-gliding perches. Paul and his son, Barry, are meanwhile buying up nursing homes (including Versa-care for $83 million) and doing real-estate deals in Mexico and England—where they've bought back a sliver of Canary Wharf, which brought them crashing down in the first place.

HANGOUTS

Bay Street has more great restaurants than great chefs, but of the many places where the brokers and traders drink and eat, five hangouts are special. *[When the Titans are looking for someplace further afield to recover their spirits and renew their energies, they go to some of the hangouts listed in Appendix 8.]*

Jump, built in an enclosed corridor in Commerce Court, combines glass and dark-walnut décor with serious but not very adventurous food. Regulars—mostly the Dominion Securities, Scotia McLeod and Yorkton crowds—swear they can tell which way the Dow is heading by the volume and pitch of its noontime buzz. A fancy pit-stop for medium-rank traders, it is a place to eat and be seen, but not if you're a top player.

Acqua, the only premium restaurant at BCE Place, is heavily booked but not always full. That has little to do with its food or ambience. The whole place is built in front of a waterfall (presumably signifying the Acqua theme) that involuntarily prompts diners of a certain age to, well, feel the need to pee. This involves a Himalayan trek up many stairs and through endless corridors to restrooms located beyond reasonable endurance.

Canoe, occupying most of the TD Tower's fifty-fourth floor, is the serious downtown business dining location. *Toronto Life* dismissed its décor as "understated butch elegance." Fair enough, but that's not what keeps this particular canoe afloat. Regulars occasionally glance across Lake Ontario to enjoy the horizon view of Niagara-on-the-Lake, but mainly they come to gaze at one another or, more specifically, at each other's dining companions, to see what mergers or acquisitions might be coming down the road. *[Among Canoe's regulars: Peter Munk, Frank Stronach, Steve Hudson, David Peterson, Ted Rogers, Joe Canavan, Blake Goldring, Trevor Eyton, Jerry Grafstein, Bob Rae, Gabe Tsambalieros, Jim O'Donnell and Brian Steck.]* Michael Bonacini, who designed the premises and invented the menu, along with partner Peter Oliver, credits the restaurant's popularity to the creation of a clublike atmosphere suitable to the late 1990s. "The new-style executives," he says, "want restaurants, like everything else in their world, to be direct extensions of themselves. That means slightly 'hip' and fashionable, yet unpretentious and understated." *[That lack of pretension has not translated into Canoe's menu, which features such dishes as "herb-stuffed breast of Ontario pheasant on hand-thrown spatzle with oven-roasted apples, Cremini mushrooms with Newfie Screech jus."]*

Another popular venue is *Far Niente* (owned by SIR Corporation, which runs the Fazoulis watering-holes) on the northeast corner of Wellington and Bay. It's the favourite hangout of the Griffiths McBurney crowd, who run up the generous tabs that keep it humming.

Prego Della Piazza (not Prego Deli & Pizza, as many habitués call it) is in a class of its own. In terms of the crowd that dines there, it is the

Winston's of the 1990s. The restaurant's appeal is based neither on its location (its spot behind the Church of the Redeemer, at the corner of Bloor Street and Avenue Road, was previously occupied by a Czech restaurant that had better food but no patrons) nor on its menu, which is rivalled by Centro, Opus, North 44, Oro, Chiaro's or even the Senator. The food is no better or worse than at dozens of other commercial pseudo-Italian spots catering to the city's jaded moderns who swear that, after one more $1-million hit, they'll sell the penthouse condo and move to a mountain shack in Tuscany—but never will.

The Prego crowd is a mixture of the city's cultural, social and moneyed élite. They are the kind of Canadians who believe that Quebec ought to be granted "distinct society" status on the basis of its great cheeses. Yet they are also acutely aware that Giorgetto Giugiaro, the designer of Italy's most aerodynamic luxury cars, has been commissioned by the Voiello spaghetti factory in Naples to produce new shapes for pasta.

Prego is *the* place to be seen, because it draws what, in this large chilly land on the very margin of the earth's meaningful geography, passes for fame. They are there, most lunch and dinner hours, the famous and near-famous, showing off their vaguely familiar countenances, listening carefully for that predatory yelp that signals the recognition of celebrity, however minor, in these misbegotten latitudes. There, too, gather the business community's big-time sharks and their pilot fish, showing their piranha-perfect teeth, scouting the room for deals. A woman of a certain age, whose hair seems to have been not so much teased as tormented, tells her luncheon companion about the former beauty queen turned newsanchor who, asked her opinion of Camus, thought it was a brand of French soap. *Quelle* fun!

The choreography of the place is simple: the publicity hounds station themselves up front; the deal-makers prefer the more discreet tables next door at Black & Blue. That more private location is the preferred dining spot of Peter and Melanie Munk, Gerry and Heather Schwartz, Galen and Hilary Weston, Catherine and David Nugent, Allan and Anne Fotheringham, Conrad and Barbara Black, as well as Eddie Cogan, the real-estate tycoon who only eats spaghetti Bolognese and smokes foul cigars. Other regulars include Mr. and Mrs. Matt Barrett, Sam Slutsky and his wife Gloria Galant, Kim McArthur, Al Cummings, Michael Levine, Pamela Wallin, Helga Stephenson, Jacquie Latimer, a sprinkle of Eatons and Siftons, Larry Bloomberg, Joe Rotman, Avie Bennett, Hal Jackman and Bruce Westwood. "The interaction here is on a mature and civilized level," emphasizes owner Michael Carlevale, who has a classics degree from Queen's and came to Canada from Boston, not Tuscany. "Prego is a place where people want to be seen. This is a restaurant with a buzz." Then he adds, as if sharing a secret, "But there is nothing inconsequential about *our* buzz."

And that serves as an apt definition of Bay Street, 1998.

15

ONE-MAN PARADIGM

"My goal in life is to be fifty and still be able to jump off my dock on one water-ski."

—*Scott Paterson, Bay Street Titan*

SOMEWHERE INSIDE GORDON SCOTT PATERSON THERE is a small, unsmiling universe, the tough carpet-trader side of him that few of his co-workers ever see, and even fewer survive. Outwardly, he is charming, smart and the most phenomenally successful of Bay Street's talented up-and-comers. At thirty-four, he is president of the country's tenth-largest investment house, Yorkton Securities, and is clearly headed for the top leagues.

What makes his future so intriguing is that, unlike most of his peers, Paterson is a multidimensional character with a search-and-destroy mentality that qualifies him as a one-man paradigm: a role model for the twenty-first-century moneymovers who are taking command of Bay Street, and therefore Canada. They are the new Titans.

On Bay Street, there is only the Old Guard and the Vanguard. Scott Paterson personifies the latter. As stock-trading volumes and prices attain frenetic levels of activity, there are more hands on the levers of financial power than ever before; some leave no fingerprints. His do. Paterson is the most intriguing member of the new group of men and women in their bursting thirties and vaulting forties who are taking over Canada's financial markets. "A lack of confidence has never been a problem for Paterson," noted Barry Critchley, who follows Bay Street's personnel daisy chains for *The Financial Post*. "In fact, he may be among the industry's most self-possessed individuals—no small feat in a business where confidence can close a deal as easily as financial fundamentals. His track record is strewn with successes."

Paterson and his peers share a mission and a destiny. Like it or not, their seniors—the bankers and brokers now in their anxious fifties and tired sixties—are nearing the end of their runs. New Titans are about to inherit the system, the money and the clout. It's their turn. Unlike Old Money, which passed on its legacy in a slow turning of generations, the Scott Patersons of the financial world are ready now, and as significant power comes their way, they are seizing it, running with it and revolutionizing Canada's fiscal universe.

Sure, they have become too rich too quickly to feel warm and fuzzy about their achievements; certainly, some are high-spirited to the point of recklessness. But mutual self-interest has always ruled Bay Street, and this new gang of Titans knows how to play that game. Out of the current roster of investment boutiques—Yorkton, Griffiths McBurney and New-crest Capital in Toronto; Canaccord and Goepel McDermid in Vancouver; and First Energy and Peters & Co. in Calgary—will emerge the industry's future leaders, and Scott Paterson will be among them.

Like most of the new Titans, Paterson pretends not to care about the increasing recognition he is receiving from the Old Establishment. Still, he loves being invited to those private tête-à-têtes in the Toronto Club, Ottawa's Rideau Club or in the deep-red-plush private conference rooms of the Mount Royal Club, where national issues are debated and discussed in solemn conclaves and where the participants are endowed with self-importance, if not much enlightenment. The exclusive number of invitees and the absence of journalists prompts a certain brand of refreshing frankness. The trick for newcomers to these majestic circles is for them to leak the fact that they were invited, without revealing what was said or decided. There's a fine line between being considered important enough to attract notice and appearing too pushy. (It's not ambition that the Establishment frowns on, it's the behaviour that ambition provokes.)

Industry whispers claim that Paterson's 1997 earnings added up to $7 million—double the compensation received by the best-paid of the Big Five bank chairmen. In the fall of 1998, Paterson moved into a $2-million mansion on Chestnut Park Drive, one of Rosedale's prime establishment addresses. He was nominated by his neighbours, David Wilson, who heads the Bank of Nova Scotia's brokerage arm, and by John Mac-Naughton, president of Nesbitt Burns, to be a director of the Investment Dealers' Association of Canada. *[His other neighbours include Charlie Baillie, chairman of the TD Bank, and Colin Watson, CEO of Spar Aerospace.]* Paterson also joined the exclusive Rosedale Golf Club (the initiation fee is $40,000), is a governor of Ridley College, plays squash at the exclusive Toronto Lawn and Tennis Club and was appointed a trustee of the Art Gallery of Ontario. *[Paterson's intercession with Steve Landry, the director of marketing at Chrysler Canada, produced a last-minute sponsor for the epic 1998 Courtauld exhibition.]* It wasn't much of a rebellious act, but on the very day the *Globe* featured the news of Frank Mersch's fall from grace, when the Ontario Securities Commission temporarily barred him from trading, Paterson invited his long-time friend to the Rosedale Golf Club, and they teed off just ahead of Galen Weston and Michael Willmot, who runs Kinghaven Capital Corp. He puffs the occasional Cohiba cigar (at $60 apiece) and buys his suits (at $2,000 a pop) from Signor Francesco on Scollard Street in Toronto's Yorkville district. (Signor Francesco Pecararo claims only thirty clients, including John Turner, Brent Belzberg and apartment tower owner Wayne Squibb. He sold his business to Harry Rosen in the fall of 1998.) Paterson has his hair done by John Efstathiou, a Greek barber at BCE Place, who also cuts Trevor Eyton's hair and knows the movers of the universe. Paterson gave him a tip ten years ago that made John a $20,000 profit, and he hasn't charged him for a haircut since. He also repays the favour by whispering market tips into Paterson's ear at every haircutting session; most of the stocks go straight up. Paterson helicopter-skis at Island Lake Lodge near Fernie, British Columbia, and has driven NASCAR racing cars around a regulation track in Las Vegas at an average speed of 148 miles per hour. ("Next to sex, this was the biggest rush I've ever had.") He received a $10,000 Cartier watch as a gift from his staff at Yorkton. On the occasional summer evening, Paterson drives down to Toronto's Island Airport, flies to his cottage at Healey Lake, near Parry Sound, and returns the next morning; on the way, he once obtained an $8-million order for Strategic-Value stock over his cell phone.

Even if at the moment his insider influence in Toronto's financial district remains one of Bay Street's safer secrets, Paterson's power is expanding exponentially, and the reach of his personal network never stops growing. In fact, he maintains his own telephone network, with ten numbers listed on his business card. Paterson is so frantically busy that he usually only answers messages left on the mobile phone in his car, a mulberry frost Infinity Q-45, because only there can he do double duty: driving while handling his priority phone traffic. In Dorothy Rogers, he is fortunate enough to employ the best executive assistant on Bay Street. True, he remains on the fringe of the inner Canadian Establishment, but he is moving up fast. This man will make waves.

What sets Paterson apart are his negotiating skills. In tight situations, he has the knack for exploiting the electric moment. During the closed-door discussions that price an initial public offering or decide the size and terms of a new issue, he is the one who breaks the impasse, sells the deal or waltzes away to a high-priority fall-back position so he can collect Brownie points for the next time round.

In his thirteen years on Bay Street, he has established an enviable record for innovation and intimidation. "At the end of the day," he says, "finance is an art, not a science, as the kids who come out of MBA schools are taught. The vast majority of opportunities in investments come about by putting together exactly the right players at precisely the right moment. It's managing the art of timing that creates the greatest plays."

Typically, Paterson leaves nothing to chance, so that, for example, both sides of the brain are represented on Yorkton's trading desk. The operation is headed by Pier Donnini, whom Scott describes as "a very right-brain trader, all guts and instinct." *[The two men met at the University of Western Ontario, when Paterson was running semi-professional betting pools on NFL games.]* To balance that approach, Paterson has placed beside Donnini a left-brain operator named Larry Farrell, who uses complicated mathematical formulas to take advantage of arbitrage plays and is constantly assessing the statistical potential of price moves in the larger-trading stocks.

Showdowns and shoot-outs are part of nearly every major Bay Street transaction. That's what gives the gunslinger culture its label and its character. Scott is a gunslinger, but not a shooter. "In presentations to management teams or to boards of directors," Paterson admits, "I find myself going out of my way to defend what I know we'll be criticized for by the Dominion Securities of the world. So I'm always on the attack. I know it's war and that at Yorkton I have a limited arsenal at my disposal." Paterson subscribes to Nietzsche's stern dictum that "if it doesn't kill you, it will make you stronger." He has never seen combat, but considers himself to be a warrior and fires verbal sallies at adversaries with the force of thunderbolts from a shoulder-held missile-firing bazooka. Robert Lantos once described him as "a heat-seeking missile."

As he increases the size of his deals, Paterson has inevitably run into the economies of scale. The brokerages owned by the big banks—the smallest of them being at least seven times the size of Yorkton—have access to relatively unlimited funds and facilities. "The guys at Nesbitt and Dominion Securities distance themselves from the market; they're just sort of standing aside and watching it," he complains. "I'm certainly not naïve enough to believe I'm larger than the market, but I sure as hell think I'm a significant participant. I can get on the line to a half-dozen people and come up with $25 million, because my relationships are directly with the institutional buyers. Brad Griffiths of Griffiths McBurney and Bob Dorrance at Newcrest could do the same thing, which I guess is why we all left the established firms."

During the extended tensions of a drawn-out bargaining session, Scott can be as tough as a latter-day Jim Connacher, whose Gordon Capital, when it was flying high, was the closest Bay Street ever came to experiencing an act of God. Scott reaches his most lethal phase when he becomes very quiet; there is a stillness at the core of the man that suggests a tiger about to pounce. "Paterson has the intuition and sensitivity that separates the merely successful from the great deal makers," says one of his frequent sparring partners. Another co-worker has a simpler explanation. "Scott," she says, "gets his buzz from the pitch."

It's true. He was born to deal. The source of Scott's power is that few of Bay Street's canniest negotiators can match him in full flight. His intellectual focus remains narrow, but his sense of timing, his tactics and strategy are remarkable. Inside the confines of what passes for Bay Street's brains trust, he holds a competitive edge. He enjoys the advantage of a highly evolved sixth sense that alerts him to competitors' nuances: the slight variation in the pitch of a voice or the speeded-up tempo of a limb movement indicate when those on the other side of the bargaining table are bending facts. "I can usually tell within ninety seconds if someone is lying," boasts Paterson. He feels most alive when he is testing his limits, flying on sheer nerve, swinging on a star. His conscience is clear, because he so seldom uses it as part of his mental arsenal. He accepts victory or defeat in any financial or personal situation only on terms that allow him to be true to himself—at whatever cost.

FOR ALL HIS APPARENT STRENGTH AND OUTWARD resolve, Scott Paterson is as insecure as a one-album country singer. Superficially self-confident, his need for the praise of his peers and reluctant admiration of his enemies is the defining mark of his character. Those unrequited longings for recognition and approval nibble at his nerve-ends like piranhas, because he will never get enough of either. "I'm highly motivated by the perception of my Bay Street peers," he admits. "I don't work for money so much as I do to pursue visions and strategies, to prove what can be done and to have the Street acknowledge that I executed what I promised."

"It's comforting to know that in an industry like yours, that is filled with misinterpretation, there is someone we can count on," wrote Brian

Semkiw, CEO of Rand A Technology, to Paterson after Yorkton completed a difficult transaction for his firm. *[Semkiw named his company after Ayn Rand, the Russian libertarian author whose theories he supports.]* It is not hard to find Paterson supporters, or critics. Established merchant bankers view him as a shameless intruder; the preening VIPs who run the bank-owned brokerage houses try hard to dismiss him as a new boy who runs on sheer chutzpah. They condemn his aggressive tactics and accuse him of expedience, which strikes a strange chord in an industry built on opportunism. Those comments are in the air, but it is impossible to find anyone willing to attach their names to such accusations. Paterson's future potential is much too menacing for that. His enemies realize that he may have an ego the size of the CN Tower and may one day overreach himself, but they also know there is little chance of slowing his momentum and that they may well end up working for him or with him. That's what keeps him safe and keeps them quiet.

He is not difficult to read. Scott Paterson may be the chairman and CEO (and largest shareholder) of an impressively expanding brokerage house, but that's only a title. What he really is, and always will remain, is an entrepreneur, a loner who makes up his own challenges as he goes along—and feels diminished if he fails to meet them. "One reason I can differentiate myself from most competitors is that I have started businesses, made and lost money on them, and know the ropes," he emphasizes. "Also, I worked three-and-a-half years in the trenches as a retail broker, so I know firsthand how hard it is to sell shares to the public, unlike most corporate-finance guys who learn to number-crunch at university but have never had to sell anything in their lives."

At heart, Paterson is a risk taker, addicted to the game as much as to the pot. Entrepreneurs are a macho fraternity, joined by only one goal—self-fulfilment—and working at only one speed—faster. They invent their own world, then conquer it. Professor Donald Thain, the University of Western Ontario sage, came up with the most telling diagnosis of the breed: "You really need to read Freud to understand their restless egos and the obsessive drive these people display. Up close, they are almost beyond human proportions—and they can carry the seeds of tragedy for later on."

Paterson's biggest problem at the moment is his youth. Worse, he looks at least ten years younger than he really is. (He turned thirty-four on January 11, 1998.) That means he was being toilet-trained during Expo '67, went to work full-time only a little more than a decade ago and earned his first million before he had to shave. "Scott is a human dynamo," says Kiki Delaney, the legendary Bay Street money manager whose company transacts significant business with him. "He's a phenomenal success, and I'm a big cheerleader for people like that." Then she leans forward and confides mischievously, "And he's only twelve years old!" Lynn Miller, Delaney Capital's small-cap manager who administers well over $1 billion in assets, is equally enthusiastic: "Scott is certainly driven, but he is one of the greatest marketing individuals I've ever met. He has something that's intangible that allows him to be successful for both the issuing parties and the buyers. The turnaround he has achieved at Yorkton is quite remarkable; it's one of the great success stories of this cycle on the brokerage side of the business."

Paterson emphasizes his youth by occasionally wearing shorts to board meetings. He can be clever rather than wise, and there are occasions when he appears precocious, untested instead of merely youthful. He thinks like a big hitter; he acts like a big hitter; he talks like a big hitter; he trades like a big hitter; he spends money and lives like a big hitter. But he doesn't yet sweat like one. He'll learn.

"The kid is a natural," says Tony Pullen, Yorkton's co-head of institutional sales, who first approached Paterson to join the firm. "Apart from the fact that Scott makes me feel like a bumbling idiot, his is the most natural talent I've seen in our industry in the past thirty years. What attracted him to Yorkton is that under Frank Giustra's leadership, its corporate culture became so entrepreneurial and outward bound that we almost became a group of franchisers, but we needed Scott to put the glue in place. That's especially true of that sensitive corporate dance of the seven veils called syndication. Scott plays that side of the business like Wayne Gretzky." Yorkton's Knowledge Industries division was revived by Paterson in 1995, earning the firm $5.6 million in its first year and double that the following year. The firm now leads the field in the number of underwritings in that category and has raised almost $3 billion for its health-care and entertainment clients. Despite his addiction to high tech, he loves to nurture little idiosyncracies about himself. "I've financed more high-tech industries than anyone else in Canada," he says, "yet I don't have any idea how to work a computer and don't want to learn. Neither do I know how to do spreadsheets and have none of the technical skills that relate to traditional investment banking." Paterson has more recently added a film and television sub-division, in which Yorkton also leads in the number and value of underwritings.

"One of my favourite moments," says Paterson, "was when Robert Lantos told me how David Kassie at Wood Gundy nearly had a coronary as he informed him that Yorkton would be leading Alliance's $61-million financing deal, and that Lawrence Bloomberg came over to his house with steam coming out of his head. *[Kassie is deputy chairman of CIBC Wood Gundy Capital; he financed Alliance before it went public and has been a director of Lantos's company ever since. Paterson is one of his fans.]* We made money out of that deal, but that meant nothing because what it was telling those guys was that we can beat their ass at Yorkton. That's why I get up every day."

"He's a real dynamo, that one," said Lantos of Paterson, when he was still heading Alliance. "Scott is amazingly energetic and a truly great salesman. Hell, he can sell my company better than I can. I've been to meetings with him and heard him tell shareholders such great things about Alliance, I would be ashamed to say them. Yet he has integrity, runs a terrific business, is tireless and a sensational marketer. But that wasn't why I chose him to do our underwriting. As everything else I do in life, I value loyalty. His firm spent an enormous amount of time getting to know the company, trading and marketing the stock more than any other firm in Canada, before they had a deal with us—just doing tremendous amounts of research, analysis and coverage. In my view, you reward performance; you reward those who do things for you. The establishment firms that we gave all our business to in the past were far more lethargic. Scott's team went at it with tremendous gusto, and after that, how can you say no? Would I do business with him again? Yes, of course."

WHAT SETS PATERSON APART is the stretch of his ambition. Watching him battle his way to the top of the world's second most ruthless trade (it ranks just behind professional croquet), it's hard to credit his ultimate ambition: he wants to be secretary-general of the United Nations. That's the kind of audacious pipedream with a limited shelf-life that young kids have when they grow up on too many Kraft dinners, but it's a safe bet that he'll not become another Boutros Boutros whatever his name was.

Yet at a surprisingly early age, Paterson is beginning to denominate his life in currencies other than money. What he values most of all is acceptance, but having attained it, he wants to put it to good use. "I don't work for money," he emphasizes. "I work for accomplishment. I work to change lives. Sure, I believe in the capital markets, but at the end of the day, you had better have something to point to: a mine in the ground, a new laboratory facility, a cure for cancer. Shuffling paper is not adding value."

There probably isn't a stockbroker on Bay Street who wouldn't declare similar intentions halfway through his third martini at Jump or Prego. Making so much money so easily makes most Canadians feel guilty, if not downright sinful, and the only way to appease the guy with the long white beard (Robertson Davies, in his final and true incarnation) is to patter like Paterson does. But with Paterson, it's not just talk. He has established several university and college bursaries and is quietly funding his private Merry Go Round Children's Foundation, which distributes free computers to financially disadvantaged but talented grade-school children who have been nominated by their teachers. *["Our entire family was pole-vaulted into the nineties in one great swoop. You've done a great thing," Meg Herbert wrote to him after a new computer arrived at her home.]* He also got Yorkton to fund TM Bioscience Corp., which nobody else on Bay Street would touch. It's a risky but fascinating start-up genetic engineering firm pioneering "biochips," which Paterson believes will be as revolutionary in the twenty-first century as microchips turned out to be in the twentieth.

Meanwhile, he knows that his own life is out of whack. He has a beautiful and talented new wife, three young daughters, more money than he ever dreamed of, yet all he does is work. *[He recently married Barbara Stoneham, a professional children's portrait photographer, with whom he has had two daughters, Adeline and Catherine. They also have a daughter, Emiline, by her previous marriage. From 1990 to 1993, Scott was married to the former Karen Albrektsen.]* In the summer of 1997, he took his first two-week vacation in six years. "What I'm beginning to realize," he says, "is that money isn't worth a damn unless independence goes with it. Time is my most prized commodity, and yet sharing in my own life seems to have become an impossible dream. That can't continue."

THE MIDDLE NAME OF SCOTT'S MIDDLE DAUGHTER is Somerville, which was the maiden name of his grandmother's grandmother, Rosina, who was married to David Young, the first practising psychiatrist in Manitoba. *[One of Young's patients was a rebellious young Métis named Louis Riel.]* Scott's grandparents played an inordinately significant role in his life, because his father and mother were divorced only three years after he was born. His grandmother died in his arms. "She'd had a stroke, and my mom called me," he remembers. "I was on my way to my cottage, and I raced home. I said, 'Tell Granny to wait for me.' And I got home, and everybody left the room, and I spent an hour with her. She had apparently stopped breathing but came back to life, arching her back and sitting up, when I opened the door of her room. My mother rubbed my grandmother's feet and held her hand and caressed her forehead, and we told my grandmother she could go. She gave so much to our lives, and now she could go. A few minutes later, she stopped breathing forever. In my eulogy, I ended by saying, 'This was the lady who when I asked, "Are there any more potatoes?" would take my plate into the kitchen and move her last potato from her plate to mine. This was the lady who stepped in as a second mother to help my mother, who was a single mom, and logged long working hours as a high-school phys-ed teacher and coach. This was the lady who corrected my grammar, typed my essays and who I could count on as a living thesaurus. This was the lady who, when I was sick, made the best chicken-rice soup I've ever tasted. This was the lady who told me to come home when the street lights came on. Friday night last, the street lights came on, and I came home to say, "I love you, thank you, and goodbye."'" It was also his grandmother who got Scott interested in the stock market by buying him five shares of Abitibi Price Paper for his fourteenth birthday.

Young Scott was raised by his mother, who had a tough time financially. His grandfather, John Stuart Drake, took him to 5:30 a.m. hockey practice and became one of his most important role models. At age nine, Scott started hawking programs (for $5 an hour) at two race-car tracks near St. Catharines, owned by the family of his good friend, the late Alex Friesen. Within three years, he was also handicapping the drivers, writing articles for the program, and reporting on the races for the St. Catharines *Standard* and for *Stock Car Racing*, an American trade journal, and he became the assistant track announcer when his voice was still changing. Displeased with his independent ways, his mother once told him, "If you don't shape up, I'll send you to Ridley!"—a nearby private school known for its discipline as well as its scholarship. To her surprise, her son jumped at the chance. He spent two highly formative years there, his tuition paid for mostly by his mother's thrift. "Ridley opened my eyes to financial success," he recalls. "Before going there, I didn't know what a summer cottage was, because we lived in part of a rented duplex, across the street from subsidized Ontario housing."

He took an economics degree from the University of Western Ontario in London, but his most important memory is of the summer job he got at Midland Doherty, through the intercession of Danny King, the father of one of his friends. King lectured the young boy on the importance of dressing correctly and how, in any office environment, you must never loosen your tie. *[If they happen to be sharing a morning elevator with Paterson, Yorkton employees are still surprised to have him lean over and straighten their ties.]* He worked for Jack Eliot at Midland on the commodities trading desk and vividly recalls thanking Eliot for taking him on, only to be told, "Cut the crap, kid. You got this job for one reason and one reason only: I owed Danny King a favour."

He landed a stockbroker job at Dominion Securities in September 1985, after graduating at twenty-one. "I was interviewed by Reay Mackay in his office on the third floor of the Commerce Court South building in downtown Toronto," he recalls. "I sat down and didn't get out a word. He just said, 'When you know what you want to do with your career, when you truly know that you're interested in being in this business, then you come and see us at that time.' I hadn't been in the room thirty seconds, and he started walking towards the door, motioning and indicating that the interview was over. I was speechless; I was scared. I kind of edged up off the seat so that I didn't look defiant and said, 'Mr. Mackay, I do know what I want to do, and I do know that I'm ready to start.' He stopped, and I went into a Scott Paterson diatribe of how long I'd been interested in the stock market, how much passion I had for it, how much I knew about Dominion Securities, how interested I was and how I needed to be given a chance. He slowly walked back to his chair, sat down, we completed the interview, and I got the job. My whole career could have gone a different path. There's no question in my mind that he was challenging me, that he wanted to see if I had the guts to stop him at the door."

Within months, Paterson earned his nickname "Cold-Call Cowboy" and became the firm's top first-year performer, earning $175,000 in commissions for 1986, mainly by phoning people he had never met and giving them his pitch. Two days before the 1987 market crash, he transferred to Richardson Greenshields as a retail broker and took most of his customers with him. "When you leave a firm," he recalls, "you tend to be treated like a vagrant, because they don't want you to take your customers with you. Prior to resigning, I went to the receptionist and knelt down on my knees. I had a $20 bill in my hand and said, 'Listen, I'm leaving tomorrow. Here's the new number you should give anybody who calls for me.' I assumed she'd rebuff the money and feel insulted. Instead, she snatched that $20 so fast it was unbelievable. It worked like clockwork." Within eighteen months, he had moved to Richardson's investment-banking division to work for Jean-Pierre Colin. This turned out to be a costly learning experience. He was a quick study, but not only were his mounting commissions ($375,000 in 1987) cut to a $50,000 salary, but he began losing heavily in his private investments.

Other kids grow up fantasizing about being explorers, movie stars, rock singers, software inventors or sex maniacs. In his teens, Paterson imagined he would lead giant corporate empires, all named after himself. There was Paterson Telecommunications, Paterson Enterprises, Paterson Life, Paterson Hotels, Paterson Trucking and many more; not just names, but prospectuses were worked out in great detail, with most of his friends named to executive positions. "I was obsessed," he now admits. "I envisioned a world where everyone I knew would be working for me. I even devised a strategy for how the Paterson Corporation would establish an army that would decide what was good for the world and for Canada, and put it into practice. I was going to settle the Jewish–Arab conflict and declare war on bureaucrats, thus setting the Canadian people free."

The trouble was that not all of Paterson's grandiose plans remained fantasies. In 1987, two years after joining Dominion Securities, he incorporated a company called Patcor Capital on the Alberta Stock Exchange and persuaded some big names of the day (Brian Hewat, then executive vice-president of Bell Canada, and Sol Zuckerman of Taurus Footwear, among others) to sit on his board. The company attempted some reverse-takeover venture-capital deals, but nothing worked, and eventually it was folded into a bingo company called Dion Entertainment Corp., with himself as chairman. It bid for the Windsor Casino licence but didn't get it, and lost so much money that at one point he only had two wearable shirts to his name (with worn French cuffs). He had to turn in his Rogers Cable selector, and ate tomato soup and grilled cheese sandwiches for a whole year. He wasn't clear of debt until the spring of 1993.

Meanwhile, he had moved to Midland Walwyn, where he started to do his first meaningful deals under Dennis Dewan, then the head of corporate finance. He led the mega-successful financing for SoftKey Software, which grew in market value from $35 million in 1991 to $2.5 billion seven years later. Paterson has had several what he calls "ten-baggers" in his career, including SoftKey, Leitch Technology (which went from $4 to $44 a share), Rand (which moved from $3.50 to $35.00) and Certicom (which moved from $3.00 to $46.50). He completed thirty-seven financings, mostly initial public offerings, during the four years he spent at Midland Walwyn, gaining initial recognition as an important player.

He also took Garth Drabinsky public.

Then Canada's most successful theatrical impresario, Drabinsky wanted to raise money for his Live Entertainment, Inc., but every dealer on Bay Street had turned him down, not because of his balance sheets (which had not yet turned sour) but because of his personality (which already had). "In April 1993, Garth and I were aboard a private jet flying from Newark to Edmonton, when he started taunting me," Paterson recalls. "'Paterson, how old are you?' he asked.

"I responded, 'Twenty-nine.'

"With a tone designed to put me in my place, Drabinsky boasted, 'When I was twenty-nine, I was chairman of Cineplex and was making $500,000 a year.'

"I shot back, 'I'm chairman of publicly traded Dion Entertainment, and this year I'll earn more than you did when you were twenty-nine!'

"Drabinsky," recalls Paterson, "was silenced. He gave me a slow smile. I had won his respect. I was more of a peer to him and not just part of his arsenal of hired help."

In early 1993, Drabinsky was acting like the world loved him, but nobody would do this deal except Paterson. "I went to my own partners at Midland, and we had an underwriting-committee meeting," he recalls. Our head of corporate finance voted against it, as did the head of institutional sales. I looked at Bob Schultz, our chairman, and Dennis Dewan, and my look said, 'I'm going to do this and if you boys won't support me, you can call me at Gordon Capital.' They finally agreed to back an initial public offering on the condition that another fully integrated mainline dealer was in the syndicate. Dewan came to my office afterwards, opened the door and said, 'If this deal doesn't get done, you're fired.'"

Paterson went to see his buddy Brad Griffiths who was at that time head of corporate finance at Gordon Capital, and he agreed to go along, but they still needed a mainline dealer. Burns Fry had turned the issue down, as had Richardson, Nesbitt Thomson and Dominion Securities. George Dembroski, vice-chairman at Dominion Securities, chewed Paterson out for having nothing good to say about Garth Drabinsky. Paterson went back to Wood Gundy anyway and found himself facing seven dubious executives, all bombarding him with questions. "I'll never forget the setting," he says. "I sat in a chair facing the seven interrogators, while one of them, David Kassie, was signing Christmas cards as we talked. There were huge accounting issues involved, because it was live theatre and Garth had been accused of being too aggressive with his accounting at Cineplex. After I left the meeting, Wood Gundy reluctantly agreed to be in the deal."

Lawrence Bloomberg said he wanted to get involved, so the final syndicate included Midland Walwyn, Gordon, Wood Gundy and First Marathon. Paterson finally had a syndicate and then began to call institutional investors. Every single institution said, "We don't want to see this stuff.

Don't even send us the information. Are you crazy? It's live theatre, and it's Garth Drabinsky!" Paterson went out on a limb, predicting that the shares would double in six months, and $30 million worth were sold, moving from their issue price of $9 to $18.25 in precisely six months.

Drabinsky was pleased by Paterson's efforts and promised he would mention him in his autobiography, which he was then writing. But he never did. "Garth never understood or cared that I risked my career," says Paterson. "I respect Garth and acknowledge that he has been one of Canada's great cultural visionaries, but he'll never acknowledge that anybody can add value to Garth Drabinsky's life except himself."

Worse, when *Ragtime* opened in Los Angeles, and Scott realized he would be in the city at the same time, he asked the Drabinsky organization to arrange for a couple of tickets and was allocated seats in the back row of the second orchestra level, just high enough so he could look down at the fifth row, which was filled with grinning guys from Wood Gundy.

In November 1994, Paterson went back to school, taking a Business School executive program at the University of Western Ontario, and then began negotiating to become the head of Thomson Kernaghan, a boutique brokerage. One of the senior people he sounded out about joining him was Tony Pullen, then a sales rep at Yorkton's fledgling Knowledge division, who immediately tried to persuade him to join Yorkton instead, a company then run out of Vancouver by Frank Giustra.

At the time, Yorkton was the Canadian leader in financing small-cap mining companies and had been doubling its staff and revenues every two years since 1988. Under Giustra's leadership, the one-time bucket-shop had been reformed, not only in terms of breaking away from its Vancouver Stock Exchange origins and ethics, but as a profitable and increasingly significant international player. "Yorkton has some really superb warriors on its staff," commented Wally Berukoff, CEO of Vancouver's Miramar Mining Corp., which at the time was being financed by the Yorkton group. "They're true warriors in the sense that they know when and how to move out and seize opportunities. They come to their desks every morning ready for battle. One reason for Yorkton's success is that they have never belonged to the old boys' network."

That was true for a very good reason: Yorkton had no old boys. Giustra, the firm's chairman and CEO, was thirty-nine; Bob Cross, its president, thirty-seven. The company was run in a highly unorthodox manner, obeying few rules of standard corporate hierarchies. Yorkton operated as a loosely organized umbrella organization for a group of entrepreneurial wizards who exercised accountability to their clients—and made a lot of money doing it. The firm's pay incentives rewarded individual as well as collective effort with a flat and fuzzy management structure: every employee was a shareholder. "I hire people who are creative, driven and tough," declared Giustra, who was allergic to quiet offices, preferring the noisy clash of energy and intelligence that characterized his firm, which raised $2 billion to finance the discovery and extraction of mineral deposits on five continents. It had also started a fledgling advanced-technologies division under David Allen.

When Giustra and Paterson finally met, Scott was already semi-committed to Kernaghan, so he made a proposal, outrageous even for him, that was bound to be refused. In order to join Yorkton, he demanded that he be placed totally in charge of the firm's Toronto office and that he be an equal shareholder to Frank, who had built up the firm. Giustra, who had carefully studied Paterson's record, was so impressed with his potential that he replied with one word: "Done."

"I have a theory that numbers speak for themselves," recalls Paterson, "and when I was shown Yorkton's profit-and-loss statement, I realized that somebody was doing something very right. I was blown away when I saw the revenue side and return on equity." His welcome wasn't unanimous. David Allen, who had been in the industry thirty-five years and headed the Knowledge Industry Group before Scott's arrival, went to see Paterson three days before he was due to take over, and flatly told him, "I woke up at 3 a.m. a couple of nights ago and realized that a red-haired prick as young as my son was going to be my boss, and I thought, Should I be pissed off at that?" He not only stayed on but handled the transition gracefully. By the spring of 1998, Paterson had been promoted to president of Yorkton, and his divisions were generating monthly revenues of $4 million.

One of his first Yorkton deals was a private placement for OpenText, a $12.5-million deal done in two days. "There was no offering memorandum, no financial statements, nothing," he recalls. "We took Tom Jenkins, the CEO, around with his laptop and tried to demonstrate their Internet search-engine capabilities, which wouldn't even work in most offices because their telephone jacks were not Internet-capable at the time. So here we were walking around with no offering memorandum, no financial statements, a guy with his laptop that didn't even work in most of the offices, and in two days we raised him $12.5 million." There followed an initial public offering at $15.00; six months later, OpenText went public on Nasdaq in the U.S., with Montgomery Securities leading the deal and Yorkton as a co-manager, and it opened at US$26.50. "By the winter of 1998, we were in the throes of proposing a bought deal,"

Paterson recalls. "I was flying from Toronto to Vancouver, and there were a couple of heated issues yet to be decided: one was the price of the deal, and the second one was whether Helix, which was a significant share-holder in OpenText, should be permitted to sell any shares as part of the offering. I felt that it would be unfair to general buyers if they had a hold period, and yet Helix had the right to sell shares. So I ended up in a heated four-and-a-half-hour discussion from my Air Canada seat, princi-pally with Tom Jenkins and Richard Black, who is a Helix principal. I was screaming and yelling at one point about the philosophy and the ethics of it not being at all appropriate for Helix to be in a position to sell stock when other investors, who were putting hard cash on the line, couldn't. Helix was taking a very strong position, and Jenkins was trying to soften me up. I had two Yorkton people on the line for much of the call—Tony Pullen, our head of sales, and Brian Campbell, who was the investment banker on the file—both anxious to do a deal. Jenkins hung up at least three times, with such comments as, 'I'm not dealing with you, Paterson. Forget this,' click.

"Finally, when we were literally touching down in Vancouver, I was still on the phone, and Helix agreed that they wouldn't sell any stock without our approval, and we agreed to the price. But it was funny: throughout the flight, people were looking around for different seats and looking back at me, and I'm sure they thought, Who is that asshole who thinks he's involved in something big? At the end of the call, Tom Jenkins said, 'The next goddamn time we do a deal, there's a condition, and it's that Paterson's got to be in Toronto, not all over the world where I can't get him. He just went bananas on me.' The phone bill, which ran to $3,910, stated that the flight time had been four hours and fifty-five minutes, and my call had been four hours and thirty-one minutes. It was presented to the client at the closing ceremony."

OCCASIONALLY, LATE AT NIGHT, when he's driving home from yet another strategy session with Bay Street's money traders or from some VIP dinner, Scott worries, Am I going to be the kid who peaked at thirty-four?

Life is unpredictable. But that's not a likely scenario. Paterson now leads the pack on Bay Street in nearly all the investment categories that will become the driving forces of the twenty-first century: the knowledge industries, technology, life sciences, leisure and entertainment. His current ambition is to float a billion-dollar deal. That may happen, or he may go another route and become a bank chairman. Meanwhile, he's transforming Yorkton into his own firm.

Scott Paterson will be heard from, soon and often, and probably in some context that will enrich him and whatever institution claims his loyalty. Dennis Dewan, who was the head of investment banking at Midland Walwyn when Paterson was there doing more initial public offerings than anyone on Bay Street, once took him out for a drink at Jump, and after a few rounds, Dennis looked at Scott and pronounced his verdict: "Kid, if you knew how good you are, you'd be scary."

Paterson looked properly startled, half believing the senior investment banker's assessment, but doing his best to look humble just the same. Dewan then delivered his parting shot. "I mean it, kid," he said. "When you wake up and look in the mirror, you don't really believe it. But someday you will, and *you'll* be scared."

4 WORKING THE SYSTEM

16

THE POTEMKIN VILLAGE

"I see more French money moving out of Quebec than Anglo. A lot of my practice is involved in establishing protective devices whereby you can live in Quebec, but should the province separate . . . its government couldn't seize your worldwide assets . . . Many of Montreal's leading citizens want to stay and leave at the same time."

—*Heward Stikeman, Montreal establishment lawyer*

I AM SITTING IN A MONTREAL BISTRO with a friend of many years, reminiscing about the city we both love. He is Michael Pitfield, once Pierre Trudeau's Clerk of the Privy Council in Ottawa, now director of Paul Desmarais's Power Corporation. He is one of those wonderfully bicultural interlocutors of the political wars between Canada and Quebec, who over the past three decades has negotiated many a compromise that kept the country united and more or less intact.

Pitfield's customary good humour is tempered by remorse for his city. *[Pitfield has more than three hundred cousins. Most have moved to Toronto. He recalls spotting five of them waiting for their enormous cars, while watching a ballet opening at the Hummingbird Centre on TV.]* We talk long into the afternoon, many a cup of cappuccino growing cold between us, as we trade memories and debate reasonable solutions. "The situation is very serious, and I am speaking from a good information base," Pitfield is saying. "The way people are moving in the Parti Québécois government is to court confrontation at future strategic moments. We must recognize that nationalism in Quebec is a deeply rooted movement that will not go away, no matter what we do. My own inclination is to stop trying to woo the sovereignists and instead to facilitate their leaving so there isn't irreversible damage inflicted on either side."

It had been so easy once. In the past, the arrangements that allowed Confederation to survive had been concluded on the basis of friendship and common memories. Participants in those early negotiations shared times at Laval seminars, casual summer encounters in Provence, or a passion for Pouilly-Fuissé 1972.

That spirit of what used to be called *bonne entente* has long since been replaced by the hard-edged threats of separation and fiscal mayhem—the end-games of Messrs. Lévesque, Parizeau and Bouchard.

In the days that followed our conversation, I encountered many laments about the city's continuing decline. Instead of the joyful destination it once was, Montreal has become a place to escape from for anybody but the *pure laine* nationalists, a besieged city in a state of suspended animation. Even in our bistro, on one of those formerly busy avenues that run downhill from Sherbrooke Street, people are trading apprehensions, nervously plotting escape routes for themselves, their families and their cash. I overhear a woman, as she sips her latte, use the phrase *"faute de mieux,"* which roughly translated means "in the absence of anything better," in reply to her companion's query whether she intended to vote yes in the next referendum, whenever it's held.

The latest trend among some of Montreal's wealthy is to set up asset-protection trusts in overseas jurisdictions, not to escape taxes, but to have their fortunes safely tucked away in case some future, newly independent Quebec republic decides to tax private capital or slaps on exchange controls to cut off the expected gush of currency outflows. "I see more French money moving out of Quebec than Anglo," says Heward Stikeman, a bedrock of Montreal's Anglo-Saxon establishment and head of the city's largest legal firm. "A lot of my practice is involved in establishing protective devices whereby you can live in Quebec, but should the province separate and be accepted as a country by international law, its government couldn't seize your worldwide assets. People are afraid that to stop the transfer of funds, the government of an independent Quebec would levy an exit tax of 50 percent, so they're protecting themselves with overseas trusts. Many of Montreal's leading citizens want to stay and leave at the same time. It's particularly true of the Québécois, because if they stay and then try to leave after independence, nobody will believe that they weren't part of the other side."

Is there still an Anglo establishment in Montreal? "Sure," says Stikeman. "But with a few exceptions they don't carry much weight any more. As for the French, they're more like a clique. They're very effective; they move in a pack. I don't know whether we can ever rescue Montreal, but we might be able to keep it alive." The Québécois are now following the pattern set by the Anglo and Jewish communities.

There are problems. For example, it's no longer enough to be bilingual. In fact, it's almost irrelevant. Everybody is. You must be *pure laine*. One of the difficulties for outside investors is the insistence of the Quebec government that any business with more than fifty employees must "use French as the common language of communication on the job." No wonder most international capital is flowing elsewhere.

I WAS STATIONED HERE AS A JOURNALIST IN THE 1950s when Montreal was still Canada's largest, most vibrant and most romantic city. In a country restrained by its Presbyterian roots, this was a wide-open town, with characters like Anna Beauchamp, the flamboyant madam who operated a dozen brothels on Berger Street. Whenever her establishments got in trouble with the law, she would climb into her chauffeured Cadillac, arrive at the courthouse, stride into the trial and, decked out in a full-length mink coat, bail out her girls, loudly inviting the arresting officers to drop in for a freebie. The sex trade boasted its own brand of morality. "We always close on Good Fridays!" she indignantly exclaimed, when a prosecutor questioned her ethics.

Montreal was a place where people enjoyed themselves, stretched their morals to fit the times and never regretted very much. As Bill Weintraub has noted, you could have a passionate debate, which might last an evening or a year, about which of the city's many delicatessens made the best smoked-meat sandwiches and whether it was Old Man Kravitz or Old Man Weismann who first introduced the noble brisket of beef from Romania to Montreal. Poets flourished, live theatre thrived, people danced all night, the coffee-house debates never stopped—then or now—and novelist Hugh MacLennan's prophetic *Two Solitudes* was still new.

Walking the streets of Old Montreal in those days—up the mountain to view the St. Lawrence River, past the archbishop's palace, around Bonsecours Market, stopping at restaurants such as Chez La Mère Michel and St. Amable—I could feel the tingle of history. I met Montrealers whose great-grandfathers had auctioned beaver pelts, run the sawmills, built the railways, dredged the rivers, founded the élites who first exploited the Canadian hinterland.

During most of Canada's history, Montreal was the nation's dominant financial centre; the influence of the St. James Street money barons far outweighed the upstarts of Bay Street. Headquarters of the two largest Canadian banks—the Royal and the Montreal—and most of the influential investment houses, such as Nesbitt Thomson, Greenshields, Royal Securities and others, were located within a square mile or two of Mount Royal's brow. Most of the big deals were put together by what was known as the Holy Trinity: Sun Life, the CPR and Bank of Montreal. *[The Montreal, which once issued its own currency, regarded itself as caretaker of the national economy, so much so that in 1907, it independently raised its interest rates.]* The country's defence effort during the First and Second World Wars was run out of Montreal, with the Angus locomotive shops producing tanks and a fledgling aircraft industry turning out many of the fighters that won the Battle of Britain. The city's largely Anglo establishment operated out of the Ritz, lunching in the Oak Room, taking tea in the Palm Court or dining in the Oval Room.

In those days, the main issue of contention between the French and English was language. Neither group was particularly anxious to adopt each other's tongue. The twin lassitudes remained distant and cool, but there was little chaffing of elbows. The experience of Guy Saint-Pierre, who later became CEO of SCN-Lavalin Inc., as well as serving on the boards of BCE, Royal Bank, GM and Alcan, was typical. He grew up in rural Quebec and studied English in school but had hardly ever spoken it conversationally when he joined the Canadian army at nineteen. Along with a group of 300 Quebec recruits, he was sent for training in Chilliwack, British Columbia: "The first night we were there, the Colonel who was in charge of the base got everyone assembled. For most of us it was our first night in the army. He said to us, 'I know a lot of you don't speak English very well and you may have difficulty understanding what we're trying to say. I've got a plan called the buddy system: each one of you who needs help with English is going to be assigned to someone who will explain to you what's going on. Anyone who needs assistance, stay behind and the rest of you are dismissed.' Of course, they all went because none of them had understood anything he said except myself and one other fellow. So I stayed behind, and the colonel asked me, 'What happened? I thought a lot of these recruits didn't speak English?' I said, 'Well, my Colonel, they left because they didn't understand a single word you said.' So the next night, he called everyone in, and the buddy system was implemented for real."

Nothing much happened regarding the anglo-francophone balance of power until 1960. Then, with the election of the progressive Liberal Jean Lesage as premier, everything changed. He launched the Quiet Revolution, which had precisely the opposite objective of most of history's social upheavals. Instead of being dedicated to the destruction of the upper classes, it aimed to create an indigenous francophone élite so its members could seize control of the province's major institutions. Quebeckers would then, at last, command their own economy.

Few Canadians outside the province realized how fundamental, almost revolutionary, a change that required. For more than a century, the resident cardinals, speaking for the Vatican and cocooned in the splendid isolation of their celestial palace at the foot of Montreal's Dominion Square, had decreed that material matters be left to the English. By default, this allowed the Anglo establishment that operated mainly out of Montreal's Mount Royal Club, aided by the more mundane power wielders at the St. James, University and Mount Stephen clubs, to run most of the province's economy.

Within the French community, Lesage's victory over the remnants of Maurice Duplessis's Union Nationale meant that the Catholic Church began to lose its control over people's lives. A genuine middle class of Québécois began to emerge, consisting at first of an adventurous few who branched out of the traditional career paths of priest, notary or doctor into business and its ancillary pursuits. That trend, encouraged by every Quebec premier who succeeded Lesage, was specifically aimed at creating a managerial class, a policy aptly summed up in Lesage's slogan, *Maîtres chez nous*. The new business tycoons were mostly trained at Montreal's École des Hautes Études Commerciales, though many followed up with Harvard MBAS. (Founded in 1907, at first its dean reported directly to the premier's office in Quebec City, and the school was treated as a department of government. The school is now an independent faculty inside the University of Montreal.) Within one generation, corporate CEOs had become Quebec's role models, and a new and vibrant bourgeoisie was in the process of taking over. By the mid-1980s, fully 40 percent of Canadian university students taking business courses were Québécois, with an incredible twenty thousand full- and part-time MBAS enrolled in the province's six major faculties of business administration. (Only ten years earlier, Quebec had graduated fewer than four hundred MBAS.) "Our businessmen have replaced the bishops as the new Quebec heroes," declared Pierre Pettigrew, then a Montreal accountant and later one of the Chrétien government's more enlightened ministers.

Heroes they may have been, but their accomplishments required a significant shove from Ottawa, which regarded a thriving Quebec business community as a bulwark against separatism. For example, Bombardier, which eventually evolved into the world's third-largest aircraft manufacturer, got its start in the industry by absorbing Canadair, but only after

Ottawa swallowed its $1.2-billion debt load. Bombardier's purchase price was $120 million, which the company could have easily recouped through sale of the land it acquired in the deal. It also got the rights to manufacture the spectacularly successful Challenger aircraft. The Mulroney government then handed Bombardier its operating cash flow by awarding it the $1.3-billion CF-18 maintenance contract, despite the objections of its own experts that Winnipeg's Bristol Aerospace could do the job cheaper and better.

Québécois quickly took over the economy, but there were some spectacular stumbles: Claude Castonguay never did realize his dream of building the Laurentian Group into a world-class financial institution. Bertin Nadeau's $7-billion Unigesco Inc. became Canada's twelfth-largest company (including the Provigo and Loeb grocery chains), but was overwhelmed by accumulated debts. *[Nadeau lived happily ever after. He has entered what he calls "the serene phase of my life" and is content to run two private companies: Kiri, a soft-drink beverage firm, and Casavant Frères, a major church-organ manufacturer.]* The Rolland family sold out its fine-paper mills, ending its family dynasty. Raymond Malenfant, an entrepreneur who indiscriminately purchased hotels and other real estate, ended up in bankruptcy court. *[In two years of court battles he attempted three hundred separate manoeuvres to stave off bankruptcy, including offering creditors free rooms in his hotels. At one point he had his hotel chefs carve larger-than-life busts of himself in lard as lobby displays, but he went bellyup anyway.]* Bernard Lamarre's $1.2-billion Lavalin Group hit the sawdust after he overexpanded to satisfy his ego instead of his bottom line. Michel Gaucher, who came out of nowhere to become Montreal's largest merchant fleet owner (fourteen ships) and in 1989, with the help of the Caisse de dépôt, took over the floundering Steinberg grocery chain, was on the ropes by 1996.

Still, by 1995, a solid platoon of impressive Québécois executives was solidly entrenched in power. When the authoritative business magazine *Les Affaires Plus* published its annual list of the fifty most powerful Quebeckers, all but four of those named were Québécois; two were Jewish. The once-dominant WASP influence had not just waned, it had vanished.

In a very real way, the Québécois are Canada's purest Titans, because in the process of creating their own Establishment, the power structure that emerged *had* to be a meritocracy. There was no entrenched Old Québécois business élite to speak of, so the Titans had no other criteria for their acceptance except merit.

To blame "the separatist menace," as the *habitués* of the Mount Royal Club continue to call it, entirely for the decline of Montreal to

Philadelphia status is tidy and simple. It is also wrong. In truth, the energies of Anglo Montreal had peaked in the 1920s. The Square Mile, where the English-speaking élite lived, was decimated by the First World War, with its best and brightest, a whole generation, wiped out in the trenches of France. Meanwhile, the CPR fortunes, which had originally dominated the city's move into major projects, such as building the Beauharnois Canal and the Canadian Pacific Railway, moved into third-generation hands and ceased taking investment initiatives.

The start of the business shift to Toronto dates back to the early twenties, when Sir Henry Thornton formed the CNR out of the bankrupt shells of the Canadian Northern, the Grand Trunk and the Grand Trunk Pacific, and allowed Toronto's Bank of Commerce (instead of the CPR's usual standby, Bank of Montreal) to become a major force in national railways. Meanwhile, the Ontario government had been financing railway construction into its own Northland as early as 1902, which triggered the Cobalt, Porcupine and Kirkland Lake mining booms. The riches of the Canadian Shield thus came under Toronto's dominance, especially because Montreal continued to regard the mining market as "a bit undignified," allowing speculative wealth to pour into Toronto. The Standard Stock and Mining Exchange was amalgamated into the more senior Toronto Stock Exchange in 1934. That contrasted with the insistence of the Montreal Stock Exchange on relegating mining stocks to trading on the floor of the decidedly junior Montreal Curb Market, where they languished. The upstart Toronto stock market became the main trading pit for the country's burgeoning resources, also giving investors access to the surging New York market. Montreal smugly rejected such extravagances and remained content to keep trading blue-chip shares, preferably bearing British pedigrees.

St. James Street, once the chief metaphor for Canadian capitalism, suffered the most ignominious decline. The floor of the old Montreal Stock Exchange was eventually abandoned and turned into a theatre. Rue St. Jacques now features only empty palaces—a forest of Corinthian columns—sporting hopeful For Rent signs, T-shirt emporiums and greasy restaurants. Business has moved up the hill to cluster around Place Ville-Marie, along Boulevard René-Lévesque and Rue de la Gauchetière, or Place Victoria, near the new stock exchange.

Montreal continued to look inward. Whatever outside influences its citizens recognized as relevant tended to come from England or France, which kept alive dreams of past glories for both dominant language groups. Toronto, meanwhile, looked outward, south to the United States for markets and ideas, and west to a hinterland willing to buy its goods and pretensions. Ontario dreamed of the future; Quebec dreamed of the past. The slogan on the province's licence plates—*Je me souviens*—said it all.

Instead of worrying about what was afoot, English Montrealers of the 1950s and 1960s lived out their lives with an imperviousness that Dickens would have found entirely contemporary. Then, in the fall of 1976, René Lévesque was elected on a separatist platform and the exodus started in earnest. The corporate flight began with Sun Life, the Royal Bank and especially the Montreal, which by 1998 did not retain a single senior executive in Montreal, though its titular head office remained there. In line with the time-tested doctrine that economic power follows political power for its own protection, Montreal's cash caches and corporate charters headed westward along the Macdonald–Cartier freeway to the safer havens of Bay Street. Eventually, ninety major head offices— including Trizec, Royal Trust, Redpath Sugar, Molson and Northern Telecom—and 13,000 corporate refugees left the province, plus another 140,000 Anglo civilians. It was the largest exodus in Canadian history— and it continues.

Even companies that officially remained in Montreal had vanished. At the time of the first separatist crisis, I remember interviewing CPR chairman Ian Sinclair about rumours that his corporate files and main-frame computer had already been shipped out of the province and that he would soon follow. In those days, the railway's headquarters was in the cavernous back rooms of Windsor Station, and I had to walk down echoing corridors of empty offices to reach the chairman's lair. Sinclair was sitting behind a massive, hand-carved oak desk that had originally belonged to Sir William Van Horne, father of Canada's first transcontinental railroad. "Tell me, Ian," I enquired, "how much of the CPR is actually left in Montreal?" I didn't think the CPR chairman would say much, because the separatists were hounding him to declare his intentions. Sinclair looked up, his face twisting into the rage that he felt at having been forced by the province's political crisis to act against his will. Then he answered my question by grimly pounding his jackhammer fists on the polished surface of the Van Horne relic. "What's left in Montreal?" he bellowed. "This desk. This damn desk!"

"Montreal," said Liberal guru John Payne at the time, "is at once a city in decline and in transition. Her national stature has dwindled. Her financial clout is gone. Her port, once the gateway to half a continent, is no longer dominant. Her manufacturing sector struggles for survival. Her airports are no longer the gateway to Canada. Her cosmopolitanism, which she wore so proudly for so long, is condemned. Her hotels, always a barometer of a city's commercial activity, are half empty. Once the commercial matriarch of the nation, she has become a frail, frayed dowager of a French-speaking region." Of the twenty-five North American cities with a population of over two million, Montreal had the highest rate of unemployment, several percentage points worse than that of the worst performers running at 13 percent, which is typical of a permanent recession.

Certainly, Montreal's prosperity was a victim of Toronto's economic dominance, Ottawa's political stupidities and Quebec City's terminal schizophrenia. But much of the pain was self-inflicted.

MONTREAL MAY BE IN THE DUMPS, BUT individual companies are flourishing, giving birth to an exciting and creative cadre of twenty-first-century Titans. "What's happening here," says Heward Stikeman, "is the dramatic rise of a new entrepreneurial group of young French Canadians who doesn't want to be locked into Quebec, even as a separate country. They're world traders."

"What is emerging," points out Professor Tom Naylor, the McGill savant who studies the province's élites, "is a new francophone group that does, in fact, have many of the attributes of the old Anglo establishment in the sense that it's trying to create family dynasties, and that's accentuated by the fact that Quebec society has always been very incestuous. It doesn't matter who you are or where you are, the jobs go to who you know. There's no open labour market, there never has been. So we have a self-perpetuating élite in a society that has always accepted self-perpetuation and nepotism as defensive necessities, essential for a time when people were largely excluded. But now that they're included in the power structure, it can be actually quite menacing."

The most thoughtful Montreal Titan I visited was Philip O'Brien, CEO and majority owner of Devencore Ltd., a real-estate servicing house that manages buildings and takes care of the property problems for large companies. "One reason these guys are doing so well in the global economy," he says, "is the multicultural thing. It's that ability we have, those extra sets of antennae we develop because we're so conscious of the fragility of cultures. That makes us listen more closely and realize that we all live in a world of minorities, which gives us a better ability to communicate with people in other countries. That's why a lot of our guys do so well, rather than being just functional in one language and one culture and saying, 'I'm North American, and I think North American.' We have had to think differently and, therefore, we're at ease in foreign situations. The other thing is that most of the guys in Montreal have found it difficult to penetrate the Canadian marketplace because people say, 'Quebec is a pain in the ass. They're dragging us down, these goddamned separatists.' So we have to deal with a hell of a lot of negative energy in Toronto and elsewhere in Canada, but you don't have to do that in other places."

Then O'Brien grows very serious. "The sad part is that we have already divorced ourselves from the rest of Canada," he maintains. "We feel Canada has abandoned us. First, it was the big companies that left in the 1970s. From then on, the brain power, the grey matter, the energy and the money have been invested elsewhere. Then the banks left, even if technically they're still supposed to be here. Try to get a loan for a Quebec speculative project; you're not going to get it. You'll get it if you're in Toronto or Alberta, but for political reasons, we're treated as if we lived in a developing country. It's a form of abandonment. Canada is not engaged in Quebec. To be engaged in something, you participate in the good and the bad.

"Sovereignty is a form of achievement, because it means you have gained respect, and I think in that sense we have become sovereign. We don't need a contract that spells it out. If Quebec ever said, 'Okay, it's over with. No more separation; it's finished; we're not talking about it anymore,' would Canadians want to come back and do things in Quebec? I don't think so. The times have changed too much for that. We already have a form of separation."

He doesn't like his own conclusion, but O'Brien goes on: "That's why we had a country. Montreal was a domestic purveyor of services for that country; it no longer is and never will be again. So why put our energy into trying to help Calgary build itself into a place with a million population when you can go to South America where there are 350-million people, and it's in the same time zone?"

This is depressing. Philip O'Brien is no mere real-estate operator. He is an ardent and dedicated federalist who was co-chairman and chief organizer of Citoyens Ensemble, the great rally held on the eve of the 1995 referendum that saved the day for Canada. Its tens of thousands of flag-waving patriots spoke for the millions of Canadians who declared that they wanted to keep a country. "That was a magical engagement; there's no question about it. It was really quite special," he reminisces. "It was a show of love. But then everybody went back home and got bored with Quebec, and I don't blame them. If I were living in Calgary I'd say, 'I've had enough of this crap.'"

THE CITY, OF COURSE, IS STILL BEAUTIFUL—no one can rob Montreal of its majestic setting. But in many ways, it has become a Potemkin village. The term dates back to Grigory Aleksandrovich Potemkin, who for seventeen years was the most powerful man in the eighteenth-century Russian empire of Catherine the Great, and incidentally was her lover. He built the first Black Sea fleet, planned to restore the old Byzantine Empire, and attempted to colonize the Ukrainian steppes. But he overreached himself by disguising the poor state of the Ukrainian economy. During Catherine's 1787 tour of the region, the story goes, he built false fronts on some of the buildings in the towns and villages she inspected, to create an atmosphere of false prosperity. As in Potemkin's villages, in Montreal these days, nothing is as it seems.

NO ESTABLISHMENT IN CANADA HAS BEEN UNDER more intense pressure than Montreal's Jewish community. The young generation has fled, most of its elders have removed their funds to safer havens, and they face renewed prejudice. Harassment by the Parti Québécois has included the insistence in 1996 that kosher Passover products had to be labelled in French. The PQ language police seized gefilte fish and matzo off grocery-store shelves, which was particularly absurd, since these products are imported strictly for the eight days of the celebration, and not made in Canada. Yet they not only carry on, but partly because so many Anglo Quebeckers have fled, the Jews have taken over leadership of the province's non-francophone population. Once banned from attending McGill, they now dominate its board of governors and have appointed its principal (Bernard Shapiro) and dean of medicine (Abe Fuks). Despite their smaller number and many internal problems, they still raise $30 million a year in the annual Combined Jewish Appeal.

There was only one leader of Montreal's Jewish community, *Rex Judae* Charles Bronfman, but he has pulled up stakes, selling his house and moving to his several other residences in New York, Palm Beach and Israel. No one has taken his place. The other vacuum is the absence of the Steinberg family, who were community leaders until sibling rivalry ruined their grocery business and drove them into exile. The only Steinberg still active is Arnold, the son of Nathan, who is a director of Altamira, Provigo and Teleglobe. Some of the other significant players include Max Bernard, Casper Bloom and Tom Hecht.

Max Bernard sits in his office, a ten-window command post that juts out like the bridge of a ship from the high-rise occupied by his law firm, and he pontificates. "The sense in the Jewish community is that we really are losing our best and brightest, the young well-educated mobile people who are either looking for where they're going to start their careers or have already left," he says. "It's very sad. We are really going through a very significant demographic change in the Jewish community. I don't think fear of anti-semitism really comes into play, but it's more a sense of exclusion because of the ethnocentrism that seems apparent in the nationalist dogma, a sense of just being tired of the politics, wanting to get away from it, wanting stability and some kind of assurance for the future. The double whammy of having the politics play havoc with the declining economy is just more than a lot of people choose to stand."

We look around through the panoramic windows of his eyrie, and there isn't a single construction crane in sight. "What is impacting on business is the constant disharmony arising from the separation option," he says. "The damage is permanent but not irreversible. The head offices have moved out are not coming back but that doesn't mean that we're not going to have the next Microsoft with a head office here. It could happen."

As co-chair of Renaissance Montreal, Casper Bloom would love to see that dream realized, but he's not overly optimistic. "It's not the recognizable names who have left, it's our progeny, it's our young brains," Bloom laments. "They're the ones with the education; they're the ones who have the ability; they're mobile, and they have no reason to stay. I've been here all my life. I'm reasonably fluent in French, I work basically always in French, because I do labour law, and even I'm not feeling comfortable at all. The children are leaving, and their parents are following them. Our roots are here; we have deep roots, many of us, particularly myself. My grandfather came over in 1860 from eastern Russia. So my roots are very deeply entrenched here. That's not the case, of course, with our children, and that's why they are leaving."

The most interesting character in Montreal's Jewish community is a Titan in pharmaceuticals named Tom Hecht. In the spring of 1997, he stepped over the line and took on a position never before open to Jews: a directorship in the all-powerful Caisse de dépôt et placement du Québec. With assets of $58 billion, it dwarfs all other Canadian financial institutions, including the banks, which operate under much tighter mandates and regulations. (The Caisse is also much more profitable, churning out net earnings of $6 billion, compared to the top banks' $1 billion-plus.) The paradox of this fiscal giant was that none of its twelve directors had ever run an independent business. They were either Caisse insiders, militant union leaders or Quebec City functionaries named to their positions by the Parti Québécois. They were militant separatists, including Roderigue Biron, who ran for leadership of the Bloc Québécois and Gilles Godbout, who is deputy to Finance Minister Bernard Landry, the most ideological of the PQ's sovereignists. Hecht broke the spell when he was unexpectedly appointed a Caisse director in March 1997. Hecht is not well known within the Canadian business community, but he built up Ibex Technologies Inc. into a multimillion-dollar enterprise.

Although he has never been bar mitzvahed and is not strong on religious ceremonies, Hecht is a vocal member of Montreal's Jewish establishment and has chaired the Combined Jewish Appeal and the United Israel Appeal of Canada. His appointment to the Caisse, which was sponsored personally by finance minister Landry, was the first positive signal by the Bouchard government to the province's Jewish community. Hecht first met Landry twenty years ago, when Landry was a junior minister in René Lévesque's separatist cabinet and officially represented the first PQ administration at a memorial service held in Montreal's Shaar Hashomayim Synagogue, chaired by Hecht. "Landry walked in with a yarmulke on his head and paid his respects, and I've had a good and respectful relationship with him ever since," Hecht recalls. "I find him to be intelligent, even if he is very much the ideologue. We've worked together on some questions that unite us, though the main issue of independence divides us in a very pronounced way. Still, we can't allow ourselves to remain in a ghetto."

Other leaders of the Jewish Establishment include Manuel Batshaw, the Cardinal Richelieu of Claridge Investments, who is a former executive vice-president of the Montreal Jewish Federation. His power base is enhanced by being Charles Bronfman's devoted spear carrier. Joseph Benarrosh, head of the Canadian Sephardic Federation, has brought his members more into the mainstream. Neri Bloomfield, grande dame of the Lady Davis Foundation, is a philanthropic dynamo, active with the Jewish National Fund. Irwin Cotler is a professor in McGill's Faculty of Law and an internationally recognized human-rights activist. Steven Cummings, scion of the wealthy Cummings family, is the best and brightest of the new generation. He is also president of the Jewish General Hospital, the largest English-speaking hospital in Montreal (only after they start each conversation and answer telephones in French). Sheila Finestone is a Trudeau Liberal, a long-time social activist and daughter of the late Monroe Abbey, former president of the Canadian Jewish Congress. Dr. Phil Gold is a physician and highly regarded guru of the Jewish community. Yoine Goldstein is a prominent lawyer and head of the central organization of Jewish activities. Senator Leo Kolber, because he is so close to them, is often called "the only non-Bronfman Bronfman." He is actively involved in all aspects of Jewish communal life and enjoys undiminished clout. Sheila Kussner is a successful fund-raiser and founder of Hope & Cope, an internationally recognized concept to assist cancer patients. Herb Marx is a judge of the Supreme Court and a former Bourassa cabinet minister. Stanley Plotnick, president of the Federation Canadian Jewish Appeal, pioneered the Pro-Montreal Movement for Youth Retention in the city (it didn't work). Reuben Poupko, Montreal's most influential rabbi, is the spiritual leader of Congregation Beth Israel Beth Aaron and a magnetic force that attracts Jewish university youth to Jewish causes. Bernard Shapiro, principal of McGill University, has become involved with Jewish communal life as a result of the controversial proposed merger involving the Montreal General Hospital, the Royal Victoria Hospital and the Jewish General Hospital. Stephen Vineberg is a former president of the Jewish General Hospital and active in all aspects of Jewish communal life. Jonathan Wener, a major developer in high-rises, is remaking the old Forum into a $70-million mega-plex with thirty screens and 7,250 seats. He co-chaired the 1995 federalist rally. Harvey Wolfe is an architect who is national president of the United Jewish Appeal in Canada. Publisher Michael Goldbloom has resurrected the Montreal *Gazette*.

THE MONTREAL JEWISH COMMUNITY's only multibillionaire, Charles Bronfman, left the city in the autumn of 1997, when he sold his Westmount house for $2.8 million—$700,000 less than his asking price. It wasn't the sale of the house that had Jewish Montreal upset, but its owner's departure.

Bronfman *was* Montreal. His daring 1968 purchase (with his own, not corporate money) of the Expos baseball team gave the city something to cheer about. He was the touchstone that Montreal Jews looked to, to be there when money was being raised or the community needed some quick advice. He was not only a good Jew but an avid Canadian. Not emotionally demonstrative, Charles loved Canada and spent a good deal of time and money educating Canadians about their own country. This was the country that had allowed his family to accumulate one of the world's great fortunes—a large and magical land where being Jewish was no handicap to realizing your dreams. He could easily be brought to tears by a good (or primitive) version of "O Canada." In the 1976 provincial election, when it looked as if René Lévesque might win, Bronfman departed from his customary reticence and spoke out in public: "If the Parti Québécois forms the next government, it will be pure, absolute hell. I see the destruction of my country, the destruction of the Jewish community." He then threatened to move Seagram out of Montreal, and the day after his speech, when Lévesque was elected with a resounding majority, he went into a protracted sulk. His threat was a bit of a reach. Five years previously, Bronfman had moved Seagram's Canadian head-quarters to Waterloo, Ontario, in case the separatists ever got power. Seco-Cemp Ltd., which then controlled most of his holdings, had already been moved to Toronto, and by 1978 less than 4 percent of Seagram's assets remained in Quebec.

He remained in Montreal, off and on, for another dozen years, but he never really recovered his enthusiasm. In 1986, Bronfman sold his hold-ings in Bow Valley Industries and in his main real-estate company, Cadil-lac-Fairview, to a Chicago developer for US$2.6 billion, and five years later moved most of his money (US$2 billion) out of the country. That was the infamous transfer, choreographed by New York lawyer Garry Gartner, that avoided payment of any capital-gains tax, which prompted Ottawa to change the rules so that it could not happen again. The sale of his house was only the final act in Charles's de-linking with Montreal, though his merchant bank, National Claridge, remains stationed there. Seagram is now run entirely from New York.

In 1994, the direction of Seagram, the Bronfmans' main company, was handed over to Charles's nephew, Edgar, Jr. "My father taught us to think in generations," declared the young Bronfman. "He always expected each generation to surpass the past generation."

Edgar, Jr.'s US$10.6-billion purchase of PolyGram NV—the world's biggest record label—in the summer of 1998 turned Seagram from a liquor company with subsidiary interests in music, TV and film, into a global entertainment colossus. Edgar, Jr. bet the farm. Alain Levy, the outgoing CEO of PolyGram, rightly called his business "more dangerous than astrology." The purchase was a big gamble. At stake was the future value of the family's 120 million shares of Seagram stock, then worth more than $7 billion.

Edgar, Jr.'s most serious previous move was his 1995 decision to sell the company's stake in E.I. DuPont de Nemours and Co. in order to buy an 80-percent share of the entertainment conglomerate Music Corpora-tion of America. One of Charles's significant functions had been to act as chief liaison with the board of DuPont, and he was profoundly upset by the switch. Scuttling the DuPont investment was severely criticized by

Seagram shareholders, because under CEO Chad Holliday, the once-dormant chemical firm became a world leader in pharmaceuticals and biotechnology. The stock that Bronfman sold for $11.7 billion was worth double that three years later, and investment analysts were predicting it would double again within eighteen months.

"The deal turned Charles Bronfman's stomach," reported *The Financial Post*. In the spring of 1998, the Bronfman trusts, under Charles's direction, sold 4.76 million common shares in Seagram. But as a loyal Bronfman, he cast his influential vote as chairman of Seagram's executive committee behind the move, only because he didn't want to start a family feud. This was a traumatic experience for Charles. Perhaps he forgot to remember that Edgar, Jr. was just following in his father's footsteps. Charles's brother, Edgar, Sr., was tickled by similar fancies. During the late 1960s, Edgar, Sr. aced his reluctant father, dynasty founder Sam, into paying $40 million to acquire 15 percent of Metro-Goldwyn-Mayer, the largest single block of one of Hollywood's major studios. The deal actually took place during a phone call to Leo Kolber, his father's financial adviser ("Listen, Leo, have you got any money?" the then thirty-nine-year-old Edgar, Sr. enquired. "I've just bought $40-million worth of MGM stock.")

Sam, whose temper could make boys out of men, ruled his empire with an iron will, but he seemed to be a puritan at heart—that is, if you forgot that his fortune was based on having been Canada's most successful bootlegger during U.S. Prohibition days, when his whisky flooded over the border to wet American whistles. Though Sam hated the idea of being involved with the sleazy Hollywood glamour game, he allowed the movie deal to go through, but repeatedly expressed his displeasure with Edgar's impetuous idea. "Tell me, Edgar," he once asked him, "are we buying all this goddamn MGM stock just so you can get laid?"

"No, Pop," Edgar assured him. "It doesn't cost $40 million to get laid." It may have started out as a lark, but by May 1969, Edgar had gained enough clout on the MGM board to be named the studio's chairman. Ahead of his time, he intended to merge it with Time Inc., which had quietly accumulated 6 percent of MGM's shares on its own. Only weeks later, Kirk Kerkorian, a high roller out of Las Vegas, bought an even larger block of MGM shares and forced Edgar out. Edgar's most embarrassing sequel was walking into a New York nightclub, where he was spotted by comedian Don Rickles, who stopped the show by saying, "Hey, there's Edgar Bronfman. He was chairman of MGM for ten minutes!"

What outsiders don't realize is that the Bronfmans, unlike the Eatons, Southams or most of the other once powerful Canadian clans, discovered the secret of how power can be passed on from one generation to the next: only one member in each generation is charged with running the business; the exercise of authority by the chosen successor, while carefully monitored, is supreme. There has never been any question of split loyalties at the top. When Sam died in 1971, Edgar and Charles made a private odyssey to his grave on the morning after his funeral, which is against Jewish tradition that forbids family visits for thirty days after interment. As Charles explained at the time, "We wanted to make a vow over Pop's grave, that we'll always stick together as one unit."

Charles Bronfman certainly is a Titan, but despite his professed love of Canada, he now wears the title *in absentia*.

MONTREAL'S TITANS ARE AN IMPRESSIVE CREW, but with a few significant exceptions, their power is local, not national. Unlike the Titans in Canada's other industrialized provinces—both of them—their influence is enclosed by their culture and their domestic constituencies. There is a full list of Quebec's new establishment in Appendix 9, but the following are some of the most important players. *[Paul Desmarais, one of Montreal's most important and most durable Titans, is profiled in Chapter 8.]*

Laurent Beaudoin runs Montreal's most important multinational manufacturer. He has created a unique, world-class corporate machine that spews out jet aircraft, subway cars, Ski-Doos and every other mode of transportation known to man, but has deliberately curtailed his national influence by refusing to sit on any boards but his own. Still, running the transportation conglomerate keeps him gainfully occupied. The Bombardier family, which Beaudoin leads (he married Joseph-Armand Bombardier's daughter, Claire) has an iron grip on the company, holding 60 percent of the voting shares and 20 percent of the equity. That's not a bad investment, considering that Bombardier's revenues have doubled to $8.5 billion in the past five years, and profits have zoomed at a compounded annual growth rate of 26 percent. Beaudoin's secret is to never step beyond the directions he carefully sets out for the company's future. His organizational charts reflect his decentralization priorities. Each of the presidents of his five operating groups is fully responsible for setting targets and achieving them. Bombardier is so decentralized that its head office on Montreal's Boulevard René-Lévesque employs only 140 people. "Laurent is the best deal maker I've run into," says Bill Turner, a Bombardier director. "He listens very carefully to what the other side wants and usually constructs something that meets their objectives as well as being good for him. His other imperative is to gear everything to the future. When we bought Learjet out of an American bankruptcy court, he immediately flew to its headquarters in Wichita, Kansas. Bill Farlinger, who had owned it previously, never visited the place. Laurent toured the plant, then asked to see the chief engineer, sat down in his office and said, 'My name is Laurent Beaudoin. I think this is a great company. What are your plans for the next generation of Lears?' I was told at a dinner about four months later that no previous owner had ever asked what they were planning to do. That one sentence reverberated right around the place like lightning. It made a hell of a difference, because the employees realized that here's a guy who cares about the future of this thing. He's not here just to merge it and cut out half the people."

Since his quadruple bypass, Beaudoin has religiously been taking one day off per week, when he hunts and fishes and rides Ski-Doos and horses, but his most obsessive hobby is his Thursday-night poker sessions. "In running the company, Laurent uses his poker face and all the legal tricks you could imagine, and he's very good at it," says Jean-Pierre Goyer, a former Trudeau cabinet minister and one of Canada's in-house directors. "He runs a team of people who always bear in mind what will be the long-term outcome. So he is not a single player as he is in cards. That's the difference. But fundamentally he is a guy who loves to be active and is always looking for new methods, new frontiers. He loves visiting his manufacturing plants and can talk with people on the floor and say, 'Tell me why you're doing things this way.'"

Despite its global holdings, billion-dollar payroll and half-dozen large factories on two continents, Bombardier is still a family affair. There are two classes of shareholders, the multiple-vote class A shareholders and the equity, class B shareholders, and the Bombardiers own a majority of both. In fact, the public float is so small that large American investment funds don't bother with it. The original Bomdardier's son and three daughters are on the board directly or indirectly through their husbands. There are twin levels of decision making: by the family itself, who usually meet before the corporate directors, and the corporate board, which only has four outsiders on it. Beaudoin takes little interest in politics, except to speak out strongly for the federal cause during referenda. But when Leo Kolber and André Desmarais asked for a contribution to a fund that would help re-engineer Jean Chrétien's poor image in French Canada, Beaudoin turned them down.

Bombardier has a major new aircraft coming on stream annually from 1997 to 2001. One estimate for future demand of its regional jets is 8,253 units worth US$114 billion over the next twenty years. Its new Global

Express, the world's most luxurious executive jet (at US$37.5 million a pop), will fly from New York to Tokyo non-stop in any winds, at Mach .80. "We've doubled our aerospace sales in the past five years," says Bob Brown, head of the company's aeronautics division, "and we'll double them again in the next five. At the moment, we have at least a 50-percent world share in most of the aircraft we make. We have the critical mass in a business that allows us to be a global force." The winter of 1997, when Canada triumphantly led the effort to negotiate a treaty that would outlaw land-mines, provided a small case history of Bombardier's dedication to business. The very day politicians were congratulating each other on their great achievement, in a room off the hall where the treaty was being signed, Bombardier already had on display brand new air-borne mine detectors (four for $6.7 million) that could sweep twenty-six square kilometres in three hours. After all, there are 100 million unexploded mines in the world, and that means profits.

At a time when Quebec is a killing ground for business expansion of any kind, at least one Montreal entrepreneur—Charles Sirois of Teleglobe Inc.—is making it so big that he has virtually overnight become a major international factor in the exponentially expanding world of international communications. Until recently, Teleglobe was limited to providing long-distance telephone service between Canada and 240 overseas locations through submarine cables and satellite links. By staging a successful *coup d'état* (backed by a personal investment of $83.3 million in Teleglobe stock) against the firm's sleepy incumbent management early in 1992, Sirois took over direction of one of the country's most international companies. Teleglobe then held the monopoly on telecommunications traffic in and out of Canada, including transmissions by satellite, undersea coaxial cable and by fibre-optics. He soon figured out that this had no future: with 100 percent of Canadian traffic, he would have only 7 percent of North America's overseas communications. He wanted at least 20 percent.

"I believe the biggest competitors of the airlines in the future will be such telecommunications companies as ours," Sirois contends. "Can you imagine a Vancouver-based businessman—who now has to spend twenty hours a week or more on a plane to keep track of his factory in Hong Kong—being able to push a button on his computer and through the new telecommunications systems be, in effect, on his shop floor, talking to the local foreman who can show him everything that's going on?"

The company's biggest breakthrough was the 1996 approval by Washington's Federal Communications Commission to allow Teleglobe to operate as a global carrier from new facilities in the United States. It thus gained identical footing to American firms and has since signed long-distance agreements with 275 carriers in 140 countries, the largest network next to AT&T. This summer, he merged with Excel Communications of Dallas, the fifth-biggest U.S. long-distance carrier. To offset that favourable ruling, Teleglobe agreed to the end of its Canadian monopoly. The growth potential is impressive: last year North Americans placed 12 billion over-seas calling minutes, with Canada accounting for only 960 million minutes of the total. "I would rather have 10 percent of the U.S. market than worry about losing 10 percent of the Canadian market," Sirois com-mented sensibly. One reason for Sirois's success is that his company is based less on its assets than on the individual talents of its executives. "We've created an environment of openness," says Sirois, "where every-body can challenge everyone else, including myself. I don't own the truth. I just make judgments and can change my mind. I prefer to hire more competent people than me, so when I go to sleep at night, I know that the store is in good hands. I don't want to look good, I just want the stock price to go up." That's understandable, since with 11 million shares in his name, Sirois is Teleglobe's largest individual stock holder. The shares have gone from $5 to $75 and more. As it happened, on the day I interviewed him (November 4, 1996), Teleglobe shares jumped $3.70 on the Toronto Stock Exchange, instantly making Sirois $40 million richer. "Good day, but so what?" was his reaction. "I'm a long-term investor."

Sirois was born in Chicoutimi, where his family ran a small paging company. When he was twenty-four and had earned a master's degree in finance at Laval, his father and uncle expressed their faith in young Charles's future by backing him with $1.5 million in cash and bank guar-antees. Sirois has since spun that stake into a personal fortune well into the billion-dollar range. It's owned mainly through National Telesystem Ltd., a personal holding company that controls more than a hundred telecommunications firms. Remarkably, less than half of Sirois's personal fortune stems from his Teleglobe holdings. He also owns majority inter-ests in a half-dozen private telecommunication companies, including the Quebec version of Much Music, Canada's largest burglar-alarm and digital cellular companies, plus a Luxembourg-based TV and radio station partnership with Time Warner.

Sirois divides his time between a Westmount mansion, a luxury flat near the Arc de Triomphe in Paris, his summer place at Magog in the Eastern Townships and a Florida condominium. His favourite pastimes are high-risk sports: scuba-diving, downhill skiing and racing his BMW or

Harley Davidson motorcycles. A harried-looking gent with a Brillo-pad hairdo and laughing eyes, Sirois is one of those rare birds (like Peter Munk, Ted Rogers and Conrad Black) who believes that destiny has chosen him to be a master of the universe. Sirois is convinced that he is fated to turn Teleglobe into the world's third-largest telecommunications carrier, just behind AT&T and British Telecom. Since he has reached fourth spot from a standing start only four years ago, no one is betting against him. Seldom pausing to catch his breath in a frantic daily schedule that seems to be choreographed rather than planned in any recognizable, linear fashion, his work habits rival the legendary time-allocation acrobatics of Ted Rogers. (So they could keep track of one another, until recently Rogers owned 5 percent of Sirois's company.) He seems to have mastered everything—except the basic tools of his trade. "I'm not a techie," he admits. "The cellular phone in my car dates back to 1985, and any phone that has more devices on it than a dial is too complex for me to handle. I've never had a computer, and I don't know how to use one. I keep my work schedule in an old-fashioned book, and if it changes, I write in the new items. At the moment, we're creating not just a whole new industry but a new way for people to live and do business. Five to ten years from now, people will no longer remember that a telephone ever had a wire."

Yves Fortier is in demand. Not just by other Titans who know a great lawyer when they manage to snare one, but by just about everyone he has ever represented. During the 1997 salmon-treaty negotiations on the West Coast, where he acted as chief Canadian negotiator until he quit—because the prime minister wanted him to represent Canada's case to the Supreme Court in the pivotal trial on Quebec's right to separate—it was the fishermen who demanded his return. The thirty-odd industry members and unions that were involved unanimously called for Fortier to resume heading the Canadian side of the talks. As usual, he had homed in on the root of the problem: it was naïve to expect American cooperation in the fishing grounds unless Canada put more pressure on Washington, which the frightened nellies in Ottawa refused to do.

He does impress. A Rhodes scholar, married since 1959 to the former Carol Eaton (of *the* Eatons), a board member of Montreal's seventeen marquee institutions (as well as a director of the Hudson's Bay Company, DuPont of Canada, the Royal Bank, Southam's, Nortel and TransCanada PipeLines), he often represents Canada before the International Court of Justice in The Hague. He was an usher at Brian Mulroney's wedding and was offered a seat on the Supreme Court of Canada when the groom became PM. Fortier now heads the Montreal law firm Ogilvy Renault, where Mulroney works. Between 1988 and 1992, Fortier was Canada's ambassador to the United Nations and earned a sterling reputation during his two terms as president of the Security Council. What's most remarkable about Fortier is that everyone takes him more seriously than he does himself. His eyes dance with private humour, no matter what he's discussing. Regarding Quebec's constitutional problems, he says, "I hope that people in the rest of Canada realize that the issue is also a bore for us. I travel a lot outside Canada, and nothing bores me more than reading my last issue of *La Presse* when I get back. It just turns me right off."

Jacques Bougie runs Alcan, which mints a fortune turning out grey gold, known as aluminium. A twenty-year company veteran, he has reoriented his firm from operating in a relationship-based management style to an evidence-based style of administration and turned it into the world's lowest-price ingot producer. Sales of $8 billion a year are spread over fifty countries; one-fifth of the firm's 34,000 labour force is in Quebec in heavily capitalized facilities that will stay in place, no matter what happens politically. Bougie visits Buenos Aires more frequently than he does Toronto and spends his prime leisure time at a cottage near Mont Tremblant. Since it is Lucien Bouchard's constituents who live in the riding where Alcan has its largest installations, "it doesn't take three hours for the premier to return my calls." Bougie is a multi-national Titan—even if he wears blue, not red, suspenders.

Paul Tellier wasn't supposed to succeed. Placing the Canadian National Railway, a corporate cripple weighed down by generations of tradition and unused rail lines, in the hands of a civil servant seemed like a recipe for disaster. Instead, once freed of Ottawa's restraints, Tellier turned into a whirling dervish. He has turned the near-moribund sunset business into a profitable and exciting enterprise. Supported by Michael Sabia, a fellow exile from Ottawa who invented the GST, as his chief financial officer, he is having the time of his life. Tellier has paid his dues. He became a lawyer, graduated from Oxford in literature, was Pierre Trudeau's point man on national unity, Jean Chrétien's deputy minister in the difficult energy department (where he initiated the National Energy Program) and Brian Mulroney's Clerk of the Privy Council and haberdashery adviser. He turned CN into an efficient company by laying off 14,000 workers and paying those who remained 90 percent of their wages for six subsequent years. In October 1995, in the middle of Quebec's referendum, he privatized CN with the largest initial private offering ($2.2 billion) in Canadian history. The price of the stock doubled in the next twelve months. Most of the shares sold to Wall

Street. "We didn't have to overcome a negative image there," he explains. "Nobody knew us." Then, Tellier began transforming CN from a Canadian to a continental railroad, which may be the most dramatic shift of all. Known around Ottawa for using a chauffeur-driven Jeep, he has owned a 750cc Honda motorcycle, but now mounts a muscular 1000cc BMW bike for recreation—and once rocketed the five hundred kilometres from Montreal to southern Vermont in one day.

Gil Rémillard is an ardent nationalist whose three books on constitutional law have become standard university texts. A man of conscience, Rémillard was both Quebec's minister of justice and minister of intergovernmental affairs during the crucial Meech and Charlottetown accord debates, acting as his government's hard-line bad cop, pushing the province's demands almost to a breaking point. Neither a convinced federalist nor a determined separatist, he was one of those deep thinkers who, when pressed, would come down on the side of wanting Quebec to be a nation, but not an independent state. Such ambivalence vanished during the Charlottetown referendum, which he strongly supported. He studied law at the University of Nice, has taught at Laval and now teaches at the University of Montreal, and has been senior counsel at Byers, Casgrain. He is often consulted on interpretations of Quebec's new 1994 Civil Code—which is handy, since he wrote it.

Jacques Menard is a triple-threat Titan: the Quebec head of Nesbitt Burns, chairman of the mammoth Hydro-Québec and chairman of the Montreal Expos. He has turned Nesbitt Burns into the leading mergers and acquisitions facilitator in the province and was asked by Charles Bronfman, when he was selling the Expos, to try and restructure the team. He put together a $100-million consortium (which included Toronto publisher Avie Bennett and the maker of Guess jeans, Mark Ruttenberg) to buy the baseball club, and as he puts it, "I accidentally became chairman of a baseball team." (He uses his time during games at the ballpark to be briefed by the Expo management people, because there are no other opportunities in his crazy schedule to run the club.) He has been the Canadian head of Oxfam, and while not politically active, he cared enough about the Meech Lake Accord to fly to Newfoundland and to try to personally persuade then-premier Clyde Wells to honour his signature on the accord. He relaxes by playing golf in Provence or spending time at his log cabin near St. Sauveur in the Laurentians. He is totally accepted by both the French and English establishments in Montreal, but strangely has not reached out for a national role. "To be busy in my mind helps make me more efficient," he says. No kidding.

Jean Monty heads Canada's largest corporation, BCE Inc. A sure-footed, impeccably credentialed student of process, Monty fits the 1990s mode of decentralized management. Less of an icon than a catalyst, he recognizes that no company the size and perplexity of BCE can be run by one man exercising his wisdom and divinity. Instead, he rules by his gut, leading a cadre of brothers and sisters in arms—*confrères*—intent on planting the flag of its operational subsidiaries—mainly Bell Telephone, Bell Mobility, Bell Canada International and Nortel—on yet-to-be-scaled heights. His background has little to do with communications or science. After receiving a master's degree in economics from the University of Western Ontario in London, Ontario, he switched to the University of Chicago, intent on getting a Ph.D. in finance, but settled for an MBA, when he grew impatient to get out into the world of commerce. What qualifies him to run BCE is none of this. Instead, it's the attitude he brings to his position, an approach best expressed during an interview I had with him, when I began to press him for a scenario about how rapidly his companies could adjust to the lightning shifts in their technological environment. After taking several runs at an answer, he interrupted himself, and shrugged. "I love change," he admitted, as if that said it all. And in the digital world of the telecommunications industries these days, it does.

Lynton Ronald Wilson moves with the grace of a swordsman, smokes fragrant Rey del Mundo cigars and over the past decade has achieved the impressive turn around of BCE that gave Jean Monty such a magnificent head start. He moved the company's market capitalization from $14 to $40 billion. When he joined, the stock of the communications giant was at $36.75; when he moved upstairs to become BCE's chairman in the spring of 1998, it was selling at $62, including a two-for-one split. In 1990, when Ray Cyr was BCE's chairman, he came to see Wilson in Toronto to offer him what is now Monty's job. He mentioned two priority issues: the urgent need to extricate BCE from its non-telcom, asset-buying binge of the late 1980s, which was draining its profits and cash flow, and his wish to launch the company into the international services arena. "After that," Cyr confided, "you can take it easy, because Bell Canada is a regulated monopoly and Northern Telecom is moving from success to success." Within months after Wilson arrived in Montreal, Bell had been deregulated and Northern Telecom, as Nortel was then called, was in big trouble. Bell was about to lose 40 percent of its long-distance revenues to Murphy Brown and other alternate servers. Wilson spent the next eight years diplomatically turning BCE into a winner, and as chairman continues to strive in that direction.

Luck made Herbert Black a Titan. The son and grandson of Montreal scrap dealers, he sold huge quantities of copper short on May 17, 1996, and came away with an estimated $50-million profit. With his father and brother, he built their company, American Iron & Metal, into a $250-million business. He flies his own helicopter, collects Gauguins, Dégases and Renoirs (he paid $1.76 million for his *Little Gypsy Girl*) and owns one of John Lennon's guitars. He is currently building a new Westmount mansion, which will have a computerized watering system for the ivy expected to climb its walls. It will be filled with $8-million worth of his Chippendale furniture. What keeps Black amused is taunting separatist cabinet ministers. At a legendary private lunch, one of these ministers asked him, 'So, Monsieur Black, you're an employer of a lot of people. What do you think of our policies?' Black surprised the politician by replying, "They're great. Keep it up, especially that language business. I've got a lot of employees who are unilingual, so they're trapped here, and I don't have to pay them very much." The minister blanched, but later in the meal, he returned to the subject by asking Black whether he was worried about separation. "Hell no," was the reply. "It'll just ensure those guys remain trapped."

David Angus is a Tory senator and was Brian Mulroney's bagman for ten years, but he survived intact and has become a Titan of his own making. Probably Canada's best-known practitioner of maritime law, he is a senior partner at Stikeman Elliott, which he took over from a young lawyer named John Turner, who left to make a career in Ottawa. Angus also heads the Montreal General Hospital and has been an Air Canada director for twelve years. He graduated from Lower Canada College at age fifteen and was too young to attend university, so he shipped out on British freighters as an apprentice deck-hand before attending Princeton University. His influence in Montreal's Anglo community stretches beyond his cv. Whenever there is a problem, he is called to intercede.

Bill Turner carries a similar mandate. The former head of Consolidated-Bathurst, once the mainstay of the Desmarais empire, he remains a director of Power Corp. and also sits on the boards of Bombardier, Celanese Canada, Provigo, SNC-Lavalin, Newmont, Schroeders Bank, Axel Johnson, and Alexander Proudfoot, an international management-consulting firm that he chairs. He is vice-chairman of the Davos World Economic Forum and runs his own investment company, Exsultate Inc. "I'm sort of a corporate gadfly," he explains. Recently he helped the U.S. Federal Reserve set up an efficient way to clear cheques, he reorganized the management at Toyota in Japan, and revitalized Caterpillar Tractor in Peoria, Illinois.

André Bisson is a kind of floating ambassador at large for Quebec business, impeccably connected, personable, smart and well informed. He provides a comforting presence for international outfits seeking a Québécois domicile, such as Axa Assurances, Julius Baer Bank, Donohue Financial, Pirelli, BJB Global and the Maxwell interests—all of which have been his accounts and directorships. Chancellor and chairman of the board at the University of Montreal and a director of Paul Desmarais's Power Financial group, he belongs to seven clubs and uses them all. A Harvard MBA who became head of the Business Administration Department at Laval University, he was once offered the ministry of finance by Robert Bourassa, but was too busy to take it.

David Culver's glory days were during his extended period as head of Alcan. When he assumed its presidency in 1977, he declared that Canada needed "more people who revel at the sight of their competitor's blood running down the streets," and he has followed that gospel ever since. He has tied to forty other companies and trade and volunteer organizations but spends most of his time running the $250-million CAI Capital Corp., which invests in mature venture companies such as Bio-Research Labs, Sunquest Vacations and Aster-Cephac, a Paris-based cosmetics and pharmaceutical company. Culver was one of the most dedicated chairmen of Tom d'Aquino's Business Council on National Issues, heading its offensive on behalf of the Mulroney free-trade initiative, and has built up a cadre of special advisers to his firm that reads like a gathering of BCNI alumni, including Ralph Barford, Roy Bennett, Peter Bentley, Rowlie Frazee, Adam Zimmerman and d'Aquino himself. He is a director of American Express and Seagram, and lives very well.

Jean Dupéré, a lawyer with Byers, Casgrain, went on to work for Bell Asbestos as legal counsel. He then engineered a buyout, ending up as the sole owner, and bought back several small mines in the Thetford Mines area. He created LAB Chrysotile, a limited partnership with the Asbestos Corporation, thus controlling all the mines in the Thetford Mines area, of which he is a 70-percent beneficiary and, therefore, worth more than $200 million.

Jean-Claude Scraire, who runs the Caisse de dépôt et placement du Québec, which manages the largest jackpot in the country ($58 billion), has demonstrated some welcome independence by refusing a request by Quebec's auditor-general to review his transactions. He set a precedent by being the first insider to get the top job and has used it as less of a nationalistic cockpit than any of his predecessors.

Stephen Jarislowsky is a Berlin-born aristocrat who graduated as a mechanical engineer from Cornell and went to Japan as a member of the U.S. Army's Counter-Intelligence team, and has the best national network in Montreal. He is close to Conrad Black, holds or has held fifteen hefty directorships and at seventy-four is going stronger than ever. He occasionally doubles as Canada's unofficial ombudsman for mistreated minority shareholders, but has reached the stage when he has been right so often that he can be as arrogant as he likes and enjoys the mixture of awe and irritation that greets most of his pronouncements.

Jean Coutu, who invented cut-rate drugstores in Quebec (where he now owns 230) has expanded into the U.S. through Maxie Drugs and the acquisition of Brooks and other drugstore chains. Coutu is the only Canadian Titan who spends part of each year living in tiny African villages, helping locals protect their land by financing the mass planting of trees (his current project is in Mali). Grégoire Golin is one of the province's best-informed pollsters. Paul Lowenstein has now been in business twenty years providing mezzanine financing of more than $500 million, plus private placements of about $800 million. His Canadian Corporate Funding Ltd. competes successfully with banks in long-term financing. Conrad H. Harrington, part of the new generation of Titans, is serving his apprenticeship with the Canadian office of a Swiss bank, Lombard Odier of Geneva. Claude Frenette makes mysterious real-estate deals in Paris and remains a power. Marcel Côté, a partner at Groupe Sécor, is the Establishment's favourite consultant. Norman Webster, the former editor of *The Globe and Mail* and the *Gazette*, has almost automatically assumed leadership of the Anglo community. He spends most of his time administering the affairs of his family trust and of Bishop's University in Lennonxville and the University of Prince Edward Island in Charlottetown. He is a voice of moderation and wisdom in a turbulent environment.

THE AFTERNOON I MET MICHAEL PITFIELD at that bistro, the autumn leaves were blowing down Montreal's emptying streets and the city seemed comatose. I left the bistro and walked down Drummond Street, once a boulevard of luxury boutiques. There I noticed the display window of a shuttered luxury-furniture store, which accurately conveyed Montreal's economic temperature. Perched on the back of a fine, taffeta armchair left behind by the proprietors of the shop was a hand-lettered sign that read, *Au revoir.*

17

THE SECRET GARDEN

"It all comes down to networking, to connections, whereas everything used to be much more preordained and unchanging."

—*Bill Mingo, Halifax's Establishment lawyer*

ONCE UPON A TIME, THERE WAS A CHARACTER named Major-General Kenelm Appleyard who toured the Annapolis Valley, liked the region's "New England" atmosphere and decided to take up the cause of industrial recovery in Nova Scotia. He became known as the midwife of Industrial Estates Ltd., the provincial Crown corporation set up in 1957 by then-premier Robert Stanfield to drag Nova Scotia into the twentieth century. The good general had been contemplating for years the fact that Halifax was falling precariously behind other Canadian cities. It boasted no shopping destination, nothing but suburban strip malls and the odd row of downtown stores that had no cohesion, no appropriately attractive focal point devoted to retailing and commerce.

One summer noon-hour in 1965, fed up with waiting for local financiers to grasp the initiative, Appleyard marched into the Halifax Club and more or less commandeered nine of its members to get off their elegant butts and kick off the project. Either his choice of vintage Establishment candidates for the assignment was brilliant or he had been well briefed. His dream team included Roy Jodrey, Frank Sobey, Charles Mac-Culloch, Sid Oland, J.C. MacKeen, Russell Harrington, Harold Connor, J.H. Mowbray and Halifax mayor Leonard Kitz, who all happened to be having lunch at the club that day.

Suddenly, things began to happen. In the end it was the combination of Sobey money from Stellarton and Jodrey funds from Hantsport that put up the necessary $60 million to build Scotia Square. That was only right. At the time, they headed Nova Scotia's reigning dynasties, and if the province's capital city needed a downtown shopping destination, why not use local funds to turn the expected profit, instead of waiting for some Upper Canadian smartass to come up the road and put in a miniature Eaton Centre?

There was an interesting sidelight to the story. A Halifax builder named Ralph Medjuck, who was then the single most powerful real-estate operator in the Maritimes, had the same idea. He had, in fact, presented his grandiose plans to City Hall for what he called Cornwallis Square, and was turned down flat. No Jews need apply. "Architecturally, our concept was far superior," claims Medjuck. "But we were politely informed we were number two to what was clearly the Establishment group, and everybody told me, 'Look, if you had a choice, who would you go with—their sponsorship or yours?'"

What's relevant about this story is that none of it could happen today. The religion of builders is no longer a factor in issuing municipal building permits. More significantly, only one of the family dynasties represented by the nine partners—the Sobeys—is still in contention in Nova Scotia, which has become a kind of secret garden inhabited by as inventive and fascinating a group of Titans as operates anywhere in Canada.

At the time of the Scotia Square incident, Nova Scotia was pretty well the private preserve of R.A. "Roy" Jodrey and Frank Sobey, who ran an impressive string of movie theatres and grocery stores. Sobey was a gent of sober mien who loved listening to records by the Tijuana Brass and lived in a magic red house with high beams and a porch from which he could see Prince Edward Island. He was a kindly man but he couldn't stand most politicians, particularly if they invaded his living-room. Whenever he caught a politician on TV in an obvious lie, he would start hurling ashtrays at his image, till it vanished into the broken glass of the tube. When I met him, he had already gone through three TV sets, but nobody was counting. He and Jodrey were modest spenders, especially on their regular trips to Toronto to look after their multimillion-dollar investments. On one expedition, they both did so well that, on the way to the airport, Sobey said, "Listen, R.A., now that we've made so much money, how about flying first class back to Halifax?"

"Hell, no," was the reply. "They'll know in Hantsport before the plane lands that I arrived first class." Jodrey at the time owned Minas Pulp & Paper, which was what allowed Hantsport to exist. A blocky, pasty-faced Baptist, Jodrey had left school at thirteen to become an apple-picker. He found a book that explained how electricity is produced and built a primitive dam across the Avon River, off the Bay of Fundy, then sold it to the provincial power authority for $250,000, which was the foundation of his fortune. Eventually, he became a director of fifty-six companies (including the Bank of Nova Scotia, where he was the largest shareholder) with assets of $3.5 billion. He got so lucky picking stocks that the Bay Street trend-setters started to watch what he was buying and followed his example, which of course drove up his stock values even more.

THE HALIFAX ESTABLISHMENT HAS GONE through several incarnations since those early days, but except for the absence of the family dynasties, its essence hasn't materially altered. "The Establishment hasn't changed that much in this area," says David Hennigar, Roy Jodrey's grandson. "There have been some newer people come along and make their mark, like John Bragg, Joe Shannon, John Risley and others. But that's what the system is set up for. I mean, if you're good, you make your mark, and you make some money." Risley, who is the most interesting of the new bunch, supports that concept. "I believe there's still very much an Establishment," he says, "and I think that's part of our unique character. To some extent the sanctity of the Establishment has been eroded by virtue of the tremendous change the world has gone through, which has redefined everything—but it still exists."

Bill Mingo, the lawyer with the wonderful white mutton-chop whiskers who is the Halifax establishment's unofficial gatekeeper (while holding down directorships in nearly every important Nova Scotia company, as well as Onex and Sun Life), does believe there has been a fundamental shift. "It's very different," he says. "If you just look around at our board and some of the things that I'm trying to do in our firm in terms of getting into new businesses and opportunities in gas and all the new plays, I've got to start searching out for different people, like the Jim Grays of this world from Calgary and others. It all comes down to networking, to connections, whereas everything used to be much more preordained and unchanging. The collapse of the fishing establishment in Newfoundland was a good example. We had to go in and buy up all those family companies, all of which were bankrupt, and I went through a process of amalgamating them and then going to the public with a share offering, and we ended up with Fishery Products International. We had to deal with the Lake family and the Penny family and all those establishment families that have been involved in the fishery for 150 years. Oh, the gnashing of teeth and the emotion involved and all of that, it was terribly difficult."

Bill Mingo is the dean emeritus of the Halifax establishment. He has been in the city all his life (more than seventy-one years), and is still called upon as a corporate and government troubleshooter. Mingo's moral authority in Halifax business and political life is unmatched.

Mingo is also a central figure, along with Purdy Crawford, in the Atlantic Institute for Market Studies (AIMS), which is a sort of down-home version of British Columbia's Fraser Institute, founded by Brian Crawley, who left to join the editorial board of *The Globe and Mail*. The think-tank's directors come from every Atlantic province, and provide a good guide to Canada's eastern establishment—plus one westerner, Jim Palmer, a Liberal establishment lawyer from Calgary.

One of AIMS's most controversial studies—which caught precisely the mood and thrust of the local and regional Titans—was the 1996 booklet *Looking the Gift Horse in the Mouth: The Impact of Federal Transfers on Atlantic Canada*. Written by its senior policy analyst, Fred McMahon of Halifax, it claimed that regional subsidies inhibit growth instead of spurring it. "We need not remain dependent on the rest of Canada for our economic future and well-being," wrote McMahon. "Canada's experiment with massive regional subsidies has done us more harm than good by raising costs, slowing down private investment and widening the unemployment gap with the rest of the nation."

If that kind of thinking is recognized as conventional wisdom, as it is in the process of becoming, it will mean a revolution. Ever since their province reluctantly joined Confederation in 1867, Nova Scotia businessmen have sought to be heard by forming alliances with their local governments, because that seemed to be the only voice loud enough to command the attention of Upper Canadian political authorities. Now they are saying, led by their very own Titans, that they want to command their own destinies and that they don't need any patronizing dollars from Ottawa. "Jean Chrétien has said that you can't solve every problem by throwing money at it, and that sort of rang true to me," says George Caines, head of the Stewart McKelvey law firm, the best in town. "Handing out money does not solve the problems." The province will be the scene of some heavy job-creating action soon, including Mobil Oil's giant $3-billion Sable Island natural gas project.

Apart from AIMS, the board of Nova Scotia Power is a useful meeting point for the Halifax establishment, plus Derek Oland, the talented CEO of Moosehead Breweries who left the Nova Scotia capital in 1997 to run his family's brewery in Saint John. The most essential gathering place for the business Titans is on the board of governors of Dalhousie University. With an astounding eleven universities in the province (one for every 81,000 citizens), there is fierce competition for prestigious chancellors and governors. There is no question that Dalhousie got the pick of the litter, so much so that its roster of board members includes almost all of the Titans described in the pages that follow.

Except for Newfoundlanders, there are few regional patriots in Canada more fierce than Haligonians. Every aspect of life is examined and boasted about. Like their cousins in other parts of Canada, they are doing most of their deals outside the country, but, unlike some of their cousins, they wouldn't trade their home base for anywhere (even though the Nova Scotia market numbers less than a million people). Halifax is a proud and happy place, because it long ago gave up trying to become a small Toronto. Joggers wave good morning to commuters who wave back; you can hear the "thock" of tennis balls as you pass the Waegwoltic Club, or watch the sailboats beating up the Northwest Arm. Seagulls wheel over the city. As Joseph Howe, the province's founding father, once put it, "You don't need a big field to raise a big turnip."

THE PARAGON OF THE NEW HALIGONIAN TITAN, who takes destiny in hand without ignoring the city's sense of tradition and history, is John Risley, the founder and CEO of Clearwater Fine Foods. Risley was a bored student who dropped out of Dalhousie University in the early 1970s and promptly lost what little money he had in bad real-estate deals. In 1976, he and his brother-in-law, medical student Colin MacDonald, raised $15,000 privately to turn a Bedford Basin seafood restaurant into a retail fish market. "We didn't know what we were doing," he recalls bluntly. They branched out into the fiercely competitive wholesale business. It was a seller's market: he needed a premium product and a market willing to pay for it. The answer was to truck live lobster to Boston, bypassing U.S. distributors buying directly from Nova Scotia fishermen. "It was one of those situations where somebody who doesn't know what they're doing asks stupid questions that the industry probably should have asked itself some time ago and never thought to," he says.

Soon, Clearwater Fine Foods was selling live snow crab and other gourmet shellfish to markets in Europe and Japan as well as the U.S., mastering the tricky business of live air cargo shipments. "Over time, our biggest asset was our customer base; a restaurant that bought crab would also buy mussels and clams. So we branched out into other segments of the seafood industry and built a business. My first trip to Europe, I had no contacts so I basically worked the Yellow Pages."

Great fortunes are small ones that survive big crises. When Clearwater nearly sank in the stormy recession of the early 1980s, it survived its worst years "because our lenders never quite figured out how bad things were." In the teeth of the storm, Risley brilliantly invested money (which was needed to pay other bills) in new technology to harvest an obscure clam species called *hokki-gai*, used in sushi. The gamble worked, and he captured a lucrative new market in Japan. Virtually all the company's business is now outside Canada. In another decision that demonstrates his keen sense of the market, he moved into scallops ahead of most potential competitors; it is now a mainstay for Clearwater.

The company's two thousand employees harvest its products, with the exception of lobsters, operating seven packaging and fish-processing plants including one in Argentina and a fleet of twenty-five small vessels. Clearwater is repeating its *hokki-gai* R&D success in a biotech venture called Ocean Nutrition Canada, which studies marine organisms to find natural products with health or nutritional value, and develops ways to prepare and consume these products. The core scientists were recruited from government-funded research that ended with federal and provincial cutbacks.

Risley is bright, energetic and, well, quirky. He has the lean, supple look of a tennis pro (actually, he is a competitive sailor who has raced in the Admiral's Cup). "I don't fit the mould of the classic Nova Scotia Establishment," says Risley, who long since gave up wearing ties and quit the Halifax Club after two years of membership because he never went there. He has an ambivalent relationship with his city. He chose long ago to keep the business in Halifax, although its sales are all international and there'd be advantages to a U.S. or West Coast base. He is also a generous philanthropist, giving for example $1 million to Dalhousie, the university he spurned as a student.

However, his business growth is taking place outside the country and his principal recreation, sailing, is undertaken anywhere in the world but Atlantic Canada. He competes in IMS-class sailing—a grand prix category in which one designs and builds one's own craft to exacting technological specifications. Several members of his crew work in the company; it creates, he says, a championship business culture. Nothing speaks to his offbeat style more than the multimillion-dollar castle he is building at Lobster Point near Chester, Nova Scotia. The 29,000-square-foot monolith must be his odd-days-of-the-week house (not including Sundays), since he already owns two other mansions, one in Halifax and yet another in Chester.

SPRINGHILL-BORN JOHN L. BRAGG, Nova Scotia's second-ranked new Titan, is a decade older and a generation more conventional than his leading counterpart, John Risley. Bragg is the fourth generation in the lumber business based in Oxford, in Nova Scotia's Cumberland County, north of the Bay of Fundy. In the mid-1960s, he switched the family's focus from lumber to food processing and exporting by establishing a wild-blueberry business. Oxford Frozen Foods has remained his flagship, although he has also invested in a Maine-based counterpart (Cherryfield Foods), Bragg Cable television, real estate, hotels and new-technology enterprises. Bragg talks a lot about focus, yet he has two big businesses that aren't connected at all: a $150-million-a-year food-processing business and a $250-million-a-year cable TV empire with 150,000 subscribers.

The family also maintains the original building supply, lumber and real-estate holdings, and a newer fresh-and-frozen-lobster business. The focus is partly on profitability and success. But there is a larger, more important concern: the welfare of Nova Scotia and the Atlantic region. "We have to create an environment in Atlantic Canada that allows business to grow and wealth to be created to have all the good things in the world we want," Bragg says.

John Bragg is the wild-blueberry king of the world (he also grows and sells more carrots than anyone else in Canada), but he describes himself as a small-towner. "I play tennis, but mostly I work; the Establishment means nothing to me," he says. He lives in Collingwood, a village of 350 people, and works in Oxford, a small town of 1,200, and has a summer cottage on the Northumberland Strait. He dismisses his importance in the Nova Scotia network of new Titans, but is a vice chairman of the board of regents at Mount Allison University, his alma mater, and sits on seven other business and community boards, including the Canadian Chamber of Commerce. "You call it networking, I call it hard work and a lot of travelling," he says.

He loves to talk about finding a wild stand of blueberries on his 12,500 acres of land in Nova Scotia or Maine and "encouraging them to grow by doing everything you would do to any other crop: fertilize them, take bees around to pollinate them, and use herbicides and fungicides."

Bragg's take on Nova Scotia's future is a completely sophisticated, Titan's-eye view of a competitive continental and global economy thriving on technology and information systems. "We are twelve hours from Boston and fifteen hours from New York by road and the world is getting smaller and we should have real potential. My real concern is whether we can get the people and the government to understand the potential and develop the political, commercial and regulatory environment that will allow the province to grow. We are in transition. We have been too dependent upon Ottawa, but I am a supporter of regional development: you can't just leave us hanging out to dry. We can do it on our own, but we can't until we change the attitudes of government and the bureaucrats to create an environment that is friendly to business."

KEN ROWE'S UNFLAPPABLE BRITISH POISE is the product of a British grammar-school education, a first career as a navigator and later first mate at sea, and an apprenticeship in marine equipment manufacturing in the United Kingdom. He has the good looks and perfect-martini cool of television's Avenger, Mr. Steed, and the sense of humour to match. He built Halifax's first Holiday Inn, he says, because "I didn't like drinking hours in this town, so now I have my own hotel and I can set my own drinking schedule." He built up his privately owned IMP Group conglomerate—secretive, obscure and worth $500 million—from a modest 1967 investment with three partners in marine supply manufacturing.

Now IMP is a major group involved in aerospace, aviation, industrial supply, petroleum products distribution, medical supplies and hotels. While he often describes his business as "manufacturing for manufacturers," his scheduled line (Air Atlantic) and chartered executive jet services (Innotech and Execaire) have a public profile. Can-Med is the largest supplier of surgical and medical equipment east of Montreal. However, it is the hotel business where his nerve has had its toughest test, and IMP has achieved its notoriety.

In the late 1980s, IMP invested $60 million to refurbish and upgrade Moscow's Aerostar Hotel, built for the 1980 summer Olympics that half the world boycotted because of the Soviet invasion of Afghanistan. Rowe sought out Russian partners and signed on Aeroflot, the national airline. By 1994, the hotel was in the black—a showpiece of Western investment in the new Russia. Then the trouble began. Canadian executives were refused work permits, or harassed and intimidated. The Russian partners tried to squeeze IMP out of the business.

Rowe sued for breach of contract in the International Arbitration Court in Stockholm and won an $8.2-million judgment against Aeroflot and a $4.9-million judgment against a second Russian partner. The Russian Supreme Court upheld the ruling, but IMP couldn't collect; in fact, Russian legal authorities actively blocked his efforts. On a Team Canada trade mission in 1997, Prime Minister Jean Chrétien raised the file with President Boris Yeltsin—to no avail. Finally, in April 1998, IMP had a Quebec bailiff seize an Aeroflot Airbus-310 jetliner at Dorval Airport to enforce the judgment; the plane was released after Aeroflot promised to pay. However, IMP is still owed millions by others in the case. "It just drags on and on," says Rowe, who estimates damages to IMP's interests at $70 million and won't quit until is collected. It isn't just the money, it's the rule of law in a country that needs foreign investment, he claims.

Rowe is sanguine about the dispute. IMP has other irons in the fire, and as the CEO and largest shareholder of the family-owned conglomerate, he continues to preside over its expansion and growth. "I'm pretty autocratic," he admits. The board, made up of his three children and three senior executives, doesn't make decisions; the meetings are open forums on results and opportunities, but Rowe calls the shots. And he does so before five-thirty each afternoon, after which he heads for his country home on the ocean at St. Margaret's Bay, with his briefcase empty. His only detours are to golf or ski. "I use up my full ration of holidays," he says. Decisive, confident and sure of his goals, Rowe is a formidable Titan—a man his Russian partners no doubt wish they'd never crossed.

THE LAST OF THE JODREY DYNASTY who, with the Sobeys, once defined the Nova Scotia establishment—is David Hennigar, grandson of clan patriarch R.A. Jodrey and nephew of John, who ran the dynasty before David took over. He speaks with the tongue of the Jodrey family.

The Jodreys' public holding company is Scotia Investments, which owns interests in CKF, a moulded paper and foam manufacturer; COBI, a frozen-food and food-processing concern; Maritime Paper Products in Dartmouth; and Annapolis Basin Group, a real-estate enterprise. Hennigar also manages public companies in which Scotia Investments holds minority interests, including Extendicare (50 percent voting interest and 10 percent of the equity), Crown Life (34 percent of the votes and 19.8 percent of the equity) and National Sea Products (35 percent voting interest).

Hennigar, who was once fired by Nesbitt Burns, personally owns and is chairman of Acadian Investments, which owns such interests as Cougar Helicopters, an offshore oil service, and Aquarius, a painting and coating business. The Jodreys are intensely private people, and Hennigar is extremely guarded about the full extent of his business dealings and about his personal life. He personifies the bridge between the Old Guard and the new Titans: on the one hand, custodian and overseer of the family's old money and on the other, an entrepreneur and investor in his own right, making his quiet mark and running with his network of Canadian contacts.

THE OTHER GREAT HALIFAX FAMILY DYNASTY is presided over by Donald C. Sobey, chairman of the family's principal investment holding arm, Empire Ltd., and his brother David F. Sobey, chairman of Sobeys Inc., the division of Empire that runs the family's original grocery business. Donald and David each own 19 percent of Empire; the estate of their brother, Bill, who died in 1989, owns another 14 percent—representing majority control of the family consortium.

The grocery, real-estate and investment business, which had a $144-million income in 1997, was turned over to professional managers about the time Bill died. It consists of company-operated Canadian food distribution and retailing, with annual sales of $3 billion. Prime retail properties—shopping plazas and grocery stores across Atlantic Canada—generate rents of $140 million a year. Empire's $786-million investment portfolio includes a 25-percent equity stake in New England food retailing giant Hannaford Bros., 43 percent of heavy-equipment company Wajax, a chain of movie theatres, and automotive and oil-and-gas interests.

THERE IS ONE OTHER HALIFAX DYNASTY WORTHY of the name: run by newspaper publisher Graham Dennis, the tyrannical, elusive and hopelessly dull owner of the Halifax Herald Limited, which publishes the *Chronicle-Herald* and *Mail Star*. A curmudgeon, to use the politest term possible, Dennis appropriated the phrase "publisher's clearinghouse" when he cleaned out the entire senior level of his newsroom and crushed a unionization drive in 1977.

"He has held the franchise on Nova Scotia newspapering," says a critic with grudging admiration. Although his newspaper may have been the worst in Canada (until challenged by the lightweight tabloids of the nineties), it was profitable and therefore endurable. But his domination over Halifax print media is under challenge by the feisty *Daily News*, a paper so aggressive in spite of its distant number-two slot in the market that it created Canada's first online newspaper Web site. Conrad Black wanted to take Dennis out, but he settled for the *Daily News*, which he purchased from Harry Steele for $20 million after fifteen minutes of negotiation. The *Daily News* has made the *Herald* a better product, says Haligonian public-relations man Steve Parker. "But the *Herald* has real issues to deal with. The afternoon newspaper is going nowhere, they've got old press technology and they haven't got editorial personality."

The *Herald*, which Nova Scotians have always loved to hate, has finally reached a stretch of the road that has been mined by a formidable competitor. It's a problem Dennis must deal with, for he apparently intends to pass the paper on to his children.

THE LEADING CAPE BRETONER among Nova Scotia's new Titans, Joe Shannon, is a self-deprecating grandfather who insists on describing himself as "a truck driver who lives down in Cape Breton." As president of privately owned Atlantic Corp. in Port Hawksbury, he is no mere trucker. Atlantic employs 1,500 people and, in addition to its middling-sized fleet of trucks, has several nursing homes, a cable TV operation and real-estate and technology interests. "It pretty well keeps a guy off pogey, running Atlantic and doing odd jobs for the government," he says laconically.

Shannon made his name with the Cape Breton Development Corporation, a long-running attempt to restructure Cape Breton's beleaguered coal-mining and steel-manufacturing economy through a Crown corporation. Shannon has been, at various times, the chairman, the acting president and a director of the Corporation. He's the guy Ottawa always turns to; now, with another Cape Bretoner, former North Sydney MP Russ MacLellan, sitting in the Nova Scotia premier's office, the calls are as likely to come from Halifax. Shannon is also the chairman of the board and chief bagman for University College of Cape Breton, most recently raising $10 million, paying off its debt and installing a new president. "The university will play a major role in the future of Cape Breton," Shannon says, "as will the Swedish-owned pulp mill and board mill at Canso."

Joe Shannon is a major player in determining Cape Breton's future; and so it's not surprising that his chief pleasure is to leave Halifax ("it's too fast for me up there") and drive north. "I'm glad to get home. You come over the hill at Havre Boucher and see the causeway [from the mainland to Port Hawksbury on Cape Breton Island] and it's pretty good. Home is another twenty minutes along, at Long Point on the way to Judique, and it's good to be there." When he drives the last mile down the lane from the highway, he looks forward to a bottle of wine with his shark steak.

A HUNDRED YEARS AFTER THE HALIFAX SHIPYARDS reached their zenith as a place where tall masted ships were built and launched to sea, there is still one man who actually makes a living from the sea. He runs a fleet of tugs, as well as cargo vessels, container ships and a fibre-optic cable-laying vessel. Fred Smithers of Secunda Marine also sails recreationally and has his own cadet corps. He may be the last old salt of Halifax Harbour. In this era of Libyan and Barbadian registry, 70 percent of Smithers's fleet fly the Canadian flag and all his crews are Canadian.

Smithers launched his career as a fleet owner in 1981 with Offshore Logistics of Lafayette, Louisiana, which needed a Canadian partner to meet Foreign Investment Review Agency regulations for oil service vessels supporting Canadian east-coast offshore drilling. Smithers formed a fifty–fifty partnership for Offshore Logistics' Canadian operation, then in 1983 began to acquire wholly owned vessels. His involvement in off-shore-drilling support led to acquiring, with Shell Canada, a 62-percent stake in the Panuke gas field offshore from Nova Scotia, through a company called Iona. "A lot of people in the Nova Scotia government just couldn't believe that upstarts from the Dartmouth marine slips could be that involved in the oil business," Smithers chuckles.

A lifelong interest in recreational sailing prompted Smithers into his signature community venture: a cadet corps that trains young people for work on his vessels. For the cadets, he refitted a schooner called *Caledonia*, recovered by Smithers after it was beached at St. Maartens in a hurricane. He floated it home to the Dartmouth yards, where it was repaired and restored.

To train Canadians for work on his vessels, Smithers put together an in-house cadet program. "We put these kids through the Nautical Institute; they get their tickets—engineering, master or whatever—but they never really get a feel for the sea. We get the cream of the crop coming out of the Institute and put them on the *Caledonia*," Smithers says. Each crew of twelve newly minted cadets takes the *Caledonia* down to the Caribbean. "Our first group going to Bermuda went through some weather when they left Halifax, and boy, they had to run out in front those seas for a day and a half. That's where you learn how to be a sailor."

Richard and Ruth Goldbloom are Halifax's favourite power couple—smart, engaging and totally passionate about the community's development. After a long and brilliant career as a pediatrician in Montreal, Boston and Halifax, Richard is now a professor of pediatrics at Dalhousie University's medical school. Ruth is a McGill graduate, a physical education teacher who made her career as a community and non-profit association organizer. She is now the fund-raiser that everyone wants for their community campaign and she never lets anybody down.

David and Margaret Fountain have inherited wealth: he is the heir to the Fred C. Manning fortune and she is of the Cape Breton Smiths, an industrialist family. Now they are the leading philanthropists in Nova

Scotia and long-standing patrons of the Neptune Theatre, to which they once gave $1 million so that it wouldn't bear their name, or anybody else's.

"My wife and I each have a deep and long-standing interest in the arts and have been patrons of the Neptune for twenty years, well before we met, in fact," says Fountain. "When the Neptune was rebuilding, I was a member of its capital campaign, and we began to ask ourselves what we would do if a large donor materialized who wanted to change the theatre's name to his, as has happened in so many other places. Because of the Neptune's substantial history and excellent reputation in Halifax and beyond, everyone connected with the theatre wanted very much to retain the name Neptune. So, before the capital campaign was launched we donated a million dollars to the project, with the belief that ours would be the largest contribution to the campaign and that we could therefore prevent any other donor from changing the theatre's name. Today, although one segment of the new complex is called Fountain Hall, the name Neptune Theatre remains."

The Fountains' home, a French-style château that accommodates large gatherings, has become a Halifax landmark. From the outside, it looks like a forest of columns. "My philanthropy," says Maggie Fountain, who has blossomed in her new incarnation, "is very much the continuation of a family tradition began by my grandparents."

Colin Latham is president and CEO of Maritime Telephone and Telegraph, and presided over the breakup of the hundred-year-old MT&T monopoly and the introduction of long-distance competition. He restructured the company and got it into the development of half a dozen new ventures. He once conducted a ceremonial burning of company policy manuals, to impress upon his employees that the old phone company was dead. Latham, an electronics engineer, ("I was the black sheep in a family of teachers"), immigrated from England in 1968 and worked his way up the ranks, becoming president in 1995. When a squash injury forced him to curtail his competitive rugby, tennis, cycling and swimming agenda, he took up marathon running. It's an apt sport for a man running a deregulated phone company.

Allan C. Shaw, the chairman and CEO of the Shaw Group, turned the family's clay brick business into a conglomerate of construction materials, land development, transportation and resources. The company was founded in Hantsport by Allan's great-grandfather, Robert W. Shaw, a clay brick and tile maker nearly 140 years ago. In 1967, the company brought in outside shareholders, and it went fully public in 1977. Now, it manufactures a thousand products in eight factories. Clayton Developments, a subsidiary, built communities that house thirty thousand people in Nova Scotia. "I learned the business bending steel and pushing wheelbarrows for $1.52, an hour even though I had a bachelor of science degree and was a family member. I eventually became a foreman and then a manager and then a general manager," Shaw recalls. He's currently the chairman and CEO of the Shaw Group, chairman of Dalhousie University's board of governors and a director of the Bank of Nova Scotia. He has connected the company to Nova Scotia's network of Titans by bringing onto the board of directors John Risley, Sir Graham Day, Ken Rowe and Gordon Cummings.

BAY STREET REFUGEE JIM MOIR JUST announced his retirement as president and CEO of Maritime Medical Care, a health-services corporation that provides supplemental health insurance, runs 90 percent of Nova Scotia's ambulances and manages a $350-million government health-care budget on contract. Moir will continue to be one of the important entrepreneurial sparks in the province. Maritime Medical was founded in 1948 as a group health insurer, and got the contract to administer the provincial medicare program—the only such arrangement in Canada. Like several other such companies in North America, Maritime Medical has no equity owners; the profits are returned to the company, so that no individual profits from medical insurance.

Moir's career started with Merrill Lynch in Toronto, where he worked for twenty-one years. After Merrill Lynch's Canadian arm dissolved, he went on to create Midland Walwyn. "My wife and I took a two-year sabbatical to smell the roses, and I looked around for something that had nothing to do with Bay Street. I wanted to go back to Nova Scotia, my original home. We purchased our dream property, down in Lunenburg County on the ocean, when we were still living in Toronto," he says. "When this opportunity came up in the health-care field, we took it."

HALIFAX'S COMEBACK TITAN IS RALPH MEDJUCK, who is in the game again after a few years of "growing grey and worrying." All too accustomed to life on the business edge, Medjuck's favourite tale these days is of Jean Chrétien paying a call. "'Mr. Medjuck, this office is nicer than mine,' the Prime Minister said. And I said, 'I'll trade you,'" Medjuck recounts.

He had extensive real-estate interests and so took a beating when the bottom fell out of the market in 1981. That was about the time of his frustrating run at natural-gas drilling off Sable Island. Using the National Energy Program's Petroleum Incentive (PIP) grants, Medjuck did a joint venture with Husky Oil and Bow Valley Resources, discovering reserves that are not likely to be produced for many years. An investment in Star Choice pay television failed to fly. Now, however, several investments by his Centennial Properties and Centennial Hotels real-estate arms have paid off. He sold interests in the Halifax Citadel Hotel and the Citadel in Ottawa (formerly the Skyline) to real-estate investment trusts, but has purchased the Lord Nelson Hotel in Halifax. His Cambridge Suites business hotel in Toronto is profitable.

"It wasn't much fun for a few years," he admits. "It was total application, but the real pleasure in my life is having brought it back together," he says. He is out of the Halifax network: he has resigned from the Halifax Club— a membership he prized because he was one of the first Jewish businessmen admitted. He has plenty of detractors around town. "He is intensely disliked," says one insider, although lots of folks admire his tenacity. At the end of the day, Halifax is a body without too many mean bones.

Medjuck now divides his time between business and family. The highlight of the family year is summer at his ocean-front place in Chester, Nova Scotia, where he sails a bright red, 38-foot Chinese junk.

THE NATIONAL TITAN OF HALIFAX'S BUSINESS network—in fact, *the* international Titan—is Sir Graham Day, who in another movie was the chairman of Cadbury Schweppes, PowerGlen and British Aerospace, and the former chairman and CEO of British Shipbuilders and the Rover Group. That was London and this is Nova Scotia, where Day is counsel to the law firm Stewart McKelvey Stirling Scales, Herbert Lamb Chair in Business at Dalhousie Business School and chancellor of the university. Just for variety, he consults to the London-based international law firm Ashurst Morris Crisp and advises the Boston Consulting Group.

It is his assiduously maintained directorships, however, that best reveal the three layers—Nova Scotian, Canadian and international—of his carefully constructed business life. In the province, he sits on the boards of the Sobeys' Empire Company and Allan Shaw's Shaw Group and Moosehead Breweries (now removed to New Brunswick). National directorships, with obvious Atlantic connections, are the Bank of Nova Scotia, Extendicare, the CSL Group and (until its merger with Trans-Canada PipeLines) Nova Corp.

Day is the hometown kid (in his case, Windsor, Nova Scotia) who made good and came back. His father was an immigrant from London's East End. To pay his way through school, he sold shoes at Sears and picked up some extra money singing in the popular CBC variety show "Sing-Along Jubilee." He graduated from the faculty of law at Dalhousie and went to work for Canadian Pacific, who sent him around the world doing legal work for its steamship line. He landed up in Mersey, near Liverpool, running a bankrupt shipyard, Cammell Laird, that had contracted with CP for three vessels. He found himself, at thirty-eight, responsible for thirteen thousand employees building nuclear submarines, attack destroyers and petroleum carriers. In the late 1970s, he was back in Canada teaching at Dalhousie, working for Dome Petroleum and putting his daughters through university.

He might have stayed, except that Prime Minister Margaret Thatcher invited him back to the U.K. to denationalize the shipping industry. "She will go down in history," says Day, "as the foremost leader of a democratic country at peace. She transformed the U.K. economy." When Day had privatized shipbuilding, "she wanted me to go into British Leyland and do the same thing." His success with what became the Rover Group led to an assignment to run British Aerospace during the Gulf War. Later, Mrs. Thatcher sent him in to privatize PowerGen. He was chairman of Cadbury Schweppes when he was knighted. In 1990, Day came home to Canada and re-immersed himself in Dalhousie, Nova Scotia business and his Canadian connections.

Sir Graham Day is regarded by many as a British administrator serving time in the colonies; in fact, he is a quintessential Canadian. He has deep roots in his father's country, but his roots are here: in Windsor, at Dalhousie. He is still the kid with no advantages who sold shoes at Sears until he earned his degree, then carved out his place in the world as a protégé of no less a Canadian institution than CP.

He is regarded as a figure of the Establishment, but he is the quintessential Titan: forward-looking, connected, a man whose success lies in his network and in his ideas for changing and advancing business in the confusing world of the late twentieth century. "There are pools of capital and individuals who have perhaps disproportionate influence, but the sort of business equivalent of the Family Compact is not to be found," says Day. "Once, you could get a relatively small group of people in a room and cover the critical levels of Canadian business. You couldn't do that today. Now you work with connections, in Montreal, Toronto, Calgary, with people who are self-reliant, self-sufficient and a little self-effacing but get together when something needs to be done."

THE HALIFAX TITANS' MOST IMPORTANT network is Dalhousie University, and the university's most passionate voice is Dale Anne Godsoe, sister-in-law of Bank of Nova Scotia chairman and CEO Peter Godsoe and widow of his brother Gerry, the former head of Nova Scotia Power. Mrs. Godsoe sits on the boards of Maritime Telephone and Telegraph, Viacom Canada, investment bank Hambros Canada and the Canadian Centre of Philanthropy. Her day job is vice-president of external relations, development and alumni at Dalhousie University, making her the university's public advocate and placing her in control central of its fund-raising and at the virtual nerve centre of the province's network of Titans. The talk on the street is that she could be president of a Canadian university someday. As already mentioned, Dalhousie brings together the local Establishment.

She ticks off the names. "Our chancellor is Graham Day, the chairman is Allan C. Shaw and vice-chairman is Jim Cowan of the law firm Stewart McKelvey Stirling Scales. The treasurer is John Risley. Governors include Murray Fraser…, who is Robert Stanfield's son-in-law, Ian Dixon, the chairman of Maritime Telephone and Telegraph; Fred Fountain; Andrew Eisenhauer, chairman of ABCO, an engineering and technology firm in Lunenburg; and Ken Rowe and George McDonald of McInnes Cooper and Robertson." Donald Sobey was chair of the last financial campaign. Undergraduate drop-out John Risley, she says, has transformed fund-raising. "He isn't reluctant to ask for a million from someone who can give it." His bagmen include men like Purdy Crawford. Godsoe argues that Dalhousie University's future is the future of the economy, a role never clearer than in its research function. "Dalhousie is the biggest research engine in the province (medicine and computers are key areas). It does 80 percent of university-based research and 30 percent of all research in the province."

HENRY DEMONE, THE SON AND grandson of Lunenburg trawler captains and descendant of Huguenots who came to Nova Scotia more than two centuries ago, was appointed president and chief operating officer of National Sea Products in 1989 at the unripe age of thirty-five. Hard-bitten fishers and financiers dismissed him. He was too young and taking on an intractable problem: the restructuring of a fishery as well as a company. Had the normally savvy shareholders (including the Jodreys, the Sobeys, the Bank of Nova Scotia and the federal government) taken leave of their senses after watching the company bleed $32 million in losses as the Atlantic fishery collapsed in the 1980s?

Could this gaunt boy with his outdated slicked-back hair do anything useful? He seemed the complete antithesis of the weathered, white-bearded Captain High Liner, salty icon of the company's best-known frozen-fish brand.

Nine years later, the critics are mute. Demone has earned his place as a Titan, the prodigy Fisher Boy, a brand name he introduced for National Sea's U.S. products. He lived through some bitter years in which he held the bloody knife that closed fish plants, idled trawlers and cut the company's workforce by almost five thousand people. Demone is a fitness nut who worked the trawlers in summers as a student, developing a physical toughness well suited to the determination in his Huguenot blood. He also came from National Sea's international and export business arm, where he had seen a bigger world and the new possibilities of global trade and commerce.

He went into National Sea with a plan. The company was a free-trade test case, a resource harvester, processor and seller; it could continue to hold its dominant position in the Canadian market and still die. It had to export. With the Atlantic ground fishery in triage, it had to diversify its product line. Demone restructured the company's finances to absorb the restructuring of the Atlantic Canada fishery. He cut costs. He started to look for new products and new markets. He developed a U.S. operating arm. The telling symbol of the changes he made was the transformation of reliable old Captain High Liner, the purveyor of reliable, predictable fish sticks, into a gastronome with the introduction of a product line called Gourmet Fillets, prepared in trendy flavours such as lemon pepper.

He restored very modest profits within two years, then through the mid-1990s settled into the grinding routine of his plan: lower costs, new products, new markets, new operations outside Atlantic Canada. Through 1996 and 1997, the financial markets and the fishers of Nova Scotia began to see real results, in quarter after quarter of growing profits, buoyed up by rising commodity fish prices. In November 1997, he raised US$17 million and C$24 million in conjoint equity transactions, combined with C$35 million and US$10 million in new credit lines. This was quickly followed by the first in what is likely to be a string of acquisitions: a company called Deep Sea Clams, which gives National Sea access to the Asian market for Arctic surf clams.

National Sea Products is back from the dead. Henry Demone made it happen, and he kept the company in Nova Scotia while he was turning it into a global business.

Peter Munk: a
charmed life —and all
of his own making

Robert Friedland: the
great fortune hunter
at work, with
Norman Keevil

Scott Paterson: those red suspenders bring fame and fortune

Peter Redman/Financial Post

Terry Hui: the Canadian Chinese community's "Establishment Man"

Bill Keay/Vancouver Sun

Christopher M⊓⊓is

Laurent Beaudoin:
to dominate anything
that moves

Bryce Duffy

Gerry Schwartz with
Heather Reisman:
Toronto's favourite
power couple

Conrad Black &
Barbara Amiel:
the Canadian
Establishment's
royalty

Matthew Barrett
with wife, Ann-
Marie: the marriage
that shook the
Establishment

Issy Sharp with Rosalie: partners in life and love

Prince Al-Waleed: the Muslim who rescued the Jew

John Risley: new-style international Titan

Dan Callis

Terry Matthews, with friend: serving the high-tech gods

Fred Chartrand/Canapress

Dick Thomson hands
over T-D chairman-
ship to Charles Baillie

Michael Phelps:
dynamism on the
west coast

Yves Fortier: the legal gun everybody wants

P. Roussel/Publiphoto

Hilary Weston: the Canadian Establishment's reigning beauty, with friend

Greig Reckie/Toronto Sun

HENRY STEELE — THE LOW-PROFILE SPORT fisherman and chairman and CEO of Dartmouth-based Newfoundland Capital Corp.—spent most of his career as a professional naval officer. In his second life, as the head of a $264-million-a-year consortium with 2,400 employees, Steele has become an Atlantic Canada Titan with a long reach, including the chairmanship of Canadian Airlines International and directorships on Southam newspapers, Fishery Products International and Dundee Bank Corp.

He brings a navy-style gung-ho attitude to everything he does. Close friends are "great guys" and "great old gals." Canadian Airlines may not yet be out of the woods but its chairman knows "things are great, doing fine, we're moving along very, very good." Conrad Black, to whom he sold his Halifax *Daily News*, "is a great guy to be associated with."

Steele's post-naval flagship, Newfoundland Capital Corp., is also "doing fine, fine, fine." It has Canadian transportation operations including rail cars, ferries, trucks and seventeen freight terminals, plus coastal container ships with maritime terminals in Halifax, St. John's and Corner Brook. Its media interests incorporate forty-two newspapers (most are weeklies) and fourteen radio stations.

With connections that include Toronto mining magnate Seymour Schulich, Calgary oil veteran John Flemming and newspaper magnate Conrad Black, Steele is rapidly becoming a national power. Of all Canadian Titans, he must have the best sense of perspective: "I don't belong to clubs, I don't like them," he says. He lives modestly, with unpretentious homes in Gander, Newfoundland, and Dartmouth, to mind his business interests there. He has a cabin near Gander but "I never go there." What he does is fish—sometimes for salmon along the coast of Labrador with Newfoundland Titan and old pal Craig Dobbin. Some of his favourite hours are spent swapping yarns with Mordecai Richler at Frank Moores's Labrador fishing camp as they wait for the fish to bite.

THE NEW TITANS OF NOVA SCOTIA'S BUSINESS NETWORK include men and women attracted here by a new thrust of Atlantic Canada economic development, including offshore oil and gas and Labrador mineral exploration. There are also bluenosers, Nova Scotia born and raised, who don't want to leave the ocean and cities in which a traffic jam is a one-light wait.

Here are some of the other highlights of Halifax's Who's Who: George Caines is the CEO of Stewart McKelvey & Stirling Scales, the province's largest legal mill. Caines personally specializes in corporate work with private, small-to-medium-sized companies. Stewart McInnes, the senior partner of McInnes Cooper and Robertson and a former minister (Supply and Services, and Public Works and Housing) in the Brian Mulroney cabinets, is the leading Tory power broker in Halifax. He and his wife, Shirley, are also the city's gardeners extraordinaire. Their property boasts thousands of bulbs: tulips, daffodils and hyacinths planted in imaginative designs. It is *the* social setting in the spring, and the McInneses use it as a fund-raising venue.

Other influential lawyers include: John Young, a heavy Liberal gun at the firm of Boyne Clark; George Cooper, the managing partner of McInnes Cooper and Robertson; and Fred Fountain, who never got round to practising law but runs a fabulous Mercedes Benz dealership for all his law-school pals who joined the bar. Steve Parker, head of the CCL Group of integrated advertising, opinion research, marketing and communications operations, founded Corporate Communications Limited when he was just twenty-six. With billings of $20 million a year, he is now the biggest, best-connected PR man in town.

Hector Jacques is the principal of Dartmouth-based Jacques Whitford & Associates, an environmental, geo-technical and geo-science firm with 670 employees across Canada and also operating offices in New England. Jacques Whitford has about $70 million a year in revenues from contracts in major developments such as the Voisey's Bay nickel discovery in Labrador and joint ventures from Argentina to Russia. It conducted the geo-technical studies for the enormous Hibernia gravity-based production platform.

Bill Black is president and CEO of Maritime Life Insurance Co., a seventy-five-year-old Halifax business institution with $1 billion in annual sales and $5 billion in assets under administration. "We do only 10 percent of our business in the Maritimes; we have more sales in Alberta than in the whole of Atlantic Canada," Black says.

Paul O'Regan is the province's wealthiest car salesman, with six GM dealerships in Halifax, Dartmouth and Bridgewater, an auto leasing empire and a used-car superstore: total annual sales $100 million. Charlie Keating, the 6-foot 7-inch, 280-pound former New York opera singer, owns Access Cable and a string of taverns, strip malls and grocery stores. David Read, owner of a dozen McDonald's restaurant franchises and Maritime oil and gas investor, is a prominent Conservative bagman. Robert Dexter's Maritime Marlin Travel has forty-eight storefronts throughout Atlantic Canada and $100 million in sales. Senator Michael Kirby is Halifax's pet Upper Canadian. Nominally his Senate seat is Chester. He is rarely seen locally, but smart Nova Scotians don't waste their political assets; when they need him, Kirby is a true bluenose.

18

THE LUCKY
SPERM CLUB

"The flooding of the Nile nourishes Egypt's crops; the Red River floods
nourish Winnipeg's soul."

—*Tom Ford, journalist and former Winnipegger*

WINNIPEG SITS THERE, an inviting and forgiving place, proudly
holding down the territory between East and West, waiting its turn. This
is what Torontonians call "fly over country," demonstrating their usual
sensitivity for the hinterland that maintains them in bagels 'n' lox. They
dismiss Winnipeg as being part of that "boorhing" cultural desert between
Prego, Toronto's in-nosher, and the Polo Lounge at the Beverly Hills
Hotel in Hollywood.

It's true. The West isn't caught up in the self-indulgences that mesmerize
those in Toronto, Ottawa, Montreal or Hollywood. By opting out of the
Perrier agenda, western Canadians have retained an institutional memory
of sorts. They can actually remember back to 1988. The citizens of
Canada's heartland—the plains of Manitoba, Saskatchewan and
Alberta—understand the country's heartland. They live in the heart of it.

To appreciate Manitoba, it is essential to sympathize—or much better,
feel—the emptiness that is at the core of the western experience. Joan
Didion, the western American novelist, best evokes that mood as she
follows the trail of those "human voices that fade out, trail off, like sky
writing." Her description of the American Midwest and its drifters has
little to do with Winnipeg, but it catches the essential loneliness of being
a westerner. "People here," she writes, "sense that their hold on their
place in the larger scheme of things remains precarious at very best.

405

People get sick for love, think they want to die for love, shoot up the town for love, and then they move away, move on, forget the face. People get in their cars at night and drive across two states to get a beer, see about a loan on a pickup, keep from going crazy, because crazy people get committed, and can no longer get into their cars and drive across two states for a beer. The women do not on the whole believe that events can be influenced. A kind of desolate wind seems to blow through their lives."

Winnipeg isn't like that, not now, but the sense of exclusion from the larger scheme of things abides. It gets translated into a mood of relaxed fatalism, a feeling that whatever happens here doesn't really matter very much, because no one will stay mad or happy for very long. To the loving eyes of its burghers, the city's attractions are the best-kept secret in Canada, and they prefer it that way.

Their love of Winnipeg regularly gets tested in bitter contests with two of nature's most potent terminators: frost and flood. The former is a chronic condition, since Winnipeg only has two seasons—winter and August—but the decennial floods are no joke. The city is built on the bottom of the ancient glacial-age Lake Agassiz, which every once in a while reclaims its original shoreline and turns the Red River Valley into a nightmare. "In a strange way, Winnipeggers need the Red River floods," mused journalist and former Winnipegger Tom Ford, at the time of the last one in the spring of 1997. "The swirling waters pull together people with many different ethnic backgrounds into a common cause— the saving of their city and homes. The floods have made Winnipeg, which is a good city, into a great city. The flooding of the Nile nourishes Egypt's crops; the Red River floods nourish Winnipeg's soul."

No other municipal jurisdiction in Canada has so much history to live down. No matter how brightly its Chamber of Commerce and other Winnipeg boosters view the present and extrapolate the future, they can't match the past. Winnipeg is the Vienna of Canada, a city-state without an empire, the Chicago of the North that never made it. What might have been and should have been is best summed up in a dispatch to the *Chicago Record Herald* by William E. Curtis, its special correspondent who visited the city in September 1911: "All roads lead to Winnipeg. It is the focal point of the three transcontinental lines of Canada, and nobody, neither manufacturer, capitalist, farmer, mechanic, lawyer, doctor, merchant, priest, nor labourer, can pass from one part of Canada to another without going through Winnipeg. It is a gateway through which all the commerce of the East and the West, and the North and the South must flow. No city, in America at least, has such absolute and complete command over the wholesale trade of so vast an area. It is destined to become one of the greatest distributing commercial centres of the continent as well as a manufacturing community of great importance."

Instead, the Panama Canal was completed in 1914, and it allowed much of the traffic that had once gone overland through Winipeg's gateways to short cut its way across the continent. Curtis's glibly optimistic description was written well before the 1947 oil strike at Leduc in Alberta, which diverted the flow of money and attention in that direction. And before the arrival of American- and Toronto- or Montreal-based branch plants, and the mentality that accompanied them, took over much of the Manitoba economy. He wrote at a time when Winnipeg could boast (and did) of having more millionaires per acre than any other Canadian city. In its edition of January 29, 1910, the *Winnipeg Telegram* proudly reported there were nineteen millionaires in town, but that the list "could be extended to twenty-five without stretching the truth," and then pointedly added, "The *Telegram*'s Toronto correspondent in writing it list of the millionaires of the domain city only put the list at twenty-one." It was a time of knighthoods, when the British sovereign honoured Winnipeg's princely businessmen with British titles.

It was, above all, a grand time for the grain trade. James Richardson & Sons delivered the first lake shipment to Port Arthur in 1883, and the business spawned the Grain Exchange five years later. It was there, amid the raucous bidding of its trading pit, that new fortunes were made. The great grain families, merchant princes all, included the Bawlfs, Sellerses, Searles, Leaches, Gooderhams, Hargrafts, Gillespies, Heffelfingers, Patersons, Purveses, McCabes, Crowes, Parrishes and Heimbeckers. "In its heyday during the 1920s and 1930s, when the action in the trading pits was hectic, the Winnipeg Grain Exchange epitomized the capitalist spirit that had built the city," wrote the Exchange's historian Allan Levine. "This was free enterprise's finest hour as millions of bushels of wheat were traded daily. Then, exchange seats went for nearly $30,000. The Exchange put Winnipeg on the international map. As a leading North American commodity market, it linked the city with the other great world grain and financial centres of New York, Chicago and London."

When the Canadian Wheat Board took control of the trade away from the Winnipeg Grain Exchange in 1935 and the unbridled growth of the Wheat Pools and co-ops cut into private trading profits, the city's great families began to feel the pressure. Winnipeg's residual mystery is why, with the remarkable exception of the Richardsons, these once vibrant grain enterprises vanished in one generation, as if they had never existed. *[Bill Parish, as well as Andrew and Robert Paterson, still carry on small-scale grain trades.]* Few of the great grain merchants or their progeny had the foresight to look further west and grab a stake in the oil and gas fields of Alberta or in the rich forests of the Pacific coast. Winnipeg money just sat there and worried about itself or was dissipated by the sons and daughters of its original families. Two of the last individually owned grain companies—Federal and National—were sold in the early 1970s, and the contemporary generation of the grain clans scattered, some joining the international jet set, others retiring to Caribbean tax havens, others still just sitting out their lives, clipping bond coupons.

The most telling sign of how far agriculture has slipped as a major or even minor concern of the business and political establishments was how easily Finance Minister Paul Martin disposed of the historic Crow Rate in his 1995 budget. *[While the February 27, 1995, budget announced the end of the Crow, it didn't bite the dust until August 1, 1996, the first day of the new crop year.]* That momentous decision altered the character of the $12-billion agricultural economy of western Canada in terms of which crops could be grown on how much acreage, which farm operations would survive and which would fail. Loss of the Crow shifted Canada's grain compass to a north-south direction, creating an entirely new delivery and distribution system. "This is almost like the theft of the chalice from a church," declared Jim Fulton, a former NDP member of Parliament for Skeena, who specializes in the politics of transportation. "The history of the Crow Rate is bedrock Canada. The railways were given a king's ransom to participate in this over time, with the Crown taking on more and more of the responsibility. Destroying that arrangement was an incredibly stupid decision, because it destroyed much of the West's economy." The subsidized Crow Rate had paid 50 percent of grain-shipping costs; in the future, farmers themselves would have to pay the full transportation tariff to tidewater ports.

On budget day, February 27, 1995, perpetuity bit the dust. The transportation subsidy that had created the western agricultural economy and that Ottawa had pledged to maintain forever, vanished overnight. Next to go will be the Canadian Wheat Board, which still exercises a monopoly on wheat sales. Ottawa's regulations prohibit growers who live close to the border from trucking their produce into the United States. Manitoba farmer Bill Cairns, who tried it, was arrested and had to spend a night at the Brandon Correctional Institute before being sprung on bail. When a youthful inmate asked him what he was in for, Cairns replied "smuggling wheat," which his fellow prisoner mistakenly heard as "smuggling weed." So he asked the farmer, "How much did you sell? "He was stunned when Cairns told him that it was 50,000 bushels. "Wow," the young man exclaimed, "all I sold was six grams, and I got two years. They're going to put you away for seven hundred years, man." The annual federal payments of at least $560 million and the east-west transportation system they supported were history. But nothing much happened. If the farmers could only have manned lighthouses on the Prairies, there might have been a national outcry. As it was, Martin's revolutionary act was met mostly by silence. One dramatic indication of agriculture's decline on the Canadian plains has been the drop in the number of grain-storage elevators from a peak of 5,758 structures in 1933 to less than a thousand that remain in operation. The W.W. Ogilvie Milling Co. erected the first unit beside the CPR tracks in Gretna, Manitoba, in 1881, though no architect has ever claimed responsibility for the unique design. At the moment, there are six thousand miles of branch lines that earn 90 percent of their revenue from hauling grain, according to University of Manitoba agricultural economist Daryl Kraft. Under the current distance-based freight-rate structure, the railways earn enough to run their entire rail network. There's also a cap on how much the railways can charge. If rates become cost based and deregulated, as many as half of the branch lines will cost more to run than they earn. They will be abandoned within ten years, even though they handle half the grain shipped from the Prairies. "Of the 648 elevators on those lines, 100 may survive," Kraft said. "You're likely to see the grain companies positioning themselves already. The number of branch lines abandoned so far has been minimal. I expect to see that accelerated over the next ten years." "I am optimistic about agriculture in the West," wrote Allan Dawson, a reporter with the *Manitoba Co-operator*, a weekly farm newspaper, "but uneasy about the future of farming." Agriculture is vertically integrating with processors at one end of the food chain and giant biotech firms at the other. If the trend continues, farmers will evolve into employees and farms into corporate branch plants. It's called progress. If consumers want food from farmers instead of from factories, they'll have to pay more. I can't see that happening any time soon, especially in the West where we rely so heavily on exports."

THE MONEY TRAIN DOESN'T STOP HERE ANY MORE. The abrupt, Toronto-dictated 1980 shut-down of the *Winnipeg Tribune* (by the Southams) and the previous acquisition of the *Free Press* by absentee Toronto landlords (the Thomson organization) cruelly underlined the Winnipeg dilemma.

More recently, the inability of the local establishment to raise the necessary cash or exert the required political will to retain the Winnipeg Jets hockey team in the city defined the limits of its disposable power. It was not an inspiring performance. Hockey matters in Winnipeg, yet in 1996, the Winnipeg Jets became the Phoenix Coyotes. No one had to spell out the obvious conclusion: the capital of Manitoba no longer ranks as a major market.

"The fate of the Jets is an instance in microcosm of the plight of Winnipeg," wrote Jim Silver in *Thin Ice*, a book about the incident. "The same powerful market forces that marginalized the Jets in a rapidly changing NHL are marginalizing Winnipeg in an increasingly continentalized economy. The failure to save the Jets is a symptom of Winnipeg's economic decline and provides further evidence of the perilous state of the city's corporate business class. As Spirit [the group formed to saved the team] chairman Alan Sweatman put it, the fear of being identified with failure 'permeates the institutional people in Winnipeg.' And this defines the problem: Winnipeg is an economically marginalized and declining city with a weak, fragmented and fearful business class—a class lacking in leadership or a coherent vision."

Others saw the crisis in much more bottom-line terms. "If the Winnipeg establishment had been more powerful, the Jets would still be here," maintains John Fraser, the Air Canada chairman, who lives here and is one of the local Establishment's charter members.

Much of Winnipeg is a shell populated by ghosts. Except for the Richardson family and Izzy Asper's improbable empire, the city is no longer major head-office country. Even the few significant corporations that still maintain their homes here, such as Great-West Life and Investors Group, owe their allegiance to proprietors in the East or, in the case of Cargill and United Grain Growers, to the South. Those Manitobans who do most of the big deals conduct their business elsewhere.

Still, as in most parts of Canada, a squad of Titans has appeared to stir things up. They are determined to prevent the city from becoming a monument to the past. Instead of bothering with agriculture and natural resources, the new group is concentrating on financial services and manufacturing goods for the American market. Tractors, commuter buses, auto parts, furniture, women's and children's clothing and many other ready-made items are flowing along the NAFTA superhighway—through the Midwestern states, past Chicago, down as far as the Rio Grande. So many trucks are queuing up at the Manitoba–U.S. border that customs facilities have had to be doubled.

In today's globalized economy, Winnipeg is doing its best with what the deity has dealt it: a mid-continent location away from mountains and oceans. That means no fog and a user-friendly time zone, which in turn means an airport that is accessible twenty-four hours a day, 365 days a year, which its boosters want to convert into a major international cargo hub. (Via the polar route, it's closer to Tokyo than Los Angeles.) Backed, not surprisingly, by Hubert Kleysen, who owns a major trucking company, the idea is to land 747 cargo carriers, then truck their contents to Chicago and points south and east. It may even work.

The province's exports have increased by 100 percent since 1990, and, as Rick Neilson, operations manager for Digital Chameleon, a high-tech firm that digitizes Superman comics for its New York clients, aptly puts it, "Nobody ever expects this stuff to come out of Winnipeg."

While most members of the Winnipeg Establishment belong to the Manitoba Club and enjoy its various functions, they mix much more freely and frequently at the Royal Lake of the Woods Yacht Club, which is actually located in north-western Ontario. Most of the Old Establishment, as well as the new Titans, have cottages on Coney and Treaty islands in the immediate area of Kenora, Ontario. The Royal Lake of the Woods Yacht Club is the last place on earth where the survivors of the great Winnipeg grain-trade families still gather. As well as such distinguished out-of-town members as John Turner from Toronto, Dick Bonnycastle from Calgary and Steve Funk and Stephen Owen from Vancouver, club membership includes sixteen Richardsons, eight Parishes, seven Patersons, five Smiths, four Leaches and two Purveses. Some other prominent members include Jim Burns, Arni Thorsteinson, Melanie Sifton, Graham Lount, Bill Konantz, Paul Hill, Kevin Kavanagh and John Kilgour. "Same people, same crowd," says Alan Sweatman, one of Winnipeg's wisest lawyers, who still sails his Redwing-30 on the lake. "Had the best sail ever last summer, one of those fifteen-mile, one-tack-in-a-slot reaches with my wife and second daughter. But the Establishment has given up on sailing. Why? Because it's become too popular. It sounds sort of cynical. But there's a big population of sailboats on Lake of the Woods now—three hundred anyway, and I mean up to forty feet—and people live aboard them. So the Establishment doesn't sail any more; they go out in their runabouts, and that's all."

One exception is H. Sanford "Sandy" Riley, who has been summering at the Lake of the Woods since he was three. He owns a place on Coney Island, as do his brothers and his parents. A member of Canada's national sailing team for eight years, he skippered a Finn at the 1976 Olympics in

Kingston, Ontario. "You learn a lot about winning, a lot about losing, a lot about yourself," he says.

In his professional life, Riley heads Investors Group, the Winnipeg company that operates Canada's largest collection of mutual funds—worth $31 billion, up from $8 billion when he took over three years ago. He runs the largest financial institution outside Montreal and Toronto, but has no power of ultimate decision because Investors is a wholly owned subsidiary of Paul Desmarais's Power Corp. Sandy is the third-generation Riley to run a financial-services firm. The English-born founder of the Riley dynasty, Robert Thomas (Sandy's grandfather), came to Winnipeg in 1881 and soon established Great-West Assurance, Fire Insurance Co., Northern Trust and the Canadian Indemnity Company. Robert was a Conservative and a Methodist who, if asked, cited those allegiances as the reason for his remarkably long life (he died at ninety-five). It was his second son, Conrad, who consolidated the family business, as well as becoming an Olympic-class rower.

"One of the reasons I love Winnipeg so much is that living here, you get to know all the pieces that make up the community," Sandy Riley rhapsodizes. "You get to know there's a political piece, a business piece and there's a not-for-profit piece, a cultural piece and a labour piece—and it's when you add them up that you begin to understand how the community works." Such comments make H. Sanford Riley (as well as Hartley Richardson, Randy Moffat, Brent Trepel, Richard Andison, Bob Chipman, Ashleigh Everett and several others) charter members of Winnipeg's Lucky Sperm Club—a gene pool of Canadian Establishment offspring who remain prominent on the Manitoba business scene.

THE CONTINUING PRIMACY OF the Richardson family is one of the Winnipeg establishment's most puzzling phenomena. With the modest silence that is their trademark, the family has passed a significant milestone: their various private companies exceeded $1 billion in revenues for the first time, though they didn't tell anybody. (Revenues are at about $1.5 billion now.)

Their most dramatic recent gain was the purchase of the Montreal-based Greenshields brokerage house in 1982, and its sale in 1996. Included in the $480-million sales tag was a substantial number of Royal Bank shares, which have since doubled in value. It was a billion-dollar bonanza. "Anyone who works in this business knows that price counts," said Chuck Winograd, the brokerage firm's chairman at the time of the sale. "This was the highest price ever paid for a Canadian investment dealer." Richardson Greenshields faded into history, becoming part of the ever-expanding stable of firms that make up the RBC Dominion Securities behemoth. Integration costs exceeded $40 million.

Among the Richardsons' remaining assets are three large seed and fertilizer companies (Buckerfields, Topnotch and Green Valley); 125 orange-and-yellow grain elevators owned through Pioneer, the largest private grain company in the country; major grain terminals in Vancouver, Sorel (Quebec), Hamilton and Thunder Bay; a 302-unit time-share development in Lake Tahoe, Nevada; several major real-estate holdings in Winnipeg, including the city's largest hotel and office building at the corner of Portage and Main; and Tundra Oil and Gas, a growing energy company that operates in Manitoba and Saskatchewan.

Historically, the Richardsons have depended on their combination of Irish shrewdness and Loyalist sobriety to spin the dollars, enlarging their fortune and multiplying their influence through five generations of astute dealing, yet they seldom stray into public view. The dynasty was founded in 1857 in Kingston, Ontario, by James Richardson, who went on to make a killing during the American Civil War by providing grain to northern New York State from his wooden storehouses around the Bay of Quinte. Although he was the region's leading entrepreneur, he launched the family tradition of never appearing in print. The Richardsons broke their public silence only once: when they commissioned Professor Donald Creighton, the most distinguished historian of his day, to write the family story. They approved his manuscript, but just before publication, George Richardson changed his mind and the book was never issued. His name was mentioned in local newspapers only twice: when he attended a champagne breakfast for the local member of Parliament, Sir John A. Macdonald, Canada's founding father; and when he died.

The Richardsons' first Manitoba office was opened in 1883, before the CPR reached the city, and for most of the next century, the family dominated the western grain trade. James's sons George and Henry succeeded him, then another James Richardson ran the firm from 1918 to 1939. He expanded its Pioneer grain division into world markets, built radio stations, grubstaked prospectors, established Canada's first commercial airline (which became CP Air and is now Canadian Airlines) and helped finance early experiments with Technicolor movies. This was the company's heyday, and even though the Richardsons, among other Winnipeg grain merchants, were minting exorbitant profits, the firm's chairman, James, stoutly maintained that the commissions his firm collected from selling wheat added only a quarter of a cent to the price of a bushel.

When a Saskatchewan farm leader came to town, James drove him around Winnipeg's Wellington Crescent to show off the grain dealers' mansions. "All this!" the astounded farmer exclaimed. "All this, on a quarter of a cent?" When James died in 1939, the Richardson men went to war, and the family's leadership passed to his widow, Muriel, who successfully ran the firm for the next twenty-seven years. In 1966, she was succeeded by George Taylor Richardson, who stayed in charge for the next three decades. A moody introvert who exuded the institutional grace of a clan chief, George had a private joy that few but his best friends knew about. One of the country's most experienced helicopter pilots, he loved guiding his Bell Jet Ranger across the Canadian landscape, skimming low over the night terrain, following the moving lights along the railway tracks and highways. Like a mechanical hummingbird, he journeyed from coast to coast, symbolically dipping his skids in both the Atlantic and the Pacific. He knew most routes well enough to navigate by sight, comfortable because he could always, for example, follow the pipeline that one of his subsidiaries threw across the Rockies.

By 1993, George's eldest son, Hartley, had been appointed president of James Richardson & Sons, the family's holding company, while his nephew Jim was named a vice-president. George's other son, David, moved to Vancouver, where he became a successful financier. Hartley's aunt, Kathleen, remains Winnipeg's most generous, most discreet and most imaginative philanthropist. According to local lore, whenever a city cultural organization receives a sizeable anonymous donation, the odds are that it's from Kathleen, delivered in her own, understated way. In the late 1980s, when she bailed out the faltering Royal Winnipeg Ballet with a major cash gift, the only condition attached was that the source of the funds not be divulged.

A clause in the contract to sell Richardson Greenshields to RBC Dominion Securities provided that Hartley Richardson become a director of the Royal Bank. By joining the Royal at forty-two, and standing six feet, four inches in his bare socks, he considerably increased the board's average height and even more significantly lowered its average age. Hartley, his nieces Carolyn Richardson and Kris Benidickson, brother David and the four members of his father George's generation, make up the board of the family holding company, which meets in Winnipeg four times a year.

Hartley, who is the eighth Richardson to head the firm, is unpretentious and accessible. Instead of skipping over to the Manitoba Club at noon, he usually has a working lunch at his desk: a ham sandwich and butter tart. He backs community projects, such as the successful attempt to bring the 1999 Pan American Games to Winnipeg, is helping to restore the pavilion at Assiniboine Park and is part of the group that is building a new baseball stadium in Winnipeg. He lives in the city's West End, near the St. Charles Golf & Country Club, and loves being a Richardson. "There's still an Establishment in Winnipeg," he says, "but we share information more readily, support each other in more active ways, network and talk things out. There's still a club, but it's not nearly as hard to get through the door."

A clutch of significant and imaginative entrepreneurs is, in fact, emerging here, and their record is impressive enough that Winnipeg's prospects are climbing instead of receding. The leading players include:

David Graves built one of the most remarkable high-tech companies in the land in just three years, and then, in the fall of 1997, sold his Broadband Networks Inc. to Nortel for $593 million. The sale of his invention—a digital wireless network using high-frequency microwaves to provide cable-style entertainment—yielded him a personal profit of $157 million. He is one of the very few high-tech pioneers anywhere who managed, not only to make a technological breakthrough, but also to retain control of the process until it was pay-off time. He stayed with the company following its sale. Significantly, the company's marketing and support organizations are based in Dallas.

Gerry Gray is Winnipeg's mystery millionaire. He dropped out of school at age sixteen, built up Blackwoods Beverages, a Pepsi franchise, to cover most of western Canada and then was bought out by the parent company for an astronomical sum. He has since been giving millions away to good causes. He lives modestly in a Tuxedo condo, owns another in Palm Beach and has a fishing hut on the Lake of the Woods.

A WASP mini-Asper, Randy Moffat inherited the business from his father, Lloyd, who started out as a radio pioneer in Prince Albert, Saskatchewan, moved to Winnipeg in 1949 and launched CKY, but died at fifty-three. That left young Randy, then only twenty-one, in charge. He has since expanded into television (including ownership of the Women's Network specialty channel) and cable (as far away as Tampa and Houston), and has a board that features two of Winnipeg's most illustrious expatriots: Bob Graham and Blair MacAulay. Moffat Communications Ltd. is the only publicly traded company in Winnipeg that has a full-time psychiatrist—Dr. Bennet Wong—on its board. Moffat is one of those anchor people who is always in demand.

Deep into his eighties, Albert Cohen made dynastic history of sorts by cutting out his twenty-one heirs and leaving to professional management

the 66 percent he and his brothers own of Gendis Inc., the family holding company. Sons Danny, Mark and Charles work for the company, but
Allan MacKenzie was appointed to the presidency, a former Canadian
Air Force chief of staff who received seventeen job offers on the day he
retired from the service at forty-eight. He operates the cut-rate SAAN
mini-department stores, owns real estate valued at more than $40 million
and, until recently, was the Canadian agency for Sony products. The
Metropolitan and Greenberg chains owned by Gendis went bankrupt.
The Cohen family also owns energy assets through Chauvco Resources
and Tundra Oil and has a large investment in the Alliance pipeline.
Despite his advanced years, Cohen hasn't stopped running. He once
complained that he "never had a youth. I went straight from childhood
into business, and I missed that part of my life." Now he's missing his old
age, too.

Decidedly un-establishment, Kerry Hawkins is the Canadian ambassador of the Cargill empire, a mysterious but humongous trading and
processing conglomerate. It is not only America's largest food
company—with forty-seven businesses that employ 80,000 people in
seventy-two countries on six continents—but the largest privately held
company of any kind, with assets estimated at well over $75 billion. "If
you are what you eat," wrote Ronald Henkoff in *Fortune* magazine, "then
part of you comes from a 133-year-old company you may never have
heard of, Cargill Inc. Chances are good that it supplies the flour in your
bread, the oil in your salad dressing, the concentrate in your orange juice,
the beans in your coffee, the sweetener in your soft drink, the malt in
your beer, the peanuts in your peanut butter, the cocoa in your candy bar,
the salt on your table, and the steak on your barbecue."

Still owned and managed by descendants of its two founding clans,
the Cargills and the MacMillans, the company's executive office is
housed in a French-style château in Minnetonka, an old-money suburb
of Minneapolis. The company publishes no financial data and discloses
only a modicum of financial information to anybody—even to its
bankers.

A Cargill veteran, Hawkins arrived in Winnipeg in 1977 and five
years later was appointed the first Canadian president of the corporation.
A faithful member of the Business Council on National Issues who serves
on a dozen local boards, he has expanded Cargill's operations by building
a large meat-processing plant in High River, Alberta, a fertilizer plant in
Saskatchewan and new elevator capacity in Prince Rupert, British
Columbia. An avid sportsman, Hawkins casts for Pacific wild salmon in

the Queen Charlotte Islands, off Bob Wright's *Charlotte Princess*, and shoots ducks at Lakewood, a small jewel of a lodge in Delta, Manitoba, which is decidedly an Establishment hang-out. Members include two Rileys, George Richardson, Jim Burns (Power Corp.), Ross King (the owner of a local optical firm), Allan MacKenzie (Albert Cohen's successor), Stewart Murray (son-in-law of former member, Doug Everett), Sterling Lyon (a former Manitoba premier), Jim Connacher (Bay Street's oldest whiz-kid) and his brother-in-law Bill Bell.

Hawkins is a major player, though like Sandy Riley, he doesn't enjoy the exercise of ultimate authority. "It's really tough," he says, "to explain to somebody from Toronto that people really like to live here . . . Christ, those winters! If it's ten or twenty or thirty below, you put up with it, because then we get those wonderful summers. It's an easy place to live; everybody knows everybody else."

An immigrant from Saskatchewan, John Fraser tried for fourteen years to turn a local conglomerate he called Federal Industries Ltd. into a major corporate player, but lost out in 1992. He remains an influential presence through his many directorships—at Bank of Montreal, Centra Gas, America West Airlines, Coca-Cola, Shell Canada and the Thomson Corp.—plus various chairmanships of every Winnipeg association except Gay Pride Day. He is one of the few Canadian members of the Royal Poincianna Golf Club in Naples, Florida. He was appointed chairman of Air Canada in the summer of 1996, and that has been his main preoccupation. Partly due to Fraser's efforts, Air Canada has moved most of its accounting and call-centre functions to Winnipeg. It was Fraser who put together The Associates, an advisory body to the Faculty of Management at the University of Manitoba, which has grown into the city's key establishment network. "I'd say 90 percent of the business-establishment people who count are on that list," Fraser estimates. *[Members of The Associates are listed in Appendix 11. As well as its Winnipeg roster, the group includes Michael Phelps of Westcoast Energy in Vancouver and Paul Hill of McCallum Hill Companies in Regina.]*

Brent Trepel is a third-generation entrepreneur who took over the Ben Moss jewellery chain in 1986 and has since doubled its outlets to thirty. That growth was accomplished at the same time that Birks and Peoples were taking gas and declaring themselves bankrupt. Trepel is one of the few Winnipeg establishment types who summers at West Beach instead of Kenora. His wife, Brenlee Carrington Trepel, a former broadcaster with 1290-FOX, is the smartest and feistiest woman on the Winnipeg scene.

Ostensibly CEO of Great-West Life, Winnipeg's largest company (which administers assets of $45 billion), Ray McFeetors is really the colonial administrator of Paul Desmarais's Canadian empire. Power Corp. holds not only 86.5 percent of the shares of Great-West Life, but its officers occupy seven of the board's twenty seats. Excluding company insiders, only one Winnipegger, Randy Moffat, sits on the board of this, the city's largest company. McFeetors is totally colourless, even among insurance executives, which is saying a lot. Some speculate that whenever he gets a call from Montreal head office, McFeetors stands up and snaps to attention at his desk.

Marc Raymond, a former architect and singer in a rock band, may run the unlikeliest business to be located, against all odds, in Winnipeg. His company, West Sun Media, designs and manufactures all of the staging and lighting for the plays and musicals put on by Livent Inc., the company that until recently was artistically directed by Garth Drabinsky. That Livent would pay the considerable expenses involved in shipping sets and lights from Winnipeg to New York, Los Angeles, Chicago, Toronto and wherever the *Phantom* roams, says a lot about Raymond's talents. He recently negotiated a sizeable contract with Disney and staged rock-star Bryan Adams's world tour.

Arni Thorsteinson is ferociously busy turning Shelter Canadian Properties into a major player. He is one of the best-connected doers in Winnipeg (close to both Izzy Asper and Gerry Schwartz), a director of a dozen companies and an all-round *mensch*. A self-starter, who organized a web of paper routes and a lawn-mowing business when he was nine, Arni worked for Richardson's as a stock analyst until he became a partner of Lount, a third-generation Winnipeg builder. His most recent acquisition was the old Winnipeg *Free Press* building. Among his hobbies is taking his Heritage Soft Tail Harley motorcycle spinning towards the flat horizons of the Prairie nights. His wife Susan, who also rides Harleys, is the driving force behind the Royal Winnipeg Ballet. Proof of Arni's organizational clout and pragmatic stance is the fact that he is a bagman for *both* the Liberals and Conservatives.

A few other impressive Winnipeg entrepreneurs include Gary Coleman, a low-handicap golfer and husband of Jake Epp's daughter, Lisa. Coleman runs Big Freight, a major national transport company. Art DeFehr operates the privately owned Palliser Furniture Group, the city's—and country's—largest furniture manufacturer with 2,500 employees and 8,000 sales agents across North America and Europe. A strong Mennonite, he devotes personal prime time to helping out in Somalia and Bangladesh. Bill Fast runs the largest window manufacturer in the West and is a silent partner in at least five other Manitoba manufacturers, through the super-secret Mennonite Group. Bob Vandewater is the local head of Wood Gundy and a significant supporter of the Filmon government in more ways than one. Marty Weinberg, president of Loring Ward, a local investment-counselling firm, is a young Turk with chutzpah to burn. Marjorie Blankstein, a minor Bronfman, is a well-connected fund-raiser, particularly active in the new Jewish Community College, a joint production of Izzy Asper and Gerry Gray.

Former president of Great-West Life and chancellor of Brandon University, Kevin Kavanaugh has been a significant fund-raiser. Lloyd McInnis is chairman of Wardrop Engineering and an articulate advocate of sustainable development. Active in the venture capital field, Jim Osborne also runs large pension accounts, including the Manitoba Teachers Retirement Fund. Bill Watchhorn is president of ENSIS Corp., a private venture-capital fund linked into large money schemes. Charlie Spiring is head of Wellington West Financial, which does local initial public offerings. Terry Smith heads a national chain of automobile-body repair shops that he is moving out of the mom-and-pop mode into the twenty-first century. The heirs of Winnipeg's noblest corporate crown, Gail, David and Leonard Asper are becoming highly visible in the community, especially through their family foundation. Randy McNicol is the town's toughest litigator. Richard Andison is president of Powell Equipment, which covers the largest territory of any Caterpillar dealer on earth, since it includes the Canadian Arctic. He still races cars and was recently married, for the third time, to the beautiful Nancy Brandt. This is one clever fellow: he winters in San Diego.

Ashleigh Everett, head of Domo, a medium-size western gasoline retailer, is also president of Royal Canadian Securities and a director of Bowering Gifts, run by her sister Sarah. Everett was recently appointed a director of the Bank of Nova Scotia. Martin Freedman is the best corporate lawyer in town. Dennis Riley runs Business Furnishings Ltd. Ian Sutherland is chairman of the North West Company, which inherited the Northern Stores division of the Hudson's Bay Company and has since expanded into Alaska. Paul Albrechsten runs Paul's Hauling, but after his heart attack, he decided that he couldn't take it with him, so he purchased a $30-million Canadair Challenger and built himself a private hangar in which to house it. David Friesen, one of North America's largest and most efficient printers of books, is an acknowledged leader in colour separation printing and has thus earned a worldwide customer base. The headquarters for David Friesen's book-publishing enterprise is in Altona, 96 kilometres south of Winnipeg, in the heart of Manitoba's Mennonite Bible belt. He is a Mennonite with a modern work ethic. Bob Kozminski has many roles: automobile dealer, CBC board member and Tory bagman, topped off by chairman of the Development Council at the University of Manitoba. Mark Chipman, eldest son of Bob Chipman and now head of the Birchwood Automotive Group, is another one of the business community's young Turks. He is busy nurturing a new IHL hockey team, The Moose. Ross Robinson heads a large heating-supplies and bathroom fixtures chain. Bob Silver runs Western Glove Works in partnership with Vancouver's Ron Stern. Although the Craig family publish no financial results, they probably take in $25 million a year and enjoy increasing their clout as they expand their fledgling TV empire into Alberta and pioneer wireless technology. John Boyd Craig, a retired Scottish hockey player who bought CKX Brandon, started the dynasty. Laurie Pollard, head of his family's bank-note company, prints most of the country's—and much of the world's—lottery tickets. Richard Kroft is an active Liberal senator, a director of CN, financier and controlled-environment freak. An angel of the Royal Winnipeg Ballet, he is well connected to power. Politics is his game, but Lloyd Axworthy's two decades of high-level participation as Winnipeg's minister to Ottawa has endowed him with considerable influence in his hometown. He believes that Canada matters, and is doing something about it.

Winnipeg has long battled the economic and geographic loneliness that comes with its territory. But in the late 1990s, its very marginality has turned into an asset. Suddenly it seems that NAFTA has made the city a logical centre for export manufacturing. The fast, free flow of electronic money has made it a perfectly reasonable site from which to direct billions in mutual-fund investments. The boiling ambition of Izzy Asper has made Winnipeg as good a place as any to base a world-class television empire.

The old bank buildings along Portage Avenue stand empty and King Wheat has been dethroned, casting doubt over the region's farming culture. But as the floodwaters of one economy recede, they leave fertile ground for the next. What can seem to be a cataclysm may yet, like the rogue Red River, nourish Winnipeg's soul.

19

THE LEXUS RANGERS

"Nobody ever drowned in their own sweat."

—*Doug Mitchell, Calgary lawyer*

IT IS 7:30 P.M. ALONG CALGARY'S MACLEOD TRAIL. Southbound is a blur of Lexuses, Beemers and Range Rovers. The traffic is practically invisible by Toronto or Vancouver standards, but this is the last rush hour of the day. The bumper-to-bumper flow of Jimmys, Jeeps and Ford Explorers that ferried home the second and third tiers of Oil Patchers to the neighbourhoods sprawling across the shoulders of the city ended hours ago. They are now safely tucked into their bum-to-bum bungalow subdivisions. On the other hand, the Titan tier of Calgary—the Lexus Rangers—ears stuck to their cell phones and bulging briefcases with night reading crammed beside them, still have a ways to go. They are retracing the journey they took fouteen hours earlier, when they raced to the Petroleum Club for some crack-of-dawn networking. They will drive for another half-hour or more along darkening roads, past the flaring natural-gas wells and pump jacks, the gushing symbols of the cash flows making them richer by the hour. As they wind their way home, they feel masters of all they survey. Their turbo-sixes or eight-cylinder engines purr as they wind their way up their driveways, past their children's $250,000 riding stables, past the swimming holes lined in Italian marble and finally slide into the garages of the ranch houses that circle the city with a diamond tiara of light.

This is home. Out here on the edges of town, Calgary's newly powerful Lexus Rangers are neighbours to the Old Establishment of the 1970s oil boom. Canadian 88 Energy founder Greg Noval's 24,000-acre Bar N Ranch and Cattle Company, west of Turner Valley, with its six thousand head of Herefords, borders the 24,000-acre spread of Calgary Flames co-owner Daryl "Doc" Seaman's OH Ranch, which was established in the first tranche of federal open-range leases 120 years ago by a partnership of reformed whisky trader Lafayette French and frontiersman O. H. Smith. Seaman has two other ranches with an additional 30,000 acres. "I'm comfortable with cowboys," he says, looking like it with his bolero tie and boots too well worn to have retained any evidence of their original labels. Like a great many of Calgary's most influential new Titans, Noval and Seaman grew up as farm boys: Noval, west of Red Deer, Alberta, and Seaman in Saskatchewan.

SINCE IMPERIAL STRUCK ITS HISTORIC gusher at Leduc in 1947, oil has been Calgary's ticket to ride. The Petroleum Club crowd, who managed most of the action, have always acted more like pioneers than pilgrims, tentative in their claims to their province's future, because too often at strategic moments, outsiders moved in and imposed their own priorities.

Of all Canadians, Albertans are technologically the best equipped for the twenty-first century, but their power base is far from secure. The Great Depression of the 1930s was harder in Alberta than almost anywhere else in North America. There was no relief available because the province was insolvent throughout most of the 1930s and 1940s. When the evangelist Bill Aberhart came to power in 1935, the province was $385 million (in 1935 dollars) in the hole and had no means of repaying or servicing that colossal debt. It was Ernest Manning, Preston's father, who as minister of trade and industry, was charged with the hapless task of trying to raise money through commercial bond issues. Given that Aberhart declared the banks his mortal enemies and that the province's securities were barred from the London Stock Exchange, Manning's job was a little like trying to float bonds on Wall Street for Fidel Castro's Cuba.

Similarly, the sudden imposition of the National Energy Program on October 20, 1980 taught the Oil Patch that fear and rage does nothing to impress the truly powerful in this country. Only mathematics does that. As long as Alberta has fewer seats in the House of Commons than the Greater Toronto Area, forget fear and rage. Ralph Klein, then Calgary's mayor, waved his hands over the skyline with characteristic optimism and said, "Well, at least the sheriff can't haul away the buildings." To attempt even the smidgen of a case in support of the NEP can still get you lynched in Alberta. And yet it was the hardships engendered by that policy that forced the province to rely on the private sector and individual initiatives to save the situation. That's the spirit that still drives the Oil Patch in the 1990s. Similarly, it was the punitive effects of the NEP that caused those personal initiatives to go global, which, it turned out, was where most of the big action was. Thanks to the infrastructure put in place during the Lougheed years, partly as a reaction to the NEP, the province had the management and technical expertise to market itself internationally; thanks to the federal government's misjudged nationalistic initiative, Alberta had the motivation.

GOING GLOBAL FORCED THE OIL PATCHERS to drastically change their methods. Before they took on the world, most business deals were calculated on the backs of envelopes and sealed with a handshake. While the qualities of simplicity and trust never stopped being held in high regard, the cold shower of the NEP prompted business to make a more sophisticated approach. For one thing, Ottawa-sponsored Petro-Canada was suddenly a big player in Alberta, underwriting exploration in the Canada lands of the extreme north, which put in play a form of bureaucratic finesse not usually associated with the Oil Patch.

The feds still shake their heads in disbelief as they tell the story about the first time Prime Minister Brian Mulroney came to Calgary after Ralph Klein became premier in December 1992. After everybody had left the Westin Hotel suite where the conference was held, the new premier and his buddy Rod Love snuck back to the room and filled their pockets with flasks of federal booze, then happily rode down the Westin Hotel's elevator, their pockets clanging with their booty. The Ottawa emissaries never came close to understanding that this was not a prank, but an essential statement.

IT'S BEEN A VERY LONG TIME SINCE ALBERTA was a sweet backwater, generations since mutual trust ranked ahead of legal precedent. It's not really fair to accuse eastern Canadians of having forgotten the history of the western plains, since they never knew it in the first place. But in dealing with the Alberta of the late 1990s, they must realize at least this: Canada's West was never a child of Canada's East. While it was the movement through Quebec and Ontario that settled western Canada at the turn of the twentieth century, the actual founding of the Prairie provinces was connected with the westward expansion of the Hudson's Bay Company and later the Canadian Pacific Railway. That dynamic was independent of the historical pressures that gave birth to Quebec and Ontario as offspring of the Empire of the St. Lawrence. Such historical conjecture may seem irrelevant in the digital world of the 1990s, but Albertans want one thing understood, plain and simple: they are nobody's country cousins—now or ever.

WHAT MAKES CALGARY SO DIFFERENT is its most obvious and most celebrated feature: its past as a cow town. That endows it with an instant and unique history, plus a cultural style all its own. Guy Weadick, an American rope trickster and showman, founded the Calgary Stampede in 1912. His proposal was rejected by the annual agricultural fair organizers, but CPR livestock agent H.C. McMullen called on the Big Four of local ranching—A.E. Cross, George Lane, A.J. McLean and Senator Patrick Burns—to see if they were interested in backing Weadick. These pioneers invented business networking, Calgary style. In addition to cattle ranching, Cross established the Calgary Brewing and Malting Co., and Burns created one of Canada's great meat-packing empires. The success of their cozy business relationships inspired the formation of the city's first private club, the Ranchmen's, which they co-founded a mile from town in a wealthy suburb that included the country mansions of William Roper Hull and Sir James Lougheed. The Big Four staked Weadick's Stampede with $100,000 and, in typical Calgary style, ran it so well it turned a $120,000 profit in its first year. Just about every barber shop or western-wear store in southern Alberta sported black-and-white photos of the early Stampede, showing Weadick in sheepskin chaps and a tall, ten-gallon hat.

Billed as "The Greatest Show on Earth," the organizers added chuck-wagon races in 1923, which did more than the rodeo, agricultural fair or amusement fair to secure the Stampede's wild reputation. In this event, which resembles the chariot races of the Roman Coliseum, fatal accidents became common. It is a fitting comparison, since Calgary during the Stampede resembles nothing so much as the Roman Saturnalia. It's the Mardi Gras of Canada, even though it has tamed down quite a bit from a few decades back, when riding horses into hotel lobbies was a routine opening-day gambit. The Stampede has now been going for eighty-six years, but it still allows buttoned-downed executives, who seldom get closer to cattle than those medium-rare T-bones at Hy's, to resurrect their rural roots and wear cowboy hats, boots and jeans to work. It also allows a certain licence in their behavior towards wives, partners, girlfriends and even female co-workers, who sometimes take advantage of

Stampede week to wear push-up bras and jeans that have to be painted on. A certain degree of loutishness and drunkenness is tolerated, but that attitude is wearing thin.

For a week, people come to work in western wear, and the big companies take turns hosting pancake breakfasts in the downtown core, complete with country-and-western bands, dancing and hay bales. By noon sobriety is in short supply. The 400 Club, home of the service layer of the oil patch, was the place to be for five consecutive years. They headlined Duane Steele; once he became famous, he was expropriated by the Petroleum Club. The streets of fashionable Upper Mount Royal are redolent with the smoky tang of barbecued ribs wafting from the American Consulate during afternoon and evening lawn parties. The Hays Breakfast, named for the late mayor Senator Harry Hays, who founded it along with three neighbours in exclusive Eagle Ridge, is in its second generation under the auspices of his son, lawyer and cattleman Senator Dan Hays. Its high point is the brewing and drinking of an appalling and highly intoxicating concoction made of "secret" ingredients commemorating an old cowboy dare-to-drink beverage that was basically fermented cow piss. Brett Wilson of First Energy Capital Corporation hosts an annual adult-participation rodeo in which upwards of nine hundred clients get into the ring and simulate competitive rodeo events with cattle but no horses. Lexus Rangers sue.

Yet the tendency to go cowboy is stronger than ever. It's not so much the realities of the Old West that are on display during Stampede Days, but the rugged individualism, the value of personal freedom, instead of the actual connections to horses or ranches. These traits are treasured in direct contrast to established, anal-retentive Central Canada and its uptight ways. In a very real and not necessarily nostalgic sense, the Stampede is a celebration of horses over trains, of sex over decorum, of tents and tepees over bank towers, of socializing over workaholism, of being open and transparent over being beholden to lawyers and number crunchers. The more successful corporate Calgary becomes, the more it needs to cultivate its roots. (Yet it is not unusual to find a beautiful woman of *pure laine* French heritage, recently arrived from Montreal, as the most hootin' and hollerin' cowgirl at the Stampede.) What's it all about? Not the need to remember, certainly, but the need to perpetuate the spirit of the West, to differentiate Calgary from lesser places that know nothing about the essential connection between meeting a payroll and breaking a horse.

There are many theories why that western spirit is uniquely alive in Alberta, but the obvious one deserves the most attention: while British Columbia and the other Prairie provinces were settled primarily from

British, German, Scandinavian and northern European stock, Alberta drew more settlers from the northern United States and east-central Europe. Their notion of society was more anti-collectivist to begin with. Meanwhile, the wheat monoculture dominated Saskatchewan and Manitoba, having a profound impact on their political cultures, while Alberta was always more economically diversified with its mixed agriculture and, later, its natural gas and oil. By their natures, both cattle ranching and oil exploration are solitary endeavours.

These producers never organized a cartel, unlike the wheat and other grain growers elsewhere on the Canadian plains. Such a collectivist tradition, set against Alberta's cult of the individual, is responsible for the time-worn adage that Saskatchewan politics is about big ideas and empty wallets, while in Alberta, it's the reverse.

Looking West, the difference between British Columbia and Alberta is that the Pacific province entered Confederation as a self-governing colony while Alberta did not; Alberta was created out of the North-West Territories in 1905 by federal legislation, so that colonial London was simply replaced by colonial Ottawa. This meant that the federal government continued to own Alberta's resources and Crown lands and used them to attract immigrants of their own choosing. It wasn't until 1930 that Alberta gained the same constitutional control as other provinces over its natural riches. For this and many other good reasons, Albertans are like elephants: they tend to move in the same direction and never forget a thing. The memory of the struggle, more than a-half-century ago, to gain control over its resources lives within the province, as do other slights and injustices magnified over the years. These and so many other insults amply demonstrate that the roots (and living branches) of Alberta's discontent were and are economic in nature, though they found political expression, first with the founding of the Social Credit Party in the 1930s, and more recently in Preston Manning's Reform movement. The line between politics and business has always been blurred in Alberta.

Among other issues, the colossal unfairness that Albertans feel the federal system has burdened them with has centred on Ottawa's official bilingualism policies. Four percent of Albertans are bilingual, about typical for the West, which is one-third the national average. There is a hugely disproportionate paucity of Albertans in significant federal posts in Ottawa, where their glass ceiling is somewhere at a level between that of janitors and backbenchers' legislative assistants. The average Albertan's knowledge of Canadian history is as shoddy as that of most Canadians, but you can bet your Tony Lama boots they can recite from hard, cold memory the alternation of prime ministers from Quebec and the West since 1968, when Quebec's ascendancy first began: Pierre Trudeau (Quebec) fifteen years; Joe Clark (West) nine months; John Turner (West) three months; Brian Mulroney (Quebec) nine years; Kim Campbell (West) four months; Jean Chrétien (Quebec) five years and counting. The score for the past three decades? Quebec-based prime ministers have run the country for twenty-nine years; Western prime ministers, for sixteen months. Says it all, *n'est-ce pas?* (That means, "Don't it?")

The transition from the Ernest Manning years, through Peter Lougheed's reign, to Ralph Klein's nachtmusic has almost been a form of dialectic, as one government paved the way for its successor, from state involvement in province building, to the period of expansion and intervention through to Ralph Klein's *lasso-faire* approach.

So much of Alberta's view of the world springs from its remembered or retold sense of history, with each affront by Ottawa circled on Calgary's perpetual calendars. As Roger Gibbins and Sonia Arrison observe in *Western Visions: Perspectives on the West in Canada*, "Although western Canadians may be forward looking as individuals, the regional political culture is often framed in terms of historical discontent."

CALGARY IS STILL, SINGULARLY, A MERCANTILE city, devoted exclusively to commerce. Everything else about its identity and sense of style—its politics, child rearing, sexual congress, finding and losing faith and the books read and written—is governed by the gravitational pull exerted by creative corporate enterprise. Peculiarly, even making money is secondary. Enterprise is the game; income and net worth are no more than marks on the score card. If the city has failings, it is its lack of perspective and that its people are too damn humourless; the toughest jobs in town belong to the standup comics at Yuk Yuks Komedy Kabaret, not the $40 whores of Victoria Park.

The business ethic of the city's Lexus Rangers remains grounded in the core values of the open-range ranch. In 1997, restaurateur Stuart Allan retraced Guy Weadick's journey when he turned his restaurant into an eatery called Buzzard's Cowboy Cuisine, which preserves the flavours of open-range cooking. Around town, chefs were recreating local culinary traditions by finding suppliers of traditional, locally produced foods and resurrecting their grandmother's recipes. "We had three choices in Calgary: aboriginal, rancher or homesteader," says Allan. He chose the cuisine of the open range and dug through the Glenbow archives for letters and documents that contained information on ingredients, menus and recipes. "I didn't want cactus and batwing bar-room doors; I wanted the real thing." He serves fresh buffalo meat and holds an annual Testicle Festival, named for the ubiquitous prairie oyster enjoyed by cowboys when they branded and castrated their steers.

CALGARY IS SPECTACULARLY ENERGETIC, electric and dynamic. It encompasses a million people, if you cast a wide net to include bedroom communities that fill in-bound highways with commuters every morning before 7:00 a.m. More significantly, it has more head offices than Montreal and Vancouver combined. In recent years, its companies have been investing upwards of $30 and $40 million a year in hosts of enterprises, including new airlines, pipelines, rail lines, telecommunications networks, oil-sands plants, refineries, chemical complexes, agri-systems, computer research, coal mines, power plants, wind farms and oil wells. Those dollars are spent anywhere on the earth's continents.

Business, in this cauldron of entrepreneurship, produces an endless stream of candidates for the evergreen ranks of the new Titans. This has been a wonderful town in which to get rich. Membership in the commercial and social élite is one and the same. You are what you do. People don't want to earn a living or be merely wealthy. They aspire to discover, to innovate and, ultimately, to build enduring fiefdoms.

The prevailing liberalism of Canadian politics, as shaped by the economic ideas of John Maynard Keynes, Walter Gordon and John Kenneth Galbraith, has been rooted out here. Yet this town lives by another Keynesian dictum, the one he repeated every day before breakfast and used to make a vast personal fortune as a stock and commodity speculator: "Business life is always a bet."

The pace of history is frenetic. Had you gone away for any two decades in the past 125 years, the place you found when you returned would have been transmuted; only the reassuring hubbub of the marketplace is constant. Southern Alberta's first establishment consisted of 126 wealthy ranchers and their partners, who settled on leases covering 2.3 million acres of prime cattle and sheep pasture on the apron of the Rocky Mountains. The very rich emulated the free-wheeling lives of the cowboy drifters. Edward, Prince of Wales, who bought the EP Ranch in 1919, borrowed the virtue of prominent women and stole the virginity of their daughters during his periodic, alcohol-soaked visits. His neighbours included shadowy remittance men from London and Montreal. The sardonic newspaper editor Bob Edwards claimed that the offences for which they were banished to the wilds of Alberta would not have afforded ten minutes of gossip had they been committed in Calgary. The cowboys included notorious Americans such as Butch Cassidy and the Sundance Kid, who found that the authorities north of the forty-ninth parallel accommodated their antics. The ranchers shipped seventy thousand head of cattle to Britain annually—their principal market and the source of such nostalgic cultural trappings as polo and cricket, as well as the bizarre sight of rich men in cowboy duds riding to hounds with coyotes standing in for foxes.

Technology, railways, telegraph poles and barbed wire fences broke up the open range, and the immigration initiatives of the Canadian government brought a flood of homesteaders and squatters to tame the land for agriculture. A brutal seven-day blizzard in May 1903 and the deadly winter of 1905–06 twice destroyed most herds of cattle and sheep. By 1907, the days of the open ranges ended as suddenly as they had begun. From now on, to succeed, cattle spreads had to operate like more conventional farms. For a time, the land was still owned by wealthy aristocrats, however, the sons of too many ranch families sacrificed their lives in the First World War. As much as anything, the premature end of those bloodlines marked the end of ranching as an outpost of the British Empire.

Twenty years after Calgary was founded, it was a city of rail yards, coal money and lumber yards. Twenty years later, the province had been chartered and oil had been discovered at Turner Valley. Twenty years after that, the United Farmers of Alberta and the Progressives had come and gone, the Depression was crushing the province and Social Credit was sweeping through like a prairie fire. Twenty years beyond that, there'd been a war and a decade of modern oil development, and the Trans-Canada PipeLine was being mapped out. In another twenty years, an upstart cartel called OPEC had emerged from obscurity to transform the oil industry into a pool of apparently limitless wealth and opportunity. Twenty years on, the city has lived through and recovered from its worst economic calamity (the NEP), hosted the 1988 Winter Games of the XV Olympiad and diversified itself into a financial, transportation, research, computer and communications centre.

Now, everything is new again. The borders of the city are pushing ever outward, the economy is diversifying into new endeavours as old buildings are torn down and new ones are thrown up against the sky.

TRYING TO DIVINE CALGARY'S CHARACTER is difficult, because paradoxically, it is a place enclosed by its very openness. That's true in a physical sense because of the surrounding Rockies, but it's also true in an allegorical sense. As elsewhere in Canada, what holds Calgary together is its Establishment, which any stranger will tell you is tough and impenetrable, and any insider will admit is mushy and wide open. There is nothing much sacrosanct here, nowhere to hide from the sun or shelter from the sky.

THE PAIN OF THE NATIONAL ENERGY PROGRAM has faded. The experience survives as a residual superstition that Albertans ought never to use the term "oil boom" lest it anger the Gods of Commerce, causing them to hex the chances of future prosperity. The casualties of 1981 to 1986 still influence Alberta's attitude to the political nether world called Ottawa. "The Trudeau Liberals lived in a completely different country. There is still that feeling of separation," says John Shiry, president of Woodside Research.

Some Liberals claim that the creation of Petro-Canada was a success of the National Energy Program. Certainly, under the iron fist of Bill Hopper, it did accomplish more than it is retroactively credited for achieving. As a publicly traded company headed by Hopper's successor James Stanford, it became a mainstream player, even though the Crown still owns the control-equity block. It actually came into existence four years before the NEP and had been conceived of as early as 1972 by westerners such as Senator Jack Austin, then a deputy minister in Ottawa, and Bob Brown, Jr., of Home Oil, for very different reasons than those that prompted the NEP. Hopper worked at warp speed for thirteen years to expand and extend every aspect of Petro-Canada's integrated exploration, production, refinery and marketing. He brought good people into the business: Canadian Pacific chief David O'Brien started his petroleum career at Petro-Canada as Hopper's second in command.

Hopper was forced out in 1993 by directors appointed by Brian Mulroney, who distrusted his Liberal connections, and segued back into the world of international oil investment. He now travels the globe from Bolivia to Singapore, vacations in Florida and calls Ottawa home, but maintains a condominium in downtown Calgary.

Rich and powerful men may be immune from the concerns of ordinary mortals, but death is still the great leveller. Philanthropist Harry Cohen, who made his fortune from distributing Sony products, construction magnate Fred Mannix, Sr., Burns Food chairman Arthur Child and *Oilweek* co-founder Les Rowland were elderly men at their passing. To the delight of those who appreciated his often acerbic political instincts,

Child left $1 million to the Reform party and another $1 million to the Alliance for the Preservation of English in Canada. Both gifts created the kind of controversy that would have appealed to Child's well-developed sense of the absurd. Cohen's wife Martha carried on the family's philanthropic legacy. Mannix, never in the public eye, became even more remote as his carefully constructed succession plan moved control of the family's business interests into the hands of his sons Ron and Fred. Land developer Ralph Scurfield, of NuWest Group Ltd., died at fifty-seven in an avalanche while he was skiing in 1985. He had taken severe financial hits through his 1979 acquisition of Voyageur Petroleum and the collapse of Calgary's housing market. Toronto financier Bob Wisener brought a venture-capital pool called Merbanco Group to Calgary and expanded the local establishment's mental visions, but died before it could mature into the equity powerhouse it might have become. Drilling contractor and one-time MP Peter Bawden was wasted by cancer, his Arctic oil-exploration and development dreams unrealized. Ranger Oil founder, professional iconoclast and amateur historian Jack Pierce suffered a fatal heart attack while on a cattle drive on his foothills ranch, where he kept 1,800 head of beef and his Beaver airplane. Carl Nickle, the flamboyant, cigar-chomping radio and television broadcaster, who made his first oil investment in a lease at Leduc the day after he covered the story of Imperial Oil's historic discovery, died in 1992 after a long, degenerative illness. The petroleum industry's worst-dressed and most passionate ambassador, he was a true patriot: the discovery of the Hibernia oil field thrilled him as much as Leduc because it finally made the Oil Patch truly national. Nickle was second-generation oil money. His father Sam had been a shoemaker and Depression-era Campbell's Soup salesman who staked his last $500 on a trip to Chicago to raise equity for a touch of wildcatting in Alberta. Sam bought a return train ticket, a new suit and rented a hotel room in the city's financial district. He spent his time in the lobby and bribed a bellboy to page, "Mr. Nickle of Calgary, you have an important long distance call" several times a day. On his last day, down to nearly his last dollar, a financier finally asked the bellboy to point out the obviously very important, very busy "Mr. Nickle of Calgary." Sam got his financing and started the company that became Ashland Canada. An elegant, generous and unpretentious man, he most often ate lunch in a humble Eighth-Avenue eatery called Bennett's Family Restaurant. There he circulated among the regulars, including young author and columnist Frank Dabbs, then a cub reporter with *The Albertan*. Sam's tales of the Oil Patch prompted Dabbs to become an energy writer for *Oilweek* and *The Financial Post* as well as writing seminal books on Ralph Klein and Preston Manning.

One Oil Patch character who couldn't come to terms with life after the NEP was Charles Hetherington, the extravagantly spoken, polo-playing, wine-swilling connoisseur who ran PanArctic Oils, a company made up of pooled northern-island exploration leases and federal dollars. Hetherington believed there were immense energy reserves in the Arctic archipelago, but gas prices never supported the enormous costs of the proposed Polar Gas pipeline to central Canada. He died despondent, believing that he would be vindicated when environmentalists and governments got over their fear of transporting liquefied natural gas through Arctic waters. Hetherington was mentored by promoters Frank and George McMahon when they opened up oil and gas exploration in north-east British Columbia. Appearing before California regulators in the early 1960s to pitch a natural-gas pipeline from Fort St. John, Hetherington was asked about the BTU value of the gas from his field, which at that point existed mainly in the minds of geologists. That didn't faze Hetherington, who admitted that he didn't know the field's BTU value, but reassured the panel that "if you put a match to it, it'll burn."

"In Calgary, you are what you do, and you're weightless behind that. It doesn't matter what you were last week," says journalist Robert Mason Lee, who was raised in Alberta and educated at the London School of Economics before returning to the city to launch his career with *Alberta Report* and later as a star CTV commentator.

Former Trizec CEO Harold Milavsky regained social and business leverage and access through volunteer community activities. He is Ralph Klein's leading fund-raiser, runs a network of seventy bagmen across the province. His private company, Quantico Capital Corp., operates expanding real-estate holdings, including the former Bentall Building (later Amoco Canada's headquarters) and the IBM buildings renovated in 1997. Of his life after Trizec, he says, "I just wanted to stay involved." He is one of many such Old Establishment cowboys who won't hang up his spurs. Bob "Bossa Nova" Blair, the ex-CEO of Nova Corp. and the Oil Patch's floating conscience, has numerous investments in restaurants and is pioneering the business of turning grain chaff into newsprint. His son Jamie is a vice-president, running international investments for Husky Oil. Bob still mentors a ginger-group network of politically inclined Alberta liberals, including the former managing editor of the *Calgary Herald*, Gillian Steward, former New Democrat MLA Barry Pashuk and political consultant Don Lovett. The self-styled Western Advisory

Group meets Monday mornings at the trendy Mission-district Starbuck's coffee shop to keep a torch burning for Canadian nationalism, improved public education, gender equality and other lost causes.

Bill Richards, the former president of Dome Petroleum, has become something of a legendary character for having a stock-promotion idea every morning. His antics remind friends of the ginger group of business developers he fostered at Dome Petroleum; they produced several ideas each day before breakfast, and at least one survived by lunch. After backing an unsuccessful attempt to build an international-trade centre, Richards settled down to invest his capital in lower-profile pursuits. He emerges occasionally to sustain his reputation by promoting odd causes such as charitable work in Bangladesh.

Dome founder Smilin' Jack Gallagher exerts his ever-dignified presence around town. He fought a valiant but hopeless skirmish against the acquisition of Dome by Amoco Canada Petroleum, because he preferred Canadian ownership. After Dome collapsed, he staged a quiet, short-lived lobby to be appointed to the Senate. A brave reminder of another time, his famed smile undiminished, he is mentor to his son Tom, who has a promising energy career in oil and wind power.

The refreshing John Masters, co-founder of Canadian Hunter Exploration, has retired, and David Mitchell, founding president of Alberta Energy, concentrates on community projects. Bill Siebens, while still visible, has wound down his daytimer and now defers to other, younger men. Others accede to their children, most notably Ocelot Energy's Verne Lyons, whose son David is now at the controls. After being dumped by Sceptre Resources, Dick Gusella founded Carmanah Resources, searched for overseas opportunities and established an exploration program in Indonesia. Gus Van Wielingen picked up the pieces following the sale of Sulpetro to liquidate its bank debt, rounded up financing from several friends and founded NuGas Limited, a natural-gas junior. Bob Brawn, who ran Turbo Resources in its glory years as an aspiring independent integrated oil giant, is now chairman of the much more modest Danoil Energy.

After taking a beating on his high-profile investments in Texas, Bob Lamond, founder of Czar Petroleum, regrouped and continued to carve his zigzag course as a specialist in junior companies that combine sound geology, an uncanny sense of the equity markets and a wonderful ability to unnerve his competitors. Lamond had the backing of a large pool of German and Swiss drilling-fund investors, who lost large sums of money with him. While he is not the influence he once was, the Oil Patch has made him very wealthy. In 1997, he pocketed $8.2 million from the sale of Orbit Oil & Gas to white-knight bidder Sunoma Energy. He hands out invitations to the most coveted New Year's Eve party in town, a Scottish gala at his sprawling Mount Royal mansion, built early in the century by Eugene Coste, Alberta's first natural-gas transportation and marketing czar. Kilted in the tartan of the Black Watch, Lamond leads an annual Highland fling across the tiled floors to the skirl of the pipes and worries not one bit.

German industrial heir Baron Carlo von Maffei, the oil boom's most intriguing and secretive character, invested in Calgary land and oil and went elephant hunting in Africa with Fred Eaton, but after losing most of his investments returned to Europe. In the 1970s, he had assembled an 18,000-acre ranch on lush, prime lands north of Calgary, built one of the biggest private residences in North America and wanted to close off half a county to create a private hunting preserve with high-security fences, armed guards and patrol dogs. His compound included a baronial 23,141-square-foot home built for $2.5 million with a 2,400-square-foot master bed chamber, squash courts, a vast wine cellar, servants' quarters and eight fireplaces with heat converters. It was subsequently purchased by Grad & Walker Energy Corp.

"WE DANCE TO THE MUSIC of the market," Hans Macjie, economic analyst for the Canadian Petroleum Association, warned in the late 1970s, when reality was suspended and the fountains of Shangri-la were flowing with sweet, light crude oil. Later, in the worst of times, the dance music became a funeral dirge for the most impractical dreams of a brief age gilded with fool's gold.

The decline of the 1980s and the recovery of the 1990s were equally slow processes, the interval taking a generation with it in the same way that the First World War wiped out a generation of the old-ranch establishment. Now a new batch of young Titans has emerged, with a different view of the world and a decidedly different style of business. They stand on the shoulders of their predecessors, but they follow their own dreams, their own timetables and their own destinies.

The Oil Patch has moved from being an exploration to an asset-management culture. Big strikes are not made with drill bits, but with teams of lawyers, tax advisers and accountants. Equity still pours in, but the myth of the wildcat well only exists, if at all, on Bay Street or Howe Street. The term "gusher" now raises the heartbeats of only the bucket shop promoters and their victims. Serious money is fundamentally motivated by, well, fundamentals, not by large visions, and it waits for results on income statements, not drill-stem tests. Permanence is pre-eminent. "Sustainable growth" has become the desired description of a company's balance sheet, not a comment on its environmental record.

"When they hit the wall in 1981 and again in 1986, the major oil companies did a lot of downsizing, got rid of assets as well as people," says Harold Milavsky. "There were blocks of assets that were put out for tender, and some of the people who were downsized or took early retirement bought these packages and started smaller companies." Many were "nickel companies" that used the initial public offerings in the junior capital pool of the Alberta Stock Exchange.

With such obvious exceptions as Bre-X, Timbuktu and Cartaway, the Oil Patch adopted intense fiscal discipline that concentrated on strong balance sheets and used borrowing only as a last resort, balancing cash flowing in from crude-oil production with natural-gas sales and midstream oil- and gas-processing revenues. When oil prices were cut by one-third in 1998 and market capitalization followed the down trend, most Lexus Rangers weathered the storm with surprising resilience. Some of the brasher members of the herd even spit in the eyes of the defeatists who drew comparisons with previous slumps in the now-familiar roller-coaster ride of world commodity prices.

Rising natural-gas prices and processing fees helped, as did a well-developed mergers-and-acquisitions market that took care of the most threatened public companies. Husky Oil exorcised the demon of another oil bust when it announced a $500-million investment to expand its Lloydminster upgrader. Heavy oil is the poor cousin of the Oil Patch, and Husky's decision to place a $500-million bet on its viability was the strongest signal possible that the new Titans would not be overtaken by events.

At the same time, the genes of financial success have fathered a new breed of demanding shareholders. Fund managers and retail investors expect companies not to deviate from the quest for accelerating quarterly and annual growth percentages. Executives walk an impossible line between risk and reward. These new Titans consider the establishment oil barons of the 1970s, who were mostly geologists and field engineers, as largely responsible for their own demise because of their indifference to financial and managerial discipline.

If any good came from the depredations of the National Energy Program, it was that the biggest companies—mostly multinationals such as Imperial Oil, Mobil, Chevron and Shell—turned their attention away from the conventional oil fields of the Western Sedimentary Basin towards the deep natural-gas reserves of the Rocky Mountain foothills, the oil sands and the deposits off the Atlantic coastline. On these geo-logical and geographical frontiers, they developed new technology and found new basins that extended and expanded Canada's abundance of hydrocarbon energy. Added to the lexicon of Canada's elephantine energy deposits were new names such as Hibernia, the Jean d'Arc Basin and Sable Island on the East Coast, and in Alberta, the Caroline gas field and Cold, Primrose and Pelican lakes.

That reorientation has also shifted the balance of power in Canadian energy politics. John Shiry, presisent of Woodside Research, points out, "The majority of provincial premiers [of British Columbia, Alberta, Sas-katchewan, Manitoba, Nova Scotia and Newfoundland] now have some kind of investment in the oil- and gas-producing industry and that changes the political dynamic in a positive way." To impose the NEP today, a federal government would incur the rage of two Atlantic premiers, as well as four from the West. Shiry rightly believes it simply could not happen.

In a second seminal shift, the Canadian independents moved in to fill the vacuum after the departure of the majors. Experienced oil finders, such as Jim Gray at Canadian Hunter, Dick Gusella at Sceptre Resources, Ron Greene at Renaissance, Guy Turcotte at Chauvco and David O'Brien at PanCanadian Petroleum, set the stage for the Lexus Rangers of the late 1990s.

Lawyers, MBAS, engineers and chartered accountants, such as Murray Edwards, Brett Wilson, John Brussa, Grant Billings and Greg Noval, have built senior producing companies by buying and selling assets first, then exploring for new oil and gas resources. They also developed a taste for international exploration. After the roof fell in on Alberta, "Peace broke out all over the world, opening up new basins where new political regimes seemed stable and were prepared to encourage foreign invest-ment," said the late Bob Wisener, describing the first exodus of Canadi-ans to foreign fields. There were successes—Canadian Occidental found favorable reserves in Yemen—but there were failures, too—Gulf Canada Resources got skinned in Russia.

By the end of 1997, fifty-six Canadian companies were producing 479,570 barrels of oil a day and 597-million cubic feet of gas a day outside the country. Dozens of others were wildcatting or lobbying to per-suade unexplored countries to open their borders and create economical tax regimes for exploration.

So spectacular was the impact of science and technology on oil sands that synthetic crude oil from the upgraders became cheaper than con-ventional production from new fields. For example, by 2010, the oil sands could be producing half of the crude output of Western Canada. Three men and a woman—Eric Newall, president of Syncrude Canada; Erdal Yildirim, vice-president of Canadian Occidental Petroleum (and a long-time Syncrude co-owner); Rick George, CEO of Suncor Canada; and Dee Parkinson-Marcoux, a vice-president of Suncor—provided the leadership and inspiration that drove the oil sands into the twenty-first century. George staked his presidency on the turnaround of Canada's first oil-sands mega-projects, which had been a drag on Suncor's fortunes for a quarter century, and expanded the company to drive corporate profitability for the next fifty years. Parkinson-Marcoux, an engineer and former Ontario Hydro executive, delivered a spectacular overhaul that not only vindicated Suncor's long commitment to the oil sands, but broke the glass ceiling for women in the Oil Patch forever. Now she is heading up Ensyn Energy Corp., which is developing new upgrading technology that will give smaller companies access to the vast heavy-oil and oil-sands deposits of Alberta and Saskatchewan by reducing the capital-requirement threshold.

Yildirim led an Alberta Chamber of Resources task force on oil-sands strategies that wrote the defining study for the resource as an integrated, self-sufficient, industrial complex, producing, refining and pipelining light-crude oil, mineral co-products and commercial by-products. Newall, an effervescent executive trained by Imperial Oil, grabbed the strategy and sold it to the Alberta and federal governments, which overhauled the tax system to make it fly.

The 1980s taught brutal lessons in corporate and economic diversification. The Oil Patch mastered the art of commodity-price hedging. It split conventional oil into four distinct pursuits: crude oil, natural gas, oil sands and heavy-oil development. The cash flows and profits from these investments move in different cycles, driven by different fundamentals, so that good performance in one offsets poor performance in another. During the 1990s, Alberta diversified its economic base into finance, forestry, chemicals, transportation, communications, aviation and software. The economy of southern Alberta developed a coherent integrated market of a million-and-a-half people centred in Calgary. While it isn't able to sustain itself in the way of southern Ontario, it has sufficient critical mass and momentum so it doesn't lurch from start to stop and back again as oil markets move through their unpredictable cycles.

"The price of oil turns on a dime and Calgary with it," Bill Richards, former president of Dome Petroleum, said following the 1986 price collapse. That's no longer true. What better proof than the pinch of the 1998 oil-price collapse. After prices dropped by as much as 50 percent and settled into the $12 to $15 a barrel range, the buoyant natural-gas market levelled off and replenished some of the losses for the sector, as many oil-weighted companies added production volumes to offset the sector's sagging cash flows. Calgary no longer had a one-horse industrial base.

IN ONE AND THE SAME MOMENT, CALGARY CAN be joyfully transparent, yet opaquely inscrutable. One of its current paradoxes is that its arguably most significant Titan has no personal wealth. Premier Ralph Philip Klein—a former television news man, professional mayor of Calgary, schmoozer and drinker—is no Lexus Ranger. He has no pension beyond a few RRSPs, has only a limited income and wouldn't know a financial hedge from a flowering bush or an initial public offering from a bar tab—even if the latter sometimes reads like the former. He is seemingly indifferent to the fact that when he leaves office as premier, he'll be poor. For him, life isn't about money; it's about achievement.

One of Klein's rivals for the Conservative Party leadership in 1992 was Minister of Energy Rick Orman, who promised to balance the province's budget by returning Klein's empties. In 1997, at the behest of his doctors, Klein cut hard liquor out of his diet. A few days after he made the decision, he responded to a toast at a fund-raiser by hoisting a glass of water. "Until tonight," he quipped, "I didn't know you drank this stuff from a glass."

As the embodiment of rejuvenated conservatism, Klein has had a greater influence on Calgary or Alberta than anyone else. His great experiments in fiscal responsibility—balanced budgets and repayment of debts—and minimalist government have been paramount influences on the commercial resurgence and social renaissance that define his time in office. Alberta's advantage includes being the most favoured tax regime in Canada for corporations, having the most lenient regulatory environment, maintaining an open ear to business, and having consultative processes which have de-fanged environmental and aboriginal conflicts. Klein is synonymous with stability. He has demonstrated that entry to Calgary's New Establishment isn't about school ties or personal fortunes. Calgary's remarkable renaissance is about the convergence of merit, money and power, and Klein is the master animator of all three.

The Premier seems to have only one name—Ralph. He encourages informality; after being sworn into power in December 1992, he danced in the lobby of the legislature with Blackfoot Indian chiefs, eagle feather in hand. His religion, such as it is, is Native-American, and he keeps sweet grass in his office. Ralph is bilingual: English and barroom. He also

understands Blackfoot, which he learned as a journalist covering the
100th anniversary of the signing of Treaty Seven, and has mastered
touches of Cantonese while travelling in China to drum up contracts.

An unsophisticated man with an antenna for sniffing out the public's
moods, Ralph dropped out of high school and joined the air force, but
was asked to leave because he couldn't cut the discipline. The closest
he'd been to business was during his brief teenage tenure as teacher and
principal of a private business school in Calgary. It was a dusty, downtown, walk-up sweatshop that trained entry-level secretaries and insurance clerks the rudiments of shorthand, typing and bookkeeping. His
students remember him as a spectacular teacher, and many later volun-
teered for his political campaigns.

Despite his lack of education or training, Ralph possesses amazing
commercial instincts blended with political savvy, from which he
evolved the mix of tax, regulation and public policy that has created a
cozy atmosphere for the province's current business resurgence and social
renaissance. Under his stewardship, Alberta became the nation's lowest
taxed jurisdiction. His laid-back, rumpled style breeds confidence.

Ralph is the grandson of a five-star European chef, turned Alberta
homesteader and sawmill proprietor, and son of a construction foreman
and weekend wrestler, Phil "Killer" Klein. Ralph's first job was ringside
water boy at his dad's Saturday wrestling matches. The Klein family is
steeped to its marrow in the politics of dissent. Andrew, a Mennonite
pacifist, fled his lucrative career in the kitchens of Germany's finest
hotels to avoid the military draft. As a young man, Phil survived the
bloody Regina Riot, which ended the 1935 "On To Ottawa" trek of
unemployed western Canadians. In spite of his humble roots, Ralph's
revolution was of the blue-chip variety. He won the Alberta Progressive
Conservative leadership campaign in December 1992 with the backing
of a group of senior politicians and business people sick of big-govern-
ment, liberal-style intervention in the market. These included resort
developer Hal Walker, who was his constituency president; Jim Gray, co-
founder of Canadian Hunter; Sherrold Moore, senior vice-president of
Amoco Canada Petroleum; Patricia Black, who became his energy minister; Rob Peters, president of Peters & Co., an independent brokerage
firm that finances junior independent oil companies; former federal
energy minister Bobbie Sparrow, herself the head of a small oil-service
company; Marshal Williams, chairman of TransAlta Utilities and former
CEO; and farmer-entrepreneurs Steve West, Peter Tynchy and Walter Paszowaki. Klein's personal lawyer, Jack Donahue, was a member of the

inner circle. Brain power was provided by former University of Calgary president Norm Wagner, who was also chairman of Alberta Natural Gas Co. until 1995, and by business-management professor George Cornish. Powerful lawyers in the group were Web MacDonald, Jr., Bruce Green and Paul Rondeau.

This coalition of Klein supporters appeared to include old friends and neighbours, political hangers-on and the usual lot of land developers and oil explorers. However, as Frank Dabbs wrote in Klein's biography, *A Maverick Life*, "A layer below the surface, the Klein Gang was a cadre of the most powerful and wealthy in the Calgary establishment. Almost without exception, they were men in high positions in business, and they had a great deal to gain in personal wealth from the success of fiscal reform: reduced corporate and personal taxes, lower minimum wages than in other provinces, in fact, among Klein's first acts was to reduce the minimum wage to $5 an hour; the lowest in the country and a $2 advantage over neighbouring British Columbia."

A shrewd judge of character, Ralph reached into the heart of the Calgary Establishment to find dedicated individuals who could help save the Conservatives from certain defeat in the 1993 (post-Getty) election. He asked James Dinning, the provincial treasurer, to enlist Marshal Williams and George Cornish to lead the nine-member Financial Review Commission that made the case for the transformation of Alberta politics. Dinning, a Queen's University graduate in commerce and public administration, started in business as Dome Petroleum's manager of government affairs. He became the director of Peter Lougheed's southern Alberta premier's office and joined Don Getty's Cabinet after being elected in 1986. He remains the betting favourite to succeed Ralph; he is young, telegenic, articulate and ideologically correct. In 1997, he temporarily left politics to join TransAlta as vice-president of corporate development, but continues to exert his influence on the Conservative Party.

"Wind me up and point me in the right direction," Ralph told his inner circle of business and political operatives to whom he entrusted the task of writing the script for the 1993 election. For five years, as he balanced the budget and reoriented the function of government, he welded his gut instinct for public opinion to his gift for expressing it. In opinion polls he has consistently scored approval ratings in the 60- to 75-percent range.

Ralph works best with groups. His retinue, the most influential establishment in Alberta, is composed of three interlocking circles. The voters picked his cabinet and caucus for him. He is free to select, or banish, the members of the loosely organized Friends of Ralph Klein, or FORK, as the initiates affectionately know it. FORK began life as the Klein Gang, the group of Calgary family friends and community activists who, as volunteers for his first mayoralty campaign, propelled him into political office. FORK's gatekeeper is Ralph's closest confidant and best friend Rod Love, his chief of staff for seventeen years. Love was a *maître d'* at the Keg Restaurant who dropped out of studying political science because he wanted to do the real thing. Love made Ralph Klein's career, his career. So integral are they to each other that when Love, weary of the constant commute between his home in Calgary and Edmonton, resigned from the premier's office to establish a consulting practice and be a full-time dad, Ralph signed up as his first client. "We are like brothers," Ralph said, on the day he announced Love's putative departure from public life.

FORK operates behind a veil of camaraderie and the instinctive discretion characteristic of wealthy men of affairs. There are more leaks from the Cabinet than from its meetings, which are often held on Fridays, complete with cold beer and a table groaning with tasty snacks. The group also communicates by phone daily; Klein is addicted to wide consultations conducted with the help of his Rolodex. The dean of FORK is the peripatetic Arthur R. Smith, one of Alberta's most eccentric political characters. He comes from a remarkable political template. His father, also called Arthur, was a tough and streetwise Prairie lawyer who in 1934 successfully defended Premier John Brownlee, of the United Farmers of Alberta, in a seduction lawsuit involving an eighteen-year-old government secretary. In 1941, he won an acquittal in the murder trial of a young couple who were accused of killing their incurably ill infant son, by using euthanasia as their defence. Using a notepad fashioned from the backs of cardboard cigar boxes, he wrote the province's first Water Conservation Act, while stretched out on the living-room sofa with a bottle of Scotch handy.

His son Art was a decorated war hero, serving on secret missions in occupied France, and the *sine qua non* of his modesty is that when the war was over, he told no one of his exploits. He served as a member of Parliament in the 1950s and has raised the art of business schmoozing to such a high level that a working relationship with him is regarded as better than an MBA. When SNC-Lavalin created an international Oil Patch engineering unit and based it in Calgary, Smith was its chairman and rain maker. Now in his late seventies, Art Smith is, next to Rod Love, Ralph's closest friend and mentor.

Other prominent members of the magic circle include his personal attorney Jack Donahue and RGO office-furniture millionaire Ross

Glen, as well as Skip MacDonald, a real-estate investor. Barry Stiles, president of Highwood Communications, and lawyers Bruce Green, Brian O'Ferrall and John McCarthy have played key strategic roles in elections and in resolving some of the more serious crises of the government. Hal Walker, golf-course and resort developer, was for several years the constituency president of Ralph's riding. Scobie Hartley, the chief executive officer of Prism Petroleums, doubles as Alberta Conservative Party communications vice-president. Roddie Mah, a travel agent and restaurateur in Chinatown, has been an associate since Ralph's television-reporting days. Strikingly, there are no women on the inside team, perhaps because Colleen Klein is the shrewdest and most effective political wife in the country.

Certainly, crossing swords with Colleen can get the staunchest member of FORK expelled to the penalty box. Communications consultant and corporate director Thompson MacDonald was Ralph's boss at CFCN-TV, but earned Colleen's displeasure. MacDonald was a director of Multi-Corp., a software developer in which the Loves and Kleins made a private-placement investment. When the deal soured because of political allegations that the Kleins had benefitted unfairly from their political influence, MacDonald had to drastically lower the profile of his contact with Ralph for a time. One element in Love's desire to get out of the premier's office was the coolness between him and Colleen after the Multi-Corp. affair, the only serious blot on Ralph's personal reputation in seventeen years of public life.

Colleen and the Loves invested $10,000 each in a private placement for a junior capital-pool company called Multi-Corp., a software developer working on the complex problem of developing computer keyboards with Chinese characters. On a trade mission to Hong Kong, the premier attended a cocktail party at which Multi-Corp. met with prospective customers. This led to allegations that the Klein and Love shares represented a conflict of interest. Colleen sold her shares and gave the profits to several charities. Love took a knock for not being more astute in recognizing a possible controversy.

It was on a social issue—the legalization of video lottery terminals—that Ralph had his worst run-in with Calgary's business leaders. As a result, Jim Gray, co-founder and chairman of Canadian Hunter Exploration, was kicked out of the FORK club. A Mormon, Gray decided in 1997 to lead Citizens for Democratic Action against the province's use of addictive video lottery terminals, located in bars and hotels, as a source of $500 million a year in provincial revenue. Once a primary influence in the Klein revolution, Gray found himself out in the cold. The man who moved into FORK to take his place was Frank Sissons, a scrappy bowling-lane operator who turned his Silver Dollar Lanes into a major casino and entertainment palace for such down-market pursuits as gambling. Sissons is a great self-promoter. When masked gunmen, looking to nab his huge cash deposit, held him up in the parking lot outside his bank and shot him in the leg, Sissons called a photographer and reporter from *The Calgary Sun* into his hospital room before the anesthetic wore off. Sissons is the front man for the Calgary campaign to keep video lottery terminals in bars and casinos. One of his arguments is that without the $500-million revenues, the provincial government might have to resort to a sales tax, which is such a forbidden topic in Alberta that most citizens would prefer a return to child labour. Klein, however, has no intention of creating new taxes or even raising existing ones. So powerful is the weight of commerce against the social impulses in the new Alberta that Ed McNally, president of Big Rock Brewery, nearly lost his business on the issue of VLTs. In early 1990, when McNally expressed his personal concerns about the impacts of VLT gambling addiction, his remarks got some media coverage, but his delivery vans were turned away the next morning from scores of hotels and bars. He had to back down publicly or face a devastating boycott that could have ruined his company.

Ralph's Cabinet is the premier's day-to-day working circle. He puts so much time into chairing the executive council and studying the work of its standing committees that opposing politicians accuse him of trying to govern without the nuisance of the Legislature, a charge that rings true. In Cabinet, veterinarian Dr. Steve West, a native of London, Ontario, dominates. He has cleaned up the key economic departments of transportation, municipal affairs, economic development and energy, and also served as solicitor-general. Red Deer auctioneer and evangelical Christian lay pastor Stockwell Day is treasurer and the premier's link to the social-conservative movement in central Alberta. His son Logan is an important Reform Party aide and practical joker in Ottawa. The Days are the provincial Tories' hyperlink to the Reform Party. Stockwell Day gave a speech to Assembly '98, a meeting of the Reform party in London, Ontario, and held out the olive branch for an alliance of interests of the Conservative and Reform parties in Alberta. It was the first overt gesture made by the provincial Conservatives for the merger of the two federal parties, a move that Ralph quietly but actively supports. High school principal Halvor Jonson, dryland farmer Shirley McLellan, rancher Ty Lund and seed farmer Walter Paszowaki complete Ralph's Cabinet-level rural network. His big-city confidantes include Edmonton lawyer David Hancock, QC, and Jon Havelock, legal counsel for Amoco Canada Petroleum, who brought to Alberta for a short-lived run the minor-league Calgary '88s, Canada's first professional basketball team. Havelock was an alderman on Ralph's last city council. Calgary small businessman Murray Smith and junior oil executive Patricia Nelson round out the inner circle of the Premier's Cabinet.

The Conservative caucus provides Klein with a secondary political forum. Members of the Legislative Assembly with an inside track include caucus chairman Mark Hlady, a Calgary stockbroker who co-chaired the premier's leadership race in 1992. Another Calgary MLA, advertising and marketing executive Heather Fisher, also exercises substantial influence. One of the strongest pair of hands in caucus belongs to Whitecourt farmer and entrepreneur Peter Trynchy, who, at sixty-seven, is the elder statesman in the Legislature, though he has been involved in several ethical controversies.

"Ralph Klein is a trick of light," wrote Frank Dabbs. "At a distance he is transparent; he keeps an open book on his drinking, prankish humour, maudlin, affectionate loyalty to family, friends and colleagues. Up close the light changes. Klein is guarded, secretive, insecure, impenetrable, a complex, brilliant, brooding man." His politics are correspondingly complicated and perplexing. For all that, his relations with business are amicable because their goals are in harmony; he has made choices that have produced real tension. In politics as in marriage, prolonged tension tends to erode relationships. At the root of the difference is Ralph's strategic decision that "social issues have no traction." He airily dismissed opponents to his deep budget cuts and the arbitrary way they were made. (The government gave departments and services a reduction target to hit and an envelope of money they could keep, and ordered them to figure out the details.) Klein labelled the complainers "mush"—municipalities, universities, schools and hospitals—not good enemies to attract, but that's his way.

Ken King, publisher of the *Calgary Herald*, whose social conscience derives from his profound Catholic faith and expresses itself in the community issues he deals with in his newspaper, says, "The government has done a marvellous fiscal house-cleaning job. What they did needed to be done and set the tone for the rest of the country. But health and education remain very strong priorities and key to the quality-of-life issue, and they are going to have to deal with that. They won't be permitted to count their shekels in the back of the Legislature hallways."

Alberta Report, the prickly voice of social conservatism, accuses Klein, his Cabinet and his cronies of having a smaller, meaner view of the world than the rest of the community. Ted Byfield, the magazine's founder and columnist, coined the dismissive term "glass-tower conservatives" to make the point that too many of Klein's gang don't have any feel for the world beyond their comfortable downtown towers. The standard to which social conservatives such as Byfield hold every premier is that of the late Ernest Charles Manning.

To commemorate Alberta's 1965 Jubilee, the province built magnificent twin auditoriums for the performing arts in Calgary and Edmonton. At Manning's behest, these words from the Roman emperor Augustus are carved on their portals: "I found a city built of brick and left it built of marble." Some of Ralph Klein's strongest supporters are waiting to see the quality of material in his monuments.

THEY ARE ALSO CLOSELY OBSERVING THE SECOND new Titan of Alberta politics, Preston Manning. Like Klein, Manning's inner circle consists nearly entirely of local business leaders. One of the most fascinating is independent brewer Ed McNally, who bridges the Old Establishment and the new Titans by being in both. By virtue of his age, social circle and long-time presence in the city, McNally is establishment. His company Big Rock is also an integral part of Calgary's new culture. No self-respecting Lexus Ranger would turn down a Big Rock Traditional (the brewery's flagship ale label) or fail to have an opinion on the merits of Wart Hog or Grasshopper, two of its other leading beers. Calgarians have a fierce pride of ownership for local businesses. Big Rock's success is communally embraced and shared. People cheer for businesses, even as they battle it out in the marketplace, just as they do for sports teams. McNally has earned the right to be called by his first name in circles that he's never met. Big Rock's story bears an uncanny historical similarity to the Calgary Brewing and Malting Co., founded before the First World War by rancher A.E. Cross to slake the thirst of open-range cowboys. Its buffalo-head logo was usurped by countless amateur sports clubs.

McNally is a cerebral, courtly man and Big Rock is a gem of a brewery. With private partners, McNally has methodically built it from a single label into a full array of quality beers, pursuing licensing arrangements in international markets. His idea of a good long weekend in London is to drop into Foyle's and ask what's hot in British publishing. One of his finds was Cambridge historian Orlando Figes's monumental 912-page *A People's Tragedy*, the first chronicle of the Russian Revolution to be completed after the fall of the Soviet Union with open access to Soviet documents. For McNally, it was a quick read. He mixes with academics, journalists and authors. His friends include University of Calgary political scientist Barry Cooper and the city's freelance political mentor, Ralph Hedlin.

As the only man in Calgary who actually understands most of what his friend Preston Manning says and writes, McNally is a founding member of a second political circle of wealthy Calgarians, whose network has been almost as influential as the Friends of Ralph Klein. He was among those in the mid-1980s who staked Preston Manning's nascent political movement, which grew into the Reform Party of Canada. That second circle included independent oil executive Jack Pirie, who loaned Manning space at Sabre Petroleums for his first political storefront. The inner group cut across the Oil Patch: R. Campbell Todd ran tiny Prairie Pacific Energy, Gordon Shaw was with Imperial and Robert Muir, with Dome. Peggy Muir and Ellen Todd rivalled their husbands' influence. Doug Hilland was one of the city's largest private financiers; David Elton was executive director of the prestigious Canada West Foundation; Cliff Fryers was a corporate lawyer, and Ron Wood, news director at CKXL. Jack and Sheila Mackenzie made a fortune in oil and used it to endow the Marigold Foundation, which did a lot of research and groundwork before the party was formally created. Jim Gray encouraged Manning's political career while keeping his membership in the federal Conservative Party. In the 1988 election campaign, Manning—who is a superb horseman and an experienced cowpuncher—came up with an appropriate nickname for his core group: the Posse.

Of the founding influences in the Reform party, only a handful came from outside Calgary. In 1986, Edmonton financier and philanthropist Francis Winspear staked the $50,000 seed money for the movement. Ted Byfield, founding publisher of *Alberta Report*, played a sponsoring role in the 1987 Western Assembly on Canada's Economic and Political Future that led to the party's founding assembly. Dr. Charles Allard, the Edmonton communications czar and personal friend of the Manning family, spotted Preston's political potential when he was still a business consultant. After the 1988 federal election in which Manning ran unsuccessfully against Joe Clark in the Rocky Mountain riding of Yellowhead, the Posse persuaded him to move to Calgary.

Calgary is unique as the home field for the new conservative movement in Canada. Klein and Manning have their constituencies here. The headquarters of the Reform party shares a small office tower with the downtown extension campus of Mount Royal College on Fourth Avenue in the west end of the city centre, only a block away from the premier's southern Alberta office. Ralph's *pied-à-terre* in Calgary is in the elegantly restored McDougall Centre, which was a sandstone school built after the First World War. In a real way, the entire legislative and bureaucratic apparatus in Edmonton is a branch plant of this building, which is testament to the overarching influence of the Friends of Ralph Klein, who hold some of their rare formal gatherings here.

THE ESTABLISHMENT'S GRAND OLD MAN — DARYL "Doc" Seaman — is also the capo of its most-important network: the Saskatchewan mafia of farm and small-town boys who swarmed over the Alberta border like a marauding guerrilla force to take charge of the promised land. At seventy-six, Doc is more than a businessman; he is the Totem of the Titans, a symbol of the long siege during which Canadians wrested dominion over the Oil Patch away from the multinationals. The senior executives of companies like Imperial, Shell and Amoco may have lavishly paid jobs, but the Lexus Rangers on whom Doc Seaman is the role model are in charge of Calgary's destiny.

Doc and his two brothers, B.J. (Byron) and Don, grew up in the small farming town of Rouleau just outside Regina, where the essential talent of boyhood was hard work; the Holy Trinity was land, family and God; and the male rite of passage was hockey. Doc finished high school in time to see combat in the Second World War as a pilot with RAF squadrons in Britain and Italy. He studied engineering at the University of Saskatoon and started his oil career as a hand on a geophysical crew in the bucolic farmland south of Edmonton during the exploration frenzy immediately after the Leduc oil discovery. He used the first $2,000 he saved to start his own seismic survey operation a year after Leduc. In 1951, he arrived in Calgary and, with his brothers, created Bow Valley Industries, which in the next 30 years grew into a $2 billion geophysical and drilling contractor and independent oil- and gas-producer. Bow Valley was one of the first Canadian independents to go overseas— exploring successfully in the North Sea and Indonesia. The Company was the premier prize of the acquisition-crazy 1980s, so the Seamans brought in Charles Bronfman as an ally to help them keep control of the company. The Seamans and Bronfman held a 30-percent equity block until they sold—on their own terms—to British Gas in 1989. *[In a three-step transaction in 1989, British Gas injected $800 million, acquired the Seaman-Bronfman block and soaked up other equity to hold 51 percent of the company. British Gas's stay in Canada, which included acquiring Union Gas, was short-lived. It sold Bow*

Valley's oil and gas assets to Talisman Energy for $1.8 billion in 1994. One of Talisman's early successes was to capitalize on the natural gas discoveries that Doc had made in Indonesia.]

Doc led the group, which included his brothers and developers Norm Green and Ralph Scurfield, that purchased the Atlanta Flames National Hockey League franchise in a flip from Nelson Skalbania. The transaction established his place at the pinnacle of community leadership. He has become the oil guru and silent philanthropist, participating in major projects like the $50-million Partners for Health hospital campaign and giving $1 million to Notre Dame College, but never acknowledged for his good works.

Doc used his fortune to become a leading rancher, with the purchase and development of the historic OH Ranch. His ranching operations are a family affair: his son manages the day-to-day operations, including international breeding and consulting.

"When we sold Bow Valley Industries, I didn't want to stop working. I was close to seventy, but I'd seen so many of my friends that had busy jobs lay down the tools and boy, they went downhill in a hurry," Doc says. "You got to have a reason to get up—you can't lay in bed until 10 o'clock or so and then head down to the club for a couple of drinks and to play cards. *[I just came back from a shooting trip in Scotland. We go goose hunting in the Peace River Country. A friend of mine has a spot in central Alberta great for ducks; I get out there a couple of times each season.]* Instead of that dismal life, Doc became a launcher of new ventures and a corporate mentor. *[Encal Energy attracted support from the Fort Worth, Texas, Bass Family and had $600 million in market capitalization by the end of 1997. Abacan Resources Corp. is the notable flameout in his stable; it launched a high-profile Nigerian offshore exploration program, collapsed and has relocated to Denver. Things don't get much worse than that.]* "His thing in life is to start young up-and-comers; he seems to take delight in funding people; he's been successful at it and has his finger in eight or ten ventures," says Ron Coleman, president of Dominion Equity Resource Fund.

When he divested himself of Bow Valley Industries, Doc retained the right to the name. In June 1996, he accepted a proposal from three of his old friends, Walter DiBoni, Ken Stiles and Jim Cummings, to relaunch Bow Valley Resources as a junior TSE listing. *The Financial Post*'s Calgary bureau chief, Claudia Catteno, dubbed it "Baby Bow." Its first IPO was for $16.5 million in September 1997.

Doc Seaman is the most successful member of Calgary's Saskatchewan mafia, and its most influential elder statesman. Members include Harold Milavsky, Bud McCaig, the controversial ladies' man Ed "Winston"

Molnar, Imperial Oil's Doug Baldwin and gas marketer Scotty Cameron. The core group of Saskatchewan Oil Patchers is inextricably connected to the legendary Notre Dame College at Wilcox, Saskatchewan—and its hockey team, The Hounds.

The Seamans boys attended Notre Dame and played hockey with TransCanada PipeLines chairman Gerald Maier and his brother. Lexus Ranger lawyer Brian Felesky is a younger alumnus. Not all graduates left home: Fred Hill of the MacCallum Hill oil, broadcasting and real estate group stayed in Regina.

Notre Dame was a rugged place; the residences were dilapidated threshing crew sheds and the hockey team travelled to games in horse-drawn sleds—no matter how far the destination or how cold the night. College founder Père Athol Murray's classical curriculum, religious discipline and hockey-as-a-metaphor-for-life philosophy produced the toughest (not meanest) cadre of Oil Patch executives and entrepreneurs that Calgary will ever see.

In its way, Notre Dame was as much a distillation of the Saskatchewan ethos, style and world-view as Upper Canada College was for Toronto. Members of the Saskatchewan mafia who didn't attend it nevertheless have many of the qualities instilled there. They were the predecessors of the Murray Edwards, Brett Wilson and John Brussa network who attended the University of Saskatchewan's Saskatoon campus with similar results.

THE OLD ESTABLISHMENT CONSISTS of serious players who provide civic continuity and corporate wisdom. They were the anchors that kept the city from drifting into oblivion while the oil industry languished in the abyss between 1981 and 1986.

Alberta's reigning Titan is Ron Southern. It's not just because of his regal $4.5-billion manufacturing and utilities empire, the ATCO Group, founded fifty years ago. And it's not only because of his princely show-jumping facility on the south edge of Calgary, although Spruce Meadows is the 300-acre heartbeat of every corporate network in Calgary worth following. Spruce Meadows made Ron and his wife Margaret, the daughter of a family that homesteaded twelve miles away, household faces as the central figures of its well-televised season of international jumping competitions each summer. The premier event, the Masters, is the richest such competition in the world with a purse of more than $1.5 million; it celebrated its twenty-third season in 1998.

No, this is the first family of Alberta business because Ron Southern is Ron Southern. Everything the Southerns touch is family business.

Spruce Meadows is Marg's domain. The Southerns' primary occupation is the succession plan that will ensure their two daughters control their destinies by controlling their inheritance. The eldest, Nancy, at forty-two, is beginning to run the ATCO Group. When she takes over, likely after her father's seventieth birthday, she will be Canada's most powerful woman executive. Her thirty-six-year-old sister, Linda Southern-Heathcott, will assume responsibility for Spruce Meadows.

Ron Southern—whippet-like and intense—has spent a lifetime understanding and perfecting family-controlled enterprise. ATCO began in 1947 because his father Samuel Donald Southern, a Calgary fireman and son of a long line of English firefighters, couldn't afford to send Ron to the University of Alberta to study medicine. He invested his $2,000 army-demobilization payment in a holiday trailer rental business run out of the family's backyard. Ron chipped in the $2,000 he had saved as a teenage bus boy and night porter at the Banff Springs Hotel. The purpose of the business was to raise Ron's tuition, but the company did not have an auspicious start, losing $600 on $1,077 of revenue in 1948. Ron completed his pre-medical bachelor of science degree, but by then the business had flourished, so in 1955 he started to work full-time. ATCO's first big break came in 1959 with a contract to provide Boeing Co. with housing facilities for thousands of workers building missile silos on the empty plains of Wyoming, Utah and North and South Dakota. The company prospered when the energy industry needed similar facilities for wildcat drilling in Northern Alberta, for the oil sands, the great Quebec hydroelectric projects of the 1960s and for the development of the Prudhoe Bay oil field and the trans-Alaska pipeline to Valdez in the 1970s.

Southern celebrated his success by becoming an alcoholic. In the process, he almost lost his most precious asset, his family. In the early 1970s, a confrontation with an executive who had the courage to point out the damage booze was doing to his credibility forced Ron to face his demon. He quit drinking, then sat down with his wife and daughters and apologized. He asked them to invite him back into their lives, to spend time together so they could build a healthy relationship. "What can we do together?" he wanted to know. "If they had said, 'Let's go bowling,' we'd have built Alberta's biggest bowling alley, I guess," he told me. "But it was horses, so we started Spruce Meadows." That was his way out of the alcoholic fog.

Southern is not a rider; he once cracked a couple of vertebrae when thrown by a horse and has never forgotten the painful experience. What he did for Spruce Meadows was to convince the government of Alberta to back it and major corporations to sponsor the events and lease club boxes to entertain clients, bankers, executives and employees during competitions. Spruce Meadows quickly became the place to be seen, with all the high-tone atmosphere of the sport. It has a cachet that many preferred to the raucous Stampede or to the tensions of hockey at the Saddledome. In 1991, Spruce Meadows hosted a Canada–Netherlands trade and investment round table built on the relationships competitive horse jumping had created with the highest levels of Dutch business and its royal family. The Congress Hall was constructed and, beginning in 1994, annual round tables became the premier intellectual occasion for Alberta business and political leaders. Southern now has the reputation to draw speakers from the highest levels of government and business anywhere in the world, including men such as Hugh Fletcher, the CEO of Fletcher Challenge of New Zealand, Conrad Black of Hollinger Corp., Lo Van Wachem, chairman of Royal Dutch Shell and, in 1998, Edgar Bronfman, Jr.

Meanwhile, ATCO went through a troubling time. In 1984, it lost money for the first and only time. Southern's banks leaned on him, an experience so unpleasant that for many years the desire for a drink of Scotch and the fear that the company would run out of cash were daily torments. Southern cracked the whip and reversed the conglomerate's ill fortune, returning it to profitability in a single year, thus picking up a tough-guy reputation that belies his generous nature.

"I figured out that Hemingway's novel *The Old Man and the Sea* evocatively echoed the message that to be great you have to last," he recalls. "It's a simplistic thing, but in every walk of life we see something come up and then disappear, like a shooting star. To create something of permanence means having one's own objective, a reasoned judgment of what you can accomplish—not a fad and not an unreasonable hurdle for your people. You don't let yourself get knocked off the ball by somebody else telling you that you should achieve something else. A company can achieve unreasonable growth for two or three years, but you compound the business process and add to the complexity of the business immensely so that eventually you can't cope."

His accomplishments are deceptively easy to enumerate: the family controls 77 percent of ATCO, a $4.5-billion company that has international industrial-housing and electric power utility holdings. The company enjoyed a 45 percent total return on investment in 1997. At age 68, Southern still works a seventy-hour week, and it's hard to identify a point in his life that could be called leisure. He is always in the ring for

Spruce Meadows' competitive events. The family takes Christmas vacations in Hawaii, but has never gotten around to buying a residence there.

He enjoys an eclectic range of music and has formed a solid friendship with Luciano Pavarotti, whose second love is horses. "Pavarotti telephoned one day, unexpectedly, needless to say," Southern reminisces enthusiastically, "and said, 'I've heard of Spruce Meadows, and I'm building something similar in Medina. Would you come down to San Francisco—I'm performing at the Cow Palace—to look at the plans?'" Ron and Marg Southern met the opera superstar in his hotel at one-thirty in the afternoon, expecting to be about an hour. Pavarotti spread out his plans and they worked until about nine in the evening. Since then, they've travelled to several cities to meet the singer, hear him perform and have become friends.

Ron Southern's preoccupation is the future of the firm. "Most world-class corporations started as family companies, but many don't survive," he points out. "In our particular situation, Nancy and Linda have been children of commerce; they've been involved in this business from the time they were born. They know more people in the company than I do. They've been involved in all the audit committees, all the workings of the company and are wise enough to know that they must have professional managers. They have already put in place how the next generation after them will run with the company."

Ron Southern does what he does because he can. His wealth allows him to indulge in the luxury of staying at the office until midnight. Calgary is a meritocracy and he has the merit to be what he is and to keep doing it as long as he wants. "I don't think it's in my shareholders' interest for me to be here when I'm eighty-two," he muses. That doesn't necessarily mean he'll be shuffling around the house in his slippers, either.

PETER LOUGHEED'S AS YET UNFINISHED CAREER has intersected with every significant aspect of Alberta's mercantile and political life since he came home from the Harvard School of Business Administration in the autumn of 1954 and went to work in the blue-chip law firm of Fenerty, Fenerty McGillivray and Robertson. As a premier during the critical years in which the province won its spurs as a centre of power, he was engaged with every important aspect of Canadian nation making. Ralph Klein may be the most significant Albertan in the province's commercial life; Lougheed remains its most influential national icon.

As a lawyer and business executive with the Mannix family's Loram Group, which he joined in 1955, Lougheed was the quintessential young professional of the 1960s—confident, competent, yet feeling stifled by Alberta's caution and the insularity of its close-knit towns. As its political leader, he was the province's most important catalyst for the defining changes of the 1970s and 1980s. He gave voice to the energy and ambition of his time and demonstrated that sophistication and urbanity were acceptable character traits. His creative focus and indefatigable spirit became the hallmarks of Calgary's metamorphosis into a worldly urban community. His optimism and courage kept a wounded community from dying in the dark years between 1981 and 1986.

Lougheed has accomplished more in the last fourteen years, since relinquishing political power, than most businessmen achieve in a lifetime—making him the poster boy for Canadians of late middle age facing a career change. No contemporary premier has led a more successful or more influential post-political life. He has been a superstar director, sitting on eighteen major corporate and advisory boards. He is an energy and international trade strategist for a long list of corporate clients and rain maker for Bennett Jones, the law firm founded by Richard Bennett, the bachelor lawyer who made his fortune in Calgary and went on to become prime minister. "I don't really do any more legal work," Lougheed says, describing himself as a negotiator and marketer. Most recently he was appointed chancellor of Queen's University, but his real title ought to be "National Treasure."

A restless overachiever, he is so busy that his secretary Pat Welsh set up three-ring binders for his four children—Stephen, Joe, Pam and Andrea—detailing his schedule three years out, and she regularly sends them pages with updates and changes. After triple-bypass surgery in 1995, he moderated his pace only a little. He is a child of the Depression, whose family lost the magnificent sandstone home Beaulieu House, built by his grandfather, Calgary founding father Sir James Lougheed. He has always been sensitive about living up to the Lougheed name, established by Sir James, a lawyer and businessman who arrived in Calgary on a railway-construction handcart in 1883 and stayed to prosper as a lawyer and investor, a founder of the city's social and political life.

Lougheed's natural toughness shone through on the football field, where he successfully played in the defensive backfield for the junior Tornadoes in Calgary, for the University of Alberta Golden Bears and for the Edmonton Eskimos. He demonstrated his tenacity on campus while courting his future wife, Jeanne, the most forebearing partner in the Calgary establishment and an influential community and business director in her own right. Lougheed is relentless, systematic and thorough with his follow-ups. When he was premier, he had a direct line to the offices of all his cabinet ministers, and they quaked when the white phone rang, because the boss usually knew their job better than they did.

Lougheed's job (apart from advancing provincial rights at the federal level) was to take a basic level of modernization and attempt to turn Alberta into an economic strength. When Lougheed came to power in 1971, the province had a 1950s level of development, and it was left to the new Conservative premier to expand upon the infrastructure; namely, hospitals, schools, airports and highways. Social programmes, the most lavish in Canada, were instituted to deal with the boom-economy issues of family breakdown and affordable housing. Lougheed also attempted to diversify the economy through a significant number of ventures: directly through provincial assistance and indirectly through the risk-capital investment arm of the Heritage Trust Fund, Vencap Equities. The entire province-wide network was underwritten with oil money.

LOUGHEED'S KITCHEN CABINET CONSISTED almost entirely of political loyalists: an amalgam of his football buddies (Don Getty), law pals (Merv Leitch), Calgary oilmen (Frank Spraggins, Rod Daniel and Bill Payne) and Edmonton business movers (Peter Macdonnell, Eric Geddes, Hoady Mitchell and Stan Milner). Ralph Klein's St. Louis Pub cabinet reflected the changed nature of corporate Alberta. They are very different from Lougheed's troops. For one thing, Klein doesn't care a whit for the ethnic politics of Edmonton and has reached over the city's traditional leadership to appeal to its blue-collar sentiments. (Lougheed was always careful to cultivate a number of Paproskis and Kowalchuks in his cabinet; Klein fired them.) While Lougheed's closest advisers were active in oil and gas exploration, Klein's were just as likely to be asset managers or lawyers, executives active in the service and supply industries, as well as in the related fields of environmental clean-up.

Peter Lougheed the patriot is out of formal politics, but still in the game, goading and prodding his fellow citizens to deal creatively with Quebec and the unity portfolio; he fears we are sleepwalking through the breakup of the country. It's a tough call to pinpoint Lougheed's greatest current influence. He played a pivotal role as a director of Canadian Pacific Limited in the 1996 decision to move CP Rail's headquarters to Calgary. He had a hand in the relocation of Shell Canada and TransCanada PipeLines to the city and, again as a director, was involved in the development and expansion of Nortel's base in Alberta; it now has a work force of 3,500 in the province. As premier he brought Canadian

Pacific, now Canadian Airlines International, to Calgary and fostered the development of Nova Chemicals, which emerged as a stand-alone company from the merger of TransCanada PipeLines and Nova Corp.

In Alberta's public life, he has been a voice for moderation as the pendulum has swung to the right, pushed by Klein and Manning. His point is as penetrating as it is simple: good government comes from the middle of the ideological spectrum, and the basic philosophy of sharing must endure and inform social policy. He is constantly warning Canadians, especially the wealthy and powerful who run its economy, that the country will not remain united if its status quo is undisturbed; there is hard work ahead, requiring compromise, flexibility and the courage to try new ideas. He has become a one-man nation builder; his network commands attention and crosses regional barriers. "What is startling to me is that prominent people in one region have little or no contact with other parts of the country," Lougheed says. "There are exceptions: Nova Chemicals chairman Ted Newall and Guy Saint-Pierre, for example, working through organizations like the Business Council on National Issues. But there aren't many, and we need more."

There are revisionists, doctrinaire Kleinists, who challenge Peter Lougheed's place in Alberta's evolution. The ideology of the new conservatives is out of tune with the small-*l* liberal values that dominated Lougheed's politics. He refused to short-change people when it came to the hard choices about government's roles and responsibilities. His diversification investments and strategies produced losers—the $650-million loss on Novatel comes to mind—as well as winners, and that they seem unable to put into perspective. He is often damned for having been too liberal. Klein complains about "repairing the fiscal damage Lougheed created."

The slump in oil prices of the late 1980s had a dramatic impact on provincial finances. Almost a decade later, after the spendthrift interregnum of Don Getty, most Albertans found it unbelievable that Klein had inherited a debt-to-population ratio then ranked among the highest in Canada. Apart from his ruthless slashes of public expenditures (which included dimming of the lights that usually shine on the provincial legislature), there was a very different quality to Klein's economic interventions. For example, when Lougheed bought Pacific Western Airlines, it was a controversial move because Conservatives are not supposed to believe in state intervention in the economy. (It was Bob Blair, then the boss of Nova, who pointed out that a Prairie Conservative is a federal Liberal. Lougheed purchased the airline on the grounds it would connect places such as Fort McMurray and Grande Prairie to Edmonton, and

Lethbridge to Calgary, better than Air Canada. Besides, there seemed nothing more potent at the time than an airline to send the signal of the New West's rising strength and currency. (CP, the forerunner of Canadian Air Lines, then belonged to Canadian Pacific and was run out of Montreal and Vancouver.) Ironically, one of Klein's first moves in office was his decision to extend $50 million to Canadian Airlines as short-term financing so the company could form an alliance with American Airlines.

Still, according to the light of his day, Peter Lougheed performed brilliantly, and ranks with C.D. Howe as one of Canada's great economic-political strategists. They recognized that there is no logic in trying to run Canada as a pure free-market economy (that approach would make us another Puerto Rico, Lougheed says), and they recognized that market forces have their limits, just as they acknowledged that the powers of government have their shortcomings. They set about using the powers of the public sector to make the market-place more effective and efficient, not just as a favoured milieu for business, but as a vehicle that delivers on the aspirations of all Canadians.

Peter Lougheed transformed Alberta, and he did so with much less pain than Ralph Klein's revolution. The Lougheed reforms of Alberta politics have stood the test of time; their benefits far outweighed the costs. His permanent legacy is that he redefined the potential of lawyers, businessmen and corporate directors. Imagine the economic tiger Alberta and Canada would be if all its Titans took their jobs as seriously and did as well as Peter Lougheed. We would be unstoppable.

LIKE THE HEIR TO THE BRITISH THRONE, Ron Mannix has spent most of his adult life apprenticing to take over the family business. The difference is that, for Mannix, it's a real job, one that he assumed in 1995 when his father Fred C. Mannix died at eighty-one as the result of a long, painful heart disease. The extent and size of the Mannix holdings are tightly guarded secrets, but in 1997, the family cashed out their coal, oil, gas and pipeline interests, held by Pembina Corp. and Manalta Coal, for $2.2 billion. They continued, at that point, to own a network of twenty significant-sized private companies and another hundred or so lesser concerns involved in railway maintenance, manufacturing, real estate and investment banking. The Mannixes have one obsession: they never give interviews. Any contact usually consists of submitting written questions and receiving written answers. When I requested an interview with Ron Mannix, I received a reply from lawyer and senior vice-president W.M. Bone, setting out nine conditions under which such an interview would be granted. I accepted them all and received a letter, dated December 8, from the Loram Corporation, signed by Ron Mannix, in which he agreed to have the interview as per our arrangement. I signed that letter pointing out that this constituted a legal agreement between us. Ron Mannix then phoned to tell me to go to hell, despite the fact that I had met the conditions that he, himself, had set. He is one of the only two individuals I approached who refused any form of cooperation. His father's public-relations man David Wood had his pay docked whenever the company or family name appeared in a news story. The Mannixes even give their alms in secret. When their charitable arm went through three name changes—Mannix Foundation to Mannis Foundation to Carthy Foundation—journalists began to pry into matters. The veil of secrecy was lifted only once. In a seven-month trial in the early 1980s, they sued the Alberta government for $35.8 million after their 327-acre estate along Fish Creek Park was expropriated. The family won an additional $2.5 million, but the price was the revelation of fleeting details of their life, including a diary kept by Fred C.'s first wife, Margaret.

Ron, his brother, Fred, Jr., and sister, Maureen, are the third generation of an industrial empire founded in 1898 when their grandfather—a seventeen-year-old Stonewall, Manitoba, farm boy son of Red River homesteaders—got the contract to build a railway grade for the CPR. Frederick Stephen Mannix, his team of horses and his dirt scraper followed the railway west, along the way picking up contracts on the construction of CPR branch lines as they bristled out across the Prairies. He stopped in Calgary, where he started a construction company that built roads, irrigation ditches and hydro dams and diversified into Prairie coal-strip mines. Ambitious and usually over extended, Fred S. made and lost two fortunes and destroyed his health in the process. In 1942, during the Second World War, he sold controlling interest in his business to U.S. construction giant Morrison Knudson, on the condition that his son Fred C. be appointed president.

Fred, who had dropped out of school, bought the family's equity back from Morrison Knudson, grabbing a piece of every heavy-construction project worth looking at, from TransCanada PipeLines to the St. Lawrence Seaway. By the mid-1950s, Fred had a secret to keep: now in his early forties, he had serious heart problems and didn't want widespread knowledge of his illness to affect the business.

Ron Mannix was barely out of his teens when he was handed into the keep of his father's most loyal senior executives: Eric Connolly, Everett Costello and Stan Waters. His training reflected the possibility that his father might drop dead at any time. He was slated to head the Loram Group, an umbrella for the company's main concerns in coal, construction and railway maintenance. By the late 1970s, he had become his own prince regent, replacing in all but title, his father—who could now spend most of his time away from the office on pursuits that included marrying the delightful young Janice Florendine, forty years his junior.

Ron's brother Fred P. was given a formal education at the University of Alberta and then assumed responsibility for the company's real estate and investment banking. The two brothers have never been close, and friction between them was skilfully resolved by separating their responsibilities. Fred, Jr.'s public face became Bowfort Capital. Maureen, an avid horsewoman, was groomed to run the charitable Carthy Foundation.

When Fred Mannix died in 1995, he had sons and heirs, but no successor. His sons were unknown. Ron was forty-seven and very few people had any notion of the extent to which he'd been in charge because of his father's physical frailty. The man behind the wall is tough, explosive and abrasive, and has had two failed marriages. He may well be one of the prickliest presences in the Oil Patch, which makes him stand out in a field of well-mannered gentlemen. Loyalists on his staff spend a great deal of time apologizing for his intemperate outbursts.

School classmates nicknamed Ron "Fat Red" and Fred, who is dark, was called "Fat Black," reflecting their hair colour and body shape. When he arrived at work one morning sporting "Fat Red" vanity plates on his candy-red Corvette, the company's security chief forcibly removed them to protect Ron as much from the wrath of his privacy-loving father as from anyone who might target the young man as a kidnap victim.

Ron Mannix rejects the idea of a Canadian Establishment. "There are so many major changes and shifts in organizations across the country that anything like this has long since broken down," he says. What's taken its place is a network of networks. "There are many different groups and organizations that ebb and flow with the change of time and good or bad fortune across the country. The people who are doing things know who else is involved."

When the Mannix empire celebrated its hundredth anniversary with a lavish but laid-back soirée at Calgary's pioneer-village-style Heritage Park on June 16, 1998, Ron Mannix celebrated his own personal milestone. Through a company called Balboa Investments, the Mannixes are financing a Hyatt hotel as part of the expansion of the Calgary Convention Centre. Property they owned was needed for the project, including a protected heritage building that has been incorporated into the design, giving them influence over the most important civic project since the Olympics. Despite the assets they have spun off, they remain powerful and mysterious—reminders to one and all that being civil was not necessarily an attribute of the Oil Patch.

MIMICKING THE BOUNCY ENERGIZER RABBIT IN THE BATTERY ADS, Jim Gray keeps going and going and going and going. The chairman and co-founder of Canadian Hunter Exploration passed the chief executive officer's job over to Steve Savidant in 1998, but continued his high energy executive lifestyle. Savidant is a member of one of Calgary's most powerful invisible networks, the Domies. These expatriates of Dome Petroleum's dynamic business culture pervade the Oil Patch. They keep in touch and take care of each other when jobs are needed or charities require support. Surprisingly, few left the city after the company collapsed in 1987. Current members include TransAlta vice-president Jim Dinning, who may be the next premier of the province; George Watson, the CEO of TransCanada PipeLines; financier Mike Grandin; and former Alberta Natural Gas chairman John Beddome. Watson has his own private nest of Domies, including Steve Letwin, his chief financial officer, and Garry Mihaichuk, the CEO of TransCanada International.

Gray leads the Calgarians for Democratic Action campaign against gambling and also heads other community projects, including fund-raising for the Calgary Women's Emergency Shelter and the Calgary Academy, a school for learning-disabled kids. The discoverer of perpetual motion, Gray starts his day with a 5:30 a.m. mile-long morning swim at the YMCA (next door to his Eau Claire condominium), which he finishes in time to meet late-rising executives for a 6:30 spin on the exercise cycles.

A devout Mormon who lives by the mantra "family, work, community," Gray is home every night by six o'clock for dinner and spends the weekend with his wife Josie at their getaway properties in Canmore or Kelowna. He rarely works more than fifty-five hours a week (what a slacker!) and never takes on more than four projects at once. His high success rate with those projects and his willingness to turn them over to others once they are in progress, give the impression that he does nothing with his life except go to the office. On the contrary, he is a close friend of his three grown children, in a generation whose preferred child-care option is to exile their offspring to some fancy boarding school in Switzerland or New England.

Gray's parents, a Kirkland Lake, Ontario, mine manager and a nurse who'd studied piano in New York, sent him to Ridley College in St.

Catharines; he later studied geology at the University of British Columbia. Gray came to Calgary in the winter of 1956–57 to learn the exploration business "sitting on wells"—the jargon used to describe exhausting days and nights on the drilling-rig floor examining drill cores and pouring drilling mud through sieves to find clues of oil and gas. He worked for the oil and gas subsidiary of American uranium mining giant Kerr-McGee Corporation. He met John Masters, a mineral explorer educated at Yale and at the University of Colorado who had discovered the Ambrosia Lake deposit in New Mexico, the biggest U.S. uranium find, and was sent to Canada in 1966 as a reward.

Masters and Gray became best friends, and when Kerr-McGee refused to back the daring new natural-gas exploration concept, Masters went to the company's U.S. headquarters and resigned for both of them. They set up Canadian Hunter Exploration after their request for backing was turned down by seventeen oil and gas companies. Masters and Gray were the first to understand the pervasive nature of natural-gas deposition in the deep sedimentary basin on the eastern apron of the Rocky Mountains. It defied conventional wisdom about the origins of natural gas and the way it was trapped in the earth.

Rather than wait on the answers to those fascinating but academic scientific issues, Canadian Hunter assembled a vast spread of mineral rights in western Alberta and eastern British Columbia and started drilling. Their discovery—the Elmworth Deep Basin—made Canadian Hunter a senior independent gas producer overnight. Still, they battled for acceptance; when they presented a paper explaining what they'd found at a 1977 international geological convention in Calgary, a thousand other geologists booed and heckled them off-stage.

It was only when Imperial Oil invested $15 million in a joint venture with them, that they became icons of the exploration culture. Their personal fortunes and the legacy of Canadian Hunter became assured when Noranada acquired control in the late 1980s. The knock on Canadian Hunter is that it has never had the profit margins of less daring companies. It's true that they spent a great deal of money on very expensive gas wells, and their benchmark of success is reserves and production volume. Cash flow and profit come later. Their long-range strategy was understandable to a mining company, however, and Canadian Hunter attributes that repelled the Oil Patch attracted Noranda. Gray applied the credibility he'd earned in business to community leadership. He and Masters led the fight against the National Energy Program. So vociferous was his voice that Marc Lalonde sent him a personal photograph signed,

"You are always in my thoughts." "You can take that any way you want," Gray chuckles. He is the man aspiring Alberta politicians must see before launching their careers, a sort-of ayatollah of moderate conservatism. He mentored both Ralph Klein and Preston Manning and was consulted on Joe Clark's political comeback. His executive secretary Patty Grier became a successful city of Calgary alderman with his encouragement. One of Gray's first great community successes was to launch the Calgary Science Centre. Education is a central part of his community focus, and in typically eclectic style, he supports both public- and private-education initiatives. He doesn't think that rich Calgarians who aren't involved in the community have earned their spurs: "Calgary is fascinating. It's caught up with people; there's money; there's intrigue, there's the future; and there's history. The Stampede is the defining cultural event—it connects us to our roots and defines the difference the idea of the cowboy makes. The city's become a much more cosmopolitan place, because we do a lot of work around the world. There's a broader group of people. The old personalities include people such as Ron Southern. The newer ones have done well in business, but they haven't defined their persona in terms of their relationship to the city and to society. They are going to do that next, and they have a rich reservoir to draw from." "Murray Edwards just works," he says worriedly, to illustrate that the new generation has yet to take on its full responsibilities. Nor does he think that giving money is enough. "Community leadership also takes time and brains," he stresses. Gray has breakfast at least once a month with a newcomer under thirty, so he can stay connected with the mind set of the Oil Patch's demographic centre of gravity. "I can remember when there was me and maybe one other guy who fought to persuade people to have breakfast meetings. Now you often can't get a seat at the Petroleum Club or the Westin. It's a little intimidating when I go and only recognize a half-dozen guys, and all the rest are twenty and thirty years old.

"We live by alliances, partnerships, networks, friends," he emphasizes. "You don't do anything on your own. Things move fast here. We're in a virtual world with people and research all over the world available to us through the Internet. It isn't what you know any more, it's how you use what you know and what everybody else knows."

The Oil Patch, he says, has gone through a transition in leadership. He is from a generation that won its spurs by finding oil and gas. Now, financial whiz-kids are leaders of the pack. Gray's influence as a corporate director is national: he sits on the boards of CNR, Edper, Brascan and Nova Scotia Power, and his private investments include successful start ups such as Calgary-based BW Technologies, which has cracked the international market for hydrogen sulphide and carbon dioxide safety-detection equipment. But his identity is wrapped around his role as community leader and mentor to a new generation. He is one of a kind—the type of citizen any community would hope others will emulate.

WHEN RALPH KLEIN COINED THE CATCH PHRASE "severely normal Albertans," he must have had the McCaig family in mind. The premier was describing the kind of "good-attitude" people who backed his political revolution at the polls, created Alberta's entrepreneurial cauldron and who gave the province its human advantage in the competition for investment and growth. Bud McCaig, chairman of Trimac Corporation, quit Moose Jaw High School in 1945 to help out at his father Jack's local trucking company, where he drove his own rig and ran the dispatch operation. Jack McCaig and his pal Al Cameron called their company Maccam (an amalgam of their surnames) Transport. They acquired a Ford dealership and established a cement company. In 1960, Trimac (for Jack's three sons, Bud, Roger and Maurice) was formed, and it purchased Calgary-based H.M. Trimble to acquire trucking operations in Alberta and British Columbia. Trimac went public in 1971, and in 1976, it diversified into oilfield operations with the purchase of Kenting Limited, a drilling and earth-sciences company. Along the way, the company made a joint investment with Canadian Pacific in the transportation and waste-management concern that was spun off to become Burlington-based Laidlaw Inc. It is now the largest highway bulk (that is, wood chips, fuel, minerals and wastes) transport company in North America. At age sixty-nine, his hands so crippled with arthritis that he can't hold a pen, he still puts in the seventy-hour week of a road trucker. He is the Albertan that Ralph Klein respects the most and chairman of the boards everyone wants to join. His directors are a Who's Who of the Down To Earth Gang, including former Shell Canada CEO Jack MacLeod, former Canadian Airlines chairman Rhys Eaton, developer Hal Wyatt, and lawyer and management adviser Murray Dubinsky. Taken together, you couldn't find ounce of pretension in the whole group. But the highlight of his week is the regular Saturday-morning doughnut binge with his grandchildren, followed by skiing or a trip to the zoo or the Science Centre. Once he flew them to Toronto for a baseball game and had them home in time for bed.

The McCaigs are not the richest family in town. Their principal asset is 14 percent of Trimac, worth about $55 million. Trimac is an industrial-transportation business with a fleet of about 2,500 trucks and 5,000 trailers in bulk hauling and another fleet of 5,000 leased heavy-transportation vehicles. It has waste-management investments in Alberta-based Bovar, and in Newalta Corp. Energy. The McCaigs have other holdings, including a 15-percent stake in the Calgary Flames and an exclusive vacation home in Barbados. Their influence comes from the leverage of their community activities. Bud's forty-six-year-old son Jeff, from his first marriage, was educated at Harvard, Stanford and Osgoode Hall. He is an influential Reform party insider and organized Manning's leadership dinner in Calgary—the city's biggest annual political fund-raiser, which draws two thousand supporters. Jeff is the CEO of Trimac, while cousin Maurice runs privately owned MoMac Investments.

Bud's former sister-in-law turned second wife is Ann McCaig, the owner-operator of Presenting Italy, a super-chic women's boutique. She is also active in the community and is a director of Suncor, chancellor of the University of Calgary (on the recommendation of Peter Lougheed) and a director of the Calgary Foundation and of the Killam Foundation. The daughter of a Russian mother who fled the Revolution and worked as a housemaid in Saskatoon before obtaining a nursing degree, Ann was granted a teaching certificate from the University of Saskatchewan and married Bud's brother Roger McCaig. After Roger's early death from cancer, she struggled to raise her children alone but found a kindred spirit in Bud and subsequently they married. In these circumstances, residual tensions abound, and the two McCaig families have not survived unscathed.

Since retiring as CEO of Trimac, Bud has been chairman of the Calgary Regional Health Authority, which with an annual budget of $760 million provides public health care to 850,000 Albertans. The CRHA was formed in the reorganization of the Alberta health ministry to decentralize hospital and public health-care management. It also provided a lightning rod to take the heat for the 20 percent cuts to health spending ordered by the government. He is not a crony of the premier; his thankless task was no patronage plum. Bud McCaig continues to be an astute follower of Oil Patch affairs. He points out that "the major oil companies—Imperial, Shell, Amoco and Chevron—are a lesser part of the overall scene now than in the past. The drilling plays are much smaller, and the big companies had high overheads and big structures and needed to make very significant finds in order for them to be worthwhile. They still do the tar sands and heavy oil and those sorts of things, but there are literally dozens and dozens of small companies that have done extremely well, and they tend to grow into big companies doing it. Renaissance, for instance, is bigger than Petro-Canada."

The toughest thing to do with Bud McCaig is to get him to talk about himself. The defining events in his life are lunch at his desk (a ham sandwich) and the family sports day that's held on his lawn each June to celebrate his birthday. The McCaigs and the Southerns were the only business families in Calgary to win more than one place in a *Calgary Herald* ranking of Calgary's most influential citizens. Bud, Ann and Jeff all made the list, as did Ron, Marg and Nancy Southern. The affection lavished on him that day is the dividend paid to a man who has done everything it is possible to do in business and the community (except retire) and who has never lost track of why he was doing it. Lots of men claim to be "doing it all for the family," but that boast is the usually the last refuge of failed fathers. Bud McCaig doesn't need to boast. His family knows what they mean to him, and that's enough for him.

THERE IS A BRANCH OF THE OIL PATCH ESTABLISHMENT that lawyer and financier Ron Coleman describes as "the silent players who move about life quietly and do their thing privately." Some are men who have reached seventy and are forced off boards and out of executive offices because of their age. Others have never been in publicly traded companies. They are, however, a pervasive presence in community affairs and remain the gurus to whom the Lexus Rangers turn for serious advice. They stay out of the media, don't trumpet their charitable doings and pass anonymously along the Plus-15 pedestrian walkways that connect Calgary's downtown corporate headquarters.

Coleman, now president of the Dominion Equity Resource Fund, is one of them. He provided invaluable outside counsel to Dome Petroleum and other senior public companies for more than two decades and is credited as the real brains behind Home Oil. He has collected a handful of prize corporate directorships, including most recently Nova Corp., before its merger with TransCanada PipeLines. "Ron turns up in the most surprising places," says another member of the quiet Establishment, John Beddome, who was the former chairman of TransCanada PipeLines and Dome and was CEO and a director of Alberta Natural Gas and Polar Gas, and who is now a consultant to independent Canadian companies.

The most influential of the quiet establishment is Harley Hotchkiss, a former Tillsonburg, Ontario, farm boy. He earned a geology degree at Michigan State University on an athletic scholarship, came to Alberta in the 1951 oil boom and made his money in a series of private oil companies, most recently Spartan Resources. He holds senior corporate directorships at Alberta Energy and Nova Corp. He is also chairman of the National

Hockey League and an owner of the Calgary Flames. A quiet man who has a farm (emphatically not a ranch) and gardens around his home, Hotchkiss co-chaired the high-profile, $50-million Partners for Health campaign.

A fellow Calgary Flames partner, Al Libin, is principal owner of the Extendicare nursing-home company and a prominent Liberal. He has investments in real estate, hotels, oil and gas. The Libin family is one of the prominent Jewish clans in Calgary, and his sister Muriel Kovitz was a chancellor of the University of Calgary.

The other leading Liberals in Calgary are lawyer Jim Palmer and Senator Dan Hays. Palmer is a Maritimer whose elegant sense of style borders on being a Brahmin knock off. Burnett Duckworth Palmer ranks with Bennett Jones as one of the premier home-grown law firms in Calgary. Next to Peter Lougheed, he has the best collection of corporate directorships and sits on the boards of, to name about half: Telus, Westcoast Energy, Peters & Co., the Bank of Canada and several of financier Murray Edwards's companies (he is, in fact, Edwards's principal mentor).

Dan Hays is the only western Canadian to have inherited a Senate seat, having been appointed to the Upper Chamber by Pierre Trudeau to replace his father Harry, a former mayor of Calgary and Social Credit-turned-Liberal MP. The Hayses introduced Trudeau to cattle ranching in Alberta, and the prime minister had a registered brand for the herd, which was maintained on the Hays ranches. Dan is a lawyer in the firm of Macleod Dixon and a past president of the Liberal Party of Canada. His Stampede breakfasts are the best attended in town.

Rod McDaniel, the geologist who founded and still chairs the city's pre-eminent petroleum engineering firm, McDaniel & Associates Consultants, had ringside seats at Peter Lougheed's kitchen cabinet, and continues to influence political as well as business affairs. Donald Harvie, heir to philanthropist Eric L. Harvie's Leduc-era oil fortune, also inherited his father's unpretentious ways. Eric drove a battered Studebaker; his son avoids having his picture published even in the annual reports of companies of which he is a director. Now seventy-four, Don presides over the $73-million Devonian Foundation, which launched the Glenbow museum, gallery and archives, built dozens of parks and commissioned dozens more sculptures in public places in western Canada. His daughter Mary Ann is a governor of the Glenbow Foundation; sons Ian and Pat are ranchers. Another quiet philantropist, Lady Ouida Touche, continues to be an important arbiter of taste and style in the arts community, although she and her baronet husband Rodney are less active in business affairs and winter in the Caribbean.

Gord Stollery, son of a Bloor Street, Toronto, tailor and founder of
Morrison Petroleums, has kept a low profile since selling out to John
Hagg's Northstar Energy, but maintains an extensive network through
his investments and hosts one of the premier Stampede week breakfasts
on his Mount Royal lawn. Petro-Canada president and CEO James Stanford has almost no profile compared to that of his flamboyant predecessor, Bill Hopper. The sixty-year-old petroleum engineer has smoothed
out the company's relationship with its Oil Patch critics. *[Even Jim Gray
buys gasoline at Petro-Can's pumps.]* He has delivered earnings, but hasn't yet
been able to persuade Ottawa to relinquish its block of controlling
shares. His courtly style has extended outside the company to a number
of community enterprises, including the Calgary Philharmonic.

Geologist J.C. Anderson is Stanford's stylistic opposite: brusque, blunt
and abrupt. Anderson Exploration made him a fortune in the late 1960s
when he found the Dunvegan gas field, but like many other independent
oilmen, he lost significant net worth because of the National Energy
Program. He persisted in the business because of his aptitude as a financial manager—a surprisingly rare attribute among the geologists and
engineers who founded junior companies in the 1970s. By 1996, Anderson had grown big enough to take over Home Oil when the Reichmans
divested it in 1996. The deal made him a player; he is now worth at least
$300 million and is regarded as one of the underrated influences in the
Oil Patch. Though his company remains the most courted acquisition
target on the street, few are willing to mount a hostile bid against this
formidable strategist. Anderson has no significant role in the community,
but has launched and mentored a number of careers.

Dick "Bones" Bonnycastle was one of the great powers of the 1970s
whose influence is now quiescent but is still a private financial power
broker. *[Bonnycastle no longer hosts the most famous of the Stampede breakfasts.
"Those went on for a long time and it was time to go," he told me. "We started gettting
lots of people coming that we didn't know."]* As the chairman of Cavendish
Investing, he made a fortune in publishing through the sale of Harlequin
Enterprises to Torstar Corp. His oil company, Rupertsland Resources, was
a powerful Canadian independent of the 1970s. His stable includes the
pharmaceutical company Patheon. He is an investor in and director of
several smaller independent oil and gas companies, including Bowridge
Resources, Windstar Energy and Canadian Conquest Exploration. He
helped stake Gus Van Wielingen's comeback company, NuGas. He also
financed Moxies restaurant chain, but his only public presence is in
international horse racing.

Bonnycastle, who was raised on his aunt and uncle's ranch in Alberta, invests in race horses mainly in the U.K., where he keeps a residence near Ascot, and in the U.S. He has Winnipeg roots and an ancestor, British army officer Robert Bolton, was brutally murdered by six of Louis Riel's men at the time of the execution of the Orangeman Thomas Scott. So Bonnycastle has cause to oppose Louis Riel's posthumous elevation to the status of Father of Confederation.

The most influential quiet men are the powerful pipeline trio of Dick Haskayne, Ted Newall and Gerry Maier. Haskayne, a chartered accountant and a Depression baby of a rural Alberta butcher, has been chairman of Nova Corp, TransAlta, MacMillan Blodel and of the University of Calgary. He was president and CEO of Home Oil until its sale to Anderson Exploration, and sits on the boards of CIBC, Alberta Energy, Fording Coal and Crestar Energy.

Ted Newall, CEO of Nova until its 1998 merger with TransCanada, is a unrepentant workaholic who spent most of his career with DuPont. He was brought into Nova to clean up the chemical side of its business, and while he was at it, he took its pipeline operations to Argentina. Born in Alberta but raised in Prince Albert, Saskatchewan, he is not purebred Saskatchewan mafia, but close enough. He spends Saturday mornings in the office, and his prized piece of office art is a bronze of a businessman on the fly, given to him by his wife, entitled *Flat Out*. In his spare time, he is chairman of the University of Calgary.

Gerry Maier, who in 1990 repatriated the headquarters of Trans-Canada PipeLines to Calgary—the city of its birth—is less well known than he might be, because he spent twenty years overseas with Conoco in Indonesia and the United Kingdom. He started his career in Calgary with Haskayne at Hudson's Bay Oil and Gas and attended Notre Dame College with the Seaman brothers. A director of BCE and the Bank of Nova Scotia, Maier founded the Van Horne Institute, a transportation-studies think-tank based at the University of Calgary and funded by Calgary's emergent transportation sector, including Canadian Airlines, Canadian Pacific and major pipeline companies.

In 1998, the Nova–TransCanada PipeLines merger brought Hotchkiss, Haskayne, Newall and Maier together in what will likely be the last great transaction of their generation. It was the biggest energy deal in Canadian history, involving $14 billion in market capitalization, $21 billion in book assets and $16 billion in annual revenues. It created two new companies: a single, seamless gas-marketing and transportation giant, and a middling-sized Canadian independent chemical company.

The deal marked the end of an era for the natural-gas business. Trans-Canada and Nova were Siamese twins joined at the hip in the 1950s. Nova, created by former premier Ernest Manning, had the exclusive right to gather gas inside Alberta and take it to the Saskatchewan, Montana and British Columbia borders. TransCanada, the product of C.D. Howe's genius at manipulating the private sector, picked up the gas and hauled it east to markets in Central Canada and the U.S. Midwest and NorthEast, as well as through British Columbia to the Pacific Northwest and California.

In 1997, Nova was in danger of being swallowed up by U.S. predators, while TransCanada had one last chance to make an acquisition that would put it into the league of North American pipeline super-giants. When TransCanada initiated the merger, using a financial and legal technique called "pooling of interests," a six-man committee, three from each side, was formed to steer the arrangement. Maier conceived the deal, but didn't want to include Nova's chemical interests. Newall cleared the way by proposing to split Nova into two companies: a pipeline supplier and a chemical producer. After TransCanada CEO George Watson made the formal offer, the companies put together another six-man group to steer it, comprising Hotchkiss, Haskayne, Maier, former bankers Ced Ritchie and Allan Taylor, and Harry Schaefer, chief financial officer of TransAlta Corp.

Maier, Haskayne and Newall are of a generation whose names became synonymous with the firms they ran, owned or controlled. The Lexus Rangers don't enjoy that kind of personal identification with their companies. Corporations are just vehicles—strategically sold or merged at such a pace that there is no room or time for sentimental attachments. In the first half of the century, companies carved their names in stone on the buildings they erected as head offices. In the second half of the century, an office tower is just so much real estate; the names of the tenants are posted with replaceable letters, although bigger firms can be counted on to outlast the careers of most of their senior people. In this carnivore era heading into the twenty-first century, names and firms are disposable, lifetime jobs are dead, and the career of a new Titan is likely to span many corporate vehicles.

THE ARRIVAL OF TWO COMPANIES IN CALGARY—Canadian Pacific and Shaw Communications—to establish their headquarters there, symbolized a shift of power and influence from the cozy Old Establishment to a posse of new Titans.

The beaver is back, reinstated as the logo of the Canadian Pacific Railway by David O'Brien, the laconic Montreal-born lawyer who tilted the country's economic centre of gravity westward in September 1997 when he moved Canadian Pacific Ltd. to Calgary. The reconnection with the railway's historic economic and social role in the West was particularly timely. CP is now Calgary's most important national company, and O'Brien is the city's leading national business figure. Under O'Brien's tutelage, the corporation that once dominated Canadian life is now blazing the path to achieve the global competitiveness that will define Calgary's next century.

The relocation of CP was a piquant moment for a city that has always had an ambivalent relationship to the railway. The CPR transformed the lonely police post and fur-trading centre into a town in 1883 by the simple act of building a railway station. Yet the company so pervaded Prairie life, as its railway, telegraph operator, land agent, grain and cattle hauler and hotel operator, that it was the lightning rod for the resentment of the free-spirited homesteader against authority. The apocryphal farmer who was told the hail ruined his crop after his house caught fire and his wife had run away with the hired man, shook his fist at the sky crying, "God damn the CPR!"

"If you really looked at it," says O'Brien, "CP has become a western-based company. Our Montreal location had very much more to do with the original financing of the company than with any of the contemporary realities. Historically, the Canadian Pacific Railway opened up the West and brought British Columbia into Confederation. The railway founded Calgary and Vancouver. Because we now operate mostly in the West, it was important to get CP Rail together all in one place—and Calgary was the right place.

"Also, there is no substantial sense of alienation left in the West. This is too vast a country not to have regional points of view, and there's still a sense that the Central Canada compact has disproportionate power, so there's still a sense of wariness, but not of the hostile nature of twenty years ago." CP's presence in Alberta levered the province's diversification strategy. Before the relocation, CP had its energy business located here with Fording Coal and PanCanadian Petroleum. With the addition of CP's hotels and transportation businesses, the texture of the city's economy is more complex and it now has a national focus to balance the inherent regionalism, the myopia, of the Oil Patch.

O'Brien has spent two decades in Calgary, but manages CP as a national network. His wife, Gail, who runs the local Holt Renfrew and sits on the board of the Glenbow Foundation, is more connected locally.

O'Brien sits on the executive committee of Tom d'Aquino's Business Council on National Issues and on the board of Tom Kieran's C.D. Howe Institute. He's also a director of the Royal Bank and of Inco.

"Calgary is not a simple city any more," he says. "It has many circles of influence. When I first arrived here in the mid-seventies, a concentrated group of people did everything, ran everything, and they were all of a like ilk. Now it's much more like Montreal or Toronto, a diversity of *kinds* of people. It's a meritocracy, but it isn't open to everyone. Women and the glass ceiling are still an issue, and I'm sure there's a racial bias. But relative to the circumstances of the mid-seventies, it's much more open."

O'Brien restructured the CPR, eliminated six layers of management and a thousand executive jobs, sold $4 billion in assets and slashed debts by $1.5 billion. He doubled the company's merchant fleet and started construction on the new Vancouver Airport Hotel. He invested several billion dollars in rail expansion and improvement. He also sold the business hotels (Calgary's Palliser, Montreal's Queen Elizabeth and Toronto's Royal York) into an income trust for $800 million, retaining management contracts and a one-third interest, while expanding the resort-hotel chain. "Size is not my target," he says. "We are making sure that we remain competitive, growing in our core areas and gradually expanding abroad, because Canada will generate only so much growth."

O'Brien is single-minded and lives a much narrower life than he'd like. "You have to create a discipline, or you can be captured and swamped by the moment. I've seen people who spend 99 percent of their time with trivia, because they let someone else set the agenda. I've never done that, but I've had to conscientiously step back to make sure it wasn't happening," he says. "I am astonished to find myself where I am," he says of his job as head of a $18-billion company that is western Canada's most powerful enterprise. "It is a very historic company that even now has interesting breadth to it, but it also has some serious challenges that have nothing to do with its past and everything to do with its future."

David O'Brien has a modulated view of power, and preaches the soft approach as the key to success for Calgary. "Influence is more important than power," he says. "Everything is more a question of persuasion than the old tyrannical ways, when somebody said, 'This is the way it's going to be.' It is not power in the raw sense that gets things done, it's influencing a whole series of constituencies from governments to shareholders to financial institutions and employees."

The first CP boss not to have come out of railroading career, O'Brien has been breaking moulds since the day he joined the company. The next step is to take a corporation that is indivisible from Canada's sense of itself—a definer of its identity and history, especially in the West—and turn it into a global powerhouse. Although he does not see himself as part of the warp and woof of the Titans' Calgary, nor as a role model for its young generation of overachievers, David O'Brien's success will strongly influence the taste the Lexus Rangers acquire for investments abroad and for his style of personal engagement.

J.R. SHAW, PATRIARCH OF CANADA'S MOST IMPORTANT media company, goes to work in Calgary's most magnificent office building, in Eau Claire near the Bow River. Shaw Court is not the biggest pile of brick in town; it's a virtual low-rise compared to its towering neighbours. But from the bronze buffalo on the spacious apron in front to the sweeping atrium in the centre, it's a glorious working environment that has the feel of the future. In terms of the electronic media, Shaw Communications is that future: a world of digital cable with Internet access, digital-music service, direct-to-home satellite television, fibre-optic networks and digital wireless phones. Shaw Communications owns a 1.7-million-subscriber cable network, which pioneered digital cable and Internet services in Canada. Depending on who's counting, it's the second- or third-largest cable service in Canada. Shaw Communications also holds a radio network with eleven licences and a digital-music service. Wholly owned Shaw Fibrelink is an access provider of data-, video- and voice-transmission services to large companies. Through Television Networks, Shaw Communications owns varying interests in six specialty channels. It has a 54-percent stake in the Star Choice direct-to-home satellite television network. Its most recent acquisition is a stake in Western International Communications, with a dozen radio stations, nine television stations, eight more specialty channels and two pay-per-view services: Superchannel and Movie Max. The takeover was bitterly contested by CanWest Global Communications, ending in what amounted to a stand off. A division of the assets was later negotiated.

Shaw Court is, ironically, an echo of the past. It was commissioned by Shell Canada before Shell rethought its corporate future and right-sized its Calgary headquarters. It's oddly appropriate that a big multinational oil company—the symbol of Calgary's Old Establishment—has ceded this space to a family of Titans who are creating the future.

However, the most noticeable furnishing in J.R.'s office isn't some electronic business gizmo; it's a pint-sized armchair between the two visitors' chairs, there for the visits of his six grandchildren—a compelling reminder that this $2.5-billion business is very much a family business. (It started with his father's industrial-products company.) J.R. is the chairman and CEO, and all his children work in key positions. His son, Jim, is the president and chief operating officer of Shaw Communications. Heather, his daughter, is vice-president and president of DMX Canada (the digital-music business) and Television Networks. His other daughter, Julie, is responsible for corporate design and maintains the family's community links in Calgary; son Brad is vice-president of Shaw Cable Systems in British Columbia. J.R.'s children all started out at the bottom of the company, working as cable installers, receptionists, clerks and the like. This may be a family business already planning for the fourth generation, but it's as in-touch a bunch of people as you're ever likely to meet.

There is a sharp edge to the competition between Shaw and its rival, Rogers. Ted Rogers and Jim Shaw made a bet over dinner in early 1997 about who would sign up more new cable subscribers by September 30 that year. The loser would treat the winner to a steak dinner and would eat beans. Not surprisingly, they couldn't agree on the final numbers. With typically Canadian panache, they decided each would host the other to a steak-versus-beans dinner in their respective home towns. Not surprisingly, the dinners may never take place. But Shaw is a healthy, focused, well-financed operation, and Rogers labours along with a debt burden and a chaotic mix of businesses. The winner in the race for overall pre-eminence was really decided when J.R. purchased 49.95 percent of the voting A shares and 14 percent of the class-B shares of Western International Communications from the market and from Emily Griffiths, the matriarch of Vancouver's Griffiths family. The controversial deal denied Winnipeg's Izzy Asper his long-time ambition of gaining WIC, because the Allard family of Edmonton, in what has emerged as an important communications alliance with Shaw, holds 49.89 percent of the voting A shares.

"I've known Ted all the way along for thirty years, and he's certainly a character. He's not really a competitor, because the cable industry doesn't compete with itself in the sense that you have different territories. You need to cooperate to strengthen the business," says J.R., whose diplomatic nature has also been the hallmark of his relationships with the Allards, the Griffiths and even bitter rival Asper.

Francis Shaw, J.R.'s father, founded Shaw Industries in Ontario, providing specialty products and services to oil refineries and pipelines. In 1961, J.R. and his brother Les were dispatched to Edmonton to build a plant for

Shaw Pipe, the world's leading pipeline-protection coating business. Shaw was also rolling tubular products for oil- and gas-exploration drilling. In 1966, he saw the potential for a new, untried business—cable television.

"Les and I believed the pipeline-construction business would end some day. Once you'd laid all the pipe, why would you need any more?" The fear may have been premature; the oil industry is drilling more wells and building more pipelines than ever before, and the coating mill that the Shaw brothers built is busier than ever most years. But the Shaws obtained the cable licence for half the city of Edmonton. As the company first in, Shaw grew by "cablizing" small towns in British Columbia, Alberta and Ontario for fifteen years. In the 1980s, they went on an acquisition hunt that netted them major markets in the Maritimes, the B.C. Lower Mainland, Vancouver Island and Saskatoon. They swapped some markets with Rogers and now control key clusters of markets in Calgary, Edmonton, Winnipeg, Toronto, rural Alberta, most of Vancouver Island and northern Saskatchewan. The 1990s have taken them into specialty television, fibre-optic links, radio, digital communications and satellite television.

"My dad was an entrepreneur, a builder, an expander. He taught us that you either grow or die; you can't stand still, and it's better to lead than follow," says J.R.—who legally changed his name last year to avoid confusion with his son and second in command, Jim. "The thing I like about cable television is that it's always changing. When I was introduced to it by my father in the early fifties, it was three channels. When we built our cable system in Edmonton in 1977, it had twenty-seven channels. Now we're building it to roughly seventy-seven channels, and if you add digital, it's two hundred. There's no end to the numbers. It's just a matter of having the eyeballs. I've always been of the view that we didn't want to be the biggest in cable, but we wanted to be as good as the best—equal at the front. We wanted good operating margins, to provide good service, and to have good customer relations. We wanted to be in the West and stay in the West, even though we have a chunk of Toronto."

J.R. lives in a nether world of electronic business decisions that are far into the future by comparison to the Oil Patch. "The customers never ask how they got the signal—over the air, by microwave, by fibre, by coaxial, by satellite. All they want is enough choice and good audio and video quality." That means Shaw must make decisions on investments that seem to be self-competitive; for instance, direct-to-home satellite may eat into the cable-subscriber base. In practice, what the Shaws do is a bit of everything, balancing out technologies by using them to reach individual customers and markets with peculiar niche characteristics—for example, an acreage may not be able to get a cable hook-up, but a direct-to-home dish could be installed. The technology allows the company to service big- and small-end markets with the same products—multiple-entertainment and information channels, Internet access and such—all with good-quality signals.

The rough and tumble often comes from decisions that the customer never hears about, such as whether to use contract satellite services from a supplier such as Telsat, which Shaw says is a frustrating relationship because he's never sure he's getting a fair shake, or investing $250 million in a private satellite.

Moving the company from Edmonton to Calgary "was the toughest decision of my life," J.R. says. He loved the capital's ambience and had a successful cattle operation outside the city. But Edmonton's air-travel connections were poor. "Edmonton Telephone would not allow us to put in fibre-optics; it wanted to build a wall around its city and not let any competition come in. We only owned half the market, whereas in Calgary, we had the whole city. We had four choices: move to Toronto, Victoria or Calgary, or stay in Edmonton."

Most important on his mind, however, was succession. "I wanted to hand the company over while I was still around. We wanted to stay in the West, and moving to Calgary allowed the next generation to take over. If we'd stayed in Edmonton, it would always be J.R.'s company. Here, the next generation can make its mark. All the children moved here from around the West to be with the business." With the Shaws getting busy on various boards in Calgary, the Lexus Rangers are now much more than a bunch of Oil Patchers.

J.R. quickly developed a liking for Calgary's informal business style: "Most days my tie is in my pocket." He is leaving the stage of the city open for his inheritors. He lives quietly, golfing a bit, taking his grand-children skiing and dining at trendy places such as Teatros and Virginia's, a tiny but chic spot in the out-of-downtown Beltline. His retreat is at his house on Lands End Road near Swartz Bay in Sidney, British Columbia, where he keeps a fifty-foot powerboat.

IN ITS 125-YEAR HISTORY, six Canadians set the direction of Alberta's Oil Patch. George Dawson of the Geological Survey of Canada started the search for petroleum in 1874. Stewart Herron correctly interpreted oily mud holes on a creek to discover Turner Valley in 1912. In the 1920s, Karl Clark turned water into wine by extracting oil from the tar sands. In the 1940s, Imperial Oil's Ted Link cracked the geological mystery of the prolific Devonian oil reservoirs at Leduc. Thirty years later, Jack Gallagher unlocked the bank for frontier exploration, incidentally creating the template for the senior Canadian independents now going multinational. And in the past decade, Murray Edwards, a pudgy, unassuming middle-class kid from Regina, who has yet to turn forty and hates getting his name in the papers, revolutionized the way wealth is created from oil.

Edwards is a financier. His astonishing success in turning $100,000 into $500 million in ten years has elevated him to leader of the city's most significant Lexus Rangers network.

"They are more money men than oil men," says Edwards' mentor, lawyer Jim Palmer. "The Old Establishment didn't worry about the economics of oil; they just went and drilled. Today, it's a different world: the economics are the big thing and the plays are much more focused. There are kids running around this town still in their thirties who have made millions and millions doing this." Edwards seems to invest in industries at the bottom of a downturn and turn them into winners as they come out of the cycle. He is chairman or CEO or both of a half a dozen major firms in which he has large stakes and sits on the boards of others. He divides his time between them as a leader and mentor, working with management groups on finance and on their strategic direction. "It's very intense and focused looking at the big picture, making sure core values, mission statements and business plans are being executed," he says. "I approach this with very great trepidation; I'm not a geologist, I'm managing assets. With proper systems and proper accountability in place, I can monitor aspects in which I'm not an expert."

Edwards is very unassuming about why he has been so successful. He invests in common-stock positions in his companies, so the size of his fortune changes at each day's market close. In September 1997, *The Globe and Mail* reported his portfolio was worth $545 million and had grown by 127 percent in a year. In June 1998, when oil prices were low, the market capitalization of his portfolio bottomed out at $475 million. He is a director and holds a 2.3-percent interest in Canadian Natural Resources, the flagship that got him started. He is chairman of Ensign Resource Services and holds 20 percent of the common stock; chairman and CEO of Magellan Areospace with a 28-percent stake; chairman and CEO of Imperial Metals holding 30.5 percent; chairman of Penn West Petroleum with 10 percent; and chairman of Rio Alto Exploration with 1.5 percent. He is a director of Canadian Foremost and owns 13 percent.

His stock positions represent 7.6 percent of the market capitalization of the seven public companies. "Personally," he says, "I never forget where I came from. You have to position yourself to go through cycles—not to get too high on the ups and too down on the lows. I have a propensity to work very hard." (He regularly gets guys out of bed at midnight.)

If you ask Murray Edwards to plot the course of his success, he'll tell you about the people who got him there. The senior members of his network are Jim Palmer; Al Markin, chairman of Canadian Natural Resources; Brett Wilson, managing director of FirstEnergy Capital, which Edwards helped stake; and John Brussa, a lawyer with Burnett Duckworth Palmer. Edwards, Brussa and Wilson attended the University of Saskatchewan together and are the nucleus of the new Saskatchewan mafia moving in to succeed Doc Seaman's group. Edwards is the bridge between the old and new Saskatchewan mafioso. As a member of the Calgary Flames owners' group since 1995, he has developed close ties with Bud McCaig and the Seaman brothers.

"Saskatchewan is a great exporter of people," Edwards says. "But Calgary is the dynamic environment, the place to do things in the West. Nowhere else in North America do you see such a concentration of capital within a seven-block area. It has the largest number of investment dealers per capita in Canada, and it delivers great economic rewards."

The son of a Regina chartered accountant, Edwards attended the College of Commerce at the University of Saskatchewan in Saskatoon, took his law degree at the University of Toronto, then joined the law firm of Burnett Palmer Duckworth, where he developed a thriving practice working with junior oil companies.

In 1988, when Edwards did his stock takings, the Oil Patch was at the bottom of its worst cycle ever, "written off as a sunset industry," he comments. "But in my view it had gone through a tremendous right-sizing, and its opportunities were just beginning to evolve." He joined Peters & Co., Calgary's home-grown oil- and gas-brokerage firm and started to develop deals. In 1992, Edward's holdings were sufficiently substantial to justify hanging out his own shingle as Edco Financial Holdings.

He and financier Jim Grenon, of Tom Capital Associates, bailed out a bankrupt mining and oil company called Canadian Natural Resources, which had $20 million in assets but couldn't cover its debt with the Royal Bank. Edwards scraped together $100,000 of his own money and persuaded the Royal to swap its loans for preferred shares. He recruited Al Markin to be the company's chairman and join its president, John Langille, in turning CNR into a $4-billion senior producer in ten years. In

1996, it acquired Sceptre Resources, an acquisition that placed it first for financial performance among all Canadian producers.

Ensign Resource Service Group had a bunch of drilling rigs and a fatal debt. Working with Ensign's CEO George Ward, Edwards reconstructed its fortunes. It now has 150 drilling rigs, ninety-five service rigs and ranks in the top five of independent Canadian drilling contractors.

In 1993, Edwards and Brett Wilson, his pal from the University of Saskatchewan ("We were involved in student politics, fighting off those Saskatchewan communists," says Wilson), established FirstEnergy Capital. While Edwards is not involved in the management of the firm, in Calgary his name is associated with it as often as those of managing partners: Wilson, Jim Davidson and Rick Grafton. They are Calgary's most essential network of young Titans.

Murray Edwards is the opposite of a corporate flip artist. "You have to be in for the long term. If you're not, then you won't create value for your shareholders, and I think you have to run the company for the benefit of the shareholders." Edwards takes compensation totalling only $60,000 a year from his positions as chairman of Ensign and Penn West companies, passing up remuneration from Magellan and Imperial Metals, where he is CEO. He doesn't cut himself in on lavish insider stock deals. He buys and sells in the market or exercises his options along with other investors. He and Al Markin, who also does not draw a salary from Canadian Natural Resources, take the same risk as Jack Gallagher and Bill Richards at Dome Petroleum, who were paper billionaires until Dome collapsed and had to content themselves with being plain-vanilla millionaires in the aftermath. His 10-percent stake in Penn West best illustrates his endurance and patience as an investor. "In 1995, we were delivering good results and had a solid business plan, but the stock was languishing. All the brokers were telling us that we should issue equity, because our debt leverage was too high. But we stuck to our plan for another four quarters until the market finally appreciated what we were doing. Since 1996, the stock has basically tripled." In 1995, he repeated his Oil Patch strategy of investing at the bottom of the cycle by buying into Magellan Areospace, a component manufacturer and maintenance and overhaul supplier to commercial and defence aircraft manufacturers and operators in North America and Europe. In 1996, he engineered a corporate refinancing and loaned the company $8 million. He now owns 28 percent of the common shares, and their value represents a third of his wealth.

Murray Edwards toils at least seventy hours a week, but regards work as his hobby. "What's work?" he asks. "I don't really know." Although his house is worth a few million, he purchased it only recently and his Ford Explorer is five years old. Unlike many of his newly wealthy friends, he has not run out and bought a ranch. He spends each Monday, Tuesday and Wednesday morning at Canadian Natural, Monday afternoons and evenings with Ensign, Tuesday afternoons with Penn West and most Wednesday mornings at Rio Alto Exploration. Every second Thursday and Friday, he goes to Magellan Aerospace in Toronto. On alternate Fridays he's in Vancouver with Imperial Metals. He's also chairman of the Calgary Flames ownership group and runs the annual $350-a-plate prime minister's dinner in Calgary. Edwards describes himself as an enthusiastic free enterpriser, but with compassion and a conscience. "That's what makes me a Liberal. For the three years I've chaired the prime minister's dinner, we've had record attendance, in excess of 1,200 ticket sales. The Calgary business community, while clearly not Liberal, understands the importance of supporting the process." His mentor Jim Palmer, who is the national party's principal bagman in Alberta, recruited Edwards as a major fundraiser for the Grits.

"He has a quick grasp of things, tremendous energy and an unbelievable memory," says Harley Hotchkiss. "He needs to balance that a little. When you work twenty hours a day, it's going to catch up to you." Hotchkiss and Dick Haskayne engineered Edwards's debut as a philanthropist in the Partners for Health hospital campaign. A friend of Edwards had breast cancer, and he devoted a significant part of his contribution to research and treatment of the disease.

"I won't describe my investment in the Flames hockey team as charitable," Edwards says. "But it is a community obligation." He attends 90 percent of the team's games, but acknowledges that, other than that, he comes up short on recreational pursuits. Edwards may not have the opportunity to slow down any time soon. "The comment is often made that the Oil Patch has moved from an exploration culture to an asset-management culture," he remarks. "That being said, we are moving back to a bit more of an exploration cycle now. The majors leaving the base couldn't compete because their cost structures were too high, so you had a lot of shuffling of assets from the majors down to the independents. Now these independents have hundreds of millions in cash flow to reinvest, and they're returning to the drill bit—which is high risk, high reward—so there are going to be winners and failures."

No doubt he will have more of the former than the latter—and one of these days, he may even take the time to trade in his Ford Explorer for a vehicle that others may regard as more suitable to his position.

THE SINGLE MOST INFLUENTIAL NETWORK OF Lexus Rangers in the new Oil Patch is a group of three men linked through their relationship with Murray Edwards. They are his dream team, the short list of guys he ranks, in addition to mentor Jim Palmer, as his closest associates and friends. They are lawyer and tax expert John Brussa, financier-activist Brett Wilson and engineer-spiritualist Al Markin.

"Forget just taxes; John Brussa is the best all-round lawyer I've ever dealt with," Edwards says. They met at Burnett Duckworth Palmer when Edwards was the firm's comer in securities law and Brussa was carving out his tax practice. Brussa grew up in Windsor, Ontario, the son of Italian immigrants. They were both drawn to business in a law firm that was a crucible of enterprise.

"Jim Palmer is a great legal entrepreneur," says Brussa. "Through prodigious legal talent, he took a crappy little firm thirty years ago and built it into something. We're the second generation of his efforts." Brussa regards himself as a fringe player, delighting in the chance to get the fly-on-the-wall perspective of his friends' business adventures. In fact, of the club around Edwards, Brussa is the intellectual lynch pin. He is a good listener, attentive to the personal as well as business and legal adventures of his pals. They all confide in him. It was he who drew Wilson into the web, begun during a chance street meeting when Wilson had decided to put together an investment firm and needed a place to hang his hat. Brussa invited him to use an empty office at the law firm where he had met Edwards.

It is Brussa, too, who sees most clearly the careers and fortunes that are spinning off Edwards's circle. He cites Keith MacPhail as the man who helped get Canadian Natural Resources tracking, then acquired moribund Bonavista and turned it around. Bruce Chernoff has taken a $10-million market-cap company called Pacalta and transformed it into a $1-billion senior producer in two years. He cites Richard Lewanski at Amber Energy and Don Hanson at North Rock as other examples of Lexus Rangers who have gone from market capitalization of $5 to $10 million to the billion-dollar range using pages from the Murray Edwards play book. "My theory is that there are two types of people," says Brussa, "those who stop when they reach a number they've picked for material success—$5 million or whatever. Then there are guys like Murray who keep going. What money can do for them has little meaning—they can't spend in a lifetime what they have—but it becomes a measure of achievement and of themselves."

As a lawyer and the kind of artificial introvert people open up to, Brussa has seen the nasty side of the incestuous nature of the Oil Patch:

"It's a wonderful game we're in, but it's a funny place. The main problem is that everyone is chasing the same apple. All these guys are direct competitors. In Toronto, one guy is in the shoe business, another guy in clothing, the other guy in the car business—it's very diversified. Here you have some diversification, but basically the world moves in the same inner circle and the same social scene. The circle is even smaller than it sometimes appears, because this is a sunset industry being extended by technology."

But there is a good side to this, too. The networking and interacting creates lifetime friendships that are part money making and part looking out for each other. "I was a good sidekick for Murray. A lot of his early deals had a big tax component, so he and I worked on a lot of things together. He asked me to sit on his boards and got me into some other opportunities. Look, you meet a guy who is a vice-president of a company and work with him as a client. Then he goes off and starts his own company, and you get involved in that. The networks just keep going and building and multiplying."

You expect him to end with a Hallejulah! but Brussa just sits there grinning.

IN HIS SHORT BUT SPECTACULAR CAREER, BRETT WILSON, the managing director of the investment firm he founded with Edwards's financing in the office borrowed from Brussa, has redefined the way equity is raised and capital is assembled in Canada's most capital-intensive city. He has gone on to redefine philanthropy in a community that has built an integral part of its identity on volunteerism and personal giving. Brett Wilson is a Titan of grand proportions, yet almost unknown even within the confines of downtown Calgary.

FirstEnergy is the epicentre of networks from both the University of Saskatchewan and the University of Calgary. "Half my engineering classmates from the University of Saskatchewan are in Calgary and most from my commerce class at University of Calgary," Wilson says. Edwards and Wilson had been faculty representatives together on the students' council at the University of Saskatchewan. Along with Rick Grafton and Jim Davidson, they seeded FirstEnergy. "That company has kicked ass all over this city," says research analyst John Shiry. "We are the number one underwriter of equities in Canada," Wilson says. "In this last year, we traded over $9 billion in equities, $2.5 to $3 billion in financings and $3 billion in mergers and acquisitions. We've come a long way in a short time. Our angle is that we are specialists in the

Canadian energy industry, experts at understanding the management teams of the local operators, and it was a very easy extension for us to follow Canadians wherever they went around the globe. As a result, we financed Vermillion when it went to France, Percalta in Ecuador and Del Mar Energy in Trinidad. If we don't know the people, we're not interested. Three quarters of our repeat revenues come from the relationships we have as partners within the business community. We're not relying on contractual rights for financing; we're relying on relationships and handshakes."

FirstEnergy is the backer of first and last resort for smaller companies. With fifty-five specialists grinding away, led by Martin Molyneaux, Wilson has also taken on financing for bigger firms such as Petro-Canada. He rejects the notion that he is breeding a generation of asset managers who will run oil companies with no idea of how to explore for more oil and gas. "The drill bit is being used as aggressively as ever, and new technologies are carrying exploration forward," he insists.

In the early going, Wilson and his partners agreed to funnel 2.5 percent of their profits into community giving. That decision made FirstEnergy the community's largest source of voluntary funds. It wasn't just the scale of dollars that changed the tempo and spirit of local philanthropy; FirstEnergy placed its money across a wide range of community causes, most of it given without fanfare.

Wilson has quietly established a new foundation that will give leadership to the endowments and contributions of some of the city's largest new fortunes. "Many people are uncomfortable with what wealth they have, and there are initiatives to start raising awareness of what individuals can do for the community in terms of full-cycle charity," he says. "Many of us are not working for ourselves any more; our material needs have been met. The work we do now is for our charities. Some of it is for ego and to keep score, but people are taking very leading-edge initiatives in terms of what's good for the community."

THERE ARE TWO AL MARKINS. One is the sweaty engineer who grew up in one of Calgary's poorest neighbourhoods and attacked his career with the ferocity of an out-of-control, type-A personality. He came to the attention of the Oil Patch while helping Bob Dixon build Merland Exploration so well that it was the most prized acquisition made by Turbo Resources in its heyday. Then, Ed Galvin hired him to run Poco Petroleum, which he took from a stock price of $3 to $17. In the process, Markin's first marriage failed, and he stepped on a lot of toes, as if he were trying to shake the spectre of the cold running water and outdoor privies of his childhood in Bowness.

The second Al Markin is the poet, philosopher and spiritual seeker who emerged from the crucible of fire when Poco overreached itself, the stock collapsed, and he was fired in a bitter dispute with his board. "He was going a hundred miles an hour when his version of success fell apart. He really questioned himself," says Brussa. "There were lots of people who told me Al Markin would never be able to build another company," Murray Edwards recalls. He, Brussa and Wilson had just gained control of Canadian Natural Resources. "In May 1988 when I was leaving Poco, Murray came to me and said, 'I'd like to go into business with you,'" Markin recounts. "I said, 'Call me in a year.' In nine months he phoned and said, 'I can't wait, I need you to take this position at Canadian Natural Resources.'"

Edwards was now talking to the new Al Markin, who had been on an internal spiritual pilgrimage and returned wanting more out of life than being the hard-driving engineer who ran into the brick wall at Poco. "My criteria were that I wanted to be a major shareholder and equal partner and only wanted to work twenty to twenty-five hours, four days a week," Markin says. "So we agreed that Murray would look after the accounting and acquisitions, and I'd look after exploration and production." He became the company's chairman and head coach. "My hours are nine to five or nine to three, four days a week. My wife Jackie and I have a board meeting every Friday morning when we visit, chat and catch up on our week."

His cubby-hole office at Canadian Natural Resources—with barely room for a bookcase and a visitor's chair, in addition to a utilitarian desk and credenza—speaks to his reoriented value system. Markin prides himself on having levelled the company hierarchy (there is no chief financial officer or chief operating officer) and on its lean and disciplined operational structure. Twice a year, he spends private time with each employee—encouraging them and abetting their work, making sure the company's vision and mission are front-of-mind. "Around here we want to have fun and do our work with integrity," he says. "It's more than just about producing oil."

When he moved into Canadian Natural Resources, the stock was trading at 10¢ and the company basically had no payroll. Its trading range in the volatile markets of 1998 ranged from $24 to $44. Even at their lowest, Markin's 2.5-million shares were worth $65 million. He now spends more time thinking about how to give his money away than how much he has. He and his wife, magazine publisher Jackie Flanagan, support the Markin Flanagan Writer in Residence Program at the University of Calgary and quietly disperse sums to other carefully considered causes. Her magazine *AlbertaViews* is an articulate voice of liberal values in a conservative culture.

Markin is low-key about his involvement as a member of the Calgary Flames owners' group. Most of his charitable work is secret. He studies karate, writes poetry and reads history, but even close friends don't know that he is usually taking courses at the University of Calgary, including philosophy, the history of poetry, the history of ideas and social psychology. He is an engineer in search of the humane side of life.

Although he converted to Catholicism when he married Jackie, attends mass regularly and is profoundly aware of the Deity, he shies away from being called religious. Spiritual he admits to, but denies being stuffy, theological or pious about it. There were men like Markin in every bunkhouse during the days of the open range—plain thinking, plain speaking, the loavon of the prairie and sometimes brutal cowboy life. Meet Al Markin, the spiritual cowboy of the 1990s.

THERE IS A FADING PHOTOGRAPH of Fort Calgary showing a group of men sitting in a circle outside the palisade, near some tepees. A man in the centre is holding forth, a frontier equivalent of the village sage by the well in some European square, or the cowboy leaning on the corral who makes a running commentary on some other man's attempt to break a horse. The Lexus Rangers rely on a handful of such gurus to cue them to important trends and the direction of opinion.

TWICE A WEEK, DAVID PARKER—journalist, ad man, film commissioner of the Calgary Economic Authority and now president of Hayborough Marketing—writes a column in the business section of the *Calgary Herald* that is the snappiest source of leaks, tips and touts in town. One mention can launch a new enterprise; it seldom breaks one, because Parker never quite got the hang of being down on things. Consequently, he's got tales to tell of personal encounters with new Titans and old Establishmentarians that can hold an audience for hours, and he does it without ever violating a confidence. He'll tell you, without any self-consciousness, about dropping in at Shaw Court to see the latest Emily Carr acquisition or Ron Southern meeting him at the Calgary airport on short notice to host a minor member of the British peerage. He'll tell you that Art Smith, "the door opener at SNC, is the best B.S.er in town," and that Roddie Mah, "the little Buddha of Chinatown," helped successive mayors Ralph Klein and Al Duerr build the city's China connection.

As senior vice-president of human resources at Nova Corp., Sheila O'Brien became the defining voice in Calgary's corporate community investments in everything from women's shelters to the arts. A witty and often irreverent advocate, O'Brien has successfully advanced women's issues by cushioning hard realities in a velvet glove of charm. As a governor of the Calgary Economic Development Authority, she helped shape a wide mandate for community and corporate relationships. A *protégée* of Ted Newall, she joined Nova Chemicals after the Nova TransCanada PipeLines merger.

A former television journalist who counselled Ralph Klein on his transition from news to politics, Grant Howard of the Howard Group is now the adviser that emerging public companies rely on to master investor relations. He made his reputation as a public-affairs adviser to the Calgary Police Service and the XV Winter Olympic Games. His wife, Judy, who also works in the family business, was a student of Klein's when he taught at a business college. The Howards' romance started during Ralph's first mayoralty campaign in 1980.

Tom Cummings, chairman of the Alberta Stock Exchange, made his reputation in Calgary business circles as a client finder for the Bank of Nova Scotia's oil and gas department. Loquacious and affable, Cummings has guided the ASE through its best and worst years with equal equanimity. He played a key role in popularizing the junior capital-pool concept—the listing of nickel shares (later dime shares) of start-up companies without active business. Junior capital pools launched a generation of successful junior oil companies and helped bring diversification capital to the city. But Cummings also has to live with the accusations that the exchange is too soft on the regulatory side and allowed Bre-X, Abacan and Timbuktu scandals to develop unimpeded.

Some Lexus Rangers regard John Shiry, the president of Woodside Research, as too much the Cassandra of the Oil Patch. He recalls ruefully that at Christmas receptions in 1997 he "spoiled a lot of conversations" when he predicted the 1998 oil-price tumble. He accurately called the $12 floor and the $12 to $15 drifting range in which prices were locked for months. A former political-science professor, Shiry named his company after the street in his hometown of Kitchener, Ontario, on which Mackenzie King was born. His intensity and conviction have earned him some critics—the penalty for being right too often. His annual "Woodside Report" is the definitive assessment of the Oil Patch's progress or lack of it. He pioneered the best databases in the industry, authored *The Financial Post*'s popular Oil Patch column for five years and is much in demand as a speaker and an analyst.

Columnist and author Sydney Sharpe is the most influential daily journalist in the city and one of the best business reporters covering the Oil Patch. After securing her reputation in the Calgary bureau of *The Financial Post* and at the *Calgary Herald*, she moved to the upstart *Calgary Sun* with her husband and sometime co-author Don Braid. Her columns alternate between acerbic analysis and folksy slices of her own life.

Martin Molyneaux, chief financial analyst of FirstEnergy Capital, plays to the toughest financial audience a man in his profession can find: 80 percent of FirstEnergy's revenues come from institutions that depend on his judgment. It was a Molyneaux report in July 1998 that made it official: low oil prices were going to make this the worst year for Oil Patch profits in the decade. To make it even tougher, his fifty-five-member, in-house congregation is the most successful money-making machine in its trade; there is little room for error. "Martin is always banging into our heads the difference between the forest and the trees," says managing partner Brett Wilson.

Blunt, opinionated and internationally consulted for his probative assessment of Canadian energy development, Ian Doig is the Oil Patch's resident curmudgeon and its most entertaining writer. His *Doig's Digest* specializes in offshore and frontier exploration and is caustically critical of the way in which the Hibernia oil discovery has been managed. A self-described bluenoser from Nova Scotia, Doig's successful career as a financial analyst and stockbroker gives him the credibility to outrage and astonish the companies and governments that he loves to hate.

One universal thinker whose influence counts alongside the Friends of Ralph Klein or the Preston Manning Posse is Ralph Hedlin, who generously shares his political instincts with "good conservatives" of any party membership. Even Liberals have learned from Hedlin. He detests their party but knows how to love the sinner while hating the sin. Hedlin graduated from every political school worth attending. He was a Winnipeg journalist with young Ted Byfield when that city produced some of the greatest political editors and newspapers in the country. He went to Ottawa with John Diefenbaker's Conservatives and worked as policy adviser to Minister of Agriculture Alvin Hamilton.

For many years, his monthly newsletter, which featured guest articles by contributors such as Peter Lougheed and Michael Walker of the Fraser Institute, was the most important political document in Calgary. He endorsed the *Alberta Report* as a much-needed alternative to the generally liberal-leaning Alberta newspapers of the 1970s, and wrote a political column for the magazine for several years until Ted Byfield made the mistake one day of telling Hedlin what to think; Ralph promptly fired his publisher.

IN CALGARY, LISTS OF RESIDENT MILLIONAIRES START with the dozen or so who've made $100 million since the last Stampede and don't bother with anybody below $5 million. The Bunk-House Gang of Lexus Rangers has more than its share of colourful characters.

In the days of the open-range cowboys, Chinese contract labour built the railway and stayed to feed the nascent European culture in countless New York Cafés and Dragon Inn Restaurants. Although they called North America the Golden Mountain, these Chinese workers laboured for their money in spite of the racism that defined their meagre lot in life. The scales have shifted. Until the recent Asian meltdown, the Asian connection was courted and fêted. It was the biggest growth market for new petroleum consumption, and it has some of the largest undeveloped oil-bearing basins.

The Oil Patch's absentee landlord, Hong Kong billionaire Li Ka-Shing, established himself as Calgary's most patient capitalist during a ten-year run with Husky Oil, the integrated producer and marketer. The Li family owns 46 percent of Husky directly and controls another 49 percent through Hutchison Whampoa, a Hong Kong public company. The CIBC owns the 5-percent balance. Li has strategic investments in the financial sector, with interests in the CIBC and in Gordon Capital.

Nova—then called Alberta Gas Trunk Lines—acquired control of Husky Oil, the Canadian subsidiary of Cody, the North American oil empire of Wyoming rancher Glenn Neilson, in a creeping takeover that included a bitter 1978 showdown with Petro-Canada. But the company foundered in the 1986 price collapse. It was starved for capital, and the acquisition tainted Bob Blair's reputation for sagacity. Bill Richards earned a $1-million fee for solving the problem with the Li introduction. In April 1987, Li acquired his stake in Husky for $487 million and pumped $1.1 billion into its coffers.

Li has steadily provided the cash to expand Husky—$280 million to acquire Canterra Energy, which had been spun out of the Canadian subsidiary of Elf Aquitaine. He financed Husky's share of the $1.3-billion construction cost of the Lloydminster heavy-oil upgrader, and the buyout of federal and provincial (Alberta and Saskatchewan) government partners.

Husky was now the premier heavy-oil producer in the country. Li also backed Husky's foray into East Coast offshore exploration and okayed the expansion of its western Canadian service-station network. By the short-term standards of most Lexus Rangers, Husky was a financial basket case all this time. It lost an estimated $1.1 billion from 1991 to 1995, when other companies were growing explosively.

Li and his Canadian point man, Husky CEO John Chin-Sung Lau, an expatriate Hong Kong accountant, were playing a long-term game. The value of their strategy became apparent when, at the nadir of oil prices in the spring of 1998, heavy oil was moving for distress prices of $7 to $11 a barrel. Husky announced a $500-million expansion of the Lloydminster upgrade and started shopping for a major acquisition. Li came into the Oil Patch in the recession of 1986 for bargain-basement prices; now he was exploiting his fiscal strength, which survived the Asian flu and Hong Kong stock-market blues, to buy other people's problems again.

On paper he is Dr. James W. Buckee, a fifty-two-year-old Oxford astro-physicist, who arrives to disprove the myth that you don't need to be a rocket scientist to succeed in oil and gas. He borrowed his career plan from Rudyard Kipling and worked as an overqualified petroleum engineer in Burma, New Zealand, Norway, Persia and in northern Alaska. On the street he is Jim Buckee, whose real science is Canadian acquisitions and foreign drilling.

The buzz on Buckee is, do not piss him off; he can be more ornery than a grizzly in spring. He was president and chief operating officer of BP Canada in 1992 when British Petroleum dumped the company without consulting him. Buckee stuck around, "to get my hands on it," and to prove that BP had made a dreadful mistake. He has—many times over.

He renamed the company Talisman Energy and took advantage of high oil and gas prices to plough drilling money into under-performing Canadian oil and gas fields. In 1994, he signed a $1.8-billion merger with Doc Seaman's Bow Valley Energy Inc., which rocketed him into the North Sea and Indonesia. In two years, the price of common shares more than doubled, from $13 to $30. People started to pay attention, and Buckee's name became associated with nearly every takeover play in town. Meanwhile, he extended and expanded the foreign-exploration programme until the annual report read like a gazetteer: Nevada, Trinidad, Algeria, Ogan Komering, Tanjung Raya, Jambi, Corridor, Brae, Clyde, Peru and Argentina.

A failed attempt in 1997 to acquire Wascana Resources was followed by a successful $501-million bid to pick up Pembina Resources from the

Mannix family's Loram Group, the biggest acquisition of domestic light-sweet crude-oil reserves in a year of accelerating takeovers. Under Buckee, Talisman's annual capital budget has risen from $153 million to $1.1 billion in five years, excluding acquisitions. Financial analyst Wilf Gobert of Peters & Co. says, "He has reinvented the company."

Buckee has also become the angry voice of the anti-climate-change movement in the Oil Patch. His scientific credentials mean that his opposition to "junk science" and to the Kyoto protocol on carbon dioxide reduction carries more weight than that of any other individual. He was furious when, in a national advertising campaign before the Kyoto conference, the Canadian Association of Petroleum Producers took the stance that the oil industry should reduce carbon dioxide emissions even though the jury is still out on the validity of climate change. Buckee, the man who poked BP in the eye by turning around Talisman, said, "[CAPP president] David Manning doesn't know a damn thing about climate change."

After studying commerce at the University of Calgary, Pat Black rocketed up the corporate ladder with a series of small oil companies. She jumped into provincial politics as a Conservative and was elected to the legislature, becoming the hardest working, and hence most visible, member of the Calgary Tory caucus. She backed Ralph Klein's leadership bid and earned the energy portfolio where she played the key role in the overhaul of taxation that triggered the current $25-billion investment boom in oil sands. She bruised a lot of other important egos and Klein shuffled her into the economic development portfolio. She considered it a demotion; Klein told her that she could turn it into a promotion if she applied herself to the task with her usual intensity. She will. Pat Black has done more than any other woman to establish the place of women in the petroleum industry. Less than two decades ago, the Oil Patch was the unabashed Canadian capital of male chauvinism and the Petroleum Club, a bastion of gender discrimination. Women were not accepted as members, and spouses could not darken the door before dinner time. By unspoken decree, one restaurant, the Top of the Summit, was off limits for wives on certain weeknights so that men could take their mistresses to dinner there. When the pendulum swung, it swung slowly. For three years, from 1986 to 1989, the Pete Club resisted the pressure to open the membership to women, even after Husky Oil and Nova Corp., where such women as Diane Hall and Sheila O'Brien were advancing to senior executive positions, canceled their corporate memberships. When she was federal energy minister, Pat Carney, now a senator, turned down its Oilman of the Year Award after a top Soviet energy bureaucrat was denied admission for lunch because she was a woman. Finally, in May 1989, the membership bar was eliminated. The old boys were lucky to have acted before Black's appointment as Energy Minister. Her toughness in a good cause is legendary, and she would have made their lives hell if they hadn't treated her as an equal. The Calgary Desk and Derrick Club, a powerful but low-key women's network, also admitted men to membership in 1989. D&D was founded in Louisiana after the Second World War by women who'd been running the refineries there but got kicked back into the secretarial pool when the men came home from Europe and the Pacific. Calgary's branch of the Desk and Derrick Club has one of the most successful job-finding operations in the city and now boasts men on its executive. In 1998 Pat Black married Stan Nelson, a retired politician and entrepreneur, in a ceremony performed by Ralph Klein.

Every herd has one—the steer who just won't stay with the herd. Texan J.P. Bryan—oil financier, western historian, art collector, rare-coin broker and sometime publisher—is of that breed. He passed through the Canadian Oil Patch like a wind in the night, and after he was going his maverick image was made over into Don Quixote with spurs.

In 1994, when Gulf Canada Resources was on the fiscal ropes, Bryan's Houston-based Torch Energy—part of the fiscal wreckage of the Reichman empire and bleeding badly from investment misadventures in the USSR—purchased a controlling 25-percent interest for $300 million. Bryan made Gulf profitable in less than two years. He doubled its daily oil production and cash flow, acquired Mannville Oil and Gas for $143 million, slashed half the staff and expanded its North American, Indonesian, Australian and North Sea production. He also restructured the company, buying an 11.75-percent interest in Syncrude from the Alberta government and flipping it into an $355-million income trust. Bryan created Gulf Indonesia Resources with a $345-million initial public offering of its Indonesian assets. He bought Pennzoil Canada's $275-million asset base, Stampeder Exploration, for $1 billion and Clyde Petroleum of Britain for $1 billion.

Bryan built up market capitalization from $600 million to $2.4 billion and raised Gulf's asset base from $1.5 to $6.6 billion. He committed a huge chunk of his personal wealth to four million Gulf shares, but his acquisition programme piled debt up to a stratospheric $2.7 billion. Then his luck turned; he failed in a bid to buy cs Resources, a heavy oil play.

Gunslinger to the bone, Bryan never did fit into the Calgary scene, even though his grandfather was a cattleman and he is an avid horseman, owns a ranch in Texas and seems like the perfect Lexus Ranger.

"My degree is in art history from the University of Texas at Austin," he says, as if to explain that an artsy guy can't cut it in the testosterone climate of Alberta. (He also has a law degree, of which he speaks less often.) "This place is a closed, fraternal community, run like a club," he complains, and he ate alone most days at the Ranchmen's Club, near the condo where he lived. "I decided to remain on the periphery and not to develop friendships that might be an impediment to doing something aggressive that wouldn't be too popular," he says.

When *Oilweek* named him producer of the year, the bruised egos complained that he hadn't yet done anything to earn it. When he decided to shift Gulf's corporate headquarters to Denver, the ego of an entire city took the news hard. Privately, he did so for personal tax and family reasons. Publicly, he wanted access to the international deal flow in Colorado's oil capital. But the decision added to his directors' anxieties about debt, softening oil prices and his iconoclastic style. On Friday, February 6, 1998, Bryan walked into the board meeting that became his own version of the OK Corral. The board dumped him and new CEO Richard Anchinleck put $850 million in assets on the block ten days later, including Bryan's corporate jet, his Nevada executive retreat, the company's coal deposits, its East Coast drilling rights, the Clyde Petroleum North Sea holdings and a package of gas plants and pipelines.

"There are people here who believe I'm brash and outspoken and wouldn't be bothered if I took a tumble," Bryan said prophetically, shortly before he was deposed. "He was undermined at the board level because he was too much a broad-brush guy," a director told Deirdre McMurdy of *Maclean's*. Strangely, once Bryan was out of the way, the Lexus Rangers discovered a peculiar affection for him. "The new broom is an awfully boring guy, a plodder," said one senior manager on the way out the door to find Bryan-style high octane somewhere else.

There are two Calgarians who hold Bunk-House Gang memberships even though they aren't in business. One is Ralph Klein, the other is Christine Silverberg. She was a senior police official in Hamilton, Ontario, when the Calgary Police Service engaged her as the first female police chief in a major Canada city. She also became the highest-ranking Jewish bureaucrat in Calgary's history. Silverberg often takes her staff to the trendy Auburn Saloon near her office for informal meetings over cappuccino and latte, and appeared on the cover of *Outlook*, the province's monthly newsletter for gays. "I believe in individualism," she said in the cover story. "When you ask me the question, 'Am I gay friendly?', what I really am, is a person who believes passionately in the rights of people to express their individualism." The chief's inclusiveness is in stark contrast to Mayor Al Duerr's refusal to associate with a major gay-sponsored choral festival in 1999. He has denied the organizers access to city funds and won't provide a mayor's letter of welcome for the programme or declare a ceremonial official day to launch the event.

Most universities don't have them any more, but if they did, Roy Greene, founder and chairman of Renaissance Energy, could always find work as the dean of men. Slightly built, bespectacled and quiet, Greene is a self-effacing, dedicated executive mentor and the quintessential shareholders' man. He has made a career of putting everyone else first. Fortunately, he's proven that selflessness doesn't have to include a vow of poverty. He is the richest young Titan whose career embraces both the boom of the late 1970s, when he founded Renaissance, and that of the 1990s decade of expansion, when it became larger than Petro-Canada. Before its 1998 acquisition of Pinnacle Resources, Renaissance had a market capitalization of $2.5 billion, oil and gas sales of about $950 million, an equal-sized capital budget and nearly 85,000 barrels per day of equivalent oil production. The inherent fiscal stability of Renaissance allowed it to expand through the bad years from 1981 to 1988, although Greene and Clayton Woitas, the CEO he personally groomed and developed, were forever apologizing about stock performance through those years.

"When I got into the industry twenty-five years ago, all companies shared equally in all projects through partnerships and joint ventures, so everybody was equally successful or equally unsuccessful," Greene says. "We realized that it took as much effort to manage a 10-percent interest in a well or field as it took to manage 100 percent, so we put together as big a working interest as we could." Greene grew the company with the drill bit, becoming the leading specialist in finding smaller, shallower oil and gas fields on the plains of eastern Alberta, where risks and costs were also lower. Renaissance punched down 1,645 wells and made more than 700 oil and 500 gas discoveries in 1997.

One thing the company did not do for twenty-five years was make an acquisition, until its friendly $1.6-billion, share-swap takeover of Pinnacle Resources in the spring of 1998. The motive was market discontent with a slipping financial performance. A cash flow of $530 million and $115 million of profit in 1997 wasn't good enough for the company's broad shareholder base, which included many hawk-eyed institutions that didn't think the company was keeping pace. With oil prices in the basement, the market withheld its approval for almost a month before the share price started to edge upward.

Greene is now a non-executive chairman and hangs his hat at his holding company, Tortuga Investment. He financed WestJet, the Calgary-based discount air carrier, which took off in 1997 in spite of stiff resistance from the big airlines and a gauntlet of regulatory hassles. WestJet is the brainchild of Clive Beddoe, a businessman with manufacturing interests in British Columbia and real estate in Calgary. Beddoe got tired of paying $500-plus for round-trip commutes between his business bases and sold Greene on the concept of establishing a lower-priced airline.

Greene understates the case when he says, "I am a very private person." He refuses to include his photo alongside Woitas's in the annual report of Renaissance, he never grants media interviews and never publicizes his extensive charitable giving. A southern Alberta farm boy, he now owns his own place, which he never calls a "ranch." He plays at the Calgary Polo Club, the oldest polo club in North America, where the game has been played for 110 years. His prowess as a hard player belies his apparent frailty in a business suit and speaks to the toughness that underpins his business style and understated success.

Fiona Read is an engineer who has carved out a reputation as a tough, ruthless corporate acquisitor, most recently snapping up Jordan Petroleum. She helped invent the concept of the oil-royalty income trust. Reserve Royalty is not an operating company; it buys and holds oil- and gas-royalty interests. "A lot of guys are sincerely afraid of Fiona. She is a shark when she goes after something she wants," says one rueful admirer, who insisted on anonymity. "It's a short life if you get on the wrong side of her." Nevertheless, she is greatly admired and her ideas are quickly imitated.

Martha Billes, the controlling shareholder of Canadian Tire, lives in Calgary and enjoys a surprising anonymity (she says she can shop without being recognized). She is the youngest child and only daughter of her company's co-founder, Alfred Jackson Billes, and niece of the other founder, John Billes. She has gained control of 61 percent of Canadian Tire's class-A shares since buying out brothers David and Alfred in July 1997 after a long feud over the future direction of the company. "My aunts worked in the business as junior clerks," she says. "There was no place for me in the company until my father put me on the board in 1980." She has a degree in biochemistry, worked as a researcher for Lever Bros., studied petroleum engineering at the Southern Alberta Institute of Technology and did a stint in the Oil Patch while waiting to make her move on the ownership of the company.

When Kevin Benson, who made his name as CEO of Trizec Corp., became the chief financial officer of Canadian Airlines International in 1995, his friends thought he was flying blind. But Benson likes the fast lane—he has owned Indy-level racing teams—so the daunting problems of the troubled airline were just so much more adrenalin. He got all the action he was craving when CAI's directors took the easy way out and resigned en masse to avoid any possible liability for their actions. An avuncular South African, Benson became CEO, and his friends wondered if that meant he was suicidal as well as blind.

For eighteen months, he navigated the airline around a succession of near-death experiences. Canadian survived. It has returned from the brink and is now carving out a niche for itself, in spite of both Air Canada's ruthless attempts to kill it and competition from upstart WestJet in some of CAI's oldest territories. Benson loves the inside track of politics as much as he loves auto racing. He is a Reform party confidante, an evangelical Christian and is prominent in Christian business circles around North America.

In the rough-and-tumble world of contract oil-well drilling, Hank Swartout is the Titan everyone has to reckon with. He built Precision Drilling, the largest drilling company in western Canada, which operates 40 percent of the five hundred rigs in the field. He became unassailable in 1997 with the $440-million purchase of rival Kenting Energy Services. The forty-seven-year-old CEO pulled down a fabulous $6.43-million pay envelope in 1997, while his share of holdings in the Company are worth more than $30 million.

A charismatic oilman was an oxymoron in the sober-sided days when you were free to wear any colour of suit so long as it was grey or blue. No more. Former rock promoter and electric-bass player John Hagg, the founder and CEO of Northstar Energy, has changed that notion for good. He is drop-dead handsome and married to a stunningly beautiful Swede, Kristin Bengtson. Oddly, considering his former career in entertainment, he is media dead, paying virtually no notice to television and ignoring newspapers most of the time. Hagg loves the golfing channel and the country-music video channel, but when he ran into Alan Thicke, he was stunned to discover that his former high-school classmate had become a TV and film star.

Hagg swings a big club in the arcane world of the Canadian Association of Petroleum Producers, where he is a driving force behind the association's annual investment conference, the premier meeting place for CEOs, analysts and investing institutions. Hagg is one of a group of independent oilmen who courted the 1988 merger between the mighty Canadian Petroleum Association and the upstart Independent Petroleum Association of Canada and turned it into what Don Stacy, then president of Amoco Canada Petroleum, ruefully called "a reverse takeover." Hagg's momentum stalled, however, after Northstar's $635-million, white-knight acquisition of Gordon Stollery's Morrison Petroleums in 1997. When oil prices tumbled, Oklahoma-based Devon Energy Corp., which had been developing Canadian production, swallowed up Northstar. In the merger, Northstar shareholders traded 4.1 of their shares to get one Devon share. Devon trades on the American Stock Exchange. The deal made Devon one of the top twenty U.S. independents, and its Alberta arm ranks in the top twenty of all Canadian producers. Devon CEO J. Larry Nicols split the Canadian and U.S. operating executives, and Hagg stayed on, running the combined Canadian operations.

When Rob Peters, the founder of Peters & Co., Calgary's oldest independent oil equities firm, moved upstairs to be its non-active chairman, he chose Michael Timms to become his successor. "Michael is an honourable gentleman," says his rival Brett Wilson of FirstEnergy. Timms is as close to a patrician as you can find among the Lexus Rangers. A graduate of the Commerce Department of the University of Calgary and a prize-winning Harvard MBA, Timms's scholarly prowess (he teaches at the University of Calgary) combines powerfully with his canny street sense. He joined Peters & Co. in 1980, two years into his career, and helped the company nab $10 billion of oil- and gas-equity offerings—45 percent of the market—between 1991 and 1997. Peters & Co. has some engaging traditions. It maintains a "wall of shame," consisting of framed press clippings on members of the firm who are featured or photographed for news articles. And members ring a handsome bronze bell when they participate in a financing deal or make a major sale. Once located on the sidewalk in front of their low-rise office block, the bell was moved with the firm to Bank of Montreal's office tower, First Canadian Place. Now that the bank is a competitor, it's ironically delicious when the bell bongs in the foyer, serenading bank customers doing business in the adjacent branch.

As CEO of Agrium, the Calgary-based chemical-fertilizer producer, John Van Brunt heads the city's tenth-largest employer with a workforce of 4,500. "We are the best-kept secret around," he says. Spun out of Canadian Pacific's Cominco mining company in 1993, Agrium now has sales approaching US$ 2 billion and is the continent's largest producer of nitrogen-based fertilizers. Van Brunt has been a key player in making the province Canada's second most important chemical-producing region, and in making his industry the province's third largest (behind oil and agriculture). Van Brunt is now going international with a US$500-million plant in Argentina. Woody MacLaren, formerly of Woodwards fame, is one of the chief investors and a member of the select group who has been invited to stay at outdoorsman Van Brunt's woodland retreat.

There are a handful of water babies in the Lexus Ranger gene pool who have been marked by their peers as entrepreneurs to watch. Real-estate holding company Boardwalk Equities is another home-grown success. University of Calgary engineering graduate Sam Kolias built the company from a single apartment block into a $1.3-billion public company in ten years. Petroleum land man (an anachronistic job title, surely) Mary Blue made her bones as a senior vice-president and director of the successful junior capital pool, Jordan Petroleum. After the company was sold to Reserve Royalty, she and former Jordan CEO Harold Petersen moved on to acquire Key West Energy. It's their third corporate construction job before Jordan they helped the now-retired Hugh Mogensen build Inverness Petroleum.

In 1997, Danish immigrant Mogen Smed built the largest factory west of the Great Lakes, a 750,000-square-foot complex to house his custom office-furniture business. Taking advantage of low wage rates and a good tax environment, Smed became Calgary's poster boy for politicians and civic boosters crowing about the Alberta advantage. Back in 1981, he had gone bankrupt, a victim of the collapse of the oil industry. The experience made him a more generous man. When he took Smed International public, he distributed 20 percent of the company to its employees. The stock is now worth $25 million. Gwyn Morgan, CEO of Alberta Energy and successor to the company's legendary founder David Mitchell, is regarded in the Oil Patch as the promising comer to watch. Ron Jackson, who took over at Burns Foods after Arthur Child's death, is also a rising new Titan.

EVER SINCE MURRAY EDWARDS rode into town in his ancient Camaro with its battered doors, the Lexus Rangers haven't gone in much for status symbols; corporate jets and gold faucets are *passé*. There are remarkably fewer trophy wives since Alberta's matrimonial law was amended in the early 1990s to automatically divide the family estate equally upon divorce. There is only one status symbol that still counts: having the best legal gun on your side of the courtroom or negotiating table.

The point spread on litigation changes dramatically if Cliff O'Brien of Bennett Jones; Neil Whitman or Al Hunter of Code Hunter; Jack

Marshall of Macleod Dixon; or David Haigh of Burnett Duckworth Palmer are in your corner. The big corporate legal guns include Martin Lambert, the managing partner at Bennett Jones, Henry Sykes of Bennett Jones, Bob Engbloom of MacKimmie Matthews and Greg Turnbull of Code Hunter. (John Donahue of Donahue Powers Pshebinski does Ralph Klein's personal work.) The tax aces include Jim McKee at Macleod Dixon and Ron Sirkis at Bennett Jones. Julia Turnbull, Wendy Best and Judy Boyes are the toughest divorce attorneys in town.

Several much-travelled businessmen-lawyers use Calgary as a home base. These include Senator Ron Ghitter, whose specialty is land development, and former cabinet ministers John Zaozirny and Milt Paul. Then there is a legal élite; John Brussa calls them "client guys"—people who make rain for their firms by combining legal skill with a presence in the community through non-profit committees, sports or politics. They don't spread advice, they dispense wisdom. Senior lawyers such as Jim Palmer, Peter Lougheed, Bill Britton, Tommy Walsh and Jack Protheroe are their role models.

Lawyer Doug Mitchell developed his profile as commissioner of the Canadian Football League and keeps above the crowd with his powerful post as co-chairman of the Alberta Economic Development Authority, which reports directly to Klein. He sets the work pace for the city at eighty hours per week. He sits on a half-dozen boards and is a trustee of the Olympic Trust of Canada. Mitchell maintains a large number of contacts and can talk on a first-name basis to more people than any other man in Calgary.

Brian A. Felesky is the ranking Canadian-tax specialist and senior partner in the firm he founded, Felesky Flynn. An accomplished legal scholar and seminar instructor, his textbooks have spawned a national reputation. He is a seasoned corporate and institutional director and champion of causes, including the Athol Murray College of Notre Dame, national unity groups and the unsuccessful drive (which he helped spearhead) to win Expo 2005 for Calgary. He and his wife Stephanie split the family's political exposure: he is the Conservative and has run Ralph Klein's premier's dinner; she is the Liberal. Felesky, an Anglican, and Doug Mitchell, an Evangelist, bring the quiet conviction and integrity of their faith to their work. It ain't worn on their sleeves, but it seems to be one of the things that make them exceptional.

Bruce Green, son of a men's-wear-store owner in the small prairie town of Ponoka, Alberta, is Calgary's leading lawyer for developers. He has ridden real-estate booms and busts for twenty years and is City Hall's memory on land development. He now raises money for Klein and remembers, "When Ralph became the mayor of Calgary, he asked me to join his team, to give him advice and assistance. I reminded him that I hadn't helped him get elected. 'That's okay,' Ralph replied, 'nobody helped me.'"

One of Green's quiet pleasures is to have watched the evaporation of anti-semitism in the city. "At one time it was well known that no Jews were allowed in the Ranchmen's Club or the Glencoe. Calgary was pretty bad in the sixties. But that was years ago," he says. "When we named a woman chief of police in Calgary, and she was Jewish on top of it, everybody reacted well. She is magnificent, an amazing woman and is right up there at the synagogue."

IN THE BURGEONING OIL BOOM OF THE LATE 1970s, the symbol of Calgary's new wealth and power was the high-rise construction crane. The flight path into Calgary's sprawling new international-airport terminal passed just to the east of a forest of these spindly structures perched atop the rising office towers that $30-a-barrel oil built.

Now the cranes are back. TrizecHahn Corp. is proceeding with the fifty-storey Bankers Hall East Tower, an 800,000-square-foot building that Talisman Energy will anchor. TransCanada PipeLines is building a 900,000-square-foot headquarters for the energy-transportation and services giant it is creating through its merger with Nova Corp. Oxford Development is erecting the 440,000-square-foot Millennium Tower. J.J. Barnicke Calgary Ltd. has decided to launch a $200-million, 21-storey, twin-office-tower complex. A Hyatt hotel is being built in conjunction with doubling the size of the Calgary Convention Centre complex, financed by Mannix money and developed by Hal Walker, Ralph Klein's first Calgary-Elbow constituency president. Another hotel, a Sheraton, is going up in the trendy Eau Claire district on the south bank of the Bow River. The site of the city's nineteenth-century lumber yards and, later, Calgary's first up-scale residential district, Eau Claire has been redeveloped. In the 1980s it served as an asphalt desert of parking-lots. Now it is a network of high-end condominiums and nightspots such as the Hard Rock Café, the Barley Mill and Joey Tomato's.

The badge of mercantilism on the march is the squash racket of George Watson, CEO of TransCanada PipeLines. An Ontario farm boy and Queen's University football star, Watson is a familiar figure on the courts of the Bow Valley Club in the Bow Valley Square office complex. A hip-replacement operation earned him the nickname "Gimpy," but hasn't kept him out of the game. Half the hard bodies of both sexes speed-cycling to work through downtown traffic with Mountain Equipment Co-op knapsacks strapped to their backs come from his stable of lawyers and marketers. Three-testicle oil boosters and their beef-eating, Scotch-swilling, cigar-chopping, $1,000-a-hand poker-game habits don't set the civic aesthetic. That era died with men like Carl Nickle. The city now gets its earnest sense of style from Jim Gray, Gordon Jaremko, Fred Peacock, Eddie Laborde, Wayne Perkins, Harold Milavsky and Grant Billings, side by side on their Stairmasters at dawn in the Eau Claire YMCA. Group sex at Friday-night parties has been succeeded, if not replaced, by tightly scheduled group jogging along the south bank of the Bow River during lunch hour. The latest merger ideas aren't mooted at the urinals of the Petroleum Club, beneath those famously witty sketches of dogs in a row peeing on a wall. Now people in sweaty T-shirts test proposals and counter proposals while running in place on street corners, waiting for traffic lights to change. Jim Gray is chairman of Canadian Hunter, Gord Jaremko is editor of *Oilweek*, Fred Peacock was a Lougheed-era industry minister, Eddie Laborde is a transplanted American oilman and one-man Calgary institution, Wayne Perkins runs the YMCA, Harold Milavsky is a land developer and Grant Billings is an independent oilman. More gallons of designer water and carrot juice are sold each year in Calgary than are quarts of single-malt Scotch.

The Porsche is still a status symbol, but so is a $2,000 mountain bike. Calgary's mayor Al Duerr, originally from a farm in Saskatchewan, rides his Harley Davidson to the University of Calgary, where he is completing his MBA in his spare time. Calgary's definition of spare time is the work you do after sixty hours a week.

"People can be dysfunctionally busy, not only with the verve with which they attack their work, but also with the verve with which they attack their social and civic responsibilities. Sixty to seventy hours in the office is nothing," worries Ken King, publisher of the *Calgary Herald*. He thinks this is recognized as a weakness and will be redressed if the city can ever learn to relax and enjoy itself.

The times have produced a new cadre of entrepreneurs: tough, intense Titans who feel strong enough to make the hard climb back up the slope from the corporate wreckage of 1986. The most popular outdoor pastimes are not the club box, spectator sports of hockey and football that entertained Alberta's rich and powerful in the 1970s and 1980s. Now the affluent and the influential participate in aggressive, daring personal tests such as white-water rafting, rock climbing, speed cycling, mountain biking, marathons, triathlons and iron-man competitions. Brett Wilson of FirstEnergy Capital Corporation takes his partners, star employees and clients white-water rafting in Costa Rica or to the Baja 1000.

When the Calgary Stampeder Football Club was community owned, it had a place on the social agenda: the games were a place to meet and mingle, club operations attracted volunteer support, and players retired to good jobs downtown. That era's gone, too. The pressures of financing marquee players such as quarterback Doug Flutie brought private ownership to the team. The first of the kamikaze financiers was Larry Ryckman, a home-town boy aflame with ambition and flexible business standards. He was driven out of business in disgrace after running afoul of Alberta Stock Exchange regulators (not an easy assignment) and getting buried by highly leveraged Alberta Treasury Branch loans.

Sig Gutsche—who made his money as a seismic data broker, owns the Hard Rock Café franchise in Calgary and is on no known social "A" list—replaced Ryckman as financier of the Calgary Stampeders. His investment in the team was a gamble that he could flip the franchise to a buyer from a major U.S. market; the strategy has stalled with the failure of CFL expansion south. The result is that football games are no longer on the social circuit, and the parties the players get invited to involve booze, not company presidents with off-season jobs to offer.

Professional hockey has fared better. The Calgary Flames, acquired in 1980 from Atlanta businessman Tom Cousins, play in the Saddledome, which has been upgraded to accommodate the corporate schmoozing that goes on around the games. "A lot of high-profile people meet either in their own boxes or in somebody else's suite at the Saddledome," President Ron Bremner says. "It's a great place to do business and socialize around a hockey game, entertainment group or recording artist."

So important is hockey's business connection that Canadian Airlines International paid $10 million to have its name attached to the Saddledome at a time when the airline was on its financial deathbed. (It has since recovered to maintain its status in the lineup of transportation companies that have given Calgary one of its major building blocks in its economic diversification.) "Owning an NHL franchise in a small Canadian market is not a business," moans former university dean and independent oilman Grant Barlett, who holds a 6-percent interest in the team. "A business is something you do to make money."

When Canada's Olympic hockey team trained in Calgary for three winters prior to the 1980 Lake Placid games, Daryl ("Doc") and Byron Seaman, the controlling shareholders of Bow Valley Industries, led a group of investors in a bid for the Atlanta Flames. Vancouver high-flyer Nelson Skalbania beat them out, then in a flip that earned him $4 million, he sold the franchise to the Calgary group. In addition to the Seamans, the original big six included Ralph Scurfield, head of the Nu-West Group land-development corporation, Norman Green of Stewart Green Properties, former Edmonton Eskimos football star Normie Kwong and private oil- and real-estate investor Harley Hotchkiss. Former Chicago Blackhawks star centre Bill Hay, who played on the team's million-dollar line with Bobby Hull and Murray Balfour and was a vice-president of Bow Valley Resource Services, controlled by the Seamans, stepped in as president of the team. Hockey genius Cliff Fletcher was hired on as general manager.

The team started out losing $6 million in the first three years and has never made money, but has sunk more than $10 million into amateur- and junior-hockey development. Ralph Scurfield died in 1985 and Norm Green split off to buy the Minnesota North Stars and move them to Dallas. Scurfield's widow Sonja and Normie Kwong wanted out, and the Seamans felt it prudent to create a succession plan that would bring in younger men with deep pockets willing to share in the risks and costs of a long-term future for professional hockey. The group bought the Scurfield, Green and Kwong interests and brought in Ron Joyce, of Tim Horton's, and oil financier Murray Edwards to each hold 15-percent stakes with Hotchkiss and the two Seamans. The remaining 25-percent stake in the team was sold in four equal pieces to Bartlett; private investor Al Libin; Bud McCaig, founder of Trimac Inc.; and Al Markin, chairman of Canadian Natural Resources. In 1997, Hotchkiss was elected by the NHL owners to a two-year term as league chairman, and Ron Bremner has replaced Bill Hay in the team's corner office. Although the Canadian Airlines Saddledome is a community facility, Bremner is also its president.

Hockey's main rival as a gathering point for business networks is Spruce Meadows. Owned by the Southern family, its series of international jumping competitions from the first weekend in June to Labour Day are serious social as well as sporting events and a key conduit for business networks. Companies who don't own a coveted club box make sure their logos are prominently displayed around the competition arena. More ambitious firms, such as fertilizer giant Agrium, sponsor events on the grounds and turn Spruce Meadows into a giant family picnic.

Charitable and political fund-raising events dot the calendar from September to June; the Palliser Hotel, the Westin and the Convention Centre are the preferred venues. More exclusive engagements include the Banff Midsummer Ball and the Oilmen's Golf Tournament at the Banff Springs Hotel. Golfing is the premier way to mix business and pleasure during the week. The Calgary Golf and Country Club and the Glenco Club's course outside the city are the favoured locations to be seen teeing off, but important golf-course meetings are as likely to take place in Phoenix or in Scarsdale, Arizona. Weekend trips to Seattle Seahawks or Denver Broncos NFL football games are used as business tools by Alberta companies who hold season's tickets for those American teams.

You can't run an oil company out of the Owl's Nest or Hy's Steakhouse any more, as some tried to do in the 1970s. The city's *maîtres d'* are its most important social coordinators, and they relish their role as keepers of reservations books and marital secrets. "Without life the universe would be nothing, and all life needs is nourishment," philosophizes Gus Christopher, who owns Benny's Bistro, a favourite lunching place for the likes of Murray Edwards and Bob Lamond. Benny's boasts the longest lunch-time waiting list in the city and has a busy office-catering service for those who can't take time to eat at a table. Everyone who is anyone chomps catered-in sandwiches for lunch most days—at their desks or in boardrooms and signing rooms. Benny's owner Gus Christopher is the brother of John Scrymgeour's second wife (now deceased). When his sister died, he helped John Scrymgeour purchase land on the Gulf of Corinth so that she could be buried in her birthplace. His regulars included the late David Walsh of Bre-X, who came for coffee in the years he couldn't afford lunch. Benny's is also the venue of the Friends of Friday, a periodic gathering of influential journalists, PR types and magazine writers for off-the-record camaraderie that keeps the lines of communication open between the media and the city's most important companies and government agencies.

The venerable Ranchmen's and Petroleum clubs have become more functional places to eat. Their surviving advantage is that their tables are too widely spaced to eavesdrop. More leisurely lunches are indulged in at Gaston's or at Caesar's, which face each other on Fourth Avenue. Teatro and Drinkwaters Grill on the Olympic Plaza across from City Hall attract a happy crowd for the *nouveau* menu and exotic martinis.

Cult lunchers still go to the St. Louis Tavern, made famous by Ralph Klein when he was the beer-swilling mayor, as opposed to the beer-swilling premier. When he's in town, Klein is now more likely to have a steak at Caesar's. The city's dean of geophysicists, Easton Wren, triggered a generational shift in 1982 when he stopped going to lunch and started to spend noon hours running.

Out of downtown, Herbert Sattlegger's La Chaumière is a magnet for the Titans. Publisher Ken King stops by in late evenings for a beer and a chicken sandwich. The original La Chaumière was a smallish place with a low ceiling. When the place required a badly overdue renovation, its popularity prompted the owners to build an entirely new structure, which mostly draws clients who have the luxury of two-hour lunch breaks. On weekends, the Post Hotel at Lake Louise—home of Alberta's finest restaurant, housed in a magnificent log pile and situated in a breathtaking mountain valley—draws the serious gourmand who like to mix menus and mergers.

Ed Galvin, founder of Poco Petroleum, recently gave the Calgary Foundation $3 million in memory of his wife, Frances. The Calgary Foundation was established 1955 by Carl Nickle, Charles Lee and other independent Oil Patchers. In 1990, it was one of the smallest community foundations in the West with barely $10 million under management, but now has more than $70 million in trust. Voyageur Petroleum founder Sid Kahnoff used his fortune to create the Kahnoff Foundation before his premature death from cancer, emulating the largesse of the city's first oil philanthropist Eric L. Harvie, who created the Glenbow museum, art collection and archives and the Devonian Foundation with his Leduc oil fortune. "I don't know if this is a variation of the old Prairie barn raising, but this community really rallies, and it's extraordinary what people give back and what they do," Ken King says.

The city's symbols were altered and its values deeply imprinted by these years in the 1980s, as hard as the midwinter ice choking the Bow River. Private jets are out; royalty trusts are in. Wildcat wells are out; investments in gas plants and crude-oil batteries are in. If you are *nouveau riche*, you try to muddy the fact by living in an older neighbourhood or marrying into social depth. Enthusiasm and adrenalin count for much less, and unbridled optimism is openly suspect. Risk tolerance is exceedingly low; perhaps that is the best marker of the great divide between 1981 and 1998. Serendipity is still permissible, but only lasting achievement is accepted as genuine. Although the price of oil is still the unelected governor of the province's economic mood swings, it is no longer the only game in town. Natural gas and the oil sands have broadened the base. A financial sector, including private merchant banking and equity-investment houses, and a major transportation sector of pipelines, rail and airlines have both grown up. Niche software developers are in the mezzanine stage between speculative startup and critical mass.

Calgary is still a city in a hurry, where bicycle-mounted cops with hand-held radar guns issue tickets to speeding cyclists on the city's bicycle paths.

The civic and business culture has a much harder edge than it did in the halcyon days of the oil boom.

It is much harder to break in here, more unforgiving if you fail. The sense of possibility and the feeling of an open, generous community tuned to the public good are attenuated by the hunger for stability and predictability. There is not much room for the vision thing, and the appetite for political risk is strictly limited.

A civic identity lacking social responsibility is a foreboding thing.

But that's why Calgary is a smaller place than it was when it had fewer people and narrower boundaries.

20

THE NORTHERNERS

"There isn't anybody in this city that you're more than one handshake away from being able to meet."

—*Dennis Erker, president of the Edmonton Eskimos*

ALBERTA'S COMMERCIAL LIFE IS A TALE of two cities: Calgary provides its mercantile heart, but Edmonton endows it with a history. Founded as a Hudson's Bay Company fort in 1795, the city's two hundred years' experience has given Edmontonians time to develop a mature sense of community. Edmonton has a gentility best expressed on the white nights of summer: dusk extends until nearly midnight in the northern latitudes, and the low elevation and further distance from the mountains ensure much warmer evenings than Calgary's. A series of cultural festivals—jazz in June and the Fringe in August—are the highlights of the season. Winter is frigid, lacking the chinooks of southern Alberta, but much more endurable than the endless snow and dampness of Montreal or Ottawa. The cold season is warmed by the magical stages of the city's twenty professional theatre groups.

This is a sports town, made so by the sterling Edmonton Eskimos, the Oilers and the Trappers baseball franchise. Fishing trips to the north and weekend golfing rounds are important to business, but the place where serious networking goes on is at Bodies By Bennett in the Marchand Mansion behind Mel Hurtig's house. Sam Bennett and his cadre of personal trainers have half of Edmonton's health-conscious Titans on their client list.

Edmonton is a city with a sense of possibilities, a place that is both the outpost and the threshold for great ventures. For its first hundred years, fur-trading Edmonton was the most important commercial centre west of Winnipeg, a lynch pin in the Hudson's Bay Company's network of forts. People boasted that the initials HBC really meant Here Before Calgary. Its muddy streets were peopled with adventurers and fortune seekers whose tales of outward-bound opportunity electrified social life. Bypassed by rail development until 1902, it lost to Calgary its primacy of place as Alberta's business community. However, its character as a staging place for great undertakings was honed at the end of the nineteenth century during the Klondike gold rush, as prospectors passed through town on their way to the Yukon.

At the start of the twentieth century, the homesteaders arrived. Unwritten immigration policy preserved the ranching country of southern Alberta for WASPs and directed eastern Europeans north to establish Ukrainian, German, Romanian, Icelandic, Jewish, Polish and Czech enclaves in the city and in a great arc around it. Some of Edmonton's blue-collar atmosphere is still attributable to the egalitarian outlook of the continental Europeans.

In 1905, the great newspaper publisher and Laurier cabinet minister Frank Oliver used his grease in Ottawa to ensure that Edmonton became the provincial capital, to the astonishment and outrage of Calgarians, thus planting the seeds of inter-city rivalry. A remarkable engineer and scientist, Henry Marshall Tory laid the foundation for the University of Alberta to become the greatest intellectual and research centre on the Prairies.

It was the opening of the North—beginning with experimentation at the oil sands between 1919 and 1945 and the Great Bear Lake uranium play of the 1930s—that branded Edmonton as the gateway to the North. Its municipal airfield was home base to Canada's greatest bush pilots, including Wop May and Max Ward. Tentacles of rail and road unravelled eastward to Athabasca and to the pioneering tar-sands projects, northward to the headwaters of the Mackenzie River and west to the great homesteads of the Peace Country.

The Second World War cemented the northern connection when two great U.S. Army enterprises—the building of the Alaska Highway and the development of the Norman Wells oilfield and the Canol pipeline— were staged out of Edmonton. After the war, oil exploration in northern Alberta depended on road and air connections in the city, and the province's main oil-related manufacturing facilities—such as drilling rigs, pipeline factories and tubular mills—were established at Nisku and Leduc, south of Edmonton. Nearby Fort Saskatchewan became the chemical and refining centre of the province, and chemicals are now the fourth-largest industry in Alberta. But mostly, Edmonton became a government city. The singular difference between Edmonton and Calgary is that the corporate decisions that affect Edmonton-based mineral exploration, oil sands, forestry, chemicals, transportation and northern exploration are mostly taken elsewhere. Northern development decisions are less and less colonial and made more and more in the indigenous communities north of the sixtieth parallel. Edmonton is a servant to industry, not its decision maker. It is Fortress North for liberal civility, intellectual and artistic life, the preserver of the northern vision and the northern connection for southern Canadians.

The Edmonton community crossed a social and cultural watershed with the purchase of the Oilers on May 5, 1998. Peter Pocklington's hyped-up business style—composed of bluff, leverage and salesmanship—had garnered plenty of ink for twenty-five years and created a Klondike-gambler image of Edmonton for the rest of the world. When Pocklington was sidelined by the forced sale of the hockey team, a more representative business leadership emerged in the thirty-five new owners. The Oilers now have more principals than players. The background and experience of this Team Edmonton accurately reflects the city as being, in the words of lawyer David Margolus, "an incubator for people who create something that is recognized, both here and in other places, as being something special."

Pocklington didn't create Edmonton's hyperbolic business image alone. The Ghermezian brothers—Nader, Eskandar, Raphael and Bahman—developers of the city's theme-park shopping centre, the $900-million West Edmonton Mall—did their bit to make the city Canada's capital of leverage. Devout Hasidic Jews who were born in Tehran, the Ghermezians immigrated to Canada in 1986 and started a rug store in Edmonton. Their flagship Triple Five Corp. was formed with the backing of 551 silent partners, Iranians who needed a secret conduit to reinvest their wealth in order to avoid Iran's notoriously capricious habit of retroactive taxation. Triple Five invested in 3,500 apartment units, office buildings, hotels and strip malls before developing the West Edmonton Mall, which opened in three stages. They once talked of cloning their monument to conspicuous consumption in Germany, China, Britain, Toronto and Niagara Falls. But the West Edmonton Mall hit a cash crunch in 1994 and was refinanced by Nomura Canada and the Alberta Treasury Branches (ATB).

The Ghermezians still control the mall, but the asset is encumbered by several tranches of mortgage financing. In the summer of 1998, the ATB applied to put the mall into receivership, sparking lawsuits and a criminal investigation into the circumstances of the 1994 refinancing. Meanwhile, the brothers are quietly expanding a family compound on Wellington Crescent. They own eight of fourteen houses, have built the first of a planned series of connecting tunnels and want to purchase the rest of the houses. They live an old-style Hasidic life. They pray rigorously, wear black even when skiing, and their children attend Yeshiva universities.

David Margolus says that land developers are bullishly projecting that, in a business-driven resurgence following the shrinkage of the government payroll in the Klein revolution, Edmonton's "employment growth, net migration and housing starts will significantly surpass Calgary's." The growth will come from Edmonton's role as the jumping-off point to the North, including the oil-sands expansion, oil and gas servicing, forestry, the chemical industry and the agricultural industries. International investors are arriving to purchase commercial and office space; there are land flips, bidding and outbidding in a dynamic run-up to anticipated business expansion.

The co-captains of Team Edmonton are Jim Hole, the chairman of the owners' group, and Bruce Saville, the catalyst of the venture. Jim, age seventy-six, is a member of Edmonton's first family, which will celebrate 100 years in the city in 1999. His father, Henry, founded Lockerbie and Hole in 1906, a plumbing- and electrical-supply concern that bears the name of the Scottish town. It flourished and allowed Jim and his brother Harry to expand into real-estate through privately owned Frobisher Development, after they turned the original business over to the third generation some fifteen years ago. Another brother Ted and his wife Lois own and operate Hole's Greenhouses and Gardens in St. Alberta, a bedroom community on Edmonton's north-west edge. With three thousand customers a day in season and a $1.5-million payroll, it may be the most successful horticultural business in Canada.

The Holes are the city's leading philanthropists, and Lois is its most important opinion leader. "Some people buy jet planes and stuff. Ours is just a different way of life, I guess, from most people," says Harry. "We're just fortunate enough to be able to [contribute]. I don't know if it's so much a sense of obligation as a sense of responsibility that you can do it, so you should. It's not stopping my wife from darning her socks."

Although she doesn't have a university degree, Lois is the chancellor of the University of Alberta. She has written widely read horticultural texts and is in demand as a speaker on gardening. She joined the 1996 Quality of Life Commission, led by lawyer and former Progressive Conservative MP Doug Roche, to examine the impacts of government cuts on social, educational and health programmes. The commission's report entitled, "Listen to Me," first warned of the "social upheaval" created by "broken families, unemployment and ravaged health and education programmes." The term "social activist" hardly covers everything Lois Hole does, but the garden and greenhouse company budgeted $250,000 in 1998 for 1,400 charitable contributions.

"My family came up through hard times, and it wasn't easy for my dad to put food on the table," says Harry. "My mom was making her own clothes and taking somebody's suit and cutting it down for me to wear to school. But I'll tell you that any time some guy came and banged on the door and wanted a meal, he got it. I guess that charitable approach rubs off on you." The family established the Annie Hole Children's Nutritional Fund, under the aegis of the Edmonton Community Foundation, to provide hot lunches and snacks for hungry kids in the schools. When they gave $5 million to the Citadel Theatre to honour their dad, the theatre board wanted to rename the building the Henry Hole Centre for the Performing Arts. The Holes insisted, instead, on a small bronze plaque dedicating the theatre to Henry's memory.

"Look here," says Harry, "the great thing about Edmonton is that the Establishment is the ordinary guy. People support one another. It's so much easier to get things done—a thing like the Oilers or the support you get for any fund drives. It's a good place to live."

Toronto-born Bruce Saville worked for Bell Canada in New Liskeard, Ontario, and fell in love with the combination of computers and telephones. He quit Bell to work for a small computer-service company in Thornhill, which served some of Ontario's thirty-five independent municipal phone companies. One of the services his employer provided was billing. In 1982, Saville set up a one-man software company to develop programming that could handle the billing. Saville Systems, which is listed on the NASDQ, developed billing software that is used by some of those tiny Ontario phone companies, as well as by AT&T, Sprint and Time Warner.

"We have 1,000 employees: 500 in Edmonton, 350 in Toronto, 100 in Ireland and the rest in customer-support offices in Singapore, London, Boston, Miami and Frankfurt. We located in Edmonton in 1986 because Edmonton Tel was our first customer when we had four or five people," says Saville. Now, most programming and research and development is done in Edmonton.

Semi-retired after pocketing an estimated $10 million from his venture, Saville won't think of leaving the city. "It's a big village. After a few years, you know everybody in town. If you go to a football or hockey game, you know half the people there. If you go to five different fund-raisers, five nights in a row, it's the same guys there every night. The village network does its first-tee deals at the Mayfair Golf and Country Club," says Saville, although the Edmonton Country Club and the Petroleum Golf Club are popular. "The Windemere Golf and Country Club is for serious players."

Saville became an Oilers booster because "I'm a wannabe athlete." Now he wants Peter Pocklington to sell him the Edmonton Trappers Triple-A baseball team, so he can turn it into a community venture.

The other major volunteer sports executive in town is Dennis Erker, who made his money in the Fairley Erker financial-advice and services group that he started with Grant Fairley in 1973. They provide retirement planning and advice on insurance and employee benefits, and are the city's leading wealth managers. Erker is also president of the Edmonton Eskimos community-owned football club. "When we hosted the Grey Cup [in 1997] we had more than 900 volunteers registered to work with us. We have more season-ticket holders per capita than any other Canadian Football League franchise." Being a director of the Eskimos is some volunteer commitment. Erker and his eight fellow directors were personally on the hook for a $900,000 loan taken to preserve the franchise through the 1997 season when the club was more than $800,000 in debt. Even before picking up $3 million in Grey Cup-event revenues, the team had made a $155,000 profit after wiping out the debt. Now with more than $2 million in a stabilization fund, the Eskimos are among the most secure franchises in Canadian sports.

"I guess the unique thing about Edmonton, compared to Calgary with its head offices, is the fact that we are in small business and we recognize that we are in small business," Erker admits. "In Calgary, social life tends to be segregated by how you make your living. All the guys in the energy business have their cocktails together and all the people in the financial business have theirs, and the brokerage community meets only together. We don't have that here because we are not big enough." Erker's Edmonton is a place of swimming pools and cottages in the summer and golfing trips to Arizona in the winter. "We have a better lifestyle and better climate than Calgary," he claims.

For all its small-business cachet, Edmonton is home to three significant corporations, and their CEOs, while relatively new to the community, are making a place for themselves. The Alberta Treasury Branches, recently made a formal Crown corporation, is undergoing a makeover from a lender of last resort and becoming a policy instrument to a competitive financial institution. Paul Haggis, its CEO and superintendent, shares credit for the turnaround with chairman Marsh Williams. Haggis is a former chief operating officer with Metropolitan Life, which has a major presence in Edmonton.

George Petty, the president and CEO of Telus Corporation, runs the third-largest and most ambitious full-service telecommunications company in Canada. Telus was government owned, and Petty has changed its identity from a stodgy phone utility to an aggressive exploiter of the Internet, of cellular and satellite phones and other advanced technology. Petty is also a director of CAE Inc., a member of the Alberta Economic Development Authority, a director of the Edmonton Opera Association and a governor of the University of Alberta.

Larry Pollock is the president and CEO of Alberta's little competitor with the major banks, Canadian Western Bank. He is also a director of the bank and president and director of its trust arm, Canadian Western Trust.

Glen Sather is the president and general manager of the Edmonton Oilers hockey club. Hockey has already made him rich, and Sather could work anywhere in the NHL for any amount of money. The fifty-four-year-old hockey genius turned down offers in 1998 from Toronto, San Jose and several other teams to sign on with the new owners of the Oilers. He cited two reasons. He worked hard to warn players who are using free-agency status to drive up hockey salaries that the game can't sustain the trend. He calls it a sweepstakes and says he couldn't turn into a carpet-bagger himself after fighting for player loyalty. The second reason is that "Edmonton is home," with a lifestyle that he and his family can't replace elsewhere.

Cathy Roozen, daughter of the late Dr. Charles Allard and co-heir with her brothers to the family media fortune, is the first lady of Edmonton business. Her personal interests are owned through Cathton Holdings, and she is secretary of the Allard Foundation and a director of Shaw Communications. Charolette Robb is the vice-president of the Alberta and Northwest Territories division of the Canadian Imperial Bank of Commerce. She also co-chairs Ralph Klein's Alberta Economic Development Authority and is an executive member of the C.D. Howe Institute. Her ranking in the parallel fields of banking and public affairs makes her the most influential economic policy shaper in the province, outside of government.

A monogrammed shirt made by the ebullient, cigar-chomping custom tailor Sam Abouhassan may cost you $150; a suit, $2,200. He golfs with

Glen Sather, and his client list includes more NHL players than any other tailor in North America. He also holds the market for Alberta's wealthiest people; he is the city's one-man Savile Row.

No account of Team Edmonton would be complete without Mel Hurtig, the scrappy publisher and social conscience of the city. Son of a Romanian tailor and furrier, Hurtig started an Edmonton book store and built it into the biggest general-trade publisher west of Toronto. His first title, A *Natural History of Alberta*, sold 77,000 copies. After the monumentally successful *Canadian Encyclopedia* was published in 1980, making him $2.2 million, Hurtig turned down an offer to sell out, gambled the farm and lost with the ill-timed *Junior Canadian Encylopedia*. The failed venture didn't wipe him out, but he had to make a living again as an author, public speaker and media personality. Always a passionate anti-poverty crusader and children's advocate, he co-founded the Council of Canadians. A past Liberal candidate, his most quixotic political adventure was to found and lead the National Party of Canada, which unsuccessfully ran candidates in the 1993 federal election. Hurtig continues to write best-selling books and to goad the national conscience.

"I was brought up to believe you should be in the newspapers three times: when you're born, when you're married and when you die," says the reclusive and very rich Sandy Mactaggart. Now seventy, Mactaggart made millions as co-founder of Maclab Enterprises, a private-investment, property-development and management business. An architect with an MBA from Harvard, he and classmate Jean de la Bruyère started building houses in Edmonton in 1952. As they prospered, they branched out into oil and gas production, venture-capital investments and apartment construction. Mactaggart has lived adventurously, ballooning, jet boating and yachting around the world. He was virtually unknown in his own city until 1990, when he served a term as chancellor of the University of Alberta, which raised his profile briefly. He lives at Soaring, a magnificent, secluded estate in southwest Edmonton named for the eagles he can see from his sprawling house. Wayne Gretzky and Janet Jones had their wedding photos taken there, and the royal family sleeps over when they're in Edmonton. The house has a deep swimming pool in a Polynesian court, and Mactaggart can swing, Tarzan-like, from his bedroom balcony into the pool at the beginning of each day: it's Edmonton's most unusual wake-up call.

Brian Hesje is the president of Fountain Tire, which has auto-repair and tire-sales partnerships in eighty Alberta communities and earns more than $130 million in sales annually. Hesje is a director of the Albert

Treasury Branch, the Western Canada Tire Dealers Association and the Northern Alberta Institute of Technology.

Joe Thompson is chairman, president and CEO of PCL Construction, following in the considerable footsteps of John and George Poole and Bob Stollery. Also at PCL is the affable Ross Grieve. And then there's Walter Makowecki, chairman, president and CEO of Heritage Foods, who built his wealth by selling 2 billion perogies. Craig Martin, the publisher of *The Edmonton Sun*, helped engineer the management buyout of the *Sun* chain in 1997. Angus Watt, a vice-president and director of Levesque Securities, is Edmonton's leading broker and financial counsellor and was his firm's top producer in 1992 and 1994.

Neil Wilkinson is chairman of the Capital Health Authority and is Edmonton's equivalent of Calgary's Bud McCaig. As the former owner and president of Barcol Doors and Windows, Wilkinson made his money as a window and door supplier to the Alberta housing industry. John Ferguson, a chartered accountant, is the founder, chairman and CEO of Princeton Developments, a significant property development and management company. He holds directorships at the Royal Bank of Canada, Suncor and TransAlta Utilities. He has been chairman of the board of governors of the University of Alberta and is a senior member of the New York-based Conference Board Inc.

David Margolus is the managing partner of the twenty-eight-member law firm of Witten Binder, whose client list includes the full sweep of the business community. He is Edmonton's Mr. Insider. Dennis McCarthy, an engineer, is president of the AGRA Construction Group, and vice-president and director of AGRA Inc., a giant Canadian construction and engineering company. Eugene Pechet is the 86-year-old patriarch of the family that is the largest shareholder group in the Canadian Western Bank. Bill Comrie is the owner of the Brick Furniture Warehouse chain and briefly owned the B.C. Lions football franchise. Ron Triffo is president of Stanley Group, an engineering group listed on the Toronto Stock Exchange.

It's a tidy community, but its ethic still reflects the toughness of the frontier exemplified by John Rowand, Fort Edmonton's original HBC Chief Factor. When several of his men came down with a serious illness, Rowand accused them of shirking their duty and decreed: "Any man who is not dead within three days' is not sick at all."

21

THE STALWARTS

"Wheat will come back. Always has from the time of Moses in Egypt.
They'll want wheat. They'll need it. They'll buy it. And we can grow
it. This is the best land in the world."

—*Bruce Hutchison (quoting a farmer named Hearn)*,
The Unknown Country, *1942*

IN HIS DEFINING BOOK ON THE FIRST HALF OF Canada's twentieth
century, *The Unknown Country*, Bruce Hutchison recounts the "magical
accident" of the wheat boom that opened up Saskatchewan. In 1843,
David Fife, a farmer near Peterborough, Ontario, planted two quarts of
wheat seeds that his friend George Essen had taken from a grain ship
unloading in Glasgow. Fife's cow ate all but two of the stalks growing
in the experimental patch. The remaining reddish grain matured ten
days earlier than anything Fife had yet grown, so he harvested forty
precious seeds in a teacup and developed them into a popular seed grain
successfully planted on the Prairies in 1876. A federal scientist, Dr. W.S.
Saunders, tested Red Fife against varieties from every plain in the world
and discovered that the wheat on the boat in Glasgow came from
Galicia. Several years later, his son Dr. Charles Saunders found a single
remaining grain in a glass bottle among his father's samples and grew it
for curiosity, then crossed it with a sample from India. The result was the
Marquis wheat, which underpinned Interior Minister Clifford Sifton's
homesteading policy that settled the Canadian plains. The result, wrote
Hutchison, was the wheat boom, "the largest economic event so far in
Canadian history that transformed the whole character and future of the
country." Had a different grain ship been in the Glasgow harbour, had
Fife's cow finished off its dinner, or had Saunders thrown out the single

grain in the bottle, Regina might have amounted to little more than that pile of bleached buffalo bones that gave it its first name.

Fifty years after Hutchison, the initiative and energy of the wheat boom had leached out of the dense black soil, taking with it Saskatchewan's optimistic and individualistic culture. During the long hegemony of the CCF and New Democrats, economic power and decision making was concentrated in Crown corporations and farmer-owned cooperatives. Private money accumulated in select, usually smaller, businesses: insurance, food processing, farm equipment and supplies, construction, the media, retail and such. Large blocks of capital were siphoned off to Alberta's oil and gas industry and to other outside investments. Some of the biggest opportunities—in utilities, telephones, food production and grain handling—were off limits. Government corporations and cooperatives competed in the potash and oil-and-gas sectors, a circumstance that discouraged outside capital, in the rare event its owners could bring themselves to trust successive socialist premiers.

In the 1980s the province experienced its worst recession since the Great Depression. All its commodities—oil, wheat, natural gas, pulp and potash—were caught in a worldwide downturn of demand for raw materials. In 1991, novelist Sharon Butala's book *The Fourth Archangel* told the story of a dying town called Ordeal, in which the central character laments, "Maybe it will all go back to the wild—be full of animals and the grass will grow again."

Grain elevators were torn down, abandoned rail lines were overgrown with weeds, and towns disappeared. Less than a quarter of Saskatchewan's million people live outside the major centres. There was many a boarded-up storefront in Regina, and locked-up school buildings dotted the country roads.

A bitter one-liner made the rounds: "Will the last person out of Saskatchewan please turn out the lights." Just the way a generation of Maritimers had gone down the road to Toronto, now Saskatchewan's brightest loaded up their cars and took their freshly printed diplomas to Calgary. The nation turned its back, except during Grey Cup season when the annual marvel was that the Roughriders were still in the game.

Then the Prairie soil stirred once more. In retrospect, the benchmarks are easy to spot. Commodity markets recovered. The long era of Tommy Douglas socialism, which had denied Saskatchewan the evolution of a business establishment, ended. First, Premier Ross Thatcher and then, after an interval, Grant Devine's Conservative government opened the door to private capital. In the Devine years, Regina-based Harco Financial,

part of the $1-billion Hill-family holdings, purchased a 42-percent inter-
est in Crown Life Insurance, and the company moved its head office to
Regina. The province shed its oil company, which became Wascana
Resources, now a subsidiary of Canadian Occidental Petroleum. Between
1989 and 1996, three giant resource companies—the Saskatchewan
Wheat Pool; the Potash Corporation of Saskatchewan, a former Saskatchewan Crown corporation; and uranium and gold producer Cameco—
issued common shares that were listed on the Toronto or New York stock
exchanges. Potash and Cameco grew out of Crown mineral assets.

Free trade transformed the grain industry, and U.S. agricultural giant
Cargill moved in to compete with the grain cooperatives. The cooperatives themselves became more competitive. Canadian Cooperative
Refineries, part of the Federated Cooperatives empire, went toe to toe
with Husky Oil in the heavy-oil upgrading business, building a $700-
million upgrader in Regina for NewGrade Energy to increase its production of synthetic crude oil to 55,000 barrels per day. NewGrade was
completed to the time the Husky Upgrader that upgrades was set up to handle
65,000 barrels a day at Lloydminster.

Saskatoon became a northern light for new business development.
The University of Saskatchewan's College of Commerce is a hotbed of
entrepreneurial effort. An agricultural biotechnology sector is developing
around the non-profit Ag-West Biotech, a research and development
catalyst. Saskatoon's economic development authority seized on the one
feature of the province that drives other Canadians nuts when they drive
through its pancake-flat topography by coining the slogan, "So flat we
can see the future."

"The economy of Saskatchewan has evolved significantly in the last
decade," says local Titan Doug Richardson of the Saskatoon law firm of
McKercher McKercher & Whitmore and one of the province's legal
bigwigs. "A new era exists, not just because of higher resource revenues
or new crops. Canola has become the number one cash crop replacing #1
Red Spring wheat, and there is expansion in biotechnology and other
fields. On the oil and gas side, the strong resource economy is a mirror to
some degree of Alberta. Oil and gas exploration is at its best levels in
over a decade. The resource sector, however, has expanded into uranium,
a substantial potash base, a smaller gold base and a strengthened forestry
industry. Clearly Saskatchewan is no longer a have-not province."

The demise of the Crow Rate has changed farming economics so
that there is an incentive now for farmers to integrate production, processing and transportation. The buzz phrase is "value added." Deals for

private companies to take over rail lines abandoned by the CPR and CNR are being evaluated. A new cooperative corporate structure, called New Generation Co-op (NGC), is being developed to create food-processing facilities such as pasta plants. The New Generation Co-ops, pioneered in Minnesota and North Dakota, are capitalized by farmers who also sign contracts to deliver production to a proposed plant. The plant is built to the capacity of the contracts. Unlike the traditional open-ended co-op, membership is capped, but the profits are still divided equally and each farmer has one vote. The Centre for Co-op Studies in Saskatoon, headed by Murray Fulton, is developing new ideas for cooperative businesses and encouraging their application through a community-development process lead by Byron Henderson. This is just one more way that Saskatoon has become the province's hotbed of entrepreneurs.

An idyllic life in Saskatchewan, as portrayed in the 1908 rhapsody written by Prairie poet and prophet Robert Stead, is coming to pass again, a Prairie of peace and prosperity surrounding joyous cities "where all is expansion and gain." Saskatchewan has developed something new: prairie Titans building commercial enterprises in Saskatchewan that add to the weight of western wealth.

Saskatchewan's oldest and largest private fortune belongs to Regina's Hill family, which once owned the land in Regina where the provincial legislature now stands. Founded in 1903 and currently run by the third generation in the person of fifty-four-year-old Paul Hill, the family business, McCallum Hill, has held real-estate, insurance, broadcasting and oil-and-gas interests. Its businesses are now estimated to be worth well over $1 billion.

Paul's colourful father, Fred, a Harvard MBA, proved his legendary grit when he was kicked out of the RCAF in 1941 because of a heart murmur. He wanted to fight in the war, so he joined the U.S. Army Air Force and piloted heavy bombers over Italy, earning the Distinguished Flying Cross and Air Medal with three oak-leaf clusters. He purchased the McCallum Hill Companies from his father in 1947 and established Western Surety a year later, in order to sidestep the takeover by the Tommy Douglas government of the family-owned Saskatchewan Guarantee & Fidelity. Under his aegis, the family developed land, acquired broadcasting licenses and drilled oil wells. Fred was a pure-bred community booster, sitting as a city alderman and as a director of the Saskatchewan Roughriders. He was an admirer of Father Athol Murray and served as chancellor of Notre Dame College when it gave former U.S. president Gerald Ford an honorary degree. But he played down his wealth, once buying up nearly all the copies in Saskatchewan of an issue of the Toronto-based *Mayfair* magazine because it described him as a "tycoon".

Fred has three sons and two daughters. His son Paul had a rigorous apprenticeship in high school at Notre Dame, and completed his studies at Western Ontario and Georgetown universities. He spent seven years learning the investment business in Toronto and Winnipeg. He became the president of McCallum Hill in 1978, on the seventy-fifth anniversary of its founding by his grandfather.

Paul expanded and extended the family real-estate interests, but the coup that put his personal imprimatur on the family fortune was the establishment of Harco Financial, formed to purchase a 42-percent interest in Crown Life, bringing the insurance giant and its seven hundred head-office jobs to Regina. For assembling the deal, Hill earned a $500,000 fee, and Harvard Developments was carried on a 5-percent interest in Haro Financial's $250-million investment in Crown Life equity. Premier Devine defended the generous compensation by saying, "When you get a multi-billion-dollar insurance office moving to Regina, it takes some jam to get a commitment. The brains are not just in Toronto and Calgary, you know." In May 1998, Crown Life sold its Canadian individual- and group-insurance operations, its Canadian reinsurance business and its international operations in Hong Kong and the Bahamas to Canada Life, which will also reinsure and administer Crown Life's U.S. business. Canada Life, which was de-mutualizing and preparing to become a publicly traded company, agreed to make Regina the headquarters of its western Canadian operations, thus preserving the jobs and economic benefits that the Devine government secured when Crown Life came to the city.

Paul has inherited his father's brass. He travels the world meeting dignitaries and politicians, and on a recent trip to South Africa, robbers held up him and his wife on a golf course. Their diamond rings, golf clubs and cellular phones were taken; however, Hill persuaded the knife-wielding bandits not to take his camera and film. On that role of film was a picture of him and Nelson Mandela.

In striking contrast to the way Paul Hill has expanded his family's interests, the Mitchell meat-packing family has devoted most of its energy fighting over their company, Intercontinental Packers. The firm has two principal assets in Saskatchewan: its pork-processing plant in Saskatoon, which generates $300 million a year, and a beef plant in Moose Jaw. The late Fred Mandel, an inventor and art collector, founded the business early in the century when he patented a new way to preserve canned ham. The feud has pitted his elderly daughter Joanna Mitchell and two of her children, sometime actors Charles and Camille, against eldest son Fred and his wife LuAn. Fred ran the company for eighteen years before he was fired in 1994, in part because of his lavish lifestyle. The squabble was resolved when Fred and LuAn made a deal to buy the pork plant while the remaining family members took control of the beef plant. In a boardroom family reunion, it was resolved that Joanna remain chairman of the company, Fred vice-chairman and Charles president. The settlement ended a series of multimillion-dollar lawsuits, but the squabbles have reduced the family's influence.

The Pinders built their pharmaceutical fortune during three generations, beginning with a corner drugstore in Saskatoon established by Bob Pinder in 1918. Second-generation brothers Herb, who has an MBA, and Ross, a pharmacist, built a dynamic fifty-fifty partnership, working from adjoining desks in a cramped office where they became "best friends," Ross says. The Saskatoon Trading Company, Saskatoon Drug & Stationery, Pinders Drug Stores, Caprice Cards and Prairieland Drug Wholesale were a dominant force in Saskatchewan and Alberta during the 1970s and 1980s. The family invested successfully in oil, and Herb became a director of TransCanada PipeLines. His sons, Dick and Herb, Jr., briefly shared the presidency of the empire, but the business devolved after Herb and Ross retired. Dick left the province and Herb, Jr., who played in the National Hockey League, retired to become a players' agent.

What other new Titans there are in Saskatchewan are the driving force behind the big, publicly traded corporations. Their CEOs and chairmen are the ranking élite of a new generation of business developers.

With a market capitalization of $3.8 billion, listings on the New York and Toronto stock exchanges, sales in 1997 of $2.3 billion and markets around the world, Potash Corporation is the premier Saskatchewan business story. In eleven years, its chairman and CEO, 65-year-old Charles Childers, turned this once listless Crown mining corporation into a profitable operator and used its cash flow to turn it into a voracious acquisitor. The stock has soared into the stratosphere, trading in the range of $120 per common share. Potash Corp. is the world's largest potash producer and fertilizer company, the third-largest phosphate producer, second-largest nitrogen producer and largest manufacturer of animal-feed phosphates. In its first seven years as a publicly traded company, Potash yielded a cumulative return of 550 percent. Childers's $3.5-million-a-year pay packet startled Saskatchewan's parsimonious farmers, who are accustomed to being long on assets and short on cash. His putative successor Bill Doyle, who was appointed president and chief operating officer in June 1998, has big potash steps to follow.

Paul Schoenals, the Devine government cabinet minister who chaired Potash Corporation from 1987 to 1989, hired Childers away from International Minerals & Chemicals to clean up Potash Corp. and take it public. In 1986, the company had lost $103 million, even though it had the lowest-cost, highest-quality potash mines in the world. "It was a typical Crown [corporation]," says Schoenals. "It was managed politically and had no leadership role in the industry. It was a sink-hole. Childers's job was to make it profitable." He had help from the Devine government, which assumed an $810-million debt, but he also provided the bottom line and shareholder focuses that formed the basis of a game plan of growth through profitability and by spending a lot of cash flow on timely acquisitions.

Bernard Michel, a former French citizen so enamoured with Saskatchewan that he took out Canadian citizenship, is the CEO of uranium and gold producer Cameco Corp. and the province's second-ranking chief executive. He was personally recruited to Cameco by Saskatchewan-born baseball star Bill Gatenby, who passed on the major leagues for a career with Texaco. When Gatenby retired, former premier Grant Devine persuaded him to come home to put Cameco together. The company produces 20 percent of the world's uranium.

The province's most controversial business move of the decade was the 1996 decision by the Saskatchewan Wheat Pool to issue equity and obtain a listing on the Toronto Stock Exchange. Deregulation of agricultural markets had created expansion and acquisition opportunities that required more capital. The goal was to get the financial resources to modernize grain-handling infrastructure and expand into value-added agri-businesses. Traditionalists, including those in other provincial wheat pools, rightly believed the Saskatchewan pool was abandoning cooperative principles, especially when its search for acquisitions threatened their turf.

Ever since Sceptre Resources successfully tested horizontal-drilling applications in heavy-oil production at the Tangleflags field near Lloydminster, Saskatchewan's petroleum sector has used the technology to drive a $3-billion-per-year pace of investment. PanCanadian Petroleum launched a project in south-east Saskatchewan in 1997 that will use carbon dioxide, imported by pipeline from North Dakota, pumped under pressure into oil reservoirs in order to increase production in a low-productivity field. The application of new refining technology at Husky Oil's upgrade capacity in Lloydminster is an important factor in a

$500-million expansion announced in 1998. After record levels of drilling (more than 2,800 wells that produce 400,000 barrels a year), Saskatchewan suffered when oil prices spiked down in 1998; it did not have a great deal of natural-gas production to cushion the 40 percent slump in prices. With 19,000 jobs to protect, the province has responded with oil-royalty reductions, the first in what is expected to be a series of industry-recommended changes to give it a more competitive investment environment.

The opening of Innovation Place, a Saskatoon ag-biotech incubator, and Ag-West Biotech Inc., a non-profit company to encourage research and marketing in the improvement of crop and animal productivity, has turned a fifteen-year do-good cause into a serious business. Ag-West played an integral part in the formation or expansion of six ag-biotech companies, representing $900,000 of investment and the creation of fourteen scientific, technological and support jobs. It merged with the International Centre for Agriculture Science and Technology to manage ICAST's eleven agri-food companies and organizations. And Ag-West and the Indonesian Institute of Sciences signed an agreement for cooperation in research and development in areas of mutual interest, including new crops, improved animal production and environmental protection.

Vaughn Wyant has several car dealerships in western Canada and one of the largest Ford dealerships on the Prairies. Terry Summach heads up one of the largest implement manufacturers in North America, run by himself, his brothers and their children. They work three shifts a day, twenty-four hours a day, selling equipment to Russia, South America and the Orient.

George McNevin built the $3.5-million Eagle Plains Hotel on the Dempster Highway in the Yukon and is expanding into the small-hotel business in northern Saskatchewan. Charlie Knight oversees a major land-holding, oil- and gas- and oil-supply company. Through the Denro Group, he worked with Paul Hill to bring Crown Life to Regina. Knight is a director of the Royal Bank. Jim Yuel has set up a mid-size chemical company with $60 million in sales and heads up the Saskatchewan Regional Economic Development Authority.

Ken Ach, a land developer who started as a hot rodder, has garnered a net worth in excess of $65 million with assets exceeding some $80 million. Robert McKercher, QC, is the Saskatchewan director for Bank of Montreal and one of western Canada's leading courtroom lawyers. His partner Doug Richardson is one of the province's best-connected corporate lawyers and keeper of confidences. Principal Secretary to former

Prime Minister John Turner, Richardson and his brother Blair own TGS Land Development Corporation, a $25-million Saskatchewan real-estate company. Harold McKay is Saskatchewan's representative at the Bank of Canada and a former senior partner of MacPherson, Leslie & Tyerman. He authored a highly constructive study of Canada's banking industry in the fall of 1998, which ought to be the plan for restructuring Canada's financial sector.

22

THE PACIFIC MYSTICS

"No matter what you do, you're always competing with God."

—*Christopher Newton, theatre director, commenting on Vancouver*

SOME SIXTEEN YEARS AGO, when I was preparing to leave Ontario for the West Coast, I sought the advice of Christopher Newton, artistic director of the Shaw Festival, where I was then a governor, about living in British Columbia. Newton had spent his early years directing experimental plays in Vancouver and knew the scene well.

His reply surprised me. "It's stunningly beautiful," he told me, "but it makes for lousy theatre." When I pressed him for an explanation, he shrugged and said, "No matter what you do, you're always competing with God."

It's true. However you occupy your days, God is out there waiting for you to ski, sail, hike, golf, surf, bat a few tennis balls or jog around Stanley Park.

Most cities are built on the histories of their inhabitants. Vancouver doesn't obey that impulse. Its citizens are not a founding people. They love the city's setting and facilities—its magical dawns and sunsets, the faring of the tides, the encircling mountains that don't brood or threaten, but blend into one another, like giant guard dogs at rest. But Vancouverites are generally reluctant to invest their emotions to make their city feel like home. Most newcomers arrive in British Columbia—as I did—as refugees from the frantic towers of Toronto or its equivalent. Having cut themselves off from their own pasts, they tend to think of the city merely as their last stop, the end of the line—as far as you can go and still have medicare. They settle into West Coast living by getting in touch with their feelings, regularly playing poker with their inner child and attending seminars on levitation to make sure they're properly grounded. They live in harmony with the seasons (there are none: the rain is either warm or cold) and are held captive by a landscape too exquisite to leave. Vancouver actually runs on two equally essential fluids: coffee and rain. Drinking refined java is an art form, and few serious conversations take place without the hiss of espresso machines in the background. Choosing the sprinkles on your double shot, low-fat, easy-on-the-foam breve macchiato is a ritual that ranks far ahead of reciting the Lord's Prayer.

Eventually, Vancouverites realize that Canada does not need to be defined by the East; that normalcy is an idea worth cultivating; and that British Columbia is 1.3 times larger than Texas.

But the Vancouver of 1998 is not the same place it was when I moved to British Columbia in 1982. The city enjoyed a decade-long boom, set off by Expo 86, that miracle of a fair that turned Vancouver into a world-class habitat. It seemed that it would never end, that the same druids who had sculpted the Utopian scenery of this blessed place would somehow guard it against bad tidings. But starting about 1995, everything changed. From being at the leading edge of the Canadian economy, prosperous yet funky, Vancouver became just funky. By the autumn of 1997, every list of favourable economic indicators ranked B.C. last. In its forecast of economic growth for 1998, the Toronto-Dominion Bank predicted a measly 0.5-percent increase for B.C., compared to 2.4 percent for P.E.I., which came in second-last among the provinces. The city's galloping growth, fuelled by a tsunami of Hong Kong dollars and immigrants, dried up as the Asian flu sweeping that part of the world turned into pneumonia. At the same time, Vancouver's head-office count kept dropping. In terms of significant corporate HQs, Vancouver now ranks just ahead of Winnipeg, but well behind other Canadian business centres. Vancouver has changed from a head-office to a branch-office economy, and that affects everything from corporate donations to the cultural life of the city. There is not a single B.C. representative in the *Globe's Report on Business* list of Canada's fifty fastest-growing companies. Capital expenditures have dropped 75 percent in the last five years. "We have a flat economy and a lousy business climate," complains Business Council of B.C. vice-president Jock Finlayson. "There is no capital investment growth in B.C. right now."

BACK IN THE LATE 1950S, WHEN I FIRST STARTED visiting Vancouver as a young reporter for *Maclean's* and *The Financial Post*, it was a busy, flourishing company town, and MacMillan Bloedel was the company. Not only did Harvey Reginald MacMillan, who ran the giant wood products firm as his private fiefdom, dominate the city, he acted as if he owned it, and the rest of the province to boot.

I visited the Pacific coast so often that, while I wasn't accepted at the Vancouver Club (being Jewish and all), I did manage to earn a badge of honour that was then considered second best. The Vancouver Hotel's Timber Club, where most of the industry's potentates gathered for lunch, rewarded my persistence with a wooden plate that had my name burned into it, which was produced every time I arrived and ordered my first martini. *[The connection between martinis and forests is admittedly vague, but if you're ever lost in the woods, the easiest way to arrange a rescue is to mix a martini. Somebody is bound to come along to tell you you're doing it wrong.]*

Strange to say that by 1998, MacMillan Bloedel, the company that used to rule Canada's Pacific coast, was no longer British Columbia's richest, or even largest, company, having vanished as a source of power in the business community and as a fountainhead of influence in Vancouver society. Like the Timber Club, its greatness exists mainly in the memory of those who recall its glory days. The company's fall from grace is an apt case history of how Vancouver became Denver with a view.

The immediate cause for the decline of MacMillan Bloedel (MB) was the leadership, from 1990 until he was fired in 1997, of an invisible insider named Robert Findlay, who almost succeeded in running it into the ground. By 1997, the once perpetually profitable dinosaur had lost $368 million on sales of nearly $4.5 billion, a precipitous drop of 822 percent from its previous, disastrous year, 1996. It says something about the bumbling company's view of reality that this profit slide prompted its board of directors to reward Findlay with two raises and a humongous bonus, so that his take-home pay reached nearly a million—$925,000, to be exact. "This is a joke," declared John Duncanson, a leading forestry analyst who downgraded his call for MB's stock from "sell" to "supersell." One reason for MB's pathetic earnings was that the company was top-heavy with thirty costly vice-presidents, more than twice as many as at B.C.'s second-largest forest firm, Fletcher Challenge, which enjoyed healthy profits. Once ranked proudly among the first half-dozen of the world's largest forest product companies, MacMillan Bloedel was down to twenty-sixth, and falling. Even the environmentalists gave up on MB. In 1997, they bypassed the company's annual meeting, where they customarily shouted insults at Findlay, to dish out the same treatment to Bill Sauder over at International Forest Products.

The downgrade appeared justified when set against the exploits and impact of the man who started the legendary firm, the late Harvey Reginald (HR) MacMillan. Born in Newmarket, Ontario in 1885, HR made his first profit from the ice-cream stand he set up for visiting farmers while he was a student at the Ontario Agricultural College at Guelph. He later studied forestry at Yale and moved to B.C. in 1907, becoming the province's first chief forester at age twenty-two. In 1919, he founded his own forest products company (in partnership with W.J. Van Dusen), and during the next four decades it grew to dominate the industry. In his heyday, MacMillan personified Vancouver's economic muscle. Having created his own empire out of the bush, he was the essential link between B.C.'s frontier and its initial flowering as home base for blue-chip business (as opposed to Howe Street's monkey business), and he made the most of it. "MacMillan usually knew what he wanted," wrote his biographer, Ken Drushka. "He wanted things his way—now. If he didn't get his way, if someone obstructed or opposed him, he would plough them under. Amazingly, he made few enemies, even among those individuals rash enough to get in his way." He drove a tug-size Bentley, owned the province's largest fish-processing plants and Vancouver Island's biggest farm, and, according to Drushka, behaved, "like a loaded freight train, thundering through people's lives."

With no male heirs, succession was HR's main problem. Major-General Bert Hoffmeister, one of Canada's most respected Second World War heroes, who had returned to Vancouver with many medals but no job, was his first choice, and he treated him like an adopted son. In 1951, HR named Hoffmeister MB's president, though he knew nothing about the industry. That was the year HR also formed a partnership with Prentice Bloedel, the province's other large forest products operator. HR summarily fired Hoffmeister six years later—establishing his claim to adopted parenthood by shedding tears as he dumped the general. HR retired from any operational role in his company at about the same time and hired J.V. (Jack) Clyne, a former B.C. chief justice, to take Hoffmeister's place. *[I only met MacMillan once. When I came through town in 1975, promoting the first volume of my* Canadian Establishment *series, Bill Duthie said that HR wanted to meet me. Arriving in his Shaughnessy house, at 3741 Hudson Street, I found HR slumped in a living-room sofa-chair, apparently snoozing. Fully ninety years old and scarcely able to move, his words faded in and out, like a short-wave radio, but there was nothing uncertain about his aim in the tirade that followed. "They never tell me anything any more," he complained. "They don't want me to know . . . They're getting into ships. That's much too risky. They're not just risking money, but our name. Tell them what I said . . . Idiots!" He was dead a year later, his message undelivered.]*

Clyne not only knew nothing about the industry, he knew nothing about business. He had grown up as a cowboy in Cariboo country and earned his university tuition panning gold in the Monashee Mountains. He then moved to London, where he first served as a strike breaker, having been sworn in as special mounted police constable during the 1926 General Strike. He later studied admiralty law and moved back to B.C., where he was eventually elevated to the judiciary. A tough *hombre* who felt he ought to be immune to criticism and believed that being nice to everybody was socially dishonest, in the next sixteen years Clyne marched MB's sales from $160 million to $966 million. His greatest coup was to absorb and obliterate Harold Foley's powerful Powell River Company, though the deal had initially been billed as a merger. It was in the midst of the ensuing squabble that Clyne performed what remains one of the few spontaneous gestures in the history of the Canadian Establishment. During a party at the house of Jack Shakespeare, a local lawyer who was trying to bring the two men together, Clyne got into an argument with the former Powell River chairman, and to make his point, he dumped the glass of liquor he had been drinking over Harold Foley's elegant head. *[I first broke this story in one of my books. As soon as it was published, Clyne was on the phone, and in his frigid, hanging-judge voice told me I had my facts wrong. "It wasn't rye that I used, it was Scotch," he growled, and hung up.]* Clyne resigned in 1972, and MacMillan Bloedel subsequently went through thirteen presidents and nine chairmen. The best of them was Ray Smith, who never went to business school but got his early training playing lead trumpet in the Dal Richards dance band. This was the gang that couldn't shoot straight. They worked hard, but solved nothing. The company moved into global shipping, aircraft manufacturing, Florida real estate and even pharmaceuticals, but failed to expand its timber holdings into B.C.'s interior. At one point, in 1976, for example, MB's merchant fleet totalled fifty-one ships, with another hundred vessels on order—yet only half a dozen of these units were required for MB's own export cargoes. This was a time when charter rates were at a twenty-five-year low, so that several of the vessels went straight from shipyard to scrap heap.

The company finally woke up in 1997, and appointed an Arkansas good ol' boy named Tom Stephens to fix things up, to see if what was left of MB could be made viable again. "We are worth more dead than alive," he wisely concluded after his initial tour of the MB premises. Whatever he achieves will not bring MacMillan Bloedel back as Vancouver's economic pace-setter. It is not a company town any more. In fact, it's not a company province.

Another high-profile corporate casualty was Vancouver's best-known department store, run by the city's touchstone family dynasty, the Woodwards.

AT SIXTY-FOUR, WHEN SHE WAS FILMING A NEW movie, Debbie Reynolds was asked by an impertinent Hollywood reporter about her sex life. She considered the question for a long moment, then thoughtfully replied, "It's not that I've forgotten how—it's that I've forgotten why." That describes perfectly why Woodwards collapsed as an economic force in western Canada. Its proprietors lost their prestigious retail chain, not because they had forgotten how to run the stores, but because they were no longer willing to invest the guts, energy and passion required to make the stores sing.

The founder of the mercantile empire was Charles Woodward, a farmer born in Wentworth, Ontario, the son of an English immigrant. In 1879, Woodward went to Manitoulin Island in northern Ontario and opened a log cabin general store that catered to a mainly Indian clientele. Twenty years later, he headed west to British Columbia, with eight children and a pregnant wife. The following year, the abstemious, tight-fisted disciple of Calvin opened a small shop in the city. He did so well that by 1903 he was able to build a department store that also did a brisk mail-order business, supplying homesteaders, trappers, bushmen and Mounties throughout the Northwest. Despite his growing wealth, Woodward never owned a car, took a trolley to his store each day, had a cheap shave at the city's barber college and, whenever he worked late, saved hotel expenses by sleeping on one of the display beds in the store's furniture department.

Two of Woodward's nine children, Percival "Puggy" Archibald Woodward and William "Billy" Culham Woodward, followed him into the business. "Billy," who later served as the province's lieutenant-governor, enjoyed the good life, touring Africa with a radio, a refrigerator and a personal servant in his tent. He was succeeded by Charles "Chunky" Namby Wynn Woodward, who recruited his cousin, Grant Woodward "Woody" MacLaren to run the stores. Tall and fit, a super skier (there is a run at Whistler named after him—*Chunky's Choice*), a great yachtsman and fisherman, Chunky rode champion cutting horses and loved tracking moose through the bush at his 164,000-acre spread, the great Douglas Lake ranch in the interior, where he felt most at home. Under MacLaren's operational talents, the chain was eventually expanded to twenty-six units.

Sales started to decline in 1981, but the big break came in 1985 when MacLaren and Woodward disagreed over the department stores' succession and direction. Woody didn't think that Chunky's son John was ready to take over—probably because he didn't have a silly nickname—and resigned when Chunky's ill-conceived scheme to sell the chain to Cambridge Shopping Centres Ltd., a Toronto real-estate syndicate, went ahead. *[Woody had an option, sealed with a handshake, to buy the controlling shares if Chunky ever sold them, and the first right of refusal if higher offers were received. Woodward ignored the process and a court battle followed.]* Chunky stayed on for another four years, but his heart wasn't in it. Expending the necessary moxie to turn the stores around was beyond the family's disposable talent or energy. The firm struggled on for another five years, mostly under court protection from its creditors, and was finally declared insolvent in 1993.

In its final decade, Woodwards could only be compared to a *Titanic* looking for icebergs; it sank, not nobly, but with its survival instincts exhausted and no one left aboard capable of reviving them. When the doors finally closed, long-term delivery drivers and senior sales staff were offered a pittance as severance pay, and unsecured creditors had to settle for thirty-seven cents on the dollar. But the nine senior executives who presided over the final collapse shared $6.6 million in pay and something called "special restructuring bonuses." Woody MacLaren went on to build one of Vancouver's most successful private investment firms, Macluan Capital, with partner Harold Ludwig. Chunky died in 1990 and his beloved ranch was sold in 1998 to communications entrepreneur Bernard Ebbers of Jackson, Mississippi.

Another dynasty that bit the dust were the Bentalls, whose four Bentall towers symbolize Vancouver's urbanization. Charles, the original Bentall, emigrated from England in 1907 as a structural engineer, designed the old Sun tower and eventually bought Dominion Construction, then one of Vancouver's largest building firms. His sons Clark and Bob joined the company, while the other brother, Howard, became a Baptist minister. The two brothers in the business split up in 1988, with Bob moving into development and going public, while Clark stayed in construction. (Clark's son David quit the business in the spring of 1998, ending that branch of the dynasty. Howard's son Barney became a successful rock singer.) The family retains a minority, 19-percent share in Bentall Corp., though they sold control of the company, which has become a major developer in Washington state, to Quebec's Caisse de dépôt for $70 million in 1996.

PAUL ST. PIERRE, one of B.C.'s wittiest commentators, once broke down Canadian politics into its regional manifestations, quipping that, "It's a disease in the Maritimes, a religion in Quebec, a business in Ontario, a cause on the Prairies and an adventure in British Columbia." In fact, it's a swamp. In most jurisdictions, provincial politicians ride the hurricane of changing public opinion by enacting legislation that solidifies their hold on some sort of solid middle ground. Not in B.C.—there is no middle ground. Polarization is the prevailing ideology. Partly it's because the province's farming population is too small to cast an ameliorating influence on the politics of confrontation. But a more likely source of conflict is that the first union leaders and founding entrepreneurs were imported from other places with other agendas. (In B.C., everything is imported except the weather.) The first cowboy capitalists were tough *hombres* out to strip the province of its resources, with no patience for organized labour and its legitimate aspirations. They fought viciously against certification and made little secret of their intention to destroy the union movement if they could. At the same time, an inordinate number of B.C.'s original unionists immigrated from Scotland and brought their shipyard class struggle with them. Their agenda—there and here—was to wage class warfare, based on the idea that businessmen were exploiters whose power had to be destroyed by the working stiffs. Instead of creating a worker's paradise, the militant unions spawned the NDP, which has been in power since 1991. It has massively altered the character and pace of the province's economy.

Glen Clark, the most ideologically left-wing NDP premier ever elected in this country, has sponsored most of those shifts in attitude. "His role models," says political historian David Mitchell, "are the politicians of the past, the old-fashioned province-builders. He is active, young and charismatic, but he is not doing anything different from what the CCF did in the 1930s." The defining moment of the NDP's turning against business actually occurred during the reign of Clark's predecessor, the amiable Mike Harcourt. His 1993 decision to expropriate, with no prepared compensation package, the Windy Craggy mine site in a remote corner of the province, in order to develop a park twice the size of P.E.I. that nobody could get to, sent a strong anti-business signal. Certainly, it put an end to the province's mining industry. By 1998, only 5 percent of the $1.5 billion raised in equity financing on the Vancouver Stock Exchange for mine expansion was being spent in British Columbia; mines kept closing and exploration expenses were cut to meaninglessly nominal levels.

The worst-hit was the forest industry—except, of course, for the fishing industry, which basically ceased to exist. Timber, pulp and paper companies' sales have been dropping $1 billion a year since 1996, and George Richards of Weldwood Canada reported that none of his fellow CEOs were any longer willing to try to convince their directors to invest money in B.C. Jack Munro, speaking for the industry-sponsored Forest Alliance, put it more succinctly: "The industry isn't even investing their goddamn depreciation, for Christ's sake." Again, the NDP government was being blamed for monumental overregulation (its dreaded Forestry Practices Code), which has boosted the cost of compliance by 200 percent, and excessive stumpage fees—$30 a cubic metre, twice the Quebec rates and three times Alberta's. B.C.'s logging costs are the world's highest, and most industry members acknowledge that they would do much better investing their corporate treasuries in T-bills than trying to operate their companies.

Government policies are driving out other sectors as well. Developers like André Molnar, who was one of the most astute, have fled to Washington State. "I've jumped through too many hoops," he complains. "We wait for years and waste hundreds of thousands of dollars getting projects approved." The developers' joke about how many people it takes to change a lightbulb: "Twelve. One to change the bulb, and eleven to do an environmental impact study." Other companies have escaped to Alberta, and an Angus Reid survey of the local board of trade revealed that a quarter of its members were preparing to move out. This was more a matter of mathematics than anti-socialist emotions. Under the NDP, not only were personal and corporate taxes hiked to the highest levels in the country, but companies were charged with a punitive capital tax, regardless of their profit positions. Politics and business don't mix in the Pacific province, and the civil war that divides them is not about to be resolved.

There is some good news: those who want work—as opposed to jobs—can still find it. Vancouver's high-tech industry is growing ten times as fast as the province's economy, and according to the B.C. Technology Industries Association, it is now B.C.'s largest employer. Tourism too is booming, with $9 billion being spent by visitors in 1998. "Beauty, not resources, is becoming the province's real engine of growth," *Financial Post* editor Diane Francis has noted. "This means British Columbia is one of the luckiest places on earth. After all, coal, timber or minerals can be exhausted. Manufacturing giants come and go. But unsurpassable scenery is a renewable 'resource' for all eternity, which attracts people and their money." Another, unexpected boom has been the film industry, which is contributing almost $750 million to the B.C.—mostly Vancouver—economy. The industry already employs thirty thousand people, which is double the size of the salmon fishery (when there was one). The reason for Vancouver's transformation into a movie lot is, of course, the cellar value of the Canadian dollar, but it would be nice if those Hollywood types didn't refer to us as "Snow Mexicans."

WHILE THERE STILL EXISTS a rearguard business establishment in Vancouver whose members can trace their blood lines to the original forestry and mining fortunes that opened up the coast, that generation is inactive, its surviving inheritors living mainly by clipping interest coupons. Most of the pioneering business families failed to benefit from second- or third-generation heirs anxious or even willing to perpetuate their fathers' or grandfathers' empires. Another group that has just about left town are the Howe Street Boys, that cold-hearted crew of stock promoters that was really a street gang hooked into selling dubious stocks to clueless customers. Their names still appear on the odd VSE listings and you see them strutting their blow-dried charms at the Hotel Georgia bar at noon, Il Giardino's on Thursday nights and Joe Fortes's singles meat market any time after five. But thanks to the initiatives of the *Sun's* David Baines and his cohorts, they are a vanishing and unlamented breed.

The Acquisitors of the early 1980s, who mistook lifestyle for character, are also mostly history. Their fate was highlighted by the rocky ride of Nelson Skalbania, that rhinestone in the rough whose glitter once illuminated the West Coast sports and real-estate scenes. The Vancouver entrepreneur who signed Wayne Gretzky to his first hockey contract was found guilty of fraud, theft and forgery, the victim of his careless exuberance and U-turn ethics.

He regarded business as a lark and the world as a giant windmill to tilt against. At the height of his success, in the late 1970s, he was flipping commercial real estate worth $500 million a year, and became a West Coast cult figure of sorts. At one point, he owned a $2.7-million private jet, a pair of Mercedes-Benz 450SLs and four Rolls-Royces, including the 1928 convertible used in the motion picture *The Great Gatsby*. He built a 1,500-square-metre Greek villa overlooking Vancouver's Fraser River and bought John David Eaton's luxurious 53-metre diesel yacht, *Chimon*. After paying $1.5 million to modernize the vessel, he cruised aboard her for only three days before putting her back on the market. He specialized in real estate, but also moved into sports (because of the big tax write-offs available) and owned the National Hockey League's Atlanta Flames (which he moved to Calgary), the Montreal Alouettes (football), Memphis Rogues (soccer), Vancouver Canadians (baseball), two World Hockey Association franchises, the Edmonton Oilers and, later, the hapless Indianapolis Racers. Skalbania signed Gretzky to boost interest in the Racers, but even that didn't help. He eventually traded the budding Great One to the Oilers, then owned by Peter Pocklington. When he folded the Racers, an Indianapolis newspaper headline read: "Nelson, go back to Skalbania."

His strength was his negotiating skill. Like the master poker player he was, he knew how to keep his emotions in check; he seldom fell in love with his properties because he seldom saw them, flipping most of them before completing the transaction. In that process, he hurt many of his fellow investors, thrived on the edge of bankruptcy and stretched the rules past their legal limits. His problem was that he wrote most deals on napkins and the insides of matchbook covers, and could never keep track of the figures.

On December 7, 1982, he ran out of money, credit and love. His second wife, Eleni, a gorgeous Greek who owns and runs Vancouver's swanky Wedgewood Hotel, which has become a prime Establishment refuge, got fed up with his antics and left him. He offered the Vancouver Opera Company $20,000 for permission to beg his wife's forgiveness publicly during the intermission of one of their performances, but settled for making his apology at a private party attended by more than 250 of his best friends. ("I'll be the most honest, loving, considerate husband possible. I just have to get rid of all the shackles that are draped over my skinny shoulders.") She agreed to a trial reunion, which is still in effect, and on the same evening he declared that he was $39 million in debt— and couldn't even pay for the dinner. (The tab was picked up by his friend, Peter Thomas.)

Instead of declaring bankruptcy, his creditors agreed to let him work out his loans—and, amazingly, he still managed to attract backers. The pattern was set with his next investment: for the first time, he officially became a pirate. Radio Caroline, a pirate broadcaster anchored eighteen miles off the English coast, was meant to mint money by bypassing British commercial radio regulations—which were promptly changed to sink the venture. There followed the purchase of a match factory, a mothballed cruise ship, a company that operated fifty miniature theme parks across the United States, a Beatles museum, something called Club West (modelled on Club Med, with horses instead of beaches), a bar in Denver and an Australian aerospace firm promising to launch satellites.

Ever the deal junkie, one of the few offers Skalbania proudly turned down was a scheme to raise the *Titanic* by filling it with ping-pong balls.

By the spring of 1996, he had run out of options. Not only were there sixty-one civil suits pending against him, but Skalbania had used a partner's $100,000 deposit in a real-estate deal for his private purposes, such as paying an overdue dry-cleaning bill. He returned the money with interest after three months, but the damage was done. The time of the Acquisitors was over.

VANCOUVER'S 1998 TITANS BELONG TO two groups: the permanent and surprisingly vital Chinese business community, plus a new platoon of bootstrap entrepreneurs who operate outside the prevailing business climate, in the sense that their impressive successes are unrelated to the downcast state of the British Columbia economy. This thin brigade of fascinating Titans is resolutely wed to staying in Vancouver, and just as firmly committed to doing much of their business in foreign parts. The following are some of the Pacific coast's leading Titans, who, unlike their more conservative central Canadian cousins, still believe in luck and that money can be won, and not just earned in a slow process of accumulation.

I once spent a few days at Jimmy Pattison's hangout in Palm Springs, and at the end of my visit he offered me a ride back to Vancouver on his jet. It was a very hot day, but his eggshell-white Cadillac slithered along the desert highway with air-conditioned verve. At the airport, we gave our luggage to a waiting porter and started ambling over to the departure gates. Suddenly, Jimmy veered away, and as we passed a long row of pay phones, he pulled open each change slot, scooped out whatever coins had been left there, and never missed a beat as we continued walking towards his waiting jet. I was speechless. Was this the ultimate capitalist, so money-minded that he felt compelled to collect pay-phone leftovers on the way to his multimillion-dollar private plane? I asked him why he had done it. "Habit," he grinned. "My first job was as a bellhop at the old Georgia Hotel, and I made more money from forgotten telephone change than from tips. So even now, whenever I see a phone, I go for it."

That's Jimmy.

Whenever I see him, I am reminded of the story about a dust-up in Zaire, when a mercenary calling himself Colonel Dominic Yugo arrived from Bosnia and started executing people on a whim. "He was the kind of man," complained one of his near-victims in *The New York Times*, "who could do you serious harm with a smile." That, too, is Jimmy.

He is Vancouver's most successful entrepreneur. His empire now enjoys total sales of $4 billion and, as Jimmy likes to boast, he employs "no partners, no shareholders and no relatives." All revenues lead to Jimmy, and he alone accrues the profits. At a low, 15 percent return, that would mean an annual pretax cash flow into Jimmy's pockets of $600 million. Who knows? It's nearly all reinvested anyway.

Though he will never leave Vancouver, Pattison no longer does much business (or "bidness," as he calls it) there. "The price of doing bidness in B.C. is too high," he complains. "Money flows where money is welcome. People will pay a small premium to live and work here, but overall, it isn't a friendly place. We are increasing investment in the U.S." He is particularly fond of the American South, where there are few unions and the average annual wage is less than $20,000.

While Pattison is an integral part of the Vancouver scene, he doesn't fit into the ambling geniality of West Coast life. When he is deal-making, he moves with the supercharged tenacity of a big-game hunter on the trail of his favourite quarry. And he is deal-making all the time. Allan Fotheringham once described him as "a freckled little buzz-saw, who dresses like Nathan Detroit and thinks like J. Paul Getty."

His secret? "I have a basket behind my desk which lists, on a daily basis, the key indicators of each industry we're in. Every bidness has a soft spot, and if you want control of what's happening, you keep watching those indices. I never wait for the weekly financial statements; there's too long a lag. I just keep tabs on things like forward bookings on my radio stations, for instance. That's the kind of thing I worry about. In the food bidness, it's volume that's critical, because when you have a high fixed overhead, you've got to keep sales high." These and many other indicators of how his companies are doing are no theoretical framework; he acts quickly on what those signs tell him. Every Friday, for example, he gets a list of every used car that has been on any of his lots more than ninety days. "I get rid of them," he says, "because that's where you get in trouble, with bad inventory."

What's unusual about Jimmy is that he is a man not only in command of his worth, but also of his soul. He genuinely believes there is some holy sanction involved in his success. "I represent what the free enterprise system allows people to accomplish," he once told me, "and I'm grateful to God that He allowed it to happen." Religious inclinations aside, it is because he is so utterly devoid of sham or pretence that his touches of self-righteousness come through as strength rather than arrogance. He makes it easy for people to supply their own reasons for liking him, and he has surprisingly few enemies.

But being Jimmy's employee is not easy. Because work to him is the only reason for breathing, he expects the same dedication from his staff. Every article ever written about Pattison repeats how, when he was starting out, he fired the car salesman with the lowest turnover at the end of each month. The story is true, but what's less well known is that the first salesman due for the chop was a middle-aged family man who broke down and cried when Pattison gave him the news. What a tragedy! Jimmy was all sympathy, he shed a tear or two—and *then* fired him all over again. When he decided to convert his CJOR radio station from all-talk to rock, Pattison fired its forty-seven employees in one day. One observer of the process compares his technique to the computer game Pac Man: he swallows companies, moving faster and getting bigger with each acquisition—yet he's never satisfied. In 1997, he bought ten companies worth $1.25 billion. His holdings include such oddments as forty *Believe It or Not* museums spread around the globe, which entertain about 10 million visitors a year, the same number as Disneyland.

Workaholics always rationalize their addiction by explaining that they enjoy their jobs; Pattison really does. It's not so much that Jimmy doesn't indulge in any leisurely activities, it's that he doesn't indulge in any leisure. He belongs to three golf clubs but has played the game precisely three times since leaving university. He has seen two movies in his life: *Dr. Zhivago* and *The Godfather*. The only two-week holiday he ever scheduled lasted no more than five days, most of it spent pacing the beaches of a Spanish seaside resort, waiting for the ordeal to be over.

He is much more interested in money than in objects, and when he splurges—as he did by trading in his Challenger 600 for the faster 601 model, it's for reasons of efficiency. He has lived in the same West Vancouver house (and been married to the same wife, the charming Mary Pattison) for the past three decades, though he did indulge himself by buying, for US$6.4 million, Frank Sinatra's estate in Palm Springs. It's next door to the spread occupied by U.S. publisher Walter Annenburg. An indication of the size of the two men's holdings is that their driveways are two miles apart. The Sinatra compound has fifteen buildings, including a spa, an art studio, a theatre, guest houses and a specially designed structure that housed the crooner's miniature train collection, where a dozen trains can run simultaneously. Jimmy's watches are legendary: Pattison's wrist-watch has three faces, set to the time zones in Vancouver, London and New York. Jimmy used to wear actionable sports jackets with the loud plaid patterns usually favoured by off-duty bartenders. No more; it's bankers' business suits now.

A side of Pattison that is seldom publicly acknowledged is his extra-ordinary generosity. He quietly donated $25 million to the Pacific Academy, a Christian secondary school in Surrey, and then, because he does so much business in the United States, gave the same amount to New York's 42nd Street Business Association, to help with its clean-up of the area. One Sunday morning, he slipped a cheque for $1 million into the collection plate at Vancouver's Glad Tidings Temple, the fundamen-talist church that he then attended and where he played the trumpet. His greatest donation was his gift of time as the volunteer chairman of Expo 86. One close Pattison-watcher estimates that in the process he lost at least $50 million worth of deals.

Three years ago, Jimmy traded his 85-foot, $1.5-million motor yacht *Nova Springs* for the 119-foot *Nova Spirit*. His pleasure cruises are limited to precisely four days a year; the balance of the time he uses the boat for entertaining staff or customers. He celebrates his wedding anniversary each summer by taking his wife and their best man and his wife to Des-olation Sound, a marine park north of Vancouver. What was not reported at the time about his boat trade was that he gave the *Nova Springs* to his good friend Peter Brown, the stockbroker who had put him into Aber (which he bought at $1.75; it eventually topped $30) and Cartaway; share swaps that had helped Jimmy Pattison's fortune multiply even faster.

"I JUST GREW UP," PETER BROWN IS SAYING. "I GUESS I was a slow grow-upper. But I'm really enjoying my privacy now. I've got a network of people protecting me, so nobody can get to me. Everything I do is con-fidential." This is The Rabbit speaking? The Peter Brown who entered UBC at fifteen and left five years later without a degree, having flunked his frosh term three times because he was partying instead of studying. The Peter Brown who used to measure the success of his trading days, not in dollars turned over, but in terms of bottles of Dom Pérignon, as in "That was a Five-Dom Day!" or "Not worth a shit. No better than a One-Dom Day." The practical joker who celebrated one Christmas by restaging the Nativity scene on Howe Street, with real donkeys and llamas, and his version of the Second Coming: Peter Brown riding in on the back of an elephant. The Peter Brown who after a stretch in Mon-treal learning the brokerage business, started out as sales manager in a VSE bucket shop called Hemsworth Turton. ("My idea of quality control was to throw a phone book at a prospective salesman. And if he could catch it, he was hired.") The Peter Brown who owned sixty pairs of

Gucci shoes, and spent most of his waking hours boozing and springing elaborate practical jokes on his friends.

Nobody was ever sure where his nickname "The Rabbit" came from, but when the staff of the vsE decided to kid him a little by arranging delivery to his office of a live white rabbit wearing a bright red ribbon, they were horrified when, just before lunch, Brown sent back a roasted rabbit on a silver platter, feet up, garnished with the same scarlet ribbon. The cooked animal had actually come straight out of Umberto Menghi's kitchen, and the original gift was very much alive, scampering in the garden of Brown's Shaughnessy house.

The Rabbit is no more. The only reminder of the good old days is a golden rabbit under glass on a shelf in one corner of his office. "We were just a bunch of guys who wanted to trade stocks, brats who grew too big and became controversial," he says. "Three years ago, I looked at our firm and the average age of our management team was fifty-five. I was fifty-one, and that's old in this business. So I found a new president, Mike Greenwood from Gordon's, and we started to put the team together. In 1997, there were seventy-five Canaccord Capital employees who took home bonuses of $1 million or more. I've got more cash than my great-grandchildren could ever spend. *[According to the whispers, Brown has something like $20 million in his RRSP alone.]* My ambition is, when I retire three or four years from now, to leave behind a first-class, national financial institution with global outreach." In the spring of 1988, Brown resigned from eight boards and committees that were taking up his time and energy, and retreated into the private world where he has spent ten happy years. He is so paranoid about staying out of the newspapers that Canaccord, his company, doesn't even run appointment ads. "I'm desperately trying to get my privacy back," he says.

Meanwhile, Brown is enjoying himself. He built a new home in Palm Springs, has a huge spread on Bowen Island and a luxury shack at Black-comb, but is restless in his Vancouver house, a 22,000-square-foot mega-mansion on Belmont Avenue that he shares with his wife, Joanne. It contains his decoy and art collections. Apart from his 4,000-plus duck decoys (a rare wooden mallard that he bought for $11,000 in 1980 is now worth $350,000), he owns the largest private Group of Seven collection—Lismer's largest canvas, the only two of A.Y. Jackson's 1926 Arctic paintings outside the National Gallery, one of the rare Carmichael oils, a number of Lawren Harris's northern canvases—and dozens more, especially from the Montreal Group. His latest toy is a $500,000 Bentley Azure convertible, black with parchment interior. (As well as a blue Rolls, a teal BMW-850i, and a Lincoln stretch limousine.)

He has cancer problems, but remains a chain smoker, playing with a blue rubber ball at his desk to try to cut down on his daily two or three packs of cigarettes. His firm is highly profitable, but he has not escaped criticism. The worst occurred in 1988, when he unwittingly became one of the figures in the civil and criminal proceedings against stock promoters Edward Carter and David Ward, who had sold $26 million worth of nearly worthless stock to a Texas mutual fund. Although Brown wasn't named as a defendant, evidence was presented that he worked with the promoters as stock trader and underwriter. Brown denied any knowledge of their scheme and was never formally accused of any wrongdoing, but his reputation suffered. Canaccord recently bought 50 percent of a London brokerage and has expanded into France, Australia and Africa, doing as many as ten thousand client trades a day.

Humourist Art Buchwald once remarked that "when you attack the Establishment, they don't put you in jail or a mental institution. They do something worse: they make you a member of the Establishment."

Even Rabbits.

IN JULY 1998, WHEN THE FIGURES FOR BRITISH Columbia's hundred largest companies were published, there was a newcomer in the top slot: Westcoast Energy Inc. It boasted an amazing 50-percent revenue increase, which shouldn't have been that surprising, since during the past ten years this little-heard-from gas transmission company leaped in revenues from $729 million to $7.3 billion, while building its asset base from $2 billion to $10 billion. The company has doubled in size three times over the past decade, and will likely do so again in the next few years.

Westcoast's CEO is Michael Phelps, an intensely political (which doesn't mean partisan) workaholic who could easily, were he so inclined, claim leadership of Vancouver's business Establishment. He runs the biggest company, is personable, well connected (when Prince Charles and his two sons went skiing at Whistler last winter, they stayed at his chalet), politically attached (he spent four years in Ottawa as executive assistant to the second-highest-ranking minister in the Trudeau cabinet) and plugged into the significant boards (as a director of the Canadian Imperial Bank of Commerce, Canadian Pacific Limited and Canfor). But he would rather eat worms than take over Vancouver's Establishment. "I'm away 50 to 60 percent of the time," he points out, "and when I'm home I tend to concentrate on family time. To the extent that economic leadership of a given community frequently bonds together, I guess I haven't really done very much. But the economic leadership of Vancouver is very diffuse. Forestry is feeling beleaguered and doesn't have quite the stroke that it used to have. Peter Bentley always represented a very significant presence in this town, still is. But he has retired as CEO, and while he's very active in the company's affairs, it's not the same as being an active CEO. There are some good young guys coming along in that business, but not quite of the same flamboyance." Phelps continues: "What you have, then, is rather a small primary-industry head-office group. Vancouver has essentially become a service economy, with a growing high-tech sector that tends to live and operate in the suburbs, and so you don't have as much interaction. This is almost too large a city now to have a closely knit economic establishment. The Chinese, of course, are an exception, and many of them are as significant to the community as Jewish families are in, say, Winnipeg or Edmonton. They acknowledge their public duty, recognize an obligation to recycle their time and money, understand that it's part of your duty to devote a certain amount of income and time to community projects. Of course, at today's combined British Columbia tax levels, you will not see much generosity in established individuals. It's not available, it's really not available—not at 54 percent tax rates. I think the government would like to be the author of the largesse rather than letting individuals lead philanthropy."

If Phelps doesn't believe in clubs, he does believe in networks—and he has one of the best in the country. *[He doesn't believe in restaurants either, preferring to eat lunch at his desk, catered by the company cafeteria.]* "I work very hard on my friendships," he says. "I prefer to do business with friends. Everybody has a different model, but Ottawa is a great training school. If you have the right job, you meet everybody in the country. And you don't even have to work that hard to meet people, because they'll find you; there's always an area of mutual self-interest. When I was in the office of energy minister Marc Lalonde from 1980 to 1982, they came by, and not just oil and gas types, but bankers, industrialists and just about anybody contemplating broad investment strategies. That's the best MBA there is, to have twenty people you can phone and pick their brains."

Winnipeg born and a lawyer by training, Phelps studied at the London School of Economics and, after his Ottawa stint, joined Westcoast as director of strategic planning. He became CEO in 1988, and his master coups were acquiring Union Gas, which distributes gas all over southern Ontario, and Winnipeg's Centra Gas. He moved the company from a single line to California into a comprehensive energy powerhouse and a significant presence across the continent, with outlying sales to China,

Mexico and Indonesia. Phelps had the advantage of joining the company and becoming its CEO when it was in a slow-growth mode, and pretty well all of the senior executive ranks were replaced at the same time. That gave him the chance to bring Westcoast into the twentieth century. In 1992, Petro-Canada abandoned its control position, so that Westcoast is now owned by the market and effectively run by Phelps.

WALTER WILLIAM LYALL DIMSDALE KNOTT is one of Vancouver's busiest and best-compensated lawyers. Occasionally, he even gets to practise law. But most of the time he is the business community's Great Networker. That's what gives him Titan status: he is at the centre of Vancouver's most eclectic and useful network. He brings people together in a way that allows their mutual self-interest to blossom. "What I do for a living," he admits, "is connect with people." He is a social butterfly, not as a hobby, but as deliberate strategy, and what it means is that, unlike most lawyers, he leads a fascinating life; rich and powerful people compete to get on his Rolodex. Recently, a Hong Kong billionaire paid him a large retainer, just so he wouldn't represent his rival in a possible court case.

He owes it all to starting out as a bus tour guide. "The happiest years of my life were my five bus-driving years," he recalls. "I had regular hours, gave sightseeing tours of the most beautiful place on Earth, had a ton of fun and didn't have to listen to lawyers' jokes. B.C. Hydro then had a company called Pacific Stagelines that hired a number of students to give Gray Line guided summer tours. There would often be questions about kinds of trees, and I knew virtually nothing except what a cedar looked like, so I'd always call other varieties 'pissonyou' trees." He lived off his tips and bagged his paycheques, and with the proceeds funded a wonderful year doing his master of law degree at the University of London.

"In Vancouver, within a ten-block radius of the Garden Lounge at the Four Seasons Hotel—that's our business community," he reckons. And that's his stomping ground. A third-generation Establishment Vancouverite, the kids he grew up with are now running the place. He knows everybody who counts, and they trust him. He juniored at Ladner Downs, had his own, successful law firm, then merged with Clark Wilson, the city's most profitable legal factory, where he is the senior partner. "Frankly," he says, "the most valuable thing a lawyer can provide a client is access to the networks that count, and I'm the baby boomer lawyer who can do that. This generation knows the value of networks, and that's why people seek me out. Any of the major firms can provide a very high quality of legal service; what I provide is that plus my network. It's sort of like being a switchboard operator. Today, I had a call from the president of a major corporation, and he was having problems with another major corporation and didn't know the president of that firm and needed someone whom they both trusted to bring them together. So I did that. I get those calls all the time. It's not really law, but it's a service, and I'm in a service industry."

His largest new client base has been recruited from Hong Kong, where he still spends two to four weeks a year. At one point, he was in such demand that his appointments were scheduled six months in advance. He is trusted by members of the Chinese community, who use him for not only corporate but family assignments. When Hong Kong migration to Vancouver was at its height, he ran a one-stop acclimatization service. His mother, Jane Knott, who earned a special UBC certificate in teaching English as a second language, was enlisted to teach the newcomers' children English. "It was a full-service operation," he boasts. "We briefed the newcomers about everything from the best beauty parlours to the lawyers, accountants and stockbrokers. They needed a network, someone who could explain the lay of the land." In the past ten years, when a major new enterprise came to Vancouver and had legal issues, nine times out of ten Knott would be on one side or the other.

Knott has become known for helping people, not just for immediate monetary gain, but as a free-floating ombudsman who invests in their future. "Today, I am helping two young men get jobs. These are people I don't know from Adam; they've been recommended to me through people I know and trust. I'll spend half an hour with them, figure out what it is they want, suggest that we get together in a month or three weeks, and during that time I'll keep my eyes and ears open to find out what the temperature is in whatever they're trying to do. If they want to be waiters in a restaurant, I'll talk to some people I know in the restaurant business. A month later, they will phone me up, I'll see them again and, unless there's a real problem with what they're up to, I'll have suggestions and some useful leads for them. They never forget. And someday they'll need a good lawyer, or they'll be restaurant managers and I'll have somebody who needs a job as a waiter . . ."

THE EAGLE SCOUT OF CANADIAN BUSINESS, Peter Bentley remains one of Vancouver's heavyweights, by virtue of his control (with 40 percent of the stock) of Canadian Forest Products (Canfor), and he is one of the few local Titans with solid links to the central Canadian Establishment.

Canfor first cracked the $1-billion mark in 1984, two years after it reluctantly went public. That was made necessary because Canfor was paying bank interest of $61 million on its $300-million debt. That was too heavy a load for its founders, John Prentice (born Pick) and his brother-in-law Poldi Bentley (born Bloch-Bauer). *[They changed their names when they arrived in Canada because of their correct perception of public prejudice against Jewish immigrants. Poldi, who later regretted it, chose the name Bentley because he loved luxury cars.]*

Peter Bentley, Poldi's son, who has worked for the company since he was fourteen, leaves no doubt about his feelings when it comes to the NDP. "They've ruined the forest industry," he claims. "In order to make the cost of capital, we have to make about 10 percent, and with what the government is doing, we're averaging about half of that. Most of our good returns happened before they were elected in 1991. The regulations are unbelievable. Renewing our tree farm licence on Vancouver Island, for example, used to involve submitting an application that ran to 800 pages; now it's 2,200 pages, and yet nobody will really read it or do anything with it."

Bentley has plenty of national clout as a mainstay at the Business Council on National Issues, a director of Bank of Montreal and Shell Oil, and a member of Chase Manhattan Bank's advisory council (Paul Desmarais and Brian Mulroney are its other Canadian members). He has chosen his daughter, Barbara Hyslop, currently group vice-president in charge of coastal operations, to carry on the family tradition. His son Michael, a graduate in business from Stanford, also works for Canfor. Peter Bentley recently ceded the CEO's job to one of the ablest of the West Coast's managers, David Emerson, the former president of Vancouver International Airport.

THERE'S SOMETHING STRANGELY DIFFIDENT ABOUT Terry Salman. He spent twenty-one years with Nesbitt Thomson, now runs his own investment house, Salman Partners (which has set yearly records since it opened in 1994) and sits on such national boards as Conrad Black's Southam Inc. David Radler, Black's *alter ego*, is one of his shareholders. He headed St. Paul's Hospital Foundation for eight years and became the most successful fund-raiser in the city. But at social gatherings, Salman seems distant, not quite in tune with the idle chatter billowing around him. No wonder. Few are aware of his military background in Vietnam's killing fields, which makes standing around any cocktail party less than life-grabbing .

Montreal born and bred, Salman's yearning for adventure led him to join the U.S. Marine Corps during the Vietnam war, straight out of high school. He was the first marine in the history of the Corps to land in a combat zone aboard a helicopter carrier—at Chulai, south of Danang. His most dangerous assignment was as a forward observer for a marine mortar squad; those are the guys who report how close the last round came to its target, so they have to be close enough to enemy lines to take an accurate sighting. Average life expectancy for the job was one week. He earned three Purple Hearts and rose to sergeant's rank. "To me, that was the backbone of the Corps," he says. "They wanted me to become an officer, but it would have required changing my citizenship, which I wasn't prepared to do.

"Vietnam was a funny kind of war," he recalls. "You'd go out on patrol and walk for hours or days, nothing would happen, and then another patrol would go out and there'd be mines or booby-traps, all hell would break loose and a lot of people would die. One Christmas Day, we had a particularly bad day as a unit, we were backed up to the South China Sea, all day long I kept watching the helicopters bringing back our dead, and I remember reading that same day in the *Stars and Stripes*, the armed forces newspaper, about Jane Fonda cuddling up to Ho Chi Minh in Hanoi. I still can't stand her. I later lived on the Ho Chi Minh Trail for a number of months, went around the perimeter at night to check my men, and if I found one sleeping, I'd put my hands around his neck, almost choke him, to jolt him into realizing how dangerous it was. All day long you'd see nobody, then in the middle of the night all these tracer rounds would come at you. You'd fire and next day you'd see some bloody patches left behind, but they always took their bodies with them. I had some wonderful kids working for me. One guy was playing Russian roulette with a 45, which is impossible to do. My radio operator, a wonderful kid from Kentucky who was a fastball pitcher with the Baltimore Orioles' farm team, put the gun to his mouth pretending it was empty, and blew his head off."

Salman later served as assistant warden at the naval brig at Pearl Harbor, in Hawaii, and regards the stint in the Marines as his most formative experience. "Vietnam taught me to appreciate life like nothing else—what it takes to survive, how much of it is luck." He perpetuates his daredevil streak by whistling down Whistler's most dangerous hills, not wearing ordinary skis but in telemark mode, which means your heel is left free and not locked into any harness. In summer, he pumps his Chinelli Super Corsa bicycle to the top of Seymour, Cypress and other mountains to relieve tension. There's a pretend move afoot among Vancouver's business élite to conscript Terry Salman into leading a squad over to Victoria, when Glen Clark's party is in session, and . . .

IF VANCOUVER ENJOYS ANY TRACE OF HIGH society, it's the Dobrzenskys, the Count and Countess, Enrico and Aline. Born to Ireland's and Czechoslovakia's "royal" sets, the two aristocrats provide an elegant counterpoint to Vancouver's keep-your-fork-there's-pie social ethic. They are so ever-present at Vancouver's best parties that they seem to live for the galas and the soirées. Not so. They own two large cattle ranches and much prime Vancouver real estate. More to the point, Enrico is an old-fashioned adventurer, shooting down to Punta Arenas in Patagonia along the Pan-American Highway by Ford Explorer; flying overseas to take part in the London–Beijing antique car rally; or hiking the onerous West Coast Trail. What nobody knows is that Aline often spends less time at parties than in the steamy kitchens of the Sisters of Atonement, a Franciscan community that runs a hostel in the East Vancouver slums along Cordova Avenue. She also helps out at St. James Anglican Church's soup kitchen. They met while Enrico, who had left his native Czechoslovakia in 1948, was serving as a lieutenant in the Italian air force and Aline was a part-time captain in an ambulance corps, visiting Rome to complete her master's degree in architecture from Trinity College in Dublin, on the work of Giambattista Piranesi. "Already she showed me that she was a rank above me," he recalls. "But I was quite full of admiration for her, and still am." She is the daughter of Sir John Aloysius Galvin, a well-known Irish industrialist. Enrico's title is inherited from his maternal grandfather, Count Zdenko Radslav Kinsky z Wchynicz a Tetowa, and his paternal grandmother, Countess Mary Dobrzensky de Dobrzenicz, who was a friend of the poet Rainer Maria Rilke.

He hasn't found Vancouver society the way he expected it to be. "When I first came here, in 1976, with a name like Dobrzensky, count or no count, I imagined that I would get nowhere because your name had to be McIntosh or McDougall or Stewart to make it. I had sort of a vision of old-time colonies, a Victorian era of some kind. It took me very little time to find out that the true power was nowhere and everywhere, but certainly not predetermined, as I thought it would be." The Dobrzenskys are a rare grace note in the Vancouver social scene.

THERE'S A MAMMOTH 150-FOOT TRAWLER being built in an unused shed in North Vancouver that may well be the most luxurious craft ever launched in Canada. It has a saucepan helicopter pad, *two* large hot tubs and every luxury known to uptown penthouses. The boat and the ship-yard are both owned by Dennis Washington, the richest and most power-ful American currently operating in Vancouver.

During the six years since he arrived on the scene, Washington has swept the waterfront. He now owns 54 commercial tugs and 260 barges (the Gates and Seaspan fleets), plus Petrobulk, which fuels local marine traffic, and the region's two largest shipyards. Listed by *Forbes* magazine as having a fortune worth $1.4 billion, Washington started out as a heavy-crane operator in Montana with a borrowed $30,000. His first prize was an undermanaged, overunionized Anaconda copper mine in Butte. He busted the union, modernized the mine and eventually spun the profits into ownership of forty construction, shipping, railway, mining and other ventures, with annual revenues of $3 billion. He has his own fishing resort on Stewart Island, has purchased a golf course on Vancou-ver Island and often flies up from his 68,000-acre Oregon ranch in his Gulfstream 4. He has made little contact with the local Titans, but could become an influential presence any time he chooses to join *le gang*.

WHILE THE ENTIRE WESTERN WORLD WAS having a nervous break-down over Washington's Helms–Burton Act, a former Doukhobor from the Kootenays, who now lives in Vancouver, was planning to invest $400 million to build a dozen hotels, a championship golf course and six hundred townhouses in Cuba. At the same time, he was exploring two significant gold-copper mines on the forbidden island, entertaining Fidel Castro in Canada—and enjoying every minute of it.

Walter Berukoff is one of those rare Canadian entrepreneurs who operates on the principle that taking risks is fun, and that taking big risks is even more fun. He believes that you are what you do, and having tried just about every trade except piracy, he is now very comfortable as a big-time resort builder and mining executive. His mines in Nevada, Cuba and Argentina boast proven reserves of more than 3 million ounces of gold, held through Miramar Mining Corporation and Northern Orion Explorations Limited. On paper, the two companies are worth $1 billion and his annual revenues top $100 million. His Cuban tourist ventures could be the biggest gold mine of them all. He has offers from the top-ranking Swiss, Jamaican, British and American hotel chains to be part-ners in his ventures.

That's a long way from his early, hidebound life. Wally, as everybody calls him because they can't spell Berukoff, simmered up in Salmo, B.C., a tiny Kootenay settlement between Trail and Nelson. "Being a Doukhobor was my main education," he recalls. "My family was expelled from Russia because we were pacifists and wouldn't go to war. It was very tough for me growing up because there was a local breakaway faction called the Sons of Freedom who set their houses on fire, didn't believe in taxes, and whose wives kept taking off their clothes in public as a form of protest. That reflected on all of us. I used to be asked by taunting kids, 'when is your fat mother going to strip?' and stuff like that. I thought very carefully, even at the age of six, what opportunities I wouldn't have because I was Russian. So, I grew up feeling very much like a second-class citizen—and that's what has made Wally run ever since."

After graduating from the University of British Columbia, he joined a Vancouver brokerage house run by Ward Pitfield, where he became a millionaire "twice by the time I was twenty-three, and was broke three times by the time I was twenty-four. I figured out how business works, especially how to use leverage, which means borrowing from the banks, something my family had frowned on, almost as a religious belief," he says. He bought a series of farm-implement plants on credit and eventually became the largest independent agricultural machinery manufacturer on the continent. He then spent most of a decade buying about fifty bankrupt businesses from receivers, rebuilding them and spinning them off for profit. His next stop was real estate, mainly purchasing hotels, shopping centres and warehouses.

"I owned a lot of businesses that people didn't even know were mine, because I've always tried to keep a low profile, and still do," he says. "Mainly I worked hard. I tell my kids, life's a trade-off. If you want to have a whole lot of leisure time, don't expect to have a lot of money. For me, it's been Wally Berukoff Inc. from the day I could walk." Berukoff drives a tough bargain and has earned his reputation as a bottom feeder. He worked his way through college as an underground driller and fell in love with the industry. He got into mining when he bought the Golden Eagle Mine near Reno, Nevada, and in 1993 he acquired the Con Mine in Yellowknife. In Cuba, two open-pit mine sites are being explored. He recently signed an $800-million contract with a state-owned Cuban corporation which will be his 50 percent partner to put up eleven new hotels containing 4,200 rooms. The deal will also include new cruise ships and shopping centres, and will earn spectacular returns, even without a single American tourist.

In his dealings with the Cuban government, Berukoff has enjoyed the advantage of a strong personal bond with Fidel Castro. The two men met in 1993 at a Canadian embassy reception, and hit it off, partly because they share a common language: Russian. Their most interesting encounter was on Canadian soil. In December 1995, Berukoff was told that Castro would be returning through Vancouver from a trip to Japan, and wanted to meet with him. Neither Ottawa diplomats, provincial ministers, airport officials nor anybody else in authority was willing to greet Castro officially, although he was a visiting head of state, and deserved special treatment.

"Despite the Canadian government telling me to stay out of it because Washington would be very upset, I moved in," he recalls. He leased a fleet of the longest stretch limousines in B.C., paid for ninety rooms at the airport Delta to house Castro's entourage, hired a platoon of free-lance bodyguards and supplied them with cell phones, in fact did every-thing to make *El Commandante* feel welcome except hire a mariachi band. The morning after Fidel's arrival, Berukoff snuck into the hotel, pretending he was part of the security net, and the two men spent a pleasant day together that included a tour of downtown Vancouver and the city's harbour, without anyone knowing about it. "Fidel is very intel-ligent, highly intuitive, very much a man who sees himself in control, yet pretends he's humble," says Berukoff. "He outsmarts the Americans because he knows exactly what they're doing and how they're going to react to his every move. How does Castro keep that well informed? He watches CNN and gets *The Wall Street Journal*, just like the rest of us."

Berukoff doesn't take the time to seek the recognition due a Titan. He'd rather do it than be it.

JOE SEGAL IS THE MOST VISIBLE TITAN IN TOWN. Promptly at twelve-thirty every working day, he appears at the southeast corner table of Chartwell's, the fine dining outlet of Vancouver's Four Seasons Hotel. He is greeted with genuine affection. He has done business with just about everybody in the room, and even when he gets the best of a deal, no one resents Joe or asks for a recount. A *mensch* by any other name, he runs a highly diversified conglomerate of formerly failed or failing manu-facturing and marketing companies that he has revived, including the Shoe Warehouse chain, a baby-crib maker, fork-lift manufacturer and steel-shelving distributor. He once owned the Fields stores and the Zellers chain, and almost took control of the Hudson's Bay Company. He is a director of the post-trauma Eaton's and the Bank of Canada.

His pride is his home. In 1988, he sold his palace at 2170 Southwest Marine Drive (for $5.5 million to Singapore's Peter Oei, owner of the global United Industrial Corporation) and moved over to Belmont Avenue, where he has a water view over the Spanish Banks. There he constructed his 30,000-square-foot dream home, which took two years to design and three to build. Its garden includes an orchard of thirty trees, each bearing one of Joe's favourite fruits; in the conservatory are grown lemons the size of grapefruits and grapefruits the size of basketballs. The place can seat two hundred for dinner and has an incredible collection of Georgian gold and silver. The new house, he confides, has four times the allure of the old one, which he described, quite rightly, as "not a mansion but a palace." The main house had ten fireplaces, eleven bathrooms and a sunken ballroom for low-life boogying.

For a man whose first job was wielding a pick and shovel during construction of the Alaska Highway, life has taken a pleasant turn. But unlike many other wealthy individuals, Joe always takes the time to hand out good advice and make significant donations to worthy causes. If the local Titans ever held a popularity contest, Joe Segal would win hands down.

SAM BELZBERG IS A SURVIVOR. HE WAS a Titan and, well, blew it. In the late 1980s, he built his First City financial conglomerate into Canada's twentieth-largest financial institution, worth $8 billion. However, there was too much debt in the equation, and he was forced out in a restructuring that saw his nephew, Brent, take over. The company collapsed amid charges that he had greenmailed his way to an empire built on blackmail, in the sense that his threat of taking over companies forced their managers to buy out his minority stakes at a premium, so they could keep their jobs.

Belzberg was one of the very few traders in the annals of capitalism who got rich by *not* buying companies. The authoritative *Institutional Investor* dubbed him "the most feared corporate raider in North America. 'Sam Belzberg' whispered over the telephone is enough to send the managers of the very largest companies into a wild-eyed panic—and prompt arbitrageurs to begin snapping up the shares of the next Belzberg victim." Sam followed what one broker called "his infallible nose for vulnerability," and had some big hits: the Bache Group (profit $48 million), Gulf Oil ($60 million, split with Boone Pickens) and Ashland Oil ($21 million). Belzberg acted as predator, but he wanted, if not to be loved, at least to be accepted. He never was, even though he is charming and genuinely philanthropic.

I am having a chicken salad sandwich with "the most feared corporate raider in North America," and he no longer has the aura of a smooth cattle baron in the third reel of an old-fashioned western, about to dislodge the salt-of-the-earth settlers. In fact, he seems downright benign. He is at peace with himself. Belzberg is seventy now and has mellowed out, lost his taste for takeover battles. But the edge is still there. He recently purchased C.E. Franklin Ltd., a profitable oil fields supply company in Calgary; he is also into real estate and is in the process of getting a charter for a bank in Bahrain. "You're looking at an area with tremendous amounts of money," he says. "We found some enlightened sheiks in the Gulf, Abu Dhabi and Oman . . ." Run for cover, guys!

FOR YEARS, THE TRAFFIC WAS ONE-WAY: the China Hands were fleeing to B.C. But there is at least one Vancouver entrepreneur who is reversing the flow, spending his skills—and $250 million—in the vast, industrially virgin territories of Asia. His name is Steve Funk, he's a former dentist, and his aim is to provide Asia with one of its rarest commodities: parking spaces. At the moment, he is building China's largest underground park aile near Shanghai's massive railway station. In partnership with the Pacific Century Group, owned by Richard Li, youngest son of Li Ka-shing, the multibillionaire who is behind downtown Vancouver's Expo lands. The $20-million structure will create parking (at $30 a day) for tenants occupying the 3 million square feet of nearby office towers that will be topped off in 1999.

"The first time I went to Shanghai, ten years ago," Funk says, "I remember standing near a travel agency, trying to figure out how to get a cab to the airport and thinking I should hop on one of the bicycles. Now there's a three-ring freeway around the city. The enormity of the demand curve for parking is astronomical; Shanghai has been growing so fast, despite the Asian slowdown, that, according to one estimate, 20 percent of the world's cranes are there, erecting new skyscrapers. Of all the mainland cities, Shanghai has the best memory bank of capitalism, having been the last stopping point where the anti-Communist nationalists holed up before skipping on to Taiwan. It's also the easiest place to get building permits, because it has the same status as a province and most of the country's governing hierarchy comes from there."

Funk, who already owns a major parking operation in Hong Kong, is also cautiously optimistic about that former colony's future. "I've been doing business in Hong Kong for thirteen years, and I don't see anything untoward happening under its new status," he says. "Hong Kong and its fiscal infrastructure simply can't be replaced. The Chinese would be shooting themselves in the foot if they were to mess it up now."

The head of Canadian Maple Leaf Financial, a controversial immigration investment fund that funnelled $250 million into the economy, Funk sold Imperial Parking, which was an outgrowth of the fund's investments, to Toronto's Onex Corp. for $27 million in February 1996. A year later, he purchased the 6,500-stall parking operation of Jardine Pacific in Hong Kong; the company's monthly net income has been doubling every six months since. That and his Shanghai operations are templates for Funk's plans to expand throughout Southeast Asia. "I am way down the road developing a $250-million fund with GE Capital, for parking construction in the region," he says. "Don't forget that Manila, for example, has 10 million people while Jakarta has 10 million-plus, and the provision of parking spaces is at a primitive level." Funk's other ambition is to establish a merchant banking operation in Asia, based on New York's prestigious Goldman Sachs. He has raised $80 million for that purpose and has five offices in place, the most recent in Singapore, headed by Chaw Chong-Foo, a Morgan Stanley graduate who holds an MBA from the University of Texas.

Funk's improbable career started in Osage, Iowa, where he was born to a fourth-generation farm family. After studying dentistry at nearby Purdue University on a wrestling scholarship (he had won the Iowa state championship), he drove up to Canada in his '68 pick-up ("a Chevy, one-ton, green, ugly") for a one-year residency at the Vancouver General Hospital. He decided to stay, and switched into business as a junior partner to Nelson Skalbania, the then high-flying entrepreneur famous for operating without a safety net. In 1981, Skalbania named him as his agent in Hong Kong, and it was there that Funk met the sons of the city's élite who now, a generation later, are its most powerful businessmen. Along the way, he became a confidant of David Tang, founder of Hong Kong's legendary China Club, who introduced him into the circles of British royalty. He dined privately with Princess Diana ("she was more beautiful in person than in her best pictures") and spent a week at Sarah Ferguson's family ranch in Argentina. "Her mother kept calling her daughter 'fishface' but Fergie's a real pistol—she's Irish, she's got a temper—and I don't know how her toes taste."

Perhaps because of his Skalbania connection, Funk has never penetrated the Establishment's inner circle, but he is moving in that direction. As a sign of his enhanced status, he recently moved into an antebellum mansion in West Vancouver that looks like it came out of the pages of *Gone With the Wind*. It sits beside a trout-filled private lake and features a curving, beautifully carved mahogany staircase that came with a guarantee that it wouldn't squeak for the next fifteen years. His hobby is riding Harleys—"growly, but hoggy machines." He has just bought a Fat Boy and loves cruising it alone or with fellow hogs across the flat prairie turf. When he did a count and discovered that in one recent year he was home for dinner exactly ten evenings, he determined to become more of a husband and father, and now spends July and August with his family at Lake of the Woods in Manitoba. He is so pragmatic that he believes only in tomorrow. "I never carry a camera or take pictures," he says, "because once something happens it's over with. I've been there, I've seen it. Pictures go into albums, then you die, and they're thrown away. It's better to look only at tomorrow."

Recalling his former profession, he says, "My teeth were cut in Asia, and in some ways I feel more at home on the streets of Hong Kong than in Vancouver. Doing business in China has no limits. The risk–reward ratio is high right now, but it's bound to come up roses."

Funk enjoys calculated risks. In 1974, he went looking for a flying instructor and finally found a grass airstrip on a farm near Burley City, Iowa, run by a seventy-two-year-old pilot who had been flying stunts for twenty-six years. "As I walked up to the plane, he said, 'Kid, do you learn quick?'"

"'Why do you ask?'

"'Because I could die any minute.'

"'I had my instruction exercise notes with me, and he threw them in the back and said, 'Forget the book.'"

Once airborne, Funk's teacher put the plane into a spin, looked over and said, "Okay, get us out of this one."

That's how Steve learned to fly. And that's how he does business.

MICHAEL AUDAIN IS PRESIDENT OF THE VANCOUVER Art Gallery, trustee of the Vancouver Symphony and a fifth-generation British Columbian, has built and sold ten thousand houses through his Polyglot Group, and is a multimillionaire. He lives at the end of an obscure cul-de-sac near Horseshoe Bay, where the bush is so thick and the road so narrow that it doesn't seem to be a street. You walk into his house and rear back. It is hung with an intensely personal collection: Gordon Smith, Jack Shadbolt, Attila Lukacs, and several canvasses by Laurie Papou. Now, the beautiful Miss Laurie is a talented artist, but her repertoire is limited, if inspired. She portrays herself and her partner, Ian Ross, in the buff, in various positions, and it's difficult to concentrate on what my host is saying.

His Establishment credentials are impeccable, yet he looks like a cashiered Sunday-school teacher, saintly yet angry as hell. The rage boiling inside him has a history. He was one of the Kerouac generation of 1960s rebels; he did it all, and isn't quite over it yet. He went to eleven different boarding schools as a youngster, departing each institution of learning either by running away, being expelled or hitting the road the day before he thought he might be asked to leave. "The only sport I was any good at," he recalls, "was boxing, because it wasn't a team sport." He failed his Grade 13 in Ontario, and his scholastic record remained unblemished at UBC, where he failed first year. At the same time, he became a campus leader of Canada's New Left, launching a nuclear disarmament movement and founding the B.C. Civil Liberties Union. Then he took a freighter and headed south to help Fidel liberate Cuba, but the ship was diverted to England. There, he marched against the bomb and brought Danny the Red over from Germany. He was jailed in Mississippi as one of the Freedom Riders, rioting for integrated schools; lived in Toronto's radical Rochdale College ("your friendly vendors would come around and ask what kind of pills you wanted, but I wasn't into that"); hung out at the City Lights Book Store in San Francisco, met Kerouac and Ginsberg, and stuff like that. "I was looking for something, but didn't find it," he recalls. "I was convinced that young people should take over the world and that students should run the universities. I thought that history was a progression of revolutions, but was never a Marxist."

He went sort of legit by becoming a juvenile probation officer in Vancouver and deputy minister of housing in Dave Barrett's NDP government. As well as his successful housing company, he taught himself Pali and has written a fascinating history of Thailand, owns a British insurance company, and generally fills the role of token rebel and art maven for the Vancouver establishment.

JACK AUSTIN, THE LIBERAL SENATOR from Vancouver, remains one of the few Titans who deserves his slot solely on the basis of brainpower. As minister of state for Social Development, he controlled the greatest share of expenditures in the Trudeau government, and ever since has exerted inordinate influence on the country's governance. To be accused of being the Liberal Party's chief thinker is a little like being a midget in a village of legless men, but Austin refuses to be discouraged. He has devoted his career to finding some mutually acceptable balance between the private and public sectors, and with Zen-like demeanour will explain why his Canada Investment Development Corporation was as close to the ideal as we're ever likely to get. Vancouver has never had stronger representation in Ottawa than during Austin's time in cabinet. That was when he created Granville Market and Canada Place as well as making Expo 86 financially viable. His more recent interests have been boosting trade with China and Mexico; he is one of the people whose brain Mike Phelps over at Westcoast picks at regular intervals. Jack Austin's brain is well worth picking.

JAKE KERR, THE HEAD OF LIGNUM, Canada's largest privately held wood company, is the only Titan in the country who has his own baseball card. Issued by a California baseball camp he attended, it lists him as "Jake the Snake," describing his talents as a relief pitcher and shortstop, and suggesting he might want to change his moniker to "The Goose." He often ends up being the forestry industry's spokesperson, negotiates with Washington and has actually had Glen Clark to his house. A friend describes his business as "cutting down trees, manufacturing two-by-fours and turning them into term deposits."

YOUSSEF NASR IS CEO OF THE Hongkong Bank of Canada, succeeding its illustrious founding duo, Jim Cleave and Bill Dalton, and making his own mark as the head of Vancouver's only head-office bank. Frank Giustra, the former head of Yorkton Securities, has blossomed in his new incarnation as a film impresario (Lions Gate Entertainment). "There just aren't enough hours in the day to take advantage of all the opportunities" continues to be his motto. He has already bought Montreal's Cinepix, and North Vancouver's North Shore Studios, Canada's largest film and TV production facilities, and made a dream deal with Paramount for the release of twenty films over the next five years. Ike Barber, who started out with one small mill in the Kootenays, has built his Slocan Forest Products into the largest lumber capacity in the province. Philip Owen, Vancouver's thoroughly establishment mayor, bats down at least half a dozen requests a day from supporters who want him to go provincial or federal. He is the best-informed man in town. Stuart Belkin, who inherited his father's wisdom and fortune ($200 million in cash), could be the next Peter Bentley. If there is a big deal coming down, Belkin is sure to be sniffing around the edges.

JACQUES BARBEAU, WHO IS THE most internationally minded of Vancouver's tax lawyers, remains a totem to good taste and great humour. He has one of the best private art collections in town, featuring the bold canvases of E.J. Hughes. "There's been a drastic change of establishment culture in Vancouver, either by necessity or by desire," he says. "People have had to reassess their work habits. You can't leave the office at three in the afternoon, as many people used to do, you can't take extended weekends, and you've got to maintain your competitive edge, which is forever changing. There's no security of tenure; if you don't perform every day, you're out."

Andy Silvester (Equinox Gallery), Andrew Graham (of *the* Grahams), and Keith Mitchell (a liberal Liberal) have great prospects. Gerald and Sheahan McGavin continue to be a generous ($2 million to the arts) power couple. Conrad Black's *alter ego*, David Radler (described in Chapter 13), is one of Vancouver most important Titans, but most of his power is exercised out of town. John McCaw, who made $3 billion when his Seattle-based family sold their cellular-telephone business, became the reluctant owner of GM Place, the Canucks and the Grizzlies when the Griffiths family went into its disintegration mode. He must wonder what the second prize was. That feeling is shared by Arthur Griffiths, the Establishment's walking afterthought. The Skidmore family, Tom and Allan, owners of Trans Canada (TCG International), run the world's largest windshield-repair franchise operation, out of Burnaby. This is Vancouver's most underestimated private fortune. They recently made $54 million selling their stock in Glenayre Technologies. Addicted to growth, Jack Poole, who used to commute in his private jet between his homes in Hawaii, Sun Valley, West Van and Newport Beach, remains a power in the development business through Greystone. *[When he was head of Daon, Poole's CEO office had twenty-two windows, an all-time Canadian record. He had the company's head office angled during construction so it would not block the view enjoyed by Vancouver Club members next door.]* He now lives in Vancouver's most spectacular penthouse, the one on English Bay, next to the Sylvia Hotel, that has a large tree growing in the middle of it.

Morley Koffman is the lawyer's lawyer, and the best mergers and acquisitions specialist in town. Nobody really knows what Ron Stern is up to, except that he owns a jeans factory that turns out twenty thousand pairs a day for the likes of Calvin Klein, three large pulp mills in Alberta, a print house and much real estate in Vancouver, as well as investments in Sault Ste. Marie and Portland, Oregon. Rafe Mair is a voice to be reckoned with, his strength based on his incorruptible independence streak. Morris Wosk owns half of Cambie Street and most of the Beach Avenue towers, and is a silent but heavy philanthropist. As are the Diamonds, Jack and Gordon and Leslie. Tom McIntyre, whose family owns something like thirteen thousand apartments in town, buys his shoes at Loebs in London (for $2,500 a pair) and only takes his Ferrari out at night. John McLernon, chairman of Colliers, enjoys expanding global clout. Brian Moorehouse, a former stockbroker, has become an important angel to local high-tech companies. Celia Duthie took over her father's book business in 1982 and has sprouted in all directions. Ron Cliff retains his considerable influence as chairman of B.C. Gas and has branched out into the greenhouse garden, through Heathcliff Greenhouses. Carole Taylor, recently named to the board of Chapters and head of the Port Corporation, is a powerhouse who lights up the scene. Bob Wyman, the only UBC benefactor who had a plaza named after him, continues to be a presence through his directorships and all-round decency.

Wendy McDonald is in a class by herself. At seventy-six, she has outlived three husbands, has a new boyfriend and remains CEO of B.C. Bearing Engineers, an industrial firm started by her first husband that she has expanded to sales of $139 million, with forty branches around the globe. A DONNA VIVENTE with honour and élan and also mdloi is she had had a wine named after her in France, but claims that she doesn't remember whether it's called Wendy's or McDonald's. Patrick Reid, who always looks as if he ought to be wearing a toga, won fame as a Second World War tank commander, made Expo 86 possible, is Rick Hanson's father-in-law and carries a personal sheen that refuses to wear off. Umberto Menghi's popularity has waned, though his restaurants remain popular, but he prefers to hang out at his Tuscany cooking school in a restored sixteenth-century estate in rural Ripoli. Darcy Rezac, who heads the local Board of Trade, claims he invented networking; it's not true—he only perfected it. His organization has become the centre of local contact-cultivation for fun and profit. Barbara Brink, who put Science World together, is increasing her already considerable volunteer profile. Brandt Louie, head of London Drugs and IGA, is married to Belinda, whose father started the first tin mine in Malaysia and was at one time the richest man in Southeast Asia. His "house" was so large that the Japanese used it as their command headquarters during their occupation. Linda Crompton, who started out as a fitness trainer, is making it big as a new-style banker, the head of Citizens Bank, which makes up in electronic moxie for not having any branches.

David McLean made his name refurbishing The Landing into *the* Gastown landmark, now chairs Canadian National Railway, is one of the chief fund-raisers for Jean Chrétien and takes pride in being an effective power broker. "My basic philosophy," he says, "is to keep life in balance.

You're never going to say, as you're dying, 'Gee, I wish I'd spent more time in the office.'" Since he became a Canadian citizen in 1980, Edgar Kaiser has always been a Titan to watch. He is one of those derring-do entrepreneurs who believe that a man reduces himself by backing away from any challenge, especially if it's self-imposed. He crashed trying to make French-fry vending machines, raced his jet around the world and set nine new speed records, took his private yacht, the 148-foot *Calliope*, up the Amazon and then began slowly opting out his business commitments. The vessel's communications equipment was so sophisticated, it had its own area code. In 1998, he broke Titan ranks by spending most of his time at Bryan Adams's sound studio, recording his own CD (*The Threads Of My Life*), a soft-rock folk album of surprising beauty.

Mike Horsey, who invented enthusiasm, is the man who put up GM Place, which has become Vancouver's entertainment headquarters. A former president of the B.C. Pavilion Corporation, which manages the B.C. Place domed stadium, he was deputy minister of tourism in Victoria and took a shot at running his own newspaper, the short-lived *Calgary Sunday*. *[Former premier Bill Bennett personally tested him out for the position. "The first time I pronounced Nanaimo correctly, I cemented my job," Horsey recalls.]* He has since become a consultant, and successfully choreographs the construction of sports/entertainment arenas the world over, as well as becoming a riverboat gambler on a grand scale.

One of Vancouver's defining corporations, Finning International, the world's largest Caterpillar dealer with revenues of $2.4 billion, sent the Clark government a stern rebuke by moving its operational headquarters to Edmonton, a particularly blunt message since its CEO, Jim Shepard, chairs the B.C. Business Council. "Vancouver is becoming just a tourist town. I think British Columbia is going to look more like Oregon than Alberta," Shepard complains.

Bruce Allen and Sam Feldman are the music promoters who count, and both have grown rich and powerful in the trade. Placer Dome CEO John Wilson has almost lived down his $6-billion offer to David Walsh to merge with Bre-X. Fellow mine-finder Norman Keevil (Vancouver's highest-paid CEO at $2.5 million) did much better when he bought 3 million shares of Voisey's Bay from Robert Friedland and turned a six-months profit of $300 million. Keevil owns a thirty-foot motor launch and loves exploring northern stretches of Vancouver Island. "It's like waking up in a different summer cottage every morning," he says.

A wry and perpetually harried sea dog, Graham Clarke's idea of a great time is to tinker with his Trimble Global Position System on his luxury cruiser, the sixty-seven-foot *Seaquel*. Head of the Vancouver Airport Authority, Clarke expends most of his efforts as a member of a dozen volunteer committees. His company operates a fleet of tour and ferry boats that is larger than the Canadian navy's Pacific fleet. Ballard CEO Firoz Rasul's magic batteries will one day replace internal combustion engines in motor cars. Rasul is also the head of the Canadian Ismaili community, appointed to that post personally by the Aga Khan. Ford and Mercedes have injected more than $1 billion into the company because they believe its drive system will win the race to manufacture the world's first practical electric car. Rasul was placed in his job by Michael Brown of Ventures West, Vancouver's leading provider of risk capital. If the Vancouver Establishment has a favoured dining location, it's Bishop's, where the host, John Bishop, knows everybody's palate and how to tantalize it.

When Arequipa Resources Ltd. was launched on the Vancouver Stock Exchange at 78¢ it turned out not to be a typical VSE listing. Its key property, four hundred miles north of Lima, Peru, actually held gold. In the summer of 1996, Barrick bought Arequipa for $1.1 billion ($30 a share) and its president, a feisty woman named Catherine McLeod who had been working for Yorkton Securities in Santiago, Chile, walked away with $9 million. She had no previous mining experience, but her father, brother, uncle and cousin are all in the game and she grew up as a self-described "mining brat." She is now trying to rewrite history with her new company, Pacific Rim Mining Corp., in Argentina. Her Whistler chalet is called Casa Barrick.

Hank Ketchum III is CEO of his family company, West Fraser Timber, and though he came to Vancouver in 1973, he has never taken out Canadian citizenship. One of his directors is David Radler, whose company, Hollinger Inc., dominates Canadian newspapers. The fit is perfect: Radler ought to be buying some of his newsprint from West Fraser—but not so. "I hope someday he will," says Ketchum, "but he's too tough. He did, but David got too tough on us." Hank Ketchum does nothing special in his spare time, takes part in no community activities and has no strong opinions on anything. "I'm a pretty boring guy, actually," he confesses. Believe it.

Howard Shapray, who used to stage manage Robert Friedland's legal battles, is Vancouver's toughest and ablest courtroom lawyer. Ed Odishaw, George McIntyre, Bill Beradino, Hein Paulus, George Hungerford, John McAlpine and Len Doust are other legal eagles worth mentioning. Bob Disdrow, at First Marathon, is the city's most successful stockbroker, certainly on his own account. His bonuses were the highest in the industry, but on top of that he owned at least 600,000 shares of Voisey's Bay before the nickel strike and probably cleared as much as $100 million with that and other deals. To be a real-estate guru is to be an oxymoron, but Ozzie Jurock, who came to Vancouver from Germany thirty-two years ago, makes a living as one, and he has an impressive following. His Web site, newsletter, faxes and speeches are never dull and seldom give bad advice. He met his wife, Josefina, aboard a ferry to Nanaimo; their first joint venture was the Chit Chat Café in White Rock. *[Nearby Kelowna has come up with at least three important Titan candidates: Chuck Fipke, whose Ekati diamond mine in the Northwest Territories will come on stream this fall (he has already bought himself a Hummer to celebrate); Ross Fitzpatrick, the Chrétien confidant and senator, who has resurrected the region's best winery (Cedar Creek); and Mel Kotler, the peripatetic founder of Fabricland Pacific.]*

In April 1991, Bob Lee (profiled below), who is one of Vancouver's most lively souls and was then chancellor of the University of British Columbia, was talking to a local developer named Peter Wall when the subject of donations came up. "What's the biggest donation ever made to a Canadian university?" Wall demanded.

"Up to now," Lee replied, "ten million."

"What about fifteen million?"

"Unheard of."

"Okay. I'll do it."

That's how UBC's Institute of Advanced Studies, modelled on the Princeton Institute of the same name, was born. It was a typical Peter Wall gambit: unpredictable, grand and mysterious. Characteristically, Wall didn't attend the dinner where his gift was announced. He is currently building Vancouver's tallest tower, a $250-million, 550-room hotel that will dwarf the other components of his centrally located Wall Centre. A Russian Mennonite who emigrated to Austria on his way to Canada, Wall arrived in 1948 with his family and no money. He used to raise racehorses on his 157-acre estate in nearby Langley, where he lives, but after his nag, Missionary Ridge, won the $1-million purse in 1992 at the Del Mar Turf Club, he abruptly gave up the sport. He owns a Challenger, maintains a New York residence, puffs Honduran cigars and enjoys everything he does. There are many stories about Wall's eccentricities—"he's right off the Wall" is a favourite comment—but they're probably not fair. Peter Wall is a loner and does things his way, including that massive gift to UBC, which was a sign of the gratitude he feels towards Canada for allowing him to carve out a grand life.

THE VANCOUVER TITAN WITH THE MOST impressive reach is a shy and secretive thirty-four-year-old Asian Canadian electrical engineer named Terry Hui. "This guy's a real player," says Bill Dalton, the former CEO of the Hongkong Bank of Canada, who was recently promoted to run its huge British operation. "I haven't met too many people I have trouble keeping up with, but Terry's one. If my brain runs at 66 mega-hertz, his is at 250. The kid is sharp. People want things from him because he's got a lot of power." Terry's an earth mover. The Canadian surrogate of Hong Kong's richest family, Li Ka-shing's, Hui commands the influence that wealth can bring. *[Forbes estimated his 1997 wealth at $11 billion, which would make him the world's third-richest individual, and reported that he owned a third of everything that moved on the Hong Kong stock exchange.]* More important, he has been applying that clout to rejig the shape and charac-ter of downtown Vancouver; Toronto is about to feel his presence in a major way as well. As CEO of Concord Pacific, Hui has been chief anima-tor and part owner of the $3 billion development transforming the former Expo 86 lands from an abandoned fair site into Canada's—and North America's—largest real estate venture. His forty high-rises repre-sent such a quantum addition to existing residential and office space— the equivalent of thirty-five new city blocks—that the project will shift Vancouver's centre of gravity to the east and south. Once completed in 2005, Concord's 12.4 million square feet of new space will be occupied by at least twenty thousand people. Remarkably, the project is almost entirely self-financing. A 10-acre chunk—the only built-up part—was sold in 1990 for $40 million to Peter Oei's Metropolitan Properties, reim-bursing most of Concord's original down payment. Not a shovel of dirt is dug on new buildings until they are substantially leased or sold.

A wispy sparrow of a man whose unprepossessing physical presence is a useful camouflage for his adroit political instincts, Hui brings to his posi-tion something more than a Darwinian desire to turn maximum profits on an acreage bought for next to nothing. In his guttural English, which suffers less from poor pronunciation than from his habit of spitting out too many words and ideas at the same time, Hui transmits the wonderful itch of youth on the trail of something big. What excites him is not so much that he is building a new city, but that it will be a new *kind* of city. One of Canada's first "smart" communities, the site is encircled by a glass tunnel six kilometres long that contains fibre-optic cables that will turn each residential and office unit into an interactive communications centre.

Nothing that happens at Pacific Place could be more controversial than its origins. Since the property accounts for one-sixth of zonable downtown Vancouver—4 million square feet of developable land—and since B.C. taxpayers had to pay an additional $20 million to clean up its post-Expo soil pollution, Li Ka-shing's purchase was the buy of the century. It was the best real-estate deal since the Dutch trader Peter Minuit bought Manhattan Island from the Indians for $24. Li Ka-shing's down payment was $50 million, with the balance of the $230-million purchase price spread over fifteen years, with no interest payments. In the first two years, the value of the property soared from $637,000 to $4 million per acre. K.M. Hui, Terry's father, is Concord's part owner. "There's a lot of understanding between the shareholders," the son explains. "It's all done among friends, so we keep each other informed on all the operational stuff. Since I have a vested interest in the company, my decisions are very much in line with those of the other shareholders." You betcha.

Mathematics aside, what Li Ka-shing's involvement in the project accomplished was to send a strong signal: Vancouver is a great place to invest. The message was loud and clear and a stream of Hong Kong dollars poured into Canada's West Coast metropolis. That flow turned into a gusher following the June 4, 1989 massacre at Tiananmen Square—with investments worth between $2 and $4 billion arriving annually for the next five years. [A not untypical reaction was the comment from real estate "sales consultant" Carolyn Feldman: "I like the Chinese. Most of them are nice, simple people. It isn't their fault that they have all this money."] During that time Vancouver's Chinese-speaking population increased by 72 percent and property values doubled, then doubled again. The joke was that the Hong Kong starter kit for moving to B.C. was "a Mercedes and a strip mall." By 1996, it was no great surprise to find, in the window of Skylight Optical, one of the city's leading downtown eyeglass dispensaries on Robson Street, a sign that read: WE SPEAK ENGLISH.

Terry Hui became a central figure in this post-Expo scenario because his best friend at university had been Tim Kwok, who had been the roommate at Stanford University of Li Ka-shing's eldest son, Victor. That was how Hui and Li first connected. They worked together on some of the project started by Terry's father, became close friends and subsequently built several developments together. Li Ka-shing had hired Vancouver architect Stanley Kwok to ride herd on Concord during its initial phase. Meanwhile both of Li Ka-shing's sons, Richard and Victor, took such an interest and were in Vancouver so often that they became Canadian citizens. Victor even married a Canadian, the former Cynthia Wong of West Vancouver. Then, Terry's great friend Victor was named to succeed his sixty-nine-year-old father, which yet again boosted Hui's power.

Very much a Titan, Hui considers himself fully bicultural and gets tired of people asking him what language he dreams in. (His answer: "Language only comes out in conversation. When you're thinking about experiences or dreaming, there's no language involved.") He appreciates having money but lives with little ostentation. What he really wants, he once confided in me, is to have one of those pivotal ideas that changes the way the world works. "If I could invent something that became a household name, I would be really happy—like Kleenex or Xerox."

The world is still waiting for a Hui.

There is somewhere deep inside Terry Hui, an existential streak that could take him in unpredictable directions. But for now, he is deciding the look, feel and future of downtown Vancouver. Actually, more than that. Over the past three years, Hui has negotiated the amalgamation of Concord with Burcon—a former VSE shell into which several large Hong Kong investors, including Terry's father, have folded their real estate holdings—and Burcon's Oxford Properties subsidiary. The combination has become a major player in Canadian real estate, with assets of well over $2 billlion. Its largest project is a glitzy $1-billion development near Toronto's Skydome. Soon the entire country will know what a Hui is all about.

Terry is also important because he represents a new generation of Chinese. He is part of the business-minded group best represented by the young Nankin physicist, Li Lu, who served as deputy commander of the student demonstrations in Tiananmen Square. Released from prison, he arrived in the U.S. in 1990, without knowing a word of English. Six years later, he graduated, for the first time in Columbia University's history, simultaneously with degrees from its business and law schools. "The Tiananmen generation of Chinese," he said at the time, "has embraced a spirit of independence. Politically, China still suppresses its people, but because the government allows some freedom in economic matters, business has become our ultimate expression of individuality."

That wasn't always the case with the older generation of the Chinese diaspora but they did emphasize business to the point that the overseas Chinese now form the world's third largest economy, after China itself and the U.S.A. They were able to achieve that awesome success because they, literally, invented networking. It's called *guanxi*, which means the connections that lubricate commercial deals and personal relations. These networks, which decide the direction of people's lives, are based on family, kinship, schools, the village from which the patriarch originated, friendship and shared work experience. Networking is central to

Chinese lives, a gift that is kept vibrant through reciprocation of favours and links into ever-expanding networks.

Once Li Ka-shing put his imprimatur on investing in Vancouver, Hong Kong's moneyed families moved in. Some came as "commercial citizens," often transferring their families, or just the kids, using Canada as an escape hatch in case the Chinese takeover of Hong Kong went sour. They did not invest their emotions into becoming Canadian, even though they claimed their adopted country's citizenship (and medicare). The most temporary of these astronauts returned once the takeover proved uneventful. Later, in 1997 and 1998, when the Asian economies went into a free fall, the balance of the temporary expats scurried back to protect their home base assets.

But there was another, more interesting group. They may have arrived as agents of opportunity, but they stayed as owners of assets. Settling mainly in Vancouver and Toronto, they became successful investors and valuable citizens. The idea of belonging to any Establishment but their own seemed strange and they have yet to reach for significant political power, but since they now form the country's third-largest language group, it will not be long in coming. Meanwhile, they concentrate on the economic side of the equation. In Vancouver, the Chinese community has moved uptown, as Oriental gentlemen acquired most of the city's valuable real estate assets.

ONE OF THE ACCEPTED DUTIES OF Vancouver's Old Establishment was to throw off, every five years or so, an appropriate candidate willing to accept exile to Victoria, where he would serve the Queen by occupying the office of lieutenant-governor. The roster of these vice-regal appointees had about them the inevitability of papal succession, without the telling plume of white smoke. Among those anointed had been such Establishment stalwarts as Walter Nichol, Eric Hamber, W.C. "Billy" Woodward, Frank Ross, Clarence Wallace, Walter Owen, Henry Pybus, "Budge" Bell-Irving (who as a Canadian general in the Second World War liberated Amsterdam) and Bob Rogers. They were all good men and true—white, Protestant and raised on porridge. They fulfilled their "overseas" posting (Vancouver Island being a place one usually visited only to fish at Campbell River) with as much grace and condescension as they could muster, which was considerable.

Then, on September 9, 1988, this self-perpetuating clique was abruptly shattered with the inspired appointment by Brian Mulroney of British Columbia's twenty-fifth lieutenant-governor, David See-Chai Lam. To

Vancouver society, it seemed a little like naming Howard Stern as convener of the Symphony Ball. Lam was, after all, Chinese, Baptist, a developer and totally devoid of social pretensions. His only club was the Rotary.

Lam's father, born in a village 190 kilometres northeast of Hong Kong, was a teacher who converted to Christianity and became the community's Baptist pastor. The family moved to Hong Kong, where young David graduated from a Baptist college and moved on to take an MBA from Temple University in Philadelphia. Returning home, he joined the family's Ka Wah Bank, where he quickly rose to CEO. In 1967, wanting to afford his three daughters a safer sanctuary, he moved to Canada. He was forty-four years old and had saved little money, but fell in love with Vancouver and opened a small real-estate office. That's when *guanxi* set in. His former Hong Kong contacts enlisted him as a channel for investing their flight capital, and he insisted they lend him enough money to buy a piece of each deal on his own account. Within a very few years, he was a millionaire. His Canadian International Properties Limited funnelled more than $500 million from Hong Kong into North America, and in the year before he assumed vice-regal office, he personally negotiated real estate transactions worth $100 million.

Lam's success was based on applying Confucian ethics to real estate—an unusual departure from the jungle tactics of Vancouver's property flippers. "Luck and my Chinese philosophy told me, enough is enough, never go for the last dollar," he says. "I always felt that I would rather lose a deal and a commission than lose a friend. Many of my clients became my friends—and many of my friends became my clients. I always paid slightly more than market and charged slightly less." Lam's hidden agenda, both in and out of Government House, was to enhance the image of Canada's Chinese community by encouraging their philanthropy. A profoundly religious man without being evangelical, he modelled his message on the Jewish community's approach to giving, donating about $5 million a year himself. *[He named his sailboat, a Hunter 42, the* Selah, *a Hebrew word for the pause between passages of music.]* "I always judge a person by what they do with their money," he says. "I never duplicate what governments should be doing, but contribute in ways that will modernize our thinking." One example was Lam's sponsorship of a series of medical and philosophical seminars in pre-turnover Hong Kong. "If I can reach a handful of intellectuals, just two dozen people," he explained, "one day, when Hong Kong is swallowed up by China, they will be scattered. But it's like sowing seeds which may blossom, keeping alive and spreading fresh ideas." He was such a successful lieutenant-governor that Ottawa kept extending his term, until he appealed to the Queen in person, to be allowed to retire and returned to private trading.

Lam's successor as the conscience of Vancouver's Chinese community is Peter Eng, a former Hong Kong academic historian who dispenses moral suasion without a trace of righteousness. The senior partner in Allied Holdings which owns half a dozen hotels around town, he is global, polished and wise. "The things one can do with money can be dangerous," he says. "But if it's looked at as a means to an end, to doing something for the good of the family or mankind, then it becomes useful." He is a computer whiz but when he writes personal letters, it's by hand: "I find it very invigorating that during the course of my working day I can compose letters that I particularly enjoy, and I like to look back again and again at them." Eng's off-duty pleasure is playing mah-jong, because it is a complicated, intellectual form of gambling that taxes your skills in reading your opponents' minds. Typical of his imaginative philanthropy was his gift of a valuable downtown corner heritage building to Simon Fraser University to be developed as a world conference centre. He was one of the founders of the University of East Asia and is a director of the Hongkong Bank of Canada. Eng first came to Vancouver during China's 1967 cultural revolution. His decision followed typical Confucian thinking. "I came," he says, "not for what was happening that year or next year, but thinking that we would live in Canada for a few generations."

The brothers Chan—Tom and Caleb—have made the most impact on Vancouver's non-Chinese community by donating $10 million cash to UBC for a 1,400-seat concert hall (the Chan Centre for the Performing Arts), following a previous $10-million donation. The brothers earned master's degrees at the University of San Francisco, where they helped multiply their family's $150 million fortune, based largely on having the Asian agency for LaCoste "alligator" clothes. In some circles, their father was known as "Crocodile Chan." The family built the famous Nicklaus golf course at Whistler (Caleb once outdrove Jack on the first tee) plus five other golf clubs as well as some of Vancouver's best designed condos. They are fanatical skiers (Caleb recently switched to snow-boarding), windsurfers and, most of all, golfers. Seventh Day Adventists, they finance the church's Canadian expansion. "I find," says Caleb, "that Canadian businessmen are down to earth and more ethical than some Americans, who are maybe a little more dynamic, but much more difficult to rely on totally." The Chans are counted among Vancouver's most valuable citizens, but they're not used to North American styles of publicity. "*Newsweek* once called me an Oriental Rothschild," Caleb complains. "Does that mean I'm some kind of wine?"

Bob Lee is a committe of one. Nearly everything that happens in Vancouver real estate of any significance swirls around him. Accessible, funny and shrewd, he is everybody's friend. Along with David Lam, he was one of the chief conduits into North America for the fortunes fleeing Southeast Asia during the political crises of the past two decades. Through his private company (The Prospero Group), he spent the 1970s and part of the 1980s, along with local partners, making serious investments in central Canada and the U.S. Sunbelt, including the forty-seven-storey Montreal Stock Exchange Tower and a quartet of office buildings in the heart of Houston. In those heady days, his syndicate's rules were simple: the partners spent $100 million a year on deals that had a 100 percent payout within twenty months. At one point, when Lee had finished negotiating for the purchase of the four Houston towers, his partners decided the occasion called for a celebratory dinner. It had been a quick and potentially profitable buy, but none of them seemed certain about precisely what they'd purchased. Finally, after a few drinks, Fred Stimpson, one of his partners, turned to Lee and said: "Bob, can you name one of those buildings we just bought?"

Lee was stuck, but put a brave face on it. "Don't be silly, Fred . . ."

"No. Come on. If you can't think of their names, can you at least think of their addresses?"

Lee was damned if he could remember such details, so he stood up and proposed this toast: "To my partners. They're so smart that if I had brains, it would be redundant! *[Lee doesn't deny this story, but says he felt even worse when he once pointed out a desirable building to one of his partners, nudged him and said, "Hey, let's buy that building!" The partner shot back. "You nut, you already own half of it."]*

Thoroughly Westernized, Lee lives in a West Van mansion and only occasionally indulges his partners and prospects by agreeing to host banquets of Chinese food. He doesn't really like the stuff, but pretends that he does. "How Chinese am I? About fifty-fifty. I was born in Canada but speak Cantonese," he explains. His kids are in the business now, including daughter Carole, who is his representative in the launch (along with Geoffrey Lau and Sam Belzberg) of a bank in Bahrain. He sits on twenty-two private and public boards and is the man to see if you're really rich or really in trouble.

In 1992, when Lee was a partner with Hemming Brasso in MCL Motor Cars, Vancouver's Jaguar, Porsche and Range Rover dealership, they had doubts about selling only luxury cars, and thought that a Honda or Mazda dealership would be a better bet.

"We sold MCL to David Ho," Lee recalls, "because I knew he was a car nut. I phoned him and said, 'David, I've got a deal here.'

"'What is it?'

"'You have a dollar?'

"'Yes.'

"'You own MCL.'"

And that was it. Ho, whose father is the leading cigarette distributor in Hong Kong and into mainland China, had arrived in Canada in 1984, following his graduation from Woodberry Forest School in Virginia (where George Bush's son is an almunus) and purchased Gray Beverages, Canada's largest independent soft drink manufacturer and distributor, from Abe Gray for $100 million. He has since sold the company, has turned MCL into Canada's top-selling dealer for the three brands he represents and recently acquired the Rolls-Royce dealership as well. Ho is not reticent about running down his competitors. ("The BMW? It's a matchbox. The Mercedes? It's cold and German, it's not built for you to drive, but for chauffeurs.") He also owns a security company and the University Golf Club. He is personally into cars and boats—has three of each. *[Including a gold, custom-made Ferrari Testa Rossa that he bought for $250,000; one of his boats is a* Miami-Vice-*style forty-two-foot cigarette Executioner open-sea racing boat. To save money, he buys identical socks so that if only one of a pair wears out it isn't wasted.]* "When I first came here," he recalls, "it was on my honeymoon and I'd never even heard of Vancouver before, but my wife was educated in Canada. We were in New York and she said, why don't we go and visit my B.C. relatives? In my mind at that time, I always pictured that when I stepped off the plane, we would find horses to ride, because it was in the West. When I first came I was most impressed, it was like being in Disneyland. But the taxes! In Hong Kong, we pay 14 percent and we have huge reserves; here, it's 55 percent—and there is a deficit. Do I regret coming here? I don't think so. Will I invest more money here? I don't think so."

Milton Wong is a Vancouver investment counsellor who manages portfolios worth $3 billion. "Investing," he says, "is an interactive art form, or should be. My investment philsophy is quite holistic and distinctive, like an artist's brush stroke. I treat each new client or situation the same way an artist approaches a new creation, without preconceived notions, and I use as much psychology as economics in making investment decisions." Unlike most of his contemporaries who enjoy showing off their possessions, Wong, who is a millionaire many times over, lives modestly. He drives a 1986 Acura that he bought second-hand for $22,000 and contemplates the universe.

Kwok Hau Hui is the head of the clan that owns the Park Hotel in Hong Kong and the Park Georgia realty group in Vancouver, run by his second son, Ernest. His first job in Canada was as a bellhop at the Georgia Hotel, which the family later bought. He is building a tennis camp and resort at Whistler and completing several other projects. Thomas Fung owns most of Canada's Chinese-language radio and TV stations and magazines, as well as Aberdeen Mall in nearby Richmond, which is the largest Asian-oriented shopping location in North America. (He also owns part of the Pacific Mall in Markham, Ontario.) When Chinese leader Jiang Zemin came to Canada, it was Fung that he chose for a private visit. He has also financed international films, such as *The Wild Geese* with Roger Moore. His son Joseph, who is still in high school, speaks English, Cantonese, Mandarin, Spanish, German, Japanese and French.

Felix Tsui got his MBA from McGill, then moved to Vancouver and became one of David Lam's partners and now runs a Vancouver merchant bank. Ernest Hui's profile is so low that he almost doesn't exist, and he likes it that way. Geoffrey Lau's family owns the main Mercedes dealership in Taiwan and all of China. He arrived in Canada in 1974 from Malaysia, established Golden Capital and Golden Properties, and became the first Chinese governor of St. George's private school. He is not fond of B.C.'s socialist government. "China is now many times more capitalist than Canada," he says. "Never in my wildest dreams did I think this was possible." Ron Shon built the $100-million Cathedral Place, the finest of Vancouver's new office towers, but had to sell off large ownership chunks to keep it viable. Eva Lee and Stanley Kwok are the Chinese community's leading power couple, holding half a dozen significant directorships between them. They are at the centre of Canada's Bamboo Network. A protégé of Vancouver architect Arthur Erickson, Bing Thom is the architect with the dream assignment: a multibillion-dollar scheme to remake China's mainland port of Dalian. At thirty-five, Henry Wu owns and operates Metropolitan Hotels in Toronto and Vancouver—all the while completing his doctorate (on artificial intelligence) in electrical engineering at MIT in Boston. David Choi heads the Royal Pacific Real Estate Group and seven other companies. Still in his thirties and a master of the Asian martial arts of Kung Fu and Tai Kwon Do, he has become a growing backstage influence in Vancouver's Chinese hierarchy.

Another of Vancouver's influential, if tiny, communities is made up of the moneyed exiles from Iran. Headed by Hassan Khosrowshahi, whose Future Shop has been a huge success, the community sticks to itself. Khosrowshahi himself is so camera-shy that at the wedding of his own daughter, celebrated at New York's Plaza Hotel, he behaved like a gate-crasher, skulking around corners and not talking to anyone. His wife, the socially active Nezhat, is chair of the Vancouver Symphony. The most Westernized and politically active of the group is Kombiz Eghdami, a lively Stanford MBA graduate, who also holds a master's degree in organic chemistry from the University of London. He may be the only introspective developer extant, loves to read and philosophize, and considers the greatest accomplishment of his life to be his successful six-year struggle to get his parents out of post-Shah Iran, by smuggling them through the mountains of Kurdistan into Turkey. As well as being developers, his family owns Rockmore International, an Oregon-based world-class manufacturer of drill bits. "Every Persian will tell you that being in British Columbia, from an economic point of view, makes no sense because of the tax levels," he says. "But there's no better place in the world to bring up children and as a culture most off us live for the next generation."

The chief representative of Lebanon among Vancouver's Titans is Joe Houssian, CEO of the phenomenally successful Intrawest. He is a tough interview. There is no softness in the man. His body seems impenetrable, hard enough to stop a bullet. Even his suits fit like armour. He clearly doesn't want to talk to me. He sits slumped in a leather chair, showing no vital signs, and it's only during odd moments, when he goes briefly off the record to tell me how much he hates being interviewed, that he shows any flashes of humanity. He drones on, editing every aside, slicing off any hints of personal colour, steering me away from his opinions, wit or playfulness. To interview Joe is to want to kill him. He is one of the most dazzlingly imaginative Vancouver entrepreneurs, owns nearly every profitable mountain top in North America, is the head of the most successful winter holiday merchandising outfit in the universe. Yet he keeps himself on such a tight leash that the "interview" is wasting his time and mine. It takes me a while to understand his game. Houssian's theory is that, if he says nothing quotable, he will not be quoted. It works. Strange bird.

Intrawest Corp., his company, now owns a dozen of the best ski resorts in North America, including Whistler (which cost him $260 million); Mont Tremblant in Quebec (where he has or will be investing $1 billion, including huge gobs of government subsidies); Copper Mountain in

Colorado; Squaw Valley, California; Snowshoe, West Virginia; and Mammoth, California, among others.

For some reason, trying unsuccessfully to interview Joe Houssian reminds me of a story about Clint Eastwood's drama coach, who kept telling the actor: "Don't just do something, stand there."

Whatever works.

Epilogue

"An era can be said to end when its basic illusions are exhausted."

—*playwright Arthur Miller*

I FIRST REALIZED WHAT GOING global really meant when an American cowboy capitalist named Joseph Culiman III, then head of Philip Morris, was taking a run at one of the larger Canadian breweries, Carling O'Keefe. As editor-in-chief of *The Toronto Star* during the early 1970s, I was very much in tune with the paper's passionately held nationalism and regularly attacked the multinationals who were gobbling up Canadian companies. That made my office a regular port of call for slyly genuflecting Genghis Khans, anxious to defang the *Star's* not very effective sting.

But I'd never met anybody like Joseph Culiman III. A John Wayne clone, the oversize Texan looked as if he made love with his boots on, and kept excusing his frequent lapses into obscenity with the winking admonition, "Pardon my French."

"Telling you, buddy," he told me, man to man, "we're gonna make a lotta beer, lotta money, lotta jobs. You know, the whole guacamole." When I enquired, in my deferential Canadian way, whether he was planning to retain Carling's Canadian board of directors, he broke up. I could tell he had been waiting for that obvious question all the way from Laredo or Cheyenne, or wherever he had come riding in from.

He moseyed over, leaned over my desk and gave me his best shot. "Listen up," he said—and I still remember that proud, "gotcha" look in his eye. *"We're going native on this deal!"*

There it was. The end of the Canadian dream. We had been reduced to tokens in our own country, and it took an American Titan wearing spurs to make that revelation clear to me.

That same fierce disregard for a nation's soul is what ultimately separates Canada's Titans from the rest of us. They are the most successful and the most cynical of this country's citizens, because they have reduced the idea of Canada to a flag of convenience—or occasionally, *inconvenience*. The once proud maple leaf is theirs to be used or discarded like a moth-eaten sweater. As Canada's economy becomes part of a homogenized global marketplace, will the Titans remain, in any sense, meaningfully Canadian? Only in their passports.

"The Titans," contends Michael Adams, the national pollster, "acted according to their own sense of integrity and principles by allowing market forces to determine the free trade deal, believing that the FTA was necessary to take them into the next century, where they would be competing globally. They had done as much as they could to exploit the Canadian hinterland. But when they saw the game was up, they made certain they would obtain access to larger playing fields."

When he said this, we were having dinner at one of Umberto Menghis's pasta palaces in Vancouver, on a cool autumn evening in 1997. I had been making the point, without too much inspiration or logic, that even if the FTA eventually brings business benefits, it was the *idea* of Canada that had been compromised, and that once that happened, no economic policies could save us, because most Canadians had such weak or ambivalent feelings about their own country. Then he came up with a fascinating epiphany.

"No!" Adams exploded—and he doesn't explode very often. "No. The point is that Canadians feel *very strongly* about their weak attachment to Canada. The essential fact about the Titans you're describing is that they've stayed in Canada. They have a strong sense of there being something unique here, that we have the freedom to be who we are, or want to become. Sure, they shoot down to Palm Beach or Palm Springs when they feel fed up, but their identity is here, and they're willing to make some free investment in their country to maintain their domiciles."

That's Canadian patriotism, 1998 style.

INTERNATIONAL CAPITALISM has no fixed address, and if it did, it wouldn't be in these chilly latitudes. Today's most valuable commodity, information, flows promiscuously through Internet webs, fibre-optic daisy chains and satellite uplinks. In the past, it was the quest for more territory that drove national ambition—whether it was Hannibal crossing the Alps, Napoleon trying to conquer Europe, or Hitler the world. Now, occupying large hunks of geography is a luxury, even a handicap. Land is the one thing that Canada has plenty of, but it has become more liability than asset. The wealthiest citizens (on a per capita basis) live in the world's tiniest principalities, whether it's Singapore, Hong Kong, Taiwan, Switzerland, Finland, Monaco or Luxembourg. Nation states are being overwhelmed by markets.

The exception for now, of course, is the U.S.A., which is both a huge nation state and *the* universal market. As the millennium approaches, we find ourselves under the gun, ambivalent subjects of an ethic that's described as global, but adheres more closely to *laissez-faire* Delaware Corporation law.

A few years ago, when I was visiting London, one of its great international bankers reminded me that the witty and prescient Irish playwright George Bernard Shaw had commented that North America and Britain were "divided by a common language."

"That's not true any more," he said. "Now, we're united, and our common language is money."

Exactly.

Whatever else is happening internationally, it's the American transnationals that are driving the global business machine. If they think of Canada at all, it's as a slightly backward extension of their northern domestic sales territories. "The boundary separating Canada from the United States," Jacques Maisonrouge, the head of IBM World Corporation, once patiently explained to me, "is no more meaningful than the equator—a line on maps, devoid of meaning."

He looked confused when I mimicked my pal from Philip Morris and replied, "Buddy, that's what going native gets you every time."

But he was right. The conquest of any nation takes place not on battlefields or in boardrooms, but within the hearts of its people and the minds of their leaders. Conquest requires surrender. The U.S. takeover owes less to American strength than to Canadian weakness. We allowed it to happen because too many Canadians—led by a timid, divided Old Establishment—thought there might be something lacking in us that the Americans might provide. So we took the chance that the invading Yanks would supply those qualities, and signed a Free Trade Agreement with them.

The Titans immediately recognized the treaty's full significance. They did not see it as a cultural sell-out, which it was, or as a threat to Canadian sovereignty, which it is. They only saw it as a chance to strengthen themselves. They knew they could grab it and run with it, make it their own, as they ramrod their way into global and continental markets. David Frum, the right-wing commentator, was the only one who spotted the true significance of the agreement. "Free trade," he wrote, "broke the élite consensus by which Canada is normally governed."

THINGS HAVE A WAY OF COMING most sharply into focus near the end of their historic cycles, which often coincide with the launch of new centuries. We're at such a moment now. "An era can be said to end," wrote the playwright Arthur Miller, "when its basic illusions are exhausted."

That's what has happened to Canada's Old Establishment, even if it will take a few more years for their decline to become obvious. The Titans are meanwhile consolidating their power, tapping new sources of energy and influence. Their pulse quickens as they enlist in the newest of frontiers: cyberspace. That's where the Titans' minds are these days, because that's where the cybermoney resides. It has three advantages: transfers are immediate, untraceable and cost 18¢.

E-cash represents the biggest revolution in currency trading since Canada's aboriginals first exchanged beaver pelts for axes and copper kettles at Hudson's Bay Company stores in the eighteenth and nineteenth centuries. Believe it. This fiscal revolution has yet to reach anything like its full impact, but international speculators—many located in Canada—spend their lives bathed in the green glow of the special monitors programmed to dispatch millions and even billions of dollars via cyberspace in search of an extra point of gain or three. In these quantities, such fast money-swaps can yield fortunes.

That weaker currencies may be further devalued in the process, and that few if any taxes are paid on these transactions, poses heavy ethical dilemmas that will one day demand resolution. Meanwhile, CyberCash software is being sold everywhere, and the numbers of subscribers to one program alone (First Virtual) is growing at 16 percent a week. Once fully operational, every imaginable—and some yet unimaginable—financial exchange will take place in cyberspace (using sophisticated encryption, of course) either over the Internet or more likely via the private satellites of several space telecommunications systems now in development.

Funds floating in cyberspace constitute the ultimate tax haven. Even the experts—or more accurately, *especially* the experts who operate in this fourth dimension—are terrified by its prospects. No one can tell how countries, provinces, cities, school districts and hospitals will finance their operations when their tax base is pushed into the ether. No one who has studied these possibilities—and all of the necessary technology not only exists, but is already on line—can figure out how governments, deprived of tax revenues, will continue to perform even such basic functions as administering their own territories, or hiring those relentless revenuers who ask you at the border how many mickeys of cheap American booze you're hiding in your shaving kit.

Rights to privacy will vanish as hackers break into the system—and they inevitably will—leaving open the possibility of staging the biggest money heist in history. There's a geographical quandary here too, because the sellers of goods or services in cyberspace will be in one country, the buyers in another, the consumers in a third, while the computer that brings them together will be operated from a ship at sea outside national jurisdictions, a submarine or a relay station on some Pacific atoll.

As currencies become unmanageable—and what's been happening to the Canadian dollar is the best example—a sense of separation will begin to appear between nation states and their economies. That will be the twenty-first-century equivalent of the church-and-state split that first allowed democracies to flourish—and it will have a far greater impact.

Predictably, one of the few modern operatives in touch with this brave new world is Bill Gates, the Microsoft king, who recognized the massive profit potential of E-cash as early as 1996. That's what prompted his $2-billion run at Intuit. The 100 million people hooked into Gates's Windows programs will be the point of entry for Microsoft's E-cash networks. At least three major American financial Institutions (First National of Chicago, Chase Manhattan and Michigan National) are already signed up as Gates's partners. Can John Cleghorn, Charlie Baillie and Steve Hudson be far behind?

A decade or so into the new millennium, there will emerge the modern equivalents of ancient trading patterns. Nation states will be replaced by alliances of city-states, such as the Hanseatic League of the Middle Ages, the trading association that combined the clout of sixty northern European cities into a powerful commercial oligarchy. Canada's latest Establishment will not escape the consequences of such drastic changes. Its members—all of us—will become children of cyberspace. And chroniclers like me will find it difficult to pin down any Establishment within the loosey-goosey anarchy that lives there. Already, "coronation of the recent Internet establishment happened so fast that there was little time for observation or even participation," notes Frank

Ogden, the Vancouver-based futurist. "If anyone ever gets the time to document that phenomenon, its original engineers will have moved on so far and so fast, that the word 'Establishment' may not be understood, nor even be of consequence any more."

Already, the profound impact of the Internet, which by the year 2000 will have more than a billion Web pages, is hard to exaggerate. It turns on its negatives: "It's not a telephone system, it's not a digital network, and it's not a five-hundred-channel universe," concludes Gerald Levin, head of Time Warner Inc. "It's the one channel that I can create. It's *me*."

"The Internet is a contemporary version of a society without rules," writes Ted Rushton, the Arizona philosopher. "It is not a sharing of voices, but a tribal debate in which every voice is heard with equal authority. William Golding described the Internet culture almost fifty years ago in his *Lord of the Flies*. His theme was the breakdown of civilized behaviour once the rules of social order were abandoned. Golding could only conceive of this happening to unsupervised British schoolboys, not rational adults. The Internet has proved that part of his thesis wrong."

Computers rigged for Internet access have already triumphed over television as the preferred and most vital means of communication. PCs outsold TVs in Canada for the first time in 1995, and convergence of the two media has been accelerating ever since. That's what the digital revolution is about. And inside some inevitable garage teenagers in sweatshirts are working on the next generation of software that will upset everything.

THERE IS NO ESCAPING THE SPREAD OF THIS NEW technology. Just before the completion of this book, I met a Richmond, B.C. entrepreneur named David Levy. He was in the process of building a vacation home on a tiny atoll off Belize called Ambergris Cay. "There's no pavement on the island and two-thirds of the population doesn't own shoes, including the guy who's doing my house," says Levy. "The predominant way of getting around is by golf cart, and there are only ten of those. There's just one pay phone, it's at the only grocery store, and to be heard you have to rant and scream over it. But they have cellular phones and Internet. So when I ask for pictures to show the progress on my house, the shoeless builder drives this decrepit golf cart to the site, takes out his digital camera, snaps off some shots, puts them on e-mail, and within twenty minutes of my request, they're in my home office at Richmond. I'm building my house by e-mail."

That, no doubt, is the how the next Establishment will rebuild itself. Electronically. Byte by byte. Voraciously.

The nervous question on everyone's mind at the end of these pages, here at the end of this century, is this: are the Titans making the world—our world—a better place, or worse? Their impact is difficult to judge because there remains such a wide gap between their magical realm and the still too "real" world they hover above.

They are in the process of establishing their networks across the globe, and they have the courage of their connections. This book documents only the beginning of the Titans' run.

Their destiny will dominate Canada's twenty-first century.

NOTHING ENDURES. That's the law of history. Neighbourhoods disappear. Cities crumble. Countries fall from grace. But establishments abide. Not as they once were, or hoped to be; but in the best Darwinian tradition. They mutate to fit the times, renewing themselves like snakes—the old body in a new skin.

IF YOU FAIL, blame the gene pool. If you succeed, run for your life or the Titans will get you.

Bonne chance, and don't say I sent you . . .

APPENDIX I

MASTERS OF THE UNIVERSE

The Trilateral Commission, founded by New York banker David Rockefeller, is the world's most powerful coalition of governing élites. They meet twice yearly to set their joint agendas with top government leaders of the world's industrialized nations, including Canada. The deliberations of these international Titans are secret, as is this list, which has not been published before. It shows the Trilateral Commission's Canadian members, past and present.

CURRENT CANADIAN MEMBERS

Chairman:

Allan E. Gotlieb, Consultant, Stikeman Elliott; former Canadian Ambassador to the United States

Commissioners:

Conrad M. Black, Chairman and CEO, Hollinger Inc.

Jacques Bougie, President and CEO, Alcan Aluminum Limited

Marshall A. "Mickey" Cohen, Counsel, Cassels Brock & Blackwell, Barristers & Solicitors

Paul Desmarais, Chairman, Executive Committee and Director, Power Corporation of Canada

Peter C. Dobell, Director, Parliamentary Centre

L. Yves Fortier, Senior Partner, Ogilvy Renault, Barristers & Solicitors; former Canadian Ambassador and Permanent Representative to the United Nations

William C. Graham, Chairman, House of Commons Standing Committee on Foreign Affairs and International Trade

Marie-Josée Kravis, Adjunct Senior Fellow, Council on Foreign Relations; former Executive Director, Hudson Institute of Canada

H. Harrison McCain, Chairman of the Board, McCain Foods Limited

James A. Pattison, Chairman, President and CEO, Jim Pattison Group Inc.

Michael E.J. Phelps, Chairman and CEO, Westcoast Energy Inc.

Ronald D. Southern, Chairman and CEO, ATCO Ltd., and CEO, Canadian Utilities Limited

L.R. "Red" Wilson, Chairman, BCE Inc.

FORMER CANADIAN MEMBERS
(with the position they occupied at the time of their membership)

Doris Anderson, President, Canadian Advisory Council on the Status of Women

Michel Bélanger, President, The Provincial Bank of Canada

Robert Bonner, Chairman, British Columbia Hydro and Power Authority

Claude Castonguay, Vice Chairman, Laurentian Bank of Canada

Louis Desrochers, Senior Partner, McCuaig, Desrochers

Claude Edwards, Board Member, Public Service Staff Relations Board

Gordon Fairweather, Chief Commissioner, Canadian Human Rights Commission

John Fraser, Minister of the Environment and Postmaster General

Donald Harvie, Deputy Chairman, Petro-Canada

Alan Hockin, Executive Vice President, Toronto-Dominion Bank

Edgar F. Kaiser, Jr., President and CEO, Kaiser Resources Limited

Michael Kirby, President, Institute for Research on Public Policy

Donald Macdonald, Counsel, McCarthy Tétrault

Mitchell Sharp, Deputy Chairman, North American Commission; Commissioner of the Northern Pipeline Agency

APPENDIX 2

THE MEAL OF THE CENTURY

On September 12, 1994, Ira Gluskin and Gerry Sheff sponsored the opening of the Barnes exhibit of French Impressionist paintings at the Art Gallery of Ontario. Invited were not merely the leaders of the Toronto Establishment, but significant Titans from across the country. The gathering, three thousand strong, was served the most lavish and elaborate meal ever served to such a large gathering. This was the menu:

HORS D'OEUVRE

Crispy Shiitake in Endive with Rosemary

Vegetable Spadini

Chicken Fillet with Yogurt & Turmeric

Spicy Prawns Black Bean Sauce

Pizza
four imported cheeses
*sundried tomato * grilled vegetable*

Pouches of Stilton & Spinach

Pears with Roquefort & Walnuts

Lobster Har Gaw Dim Sum

Tapenade Asiago
Sundried Tomato on Pappadam

Chicken in Coconut
Mango Lime Chutney

Goat Cheese on Radicchio
Sesame, Lavender Oil & Frissee

Deep-Fried Potato & Ratatouille
*(3 pepper * onion * tomato * oregano * basil)*

Tarragon Leaf

Buckwheat Blinis with Red Caviar (with sour cream-chive)

Sushi California Roll & Vegetable Futomaki

Pepper Tomato Mascarpone Foccacia
(toasted foccacia with mascarpone
*grilled yellow pepper * sundried tomato confetti)*

Kosher

⊰ ✳ ⊱

Endive with Crispy Shiitake

Vegetable Spadini

Pizza—*two types*

Pouches of Stilton & Spinach

Pappadam

Pears & Roquefort

Chicken in Coconut

Goat Cheese in Radicchio

Potato Ratatouille

Sushi ✳ Futomaki

Mascarpone Foccacia

Blini with Caviar

Vegetarian

⊰ ✳ ⊱

Vegetable Spadini

Potato Ratatouille

Pappadam

Pears & Roquefort

Goat Cheese

Futomaki

Mascarpone Foccacia

Poisson

⊰ ✳ ⊱

Smoked Salmon

Graved Lax
*(creamed horseradish ✳ sweet mustard sauce
teriyaki ginger ✳ wasabi vinaigrette ✳ sweet onion marmalade)*

The Oysters:
Pine Island ✳ Royal Miyagi ✳ Evening Cove
*peppered vodka shallot
vinaigrette ✳ freshly grated horseradish*

THE DINNER
⊱ ✹ ⊰

Chilled Tenderloin of Beef in a Peppercorn Crust

Shrimp with Tricolour Peppers, Snow Peas,
Shiitake, Bean Sprouts,

Zucchini & Ginger in Soya Oyster Sauce

Bleu Tuna in Sesame & Peppercorns

Veal Medallions in Madeira & Morels

Ragout of Salmon in Pickled Ginger & Lime Zest

Roast Rack of Lamb

Capon in Rosemary Sea-Salt Crust

Mushroom Station

Chanterelles with Chive & Shallot

Herbed Marinated Grilled Portobello

Ravioli with Goat's Cheese

Pasta

Lemon Pepper Fusilli

Citrus Infused Olive Oil with Sundried Tomato Confetti

Marinated Chicken Fillet in Garlic, Soy, Ginger and
Cilantro Sauce with Tiger-Striped Turmeric Basmati Rice

Salads
⊱ ✹ ⊰

Couscous

Lentil

Black Bean Hoisin

Chickpea

Orange Fennel

Balsamic Tomato

Wild Rice

Edible Flower

Cucumber, Yogurt, Turmeric and Cumin

Parsley Butter Orzo

Sweet Potato

Arugula Dandelion

Glass Noodle Sesame

Garlic Parmesan Tomato Macaroni

Ratatouille

Onions and Potatoes au gratin

Cheeses

-⊰ ✳ ⊱-

Roquefort ⚹ triple cream Brie
St. Paulin ⚹ sage Derby ⚹ red Leicester
Black Grapes ⚹ French Baguette

PLATED DESSERT

-⊰ ✳ ⊱-

light pink	Strawberry Yogurt Mousse
purple	Cassis Yogurt Mousse
brown	Espresso Chocolate
white	Semolina Pudding
orange	Mango Mousse
yellow	Passion Fruit Mousse
crimson	Raspberry Yogurt Mousse
sage	Crème Brûlée

DESSERT STATION

-⊰ ✳ ⊱-

Crêpes Suzettes
Shortbread with Lavender Bavarois
Chocolate-Dipped Capped Gooseberries
Miniature Cones with Ice Cream
in
Barnes-coloured Cocktail Napkins

BEVERAGES

-⊰ ✳ ⊱-

Lillet on Ice with Orange Slice
Pol Roger Champagne
Wine
Newtonian Chardonnay
Newtonian Claret
Labatt's Beer
Martinis
Evian ⚹ Perrier
Coca-Cola
Orange Juice ⚹ Cranberry Juice
Clamato Juice ⚹ Tomato Juice
Tonic

APPENDIX 3

THE DREAM TEAM

In the fall of 1997, the University of Toronto set out to collect an initial $400 million (later raised to $650 million) to help finance the shortfall in its operating expenses, build up its number of academic chairs, expand endowments, and pay for new campus buildings and institutes. The roster of the campaign's executive team, listed below, is a handy check-list of Toronto's mainstream Establishment.

Charles Baillie, President and CEO, Toronto-Dominion Bank

Claude T. Bissell, President, University of Toronto, 1958–1971

Wendy Cecil-Cockwell, Chair, Governing Council

F. Anthony Comper (Chair), President and COO, Bank of Montreal

George E. Connell, President, University of Toronto, 1984–1990

William G. Davis, Counsel, Tory Tory DesLauriers & Binnington

Jon S. Dellandrea, Vice President and Chief Development Officer, University of Toronto

John R. Evans, President, University of Toronto, 1972–1978; Chairman, Torstar Corporation

Trevor Eyton, Senior Chairman, Edper/Brascan Corporation

Shari Graham Fell, fund-raiser, Co-Chair of campaign; wife of Tony Fell, Chairman and CEO, RBC Dominion Securities

Al Flood, Chairman and CEO, Canadian Imperial Bank of Commerce

Ira Gluskin, Partner, Gluskin Sheff & Associates

Bonnie Gotlieb, fund-raiser, Chair, 1997 Brazilian Ball

Hal Jackman, Chairman and President, E-L Financial Corp. Limited

Norman Jewison, film producer

Murray B. Koffler, Chair, The Koffler Group

Dorie Lee, Vice President and Director, Nesbitt Burns Inc.

J.A. Ernest Morel, Senior Vice President, Planning & Projects

Peter Munk, Chairman, Barrick & TrizecHahn Corp.

David R. Peterson, Senior Partner, Cassels Brock & Blackwell

J. Robert Prichard, President, University of Toronto

Bob Rae, Partner, Goodman Phillips & Vineberg

Joe Rotman, Chairman, Managing Director and CEO, Clairvest Group Inc.

Susan M. Scace, Co-Chair, Foundation Division

Lionel H. Schipper, President, Schipper Enterprises Inc.

Richard E. Venn, Chairman, CEO and Managing Director, CIBC Wood Gundy

Rose Wolfe, Chancellor Emeritus, University of Toronto

APPENDIX 4

TOM D'AQUINO'S ARMY

These are the members of the Business Council on National Issues, the country's most powerful Establishment grouping. This is a roll-call of Canada's new Titans. Among them, they command assets of $1.7 trillion and employ 1.5 million Canadians. Their relentless lobbying, led by their president and CEO, Tom d'Aquino, sets the national agenda.

James C. Alfano, President and CEO, Stelco Inc., Hamilton

Stuart G. Angus, CEO, P&R Holdings Inc., Toronto

G.F. Kym Anthony, Chairman and CEO, TD Securities Inc., Toronto

E. James Arnett, President and CEO, The Molson Companies Limited, Toronto

Robert M. Astley, President and CEO, The Mutual Life Assurance Company of Canada, Waterloo

R. Jay Atkinson, President and CEO, Jannock Limited, Toronto

A. Charles Baillie, President and CEO, Toronto-Dominion Bank, Toronto

Alex G. Balogh, Chairman, Falconbridge Limited, Toronto

Matthew W. Barrett, Chairman and CEO, Bank of Montreal, Toronto

Thomas J. Bata, Honorary Chairman, Bata Limited, Toronto

Laurent Beaudoin, Chairman and CEO, Bombardier Inc., Montreal

Peter J.G. Bentley, Chairman, Canfor Corporation, Vancouver

André Bérard, Chairman of the Board and CEO, National Bank of Canada, Montreal

Lawrence S. Bloomberg, President and CEO, First Marathon Inc., Toronto

John A. Boland III, President and CEO, Dominion Textile Inc., Montreal

Jacques Bougie, President and CEO, Alcan Aluminium Limited, Montreal

John L. Bragg, President and CEO, Oxford Frozen Foods Limited, Oxford, N.S.

Dan Branda, President and CEO, Hewlett-Packard (Canada) Ltd., Mississauga

William C. Brown, Chairman, BC Sugar Refinery Limited, Vancouver

Pierre Brunet, President and CEO, Lévesque Beaubien Geoffrion Inc., Montreal

James R. Bullock, President and CEO, Laidlaw Inc., Burlington

Claudio F. Bussandri, President and CEO, Medis Health and Pharmaceutical Services Inc., Saint-Laurent

John E. Caldwell, President and CEO, CAE Inc., Toronto

Brian A. Canfield, Chairman and Director, BC Telecom Inc., Vancouver

L. David Caplan, Chairman and CEO, Pratt & Whitney Canada Inc., Longueuil

Frank Cella, Chairman and CEO, Nestlé Canada Inc., Toronto

Gordon F. Cheesbrough, CEO, Altamira Corporation, Toronto

Pierre Choquette, President and CEO, Methanex Corporation, Vancouver

John E. Cleghorn, Chairman and CEO, Royal Bank of Canada, Toronto

Jack L. Cockwell, President and CEO, Edper/Brascan Corporation, Toronto

Albert D. Cohen, Chairman and CEO, Gendis Inc., Winnipeg

David W. Colcleugh, DuPont Canada Inc., Mississauga

Thomas W. Cryer, Chairman, Deloitte & Touche, Toronto

David M. Culver, Chairman, CAI Capital Corporation, Montreal

Dominic D'Alessandro, President and CEO, Manulife Financial, Toronto

André Desmarais, President and Co-CEO, Power Corporation of Canada, Montreal

Paul Desmarais, Jr., Chairman and Co-CEO, Power Corporation of Canada, Montreal

Jean Douville, Chairman and CEO, UAP Inc., Montreal

R. Lamar Durrett, President and CEO, Air Canada, Montreal

Anthony S. Fell, Chairman and CEO, RBC Dominion Securities Inc., Toronto

Alain Ferland, President, Ultramar Ltd., Montreal

William R. Fields, President and CEO, Hudson's Bay Company, Toronto

Al L. Flood, Chairman and CEO, Canadian Imperial Bank of Commerce, Toronto

Marc G. Fortier, Chairman of the Board and CEO, Air Liquide Canada Inc., Montreal

Jun Fukuhara, President and CEO, Marubeni Canada Ltd., Toronto

Ronald G. Gage, Chairman and CEO, Ernst & Young, Toronto

David A. Ganong, President, Ganong Bros. Limited, St. Stephen, N.B.

Claude A. Garcia, President, Canadian Operations, The Standard Life Assurance Company, Montreal

Bobbie Gaunt, President and CEO, Ford Motor Company of Canada Limited, Oakville

Richard L. George, President and CEO, Suncor Energy Inc., Oil, NWT

Robert T.E. Gillespie, Chairman and CEO, General Electric Canada Inc., Mississauga

Serge Godin, Chairman and CEO, The CGI Group Inc., Montreal

Peter C. Godsoe, Chairman and CEO, Bank of Nova Scotia, Toronto

Albert Goller, President and CEO, Siemens Canada Limited, Mississauga

James K. Gray, Chairman and CEO, Canadian Hunter Exploration Ltd., Calgary

Robert J. Gunn, President and CEO, Royal Insurance Company of Canada, Toronto

Jean-René Halde, President and CEO, Livingston Group Inc., Toronto

Robert L. Harms, President and General Manager, 3M Canada Company, London

Milton E. Harris, Chairman and CEO, Harris Steel Group Inc., Toronto

Kerry L. Hawkins, President and CEO, Cargill Limited, Winnipeg

Joseph J. Heffernan, President and CEO, Rothmans, Benson & Hedges Inc., Toronto

J. Allen Hennessy, President, Bechtel Canada Inc., Toronto

James S. Horrick, Chairman, President and CEO, Aon Canada Inc., Toronto

Steven K. Hudson, President and CEO, Newcourt Credit Group Inc., Toronto

Lew C. Hutchinson, President and CEO, Co-Steel Inc., Toronto

The Honourable Henry N.R. Jackman, Chairman and President, E-L Financial Corporation Limited, Toronto

Edward S. Jurus, President and CEO, Kodak Canada Inc., Toronto

V. Maureen Kempston Darkes, President and General Manager, General Motors of Canada Limited, Oshawa

David W. Kerr, Chairman and CEO, Noranda Inc., Toronto

Thomas E. Kierans, Chairman of the Board, Moore Corporation Limited, Toronto

Joseph Kruger II, Chairman and CEO, Kruger Inc., Montreal

Bernard Kueng, President and CEO, St. Lawrence Cement Inc., Montreal

John S. Lacey, President and CEO, Western International Communications Ltd., Vancouver

Jacques Lamarre, President and CEO, SNC-Lavalin Group Inc., Montreal

J. Spencer Lanthier, Chairman and CEO, KPMG Canada, Toronto

Colin Latham, President and CEO, Maritime Telegraph & Telephone Company Limited, Halifax

Dennis A. Lauzon, President and CEO, Dow Chemical Canada Inc., Calgary

R. Jack Lawrence, Chairman, Lawrence & Company Inc., Toronto

Brian M. Levitt, President and CEO, Imasco Limited, Montreal

Paul N. Lucas, President and CEO, Glaxo Wellcome Inc., Mississauga

Gaétan Lussier, President and CEO, Culinar Inc., Montreal

Brian F. MacNeill, President and CEO, IPL Energy Inc., Calgary

Howard Mann, President and CEO, McCain Foods Limited, Toronto

Ronald N. Mannix, Chairman and CEO, Loram Corporation, Calgary

André Marcheterre, President, Merck Frosst Canada Inc., Kirkland

John T. Mayberry, President and CEO, Dofasco Inc., Hamilton

Daniel L. McCaw, President and CEO, William M. Mercer Limited, Toronto

William J. McClean, Chairman, Alliance of Manufacturers & Exporters Canada, Toronto

Raymond L. McFeetors, President and CEO, The Great-West Life Assurance Company, Winnipeg

Diane E. McGarry, Chairman, President and CEO, Xerox Canada Ltd., Toronto

Margaret H. McGrath, President and COO, PPG Canada Inc., Mississauga

Wayne M.E. McLeod, President and CEO, CCL Industries Inc., Toronto

John D. McNeil, Chairman and CEO, Sun Life Assurance Company of Canada, Toronto

James J. Meenan, President and CEO, AT&T Canada, Toronto

Susumu Miyamoto, President and CEO, Mitsui & Co. (Canada) Ltd., Toronto

Gwyn Morgan, President and CEO, Alberta Energy Company Ltd., Calgary

David L. Morton, President and CEO, The Quaker Oaks Company of Canada Limited, Peterborough

Ronald D. Munkley, President and CEO, Mitsubishi Canada Limited, Vancouver

Youssef A. Nasr, President and CEO, Hongkong Bank of Canada, Vancouver

J. Edward Newall, CEO, NOVA Corporation, Calgary

Eric P. Newell, Chairman and CEO, Syncrude Canada Ltd., Fort McMurray

David A. Nield, President and CEO, The Canada Life Assurance Company, Toronto

David P. O'Brien, Chairman, President and CEO, Canadian Pacific Limited, Calgary

Philip M. O'Brien, Chairman and CEO, Devencore Ltd., Montreal

Thomas C. O'Neill, Chairman and CEO, Price Waterhouse, Toronto

Robert B. Peterson, Chairman, President and CEO, Imperial Oil Limited, Toronto

Michael E.J. Phelps, Chairman and CEO, Westcoast Energy Inc., Vancouver

Roger Phillips, President and CEO, IPSCO Inc., Regina

Gerald L. Pond, Chairman, The Canadian Chamber of Commerce, Saint John

Alfred Powis, Founding Chairman, Business Council on National Issue, Toronto

J. Brian Prendergast, President, Monsanto Canada Inc., Mississauga

Jocelyn Proteau, President and CEO, Fédération des caisses populaires Desjardins, de Montréal et de l'ouest-du-Québec, Montreal

Sheldon Rankin, President and CEO, Marsh & McLennan Limited, Toronto

Peter F. Rankine, President, Honeywell Limited, Toronto

R. Gregory Rich, Chairman and President, Amoco Canada Petroleum Company Ltd., Calgary

Hartley T. Richardson, President, James Richardson & Sons Limited, Winnipeg

H. Sanford Riley, President and CEO, Investors Group Inc., Winnipeg

Edward S. Rogers, President and CEO, Rogers Communications Inc., Toronto

John A. Roth, President and CEO, Northern Telecom Limited, Brampton

Henri-Paul Rousseau, President and CEO, Laurentian Bank of Canada, Montreal

Guy Saint-Pierre, Honorary Chairman, Business Council on National Issues, Montreal

Serge Saucier, President and CEO, Raymond, Chabot, Martin, Paré, Montreal

Arthur R. Sawchuk, President and CEO (Interim), Avenor Inc., Montreal

Robert B. Schultz, Chairman and CEO, Midland Walwyn Capital Inc., Toronto

Isadore Sharp, Chairman and CEO, Four Seasons Hotels and Resorts, Toronto

James F. Shepard, Chairman and CEO, Finning International Inc., Vancouver

Charles Sirois, Chairman and CEO, Teleglobe Inc., Montreal

Stephen G. Snyder, President and CEO, TransAlta Corporation, Calgary

Michael D. Sopko, Chairman and CEO, Inco Limited, Toronto

Ron D. Southern, Chairman and CEO, ATCO Ltd., Calgary

James M. Stanford, President and CEO, Petro-Canada, Calgary

Brian J. Steck, Chairman and CEO, Nesbitt Burns Inc., Toronto

Lawrence F. Strong, President and CEO, Unilever Canada Limited, Toronto

Alex Taylor, President and CEO, AGRA Inc., Oakville

Paul M. Tellier, President and CEO, Canadian National, Montreal

Robert Tessier, President and CEO, Gaz Métropolitan, Inc., Montreal

David A. Tuer, President and CEO, PanCanadian Petroleum Limited, Calgary

Paul S. Walters, Chairman and CEO, Sears Canada Inc., Toronto

Colin D. Watson, President and CEO, Spar Aerospace Limited, Toronto

John D. Wetmore, President and CEO, IBM Canada Ltd., Markham

George H. Weyerhaeuser, Jr., President and CEO, Weyerhaeuser Canada Ltd., Vancouver

Donald G. Whitcomb, President and CEO, Celanese Canada Inc., Montreal

Sheelagh D. Whittaker, President and CEO, EDS Canada, Toronto

John M. Willson, President and CEO, Placer Dome Inc., Vancouver

L.R. Wilson, Chairman, BCE Inc., Montreal

Charles W. Wilson, President and CEO, Shell Canada Limited, Calgary

Robert J. Wright, Chairman, Teck Corporation, Toronto

APPENDIX 5

THE DESMARAIS EMPIRE

The three charts that follow capture the complicated anatomy of Paul Desmarais's $100-billion empire. Power Corporation of Canada controls Power Financial, which in turn controls Parjointco, which controls Pargesa Holdings, which runs most of the European operations. There are large minority holdings in most of the companies listed, but the decisions that count are made in Montreal by Paul Desmarais and his sons André and Paul, Jr.

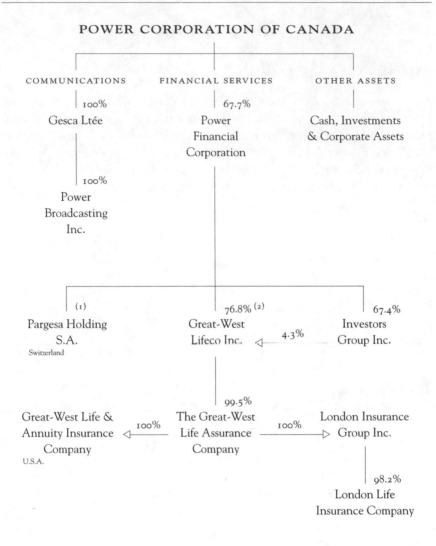

POWER CORPORATION OF CANADA

COMMUNICATIONS — FINANCIAL SERVICES — OTHER ASSETS

100% — Gesca Ltée

67.7% — Power Financial Corporation

Cash, Investments & Corporate Assets

100% — Power Broadcasting Inc.

(1) Pargesa Holding S.A. Switzerland

76.8% (2) Great-West Lifeco Inc. ◁— 4.3% —

67.4% Investors Group Inc.

99.5%

Great-West Life & Annuity Insurance Company U.S.A. ◁— 100% — The Great-West Life Assurance Company —100% ▷ London Insurance Group Inc.

98.2% London Life Insurance Company

(1) Through its wholly owned subsidiary, Power Financial Europe B.V., Power Financial Corporation held a 50-percent interest in Parjointco N.V. Parjointco held a voting interest of 62.4 percent and an equity interest of 55 percent in Pargesa Holding S.A.

(2) Power Financial held a 65-percent direct and indirect voting interest.

POWER FINANCIAL CORPORATION

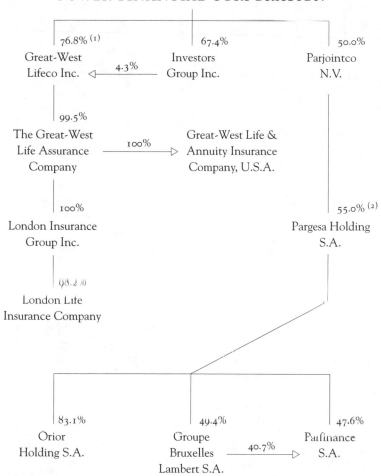

(1) 65-percent direct and indirect voting interest.

(2) 62.4-percent voting interest.

PARGESA HOLDING

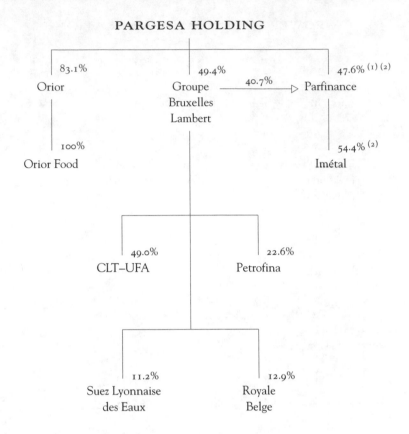

Percentages denote cumulative interests in participating equity held by subsidiaries and affiliates of Pargesa Holding as at December 31, 1997.

Groupe Bruxelles Lambert holds its interests through various intermediate holding companies including Electrafina, Audiofina and Royale–Vendôme.

(1) Parfinance held a 1.9-percent interest in Compagnie Financière de Paribas and a 0.65-percent interest in AXA–UAP at the end of 1997; these participations were sold in the first quarter of 1998.

(2) In March 1998, Parfinance and Imétal announced their intention to submit to their respective shareholders, in June, a project to amalgamate.

APPENDIX 6

THE IVEY BRIGADE

The most aggressive and most successful producer of masters of business administration in the country is the Ivey School of Business at the University of Western Ontario in London. Its graduates generally command the highest starting salaries and most often reach the top rungs on corporate ladders. Below is a selection—made by the school's Alma Mater officials—of its most successful graduates. The list includes MBAS and PhDs, but not executive MBAS, whose prime domicile of choice is Queen's University in Kingston, Ontario.

Adam, Alexander (Sandy), President and CEO, Algoma Steel Inc., Sault Ste. Marie

Alexander, Michael J., President, Loomis Armored Car Service Ltd., Vancouver

Anderson, William D., Senior Vice President, Finance, BCE Inc., Montreal

Anthony, G.F. Kym, Vice Chairman Investment Banking, TD Securities Inc., Toronto

Arnold, G. Jeffrey, Vice President and CFO, Campbell Soup Company Ltd., Toronto

Arthur, Mark L., President and Chief Investment Officer, Royal Bank Investment Management Inc., Toronto

Baillie, Aubrey W., Deputy Chairman, Nesbitt Burns Inc., Toronto

Barber, Thomas K., former President, Morgan Stanley Canada Ltd., Toronto

Baril, Pierre M., former President and CEO, Altamira Management Ltd., Toronto

Barnes, Gary R., former CEO and President, Coca-Cola Foods Canada Inc., Willowdale

Barrett, Deborah J., Senior Vice President and CEO, Harrowston Inc., Toronto

Basian, Karen E., CFO, Hostess Frito-Lay, Mississauga

Bean, W. Donald, former President and CEO, Wood Gundy Inc., Toronto

Beasley, Gerald E., Senior Executive Vice President, Canadian Imperial Bank of Commerce, Toronto

Beauchamp, Marc E., President, Novacap Investments Inc., Montreal

Belbeck, Kenneth G., former Chairman, Peat Marwick Stevenson & Kellogg, Toronto

Birks, Barry D., President, Tyringham Investments Ltd., Montreal

Black, David H., President, Black Press Ltd., Victoria

Boswell, Edward F., Chairman, E.B. Eddy Forest Products Ltd., Ottawa

Braithwaite, J. Lorne, President and CEO, Cambridge Shopping Centres Ltd., Toronto

Bras, Robert W., President and Owner, Menu Foods Ltd., Mississauga

Breen, Howard J.J., President and COO, Young & Rubicam Canada, Toronto

Breukelman, William A.A., former Chairman, Imax Corporation; now Chairman, Business Arts Ltd., Mississauga

Britton, William L., Chairman and National Managing Partner, Bennett Jones Verchère, Calgary

Brock, William T., Deputy Chairman, Toronto-Dominion Bank, Toronto

Brooks, Robert L., Executive Vice President, Investment Banking, Bank of Nova Scotia, Toronto

Brouillard, Robert V., former Managing Partner, Deloitte & Touche Management, Toronto; now CEO, Deloitte & Touche Consulting Group–Europe.

Brown, Logan Rae, former Chairman, Robin Hood Multifoods Inc., Toronto

Brown, Stephen R., former President, Alcan Rolled Products Company, Montreal; now President and CEO, Mueller Electric Company, Cleveland

Cadsby, Ted, CEO and President, CIBC Securities Inc., Toronto

Cameron, Bradley, President, Lehman Brothers Canada Inc., Toronto

Campbell, William, former President and CEO, Philip Morris Inc., New York; now Corporate Executive Vice President, Citibank, New York

Carroll, John C., Past Chairman, Molson Breweries, Toronto; now President, Clairon Holdings Inc., Toronto

Charbonneau, Peter C., President, Newbridge Networks Corporation, Ottawa

Charles, Ronald D., Managing Partner, Caldwell Partners International, Toronto

Cheng, Kar Shun Henry, Managing Director, New World Development Company, Hong Kong

Chow, Shody, Managing Director, Swire Pacific Trading, Hong Kong

Chrominska, Sylvia D., Executive Vice President, Human Resources, Bank of Nova Scotia, Toronto

Clark, C. David, former Chairman and Publisher, *Globe and Mail*, Toronto, former Chairman and CEO, Campbell Soup Company Ltd., Toronto

Clark, C. Greig, Founder & former Chairman, College Pro Painters Ltd., North York

Clitheroe, Eleanor R., Managing Director, Ontario Hydro Services Company, Toronto

Clouston, Brendan R., former CFO, Tele-Communications Inc., Denver

Clouston, Robert A., Executive Vice President and General Manager, ConAgra Frozen Foods

Colbourne, Douglas S., Chairman, Ontario Municipal Board, Toronto

Cole, Gordon A., Executive Vice President and COO, Interprovincial Pipe Line Ltd., Calgary

Colter, Gary F., Vice Chairman, KPMG, Toronto

Conn, David B., President, Colgate Palmolive Ltd., Boksburg

Connochie, Robert G., former President and CEO, Potash Company of America Inc.

Cope, George A., President and CEO, Clearnet Inc., Pickering

Cornhill, David W., former President and COO, Alberta & Southern Gas Company Ltd., Calgary

Couturier, Rosaire M., Executive Director and CEO, Institute of Canadian Bankers, Montreal

Crossgrove, Peter A., CEO and President, Southern Africa Minerals Corporation, Toronto; former Chairman and Acting CEO, Placer Dome Inc., Toronto

Crowley, Patrick, CFO and Executive Vice President, Abitibi Consolidated Inc., Montreal

Crump, C. Kenneth, Senior Vice President and CFO, BC Telecom, Burnaby

Cullen, Mark L., Vice Chairman and Director, RBC Dominion Securities, Vancouver

Dampier, J. Lawrence, former Chairman of the Board, Nabob Foods Ltd.

Dembroski, George S., Vice Chairman, RBC Dominion Securities, Toronto

Derksen, Paul W., CFO and Senior Vice President, Canada Trust, Toronto

Dodge, Edwin V., Executive Vice President, Operations, Canadian Pacific Railway, Calgary

Doran, John C., Executive Vice President, Administration and CFO, Canadian Imperial Bank of Commerce, Toronto

Dossett, Jeffrey J., former President, Microsoft Canada Inc., Mississauga; now General Manager–Internet Customer Unit, Microsoft Corporation, Redmond

Drummond, Brian P., former Vice Chairman, Richardson Greenshields of Canada Ltd., Montreal

Duncan, Gordon A., President and CEO, RNG Equipment Inc., Mississauga

Earthy, David G., President and CEO, Consolidated Fastfrate Inc., Toronto

Eckert, John F., Managing Partner, McLean Watson Capital Inc., Toronto

Eden, Ronald W., former President and CEO, Canada Malting Company Ltd., Etobicoke

Elwood, E. Peter, CEO and President, Thomas J. Lipton, Toronto

Eyton, Rhys T., former Chairman, Canadian Airlines Corporation, Calgary

Farrish, Kenneth R., President, Delta Faucet Canada, London

Ferchat, Robert A., Chairman and CEO, BCE Mobile Communications Inc., Mississauga

Fisher, Shelley, President, FBI Brands Ltd., St-Laurent

Fleck, James. D., Chairman, Flect Manufacturing Inc., Willowdale

Fortier, Marc G., Chairman and CEO, Air Liquide Canada Inc., Montreal

Fraser, Barbara H., Chairman and CEO, Citicorp Investment Services, New York

Gaasenbeck, Matthew, Executive Vice President, Sharwood & Company, Toronto

Ganong, David A., President, Ganong Brothers Ltd., St. Stephen

Garwood, Joseph J., President, Camelot Pictures Inc., Toronto

Gibson, William W., President and CEO, Mountain Equipment Co-op, Vancouver

Gill, John B., CEO and President, North West Life Assurance Company, Vancouver

Gillespie, A. Ian, CEO and President, Export Development Corporation, Ottawa

Gillin, R. Peter, Vice Chairman, Rothschild Canada Ltd., Toronto

Godbout, André D., Senior Executive Vice President, Lévesque Beaubien Geoffrion, Montreal

Golden, Kerri-Lynne, CFO and Vice President, Imutec Pharma Inc., Scarborough

Gorman, John C., Chairman, President and CEO, Enron Capital & Trade Resources Corporation, Calgary

Gouin, Serge, Vice Chairman, Salomon Smith Barney Canada Ind., Montreal

Grainger, John R., President and COO, Laidlaw Transit Inc., Burlington

Grant, Jon K., Chairman, Canada Lands Company Ltd., Peterborough

Graye, Mitchell T., Senior Vice President and CFO, Great-West Life Assurance Company, Winnipeg

Green, R. Alexander, President, Blackburn Media Group, London

Greenspan, Sheldon, President, Eco-Shred Ltd., Mississauga

Gudewill, Sam, President and Principal, Innovex Equities Corporation, Vancouver

Gulliver, René D., Senior Vice President and CFO, Royal LePage Ltd., Don Mills

Hallisey, Richard S., Vice Chairman and Director, First Marathon Securities, Toronto

Harrigan, Kenneth W.J., former Chairman and CEO, Ford Motor Company of Canada Ltd.

Hayhurst, Douglas P., Senior Partner–British Columbia, Price Waterhouse, Vancouver

Heersink, Ewout R., CFO and Vice President, Onex Corporation, Toronto

Hill, James T., President and CEO, Economical Mutual Insurance Company, Waterloo

Hill, Paul J., President, McCallum Hill Ltd., Regina

Hobbs, Richard J., Chairman and CEO, Illuminated Filmworks Inc., Freeport

Hockin, Thomas A., President and CEO, Investment Funds Institute of Canada, Toronto

Hodgins, Robert B., Vice President and Treasurer, Canadian Pacific, Calgary

Hook, William C., President, Livingston Healthcare Services Inc., Oakville

Hopper, Wilbert H., former Chairman and CEO, Petro-Canada, Calgary

Horne, James W., President and CEO, Colliers International, Toronto

Hunter, James L., President and COO, MacKenzie Financial Corporation, Toronto

Hyndman, Douglas M., Chairman, BC Securities Commission, Vancouver

Irwin, A. Scott, Senior Vice President, Irwin Toys Ltd., Toronto

Ivey, Richard M., President, Ivest Corporation, London

Ivey, Richard W., Chairman, Livingston Group Inc., Etobicoke

Ivey Thom, Rosamond A., Managing Director, JRS Group, Toronto

Jackson, Donald K., Chairman, Parkview Capital Corporation

Jackson, Terry A., Executive Vice President, Bank of Montreal, Toronto

Janzen, Rudolf H., President and CEO, Procorp Developments Inc., Calgary

Johnson, Donald K., Vice Chairman, Nesbitt Burns Inc., Toronto

Johnson, J. Edward, Vice President, General Counsel and Secretary, Power Corporation of Canada, Montreal

Joseph, J. Urban, Chairman, Career Edge, Toronto; former Vice Chairman, Toronto-Dominion Bank, Toronto

Kanovsky, Michael M., President, Sky Energy Corporation, Calgary

Kassie, David J., Chairman, CIBC Wood Gundy Capital, Toronto

Kelly, Howard L., former President and CEO, Guardian Trust Company, Montreal

Kernaghan, Edward J., Chairman and CEO, Thomson Kernaghan & Company Ltd., Toronto

Knowles, Richard L., Chairman and CEO, Jones Heward Investment Management Inc., Toronto

Knowlton, Gerald L., former Chairman, Knowlton Realty, Calgary

Kuhlmann, Arkadi R., President and CEO, ING Direct Inc., North York

Lackenbauer, Gordon S., Deputy Chairman, Nesbitt Burns Ltd., Calgary

Lagassé, Louis, Principal Partner, Lagassé Lagassé, Sherbrooke

Laird, Allan D., President, A.D. Laird Consulting Ltd., Vancouver

Lamoureux, Gilles, Managing Director, Orenda Corporate Finance, Toronto

Lang, Christopher H., Chairman, Christopher Lang & Associates, Toronto

Lang, Donald G., President, CCL Custom Manufacturing Inc., Rosemont

Laparé, Jacques, President–Transportation Services, Bombardier Inc., Kingston

Latimer, Radcliffe R., former President and CEO, TransCanada PipeLines Ltd., Toronto

Latta, Fraser D., Vice Chairman and COO, Cott Corporation, Toronto

Lawrence, Mark A., Director, Loewen Ondaatje McCutcheon Ltd., Toronto

Lawrence, R.J., Chairman, Lawrence & Company Inc., Toronto

LeBoutillier, John A., President and CEO, Iron Ore Company of Canada, Montreal

Leblanc, Jean-Yves, President and COO, Bombardier Transportation Group, Saint-Bruno

Lee, Seng Wee, Chairman of the Executive Committee, Oversea-Chinese Banking Corporation, Singapore

Lehman, Christopher W., former Chairman, Saatchi & Saatchi; former President, Hayhurst Advertising Ltd.

Lennox, R. Ian, President and CEO, Drug Royalty Corporation Inc., Toronto

Lifson, Elliot, Vice Chairman, Algo Group Inc., Montreal

Lindores, Douglas P., former CEO, Canadian Red Cross Society, Ottawa

Love, Jon E., President and CEO, Oxford Properties Group Inc., Toronto

Luba, Robert W., President, Luba Financial Inc., Toronto

Lunt, Wayne E., Senior Vice President, TransCanada PipeLines Ltd., Calgary

Lynch, Terrence F., former Chairman and CEO, Hay Management Consultants, Toronto

Lyons, Terrence A., President and Managing Partner, BC Pacific Capital Corporation, Vancouver

MacDiarmid, J. Hugh, Executive Vice President–Commercial, Canadian Pacific Railway, Calgary

MacDonald, James, Chairman and Managing Partner, Enterprise Capital Management Inc., Toronto

MacDonald, Ralph W., former President and CEO, Cooper Canada Ltd.

Mackay, Ian A., Co-Managing Director, Conquest Management Company, Toronto

Magee, Christine A., President and Co-Founder, Sleep Country Canada, Toronto

Maich, Robert S., President and COO, Silcorp Ltd., Scarborough

Maier, Gerald J., Chairman, TransCanada PipeLines Ltd., Calgary

Major, Bruce W., President, Christie Brown & Company, Etobicoke

Marshall, Brian D., Vice Chairman, Corporate Finance, Midland Walwyn Capital Inc., Toronto

Martin, Joseph P., CEO, The Company-Operators Group Ltd., Guelph

Matte, Bernard W., former President, Wajax Industries Ltd., Langley

Matthews, Christopher R., Chairman and CEO, Hay Group Inc., Philadelphia

McCain, Michael H., President and COO, Maple Leaf Foods Inc., Toronto

McCoy, Richard H., Vice Chairman, Toronto-Dominion Securities Inc., Toronto

McDonald, Stephen D., Vice Chairman of Group Administration, Toronto-Dominion Bank, Toronto

McDougall, Donald J., President and CEO, Novatronics Inc., Stratford

McMorran, Sydney R., Vice Chairman, Toronto-Dominion Bank, Toronto

McNeil, Kevin W., President and CEO, CIBC General Insurance Company Ltd., Mississauga

Menard, L. Jacques, Chairman of the Board, Hydro-Québec; Deputy Chairman and Managing Director PQ, Nesbitt Burns Inc., Montreal

Messier, Jacques R., President and
COO, Novapharm Ltd., Scarborough

Miller, Glenn A., President,
PenEquity Management
Corporation, Toronto

Mitchell, Ronald W., former
President, CEO and Publisher, The
Financial Post Company, Toronto

Moon, Alan C., President and COO,
TransAlta Energy Corporation,
Calgary

Moore, Edward G., CEO and President,
IGA Canada Ltd., Etobicoke

Moore, Ronald E., former President
and CEO, Adidas USA Inc.

Moran, Harold J., former President,
Molson Ontario Breweries Ltd.,
Toronto

Morrisette, Pierre, President and CEO,
Pelmorex Inc., Mississauga

Mullen, David F., CEO, HSBC Capital
Canada Ind., Vancouver

Muncaster, J. Dean, former President
and CEO, Canadian Tire
Corporation Ltd., Toronto

Munday, Anthony, Executive Vice
President and CFO, Inco Ltd.,
Toronto

Murphy, Helen, CFO, Polygram Music
USA Inc., New York

Murray, Susan, Founder and CEO,
SAMCI, Toronto

Needham, Michael J., Chairman and
CEO, SimEx Inc., Toronto

Nesbitt, Richard W., President and
CEO, HSBC Securities, Toronto

Nichol, David A., former President,
Cott Corporation; former
President, Loblaw Companies
Ltd., Toronto

Nininger, James R., President and
CEO, Conference Board of Canada,
Ottawa

Nourse, Robert, former President and
CEO, The Bombay Company Inc.,
Fort Worth

O'Callaghan, Patrick F., former
President and Managing Partner,
The Caldwell Partners
International, Toronto

O'Leary, T. Kevin, President, The
Learning Company Inc.,
Cambridge MA

Paquin, Madeleine M., President,
Logistic Corporation, Montreal

Patterson, Christopher W., Executive
Vice President Marketing, Volvo
Trucks North American,
Greensboro

Payson, L. Russell, President,
The Paige Group Inc., Dorval

Pearson, J. Bruce, Chairman, The
Blackburn Group Inc., London

Pelletier, Michel, Senior Vice
President, Agency Banking,
Laurentian Bank of Canada,
Montreal

Polubiec, Mark J., former Executive
Vice President, Canaccord
Capital, Toronto; former President
and CEO, Burns Fry Ltd.

Pommier, Paul, Senior Executive
Vice President, Lévesque Beaubien
Geoffrion Inc., Montreal

Poole, Thomas A., Chairman and
CEO, Sepp's Gourmet Foods Ltd.,
Burnaby

Powell, John A., former President
and CEO, Wajax Ltd., Montreal

Prevost, Edward J., President and
CEO, Para Paints, Brampton

Rastogi, Dipak K., Executive Vice
President, Citibank NA, New
York

Rattee, David A., President and CEO,
CIGL Holdings Ltd., Toronto

Reid, Bruce H., former President and CEO, Brick Warehouse Corp., Edmonton; former Chairman, President and CEO, WH Smith Canada Ltd.

Renner, Theodore H., President, Vista Energy Inc., Regina

Ridout, Derek M., President and CEO, Silcorp Ltd., Scarborough

Ritchie, Gordon M., President and CEO, RBC Dominion Securities Corporation, New York

Ritchie, John R., Chairman and CEO, IMAGO Consulting Group Ltd., Calgary

Ritchie, Robert J., President and CEO, Canadian Pacific Railway, Calgary

Robertson, Paul W., President, YTV Canada Inc., Toronto

Robertson, Russel C., Canadian Managing Partner, Arthur Andersen & Company, Toronto

Rosen, Laurance J., President, Harry Rosen Inc., Toronto

Rothschild, John A., President and CEO, Prime Restaurant Group Inc., Mississauga

Royer, Terrance E., President and CEO, Royco Hotels & Resorts Ltd., Calgary

Saunders, James L., former President and COO, Moore Business Forms International, Toronto

Saunders, Peter B., COO, T. Eaton Company Ltd., Toronto

Shaw, Heather, President and Co-Founder, Digital Music Express Canada, Toronto

Schumacher, C. John, Managing Director–Global Trading, Scotia Capital Markets, Toronto

Scott, Donald C., former Senior Partner, Clarkson Gordon, Toronto

Scott, E. Duff, Chairman, QLT Photo Therapeutics Inc., Toronto

Sharpe, C. Richard, former Chairman and CEO, Sears Canada Inc., Toronto

Shlesinger, Joseph C., Managing Director, Bain & Company Canada Ltd., Toronto

Shuparski, Mark, President and CEO, Bentall Corporation, Vancouver

Smith, N. Arthur, President and CEO, The Electronic Commerce Council, Mississauga

Smith, W. Keith, Vice Chairman, Mellon Bank Corporation, Pittsburgh

Snowden, Gerald W., President and CEO, McCormick & Company Inc., Maryland

Snyder, Stephen G., CEO and President, TransAlta Corporation, Calgary

Spafford, Paul B., Vice Chairman, CIBC Wood Gundy Securities Inc., Toronto

Speers, Douglas E., President and CEO, EMCO Ltd., London

Stevens, D. Glenn, President and CEO, Itwal Ltd., Mississauga

Stinson, William W., former President and CEO, Canadian Pacific Ltd., Montreal

Stollery, H. John, CEO, TNT North America Inc., Mississauga

Stymiest, Barbara G., Senior Vice President and CFO, Nesbitt Burns Inc., Toronto

Sutherland, Frederick R., Vice President–Human Resources, McCain Foods, Toronto

Tate, G. Robert, President, Beaver Lumber, Sudbury

Taylor, Howard W., former Managing Partner, Deloitte & Touche, Toronto

Thomas, Paul A., President, Merrill Lynch Canada, Toronto

Thompson, John, Principal, Gornitzki,Thompson & Little, Toronto

Thompson, John D., Deputy Chairman of the Board, Montreal Trust Company Ltd., Montreal

Thomson, David J., President, Great-West Life Assurance Company, Denver

Thomson, William W., former President, Norcan Engineering, Vancouver

Tolmie, Kenneth R., Chairman and CFO, Beacon Group of Companies, Vancouver

Torrey, David L., President, Torcanus Inc., Montreal

Tough, Douglas D., President, Cadbury Schweppes Beverages, Watford

Triggs, Donald L., President and CEO, Vincor International Inc., Mississauga

Twiss, Wesley R., Executive Vice President and CFO, Petro-Canada, Calgary

Van Wielingen, Mac H., President, ARC Financial Corporation, Calgary

Verdon, Raymond J., former President, Nabisco Biscuit Company, East Hanover

Vollmershausen, Dennis W., CEO, Champion Road Machinery Ltd., Goderich

von der Porten, Robert, President–North American Division, Speedy Muffler King Inc., Toronto

Waddington, Philip, former CEO, Canadian Plastics Group Ltd., Richmond Hill

Walcot, Donald T., Chief Investment Officer, BIMCOR Inc., Montreal

Wallace, Peter L., President, CT Financial Services Inc., Toronto

Watsa, V. Prem, Chairman and CEO, Fairfax Financial Holdings Ltd., Toronto

Watson, Colin D., President and CEO, Spar Aerospace Ltd., Toronto

Watson, Larry G., President, Marsh and McLennan, Winnipeg

Weldon, David B., former Chairman and President, Midland Doherty Ltd., Toronto

West, William A., former President, Petro-Canada, Montreal

Westaway, James G., President, Wescast Industries Inc., Brantford

Wettlaufer, J. Mark, President, TD Asset Management, Toronto

Wheaton, Mark G., Vice Chairman, Co-Head Investment Bank, Toronto-Dominion Securities Inc., Toronto

White, Paul C., former President, Arthur D. Little of Canada Ltd., Toronto

White, William F., President, IBK Capital Corporation, Toronto

Whitehead, Douglas W.G., President, Fletcher Challenge Canada Ltd., Vancouver

Wilgar, Stephen A., President, CAA, Toronto

Williamson, Kenneth F., Vice Chairman–Finance, Midland Walwyn Capital Inc., Vancouver

APPENDIX 7

THE BAY STREET GANG

Of the thousands of money-minded men and women who call Bay Street their spiritual home, less than a hundred "make the markets." Below are some of the leading contenders for this mark of distinction.

BUY-SIDE PLAYERS

Mark Bonham, founder of BPI— fought and lost to Jim McGovern; started Strategic Value; bought Laurentian assets for seemingly high price in 1997 and made a fortune.

Gerry Brockelsby, Marquest— ultimate momentum player; mid caps.

Gary Chapman, Guardian— momentum, growth.

Sue Coleman, Frank Mersch's *alter ego* at Altamira—friendly, confident, a good person.

Wayne Deans, Deans Knight, formerly with Milton Wong—left to start Deans Knight with Doug Knight, also of M.K. Wong. Close to First Marathon.

John Embry, RBIM—natural resource king.

Ira Gluskin, Gluskin Sheff—most astute observer of the scene.

Allan Jacobs, Sceptre—solid mid caps; made over $2 million in 1997.

Peter Larkin, king of Royal Trust— seen it all, done it all.

Lynn Miller/Kiki Delaney, partners at Delaney Capital—the smartest money managers in Canada.

Steve Misener, BPI Mutual Funds— micro-cap king; 150 percent performance in 1996.

John Mulvihill, Mulvihill Capital— formerly Canada Trust; aggressive.

Jim O'Donnell, O'Donnell— consistently underestimated; likeable and lucky.

Scott Penman, Investors—cocky and smart; strong performance.

Alan Radlo, Fidelity—decides value of stock and moves the quote there.

Rohit Segal, London Life—makes huge bets; big trader.

Ray Steele, Goodman—takes big swings.

Michael Waring, Knight Bain— eccentric, smart.

John Zechner, Zechner & Associates—manages CI Funds; big cap momentum player; aggressive trader.

MOST SUCCESSFUL POLITICIAN TURNED INVESTMENT BANKER

Ed Lumley, Nesbitt Burns—on boards of CN, Trilon, Air Canada, Magna, etc. Brings in *big* business.

BIGGEST MONEY EARNERS AT BOUTIQUES

Sprott Securities
Eric Sprott—owns 70 percent of Sprott; trades firm capital very successfully, earning over $7 million per year.

Griffiths and McBurney
Brad Griffiths, Gene McBurney, Kevin Sullivan, Michael Wekerley—four equal partners. Wekerley is the most aggressive trader on the street, period; runs trading-room like an orchestra—standing, waving his arms, screaming orders and directions. Each of the four makes $10 million a year.
Tom Budd—best oil and gas investment banker in Canada; likely paid $5 million.
David Connacher—Jim's son, who fled Gordon to join Griffiths.

Received a reported $250,000/month commission from Fidelity; has switched to Paterson's firm.

Newcrest Securities
Bob Dorrance—highly regarded, ran Nesbitt's sales and trading prior to forming Newcrest.
Jim Hinds—highly regarded capitals markets and syndicate person, ran Wood Gundy's syndication.
Scott McNicol—most gentlemanly big trader on the street.
Robbie Pryde—one of the most respected salespeople in Canada.
Newcrest has led three large deals: Baton, Canadian Firemaster and Onex. Senior partners are paid probably $2.5 million each.

MOST POWERFUL BUY-SIDE TRADERS

Stevie Craig, J. Zechner Associates—swings the bat for big positions.

OTHER TOP TRADERS

Research Capital
Tony Popowich—head trader; moved from Altamira trading desk where he was Frank Mersch's number one trader.

Goepel McDermid
Rusty Goepel—famous for annual fishing trips.
Ken Shields—strongest forest products investment banker.

Midland Walwyn
Guy Savard
Marc Deslongchamps

Carol Mitchell—best salesperson in Canada.

Wood Gundy
John Hunkin, CEO
Richand Venn—pulled off Newcourt deal.
David Kassie
Jay Smith—top retail broker.

RBC Dominion Securities
Gord Nixon—head of investment banking; likely successor to Tony Fell.
Chuck Winograd—another candidate to succeed Tony.

Mike Norris—strong Calgary-based player.

First Marathon
Rick Hallisey—nearly equal to Tom Budd in oil and gas.
Peter Jones—head of investment banking.

Scotia McLeod
Brian Porter—in charge of wholesale side.
Scot Martin—good investment banker.

Bunting
David MacDonald—strong mining franchise.

TD Securities
Steve Clarke—legendary liability trader.
Gordon Private Client
Crawford Gordon—his father was Crawford Gordon of AVRO Arrow fame; left Nesbitt after twenty-nine years as a leading retail broker.
Don McFarlane—formerly RBC Dominion Securities' biggest broker ($2 million plus annual commission); left to join Gordon Private Client.

Gordon Capital
Gerry Gravina—daring liability trader.

MUSICAL CHAIRS CHAMPION

Marc Deslongchamps, Midland Walwyn—recruited in June 1998 from RBC Dominion Securities for a reputed $1.75 million annually for two years.

MOST EFFECTIVE U.S. INVESTMENT BANKERS IN CANADA

Stanley Hartt and Rob Gemmel at Salomon Bros. They win more telecom business than Merrill or Goldman.

HIGHEST-PAID RBC DOMINION PROFESSIONAL

Roland Kuiper—heads proprietary trading group; makes more money than Tony Fell.

HOT TRADER

Stuart Smith, Wood Gundy

DERIVATIVES KING

Eric Tripp, Nesbitt

APPENDIX 8

ESTABLISHMENT HANGOUTS

Canada's Titans work hard and play harder. The world is their playpen. Everyone has their favourite hangout or hideout. The Greenhouse in Dallas is a current favourite among the Toronto crowd, with Main Chance in Arizona still popular among the slightly older crowd. These are some of the more frequently visited spots:

Amandari-Ubud, Bali, Indonesia. Sanskrit for "place of peaceful spirits." Health complex, staff-to-guest ratio of five to one.

Four Seasons, Nevis, Caribbean. The only Caribbean resort to receive the Five-Diamond Award from the American Automobile Association.

Turtle Island, Fiji. Remote and private island getaway, only fourteen couples allowed to visit at any one time.

Wickannish Inn & Sooke Harbour House, Sooke, British Columbia. Best food and cosiest rooms in Canada.

Roaring Pavilion, near Ocho Rios, Jamaica. The ultimate in luxury, privacy and expense.

Bedarra Island Retreat, Queensland, Australia. Azure waters and boulder-strewn sandy beaches backed by tropical rain forest. Off the northern coast of Queensland.

Taybet Zaman, near Petra, Jordan. A late nineteenth-century Arabic village turned into a twentieth-century hotel at the request of Jordan's Queen Noor.

Hostería La Mirage, Cotacachi, Ecuador. Set on a hillside in the Andes, a few hours north of Quito. Six hectares of spectacular gardens, vineyard, a view of two volcanoes.

The Inn at Manitou in McKellar, Ontario. Five-star resort, 220 hectares, on the shores of Lake Manitouwabing, 240 kilometres north of Toronto.

Sivananda Ashram Yoga Camp, Val Morin, Quebec. Meditation, yoga classes, lectures, a spiritual extravaganza.

Hostellerie les Trois Tilleuls, St-Marc sur Richelieu, Quebec. Favourite business meeting site, twenty-four guest suites and lounges, four-star cuisine, nearby Île aux Cerfs, pheasant hunting. Hunter's Package includes a professional guide and pointer dog plus an extra-hearty hunter's dinner at the end of the day.

Tara Manor Inn, St. Andrews-by-the Sea, New Brunswick. Twenty-acre estate was home to former prime minister Sir Charles Tupper, as well as C.D. Howe. Golf, tennis, whale-watching excursions.

Sah Naji Kwe Wilderness Spa and Meeting Place, Northwest Territories. Focus of this retreat is its therapeutical clay baths and its raw, unpolished setting on the Canadian Shield.

TOP SPAS

Canyon Ranch, Tucson, Arizona
Canyon Ranch in the Berkshires, Lennox, Massachusetts
Golden Door, Escondido, California
The Greenhouse, Arlington, Texas
Rancho La Puerta, Tecate, Mexico
Givenchy Hotel & Spa, Palm Springs, California
Miraval Life in Balance, Tucson, Arizona
Hilton Head Health Institute, Hilton Head, South Carolina
Woodlands Spa, Farmington, Pennsylvania
Aveda Spa, Osceola, Wisconsin

TOP RESORTS

Grand Wallea Resort, Hotel & Spa, Maui
Peaks at Telluride Resort & Spa, Telluride
Lodge & Spa at Cordillera, Edwards, Colorado
Ihilani Resort & Spa, Oahu
Marriott's Desert Springs Resort & Spa, Palm Desert, California
Marriott's Camelback Inn, Scottsdale, Arizona
Sandals Royal Bahamian Resort & Spa, Bahamas
La Costa Resort & Spa, Carlsbad, California
Topnotch at Stowe, Stowe, Vermont
Sanibel Harbor Resort & Spa, Fort Myers, Florida

APPENDIX 9

MONTREAL'S SUPERSTARS

Ever since René Lévesque was elected premier in 1976, Montreal's economy has been in free fall. But that hasn't stopped some of Canada's most capable and successful Titans from calling it their home base. Because the separatist threat still hangs over the city, its future remains uncertain. Meanwhile, the men and women listed below are forging a new world.

Laurent Beaudoin, Chairman, President and CEO, Bombardier Inc.

Charles Bronfman, Co-Chair, Chairman, Executive Committee, The Seagram Company

Paul Desmarais, Chairman, Executive Committee and Director, Power Corporation of Canada

Pierre Michaud, Provigo

Pierre Lessard, Metro Richelieu

Claude Lessard, Cossette Communication-Marketing

Brian Levitt, Imasco

Gilles Ouimet, Pratt & Whitney

André Bureau, Astral Communications

Jacques Lamarre, SNC-Lavalin

André Caille, Hydro-Québec

André Bérard, National Bank

Michel Vennat, lawyer

François Beaudoin, Business Development Bank of Canada

The Péladeau Family, Quebecor Inc.

Guy Saint-Pierre, Chairman, SNC-Lavalin Group Inc.

Charles Sirois, Chairman and CEO, Teleglobe Inc.

THE NEW MANAGERS

Raymond Bachand, Fonds de Solidarité des Travailleurs du Québec

Claude Béland, Mouvement des Caisses Desjardins

André Bérard, National Bank

Micheline Bouchard, Hewlett-Packard

Jacques Bougie, Alcan

Jacqueline Boutet, Château Real Estate

Claude Brochu, Expos

Pierre Brunet, Lévesque, Beaubien Geoffrion

André Calli, Hydro-Québec

David Caplan and Gilles Ouimet, Pratt & Whitney

Ronald Corey, Club de Hockey Canadien

Pierre Côté, Canadian Celenese Inc., Quebec City

Leon Courville, National Bank

Pierre Desmarais, Unimédia

Guy Desfresne, Quebec Cartier Mining

Marcel Emond, Petromont

Raymond Garneau, Alliance Industrielle

Robert Gratton, Power Financial

Jeannine Guillevin-Wood, Laurentian Bank

Gerald Lacoste, Montreal Stock Exchange

Pierre Laurin, Merrill Lynch Canada
Jacques Lemarre, SNC-Lavalin
John LeBoutillier, Iron Ore Co.
Monique Leroux, Royal Bank
Pierre Lessard, Metro-Richelieu
Brian Levitt, Imasco
Gerald Limoges, Ernst & Young
Jacques Menard, Nesbitt Burns,
    Hydro-Québec, Expos
Pierre Michaud, Provigo
Jean Monty and Derek Burney, BCE
Jean Neveau, Quebecor Printing
Jocelyn Proteau, Movement
    Desjardins #2
Robert Rabinovitch, Manuel Batshaw
    and Arnold Ludwick, Claridge
    Investments

John Rae and Michael Pitfield, Power
    Corp.
John Redfern, Lafarge Canada
Henri-Paul Rousseau, Laurentian
    Bank
Louise Roy, Geoffrion
Raymond Royer, Domtar
Guy Savard, Midland Walwyn
Guylaine Saucier, CBC
Serge Saucier, Raymond, Chabot,
    Martin
Jean-Claude Scraire, Caisse de
    dépôt
Paul Tellier and Michael Sabin,
    CNR
Michelle Turcotte, RBC Dominion
Manon Vennat, Spencer Stuart

THE ENTREPRENEURS

Louis Audet, Cogneco Inc.
Luc Beauregard, National Public
    Relations
Dr. Francesco Bellini, Bio Chem
    Pharma
Herb Black, tin magnate
Claude Bruneau, manages Desmarais
    fortune
Micheline Charest, CINAR film
    production
Jean Coutu, The Jean Coutu Group,
    PJC Inc.
Gerald Desourdy, Société Desourdy
Marcel Dutil, Canan Manac Group
Serge Godin, Groupe CGI
Paul-André Guillotte, GTC—
    Péladeau clone

Jonathan Kolber, Israeli
    Investments
Daniel Langlois, SoftImage
Bernard Lemaire, Cascades Inc.
Remi Marcoux, Transcontinental
    Group (publishers)
Robert Miller, Future
    Electronics
Phil O'Brien, Devencore
Michel Perron, Somiper Inc.
Hervé Pomerleau, builder
Adrien Pouliot, CFCF Inc.
Serge Racine, Shermag
Lino Saputo, Groupe Saputo
Alvin Segal, Peerless Clothing
Laurent Verrault, GLP
    Engineering

PROPRIETORS

René Angélil, husband and manager of Céline Dion

Philippe de Gaspé Beaubien, Chairman and President, Telemedia Corp.

Alain Bouchard, Chairman and CEO, Alimentation Couche-Tard Ltd.

Jean Bienvenue, Director, Olymet and Company

Claude Chagnon, President and COO, Vidéotron

Jean Coutu, Chairman and CEO, The Jean Coutu Group, PJC Inc.

Jean Dupéré, Thetford Asbestos Mines

Aaron Fish, Chairman and CEO (now retired) and Peter Blaikie, President and COO, Unican Security Systems Ltd.

Hugh Hallward, Chairman, Atlas Copco Canada Inc.

Paul Ivanier, President and CEO, Ivaco Inc.

Joseph Kruger, Chairman and CEO, Kruger Inc.

Paul Lowenstein, CEO, Canadian Corporate Funding

Eric Molson, Molson Breweries Ltd.

Bertin Nadeau, Chairman and CEO, GescoLynk Inc.

Robert Ouimet, Chairman, President and CEO, Ouimet-Cordon Bleu Inc.

Jeremy Reitman, President, Reitmans, Canada Ltd.

Lorne Webster, Chairman and CEO, Prenor Group Ltd.

Jonathan Wener, Chairman and CEO, Canderel Holdings Ltd.

THE LAWYERS

David Angus
Jean Bazin
Max Bernard
Casper Bloom
Philippe Casgrain
Raymond Crevier
Daniel Fournier
Francis Fox
Willibroad Gauthire
André Gervais
Jim Grant
Roy Heenan
Sydney Horn
Pierre-Marc Johnson
Marc Lalonde
Gabriel Lapointe

Pierre Legrand
Eric Maldoff
Brian Mulroney
Jean-Pierre Ouellet
Robert Paré
Alex Patterson
Richard Pound
Gil Rémillard
Jim Robb
Heward Stikeman
Jacques Tétreault
Gerald Tremblay
Pierre Elliott Trudeau
Michel Vennat
Robert Vineberg
Stephen Vineberg

THE GURUS

Yvan Allaire	Julius Grey
Drummond Birks	Jean Guertin
André Bisson	Stephen Jarislowsky
Anthony Boeckh	David Johnson
Prof. Reuven Brenner	Leo Kolber
Claude Castonguay	Henry Mintzberg
Gretta Chambers	Hartland Molson
Marcel Côté	Derek Price
Alain Cousineau	Bernie Shapiro
David Culver	Ian Soutar
Jean de Grandpré	Robert Swidler
Claude Forget	Charles Taylor
Claude Frenette	Bill Turner
Gregoire Gollin	Norman Webster

LUCIEN BOUCHARD'S SECRET DINNER LIST

In the fall of 1996, shortly after he became premier of Quebec, Lucien Bouchard held a private dinner and several secret meetings with fourteen members of the Montreal establishment, plus the mayor of Quebec City (Jean-Paul l'Allier). He was anxious to obtain approval from the business community for his plan to reduce the provincial deficit and push for Quebec's independence. He received the former with enthusiasm, but was denied the latter, which caused him considerable dismay. These were his dinner guests:

Laurent Beaudoin, Chairman, President and CEO, Bombardier Inc.
Jacques Bougie, President and CEO, Alcan Aluminium Ltd.
Micheline Charest, Chairman and CEO, CINAR Films Inc.
John Cleghorn, Chairman and CEO, Royal Bank of Canada
Gilles Jarry, Vice President, Bank of Montreal
Phyllis Lambert, Director, Centre Canadien d'architecture
Brian M. Levitt, President and CEO, Imasco
Eric Maldoff, lawyer, Martineau Walker
Ronald Y. Oberlander, President, Abitibi-Price
Pierre Parent
Pierre Péladeau, Chairman, Quebecor Inc.
Michael Rosenberg, ROSDEV
Henri-Paul Rousseau, President and CEO, Banque Laurentienne
Charles Sirois, Teleglobe Inc.

APPENDIX II

THE MANITOBA BUSINESS MAFIA

John Fraser, the former CEO of Federal Industries Ltd. and currently chairman of Air Canada, organized a group of Winnipeg establishment types to be advisers to the management faculty at the University of Manitoba. They do that as well as helping raise money for the business school's campus operations, but in this age of networking the group has quickly become an essential and influential gathering of local decision makers:

Norman J. Alexander, investment consultant.

Dr. Dennis Anderson, President, Brandon University

Richard G. Andison, Chairman and CEO, Russell Equipment Ltd.

Richard E. Archer, Executive Vice President, Investments and Trust, Investors Group

James M. Babcock, Senior Vice President, Toronto-Dominion Bank, Manitoba and Saskatchewan Division

Sheldon Berney, President, Ada Holding Co. Ltd.

Mark A. Bernstein, President, Phillips Point Products Ltd.

Richard R. Bracken, President, Royal Canadian Securities Ltd.

R.B. Brennan, President and CEO, Manitoba Hydro

Robert Caswill, Director of Education, The Institute of Chartered Accountants of Manitoba

Robert M. Chipman, Chairman, The Megill-Stephenson Co. Ltd.

Gail A. Cocker, Senior Vice President, Bank of Montreal

Norman L. Coghlan, President, Coghlan's Ltd.

Albert D. Cohen, Chairman and CEO, Gendis Inc.

Ken Cranston, Vice President, Manitoba and Northwestern Ontario, Bank of Nova Scotia

D.J.G. Cuming, Office Managing Partner, Deloitte & Touche

Robert W. Cunningham, President, Cunningham Business Interiors Ltd.

Arthur A. DeFehr, President, Palliser Furniture Ltd.

Donald A. Dick, President, Donald A. Dick Estate Planning Ltd.

Hugh G. Eliasson, Deputy Minister, Government Services, Government of Manitoba

Roger Emery, President, R&M Emery Enterprises Ltd.

Roland R. Engel, President and CEO, Atomic Transportation System Inc.

Charles Feaver, Senior Vice President, Research & Development, Faneuil ISC Inc.

Wayne Fingas, Managing Principal, Towers Perrin

John F. Fraser, Chairman of the Board, Air Canada

Martin H. Freedman, lawyer, Aikins, MacAulay & Thorvaldson

William Funk, President and CEO, Manitoba Lotteries Corp.

Freddy T. Gaspard, President, Gaspard & Sons Ltd.

Elaine Goldie, Director of Development, Department of Private Funding, University of Manitoba

Allan Grant, Partner, Lazer Grant & Company

Robert C. Hamaberg, President, Standard Aero Ltd.

Leonard W. Hampson, Executive Director, The Certified General Accountants Association of Manitoba

Gary Hannaford, Executive Vice President, The Institute of Chartered Accountants of Manitoba

Gregg J. Hanson, President and CEO, Wawanesa Mutual Insurance Company

Kerry L. Hawkins, President and CEO, Cargill Limited

Paul J. Hill, President and CEO, McCallum Hill Companies

Henry Hudek, President, IQON Financial Management

Duncan M. Jessiman, Chairman, Bison Diversified Inc.

Brian A. Johnson, President and CEO, Crown Life Insurance Company

David S. Kaufman, President, Silpit Industries Ltd.

Hubert T. Kleysen, President and CEO, Kleysen Transport Ltd.

R.M. Kozminski, President and CEO, Keystone Ford Sales

Serena H. Kraayeveld, Managing Partner, Coopers & Lybrand

Dan H. Kraayeveld, Executive Director, The Winnipeg Foundation

Otto Lang, President and CEO, Centra Gas Manitoba Inc.

J. Robert Lavery, President and CEO, Winpak Ltd.

Augustus S. Leach, President, Leachold Investments Ltd.

Garry Leach, President, MRM Steel Inc.

Dennice M. Leahey, Senior Vice President and General Manager, Royal Bank of Canada

David Loch, President, Loch Mayberry Fine Art Inc.

Nick R. Logan, President, National Leasing Group Inc.

Donald T. MacAngus, Chairman of the Board, Winnipeg Building & Decorating Ltd.

Sheryl MacDonald, President, Encore Travel Ltd.

G. Allan MacKenzie, President and CEO, Gendis Inc. and Associate Corporations

Dean Magnus, Office Managing Partner, Doane Raymond

Ken L. Matchett, CEO, XCAN Grain Pool Ltd.

Brent J. McLean, Partner, Price Waterhouse

Penny McMillan, Executive Director, Tourism Winnipeg

Glen J. Middleton, Managing Principal, The Alexander Consulting Group

Sandi Mielitz, Vice President Grain and Western Canada, CN North America

Randy L. Moffat, President and CEO, Moffat Communications Ltd.

Dale A.G. Parkinson, Executive Vice President, Investors Group Inc.

William B. Parrish, President, Parrish & Heimbecker Ltd.

John S. Pelton, Chairman and CEO, Russel Metals Inc.

Michael E.J. Phelps, Chairman of the Board and CEO, Westcoast Energy Inc.

Lawrie O. Pollard, President, Pollard Banknote Ltd.

Gerald V. Price, President and CEO, E.H. Price Ltd.

David R. Quinton, President, Quintex Services Ltd.

W. John Rae, Chairman and CEO, Novamet Development Corporation

Dick C. Reid, Vice President and Manager, Commercial Banking, Manitoba Region, Canadian Imperial Bank of Commerce

Dr. Donald S. Reimer, Chairman, President and CEO, Reimer Express World Corp.

George T. Richardson, Chairman and Managing Director, James Richardson & Sons Ltd.

Hartley T. Richardson, President, James Richardson & Sons Ltd.

Richard C. Riess, President, Geo. H. Young & Co. Ltd.

H. Sanford Riley, President and CEO, Investors Group Inc.

Conrad S. Riley, Jr., President and CEO, United Canadian Shares Ltd.

John D. Ritchie, Vice President and Director, Wood Gundy Inc.

Karn D. Sandy, Corporate Secretary and Executive Director, Corporate Services & Research, Workers Compensation Board of Manitoba

J. Douglas Sherwood, President and CEO, Crown Corporations Council

Kenneth Kidd, Vice President and General Manager, New Holland Canada Ltd.

Gary T. Steiman, President, Gemini Fashions of Canada Ltd.

Ian Sutherland, President and CEO, The North West Company

Donald G. Swanson, President, Lordon & Associates

Marvin T. Taylor, President, M.T. Taylor & Associates

Arni C. Thorsteinson, President, Shelter Canadian Properties Ltd.

Marvin E. Tiller, President and CEO, Canadian Shield Enterprises Inc.

Jim Venn, Executive Vice President and CEO, Dominion Malting Ltd.

William E. Watchorn, President and CEO, ENSIS Corporation

Richard E. Waugh, Vice Chairman, The Bank of Nova Scotia

Gordon B. Webster, Managing Partner, Price Waterhouse

Donald W. Whitmore, President, The Vector Construction Group

Paul D. Wright, Partner, Coopers & Lybrand

APPENDIX 12

THE LEXUS RANGERS, CALGARY

Calgary's Establishment ranks second in national significance only to Toronto's Bay Street. Below are some of the main players, not only in the Oil Patch, but in the city's rapidly diversifying economy:

The Old Establishment

J.C. Anderson, Anderson Exploration
Doug Baldwin, Imperial Oil
John Beddome, corporate director
Richard Bonnycastle, Cavendish
    Investing
Bob Brawn, Danoil Energy
Jim Gray, Canadian Hunter
    Exploration
Dick Guesella, Carmanah Resources
Dick Haskayne, Nova Corp.
Bob Lamond, Sunoma Energy
Al Libin, private investor
Peter Lougheed, Bennett Jones
    Verchere
Gerry Maier, Nova Chemicals
Fred Mannix, Jr., Loram Group
Ron Mannix, Loram Group
Anne McCaig, Presenting Italy
Bud McCaig, Trimac

Jeff McCaig, Trimac
Rod McDaniel, McDaniel &
    Associates Consultants
Harold Milavsky, Quantico Capital
David Mitchell, Alberta Energy
    Company (emeritus)
Rob Peters, Peters & Co
John Scrymngeour, *Alberta Report*
Doc Seaman, Bow Valley Energy and
    Dax Holdings
Bill Siebens, private investor
Art Smith, SNC-Lavalin
Marg Southern, Spruce Meadows
Nancy Southern, Atco
Ron Southern, Atco
Linda Southern-Heathcott, Spruce
    Meadows
Gus Van Wielingen, NuGas
Charles Wilson, Shell Oil

The New Titans

Grant Bartlett, oil investor and
    Calgary Flames
Clive Beddoe, WestJet
Kevin Benson, Canadian
    Airlines
Martha Billes, Canadian Tire
Grant Billing, Superior Propane
Ron Bremner, Calgary Flames
Lee Brown, Brown & Root
John Brussa, Burnett Duckworth
    Palmer

Dr. James Buckee, Talisman Energy
Jim Davidson, FirstEnergy Capital
Robert Dineen, PCL Construction
James Dinning, TransAlta
John Driscoll, NCE Resources
    Group
Murray Edwards, EDCO Financial
    Holdings
Jim Gardiner, Fording Coal
Rick George, Suncor
Norman Gish, Alliance Pipeline

T.W. Gomke, Gibson Petroleum
   Company
Rick Grafton, FirstEnergy Capital
Ron Greene, Tortuga Investment
Norm Harrison, Bannister Majestic
Harley Hotchkiss, Spartan Resources
Barry Jackson, Crestar Energy
Jim Kinnear, Pengrowth Gas
Ralph Klein, Premier of Alberta
Sam Kolias, Boardwalk Equities
John Langille, Canadian Natural
   Resources
David Lyons, Ocelot Energy
Brian MacNeil, Interprovincial
   Pipeline
Al Markin, Canadian Natural
   Resources
Ed McNally, Big Rock Brewery
Martin Molyneau, FirstEnergy
   Capital
Gwyn Morgan, Alberta Energy
Ted Newall, Nova Chemicals
Eric Newell, Syncrude
Greg Noval, Canadian 88

David O'Brien, Canadian Pacific
George Oswald, Marine Pipeline
   Construction
Dee Parkinson-Marcoux, Ensyn
   Energy Corp.
Fiona Read, Reserve Royalty
Brad Shaw, Shaw Communications
Heather Shaw, Shaw
   Communications
Julie Shaw, Shaw Communications
Jim Shaw, Shaw Communications
J.R. Shaw, Shaw Communications
Hank Swartout, Precision Drilling
Michael Tims, Peters & Co.
John Torode, Torode Realty
Guy Turcotte, formerly at Chauvco
John Van Brunt, Agrium Inc.
George Watson, TransCanada
   PipeLines
Donald Wilson, Prudential Steel
Clayton Woitas, Renaissance
   Energy
Brett Wilson, FirstEnergy Capital
Erdal Yildirim, Canadian Occidental

The Teckie Titans

Revitt Elred, Minerva
Ron George, Paragon
David Martin, Smart Tech

Frank Myers, CMG Computer
   Modeling
Hugh Stanfield, Pulsar
Adrian Zissos, Meriac Project

Personalities, Players and Opinion Makers

Stuart Allan, Buzzard's Cowboy
   Cuisine
Mary Blue, KeyWest Energy
Ted Byfield, founder, *Alberta
   Report*
Tom Cummings, Alberta Stock
   Exchange
Ron Coleman, Dominion Equity
   Resource Fund

Frank Dabbs, author and columnist
Ian Doig, *Doig's Digest*
Al Duerr, Mayor of Calgary
Jackie Flanagan, Publisher, *Alberta
   Views*
Senator Ron Ghitter, Property
   Consultants
Sig Gutsche, Hard Rock Café and
   Calgary Stampeders

Senator Dan Hays, Hays Ranches
and Macleod Dixon
Ralph Hedlin, freelance guru
Grant and Judy Howard, The
Howard Group
Ken King, Publisher, *Calgary Herald*
Pat (Black) Nelson, Minister of
Economic Development,
Government of Alberta
Gail O'Brien, Holt Renfrew
Sheila O'Brien, Nova Chemicals
Milt Pahl, venture capitalist

David Parker, Harborough
Marketing
Les Pyette, Publisher, *Calgary Sun*
Sydney Sharpe, *Calgary Sun*
John Shiry, Woodside Research
Christine Silverberg, Calgary Police
Service
Sir Rodney and Lady Ouida Touche,
investors and taste makers
Hal Wyatt, private investor
John Zaozirny, lawyer, investor and
corporate director

Legal Beagles

Wendy Best, Dunphy Calvert
Judy Boyes, Turnbull Boyes
Bill Britton, Bennett Jones Verchere
Jack Donaghue, Donaghue Powers
Pshebriski
John Donahue, Donaghue Powers
Pshebriski
Bob Engbloom, MacKimmie
Matthews
Brian Felesky, Felesky Flynn
Bruce Green, Milner Fenerty
David Haigh, Burnett Duckworth
Palmer
Al Hunter, Code Hunter
Martin Lambert, Bennett Jones
Verchere

Jack Marshall, Macleod Dixon
Jim McKee, Macleod Dixon
Doug Mitchell, Howard Mackie
Cliff O'Brien, Bennett Jones
Verchere
Jim Palmer, Burnett Duckworth
Palmer
Jack Protheroe, home office lawyer
Ron Sirkis, Bennett Jones Verchere
Henry Sykes, MacKimmie Matthews
Greg Turnbull, Code Hunter
Julia Turnbull, Turnbull Boyes
Tommy Walsh, Walsh & Co.
Neil Whitman, Code Hunter

APPENDIX 13

CALGARY'S ANIMATORS GALORE

In 1984, the Faculty of Management at the University of Calgary established an advisory council meant to help design its curriculum. They did that, but they began to network so effectively among themselves that belonging to the Management Advisory Council became a highly desirable ticket. Here is the current list of adherents:

Frank Altin, Senior Consultant and Director, The Advisory Group

Jerry Anderson, President and General Manager, Mobil Oil Canada

R. William Andrew, President, Andrew & Propp Estate Planning Corporation

Douglas D. Baldwin, Senior Vice President and Director, Imperial Oil Ltd.

Dr. Grant A. Bartlett, President and CEO, Archer Resources Ltd.

John M. Beddome, President, Epic Energy

Michael Bird, General Manager, Canadian Pacific Hotels & Resorts

Ron Blakely, Chief Financial Officer, Shell Canada Ltd.

Daniel W. Boivin, President and CEO, Novacor Chemicals Ltd.

Ken Boutilier, Senior Manager, Health Strategy, Glaxo Wellcome

Robert G. Brawn, President and CEO, Danoil Energy Ltd.

Walter P. Brock, retired from Deloitte & Touche

George Brookman, President, West Canadian Graphic Industries

Dennis R. Burns, Registered Representative, RBC Dominion Securities

Alan P. Cadotte, President and CEO, Newalta Corporation

J. David Carlson, Investment Adviser, RBC Dominion Securities

John Carpenter, Executive Director, Certified General Accountants of Alberta

E.R.R. Carruthers, Judge, Provincial Court of Alberta

Douglas A. Carty, Senior Vice President and CFO, Canadian Airlines International Ltd.

A. Bernard Coady, President, Coady Investments Inc.

Robert B. Colborne, President, Pacific Western Transportation Ltd.

Fred Coles, Chairman, Applied Terravision Systems Inc.

Dr. Allan Conway, Director, Executive MBA Program, Faculty of Management

Don J.A. Cross, President, Stockland Holdings Inc.

Alex R. Cummings, President, A.R. Cummings Consulting Ltd.

Gordon E.M. Cummings, President, Alberta Wheat Pool

Navin Dave, Office Managing Partner and Managing Partner, West KPMG

John de Bruyn, Partner, Deloitte & Touche

Robert Dittmer, Executive Vice President, AGRA Industries Limited

Ron E. Doersam, Vice President, The Colt Companies

Ross D.S. Douglas, President and CEO, Highridge Exploration Ltd.

Bonnie DuPoint, Senior Vice President, Human Resources, IPL Energy Ltd.

Victor S. Dusik, Partner, Ernst & Young

Sterling Eddy, President and CEO, Society of Management Accountants of Alberta

Peter Edwards, Partner, Conroy Partners Limited

David Evans, Chairman and CEO, Barrington Petroleum Ltd.

Richard Ferris, District Manager, Calgary North, Canadian Imperial Bank of Commerce

Charles W. Fischer, Senior Vice President, Exploration & Production, North America, Canadian Occidental Petroleum Ltd.

Edward G. Fitzhenry, President and CEO, Pelorus Navigation Systems

Murray L. Fox, President, Foxco Investment Corporation

Ron Franklin, Executive-in-Residence, Faculty of Management

Dr. Ronald George, President, Perigon Solutions Inc.

Russell K. Girling, Senior Vice President, Power North America, TransCanada Power

J. Doug Graham, President, Canadian Western Natural Gas Company

Ron Greene, Chairman, Tortuga Investment Corp.

Edward C. Grimes, Vice President and General Manager, DOSCO Supply

John A. Hagg, CEO, Northstar Energy Corporation

Eugene Hamel, Consultant, Unocal Indonesia

Rick Harrop, President, Talara Resources Ltd.

Richard F. Haskayne, Haskayne & Partners

Robert J. Herdman, Partner, Price Waterhouse

John F. Hodgson, Partner, Price Waterhouse

Bill Hodsmyth, Community Banking Manager, Calgary NW, Bank of Montreal

Bev Hughes, President, Mark Personnel Services Inc.

Dick Huisman, President and CEO, Greyhound Canada Transportation Corp.

H. Douglas Hunter, President, RFM Capital Corporation

Don Hyndman, Partner, Deloitte & Touche

Dr. Mansour Javidan, Policy & Environment Area, Faculty of Management

C. Kent Jespersen, President, Gas Services, Nova Corporation of Alberta

Alan S. John, President, Watermark Advertising Design Limited

Dr. Vern J. Jones, Associate Dean (External), Faculty of Management

Darshan S. Kailly, President and General Manager, Canadian Freightways Ltd.

Ernest Kapitza, Vice President and Manager, Toronto-Dominion Bank

Walter A. Kmet, President and CEO,
ATCO Structures Inc.
Hal Kvisle, President, Fletcher
Challenge Energy Canada
Larry B. Krause, President and CEO,
Summit Resources Ltd.
Al G. Lennox, Senior Partner, AG
Lennox & Associates
Ann MacDiarmid, President, Raptor
Communications
Dr. P. Michael Maher, Dean, Faculty
of Management
Fred P. Mannix, Chairman and
Director, Campbell Construction
Company Ltd.
Ann McCaig, Chancellor, The
University of Calgary
Trimac Limited
Graham J. McFarlane, Director,
Western Management
Consultants
Stewart McGregor, Chairman and
CEO, Numac Energy Inc.
Dr. Per B. Mokkelbost, Finance Area,
Faculty of Management
Joe Moreau, Location
Manager–Calgary, IBM Canada
Ltd.
David G. Morrison, President and
CEO, Brewster Transportation
& Tours
Harry L. Olson, Partner, KPMG
Toby Oswald, Vice President, Public
Relations & Government Affairs,
Canada Safeway Ltd.
G. Barry Padley, CFO, Paramount
Resources Ltd.
James S. Palmer, Senior Partner,
Burnet, Duckworth & Palmer
Maury Parsons, Executive-in-
Residence, Faculty of
Management

Frederick H. Peacock, President,
Peacock Investments Ltd.
G.R. Peden, Manager, Human
Resources, Numac Energy
Karen Prentice, Legal Counsel and
Corporate Secretary, Corporate
Governance, City of Calgary
Electric System
S. Ford Ralph, Vice President,
Logistics & Support Services,
Petro-Canada
R. Gregory Rich, Chairman and
President, Amoco Canada
Petroleum Co. Ltd.
Dr. Brent Ritchie, Tourism Area,
Faculty of Management
Ewald Roesler, Senior Vice President,
TELVO
Communications Inc.
Dr. Jim Robertson, retired professor
Shannon Ryhorchuk, Partner,
General Practice, Coopers &
Lybrand
Barry Sadrehashemi, Controller,
Arakis Energy Corporation
Dr. Robert A. Schulz, Petroleum
Land Management, Faculty of
Management
Stewart Scott, CFO, Calgary
Co-operative Association Ltd.
Terry Semeniuk, CEO, United Farmers
of Alberta Co-operative Ltd.
Brad Stevens, CFO, FWJ Advertising
Public Relations
Joe D.A. Struck, Partner, Felesky
Flynn
Gord G. Tallman, Senior Vice
President and General
Manager, Alberta, Royal
Bank of Canada
Paul Taylor, Vice President, Business
Development, TransAlta
Corporation

Betty Thompson, National Board Representative, Certified General Accountants Association of Alberta

R.W. Thompson, Lawyer, Bennett Jones Verchere

Stella M. Thompson, Principal, Governance West Inc.

Garth Toombs, President, Garth Toombs & Associates Inc.

Wesley R. Twiss, Executive Vice President, Petro-Canada

John D. Watson, Vice President, Finance and CFO, Alberta Energy Company

David E. Waymouth, Managing Director, Waymouth Associates Inc.

Gerry Wood, President, Woodridge Lincoln Mercury Sales Ltd.

Barbara J. Young, President, Highland Technology

APPENDIX 14

THE BAMBOO NETWORK

Many of Vancouver's Titans are Oriental, and they are transforming the city's skyline, business habits and way of life. This is a list of the city's Chinese establishment.

Yik Fung Au-Yeung, accountant

Caleb Chan, President, Burrard International Holdings Inc.

Daniel Chan, President, Chancellor Real Estate Co. Ltd.

Dr. Kai Sun Chan, family physician

Raymond Chan, Member of Parliament, federal minister

Tom Chan, Director, Burrard International Holdings Inc.

Tung Chan, Vice President, Toronto-Dominion Bank

Derek Cheng, Chairman, Chinese Cultural Centre

James Cheng, Architect, James Cheng Architects

C.K. Choi, President, Eason Enterprises Ltd.

David Choi, President, Royal Pacific Realty Corporation

Peter Eng, Chairman, Allied Holdings Ltd.

Thomas Fung, President, Fairchild Holdings Ltd.

David Ho, Chairman, MCL Motors

James Ho, President, Quantum Financial Services (Canada) Ltd.

Ernest Hui, Managing Director, Park Georgia

Terence Hui, President and CEO, Concord Pacific Developments Corp.

Maggie Ip, Founding Chairperson, SUCCESS

Andy Joe, lawyer/realtor

Douglas Jung, Lawyer (former MP)

Angela Kan, Executive Director, Chinese Cultural Centre

M.K. Koo, Group Chairman, Nam Tai Electronics (Canada) Ltd.

Jenny Kwan, MLA, Minister of Municipal Affairs

Chuck Kwok, Vice President, Anson Realty

Stanley Kwok, President, Amara International, and Eva Kwok

Allan Lai, Chairman, Henderson Group

Thomas Lai, Advisor, Hongkong Merchants' Association of Vancouver

David Lam, former Lieutenant-Governor of British Columbia

Geoffrey Lau, President, Golden Properties Ltd.

Art Lee, lawyer (former MP)

Bob Lee, Chairman, Prosperous Group

Daniel Lee, Alderman, City of Vancouver

David S. Lee, Senior Vice President, B.C. Region, Hongkong Bank of Canada

David Y. Lee, Vice President, Canada Trust

Don Lee, City Alderman, Vancouver

Jack Lee, President, Canada Syndicates Inc.

Sophia Leung, MP

Wing T. Leung, Architect, WT Leung & Architects

K.C. Liu, Developer

Mason Loh, Chairman, SUCCESS

Brant Louie, President and CEO, HY Louie Group & London Drugs

Shui Chiu Ng, Chairman, King Day Holdings Ltd.

Ron Shon, Chairman, The Shon Group

Bing Thom, architect

Yuet Tong, President, Chinese Merchants Association

Lillian To, Executive Director, SUCCESS

Francis Wong, Chairman and CEO, The Faw Group

King Wong, Past President, Vancouver Chinatown Merchants Association

Milton Wong, Chairman, HSBC Asset Management Canada

Tai Yao, President, Talsun Enterprises Corp.

Bill Yee, former Alderman, City of Vancouver

Yiu Chung Yeung (Alex Yeung), developer

Index